MEADE

AT GETTYSBURG

CIVIL WAR AMERICA

Peter S. Carmichael, Caroline E. Janney, and Aaron Sheehan-Dean, *editors*

This landmark series interprets broadly the history and culture of the
Civil War era through the long nineteenth century and beyond. Drawing
on diverse approaches and methods, the series publishes historical works
that explore all aspects of the war, biographies of leading commanders,
and tactical and campaign studies, along with select editions of primary
sources. Together, these books shed new light on an era that remains
central to our understanding of American and world history.

MEADE

AT GETTYSBURG

A STUDY IN COMMAND

Kent Masterson Brown

THE UNIVERSITY OF NORTH CAROLINA PRESS *Chapel Hill*

Designed by Richard Hendel
Set in Miller, Antique No 6, and Caslon Ionic
by Tseng Information Systems, Inc.
Manufactured in the United States of America

The University of North Carolina Press has been a
member of the Green Press Initiative since 2003.

Jacket illustration: *Major General Geo. G. Meade*,
photographed between 1861 and 1865; print made between 1880 and 1889.
Courtesy Library of Congress Prints and Photographs Division.

Frontispiece: an unpublished photograph of General George Gordon Meade,
taken by Jacob Byerly at Frederick, Md., on either 7 July or 8 July 1863,
showing Meade as he looked during the Gettysburg campaign.
Kent Masterson Brown Collection.

Library of Congress Cataloging-in-Publication Data
Names: Brown, Kent Masterson, 1949– author.
Title: Meade at Gettysburg : a study in command / Kent Masterson Brown.
Description: Chapel Hill : The University of North Carolina Press, [2021] |
Series: Civil War America | Includes bibliographical references and index.
Identifiers: LCCN 2021003640 | ISBN 9781469661995 (cloth) |
ISBN 9781469662008 (ebook)
Subjects: LCSH: Meade, George Gordon, 1815–1872—
Military leadership. | Gettysburg Campaign, 1863.
Classification: LCC E475.51 .B758 2021 | DDC 355.0092—dc23
LC record available at https://lccn.loc.gov/2021003640

To my dear wife, Genevieve,

And to my three wonderful children,

Annie Louise, Philip, and Thomas,

I love you all more than I can say.

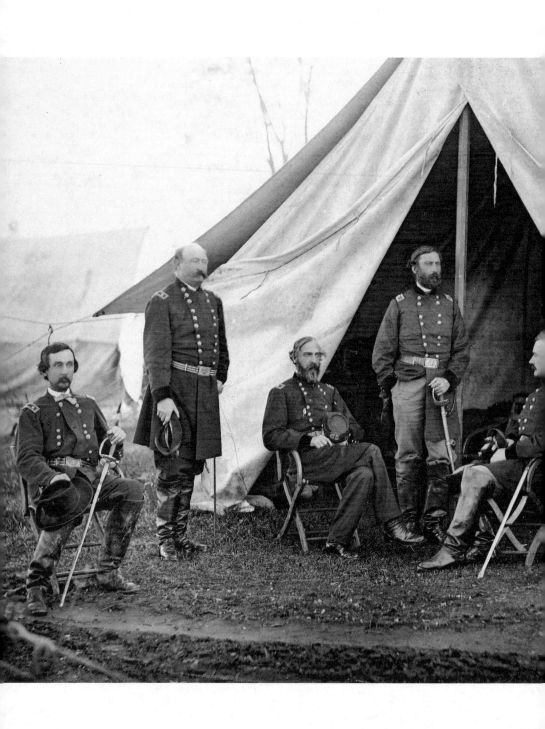

CONTENTS

MAPS & FIGURES

MAPS

FIGURES

MEADE

AT GETTYSBURG

PROLOGUE

The Union armies in Virginia followed a disheartening and bloody course for the first twenty-six months of the Civil War. The Army of Northeastern Virginia, commanded by Major General Irvin McDowell, engaged the enemy once at the First Battle of Bull Run, on 21 July 1861. A Confederate force, commanded by General Joseph E. Johnston, and comprising the Army of the Potomac, commanded by General P. G. T. Beauregard, and Johnston's own Army of the Shenandoah, defeated McDowell, who lost control of his forces. The rout turned into a panic as the fugitives from McDowell's army—along with the frightened spectators with picnic baskets who had lined the hills—fled back to Washington, D.C. Nearly three thousand Union casualties worsened the humiliation. That was President Abraham Lincoln's rude introduction to war as commander in chief.[1]

Summoned to Washington in August 1861 to assume command of what was left of McDowell's army, together with fresh volunteer regiments from many loyal states, was Major General George B. McClellan, who had successfully commanded a relatively small army in the Battle of Rich Mountain, an engagement fought in what is now West Virginia, ten days before First Bull Run. By 1 November, McClellan was named commander in chief of all the Armies of the United States, after the retirement of General Winfield Scott.[2]

A most capable organizer, McClellan soon united the fragments of McDowell's army and all the newly arrived volunteers into a force he named the Army of the Potomac. McClellan trained and drilled his forces through the winter. After much prodding by Lincoln, McClellan put his men, guns, horses, mules, wagons, and equipment on transport vessels and moved them by sea to Fort Monroe at the tip of the Virginia Peninsula, landing on 2 April 1862. The object of the ambitious campaign was to advance up the Peninsula and seize Richmond, the Confederate capital.[3]

McClellan's advance up the Peninsula began on 4 April, and his movement showed early signs of success as the Confederate defenders, com-

1

manded by General Joseph E. Johnston, withdrew from Yorktown all the way back to just south of Richmond. At the Battle of Fair Oaks (or Seven Pines), on 31 May, McClellan's drive to Richmond stalled, but General Johnston was wounded. In Johnston's place, on 1 June Confederate president Jefferson Davis named General Robert E. Lee as commander of the Confederate forces on the Peninsula.[4]

As McClellan sought to shift his base of supply from the York River to Harrison's Landing on the James River, Lee was reinforced by General Thomas J. "Stonewall" Jackson's Army of the Shenandoah, which had scored a string of stunning victories over four different Union armies in the Shenandoah Valley. The Confederate armies launched a series of attacks; over seven days, from 25 June to 1 July, Lee slammed into McClellan's forces at Beaver Dam Creek, Gaines's Mill, Savage's Station, Glendale, and finally Malvern Hill. With his army's back to the James River, McClellan's grand campaign came to an ignominious end, and the War Department directed that McClellan return his forces to Washington. The price paid for the failed campaign was nearly sixteen thousand Union casualties.[5]

Meanwhile, the Union Army of Virginia had been assembled outside Washington, commanded by Major General John Pope. Pope's mission was to move south along the Orange & Alexandria Railroad deep into enemy territory, in hopes of drawing elements of Lee's army away from the Peninsula. That did not happen. Pope soon learned that Lee was driving north. One element of Lee's army was moving directly toward Pope; Jackson's wing was moving to strike Pope's flank. As Pope withdrew back toward Washington, he was reinforced by three of McClellan's corps after they arrived at Alexandria, Virginia.[6]

On 29 August, Lee's army collided with Pope's along the very same fields where the First Battle of Bull Run was fought thirteen months before. Pope's attacks were repulsed that day. On the next day, Lee's counterthrusts devastated Pope, leaving the army with more than fourteen thousand killed, wounded, captured, or missing. In just over one year as commander in chief, Lincoln had suffered three successive defeats of his principal armies in Virginia. The total casualties by then reached over thirty-three thousand.[7]

Lincoln had to move fast, as Lee's army surged north, crossed the Potomac River at White's Ferry near Leesburg, and then marched to Frederick, Maryland. Pope was reassigned, and General McClellan resumed command, leading the Army of the Potomac out of Washington toward Lee. On 14 September, he attacked Lee's well-positioned forces at Turner Pass, Fox's Gap, and Crampton's Gap in the South Mountain range west of Frederick. It was a bloody ordeal. That same day, Stonewall Jackson's detached wing of Lee's army captured the entire Union garrison of nearly thirteen thousand troops at Harper's Ferry, Virginia.[8]

Lee fell back toward Sharpsburg, Maryland, and his army halted along generally high ground west of Antietam Creek, reinforced by most of Jackson's wing of the army. On 17 September, McClellan attacked Lee, but the attacks were launched piecemeal; he appeared to lack the skills of a great tactical commander, as had McDowell and Pope before him.[9]

The attacks against Lee's left flank, along the northern end of the Antietam battlefield around the Dunker Church, failed to break through; the fighting there was desperate and ferocious. Union troops found more success with attacks against Lee's center in a sunken road, but they were stopped by Lee's timely reinforcements. Along the southern end of the battlefield, McClellan's attacks were directed across a stone bridge over Antietam Creek; they drove Lee's right flank to the very edge of Sharpsburg, where again Confederate reinforcements—this time General A. P. Hill's Division—arrived from Harper's Ferry, stopping McClellan's last assault. It was the bloodiest single day in American history. McClellan's casualties alone amounted to more than fifteen thousand for the campaign. Although Lee subsequently withdrew back across the Potomac River and the Army of the Potomac held the battlefield, Antietam was hardly a Union victory.[10]

McClellan seemed paralyzed after the battle. He finally moved his army on 26 October, but he was relieved of command at Warrenton, Virginia, and, in his place, Lincoln named Major General Ambrose Burnside.[11]

To recover and resupply his army, as well as to protect Richmond, Lee moved to Fredericksburg, Virginia. In response to Lee's movements, Burnside drove the Army of the Potomac to Falmouth, across the Rappahannock River from Fredericksburg.[12] After constructing bridges across the river, on 13 December Burnside launched a frontal assault in cold, misty conditions against Lee's defensive positions on Marye's Heights and along imposing high ground to the south. Confederates mauled the Army of the Potomac, which suffered nearly thirteen thousand casualties. Lincoln faced yet another humiliating loss. Burnside was not through, however; he attempted to dislodge and defeat Lee by means of a turning operation. The army would march alongside the Rappahannock River and cross at Bank's Ford and then get onto Lee's rear. On 20 January 1863, Burnside got his army under way during a brutal rainstorm that lasted for two full days. Roads turned into muddy quagmires, and even small streams swelled and became impassable. The operation was abandoned.[13]

In the wake of the Mud March, Burnside was relieved of command on 26 January; Lincoln turned over command to Major General Joseph Hooker. Hooker moved the Army of the Potomac along the Rappahannock River to Kelley's Ford, where it crossed and then marched to a crossroads called Chancellorsville, well behind Lee's army. Still at Fredericksburg, Lee got word of Hooker's movement and marched his army west, closer to Hooker's, leaving a division behind at Fredericksburg to protect his rear. Dividing his army, Lee sent General Jackson and his wing around the right flank of Hooker's forces and into his rear on 2 May. The movement was concealed by the dense woods. Jackson then launched a surprise attack. He rolled up Hooker's unsuspecting forces. They withdrew in confusion to the clearings around the Chancellor House. A Union thrust against Lee's rear, led by General John Sedgwick's corps, was first resisted by a lone Confederate division, but then it was struck by a flanking force that Lee had detached, stopping Sedgwick in his tracks.[14]

The battle was a decisive victory for Lee and his army; it may have been the most remarkable tactical victory of the war. Union casualties in the campaign exceeded sixteen thousand.[15]

The repeated defeats of the Army of the Potomac and the high numbers of casualties made much of the public in the loyal states not only dissatisfied with the war but unwilling to volunteer for duty. Needing men to continue to prosecute the war, the Lincoln administration and Congress instituted a draft in March 1863. Draft enactments are never popular, and after Chancellorsville, the Lincoln administration was justifiably fearful of civil unrest.[16] Meanwhile, its principal army had been consistently beaten, and even humiliated, over the course of the twenty-one months of its existence. Among the general officers, few wished to assume command.

In June 1863, Lee's army seized the initiative, marching into Maryland and Pennsylvania. Lincoln knew he could not politically face another defeat. So he and his closest military and civilian advisers determined to order—not ask—Major General George Gordon Meade to command the Army of the Potomac. Meade would dutifully take command of an army that had never yet defeated its enemy.

As commander of the Army of the Potomac at Gettysburg, Meade delivered not only that army's first victory of the war but also a victory in what was the largest land engagement ever fought on the North American continent. But to President Lincoln and his close cabinet officials—cognizant of an upcoming election, among other considerations—and to many historians even to the present day, that was not enough. They accuse Meade of holding too many councils of war and thereby lacking the moral courage to exercise command over his subordinates. Beyond that, they accuse him of not vigorously pursuing the enemy as it retreated back to Virginia, thereby allowing it to escape across the Potomac River, even though, Meade's detractors claim, he somehow had the golden opportunity to destroy Lee's army before it escaped.

The following pages examine, for the first time, Meade's generalship of the Army of the Potomac from 28 June 1863 to 17 July 1863. Meade's decision-making during that timeframe has never before been critically examined using all the documentary evidence available, together with the necessary analysis based on that evidence. What emerges is a General George Gordon Meade never seen before, an effective operational commander and a determined and relentless tactical commander who is fully aware of the strength and capability of his enemy.

Apart from the horrific losses on the battlefield, the price Meade and his army paid for the victory at Gettysburg was a supply line that was too attenuated and too vulnerable to enemy attacks. As a consequence, by the time the fighting ended at Gettysburg, Meade's sixty thousand officers and men had not been fed for days and neither had his more than thirty thousand horses. The army was desperate for food, forage, clothing, shoes, and even ammunition, and it would take days for enough of those basic supplies to reach the army even in the absence of enemy attacks along that supply line.

Even so, once Meade verified that Lee's army was retreating to Virginia, he drove his depleted, weary, hungry, and largely shoeless army through driving rains and deep mud across two mountain ranges, in just four days, in order to confront the enemy along the Potomac River, a sixty-four-mile journey. By the time the army was in a position to confront Lee's defenses, it had lost more than fourteen thousand horses in the campaign and hundreds were dying every day. Lee's defenses were so thoroughly prepared, and so formidable, and Meade's army was so depleted and at such a tactical disadvantage, that Meade's corps commanders advised against any attack. No such golden opportunity to destroy Lee's army ever existed; Meade perceived correctly that an attack would yield only another futile killing field often experienced by the Army of the Potomac in the years before Meade took command.

The following pages present a General George Gordon Meade that has taken too long a time to emerge.

1

HE IS A
GENTLEMAN AND
AN OLD SOLDIER

Days after the Battle of Chancellorsville, Major General George Gordon Meade, commander of the Fifth Corps of the Army of the Potomac, sat in his tent not far from key fords of the Rappahannock River. There he penned a letter to his wife, Margaretta, whom he called Margaret. He saved his opinions of his fellow generals for his most private correspondence; that day he gave vent to his anger over Major General Joseph Hooker's disastrous performance. "General Hooker has disappointed all his friends by failing to show his fighting qualities in a pinch," Meade wrote. "He was more cautious and took to digging quicker than McClellan, thus proving that a man may talk very big when he has no responsibility, but that is quite a different thing, acting when you are responsible [as opposed to] talking when others are." Two days later, Meade explained to Margaret the fundamental problem brought about by Hooker's performance: "I think these last operations have shaken the confidence of the army in Hooker's judgment, particularly among the superior officers."[1]

In May 1863, Meade was well known to the army's professional soldiers, and he was in a good position to assess how his colleagues viewed Hooker's actions at Chancellorsville. But Meade was not well known in the ranks of the army beyond the Fifth Corps. Reporters did not like mentioning his name in their newspapers. Wrote one of Meade's staff officers later in the war: "The plain truth about Meade is, first, that he is an abrupt, harsh man, even to his own officers, when in active campaign; and secondly, that he, as a rule, will not even speak to any person connected with the press. They do not dare to address him."[2]

Meade was born in Cadiz, Spain, on 31 December 1815, the son of prominent Philadelphians, Richard Worsam Meade, a merchant working in Spain, and Margaret Coats (Butler) Meade. He was the eighth of their eleven children. Forty-seven years old in the spring of 1863, Meade was twenty-eight years out of West Point, where he was graduated nineteenth out of a class of fifty-six in 1835. After graduation, he was assigned as a brevet second lieutenant in the Third United States Artillery to Florida, where he fought the Seminole Indians. On resigning from the army, Meade worked as a civil engineer for a railroad in Alabama. He reentered the army in 1842 as a second lieutenant in the Corps of Topographical Engineers. He served with General Zachary Taylor at Palo Alto, Resaca de la Palma, and Monterrey during the war with Mexico; he also served with General Winfield Scott at Vera Cruz, rising to the rank of captain. After the Mexican War, Meade served assignments constructing lighthouses and improving harbors in New Jersey and Florida; he subsequently oversaw the surveys of Lake Huron and northern Lake Michigan.[3]

When war broke out in 1861, Meade was commissioned a brigadier general of volunteers in the early fall and placed in command of a brigade of Pennsylvania Reserves in General McClellan's Army of the Potomac. Commanding another brigade of Pennsylvania Reserves was a newly minted brigadier general of volunteers named John Fulton Reynolds, whom Meade trusted and liked, even though he was a professional rival. The two generals fought alongside one another against General Robert E. Lee's Army of Northern Virginia through the Peninsula Campaign in the spring and summer of 1862. Reynolds was captured during the retreat after the fighting at Gaines's Mill. Meade was wounded at Glendale; one bullet struck him in the upper right side and then ranged down, exiting out his back just above the hip, while another hit him in the right arm.[4]

Despite these wounds, Meade returned to command his brigade of Pennsylvania Reserves after about two months of recuperation. Command of the division during Meade's absence had been given to Reynolds, who had been exchanged, and that division was assigned to the Army of Virginia, commanded by Major General John Pope. Pope's forces, however, were crushed by Lee's army along the fields above Bull Run at the end of August. Posting his division across the Warrenton Turnpike near Henry House Hill, Reynolds, with Meade's brigade, prevented the Confederates from turning their victory into another Union rout.[5]

When Lee invaded Maryland in September 1862, while at Frederick, Meade was given command of the full division of Pennsylvania Reserves in the First Corps under "Fighting Joe" Hooker. Meade's sometimes rival Reynolds had been temporarily dispatched to command emergency troops in Harrisburg, Pennsylvania. Thus when Hooker was wounded at Antietam early on the morning of 17 September, Meade took over command of the First Corps on the battlefield, where he oversaw the incomprehensibly bloody ordeal of fighting in the famed cornfield between the North Woods and the Dunker Church.[6]

McClellan was finally replaced as commander of the Army of the Potomac for good at Warrenton, Virginia, on 5 November. Two days later, Major General Ambrose Burnside was given command of the army. By then, command of the First Corps had been given to General Reynolds after he returned from Harrisburg, a decision that irritated Meade. After all, Meade already had more combat command experience than Reynolds. "Frankness," wrote Meade to his wife, "compels me to say, I do wish Reynolds had stayed away, and that I could have had a chance to command a corps in action. Perhaps it may yet occur." Yet Meade understood that Reynolds possessed a presence that he did not. Reynolds "is very popular and impresses those around him with a great idea of his superiority," wrote Meade to Margaret Meade, and Reynolds, along with Brigadier General John Gibbon and Major General Abner Doubleday, visited McClellan together on 9 November to bid him farewell. The officers of the old army had a fondness for McClellan, and Meade was among McClellan's supporters, although he had questioned his lack of aggressiveness.[7]

Elevated to the rank of major general of volunteers on 29 November, Meade resumed command of the division of Pennsylvania Reserves in the First Corps. As part of Major General William B. Franklin's "Left Grand Division," the First Corps and Meade's division fought well at Fredericksburg on 13 December, though the battle was a disaster for the Union forces. Meade privately admitted to Margaret that he was displeased with Reynolds's failure to support his attack at Fredericksburg, but it did not seem to compromise an underlying friendship. Nine days later Meade was named commander of the Fifth Corps by Burnside, replacing Major General Daniel Butterfield. By 26 January 1863, Hooker was placed in command of the Army of the Potomac, relieving Burnside. Meade commanded the Fifth Corps during the ensuing Chancellorsville campaign; he had proven to be a capable tactical commander.[8]

At forty-seven, Meade had the appearance of an older man, tall but rather thin and gaunt. His face was deeply lined; his thinning hair and scraggly whiskers were largely gray. Far-sighted, he used pince-nez spectacles that hung from a lanyard around his neck in order to read. Frederick Law Olmsted, who was then serving in the United States Sanitary Commission, wrote that Meade had a "most soldierly and veteran-like appearance; a grave, stern countenance—somewhat Oriental in its dignified expression, yet American in his race horse gauntness. He is simple, direct, deliberate, and thoughtful in manner and speech and general address.... He is a gentleman and an old soldier."[9]

Meade's fellow officers viewed him as sturdy, reliable, competent, and hard-driving; one described him as "clear-headed and honest, [a commander] who would do his best always."[10] Lieutenant Frank A. Haskell, who served on the staff of General John Gibbon, noted that among the officers who knew Meade, "all thought highly of him, a man of great modesty, with none of those qualities which are noisy and assuming, and hankering for cheap newspaper fame.... I think my own notions concerning Genl. Meade ... were shared quite generally by the army. At all events all who knew him shared them."[11]

One veteran who knew Meade well described him as "a most accomplished officer." Meade, he wrote, "had been thoroughly educated in his profession, and had a complete knowledge of both the science and the art of war in all its branches. He was well read, possessed of a vast amount of interesting information, had cultivated his mind as a linguist, and spoke French with fluency." When foreign dignitaries visited the army, they almost always spent considerable time with Meade.[12]

Meade did have his detractors, however. He was called a "damned old google-eyed snapping turtle" because he had a tendency to lose his temper and lash out at subordinates. Sometimes officers would find him "in a mood to rake people" or simply "irascible." He was once described as having "gunpowder in his disposition." Lieutenant Colonel Theodore Lyman, who would later become one of Meade's staff officers, recalled that he had an "excellent" temper, which "on occasions burst forth, like a twelve pound spherical case." When the movement of his troops was on Meade's mind, Lyman noted, the general was "like a firework, always going bang at someone." It was said of Meade that "he never took pains to smooth anyone's ruffled feelings." Nevertheless, Meade seemed to wear well; the more one served with or under him, the more one grew to respect him.[13]

Of all the descriptions of Meade, Lyman gives the best glimpse into how he functioned as a commander. Meade, Lyman wrote, "is a thorough soldier, and a mighty clear-headed man; and one who does not move unless he knows where and how many his men are; where and how many his enemy's men are; and what sort of country he has to go through." Lyman then added: "I never saw a man in my life who was so characterized by straightforward truthfulness as he is."[14]

Apart from his long and loyal service in the army, Meade was a devoted

Major General George Gordon Meade. (Library of Congress)

family man. He had been married to the former Margaretta Sergeant, the eldest daughter of Congressman John Sergeant of Pennsylvania, for twenty-two years. Their marriage was consecrated on 31 December 1840, Meade's birthday. Meade fathered seven children: by the summer of 1863 John Sergeant Meade was twenty-two; George, twenty; Margaret, eighteen; Spencer, thirteen; Sarah, twelve; Henrietta, ten; and William, eight. For all that has been written about Meade over the years, few have noted how much he loved his wife and children. His letters to his family reflect effusive tenderness and devout Christian faith, often reminding Margaret and the children that events are ultimately dictated by the "will of our Heavenly Father."[15]

Unlike most of the general officers in the Army of the Potomac, Meade had significant—and rather close—family ties with the Confederacy. His older sister Elizabeth Mary had married a Philadelphian named Alfred Ingraham. The couple moved to Port Gibson, Mississippi, south of Vicksburg, where Alfred managed the banking interests in the Grand Gulf & Port Gibson Railroad Company there of the noted Philadelphian Nicholas Biddle. Elizabeth Mary became an ardent Confederate.[16]

The Ingrahams lost two sons in the Confederate service. Major Edward Ingraham was mortally wounded near Farmington, Mississippi, on 10 May 1862, while serving on the staff of Major General Earl Van Dorn. He died in Corinth. While at Falmouth, Virginia, in February 1863, Meade received a note under a flag of truce from Edward's brother, Frank, who informed Meade of Edward's death and of the death of their sister Apolline's husband, Thomas LaRoche Ellis, "from exposure in the [Confederate] service." Ellis had served in Colonel Wert Adams's First Mississippi Cavalry. Frank's note ended: "Mother and the rest are all well and wish to be remembered to [their] Yankee relations." Fighting with the Twenty-First Mississippi in Brigadier General William Barksdale's Brigade, Frank was killed at Marye's Heights on 3 May 1863 during the Chancellorsville campaign. Meanwhile, the Ingraham's plantation at Port Gibson, Ashwood, was overrun and pillaged in early May by Major General Ulysses S. Grant's forces as they pressed onward to Jackson, Mississippi, and, ultimately, Vicksburg. Major General John A. McClernand coincidentally made the Ingraham's house his headquarters after the Battle of Port Gibson.[17]

Another sister of Meade's, Mariamne, married a Thomas B. Huger of Charleston, South Carolina. She died in 1857, and her husband, a Confederate lieutenant, was killed in action defending Forts Jackson and St. Philip at the mouth of the Mississippi River against Flag Officer David S. Farragut's Union fleet in April 1862. If that was not enough, Margaret

Old Baldy, General Meade's favorite horse. (Library of Congress)

Meade's younger sister Sarah had married then congressman Henry Alexander Wise of Virginia. Wise had helped secure Meade a commission in the Topographical Engineers at about the time of his marriage to Margaret. The Meades had even named a daughter in honor of Congressman Wise, so close were they. After Sarah's death in 1850, Wise served as governor of Virginia until the outbreak of the war; in that capacity, he signed John Brown's death warrant. By the summer of 1863, Wise was a brigadier general in the Confederate service.[18]

Although Meade was an unshakable champion of the Union and deeply committed to the old army, he was also devoted to every member of his family. His fervent hope for a reconciliation of the two contending regions on the eve of war unquestionably led him to vote for the moderate John Bell, the Constitutional-Union candidate for president, in the election of 1860. After all, members of his family then had opposing views on the crisis and would undoubtedly choose opposite sides if it came to war.[19]

Like all general officers, Meade, a fine horseman, had several horses available for his use at all times. He purchased his favorite, Old Baldy, in September 1861. A big, bright bay stallion with a white face and stockings, he had carried Brigadier General David Hunter, who was wounded at First

Manassas. Old Baldy himself was wounded twice in that battle, one of the wounds being through the nose, but the Quartermaster Department salvaged the horse and sold him to Meade. With what is called a rocking gait, his walk was similar to a slow trot, making it difficult for Meade's staff officers to keep up. "The Chief rides in a most aggravating way," wrote one officer, "neither at a walk nor a gallop, but sort of amble which bumps you and makes you very uncomfortable." Meade rode Old Baldy through the fighting at Dranesville, two of the Seven Days Battles before Richmond, and Second Manassas, where the horse was wounded in the leg. In the desperate fighting in the famed cornfield at Antietam, Old Baldy was again wounded, this time in the neck, and left on the field, presumed dead. But after a Union advance, Meade's resilient war horse was found grazing on the battlefield. The general and his horse became inseparable through the Fredericksburg and Chancellorsville campaigns.[20]

The two saw hard days as Hooker's Army of the Potomac was defeated at the Battle of Chancellorsville on 2 and 3 May 1863 by Lee's Army of Northern Virginia. Hooker's army boasted nearly 130,000 officers and men on the eve of the battle. Its enemy's strength was less than half that number because two of Lee's divisions were foraging in distant Suffolk, Virginia, when the fighting erupted. As Hooker attempted to get his army behind Lee's, Lee divided his force again, sending Lieutenant General Thomas J. "Stonewall" Jackson's Second Army Corps on a flanking march on 2 May that overcame the Union right flank undetected. The ensuing attack was so surprising and ferocious that the Union lines, mostly Major General Oliver Otis Howard's Eleventh Corps, collapsed. Resistance amounted to broken elements of the stricken Eleventh Corps—and the Second, Third, and Twelfth Corps—offering what resistance they could as they withdrew to the clearings around the Chancellor House, where, on 3 May, the bloodletting was renewed, leading to a Union withdrawal. A Union thrust by Major General John Sedgwick's Sixth Corps against Lee's rear at Marye's Heights and Salem Church on 3 May stalled, bringing the horrid ordeal to an end on the ensuing day. Lee's army in victory suffered 12,463 killed, wounded, captured, and missing, including the mortal wounding of Stonewall Jackson. The Army of the Potomac, in defeat, lost 17,287 killed, wounded, captured, and missing.[21]

Hooker was forty-nine years old, a native of Hadley, Massachusetts, and an 1837 graduate of West Point. He served with distinction as a staff officer to General Zachary Taylor and, at General Winfield Scott's insistence, as assistant adjutant general to General Gideon J. Pillow, in their campaigns in Mexico, winning brevets all the way to the rank of lieutenant colonel for gallant and meritorious conduct. Hooker became assistant adjutant general of the Pacific Division in 1848 but resigned his commission in 1853 to take up farming near Sonoma, California. He sought to rejoin the army after the outbreak of the war, and on 6 August 1861, he was commissioned a brigadier general of volunteers. As a division commander in Major General Samuel P. Heintzelman's Third Corps, Hooker saw fighting in the battles on the Virginia Peninsula and at Second Bull Run. A typesetter of a New York newspaper titled a story on the fighting at Williamsburg "Fighting—Joe Hooker." From then on, Hooker was known as Fighting Joe. At Antietam, he commanded the First Corps and was wounded in the fighting; then Brigadier General George Meade assumed command of the corps on the battlefield. At Fredericksburg, Hooker commanded the "Center Grand Division." On Major General Ambrose Burnside's removal from command of the Army of the Potomac in January 1863, Hooker became its commander. He was a bachelor, a station that was unusual in the mid-nineteenth century for a man of his stature, although General Sedgwick and newly commissioned Major General John Reynolds, the First Corps commander, were also bachelors at the time.[22]

On the night of 5 May, the day after the fighting ended at Chancellorsville, and only hours after Sedgwick had gotten his troops back across the Rappahannock, Hooker, contrary to the appeals of most of his corps commanders, ordered all of the Army of the Potomac to recross the river and commanded each corps to return to the camps they occupied near Falmouth before the battle. General Meade wrote to his wife that he "opposed the withdrawal with all my influence," but without success. Several other corps commanders joined Meade in urging Hooker to advance, not retreat.[23]

Hooker wrote directly to President Lincoln notifying him of the movement. Lincoln, irritated by another general who seemed unwilling to advance on the enemy, directed Major General Henry W. Halleck, the general in chief, to accompany him to Hooker's headquarters. Halleck, a native of Westernville, New York, was forty-eight years old; an 1839 graduate of West Point, he was widely regarded as a brilliant scholar of military history and science, having published multiple works in those fields. He had been commissioned a major general at the beginning of the war on recommendation of General Winfield Scott. Halleck's early role in command of the Department of the Missouri was successful, though his personal command of that department's principal army in the field was ineffective. His movement of the army to Corinth, Mississippi, after the Battle of Shiloh was so slow that it allowed the Confederate army to escape.[24]

HE IS A GENTLEMAN AND AN OLD SOLDIER

Major General Joseph Hooker. (Library of Congress)

Major General Henry W. Halleck. (Library of Congress)

Nicknamed Old Brains and, at times, Old Wooden Head, Halleck was not well liked by many of the generals in the field or by many of those in Lincoln's administration. He was constantly in physical pain due to chronic diarrhea and hemorrhoids and took opium to relieve his discomfort; he also may have heavily imbibed alcohol to relieve the effects of the opium. He seems to have struggled with indecision, likely due to a lack of confidence. Gideon Welles, Lincoln's secretary of the navy, caustically recorded in his diary that Halleck "originates nothing, anticipates nothing ... takes no responsibility, plans nothing, suggests nothing, is good for nothing."[25] Nevertheless, after Shiloh, Lincoln directed Halleck to Washington to serve as general in chief. Even Lincoln once referred to him as "little more than a first rate clerk," but the president ultimately deferred all military questions to him, and publicly said so. Lincoln's secretary, John Hay, admired Halleck. "He is a cool, mature man," Hay wrote, "who understands himself. Let us be glad we have him."[26]

When Lincoln and Halleck arrived at Hooker's headquarters on 7 May 1863, what they said to Hooker is anybody's guess. But Meade met with Lincoln and Halleck for "a couple of hours, took lunch, and talked of all sorts of things," even as "nothing was said of [the] recent operations." The president and general in chief similarly visited with other corps commanders of the army, gauging their morale and confidence in their commander. By day's end, Lincoln returned to Washington, leaving Halleck behind to continue the assessment.[27]

When Halleck returned to Washington, he met with Lincoln and Secretary of War Edwin M. Stanton. Stanton and Halleck held one another in mutual dislike; there had even been a widely circulated story that Halleck slapped Stanton after the secretary of war called him a liar. But the trio unquestionably concluded that the defeat at Chancellorsville and the withdrawal across the Rappahannock River were inexcusable. Stanton was reported to have told Lincoln: "I have no confidence in General Hooker, though his personal courage I do not question."[28]

Stanton's opinion was shared not only by Halleck but also by most of Hooker's corps and division commanders. When Major General Darius N. Couch, commander of the Second Corps and senior corps commander in the army, met with the general in chief during his visit to the army, he asked to be relieved from command of that corps, claiming he could not continue so long as Hooker remained in command of the army. Other corps commanders, Halleck discovered, collaborated in asking that Hooker be relieved from command. One of them was Major General Henry Warner Slocum, commander of the Twelfth Corps, who, Halleck found out, asked the other corps commanders to join him "to take action" on the matter; another was General Sedgwick.[29]

At the same time, Generals Couch, Slocum, and Sedgwick, all senior in rank to Meade, sent Meade word that they would willingly serve under him. Meade explained to his wife: "I think I know myself, and am sincere when I say I do not desire the command; hence I can quietly attend to my duties, uninfluenced by what is going on around me, at the same time expressing, as I feel, great gratification that the army and my senior generals should think so well of my services and capacity as to be willing to serve under me." Later, Hooker told Meade "in a most desponding manner that he was ready to turn over to [him] the Army of the Potomac; that he had enough of it, and almost wished he had never been born."[30]

It was a critical moment for the Army of the Potomac, which not only had suffered another defeat at Chancellorsville but was reduced in size since the battle by the discharge of fifty-eight infantry regiments, totaling twenty-five thousand troops, due to the expiration of their enlistments. Those losses would be only partly replaced by the eventual addition of five brigades consisting of about twelve thousand officers and men.[31]

After the fighting at Chancellorsville, the army was made up of seven army corps consisting of nineteen infantry divisions, of which seven had two brigades, eleven had three, and one division had four. In all, the army had fifty-one brigades. The various infantry corps were commanded by some notable major generals: Reynolds commanded the First Corps; Couch, the Second; David Bell Birney, the Third (temporarily); Meade, the Fifth; Sedgwick, the Sixth; Howard, the Eleventh; and Slocum, the Twelfth. Brigadier General Henry Hunt served as chief of artillery. Under Hunt was the Artillery Reserve, commanded by Brigadier General Robert O. Tyler.[32]

The cavalry of the army was organized as a corps under Brigadier General Alfred Pleasonton, who succeeded Major General George Stoneman, an officer Hooker disliked. The cavalry consisted of three seriously undersized divisions: the First under Brigadier General John Buford, the Second under Colonel Alfred N. Duffie, and the Third under Brigadier General David McMurtrie Gregg. With the expiration of enlistments, the cavalry corps had been reduced from 17,193 officers and men on 30 April to 12,162 on 31 May. Hooker claimed that the "effective" strength of his cavalry was closer to 7,500.[33]

The army had sixty-five artillery batteries of mostly six guns each, totaling 370 guns, of which 212 were with the infantry, 50 with the cavalry, and 108 in an artillery reserve. The Army of the Potomac included 97,369 officers and men. So large was the army that the quartermaster, subsistence, ordnance, and ambulance wagon trains of its infantry and cavalry corps and artillery reserve were more than fifty miles long. Add to that the thousands of cattle herded alongside the subsistence trains of each of the army corps and one gets a glimpse of the immensity and complexity of the Army of the Potomac.[34]

Hooker arguably had a certain genius about him. Apart from the defeat and losses, Hooker's command brought about notable innovations. Notably, Hooker conceived and created the Bureau of Military Information. The bureau was formed in February 1863 when Hooker appointed thirty-five-year-old Colonel George H. Sharpe as deputy provost marshal on the staff of Brigadier General Marsena Rudolph Patrick, provost marshal general of the Army of the Potomac. A lawyer in New York City before the war, Sharpe was a graduate of Rutgers University and Yale Law School. At the outbreak of the war, Sharpe became a company commander in the Twentieth New York State Militia for three months. He then raised the One Hundred Twentieth New York Infantry, commanding it through Fredericksburg, after which he received the appointment to the staff of General Patrick.[35]

When Sharpe became deputy provost marshal, he and Captain John C. Babcock, a former employee of the detective Allen Pinkerton and, more recently, a civilian intelligence chief on the staff of General Burnside, were ordered by Hooker to form an intelligence unit. That Bureau of Military Information ultimately employed more than seventy field agents. Babcock assumed the number two position in the bureau, and a Captain John McEntee was given the number three position. Sharpe, Babcock, and McEntee also served on the staff of the commanding general of the army.[36]

The bureau showed signs of success almost from the beginning. Colonel Sharpe and his agents methodically interrogated Confederate prisoners and deserters, as well as civilians, in order to assess the composition of the Confederate army as well as its movements. This provided Hooker with a sizable amount of information about Lee's army, including detailed orders of battle, showing the composition of each of Lee's corps, divisions, and brigades. It tracked enemy movements by the use of scouts sent deep into areas controlled by Lee's army or areas through which elements of Lee's army passed, where they interrogated virtually everyone with whom they came into contact. In addition, Sharpe's scouts mapped roads. They were known to operate anywhere from thirty or more miles from the army. Although the information streaming into his headquarters back in early May did indicate a possible enemy movement toward the right flank of

The Bureau of Military Information, left to right: Colonel George H. Sharpe,
Captain John C. Babcock, unidentified, and Captain John McEntee.
(Library of Congress)

the Army of the Potomac at Chancellorsville, Hooker failed to thoroughly
address it.[37]

Lee reorganized his Army of Northern Virginia in the wake of the Chancellorsville triumph and the death of General Jackson into three army
corps of three divisions each, commanded by lieutenant generals: James
Longstreet commanded the First Army Corps, Richard S. Ewell, the Second, and Ambrose Powell Hill, the Third. Each division consisted of four
brigades, except Major Generals Robert E. Rodes's of Ewell's corps and

HE IS A GENTLEMAN AND AN OLD SOLDIER

Richard H. Anderson's of Hill's corps, which had five brigades each, and George E. Pickett's of Longstreet's corps, which had three. In all, Lee's army had thirty-seven infantry brigades. The cavalry was organized into a division commanded by Major General J. E. B. Stuart, consisting of six brigades under Brigadier Generals Wade Hampton, Beverly H. Robertson, Fitzhugh Lee, Albert G. Jenkins, William E. Jones, and William Henry Fitzhugh Lee, along with six batteries of horse artillery under the direction of Major Robert F. Beckham. An independent brigade of cavalry with a battery of artillery was commanded by Brigadier General John D. Imboden. Lee's army consisted of 196 regiments and battalions of infantry and cavalry, along with sixty-nine mostly four-gun artillery batteries, altogether 287 guns. The army numbered 77,518 officers and men, the largest force Lee ever commanded, and after Chancellorsville, it was situated on the south bank of the Rappahannock River in and around Fredericksburg.[38]

By early June, the two armies faced each other in almost the same positions they held on the eve of the Battle of Fredericksburg seven months before. Hooker's headquarters were in Falmouth on the north bank of the Rappahannock. Reynolds's First Corps was in the vicinity of White Oak Church; Couch's Second Corps was near Falmouth; Birney's Third Corps was at Boscobel, near Falmouth; Meade's Fifth Corps was situated upstream in the vicinity of Banks's and United States Fords of the Rappahannock; Sedgwick's Sixth Corps was near White Oak Church with its Second Division at Franklin's Crossing of the Rappahannock, near the mouth of Deep Run; Howard's Eleventh Corps was near Brooke's Station on the Aquia Creek Railroad; and Slocum's Twelfth Corps was at Stafford Court House and Aquia Creek Landing. Pleasonton's Cavalry Corps had its headquarters at Manassas Junction, thirty miles south of Washington, with elements of it near Warrenton Junction and Brooke's Station. The Artillery Reserve was positioned near Falmouth.[39]

General Hooker received intelligence that the enemy "had broken up a few of his camps and abandoned them" on the right flank of its line in the vicinity of Hamilton's Crossing of the Rappahannock River. After picking up some deserters from Hood's and Pickett's divisions of Longstreet's corps, Hooker opined that Lee was readying his army for a move toward the Potomac River by way of Gordonsville or Culpeper, Virginia, a remarkably accurate assessment.[40]

Lee put his army in motion on 3 June. Led by the divisions of Major Generals Lafayette McLaws and John Bell Hood of Longstreet's corps, the movement was followed by Ewell's corps on 4 and 5 June. In advance of the infantry, Stuart moved his mounted brigades to Culpeper. Stuart's movement was reported to Hooker by Colonel Sharpe's scouts on 7 June. That same day, Longstreet's and Ewell's corps rendezvoused with Stuart's cavalry division at Culpeper; Hill's corps remained in Fredericksburg in front of Hooker's army.[41]

Hooker was regularly receiving reports about enemy movements from Colonel Sharpe's scouts and from his far-ranging cavalry divisions. He ordered Sedgwick's Sixth Corps artillery brigade to open fire on the enemy that remained below Fredericksburg from its positions along the Rappahannock River on 6 June. The Sixth Corps was then ordered to cross the river on pontoon bridges to "ascertain the position and strength of the enemy" in the positions at Deep Run, south of Fredericksburg. Believing that most of Lee's infantry were still at Fredericksburg on 7 June, Hooker ordered Pleasonton to strike Stuart at Culpeper. That same day Lee reviewed five of Stuart's brigades, some 10,292 horsemen, on the plains near Brandy Station, Virginia.[42]

In the early morning hours of 9 June, Buford's Union cavalry division crossed the Rappahannock and struck Stuart's legions near St. James Church. In the melee, General William Henry Fitzhugh Lee was wounded, and Colonel John R. Chambliss took command of Lee's brigade. Generals Gregg's and Duffie's Union cavalry divisions crossed the Rappahannock and headed toward Brandy Station. An enormous engagement resulted, and the Union cavalry matched its counterpart in a manner not seen in previous battles. The Union cavalry leisurely recrossed the Rappahannock without further engagement.[43]

At Brandy Station, Hooker's scouts discovered the presence of two of Lee's army corps: Ewell's and Longstreet's. Ewell's corps left Brandy Station the day after the great cavalry battle and advanced toward the lower Shenandoah Valley. Ewell detached Rodes's Division and Jenkins's cavalry brigade to attack a brigade of Union cavalry at Berryville, Virginia, commanded by Colonel Andrew T. McReynolds, who quickly withdrew his command back to Winchester, Virginia, where Major General Robert H. Milroy's main Union force of nearly nine thousand officers and men held the town.[44]

On 14 June, Rodes and Jenkins attacked the Union garrison of about twelve hundred infantry and a battery of artillery at Martinsburg, in present-day West Virginia, twenty-eight miles north of Winchester, driving those Union troops out of the lower Shenandoah Valley. Elements of the Union force escaped to Harper's Ferry. That same day, General Ewell, with the divisions of Major Generals Jubal Anderson Early and Edward

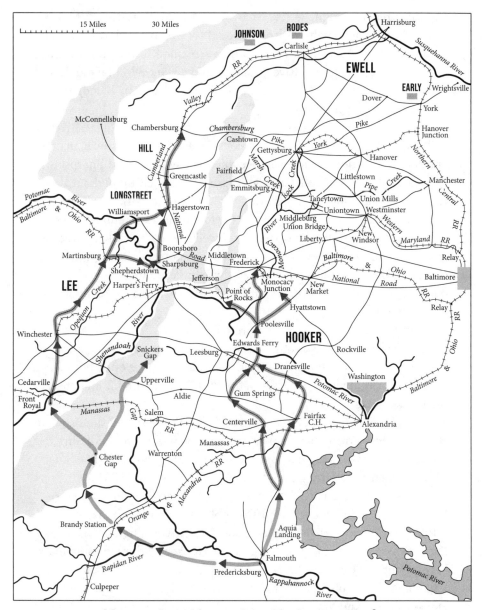

Map 1.1. 3 June 1863 to 27 June 1863: Lee moves north;
Hooker protects Washington.

Johnson, reached Winchester. At 6:00 P.M., Ewell assaulted Milroy's forces. After a tough fight, Milroy's troops broke up in the darkness. Many withdrew toward Harper's Ferry; others streamed toward Martinsburg and crossed the Potomac River winding up at Hancock, Maryland; and some, including General Milroy himself, fled as far west as Bloody Run in Bedford County, Pennsylvania.[45]

On 15 June, Ewell's victorious divisions crossed the Potomac River at Williamsport, Maryland, and at Boteler's Ford at Shepherdstown, in present day West Virginia, and then occupied Hagerstown and Sharpsburg, Maryland; Jenkins's cavalry brigade was sent up the Cumberland Valley toward Chambersburg, Pennsylvania. That same day, the Union garrison at Harper's Ferry withdrew from the town and took refuge across the Potomac River on Maryland Heights. Ewell had completely cleared the lower Shenandoah Valley of Union troops; he captured nearly 3,500 prisoners, twenty-three pieces of artillery, three hundred wagons loaded with quartermaster, subsistence, and ordnance stores, and a large number of horses and mules.[46]

Longstreet's and Hill's corps were on the move. Hill left Fredericksburg on 14 June; Longstreet left Culpeper the next day, keeping east of the Blue Ridge Mountains. Stuart's five cavalry brigades operated east of Longstreet, occupying the passes in the Bull Run Mountains and observing Hooker's army.[47]

On 24 and 25 June, Longstreet's and Hill's corps crossed the Potomac River and headed to Hagerstown. Hill's corps was spotted crossing the Potomac River by a Union signal station atop Maryland Heights. Stuart, who had been directed to guard the mountain passes until all Union troops had crossed the Potomac, was authorized by Lee to take three brigades—Hampton's, Fitzhugh Lee's, and Chambliss's—along with six pieces of artillery, and move between Hooker's army and Washington. One objective of Stuart's operation was to preoccupy Hooker's mounted commands, keeping them away from Lee's rear in the Shenandoah and Cumberland Valleys. Another objective was to interrupt communications between Hooker's army and Washington. On 24 June, Stuart's three brigades left Salem Depot, Virginia, a station on the Orange & Alexandria Railroad, and rode toward Bristoe Station. Stuart left Robertson's and Jones's brigades at Ashby's and Snicker's Gaps of the Blue Ridge Mountains that led to the Shenandoah Valley in order to protect the rear of Lee's army.[48]

On the eve of Hooker's movements, important events occurred in response to the movements of Lee's army. Governor Andrew Curtin of Pennsylvania was convinced that Lee was going to strike into the heart of the commonwealth. In response to his appeals, the War Department created the Departments of the Monongahela and Susquehanna on 10 June. The Department of the Monongahela consisted of that portion of the commonwealth west of Johnstown and the Laurel Hill Mountain range. Important to Hooker's army and its theater of war, the Department of the Susquehanna was composed of that part of Pennsylvania east of Johnstown and the Laurel Hill Mountains. Emergency infantry regiments were raised in Pennsylvania, New Jersey, New York, and elsewhere to defend Pennsylvania. The Department of the Susquehanna would grow to more than thirty thousand emergency troops over the coming weeks. On 10 June, the War Department named General Couch commander of the Department of the Susquehanna, relieving him of command of the Second Corps of the Army of the Potomac. Couch reported to his new assignment in Harrisburg, Pennsylvania, on 11 June at 1:00 P.M. In Couch's place, Major General Winfield Scott Hancock was assigned to command the Second Corps.[49]

Hooker followed a course that kept the Army of the Potomac positioned between Lee's army and Washington. For all the complaints voiced against Hooker in the wake of the defeat at Chancellorsville, no one could complain about his rapid movement north. The movement of the Army of the Potomac began on the morning of 11 June, led by the Third Corps, followed the next day by the First and the Eleventh Corps. On 13 June, the First Corps marched to Bealton, the Fifth Corps by way of Grove Church toward Morrisville, the Sixth Corps to Potomac Creek, the Eleventh Corps to Catlett's Station, and the Twelfth Corps to Dumfries. On the day Ewell's corps crushed the Union garrisons at Martinsburg and Winchester, 14 June, the rear of Hooker's long columns—the Twelfth Corps—reached Dumfries. The Second Corps remained at Falmouth, so long were the columns ahead of it. Hooker established his headquarters at Dumfries.[50]

Throughout the advance of the Army of the Potomac toward the Potomac River, General Meade was acutely aware that General Hooker had fallen from grace with the president and the War Department. Yet Hooker remained in command. Little did Meade know on 16 June that the relationship between Hooker and the president and War Department would deteriorate even more, although he probably could have guessed that it would. The ensuing thirteen days would be filled with uncertainty and anxiety for Meade and all the corps commanders of the army as he and they moved ever closer to Lee's army in Maryland and Pennsylvania with Hooker still in command.

AS A SOLDIER,
I OBEY IT

When Hooker assumed command of the Army of the Potomac in January 1863, the War Department gave him explicit instructions to protect Washington and Harper's Ferry. In the wake of Chancellorsville, the 31 January instructions became the flashpoint between Hooker and the War Department. As early as 5 June, Hooker asked the president that if Lee moved to Culpeper and left a corps at Fredericksburg, would he have permission to attack it; specifically, Hooker wished to know if such was within the spirit of his instructions. Hooker often ignored the chain of command and communicated directly with President Lincoln, rudely bypassing General in Chief Halleck. Lincoln did not respond to Hooker's request favorably but referred the matter to Halleck for a decision. Halleck quickly informed Hooker that such an attack would leave Harper's Ferry and Washington unprotected; the request was denied.[1]

Again, on 10 June, when Hooker discovered that Lee's army was moving north, he telegraphed the president a lengthy letter advocating that he be allowed to take Richmond, then virtually undefended. Lincoln objected. Over the next six days, Hooker sent a flurry of telegrams directly to the president about the Union forces at Winchester and Harper's Ferry, intelligence received at army headquarters about the movements of Lee's forces, and possible moves he might pursue to intercept elements of the enemy army. Then, on 16 June, Hooker wrote a telegram to the president ostensibly providing suggestions about a move to prevent a junction of A. P. Hill's corps with Ewell's and Longstreet's, all of which should have been sent to Halleck, the general in chief. In that telegram Hooker wrote: "You have long been aware, Mr. President, that I have not enjoyed the confidence of the major general commanding the army, and I can assure you so long as this continues we look in vain for success, especially as future

Harper's Ferry. (Library of Congress)

operations will require our relations to be more dependent upon each other than heretofore." It was a bald-faced attempt to undermine Halleck.[2]

In one of the most extraordinary letters ever sent by a president to a general of an American army, Lincoln replied that day that Hooker must directly communicate with the general in chief. Wrote Lincoln: "To remove all misunderstanding, I now place you in the strict military relation to General Halleck of a commander of one of the armies to the general-in-chief of all the armies. I have not intended differently, but it seems to be differently understood; I shall direct him to give you orders and you obey them."[3]

True to his character, Hooker was not about to be put in his place. Hooker's headquarters were at Fairfax Station, and his army occupied positions along a line from Manassas Junction to Centerville to Fairfax Court House and Gum Springs in northern Virginia. He telegraphed Halleck about whether he should exercise control over Major General Samuel Heintzelman's Department of Washington and of Major General Robert C. Schenck's Middle Department in Baltimore. Halleck tentatively agreed to put the troops of General Schenck's department that were east of Cumberland, Maryland, directly under Hooker's control, but demurred when pressed about Heintzelman's forces.[4]

After meeting with Hooker on 23 June and impressing upon him the importance of Harper's Ferry being held at all costs, the president and general in chief tightened the noose around Hooker on 24 June. Major General William H. French, of Schenck's department, was given command at Harper's Ferry. French was instructed to protect Maryland Heights and observe enemy movements. That same day, Brigadier General Benjamin F. Kelley was named commander of a portion of Schenck's department that included all the forces west of Hancock, Maryland, to be known as the Department of West Virginia.[5]

Lincoln and Halleck held at least one conference with a ranking commander in the army about taking Hooker's place. That conference was with General Reynolds back on 2 June, but he refused to be placed in command of the army. Few professional soldiers wanted to risk their careers commanding the Army of the Potomac. By 24 June, the president and general in chief had done little to find a replacement for Hooker. It appears that the president had stopped trying, resolving instead to keep Fighting Joe as commander.[6]

While Hooker's army was nearing the Potomac River, information of the enemy's whereabouts trickled into army headquarters and the War Department. One of Colonel Sharpe's scouts, Captain Babcock, forwarded a report to Hooker, dated 24 June, that Lee's army "has passed through Martinsburg toward the Potomac. The main body are crossing [at] Shepherdstown.... Nine thousand men and sixteen pieces of artillery passed through Greencastle [Pennsylvania] yesterday P.M. .... Large bodies of troops can be seen from South Mountain at Antietam Furnace, by aid of glasses."[7]

The Army of the Potomac moved closer to Frederick, Maryland, on 25 June. A drizzling rain fell in the afternoon and continued through the rest of the day, impeding the army's march on the muddy roads. Crossing on two pontoon bridges strung across the Potomac River at Edwards Ferry near the mouth of Goose Creek, the First Corps marched to Barnesville, Maryland; the Third Corps marched to the mouth of the Monocacy River; the Eleventh Corps reached Jefferson, Maryland; and the Artillery Reserve moved to Poolesville, Maryland. The Second Corps got as far as Gum Springs, Virginia, from its bivouac the previous night at Thoroughfare Gap. Meade's Fifth Corps remained at Aldie, Virginia; Sedgwick's

Sixth Corps was at Germantown and Centreville, Virginia; and Slocum's Twelfth Corps was at Leesburg, Virginia. Army headquarters remained at Fairfax Court House, Virginia, where it had been since 18 June.[8]

Buford's and Gregg's cavalry divisions covered the rear of Hooker's forces as they crossed the Potomac, moving from Aldie to Leesburg. Ahead of the Army of the Potomac was a cavalry division from Heintzelman's department commanded by Major General Julius Stahel that was galloping toward Frederick from Fairfax Court House.[9]

On 26 June, the First Corps marched through drizzling rain and mud to Jefferson, Maryland, from Barnesville; the Second Corps crossed the bridges at Edwards Ferry; and the Third Corps marched from the mouth of the Monocacy River to Point of Rocks, Maryland, on the Potomac River. Meade's Fifth Corps left Aldie and passed through Leesburg, crossing the Potomac River at Edwards Ferry, and then marched all the way to within four miles of the mouth of the Monocacy River. The Sixth Corps got as far as Dranesville, Virginia. The Eleventh Corps, under orders from army headquarters to cover the army from the west, marched all the way to Middletown, Maryland, nine miles west of Frederick, where it joined Stahel's cavalry division. The Twelfth Corps left Leesburg that day and crossed the Potomac River at Edwards Ferry, marching to the mouth of the Monocacy River near Meade's Fifth Corps. Hooker's headquarters were moved from Fairfax Court House, by way of Dranesville and Edwards Ferry, to Poolesville, Maryland, on 26 June.[10]

Hooker left Poolesville for Harper's Ferry on the morning of 27 June. There, he inspected the defenses of Harper's Ferry and Maryland Heights. Angrily, he telegraphed Halleck from Sandy Hook shortly after noon:

> I have received your telegraph in regard to Harper's Ferry. I find 10,000 men here, in condition to take the field. Here they are of no earthly account. They cannot defend a ford of the river, and as far as Harper's Ferry is concerned, there is nothing of it. As for the fortification, the work of the troops, they remain when the troops are withdrawn. No enemy will ever take possession of them for [purposes of using] them. This is my opinion. All the public property could have been secured tonight, and the troops marched to where they could have been of some service. Now they are but a bait for the rebels, should they return."

Then he added: "I beg that this may be presented to the Secretary of War and His Excellency the President." Halleck received the telegram at 2:55 P.M.[11]

Hooker's last sentence must have angered Halleck; it literally told the general in chief that his decision was of no moment. Hooker could be rude, insulting, impulsive, and insubordinate. Within five minutes of sending his first telegram, and before Halleck could respond, Hooker sent another one: "My original instructions require me to cover Harper's Ferry and Washington. I have now imposed upon me, in addition, an enemy in my front of more than my number. I beg to be understood, respectfully, but firmly, that I am unable to comply with this condition with the means at my disposal, and earnestly request that I may at once be relieved from the position I occupy."[12]

Accepting Hooker's resignation presented problems for Lincoln. Hooker had a propensity to criticize those under whom he served, and he cared little if the person he criticized knew he said it; he had a vitriolic tongue. Hooker also had powerful friends in high places, not the least of whom were Secretary of the Treasury Salmon P. Chase, along with Senators and radical Republicans Zachariah Chandler of Michigan and Benjamin F. Wade of Ohio, both of whom sat on the Joint Committee on the Conduct of the War in Congress. Even in the wake of the disaster at Chancellorsville, Chase, Chandler, and Wade called on Secretary Stanton to voice their support for Hooker.[13]

Hooker also had a following in the army, particularly in the Third Corps, which was under the temporary command of General Birney. The Third Corps commander was forty-four-year-old Major General Daniel E. Sickles, the Tammany Hall, Democratic political figure from New York City who had murdered his wife's reputed lover, Philip Barton Key, the son of Francis Scott Key, but had been acquitted on the ground of temporary insanity. One of Sickles's defense lawyers in the case had been none other than Edwin M. Stanton, Lincoln's secretary of war. Before Sickles's run-in with the law, he had served as secretary to the American legation in London and had been elected to the U.S. House of Representatives. Sickles had no military training whatsoever. Rather, he obtained his position from his ability to raise troops in New York City, and he turned that into rank through his political connections. He seized on the outbreak of war as an opportunity to regain some respectability. Sickles did bring with him significant numbers of troops and Democrat support for the war. Sickles, however, was neither respected nor well liked by the old army generals. General Meade had no respect for him. Yet Hooker and Sickles were friends; their friendship had evolved over the past campaigns. It was Hooker who placed Sickles in command of the Third Corps. Hooker knew Sickles had friends in Congress, lots of them; many were Democrats

Major General Daniel E. Sickles. (Library of Congress)

whose support the Lincoln administration needed. Sickles therefore exercised considerable influence over Hooker. Because Sickles's Third Corps included Hooker's old division, many officers and men in that corps idolized Fighting Joe. Sickles could be coarse and vindictive. He was self-aggrandizing and would use his political allies to achieve his purposes. All those factors made accepting Hooker's resignation a very sensitive matter.[14]

Beyond the rank and file in the Third Corps, Hooker surrounded himself with his friends and supporters; most were politically well connected. General Daniel Butterfield, Hooker's chief of staff, was an exemplar. Butterfield was no professional soldier; he was graduated from Union College in Schenectady, New York, not West Point. Little Dan, as he was called, was frail and short in stature; he barely came up to Hooker's shoulders. He commanded the Fifth Corps at Fredericksburg but was replaced by Meade, who outranked him. Butterfield was bitter about that. He did have friends in high places, though. One, Secretary Chase, had probably secured Butterfield's appointment to command the Fifth Corps.[15]

Meade distrusted the officers who surrounded Hooker; he believed some of them were unprofessional, though as usual he limited his opinions to correspondence with his wife. At the time Hooker was named commander of the Army of the Potomac, Meade wrote Margaret: "I believe Hooker is a good soldier ..., [but] the danger he runs is of subjecting himself to bad influences, such as Dan Butterfield and Dan Sickles, who, being intellectually more clever than Hooker, and leading him to believe they are very influential, will obtain an injurious ascendancy over him and insensibly affect his conduct." A few days later Meade wrote his wife again: "I do not like [Hooker's] *entourage*, such gentlemen as Dan Sickles and Dan Butterfield are not the persons I should select as my intimates."[16]

While Hooker was preoccupied with his squabble with Halleck over the garrison at Harper's Ferry, the Army of the Potomac was on the move on 27 June. After raining all night, the day was cloudy but pleasant for a change. The First Corps marched from Jefferson to Middletown; the Second Corps from Edwards Ferry, by way of Poolesville, to Barnesville; the Third Corps from Point of Rocks, by way of Jefferson, to Middletown; the Fifth Corps, from a site between Edwards Ferry and the mouth of the Monocacy River, to Ballenger Creek, near Frederick; the Sixth Corps from Dranesville, by way of Edwards Ferry, to near Poolesville; the Twelfth Corps from near the mouth of the Monocacy River, through Point of Rocks, to Knoxville, Maryland, on the Potomac River. The Eleventh Corps was already at Middletown, along with Stahel's cavalry division, protect-

Major General Daniel Butterfield. (Library of Congress)

*Prospect Hall, the site outside Frederick, Maryland, where
General Meade formally became commander of the Army of the Potomac,
replacing General Hooker. (Wikimedia Commons)*

ing the approaches to Frederick from the South Mountain passes to the west. While Hooker was at Harper's Ferry and Sandy Hook, his own headquarters were moved from Poolesville to Frederick that day.[17]

By evening, 27 June, General Hooker's headquarters tents were pitched on the grounds of Prospect Hall, south of Frederick, along the Harper's Ferry or Ridge Turnpike on the way to Jefferson. Prospect Hall was an imposing two-and-one-half-story brick house, complete with a portico supported by eight columns. The house was built on the highest ground in Frederick, and from its east porch the old city of Frederick was fully visible. A part of the house dated to 1775. The historic home was purchased in 1855 by a prominent citizen of Frederick County, William P. Maulsby, a slave owner, who commanded the First Maryland, Potomac Home Brigade, that would join the Twelfth Corps of the Army of the Potomac in the days ahead.[18]

Just a few miles due south of Prospect Hall, in the fields south and west of Ballenger Creek, General Meade's Fifth Corps halted after a long march through very rough terrain along the Potomac River. The headquarters tents of the Fifth Corps were set up near the two-and-one-half-story brick house of Robert McGill, built around 1780 and named Arcadia. Confederate Brigadier General William N. Pendleton had occupied Arcadia just before the battles along South Mountain in the fall of 1862. The main line of the Baltimore & Ohio Railroad from Monocacy Junction to Point of

AS A SOLDIER, I OBEY IT

Rocks ran just east of the house. Camps for the troops were set up in the broad, rolling fields between the house and the railroad.[19]

A conference was called at the War Department late into the night of 27 June. There, Lincoln, Halleck, and Stanton agreed to accept Hooker's resignation and to give command of the Army of the Potomac to General Meade, although, given the exigencies of time, he could not be approached beforehand. It was too late; they decided they would simply order Meade to become army commander. They had no other choice. Halleck and his adjutant general signed duplicate copies of Lincoln's orders, one for each general. Halleck called on Lieutenant Colonel James A. Hardie, Stanton's chief of staff and a friend of both Hooker and Meade, and directed him to carry the president's orders to the generals.[20]

Hardie, another New Yorker, was forty years old and twenty years out of West Point. He served in the Mexican War as an aide to General John E. Wool. Promoted to the rank of lieutenant colonel, Hardie served on the staff of General McClellan as adjutant general of the army on the Peninsula and during the invasion of Maryland. He was assigned to the headquarters of the "Left Grand Division" at Fredericksburg. Scholarly looking, slightly built, with gray, deeply set eyes, and wearing small wire-rimmed spectacles, he looked more like a schoolteacher than an army officer. Nevertheless, he was well known and highly respected by almost all of the general officers in the Army of the Potomac.[21]

Halleck admonished Hardie not to disclose his identity or business, directing his messenger to dress in civilian clothes. Halleck made clear that when Hardie arrived at Frederick, he was to make his way to General Meade and make him understand that the order for him to assume command was peremptory; he could raise no questions, and the order could not be refused. Hardie was then to escort Meade to Hooker's headquarters and see to the transfer of command.[22]

Hardie was reluctant to carry out the assignment. He knew Hooker and Meade and was concerned about his relationship with both men. But Lincoln abruptly told Hardie that he would take all responsibility for any wounded feelings.[23]

Hardie received passes and orders to travel on special trains of the Baltimore & Ohio Railroad to Frederick and to enter the picket lines of the Army of the Potomac, as well as Meade's and Hooker's headquarters. His superiors instructed that if he was in danger of being captured, he should destroy all of his papers and attempt to deliver the messages orally. He was given money to buy any conveyance he needed to reach his destina-

Brigadier General James A. Hardie. (Library of Congress)

tions. Hardie first journeyed from Washington to Relay, Maryland, a station about ten miles west of Baltimore, and there changed trains for Frederick.[24]

Once on the train, Hardie wound up being seated next to General Sickles, who was on his way back to the army after a leave of absence in New York due to what he called "a contusion from a fragment of a shell" suffered at Chancellorsville. Seated with Hardie and Sickles was Captain James E. Smith, commander of the Fourth New York Independent Battery in Sickles's Corps, who had boarded the train with his corps commander. Sickles recalled Hardie "chatting all the way [to Frederick], without ever revealing a word of his mission."[25]

The special train carrying Hardie arrived at the station at All Saints and Market Streets in Frederick around midnight. Entirely in civilian dress, as ordered, Hardie sought the whereabouts of Meade's headquarters. By "liberal use of money," he obtained a buggy and driver who knew the roads to, and the location of, the Fifth Corps campsites at Arcadia, south of town. It was not easy, as "all the roads leading to the camps were thronged with boisterous soldiers, more or less filled with Maryland whiskey, and many of them ripe for rudeness or mischief."[26]

At about 3:00 A.M. Sunday, 28 June, Hardie arrived at Arcadia. He walked to the tent of Lieutenant Colonel Frederick T. Locke, the assistant adjutant general of the Fifth Corps, believing it was Meade's. Examining Hardie's credentials, Locke told him that Meade's tent was next to his. Hardie stepped inside. He walked up to Meade's cot; the general was sound asleep. After some gentle nudging, Hardie told Meade he had come there to give him trouble. Meade wrote afterward that his first thought was that Hardie was there either to relieve him from command or arrest him for some unknown wrongdoing. Meade "promptly" told Hardie that "his conscience was clear, void of offense towards any man and that he was prepared for his bad news." Locke recalled hearing Meade state to Hardie: "Well, I have always tried to do my duty in any position in which I have been placed." Locke, too, thought Meade had been placed under arrest.[27]

The document Hardie gave to Meade read as follows:

> General
> You will receive with this the order of the President placing you in command of the Army of the Potomac. Considering the circumstances, no one ever received a more important command; and I cannot doubt that you will fully justify the confidence which the government has reposed in you.

You will not be hampered by any minute instructions from these headquarters. Your army is free to act as you may deem proper under the circumstances as they arise. You will, however, keep in view the important fact that the Army of the Potomac is the covering army of Washington, as well as the army of operation against the invading forces of the rebels. You will therefore maneuver and fight in such a manner as to cover the Capital and also Baltimore, as far as circumstances will admit. Should General Lee move upon either of these places, it is expected that you will either anticipate him or arrive with him, so as to give him battle.

All forces within the sphere of your operations will be held subject to your orders.

Harper's Ferry and its garrison are under your direct orders.

You are authorized to move from command and send from your army any officer or other person you may deem proper; and to appoint to command as you may deem expedient.

In fine, General, you are entrusted with all the power and authority which the President, the Secretary of War, or the General-in-Chief can confer on you, and you may rely on our full support.

You will keep me fully informed of all your movements and the positions of your own troops and those of the enemy, so far as known.

I shall always be ready to advise and assist you to the utmost of my ability.

Very respectfully, Your obedient servant,

H. W. Halleck

General-in-Chief[28]

Meade at first protested against being placed in command of an army that he believed wanted General Reynolds as the successor to Hooker; his personal relationship with Reynolds made it difficult for him to accept such an appointment. He further expressed his concern about being placed in command of the army in the presence of the enemy when he knew nothing of its positions or dispositions. Meade asked Hardie to telegraph Stanton requesting that he be relieved from the order. Hardie told Meade that all of his protests had been discussed in the council, that it had been assumed he would ask to be relieved and that Reynolds, or almost anyone else, be named commander. The council, Hardie replied sternly, determined that Hooker must be replaced by Meade alone. Hardie recalled that Meade then said ruefully, "Well, I've been tried and condemned without a hearing, and I suppose I shall have to go to execution." Meade called for his orderly and horse, dressing as hurriedly as he could in a worn army blouse over the mud-spattered trousers in which he slept and pulling on thigh-length boots. He donned his old slouch hat and quickly called upon his son, George, to "mount up" as fast as possible. Meade probably mounted his favorite horse, Old Baldy; it had carried him through all his battles.[29]

By about 5:00 A.M., the entourage reached the turnpike that stretched between Frederick and Jefferson. There, they traveled down the road and, near the toll gate, turned into the property containing the large brick house known as Prospect Hall. Hooker's headquarters' tents were pitched on the lawn.[30]

Hardie first walked to the tent of the telegrapher. Just before 5:30 A.M., Hardie dictated a terse message to Halleck: "I have accomplished my mission. Will telegraph again in an hour or two." Of concern next was how Hooker would relinquish command.[31]

Meade wanted to meet with Brigadier General Gouverneur Kemble Warren, the chief engineer of the army, first. He did not want General Butterfield to serve as chief of staff if he could help it; he thought highly of Warren. Only thirty-three years old, Warren was born at Cold Spring, New York, across the Hudson River from West Point. He entered West Point at age sixteen, graduating in 1850. Warren served in the topographical engineers, mapping many of the states west of the Mississippi River. When the war broke out, he helped raise, and then was commissioned lieutenant colonel of, the Fifth New York, serving with that regiment at the Battle of Big Bethel and then as its regimental commander during the Siege of Yorktown. He assisted chief topographical engineer Brigadier General Andrew Atkinson Humphreys during the advance up the Peninsula, and then he commanded a brigade in the Fifth Corps in the Seven Days Battles and at Second Bull Run. Promoted to brigadier general in September 1862, Warren commanded his brigade in the Battle of Fredericksburg. After General Hooker took command of the Army of the Potomac, Warren was named chief topographical engineer of the army, which position he still held on 28 June.[32]

Meade was led to Warren's tent at army headquarters around 5:30 A.M. Warren heard Meade's voice and woke up. "I am in command of the Army of the Potomac," Meade said, "and I want you to be my chief of staff." In the ensuing discussion, Warren recalled that he "earnestly advised" Meade to retain Butterfield, "because of the great help he could give [him] from his knowledge of the actual affairs and recent orders, instructions, etc." Warren further told Meade that his position as chief engineer "was really more

Brigadier General Gouverneur Kemble Warren. (Library of Congress)

important to [Meade] because [Warren] knew what to do in that place."
Meade generally accepted Warren's advice; Warren would remain, however, one of Meade's closest confidants throughout the ensuing campaign.
Warren's sharp judgment on this and other matters confirmed Meade's
justly placed confidence in him, but Meade wasn't quite through trying to
find a chief of staff other than Butterfield.[33]

One officer at army headquarters Meade would not hesitate to keep was
Assistant Adjutant General Seth Williams. Born in Maine, the forty-one-
year-old Williams was an 1842 graduate of West Point. He served in the
Mexican War and then as adjutant general of the military academy. More
recently, the balding, officious Williams served as adjutant general of the
Army of the Potomac under McClellan, Burnside, and Hooker. He was a
thorough professional and was well liked by Meade and his fellow generals. Meade met with Williams briefly and asked him about serving as
both chief of staff and adjutant general, but Williams declined to accept
the added responsibility. Meade told Williams that he would remain as
adjutant general. Meade then braced himself for the meeting with Hooker
and his staff.[34]

Approaching Hooker's headquarters tent, Hardie and Meade were
greeted by not only Hooker but Butterfield, along with a host of staff officers, soldiers, and civilian clerks. Seth Williams soon joined the gathering.
One of the officers at army headquarters was Captain Thomas W. Hyde,
an aide to General Sedgwick who was delivering dispatches that morning.
Hyde could not help looking at Meade. He was dressed, Hyde recalled, "in
his well-worn uniform, splashed with mud, with his glasses, and his nervous and earnest air; [he] looked more like a learned pundit than a soldier." Walking Hooker back into his tent, Hardie took it upon himself to
break the news to him privately that he would be relieved from command
and that Meade would replace him. Hooker likely needed no one to tell
him the news after seeing all of his visitors at such an early hour. "It was
a bitter moment to all," remembered Charles F. Benjamin, a clerk at army
headquarters. "Hooker's chagrin and Meade's overstrung nerves made
the lengthy but indispensible conference rather trying to the whole party,"
Benjamin wrote. Meade broke the tension by insisting on being regarded
as a guest at headquarters so long as General Hooker was present and by
requesting that Butterfield not exercise his privilege of leaving the army
with Hooker but, rather, stay on to continue to serve as chief of staff.[35]

At 7:00 A.M., Meade interrupted the meeting, probably at Hardie's insistence, in order to dictate to a telegrapher at army headquarters a response to Halleck's letter that accompanied the president's order placing

Adjutant General Seth Williams. (Library of Congress)

him in command of the Army of the Potomac. Hardie was anxious that Halleck get a response from Meade. Meade wrote his response on the desk of Assistant Adjutant General Williams:

> The order placing me in command of this army is received. As a soldier, I obey it, and to the utmost of my ability will execute it. Totally unexpected as it has been, and in ignorance of the exact condition of the troops and position of the enemy, I can only now say that it appears to me I must move towards the Susquehanna, keeping Washington and Baltimore well covered, and if the enemy is checked in his attempt to cross the Susquehanna, or if he turns toward Baltimore, to give him battle. I would say that I trust that every available man that can be spared will be sent to me, as, from all accounts, the enemy is a strong force. As soon as I can post myself up I will communicate more in detail.[36]

An aide galloped back to Arcadia and informed Lieutenant Colonel Locke that Hooker was relieved and Meade had assumed command of the Army of the Potomac. Locke was directed to inform Major General George Sykes, the forty-one-year-old commander of the Second Division of the Fifth Corps, that he was now in command of the Fifth Corps in Meade's former place.[37]

Outside, the drizzling rain continued to fall. From the spires of Trinity Chapel, St. John's Roman Catholic Church, All Saints Episcopal Church, and the twin spires of the Evangelical Lutheran Church of Frederick, bells pealed announcing Sunday morning services. Hooker and Meade reviewed the maps closely; Meade first needed to establish the whereabouts of all of the elements of his own army. The evening before, Meade had led his own Fifth Corps into the fields around Arcadia, south of Frederick, having marched all the way from the Potomac River crossing at Edwards Ferry. It had been a tiring march, amounting to more than twenty-five miles over hilly country. The Fifth remained at Arcadia that morning; Meade was aware that Brigadier General Samuel W. Crawford's division of Meade's old Pennsylvania Reserves would have to march from the mouth of the Monocacy River to join the corps, a distance of about seventeen miles. All of the other elements of the army were preparing to move while Meade was meeting with Hooker.[38]

Pointing to the map, Hooker showed Meade that Reynolds's First Corps was under orders to march the eight miles from Middletown to Frederick along with Howard's Eleventh Corps. The Third Corps, over which General Sickles would again assume command within a matter of hours, was ordered to march from Middletown to Woodsboro, Maryland, a village about seven miles northeast of Frederick, a total distance of about fifteen miles. Sedgwick's Sixth Corps was to move from Poolesville to Hyattstown, Maryland, a town southeast of Frederick, a thirteen-mile march, and Slocum's Twelfth Corps was ordered to march to Frederick from Knoxville, a village at the base of the South Mountain range on the Potomac River. In all, the Twelfth Corps would march nearly eighteen miles.[39]

Hooker also brought to Meade's attention the fact that Brigadier General John Buford's cavalry division had been directed to ride from Jefferson to Middletown to replace the First, Third, and Eleventh Corps in order to protect the western approaches to Frederick from Hagerstown along the National Road through Turner Pass, and to protect against enemy movements through Crampton's Gap. General Gregg's cavalry division had been ordered to take up positions near New Market and Ridgeville, Maryland, along the National Road, connecting Frederick with Baltimore, in order to protect the army to the east. After having heard Hooker's explanation, Meade, recalled Benjamin, "unguardedly expressed himself as shocked at the scattered condition of the army."[40]

Supplying the army while at and near Frederick was the double-track main line of the Baltimore & Ohio Railroad, which ran from Baltimore, sixty-one miles, to Monocacy Junction, southeast of Frederick, with its spur line that extended from that junction to the southern suburbs of Frederick. The main line of the railroad ran south to Harper's Ferry, then westward to Martinsburg in present-day West Virginia, and then all the way to Grafton. Since 1835, the Baltimore & Ohio Railroad also operated a line that led from Baltimore to Washington, terminating on New Jersey Avenue. That line diverted from the main line at a place called Relay, Maryland, later Washington Junction, about ten miles southwest of Baltimore, where there was a two-and-one-half-story hotel known as Relay House. The main line headed northwest from Relay, following the Patapsco River past Ellicott Mills, and then all the way due west to Frederick; the Washington line headed south from Relay to the capital city after crossing the gigantic stone Thomas Viaduct over the Patapsco River. It was along those two rail lines that the army was being resupplied. After the extensive marches from central Virginia to Maryland, the army was in desperate need of clothing, shoes, ordnance, horses, mules, forage, coal, steel, and subsistence stores. Along those two rail lines ran telegraph wires. That telegraph system, which the signal corps extended from the passenger station at Frederick to army headquarters at Prospect Hall, enabled the commander of the Army of the Potomac and General Halleck to

Brigadier General Marsena Rudolph Patrick. (Library of Congress)

communicate. The railroad line ran parallel to the National Road that led from Baltimore to Frederick. The National Road, a macadamized turnpike, was another main artery of supply for the army.[41]

Overseeing the supply of the Army of the Potomac was its quartermaster general, forty-five-year-old Brigadier General Rufus Ingalls. A native of Denmark, Maine, Ingalls was an 1843 graduate of West Point. He had served as a quartermaster ever since the Mexican War and was named quartermaster general of the Army of the Potomac early in the war. Ingalls had served under Generals McClellan, Burnside, and Hooker; Meade, who admired and respected Ingalls, quickly told him that he would continue in his role.[42]

Meade also desired to retain Brigadier General Marsena Rudolph Patrick as the army's provost marshal. A native of Watertown, New York, fifty-two-year-old Patrick was a classmate of Meade's at West Point. After serving in the Mexican War, he farmed in his home state until he became inspector general of New York troops at the outbreak of hostilities. He was then commissioned a brigadier general and assigned to McClellan's staff. He commanded a brigade in the First Corps during the Antietam Campaign, where he was reunited with Meade as a combat officer. Subsequently, McClellan appointed Patrick provost marshal general. He, too, continued under Generals Burnside and Hooker. He was a strict disciplinarian with a stentorian voice.[43]

The discussions between Meade and Hooker were well under way when General Reynolds and a number of his aides rode into headquarters, wishing to pay respects to their new commander. Headquarters clerk Benjamin could not help but notice how Reynolds was dressed. He "presented a neat figure" and wore a "close-fitting frock coat and a kepi which he held in his hand," a stark contrast to Meade. After observing Meade with a group of visiting officers, Benjamin reentered his own "little office tent" to continue his work. He was startled when he saw Meade ushering Reynolds into his quarters. Benjamin believed that because he was being screened by the traveling desk that he had placed on a table, his presence had not been perceived by the two illustrious visitors. He then heard Meade's and Reynolds's discussion.[44]

"Reynolds, I have been very anxious to have a talk with you since I have been put in command," Meade said. "I assure you, I never dreamed that the command was to be given to me. I had supposed, as everybody in the army did, that it would fall to you when a change was made. I never would have accepted it, but it was put upon me as an imperative order and I had to take it. I wanted you to understand this; but I am not here by my will;

and I can count on you, above all others, for the support that I would have given you, if you had been placed in the situation that I am in."[45]

"General, in my opinion, the command has fallen where it ought to fall," Reynolds replied. "If it had come to me in the same way, I should have been obliged to take it, but I am glad that it did not. I understand the difficulties of your position and you may rely upon me to serve you faithfully.[46]

After being thus assured, Meade turned to the scattered whereabouts of all the troops, most of which were then on the march toward Frederick. Meade detailed for Reynolds the nature of the communications he had received from Washington, what information he had obtained of the position of the enemy, and all that he had heard from Hooker and Butterfield. The meeting ended, and Reynolds mounted up and rode away from Prospect Hall with his aides. Meade returned to Hooker's headquarters tent, where his discussions with Hooker and Butterfield continued.[47]

Meade already understood from newspapers delivered in the camps that the enemy was in the Cumberland Valley of Maryland and Pennsylvania and that elements of Lee's army were "near" Harrisburg. The 27 June *New York Times* reported General Ewell's corps at Chambersburg, Pennsylvania, and "momentarily expected" to enter Carlisle. Governor Andrew Curtin of Pennsylvania, it read, was going to issue a proclamation calling for fifty thousand militia to defend the state. It reported vast numbers of refugees fleeing north to Harrisburg as Lee's army moved deeper into Pennsylvania. Earlier editions of the *New York Times* reported the Confederate force rapidly advancing toward the Pennsylvania capital. Those newspapers, however, were running stories that were generally twenty-four to forty-eight hours old at the time they were published.[48]

Stacks of dispatches that had been received at army headquarters over the past two days gave Meade some idea of the whereabouts of the enemy that was mostly on the west side of the South Mountain range. Hooker showed Meade all of them.[49]

On the late afternoon of 26 June, General Howard sent a report to Reynolds with fresh intelligence after his corps replaced Stahel's cavalry at Turner Pass and Crampton's Gap. A copy was sent to army headquarters. Meade carefully read it. "Fifteen of his headquarters cavalry," Howard wrote, "dashed into Boonsboro and galloped about a half mile beyond chasing out a squad of rebel cavalry." Howard reported that, after questioning the inhabitants of the town, the cavalrymen learned that Longstreet's corps camped between Keedysville and Sharpsburg, Maryland, the previous night and moved on to Hagerstown that morning. Corroborating the information previously provided by Stahel, Howard noted that

Ewell's corps had passed through Hagerstown on 16 June. On 25 June, Hill's corps passed through the area. Howard estimated Lee's army at "between 60,000 and 70,000 men," a remarkably accurate assessment. He concluded the dispatch: "Lee in person crossed the Potomac last night."[50]

Meade observed that on 27 June, Hooker's headquarters had received a report from the provost marshal of Howard's Eleventh Corps at Middletown that a "coach-load of passengers came from Hagerstown this morning"; all of them claimed that "between 90,000 and 100,000 rebels have passed on to Pennsylvania." They said that Ewell's, Longstreet's, and Hill's corps marched through Hagerstown and that Lee, himself passed through the day before. The rear guard of Hill's corps was moving through the town that morning. The passengers said that "the rebels had more than 300 pieces of artillery." They "have taken a large number of cattle, which they have sent to the rear," the agitated passengers claimed. "Foraging parties," they said, "were going in every direction picking up cattle and sheep and other supplies." General Reynolds, as the wing commander, wrote an endorsement on the provost marshal's report: "General Ewell is with Early's division in person, and their column is evidently directed on Gettysburg. They must pass Waynesborough, and have a good pike from there to Gettysburg, and from Gettysburg they have a good pike to return back to the Cumberland Valley, above Carlisle, if they design to."[51]

A report was sent to Hooker on 28 June, Meade discovered, that claimed that "the main body of General Stuart's cavalry" was spotted by Howard's Eleventh Corps outposts in Turner Pass, camping between Williamsport and Hagerstown, Maryland. Enemy cavalry began passing through Hagerstown "at the break of day." The rebels, noted Lieutenant Colonel Charles W. Asmussen, Howard's chief of staff, "are driving cattle and horses toward Williamsport." Although those Confederates were not the main body of Stuart's cavalry but, rather, elements of probably Generals Jenkins's and Imboden's brigades, they represented a large presence. Operating behind Lee's army as it moved north, those horsemen were overseeing the return to Virginia of vast amounts of quartermaster stores, as well as cattle, sheep, and horses that the army was seizing in Maryland and Pennsylvania.[52]

After reading all of the reports of enemy operations, Meade and Hooker discussed possible movements of the army. Hooker, it appears, provided Meade with "no plan of his own," nor did he offer Meade "any views that he may have had up to that moment," claimed Benjamin, the headquarters clerk. Hooker and Meade apparently conferred for a considerable time, however. After nearly eight hours, the conference ended.[53]

As the conference ended, General Hooker penned General Order No. 66, his last to the Army of the Potomac:

> In conformity with the orders of the War Department dated June 27, 1863, I relinquish the command of the Army of the Potomac. It is transferred to Maj. Gen. George G. Meade, a brave and accomplished officer, who has nobly earned the confidence and esteem of this army on many a well-fought field.
>
> Impressed with the belief that my usefulness as the commander of the Army of the Potomac is impaired, I part from it; yet not without the deepest emotion. The sorrow of parting with the comrades of so many battles is relieved by the conviction that the courage and devotion of this army will never cease nor fail; that it will yield to my successor, as it has to me, a willing and worthy support.
>
> With the earnest prayer that the triumphs of its arms may bring success worthy of it and the nation, I bid it farewell.[54]

On Seth Williams's field desk Meade then wrote General Order No. 67:

> By direction of the President of the United States, I hereby assume command of the Army of the Potomac.
>
> As a soldier, in obeying this order—an order totally unexpected and unsolicited—I have no promises or pledges to make. The country looks to this army to relieve it from the devastation and disgrace of a hostile invasion. Whatever fatigues and sacrifices we may be called upon to undergo, let us have in view constantly the magnitude of the interests involved, and let each man determine to do his duty, leaving to an all-controlling Providence the decision of the contest.
>
> It is with just confidence that I relieve in the command of the army an eminent and accomplished soldier, whose name must ever appear conspicuous in the history of its achievements; but I rely upon the hearty support of my companions in arms to assist me in the discharge of the duties of the important trust which has been confided to me.[55]

It was nearly 2:30 P.M. The conference had been proceeding, with a few interruptions, for the better part of eight hours. Lieutenant Colonel Hardie finally wrote a dispatch to General Halleck, which he handed to the telegrapher: "I shall return tonight. I have been waiting for the formal issue of the order of the late commander before telegraphing. This is now written. I have had a chance to ascertain the state of feeling and internal condition of the army. There is cause for satisfaction with it. The late commander leaves for Baltimore this afternoon." One can imagine the relief of those who received the dispatch in Washington.[56]

Around 6:00 or 7:00 P.M. General Hooker stood in front of his head-quarters tent and "took leave of the officers, soldiers and civilians" attached to his headquarters. All of those attached to army headquarters "were drawn up in line as Hooker passed along shaking hands with each one and laboring to stifle his emotions." Young Major Hyde, the provost marshal and acting inspector general of the Sixth Corps, who was standing nearby, recorded his impressions. "I bid General Hooker goodbye today and he was very kind to me," Hyde wrote his mother. "His farewell to us all was sad and I could not but feel for him." Then Hyde added: "I am glad he is going."[57]

Just before Hooker and his aides left for Relay and Washington, Second Corps commander General Hancock and his Second Division commander, General Gibbon, rode into army headquarters to congratulate Meade. "Hooker who was at headquarters when we reached there," recalled Gibbon, "did not appear in a good humor at all." Gibbon added: "We knew, then, very little of the circumstances attending [Hooker's] relief and did not feel much interest in them; all other feelings, so far as I was concerned, being swallowed up in one of relief at the change."[58]

Hancock and Gibbon apparently cheered Meade by their visit. Gibbon addressed Meade as "commander of the army," and Meade replied with a laugh: "I'll have you shot [for speaking of me thusly]." Meade had a sense of humor he would reveal only when he was in the company of those he liked and respected. "General Meade evidently felt very heavily the responsibility thus thrown upon his shoulders," recalled Gibbon, "and I think was cheered by the assurances he received of the confidence felt in his ability by the army and the predictions that we would now defeat Lee whenever the two armies came into contact." Hancock and Gibbon departed; they did not arrive at the campsites of the Second Corps east of Frederick until 10:00 P.M.[59]

General Howard, commander of the Eleventh Corps, was elated with Meade's elevation to command. He rode to Meade's headquarters to offer his congratulations. He had known Meade before the war and had served with him thus far during the war. When Howard entered Meade's tent, the new commander had his coat off, "for those June days were very warm," remembered Howard, and he noted that Meade "seemed different at Frederick. He was excited." Meade stood up and extended his hand. "How are you, Howard?" he said. Meade deflected all congratulations. Howard recalled that Meade "looked tall and spare, weary, and a little flushed, but

AS A SOLDIER, I OBEY IT

I knew him to be a good, honest soldier, and [I] gathered confidence and hope from his thoughtful face." Meade, Howard later noted, was "an esteemed, experienced regular officer, old enough to be my father, but like a father that one can trust without showing him any special regard. So we respected and trusted Meade from the beginning."[60]

Hooker and two of his closest aides, Major William H. Lawrence and Captain Harry Russell, mounted up. Lieutenant Colonel Hardie got in the buggy that was loaded with Hooker's baggage for the trip to the passenger station at All Saints and Market Streets in Frederick, where they would depart on a special Baltimore & Ohio train. Before the buggy, mounted officers, and escort got under way, the crowd moved aside as General Meade approached Hooker. Meade uncovered his head and extended his hand to Hooker. The two generals shook hands and exchanged a few words in "a low tone." With that, Hooker and his staff officers, the buggy with Hardie, and the mounted escort moved off. The necessary, orderly, and expeditious transfer of command was finally achieved. Meade had to transition quickly from a capable tactical commander to the operational commander of the Army of the Potomac.[61]

3

MY INTENTION NOW
IS TO MOVE TOMORROW

Meade walked silently back to the tent that Hooker had just vacated. He named three aides-de-camp: Major James Cornell Biddle, formerly with the Twenty-Third Pennsylvania, Captain William Jay of New York, and his own son, Captain George Meade. Joining Meade as well would be Lieutenant Colonel Joseph Dickinson and Captain Charles F. Cadwalader of Hooker's staff, Captain Addison G. Mason, and Major Benjamin Ludlow. Dickinson would serve as senior aide, a position he held under Hooker. Both Dickinson and Cadwalader were cited for their exemplary performance during the Battle of Chancellorsville by many commanders, including Meade. Young Captain George Meade was twenty years old; he left West Point in June 1862 after two years there and joined the Sixth Pennsylvania Cavalry, the regiment in which Captain Cadwalader had served before being assigned to Hooker's staff. Captains James Starr and Emlen N. Carpenter would also join Meade's staff as aides; both had served in the Sixth Pennsylvania Cavalry with young George Meade. Meade selected staff officers whom he knew well and who were members of prominent families, refined and well educated; Major Biddle, Captain Cadwalader, and Captain Jay, the grandson of Chief Justice John Jay, being examples. Young Captain Meade, Biddle, and Jay had served General Meade while he commanded the Fifth Corps. Also serving on Meade's staff would be Colonel Sharpe and Captains Babcock and McEntee of the Bureau of Military Information.[1]

Meade stepped out of his tent. Walking up to his son, he quietly said: "Well, George, I am in command of the Army of the Potomac." He then asked young Captain Meade to return to the Fifth Corps headquarters at Arcadia, bring back all of his belongings, and notify Biddle and Jay of their new assignments. General Meade asked that his African American

*Major General George Gordon Meade and staff, a photograph taken
less than three months after the Gettysburg Campaign. Pictured with Meade
are Generals Patrick, Humphreys, and Ingalls. The photograph provides a
glimpse of the number of officers and orderlies attached to the headquarters
of the Army of the Potomac. (Library of Congress)*

servant, John Marley, be brought to his new headquarters, as well as all
his other horses. In all, Meade would assign twelve commissioned officers
as aides on his staff. Beyond his aides and servant, Meade inherited from
Hooker anywhere from twenty to thirty mounted enlisted orderlies detached from cavalry regiments to assist the aides in carrying dispatches
and orders to subordinate commanders.[2]

Meade had asked Butterfield to continue to serve as chief of staff, but
as he had confided to Margaret, he was most uncomfortable with him.
Meade questioned Butterfield's character and doubted his loyalty. By contrast, Meade respected fifty-three-year-old Brigadier General Andrew
Atkinson Humphreys, then in command of the Second Division of Sickles's Third Corps. A native of Philadelphia, Humphreys hailed from a distinguished family of naval constructors. An 1831 graduate of West Point,
he served in various garrisons until he resigned his commission in 1836.
Reappointed on the reorganization of the Corps of Topographical Engineers in 1838, Humphreys had served with distinction in the Seminole

Brigadier General Andrew A. Humphreys. (Library of Congress)

War. He surveyed harbors, rivers, and coastal areas from the Atlantic Coast to the Mississippi River—and even on the Pacific railroad surveys—before finally being appointed to West Point as a member of a board to revise a program of instruction, as well as a member of a commission to examine the organization, systems of discipline, and course of instruction at the academy in 1860. After the war broke out, Humphreys served on the staff of General McClellan and as chief topographical engineer of the Army of the Potomac. Appointed a brigadier general in April 1862, he commanded the Third Division of the Fifth Corps in the Antietam Campaign and in the Battles of Fredericksburg and Chancellorsville. Humphreys and Meade had served in combat together.[3]

Hooker had apparently already left army headquarters when Meade directed Butterfield to request Humphreys, in writing, to meet with him. Humphreys rode to Meade's headquarters, where he "passed several hours" with the new army commander. During the course of their discussion, Meade asked Humphreys if he would agree to serve as his chief of staff. Humphreys "declined or deferred" the offer. He convinced Meade that he could provide greater service by retaining command of his division in the Third Corps in the impending battle. Indeed, Meade could not have agreed more that Sickles's corps was in desperate need of a competent division commander like Humphreys. Meade, however, resolved to renew the request as soon as he believed it necessary.[4]

One officer Meade retained at his headquarters was General Henry Jackson Hunt, the chief of artillery of the army. Forty-four years old, Hunt was a native of Detroit, Michigan, and an 1839 graduate of West Point. After service with General Winfield Scott in Mexico, Hunt became a member of a board established by the army to revise the system of light artillery tactics. Their report was adopted by the War Department in 1860 and was in use in the army throughout the war. Hunt had served with distinction through the fighting at First Manassas, the Peninsula, Antietam, Fredericksburg, and Chancellorsville. Most recently, he had been serving on the staffs of the army commanders as chief of artillery. He was widely credited with ensuring the victory at Malvern Hill with his placement of nearly one hundred guns, making that hill impossible for the enemy to take. Meade respected Hunt, although he was not close with him. Meade, nevertheless, would rely on Hunt's abilities as an artillery chief, as well as his related skills as an engineer. Time, however, did not permit Meade to articulate with specificity all of the duties he expected Hunt to assume.[5]

Meade's first order of business was to bring the army together to form a perimeter around Frederick to protect the men, wagon trains, supplies, ordnance, and horses and mules from Confederate cavalry attacks. Meade issued orders for the Second Corps to occupy a position "from Monocacy Junction to the bridge above Carroll Creek." The Eleventh Corps would extend the line from the left of the Second Corps "to George Schultz's [residence] on the road to Hamburg," north of Frederick. The First Corps would fill the area between the left of the Eleventh Corps and the Middle-town Road west of Frederick. The Twelfth Corps would form on the left of the First Corps extending the perimeter to Ballenger Creek, south of Frederick. The Fifth Corps would then fill the line between the Twelfth Corps and the Second Corps. The Third Corps bivouacked at Walkersville, seven miles north of Frederick on the road to Woodsboro. The Sixth Corps camped at Hyattstown, south of Frederick. A strong cavalry presence was directed to protect the Third and Sixth Corps because they were so distant from the rest of the army. In his detailed orders, Meade admonished the corps commanders to guard all wagon trains and camps and to appoint a staff officer from each corps to report to army headquarters. He urgently requested that every opportunity to replenish supplies should be taken by each corps commander.[6]

Meade closely examined maps of the area north of Frederick. Outside his tent the rain continued to fall. What limited intelligence he had already received informed him that Lee's army on 28 June was spread out along a front that extended in excess of fifty miles. From all accounts, Lee's army numbered anywhere from sixty to one hundred thousand troops, possibly more. Longstreet's corps was last seen at Hagerstown marching toward Greencastle, Pennsylvania; Hill's corps, for all anyone knew, was ahead of Longstreet, moving toward Chambersburg, Pennsylvania, forty-two miles north of Frederick. Elements of Ewell's corps had been spotted march-ing toward York, Pennsylvania, and, possibly, the Susquehanna River; some were heading north toward Harrisburg. Mostly, Lee's widely scat-tered forces were situated in the Cumberland Valley and along, or even perhaps north of, a macadamized turnpike in Pennsylvania that extended from Chambersburg, through Cashtown and Gettysburg, to York. That east-west Chambersburg-to-York turnpike in Pennsylvania appeared to Meade to be the reference line, or axis, for the disposition of most of Lee's invading forces. General Reynolds also seemed to reference the turnpike in his endorsement of General Howard's report of 27 June. Meade deter-mined that he must move the Army of the Potomac closer to that axis if he was to accomplish his mission.[7]

From the maps, Meade discovered a road network extending southeast from the Chambersburg-to-York turnpike axis and Gettysburg through

Frederick and Carroll Counties, Maryland, toward Baltimore. Four different roads ran south and southeast from Gettysburg that had to be denied use by the enemy if Meade's army was to protect the approaches to Baltimore and Washington. First, the Emmitsburg-Gettysburg Road extended south from Gettysburg to Emmitsburg, in Frederick County, a distance of about ten miles. At Emmitsburg, and nearly five miles south of that town, the road connected with two roads that led through Taneytown and Middleburg, in Carroll County, and on to Westminster, the county seat of Carroll County, twenty-two miles southeast of Gettysburg. About eleven miles east of Westminster, a road, originating in Harrisburg, led due south through Reisterstown, Maryland, and directly to Baltimore, known as the Harrisburg and Baltimore Road. Also extending south from Gettysburg was the Taneytown Road, which led to Taneytown, about thirteen miles distant. From Taneytown, another road ran another fifteen miles east through Frizzellburg, Maryland, to Westminster. Running southeast out of Gettysburg for more than twenty-two miles was the macadamized Baltimore Pike, which passed through Union Mills, Maryland, and on to Westminster. A fourth road extended from the Hanover Road, just east of Gettysburg, to Littlestown, seven miles south; at Littlestown it connected with the Baltimore Pike twelve miles northwest of Westminster. From Hanover, Pennsylvania, another road led due south through Manchester, Maryland, ten miles south of Hanover, to Reisterstown, nineteen miles south of Manchester, and on to Baltimore. To carry out the instructions to protect Baltimore and Washington, Meade's daunting task would be to have his forces occupy those roads to Baltimore and deny Confederate forces access to them. What Meade could not discern from the maps were any topographical features such as hills and ridges. Meade was using what were called residential maps, and they did not include such topographical features, although the Frederick County, Maryland, and Adams County, Pennsylvania, maps provided outlines of the South Mountain range, but nothing more.[8]

It appears that accurate topographical maps of much or all of the area across which Meade would have to conduct his campaign had been made by the War Department in the fall and winter of 1862. Recalled one topographical engineer officer: "[Those maps] showed the contour (of the ground) by lines of every twenty feet of elevation, as also every house, fence, knoll, and ravine." Unfortunately, the officer recalled, "no effort was made by those who had the matter in charge to have the maps finished and copies made."[9]

Meade not only had to protect Baltimore and Washington and, in the process, confront the enemy but had to be able to constantly resupply his enormous army with vast amounts of forage, subsistence stores, iron, coal, shoes, blankets, clothing, equipment, and ordnance. Meade observed a railroad line on the maps that led from Baltimore to Westminster, a line he was informed was operational. The Western Maryland Railroad, a company chartered in 1853, operated that line. Construction of the Western Maryland began in 1857 at another site called Relay, this one a station on the Northern Central Railroad seven miles north of Baltimore; the twenty-nine-mile, mostly single-track, rail line was completed to Westminster in 1861. It entered Westminster after passing Cranberry Station, Maryland, about three miles to the northeast. Bending southwest at Cranberry Station, the rail line ran through Westminster to Beacham's Station, New Windsor, and, then due west, to Union Bridge, Maryland, where it terminated about ten miles west of Westminster. The extension from Westminster to Union Bridge was completed in 1862. The Western Maryland Railroad operated about four trains a day between Baltimore and Westminster. It did not have a telegraph line in 1863 and would not have one in place until the following year. Yet, so long as the Western Maryland Railroad was open from Baltimore to Westminster, Meade concluded that he could use Westminster as his base of supply while occupying the road network that ran from the turnpike axis at Gettysburg south to Baltimore. The Western Maryland Railroad extension to Union Bridge, Meade reasoned, would enable him to bring supplies by rail to his forces even if elements of the army were fifteen or twenty miles west of Westminster.[10]

Meade was concerned by the needy condition of the troops and their powerful lack of even basic items, such as clothing, shoes, and socks. Meade met with General Ingalls to be brought up to date. As a result of the meeting, Ingalls ordered "10,000 pair of bootees and the same number of socks," with the aim of issuing them as the troops marched north from Frederick.[11]

Meade had been previously notified by telegraph from General Halleck, while he was meeting with Ingalls about supplies, that General Couch at Harrisburg had been placed under Meade's command. Halleck directed Couch to send to Meade any information of the enemy's movements in Couch's vicinity immediately. Up to this time, Meade's concerns about enemy activity had been directed to the west, across the South Mountain range, and to the north.[12]

As early as 1:00 P.M., 28 June, at least four hours before Hooker left, Meade received a message from Halleck: enemy activity had been spotted east of Frederick! Halleck dispatched a note to Meade by telegraph that "a brigade of Fitzhugh Lee's cavalry has crossed the Potomac near Seneca Falls, and is making for the railroad [between Frederick and Baltimore] to cut off your supplies." That was likely the same cavalry spotted in Pooles-ville, Maryland, earlier by General Sedgwick. The Baltimore & Ohio Rail-road was not all that was in harm's way. The quartermaster and subsis-tence stores that still remained at Edwards Ferry after the army completed its crossing of the Potomac River were completely unprotected, wrote Halleck, and, if that was not bad enough, a large wagon train of supplies was en route to the army along the National Road from Baltimore, liter-ally in the path of the enemy cavalry. That wagon train, it was believed, was completely exposed.[13]

Indeed, the three Confederate cavalry brigades of General Stuart that had been sent by Lee on 24 June to gallop behind the Union army had crossed the Potomac River at Seneca Falls east of the Army of the Poto-mac. Stuart's command was in fact operating between Meade and Balti-more and Washington. The brigades of Generals Fitzhugh Lee and Hamp-ton and Colonel Chambliss, along with six pieces of artillery, were heading north toward Meade's supply and communication lines of the Baltimore & Ohio Railroad and the National Road.[14]

These rapid developments involving threats to his supply and com-munication lines were followed by more bad news for Meade. Just after 3:00 P.M., while Hooker was still at army headquarters, Meade was in-formed by General Halleck that 150 wagons had been captured near Rock-ville, Maryland. Quartermaster General Montgomery Meigs angrily wrote to General Ingalls at Meade's headquarters. Meigs told Ingalls that all the bootees and socks had been ordered and that they would be sent to the army "as soon as a safe route and escort can be found." He then launched into a harsh reminder that "last fall I gave orders to prevent the sending of wagon trains from this place to Frederick without escort. The situation re-peats itself, and gross carelessness and inattention to military rule has this morning cost us 150 wagons and 900 mules, captured by cavalry between this [place] and Rockville." Meigs continued his message in a resentful tone: "All the cavalry of the Defenses of Washington was swept off by the army, and we are now insulted by burning wagons 3 miles outside of Ten-nallytown." He ended his note to Ingalls by ruefully adding: "Your com-munications are now in the hands of General Fitzhugh Lee's brigade."[15]

To compound the problem, Stuart's horsemen cut the telegraph wires for a considerable distance along the Baltimore & Ohio Railroad. Meade's ability to communicate by telegraph with General Halleck in Washing-ton or with General Schenck in Baltimore was now severed. Tracks were

Quartermaster General Montgomery Meigs. (Library of Congress)

taken up and at least two bridges along the Baltimore & Ohio Railroad, at Hood's Mill and Sykesville, between Frederick and Baltimore, were set on fire and partially destroyed. Meade now lacked any means of communicating with General Couch by telegraph as Lee's army was operating between the Army of the Potomac and Harrisburg. All telegraphic communication with Couch had been routed through Relay, Baltimore, and Washington, but that was now shut down.[16]

Necessity demanded that communications with Relay, Baltimore, and

Washington be reopened, and quickly. Still, it would take twenty-four to forty-eight hours to do so. Meade undoubtedly called upon General Ingalls. The quartermaster department not only oversaw the sock orders but also directed all telegraphic communications of the army. Telegraphic repair crews were dispatched from the army to replace the wires. Ingalls likely requested the Adams Express Company to lend its assistance. It appears that an effort was put in motion to set up mounted relays along the National Road from Frederick to Relay. As was customary, stations with fresh horses and couriers were put in place at intervals of usually seven miles. Messages would be galloped from one station to the next; at each successive station, a courier on a fresh horse would carry the message to the next station much like the Pony Express. Track crews were dispatched by Ingalls and the Baltimore & Ohio Railroad to repair the tracks and bridges. In the meantime, Meade was completely out of touch with his government. Such was Meade's rude introduction to command.[17]

Before the Confederate cavalry's interference with the telegraph lines, Meade's headquarters had received a raft of reports that originated with General Couch at Harrisburg and were forwarded by Halleck to Meade while the telegraph was still in operation. All the bridges on the Northern Central Railroad, between Hanover Junction and Harrisburg, were being burned by the enemy, Couch reported. The Northern Central extended from Harrisburg through Hanover Junction to Reisterstown, Maryland, and Baltimore. The forwarded dispatches notified Meade that General Rodes's Division of Ewell's Corps was near Carlisle. Another report announced that York, Pennsylvania, "surrendered." Yet another dispatch from Couch forwarded by Halleck announced that 14,000 Confederate infantry and 2,000 cavalry "entered" Carlisle. Couch was even gathering explosives along with combustible materials to set at places along the public bridge over the Susquehanna River to be detonated if the enemy reached there. In addition, Couch sent several reports of Confederate cavalry being observed as far west as near Bedford County, Pennsylvania. There was also word from Couch that there were "15,000 [enemy troops] in or near Carlisle, and 4,000 to 8,000 from Gettysburg to York and Hanover." Meade had to cope with a bewildering amount of information, made even more difficult to assess because of Lee's army's widely scattered movements.[18]

Army headquarters also received from the War Department a written statement of a civilian from Hagerstown, Maryland. Thomas McCammon, a blacksmith, had left Hagerstown and entered the Union lines to report what he had observed. He claimed that General Jenkins's cavalry brigade passed through Hagerstown "a week ago last Monday." The cavalry "went back and forth out of Pennsylvania, driving horses and cattle," repeating a report Meade was now seeing frequently. The first infantry passed through Hagerstown shortly thereafter, identified as Ewell's corps. "Generals Ewell and Rodes," along with two other generals, "attended Catholic Church there on Sunday," read McCammon's statement. These troops "left in the direction of Greencastle [Pennsylvania] in the afternoon." McCammon reported that all of Longstreet's corps, except two brigades, passed through town on 27 June. He said that he saw Longstreet and that Longstreet and Lee had their headquarters at a Mr. James H. Groves's farm on the road to Greencastle the previous night. They left at about 8:00 A.M. Hill's corps, he claimed, passed through Hagerstown ahead of Longstreet. A "prominent lawyer and leading Confederate sympathizer, James D. Roman, was heard saying that Lee's army is nearly 100,000 strong," McCammon wrote. "Other residents of Hagerstown," he noted, "have taken pains to count the rebels, and could not make them over 80,000." They counted the artillery at 275 guns. Some regiments, they claimed, had only 175 men; two appeared to have barely 150. Lee's army had extensive "transportation," and a great many of the wagons appeared to have been captured at Winchester. McCammon recalled seeing Brigadier Generals Cadmus Wilcox's and Joseph B. Kershaw's wagon trains; he had been informed that Kershaw's brigade was in McLaws's Division of Longstreet's corps. He saw General Hood and Brigadier General Lewis A. Armistead, and he got a glimpse of Pickett's Division. McCammon noted that Lee's men carry "lots of Confederate money; [they] carry it in flour barrels." That money, Meade must have recognized, was being used to purchase quartermaster and subsistence stores for the army. McCammon's was the most detailed and accurate description of Lee's invading forces that Meade had yet seen. At 4:45 P.M., with General Hooker nearby, Meade forwarded McCammon's written statement to General Halleck by couriers.[19]

By Halleck's 27 June orders, Meade was given command over the garrison at Harper's Ferry. It appears that the confidence Lincoln, Halleck, and Stanton had in Hooker had diminished to such a degree that they had refused him command over any forces not attached to his army. Had that been designed to drive Hooker from command? It may have been. Having been given command over the Union garrison at Harper's Ferry by Halleck, Meade sent a dispatch to General French at 6:00 P.M. asking him to provide a count of the number of men that would be sufficient to hold the heights northeast of Harper's Ferry in the event of an attack and whether the garrison would be ready to move the next day. French informed Meade later that "five thousand reliable men could make a practicable defense" of Harper's Ferry. "I do not consider the force here stronger than that," French added. He then informed Meade: "I have made no preparations beyond having three days' rations on hand, not anticipating being moved without renewed notice."[20]

At 7:00 P.M. on 28 June, Quartermaster General Meigs sent a message to Ingalls by couriers that the clothing and accoutrements ordered by Meade would leave Washington by rail. The train, Meigs noted, would carry "20,000 pair of bootees, 10,000 pair of socks, and all the coal ordered yesterday." In addition, "600,000 pounds of grain" were ready to be shipped along with the other supplies. With the telegraph wires down, it would take hours for this reassuring message to arrive at Meade's headquarters. It would take even longer for the supplies to reach the army, given the inoperable state of the Baltimore & Ohio Railroad.[21]

Next, several disturbing dispatches were handed to Meade. One came from Brigadier General Adolph von Steinwehr of the Eleventh Corps, whose headquarters had been at the Mountain House in Turner Pass. Steinwehr reported that five thousand of Stuart's cavalry had passed through Williamsport, Maryland, the day before. General Sedgwick, whose Sixth Corps was on the march from Poolesville to Frederick, reported that three thousand Confederate cavalry were in his rear. Alarmingly, it now appeared that a Confederate cavalry force was between the army and Washington! "My impression," Meade quickly wrote to General Halleck, "is that Stuart has divided his force, with a view of harassing our right and left flanks."[22]

At 9:00 P.M., Meade sent a note by couriers to Halleck providing him with the details of his intended movement of the army in the morning. "My intention," Meade wrote, "is now to move tomorrow on three lines to Emmitsburg and Westminster, having the army on the road from Emmitsburg through Westminster, or as near there as we can march." Meade then added: "This movement is based upon what information we have here of the enemy's movement." Meade informed Halleck that he was unsure of the disposition of the garrison at Harper's Ferry and then solicited Halleck's "views as to the movements proposed."[23]

Meade later testified that on 28 June he determined to move the army as fast as possible along the principal line from Frederick toward Harrisburg, "extending the wings of the army on both sides of that line as far as safety would permit," and would continue to do so until he encountered the enemy or until the enemy was about to encounter the Army of the Potomac. The object of such a movement would be to compel the enemy to "loose his hold on the Susquehanna and meet in battle at some point." Meade believed he had to "give battle wherever and as soon as he could possibly find the enemy." He then noted that "some maneuvers might be made with a view to secure advantages on our side in that battle, and not allow them to be secured by the [enemy]." If anyone thought that Meade was timid, that was put to rest on 28 June. With as little intelligence of the positions of the enemy as Meade had available, he determined to move the army toward the Chambersburg-to-York turnpike axis.[24]

At a late hour on what must have been one of the longest days of Meade's life, while perusing maps of Frederick and Carroll Counties, Maryland, Meade dictated orders to his assistant adjutant general, Seth Williams, for the movement of the army on the following day. Throughout the ensuing campaign Meade would prefer to dictate his orders to Seth Williams and not his chief of staff, Daniel Butterfield. Although some orders would be dictated to Butterfield, Meade and Butterfield "were not on good terms." Where possible, Meade maintained a distance from his chief of staff. That strained relationship only added to the difficulties facing Meade. Meade chose Williams to prepare the first marching orders he gave to the army.[25]

Meade ordered Reynolds's First Corps to march north to Emmitsburg by way of Lewistown and Mechanicstown, Maryland, at 4:00 A.M. on 29 June. Reynolds was directed to keep "to the left of the road from Frederick to Lewistown, between J. P. Cramer's [residence] and where the road branches to Utica and Cregerstown," to enable Howard's Eleventh Corps to march parallel to the First Corps to Emmitsburg. At the same hour, Slocum's Twelfth Corps was ordered to march to Taneytown by way to Ceresville, Walkersville, and Woodsboro, Maryland; Hancock's Second Corps was directed to march to Frizzellburg by way of Johnsville, Liberty, and Uniontown, Maryland, followed by Sykes's Fifth Corps and the engineers and bridge trains of the army. Sykes was directed to halt his corps at Uniontown. Sedgwick's Sixth Corps was ordered to march "to the right" of the Second and Fifth Corps to New Windsor, Maryland. Sickles's Third Corps was ordered to march to Taneytown by way of Woodsboro and Middleburg, Maryland, at four in the morning, too. Tyler's Reserve Artillery was directed to precede the Twelfth Corps to a location between Middleburg and Taneytown. All of the corps commanders and commanders of detached brigades were ordered to report to Meade by a staff officer their exact positions on the night of 29 June and similarly on all future marches. Communications, Meade directed, must be kept up all along the way. Scouts were ordered sent out in front of the columns to "bring in information," and "strong exertions [were] required and must be made to prevent straggling."[26]

"The cavalry," Meade directed, "will guard the right and left flanks and the rear, and give the commanding general information of the movements, etc., of the enemy in front." Meade conferred with General Pleasonton, the cavalry corps commander, and left it to him to provide his division commanders more detailed instructions.[27]

By 10:30 P.M., General Meigs confirmed to General Ingalls the report that the Confederate cavalry that crossed the Potomac River at Seneca Falls was composed of three full brigades, more than six thousand men, and that General Stuart was in command "in person." Stuart's command was heading north toward the Western Maryland Railroad and Westminster, Maryland, directly on and toward Meade's projected line of supply and communication and supply base.[28]

Civilian informants, organized by forty-year-old Gettysburg lawyer David McConaughy, provided what may have been the last piece of intelligence received at army headquarters that night. For sure, it was the most up-to-date intelligence Meade read that day. R. G. McCreary, T. D. Carson, a cashier at the Bank of Gettysburg, and McConaughy informed Meade by a written report dated 27 June that "about 200 cavalry, one battery, and 2,000 infantry occupied Gettysburg last night (26 June), and moved this morning toward Hanover Junction, on the Northern Central Railroad." They claimed that the force was "part of Ewell's corps under Early; the cavalry under [Colonel Elijah V.] White." Another column was "reported as moving five miles north of Gettysburg in the direction of York," and they stated that the Confederates "told the country people that another column would come from Carlisle and meet them at York." All this information seemed to corroborate the reports from General Couch.[29]

It had been an extraordinary and all-consuming day for the new commander of the army. Meade probably never retired that night; instead, he managed getting only short naps. His rude and sudden awakening that morning probably seemed to have taken place a lifetime ago rather than less than a day ago. Meade had not even found the time to write to Margaret about being named commander of the Army of the Potomac.

4

I AM MOVING
AT ONCE AGAINST
LEE

Monday morning, 29 June, dawned misty with more drizzling rain. In the dark, early hours in his headquarters tent, Meade took a few moments to write Margaret as the camp was being dismantled around Prospect Hall. He broke the news that he had been named commander of the Army of the Potomac. "It has pleased Almighty God," he wrote, "to place me in the trying position that for some time past we have been talking about." He then added:

> As, dearest, you know how reluctant we both have been to see me placed in this position, and it appears to be God's will for some good purpose—at any rate, as a soldier, I had nothing to do but accept and exert my utmost abilities to command success. This, so help me God, I will do, and trusting to Him, who in his good pleasure has thought it proper to place me where I am, I shall pray for strength and power to get through with the task assigned me.... I am moving at once against Lee.... Pray earnestly, pray for the success of my country. Love to all.[1]

The cavalry corps of the army had undergone an organizational change within the past twenty hours. One of the last orders issued by General Hooker on 28 June was a directive relieving General Stahel of command of his division of cavalry and notifying him that he was being reassigned to General Couch's Department of the Susquehanna in Harrisburg. On the heels of that order, General Pleasonton directed Brigadier General Wesley Merritt to report to General Buford, where he would command a third brigade in the First Division. Stahel's command was designated the Third Division, and command of it was given to Brigadier General Hugh Judson Kilpatrick, an 1860 graduate of West Point. To command brigades in Kilpatrick's division, Pleasonton assigned Brigadier General Elon J. Farnsworth and newly appointed Brigadier General George Armstrong Custer, who was then only two years out of West Point.[2]

Meade met with General Pleasanton late the night before, commanding him to move early in the morning. He delegated the issuance of detailed orders to Pleasanton but admonished Pleasanton to protect the army's flanks and provide him with desperately needed information of the whereabouts of Lee's army.[3]

In accordance with Meade's overall plans to advance the army, General Pleasonton issued orders for the cavalry corps on the morning of 29 June. Pursuant to those orders, two of General Buford's brigades, Colonels William Gamble's and Thomas C. Devin's, along with a battery of artillery, left Middletown and moved west of the army, through Turner Pass, to Boonsboro, and then along the western base of the South Mountain range to Cavetown, Maryland. Those two brigades were directed to recross the mountains, pass through Monterey Gap, and encamp near Fairfield, Pennsylvania, a fifty-mile operation.[4]

A third brigade—Brigadier General Wesley Merritt's, along with a battery of artillery—was ordered to march with the wagon trains of the division "by way of Frederick City, Adamsville, Lewistown, and Catoctin Furnace to Mechanicstown [Maryland]." Gamble's and Devin's brigades screened the left flank of the army west of the South Mountain range. Merritt rode along the eastern base of the Catoctin Mountain range, using detachments to "visit" Hagerstown, Cavetown, and other sites west of the South Mountain range, so as to keep the army informed of any enemy movements in the Cumberland Valley.[5]

Two brigades of General Gregg's division, along with an artillery battery, under Pleasonton's orders, were galloping east of the army, screening its right flank, "from Ridgeville, by way of Carter's [residence], to Westminster [Maryland]." The third brigade of the division and an artillery battery were to ride to New Windsor "by the way of Liberty and Unionville."[6]

To the newly installed commander of the Third Cavalry Division, General Kilpatrick, Pleasonton gave orders for one of his brigades—General Farnsworth's—to move "by way of Woodsborough, Bruceville, and Taneytown, [Maryland] to Littlestown, [Pennsylvania]," a distance of forty miles. General Custer's brigade, along with an artillery battery, were ordered to "move by Utica, Creagerstown, and Graceham, to Emmitsburg, [Maryland,]" and then on to Littlestown, just under fifty miles distant. Pleasonton's headquarters would be established at Middleburg. There, most of the wagon trains of the cavalry corps were ordered to assemble.[7]

Major General Alfred Pleasonton. (Library of Congress)

All around Fredrick, bugle signals, and "The General" from the regimental drummers, aroused the troops—more than ninety thousand of them—beginning at 3:00 A.M. There was no time to cook breakfast; the soldiers would eat hard bread on the march. Tents were taken down and baggage was loaded in wagons. Corporal Johnson of the Twenty-Ninth Pennsylvania performed a duty that was probably repeated by noncommissioned officers in most of the regiments in the army, writing: "I issued eight pair of shoes received from the regimental quartermaster this morning."[8]

"Attention" was sounded. "Fall in," yelled company commanders. At the call "Forward," muskets were brought to "right shoulder shift," and the columns prepared to march. Troops in each of the seven corps were formed in four columns all through the morning hours; two columns were ordered to march on either side of the roads. At the command "March," the long columns moved out alongside the roads. All of the artillery batteries and long lines of quartermaster, subsistence, ordnance, and ambulance wagon trains, seven to ten miles in length in each of Meade's seven army corps, rumbled along in the middle of the roads. Lumbering along in and among the subsistence trains were large herds of cattle and their mounted drovers. Mounted regimental, brigade, division, and corps commanders and their staffs rode in the center of the roads in the midst of their commands. Captain Hyde, of General Sedgwick's staff, sent his mother a letter describing the march that morning. His brief description of the Sixth Corps provides a glimpse into the immenseness of the army. "To give you some idea of an army," he wrote, "our Corps of 16,000 men with its wagons takes six hours to get in motion, and on the road is 9½ miles long." That would make the Army of the Potomac nearly one hundred miles in length if all its seven corps and its artillery reserve and cavalry corps were stretched out on one road.[9]

The army was on the move. Reynolds's First Corps, 12,157 officers and men according to the last returns, left Frederick punctually and was marching toward Lewistown and Mechanicstown on its way to Emmitsburg, twenty-six miles distant. The Second Corps, 14,373 officers and men, got a late start, due, it seems, to Meade's order not being delivered to General Hancock in a timely manner. Only by 9:00 A.M. was the Second Corps on the march toward Johnsonville and Liberty; the men had a long way to go before they would halt at their destination, Uniontown, thirty miles away. Sickles's Third Corps, its last returns showing 13,881 officers and men, marched out of Walkersville on their seventeen-mile trek to Taneytown. Sykes's Fifth Corps, in all 15,102 officers and men, followed the Second Corps toward Liberty, and Howard's Eleventh Corps, 12,096 officers and men, trudged along behind the First Corps on its way to Emmitsburg. Slocum's Twelfth Corps, 9,816 officers and men, was marching to Taneytown behind all of the Reserve Artillery brigades, a twenty-three-mile trek. Sedgwick's Sixth Corps, the largest in the army at 17,625 officers and men, left Hyattstown and was on the road east of Frederick, on Meade's right flank, heading toward New Windsor, a distance of twenty-seven miles. The army medical wagon trains were ordered to follow the army headquarters wagon trains, along with the signal corps train. The engineer train conveying bridge trestlework and pontoons were ordered to follow the Fifth Corps.[10]

Jacob Engelbrecht, a merchant and local political figure in Frederick, watched the Army of the Potomac pass through the city along Market Street on 29 June. He entered a note in his diary at 10:45 A.M.: "While I am writing this, the streets are chucked full of wagons and cavalry and infantry. To estimate the number would be more than I am able, but I should suppose to say 70 or 80,000 would not be out of the way. And wagons I think 1,000 or more would not exceed the number and I reckon 3 or 4 hundred cannon and still they are passing the door."[11]

While the city of Frederick was clogged with marching and, in many cases, alcohol-impaired troops, General Hooker and Lieutenant Colonel Hardie, along with Hooker's aides, attempted to depart for Relay and Washington. Because the Baltimore & Ohio Railroad had been shut down the previous afternoon, they had been forced to stay overnight in the United States Hotel across Market Street from the passenger station. Accompanying them was Brigadier General Gilman Marston of Heintzelman's department, who commanded troops at Poolesville and at the signal station at Sugar Loaf Mountain near the mouth of the Monocacy River. Marston was returning to Poolesville. They boarded a special Baltimore & Ohio train at an early hour in the morning. All were hoping the bridges and trackage that had been partially destroyed by Stuart's cavalrymen had been repaired enough to allow the train to pass, but no one could be sure because the telegraph wires down the tracks had been cut. The special train left the station in Frederick behind the regular morning train but got only as far as Monocacy Junction, where both trains stopped. There, they waited in the pouring rain until well after noon for the rail line to be reconnoitered by at least two other engines and cavalry commands to make sure the track was secure. Unfortunately, the bridges were not sufficiently repaired to allow the trains to pass that day. In fact, trains would not be operable along the railroad for another twenty hours. Hooker, Har-

I AM MOVING AT ONCE AGAINST LEE

die, Marston, and Hooker's aides returned to the United States Hotel in Frederick for another night.[12]

Trouble appeared at the other end of the line, too. War correspondents Whitelaw Reid of the *Cincinnati Gazette*, Samuel Wilkeson of the *New York Times*, and Uriah H. Painter of the *Philadelphia Inquirer* climbed aboard a train in Washington for Frederick. Relay, Maryland, west of Baltimore, was as far as the reporters got. "I am very sorry, gentlemen," said an official of the Baltimore & Ohio Railroad, "I would get you out at once if I could; but the rebels cut our road last night, this side of Frederick, and we have no idea when we can run again."[13]

The countryside through which all of Meade's corps were about to march was not as rugged as the region they had traversed from Edwards Ferry to Frederick the past two days. Northern Frederick County and Carroll County were situated, however, along the base of the Cactoctin Mountains; some of the terrain was relatively level, but most was rolling and hilly. All of those lands were drained by innumerable creeks and streams that fed into the Monocacy River, a fast-moving stream that ran north to south, eventually emptying into the Potomac River at Point of Rocks. Marching through that country would be rough in the best of weather; rain and mud would make it difficult in the extreme.[14]

As Meade traveled along the roads, he alternated between riding his favorite horse, Old Baldy, and working in a headquarters wagon. Meade and his entourage followed Reynolds's First Corps most of the way. Occasionally Meade's headquarters flag, the national colors, was uncased for the benefit of villagers and townspeople along the way. At 11:00 A.M. on 29 June, while in a headquarters wagon, Meade wrote a letter to Halleck directly responding to the general in chief's concerns about the army covering Washington and Baltimore:

> Upon assuming command of the army, and after carefully considering the position of affairs and the movements of the enemy, I have concluded as follows: To move today toward Westminster and Emmitsburg, and the army is now in motion for that line, placing two corps, First and Eleventh, at Emmitsburg; two corps, Third and Twelfth, at Taneytown; one corps, Second, at Frizzellburg, and one corps, Fifth, at Union; Sixth Corps at New Windsor; my cavalry guarding my flanks and rear.
>
> If Lee is moving for Baltimore, I expect to get between his main army and that place. If he is crossing the Susquehanna, I shall rely upon General Couch, with his force, holding him until I can fall upon

his rear and give him battle.... I shall incline to the right towards the Baltimore and Harrisburg Road, to cover that and draw supplies from there if circumstances permit it; my main objective point being, of course, Lee's army, which I am satisfied has all passed through Hagerstown towards Chambersburg. My endeavors will be in my movements to hold my force well together, with the hope of falling on some portion of Lee's army in detail.[15]

Replying to Halleck's anxiety about General Stuart's capture of the extensive wagon train near Rockville and his operations against the Western Maryland Railroad, Meade wrote: "My main point [is] to find and fight the enemy, I shall have to submit to the cavalry raids around me, in some measure." Meade then turned to his main concern: "Telegraphic communications have been cut off. I have no opportunity to receive a reply to mine asking your advice as to these movements, and upon my best judgment proceed to execute them." He elaborated on his critical situation. "I can at present give no orders as to General Schenck's department in Baltimore, or the Potomac in my rear; neither can I, in the absence of telegraphic communication, and on account of the great distance of Couch, exercise any influence, by advice or otherwise, concerning the cooperation of that force." But then Meade noted matter-of-factly: "These circumstances are beyond my control." Meade concluded: "Headquarters tonight are at Middleburg, 3 miles from Uniontown and 13 from Westminster. There is rail communication from Baltimore to Westminster." He gave the dispatch to a courier and sent him galloping back toward Frederick to be taken from there by relay riders to Relay, Maryland, and then telegraphed to Halleck. Rarely has a new commander been presented with such daunting and complex issues on his first day in command as was George Meade. He dealt with his limitations and deprivations with a steady head and evident equanimity.[16]

By dispatch rider, Meade finally received a response from Halleck to his telegram sent at 9:00 P.M. on 28 June detailing the proposed movements of the army. Halleck simply stated: "So far as I can judge, without a better knowledge of the army's positions, your proposed movement seems good." Meade had little more information of the whereabouts of the enemy than Halleck and had to rely on his mature judgment in the absence of facts.[17]

On the afternoon of 29 June, Meade determined what to do with General French at Harper's Ferry. He sent French a dispatch commanding him to "remove the property of the Government at Maryland Heights, etc., by canal to Washington" and to march his command "to join this army without delay." Meade directed French to detach no more than three thousand men to remove and escort the property to Washington.[18]

Lieutenant Colonel Rufus R. Dawes of the Sixth Wisconsin in the First Corps remembered observing General Meade during the march of the First Corps from Frederick to Emmitsburg. "Few of our men knew him,' Dawes recalled. "He was sometimes seen riding by the marching columns of troops at a fast trot, his hat brim turned down and a poncho over his shoulders. The only sign of rank was a gold cord on his hat." Notably, numerous mounted staff officers, some general officers, eight companies of the Eighth United States, and, at times, the Ninety-Third New York, the First Pennsylvania Reserve Volunteer Cavalry, two companies of the Sixth Pennsylvania Cavalry, and detachments from four United States Regular Cavalry regiments, served as Meade's headquarters' escort and as Provost Marshal General Patrick's guard. Meade was easily distinguishable in the army on the move.[19]

During the extensive marches on 29 June, soldiers began hearing at random of General Hooker's replacement by Meade. As the day wore on, rumor spread up and down the columns that Meade was only a temporary commander; General McClellan was on his way back to the army. Rumors were even spread that McClellan was in command of the army. Soldiers in the First Corps heard a rumor that General Reynolds was in command of the army. C. W. Bardeen, a fifer in the First Massachusetts Infantry in the Third Corps, was disgusted after hearing about Meade's appointment. He entered a note in his diary: "My division, especially my brigade, and most especially my regiment … didn't like him." Bardeen later explained: "We still felt that our reputation was bound up with Hooker's, and we resented his dismissal from command, so we were prejudiced against Meade from the start."[20]

Meade and his entourage reached the tiny village of Middleburg at around 5:00 P.M. He and his staff entered the stone two-and-one-half-story hotel owned by Joe Linn on the north side of the main street, which led from Middleburg to Uniontown, about five miles east. There, Meade finally caught up with the day's correspondence while he waited for his headquarters tents to be set up about one mile to the north.[21]

An aide to General Sedgwick reported to Meade that the Sixth Corps would not be able to reach New Windsor; instead, it stopped at a little village called Sam's Creek, several miles short of New Windsor. Meade responded by dictating a message back to Sedgwick at 5:35 P.M., stating it was "of the utmost importance that you would move early tomorrow morning, and, with your left at Westminster, occupy the railroad terminating at that place." Meade was anxious to hold the roads from Harrisburg to Baltimore on his right flank and to occupy Westminster so that the Western Maryland Railroad was secured.[22]

At 6:20 P.M., General Slocum wrote to Meade that he was unable to get beyond Double Pipe Creek with the Twelfth Corps. Still, the Twelfth Corps had marched twenty-three miles that day behind the Artillery Reserve. Slocum's delay was caused by wagon trains that, he said, "do not belong on this road." Meade knew that the wagon trains choking up the road through Middleburg belonged to Sickles's Third Corps. Those same trains had blocked Meade's headquarters wagon trains as Meade approached Middleburg. Slocum then added: "When I left Frederick, there were a great number of men from every corps in the army lying about the streets, beastly drunk. I think it important that a cavalry force should be sent back to bring them up."[23]

Receiving Slocum's dispatch, Meade sent a stern message to General Patrick directing him to "take immediate and prompt measures to have all stragglers and drunken soldiers driven out of Frederick and sent to their commands." General Patrick was setting up his own headquarters north of Middleburg when he was summoned to meet with Meade. At what Patrick referred to as "a late hour," he rode back to Joe Linn's Hotel in Middleburg. "The roads," he recalled, "were completely blocked with trains and troops." After meeting with Meade, Patrick ordered two squadrons of cavalry from his provost guard to "go back to Frederick and clean out that town, which was reported full of drunken men and stragglers."[24]

Manley Stacey, a private in the One Hundred Eleventh New York in Hancock's Second Corps, penned a letter to his father recalling the march of 29 June. "We marched thirty miles," he wrote. "We left Frederick at 10 am and halted at 11 pm. Oh how tired I was. I was completely worn out and exhausted so that I groaned at every step." He then added: "When we halted last night there was not two whole companies left in the regiment. The boys had marched just as far as they were able and then fell out. The road was lined with men for five miles before we halted." He told his father that two men in the regiment had died along the way. "God knows," he wrote, "how many there was [who died] in the corps."[25]

Meade sent a terse dispatch to General Sykes at 6:45 P.M. informing him that he was satisfied with the progress of the Fifth Corps that had reached Liberty. With General Sickles's Third Corps, however, Meade was less than pleased. At 7:00 P.M., he informed the Third Corps commander that "the train of your corps is at a standstill at Middleburg, delaying, of course, all movements in the rear." Meade informed Sickles that he ex-

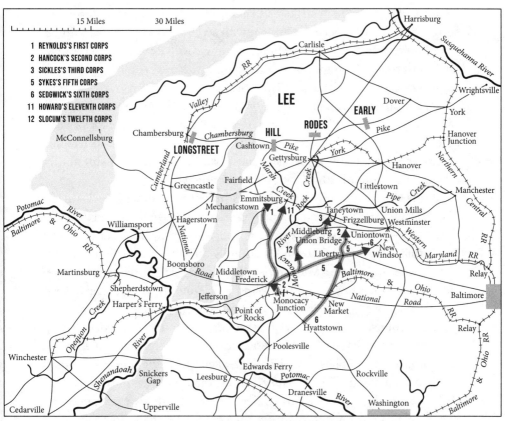

Map 4.1. 29 June 1863: Meade moves his army toward Lee.

pected him to give his "immediate and personal attention to keeping your train in motion." That was Meade's first attempt to confront Sickles, a general in whom Meade had little confidence as a soldier.[26]

Remarkably, by the close of 29 June, after just one single day's march, Meade's army was already nearly in a position that would enable it to cover all the approaches to Baltimore and Washington. By late at night, Reynolds's First Corps was at Emmitsburg; Howard's Eleventh Corps was nearby. Hancock's Second Corps was at Uniontown. Sickles's Third Corps was at Taneytown; Slocum's Twelfth Corps was at Double Pipe Creek, just west of Middleburg. Sykes's Fifth Corps was at Liberty, while Sedgwick's Sixth Corps was just south of New Windsor at Sam's Creek. The Artillery Reserve and all the army medical wagon trains rumbled on to Middleburg along with the engineer and Signal Corps trains. On the army's left flank, along the eastern base of the South Mountain range at Fairfield, were two brigades of Buford's First Cavalry Division; his scouting parties were operating north of Fairfield and east toward Gettysburg. Buford's reserve brigade was at Mechanicstown with scouting parties as far west as the western base of the South Mountain range. Kilpatrick's Third Cavalry Division, after galloping through Littlestown, was near Hanover, Pennsylvania. Gregg's Second Cavalry Division reached Westminster. The army held positions from the mountains on the west all the way to the Western Maryland Railroad at Westminster on the east, and cavalry patrols were spread out all across Meade's left, front, and right, scouting roads leading to Cashtown, Gettysburg, Carlisle, and York. But Meade was still not in telegraphic communication with his government.[27]

Meade had successfully brought the Army of the Potomac into the heart of Carroll County, Maryland. So many creeks and streams coursed through the county—and so much wheat, corn, and other grains were raised in the area—that sixty-eight flour and grist mills operated there. Some towns like Union Mills, Hood's Mill, and McKinstry's Mill were named for those enterprises. Other towns like New Windsor, Detour, Trevanian, and Sykesville began as a result of flour and grist mills.[28]

L. L. Crounse, a newspaper correspondent with the *New York Times*, traveled along with the army. "General Meade," he wrote on 29 June, "steps in vigorously, and applies himself with great energy to the task before him." Crounse then noted: "We have very little information from the enemy. The great distance between the two armies, and the rapid movement of both, have tended to lessen reports from the enemy. We shall, however, have definite information from the enemy in a day or two, and possibly a battle by the close of the week."[29]

Indeed, Meade had only spare amounts of information on the whereabouts of Lee's army. He could not be confident of any reports of the location of any of the elements of Lee's army on the evening of 29 June. Meade received a message from General Reynolds at Emmitsburg around seven o'clock in the evening. Captain Stephen Minot Weld, one of Reynolds's aides, brought the report to Meade. Reynolds reported that Edward Hopkins, one of Colonel Sharpe's scouts, had just returned from Gettysburg. Hopkins reported that elements of Ewell's corps—Early's Division—had passed through in the direction of York; Rodes's Division had been reported as far north as Carlisle. Hill's corps was said to be moving toward Chambersburg. Reynolds received nothing new about the whereabouts of Longstreet's corps; its last sighting was on the road between Hagerstown and Chambersburg.[30]

The forward movement of the Army of the Potomac under Meade's command halted generally along and below a sizable stream known as

Big Pipe Creek in Carroll County, Maryland. Finally, Meade's headquarters were set up in tents about a mile north of Middleburg on the largely level fields of the farm of a Peter Koons located on the east side of the road that ran from Middleburg to Taneytown; the farm extended to the south bank of Big Pipe Creek. There, the creek cut its way through precipitous bluffs. Koons was described by his nineteen-year-old son James as a "well known ... Union Man."[31]

In the Koons's fields south of Big Pipe Creek all of Meade's headquarters' wagon trains were parked. There, too, were the campsites and wagon trains of all the infantry and cavalry troops of the headquarters' escort and provost marshal's guard. As the evening progressed, General Pleasonton established headquarters there, and the Cavalry Corps parked its extensive wagon trains in those fields as well. General Tyler's five brigades—twenty-one six-gun batteries—of the Artillery Reserve, along with its enormous wagon trains, also parked in the Koons fields, together with the army medical wagon trains and the Engineer and Signal Corps trains. "Every field," young Koons recalled, "was occupied excepting those in wheat uncut, although on both sides of the main road was an additional road through the uncut wheat [that was] used by the cavalry, as the main road was filled with infantry for miles." He recollected that "in one field, blacksmith shops were run all night, in another field [were] General Meade's headquarters tents."[32]

James Koons remembered that the paymaster's wagon was not parked far from General Meade's headquarters tents. "The paymaster, in paying bills," Koons wrote, "used a pair of shears to clip from the sheets the money wanted, whether one, five, ten, or hundred dollar bills; each till contained a certain amount of sheets, from one dollar bills up, and all the paymaster had to do was pull out a sheet and clip off the amount wanted." What young Koons did not know was that the next day, 30 June, was payday for the army, and paymasters in every element of the army were busy similarly preparing the pay for every officer and soldier in every regiment, battalion, and artillery battery.[33]

On 29 June, along the east-west turnpike axis between Chambersburg and York were at least three sizable commands from Lee's army, but they were last seen at both ends of that fifty-mile stretch of turnpike. Gettysburg was little more than eighteen miles north of Meade's Middleburg headquarters. If enemy forces were anywhere, Meade reasoned, they likely were along that turnpike axis, east and west of Gettysburg, but Meade had no reliable intelligence of the specific whereabouts of any of them.

Unbeknown to Meade, all of Hill's corps was ordered to move toward

Cashtown on the turnpike axis from Chambersburg on 29 June; in fact, only Major General Henry Heth's Division of Hill's corps reached Cashtown that day. Longstreet's corps was ordered to follow Hill, leaving Pickett's Division at Chambersburg until relieved by Imboden's cavalry brigade. Ewell was recalled from Heidlersburg and directed to join Hill and Longstreet at Cashtown or Gettysburg as circumstances dictated. Rodes's Division of Ewell's corps marched south from Heidlersburg toward Gettysburg. Early's Division of Ewell's corps was ordered to return from near Berlin by way of parallel roads, north of the turnpike axis, to join the rest of the army along the base of the South Mountain range. Meanwhile, Major General Edward Johnson's Division of Ewell's corps escorted an enormous wagon train filled with purchased and impressed quartermaster stores back from near Scotland to Chambersburg; it was then ordered to march along the turnpike axis to Cashtown.[34]

Up to the evening of 29 June, Meade had heard little of the whereabouts of General Stuart's cavalry brigades, whose forays had seized the wagon train near Rockville, cut the telegraph wires along the Baltimore & Ohio Railroad, destroyed railroad bridges, and then moved toward the Western Maryland Railroad on Meade's right flank. For all Meade knew, the Western Maryland Railroad was destroyed. He had no definite intelligence.[35]

Unbeknown to Meade, General Stuart's three cavalry brigades had entered Westminster at about 4:00 P.M. on 29 June. For more than twenty-four hours before, the town had been occupied by only two companies of the First Delaware Cavalry from General Schenck's Department, commanded by Major Napoleon B. Knight. Alarmed citizens had alerted the Delaware cavalrymen of the approach of Stuart's legions. In a daring move, Major Knight had attacked the approaching Confederates, not knowing their vastly superior numbers. Stuart's cavalry easily dispatched the Delaware troopers in the main street of Westminster. Stuart's brigades, with the huge caravan of wagons captured near Rockville, moved through Westminster as General Sedgwick's Sixth Corps, led by General Gregg's cavalry division, approached New Windsor, only five miles away. Stuart did not tarry long; he moved his command northward to Union Mills.[36]

At 10:00 P.M., General Hancock, whose exhausted corps was arriving at Uniontown, received word that Stuart's brigades were at Westminster. He immediately notified Meade, who sent for General Pleasonton. Pleasonton denied that Stuart was at Westminster, claiming that Gregg's division was there. Gregg, however, had only reached New Windsor. Stuart not only left Westminster quickly but left the Western Maryland Railroad unscathed. As Hancock later testified, the ferocious pace, and northeast

I AM MOVING AT ONCE AGAINST LEE

trajectory, of Meade's army had "one grand effect—it placed us so near Stuart that instead of marching up to Gettysburg, as he would probably have done otherwise, he was forced over toward the Susquehanna, which ... prevented him from joining Lee." That fast pace of Meade's army, and its northeast trajectory, also caused Stuart to leave Westminster before he could do serious damage to the Western Maryland Railroad.[37]

Lacking other intelligence, and using only information provided by his engineers, Meade determined to move his army into the most defensible position possible, a position from which he could also operate offensively. Assessing the maps of Frederick and Carroll Counties, Meade dictated a circular to all his commanders through his assistant adjutant general, Seth Williams. Slocum's Twelfth Corps was ordered to pass the Third Corps and march to Littlestown, Pennsylvania, on the morning of 30 June. Sykes's Fifth Corps was, at the same time, to march to "Pipe Creek Crossing" at Union Mills, Maryland, a site on the Baltimore Pike between Littlestown and Westminster, Maryland. Sedgwick's Sixth Corps was ordered to march through Westminster to Manchester, Maryland, in the morning, forming the far-right flank of the army. If Stuart's cavalry brigades were in the vicinity, Gregg's and Kilpatrick's cavalry divisions would have to confront them. Reynolds's First Corps was directed to move from Emmitsburg due north to Marsh Creek, "half way" to Gettysburg, leaving Howard's Eleventh Corps at Emmitsburg. Sickles's Third Corps was ordered to march from Taneytown to Emmitsburg. The Artillery Reserve was directed to move to Piney Run Crossing on the road between Littlestown and Taneytown, following the Twelfth Corps. The engineer train, and two components of the bridge train that had arrived at Middleburg, were ordered to follow the Fifth Corps to a position between Littlestown and Westminster. Meade informed his corps commanders that his headquarters would move at 8:00 A.M. and be reestablished at Taneytown. The end of his circular read: "Headquarters train will have the right of way when it moves." Meade was positioning the army along and in advance of Big Pipe Creek. Given what he knew from the limited intelligence of the enemy's whereabouts he possessed and his orders from Halleck, it was Meade's most sensible option.[38]

Meade knew from experience that intelligence is often unreliable and always transient. Lee's army was on the move; where its elements were since the last reports were received at army headquarters was anybody's guess. What Meade clearly understood was that his adversary was skillful, active, and enterprising and that, like many such adversaries, his movements often presented "a perfect riddle." Because of the unreliable, fluid, and transient nature of intelligence, one great military theorist aptly warned that "war is a flimsy structure that can easily collapse and bury us in its ruins." That kind of warning would not have been lost on Meade on the night of 29 June.[39]

Meade still lacked any definitive information about the enemy's location and strength. He called Colonel Sharpe of the Bureau of Military Information and his staff to his headquarters on the Koons farm. So impressed was Meade with Gettysburg lawyer David McConaughy's 27 June intelligence report he received the previous evening that he directed Sharpe to enlist him to supply more. Sharpe scribbled a note to McConaughy at army headquarters at Middleburg. After informing McConaughy that "the General [directed him] to thank you for yours today," Sharpe wrote: "The names of the generals (and number of forces, if possible) are very important to us, as they enable us to gauge the reports with exactness. The General begs, if in your power, that you make such arrangements with intelligent friends in the country beyond you to this effect, and that you continue your attention to us, as much as your convenience will permit." It was 7:00 P.M.[40]

Shortly thereafter Meade dictated to General Butterfield a message to be handed to Colonel Sharpe: "The major general commanding desires that you send [scouts] to Gettysburg, Hanover, Greencastle, Chambersburg, and Jefferson tonight and get as much information as you can of the numbers, position, and force of the enemy, with their movements." Whatever findings Sharpe and his scouts would make would never be received at army headquarters in time for Meade to initiate an engagement with the enemy.[41]

The capital city of Washington was alarmed because of reports circulating concerning Lee's threatening movements. Reports of supposed enemy movements, dire predictions, and unsolicited and unwanted advice from politicians throughout the northeast and elsewhere were continually received at the War Department. A telegram was received by Secretary of War Stanton on the evening of 29 June, claiming: "We have information we deem entirely reliable that the rebels are marching on Philadelphia in large force, and also on points on the Philadelphia, Wilmington, and Baltimore Railroad." The telegram added: "Philadelphia once taken, they think they will be able to dictate terms to the Government." Simon Cameron wrote to the president that night claiming, "Within the next forty-eight hours, Lee will cross the Susquehanna River unless General Meade strikes his columns tomorrow, and compels him to concentrate his forces west of the Susquehanna for a general battle." Rumors circulated through the

White House and War Department that elements of Lee's army were on the outskirts of Washington and Baltimore ready to attack! Although likely not shared with Meade, telegrams flowed into the White House on the first full day of Meade's command pleading for General McClellan's return as commander of the Army of the Potomac. Governor Joel Parker of New Jersey wrote to the president a demand: "The people of New Jersey want McClellan at the head of the Army of the Potomac. If that cannot be done, then we ask that he may be put at the head of the New Jersey, New York, and Pennsylvania troops now in Pennsylvania." One S. F. Miller at far away Louisville, Kentucky, demanded the president to "call McClellan to the head of the armies of the Government."[42]

For Meade, the day was productive in regard to repositioning the army. In his headquarters tent he could hear the rain falling on the canvas. Taking a moment, he scribbled a note to Margaret: "We are marching as fast as we can to relieve Harrisburg, but have to keep a sharp lookout that the rebels don't turn around us and get at Washington and Baltimore in our rear. They have a cavalry force in our rear, destroying railroads, etc., with the view of getting me to turn back; but I shall not do it. I am going straight at them, and will settle this thing one way or the other. The men are in good spirits; we have been reinforced so as to have equal numbers of the enemy, and with God's blessing I hope to be successful. Good-by!"[43]

In those late hours alone Meade must have thought of the lessons he learned as a cadet at West Point and as a soldier. His army by the next day would be spread out on a front that was thirty miles long, from Manchester to Emmitsburg. Would the army be too spread out? Would its flanks be vulnerable to attack? The army had to cover the approaches to Baltimore and Washington. Could he force the enemy to concentrate somewhere in his front? It would take a bold move by elements of his army to force that result. "Everything in war is simple," wrote the great Prussian military theorist Carl von Clausewitz, "but the simplest thing is difficult." Meade knew from experience that "countless minor incidents—the kind you can never really foresee—combine to lower the general level of performance, so that one always falls far short of the intended goal. Iron willpower can overcome this friction; it pulverizes every obstacle, but of course, it wears down the machine as well."[44]

5

YOU MUST FALL BACK
TO EMMITSBURG

Rain fell steadily all through the night. Intelligence Meade received through the wee morning hours of Tuesday, 30 June, indicated that Longstreet's and Hill's corps were at Chambersburg and "partly toward Gettysburg." Divisions of Ewell's corps remained at or near Carlisle and York, hardly a change from the previous day's information. General Buford, however, sent a message to General Reynolds at 5:30 A.M. from near Fairfield, Pennsylvania, at the eastern base of the South Mountain range. The report demanded Meade's close attention and a timely response and, accordingly, was forwarded to Meade. "The enemy has increased his forces considerably," Buford wrote. "His strong position is just behind Cashtown." A scouting party from Buford's two brigades, he reported, ran into "a superior force, strongly posted," near Mummasburg, Pennsylvania, just north of Cashtown. Another party of Buford's scouts galloped three miles due north of Fairfield and "met a strong picket; had a skirmish, and captured a prisoner of Rodes's Division." According to that information—and the intelligence received over the past twenty-four hours—the movements of Longstreet and Hill indicated to Meade "a disposition to advance from Chambersburg to Gettysburg." Meade continued to believe that along that east-west turnpike axis between Chambersburg and York was most likely where Lee's widely scattered forces would concentrate. Gettysburg, eighteen miles north of Meade's headquarters outside of Middleburg, Maryland, appeared to be the site to which Longstreet's and Hill's troops were being directed, but there was still nothing definitive pointing to that conclusion.[1]

Meade finally received word of Stuart's Confederate brigades operating east of the army, but the information was scant. In a dispatch to General Reynolds, written at 7:40 A.M., Meade notified him that "General Gregg reports the presence of a large cavalry force of the enemy at Westminster yesterday afternoon and last night. It is supposed this cavalry force is making for Littlestown." Meade understood that General Kilpatrick's division was then "in close proximity" to those Confederate cavalry brigades. It was. He also understood, surely with some relief, that Stuart's prodigious force of horsemen had not damaged the Western Maryland Railroad between Westminster and Baltimore.[2]

Young James Koons recalled Meade's headquarters on his father's farm north of Middleburg on the early morning of 30 June. "Engineers and officers of headquarters," he wrote, "together with my father, Peter Koons, went in the rear of the barn on the hill and examined a large map." He remembered that his father "gave the engineers the situation of every hill, ravine, and crossing, every turn made by [Big Pipe Creek's] course for about four miles." Meade's engineers could see the advantages of a defense line along Big Pipe Creek by looking at the bluffs along the south bank of the stream bordering the Koons farm. The bluffs loomed formidably. Koons noted that his father "was cautioned not to disclose what took place on the hill" under any circumstance. After all, Carroll County, like Frederick County, had plenty of residents who were Confederate sympathizers.[3]

What interested Meade and his engineers were positions along Big Pipe Creek that ran west, from Manchester through Union Mills to about two miles west of Middleburg, the site of Big Pipe Creek's confluence with Little Pipe Creek, a smaller stream that originated northwest of New Windsor and ran through Union Bridge, well below the course of Big Pipe Creek. Double Pipe Creek ran west from the confluence of Big Pipe Creek and Little Pipe Creek only about a mile before it entered into the Monocacy River about ten miles south of Emmitsburg.[4]

What Meade's engineers discussed with Koons was a possible defense line that would be developed along the south bank of Big Pipe Creek; it would extend for nearly twenty miles, east to west. On its eastern end, the line would be unassailable; from Manchester to Union Mills, about eight miles west, the heights forming the south bank of the creek were generally about one hundred feet above the creek, and some of those bluffs towered upward almost from the creek's edge. From Union Mills to where the road between Taneytown and Frizzellburg crossed Big Pipe Creek, about eight miles west, the elevation of the bluffs decreased to well less than one hundred feet above the creek. Thereafter, the bluffs along the last five miles of the defense line to Middleburg steadily decreased to under fifty feet.[5]

That morning, Meade and his engineers were examining a line of de-

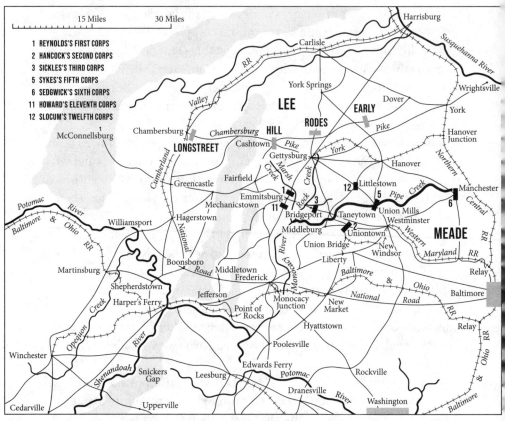

Map 5.1. 30 June 1863: The Pipe Creek Line.

fense along favorable ground that covered every approach to Baltimore
and Washington that Lee might try to force; they strategized for each
eventuality so they would be prepared no matter which line of approach
Lee selected. Meade believed that certain elements of the army should be
moved ahead of the defense line so that they would fall back onto the Pipe
Creek line if attacked. The object of occupying the advanced positions was
to lure the enemy to attack them while also masking the defense line along
the bluffs forming the south bank of Big Pipe Creek. If Lee used roads
that emanated from Gettysburg and wound their ways to Baltimore and
Washington, or if he used the direct roads from Harrisburg to those critical cities, or all of them at the same time, he would inevitably find Meade's
army strongly posted in front of and along Big Pipe Creek, blocking his
movements.[6]

Beyond the fact that the defense line would be substantially reinforced
and would cover any and all the approaches Lee's army might take toward

Baltimore and Washington, Meade determined to establish a supply base at Westminster with a direct railroad line to Baltimore and, consequently, Washington. That rail line, the Western Maryland Railroad, extended west from Westminster, about ten miles, to Union Bridge. Westminster would be only seven miles behind the right center of Meade's contemplated lines at Union Mills; Union Bridge would be only seven miles from the left flank of that contemplated defense line.[7]

Meade had decided to concentrate his army in front of Big Pipe Creek and lure Lee to advance his army against him. If the word "contingency" is defined as "an event that may occur but is not likely or intended," then preparing to receive the enemy along the Pipe Creek line was no "contingency." Rather, as of 30 June, Meade contemplated to fall back to those heights and fight Lee there. If the word "contingency" applies at all, then it is to the possibility of Meade launching an offensive movement ahead of the Pipe Creek line if developments dictated such a move. Only in that sense would the Pipe Creek line be considered an "offensive-defensive line" on 30 June.[8]

What became known as the Pipe Creek line, wrote General Henry Hunt, would afford Meade "with perfect liberty of action in all directions," as good roads led in all directions from the defense line. Indeed, the roads running east to west, connecting Westminster with Uniontown, Taneytown, and Emmitsburg—and parallel roads connecting Westminster with Uniontown and Middleburg—gave Meade complete freedom to move troops to threatened segments of the defense line. Meade's contemplated defense line could not be turned by Lee without Lee endangering his own army. Lee would not be at liberty to move his army onto Meade's flanks; he would run the risk of finding Meade's army between his own army and its line of supply and communications through Cashtown Pass to the Cumberland Valley. General Hunt may have summed up Meade's strategic thinking when he wrote: "There would then be but two courses for Lee—either to attack Meade in the chosen position, or to retreat without a battle. The latter, neither the temper of [Lee's] army nor that of his government would probably permit."[9]

In the event Meade suffered a defeat, "his line of retreat would be comparatively short and easily covered," recollected General Hunt. He would also be able to fall back on the relatively short rail line and turnpike that ran to Baltimore, where all the army's supplies originated. General Schenck's troops would be available in support. If Meade defeated Lee along the Pipe Creek line, the enemy's withdrawal would be lengthy even before it reached the South Mountain passes. Meade's contemplated defense lines

Brigadier General Henry Hunt. (Library of Congress)

were so logically organized that General Hunt remarked after the war that Meade's ultimate directives to establish the line along Big Pipe Creek were "wise and proper orders, and it would probably have been better had he concentrated his army behind Pipe Creek rather than at Gettysburg, but events finally controlled the actions of both leaders."[10]

A gentle rain continued to fall through the morning of 30 June. Meade's headquarters' tents were stricken and packed away in wagons along with all the desks, chairs, trunks, lamps, beds, bedding, and clothes. Army headquarters began moving to Taneytown, just six miles north of Middleburg, at 8:00 A.M. The headquarters train, medical wagon train, engineer and Signal Corps trains, and all of the marching and mounted troops of the escorts maneuvered onto the Middleburg and Taneytown Road to commence the relatively short journey to Taneytown.[11]

At Taneytown, the oldest town in Carroll County, the headquarters trains and escorts turned northeast onto the York or Littlestown Turnpike and continued about two miles when they stopped on the farm of a Benjamin Shunk on the south side of the road in front of Piney Creek. There, headquarters tents were pitched in the fields. Meade's own tent was set up alongside a giant sycamore. Adjacent to the site where Meade's headquarters were being established, General Sickles's Third Corps had camped the evening before on the large farms of Samuel Null, John and Jacob Thompson, and John Keviner, among others.[12]

While the army headquarters tents were being set up on the Shunk farm, Meade occupied the Trinity Lutheran Church parsonage library on the south side of Emmitsburg Street near the center of Taneytown. The Reverend Levi T. Williams, the rector of the Lutheran church, came out to greet Meade and his staff as they entered the town. The two men became acquainted, and at Williams's insistence, Meade made his temporary headquarters in the Lutheran parsonage.[13]

Meade's left flank at Emmitsburg was, to him, the most vulnerable to attack. Communications with that flank had to open up as rapidly as possible. Signals could help. The steeple of the Lutheran church across Emmitsburg Street from the parsonage served as a prime location for a signal station. Haziness and intermittent rain, however, prevented any signal communication during the day. Consequently, a party from the Signal Corps was ordered to Emmitsburg to survey the possibility of setting up a telegraph line between that place and Meade's headquarters.[14]

So immense was Meade's army—and so choked had been the roads north and east of Frederick on 29 June—that one of the bridge trains, carrying sixty-nine pontoons and all the trestles and bridging, was still

Emmitsburg, Maryland. (Library of Congress)

clearing the streets of Frederick, thirty miles distant, at the same time
as Meade's headquarters were being moved to Taneytown. Jacob Engelbrecht of Frederick penned an entry in his diary at 8:25 A.M. on 30 June:
"This morning before day a Pontoon [train] passed through our city on
their way towards the Susquehanna River. It took 2 or 3 hours to pass."[15]

Meade's troops were suffering. Many of his men lacked shoes and adequate clothing after the long marches into Maryland and the recent forced
marches through the rain and mud. The men were also exhausted and
in need of rest. Meade had no telegraphic communications with either
General Halleck or Quartermaster General Meigs. He could request supplies, but the request could not be timely transmitted, and the supplies requested could not be delivered at all. Yet, if the army was expected to fight,
it must be equipped, and it must be rested. So desperate was Meade to
get the necessary quartermaster stores for the troops, particularly shoes,
that he determined to enlist the efforts of General Couch in Harrisburg.
At 10:45 A.M., Meade sent a dispatch to Couch from his Taneytown headquarters. He informed Couch that the Army of the Potomac was "in position between Emmitsburg and Westminster, advancing upon the enemy."
Hill's corps, he wrote, "holds Cashtown Pass, between Gettysburg and
Chambersburg." He was still unsure of the "whereabouts of Longstreet and
Ewell." That was all he really knew. Meade then explained to Couch that if
there were telegraphic communication with Philadelphia, Baltimore, and
Washington, then he would "like supplies and shoes accumulated to be
thrown to me on the line of the Northern Central or the Susquehanna, as
circumstances may require or my movements may make most desirable."
Meade called on Couch to "communicate [his] dispatch to [Halleck] the

General-in-Chief." That dispatch was sent by a rider to Frederick to be carried by relay riders to Relay, Maryland, the nearest telegraph office, so that it could be sent to Washington and Harrisburg.[16]

What is certain is that Meade expected fighting to erupt soon, probably within a day or two. He dictated a circular to Seth Williams in expectation of the clash he anticipated. The circular he issued directed "corps and all other commanding officers" to "address their troops, explaining to them briefly the immense issues involved in the struggle." Meade wanted all the troops to be reminded in passionate terms that "the enemy are on our soil" and that "the country now looks anxiously to this army to deliver it from the presence of the foe." He added an appeal to the soldier's hearts: "Homes, firesides, and domestic altars are involved." To the officers, Meade noted: "The army has fought well heretofore; it is believed that it will fight more desperately and bravely than ever if it is addressed in fitting terms." Meade ended his stirring circular with a somber and strict reminder of just how pressing was the situation: "Corps and other commanders are authorized to order the instant death of any soldier who fails in his duty at this hour."[17]

Not long after Meade sent his desperate appeal to Couch, good news arrived at army headquarters. The War Department forwarded to Meade a telegram from James W. Garrett, the president of the Baltimore & Ohio Railroad, reporting from Baltimore at 11:55 P.M. on 29 June, that the telegraph line to the Monocacy River that had been cut by Stuart's Confederate horsemen had been restored. Garrett also assured the War Department that the bridges and roadbed of the main stem of the rail line would be fully repaired and operational "early Tuesday" morning, 30 June! This meant Meade could resume communicating with Halleck by means of the telegraph at Frederick and that he could begin receiving supplies, particularly shoes and clothing, through Frederick. Although riders would still have to gallop between Frederick and army headquarters to send and receive telegraphic messages, it was better than the situation had been since the afternoon of 28 June.[18]

On the morning of 30 June, Reynolds forwarded to Meade, by Captain Weld, a captured enemy dispatch. One of Buford's scouts seized the dispatch the previous night on the York Turnpike between Gettysburg and Oxford. The dispatch was written by General Early and was intended to be sent to an unnamed colonel, likely in Jenkins's cavalry brigade. The dispatch was tersely worded: "Get between Gettysburg and Heidlersburg, and picket Mummasburg and Hunterstown. Send in the direction of Gettysburg, and see what is there, and report to General Ewell at Heidlersburg. A small body of Yankee cavalry has made its appearance between Gettysburg and Heidlersburg. See what it is."[19]

According to Buford, the captured bearer of the dispatch "saw [General] Early last at Berlin." That put Ewell himself and elements of his corps at Heidlersburg, just seven miles northeast of Gettysburg! With Longstreet's and Hill's corps showing "a disposition to advance from Chambersburg to Gettysburg," it appeared to Meade that Gettysburg was where Lee was directing the movement of most of his army. Still, though, Meade could not be certain. Before he could even consider moving the army forward, he had to ascertain the whereabouts of all Lee's forces.[20]

Orders for the movement of all elements of the army were issued at Meade's Taneytown headquarters on 30 June; they restated the circular issued the previous day with notable modifications. Meade would issue actual orders to march to each corps commander only when he desired the movement to take place. Meade wanted to let up on his demands on most of the troops, who were tired, ragged, and in many cases shoeless, but he also had to align his army in front of Big Pipe Creek as rapidly as possible. Still, 30 June was payday, and all the troops had to be given some time to muster for their monthly pay, meager though it was.[21]

Sickles's Third Corps was directed toward Emmitsburg on 30 June, halting at Bridgeport, Maryland, only about five miles west of Taneytown. Meade wanted Hancock's Second Corps to move on 1 July from Uniontown, Maryland, to Taneytown, about six miles; Sykes's Fifth Corps was ordered from Liberty, Maryland, to Hanover, Pennsylvania, by way of Westminster and Union Mills, Maryland, on 30 June, a long march of thirty miles that it would complete only to Union Mills on that day. Slocum's Twelfth Corps was directed to march from Taneytown to Two Taverns, Pennsylvania, just north of Littlestown on 30 June, nearly ten miles. Reynolds's First Corps at Emmitsburg was ordered to move, not to Marsh Creek, but "to Gettysburg," and Howard's Eleventh Corps, near Emmitsburg, was directed to be within supporting distance of Reynolds. Sedgwick's Sixth Corps was ordered to march about twenty miles from near New Windsor to Manchester, Maryland, on 30 June and anchor the right flank of the army, blocking the turnpike from Harrisburg to Baltimore. By the day's end, all of Meade's corps would be situated on or just ahead of Big Pipe Creek. Even before Meade issued any order regarding a defense line along Pipe Creek, he was positioning all seven corps so that the line could be used.[22]

In that same order, Meade directed the cavalry "to the front and flanks, well out in all directions, giving timely notice of positions and movements of the enemy." He ordered "all empty wagons, surplus baggage, useless animals, and impedimenta of every sort to Union Bridge." Supplies would eventually be brought to that location by the Western Maryland Railroad. Meade directed the Signal Corps to repair the telegraph line between Gettysburg and Hanover, on the Northern Central Railroad to Baltimore, as the Fifth Corps was ordered to move to Hanover. There was a possibility that telegraphic communications with Washington could be reopened on the Hanover line. Such a line would make communications with Washington somewhat more rapid. Meade then reminded his corps commanders: "Prompt information to be sent into headquarters at all times. All ready to move to the attack at any moment." He informed his corps commanders that General Couch believed that enemy operations on the Susquehanna were designed to prevent his cooperation with the Army of the Potomac, rather than being an offensive. Meade noted that he believed Harrisburg and Philadelphia had been relieved.[23]

When the Sixth Corps departed New Windsor that morning it left behind some stragglers, including a few who had become intoxicated. One Sixth Corps soldier had died of exhaustion the night before, grim testimony to the grueling thirty-mile march from near Hyattstown to New Windsor the previous day. That soldier was buried in the Presbyterian graveyard in New Windsor by a cousin, a fellow soldier who remained behind to tend to his stricken kinsman.[24]

Hancock's Second Corps remained in bivouac mostly south and east of Uniontown throughout 30 June; troops camped either along the John Babylon farm or on farms of Babylon's neighbors to the south. General Hancock set up headquarters south of Uniontown, in the home of Dr. J. J. Weaver, along a tributary of Little Pipe Creek; some of Hancock's staff occupied the Segafoss Hotel of Levi Grise, built in 1802, in the west end of the village.[25]

General Gibbon, Hancock's Second Division commander, sat down in his headquarters tent on the Babylon farm on the morning of 30 June and composed a letter to his wife. "We are now rapidly approaching the enemy and under our new commander, I believe, can whip him. The spirit of the army has been much improved by the change and we all now congratulate ourselves that we shall, at least, have an honest administration of affairs at Headquarters." Gibbon admired Meade, and he was not alone; many of the regular army commanders were also pleased that Meade was in command.[26]

Although General Reynolds was ordered to take his First Corps "to Gettysburg" on 30 June, for reasons unclear to history, he did not receive

Meade's order until late that night, by way of General Howard. Meade thought highly of Reynolds's skills; the First Corps commander was both competent and reliable. Forty-three years old, Reynolds was a native of Lancaster, Pennsylvania, and an 1841 graduate of West Point. After service as an artillery officer along the Atlantic Coast, the Texas frontier, and the Mexican War, he became the commandant of cadets and an instructor of tactics at West Point just before the war broke out. Captain Weld described Reynolds as "brave, kind-hearted, modest, somewhat rough and wanting polish, he was a type of the true soldier." Reynolds had a tendency to ride out alone ahead of his staff; he also had an annoying propensity to issue orders about minutiae that annoyed and, at times, insulted his subordinates. Meade and Reynolds had served alongside each other since the beginning of the war. They were close confidants despite being professional rivals. So pleased was Reynolds with the news of Meade's appointment as commander of the army that a "mark[ed] change took place" in him, said members of his staff to Reynolds's sister, Ellie. "Before," they all remarked, "he had been so depressed, and never said an unnecessary word; [after Meade's appointment] he at once seemed to throw off a load and his spirits were bright and he talked and joked as he had not done since [before] Chancellorsville." Meade may have known that Reynolds was engaged to be married to a woman named Catherine Hewitt, a native of Stillwater, New York. Kate, as she was known, wore Reynolds's West Point class ring on a necklace; in Reynolds's coat pockets were handkerchiefs embroidered by Kate with the initial "R." Around his neck he wore two emblems of Kate's Irish Catholic faith, a heart and cross and clasped hands, the claddagh. Reynolds even wore a gold ring on his little finger that bore the inscription, "Dear Kate."[27]

It was no accident that General Reynolds commanded the lead corps on the road to Emmitsburg the previous day. That position, anchoring the left wing of the army as it moved north, was closest to what appeared to be the heaviest concentrations of the enemy. If Longstreet's and Hill's corps were heading toward the Cashtown Pass on the east-west turnpike axis and threatening the left flank, Meade needed a trusted commander to be the first to meet that threat. With Reynolds at Emmitsburg, Meade was confident that his vulnerable left flank was secure. It was the importance of the left wing that prompted Meade to send members of the Signal Corps to Emmitsburg to see if they could set up telegraph wires between there and army headquarters at Taneytown that morning.[28]

Meade underscored the hefty reliance he placed on Reynolds by formally appointing him to command the left wing of the army, consisting

Major General John F. Reynolds. (Library of Congress)

of the First, Eleventh, and Third Corps. Meade dictated the order to Seth Williams. Meade directed Reynolds to "make such dispositions and give such orders as circumstances require, and report from time-to-time to the commanding general." Meade placed implicit and total trust in Reynolds's judgment. Upon Reynolds being named left wing commander, Major General Abner Doubleday, commander of the Third Division of the First Corps, took over as corps commander.[29]

Emmitsburg, the northernmost community in Frederick County, Maryland, was a thriving town up until it was devastated by fire in mid-June 1863. Located at the base of the Catoctin and South Mountain ranges, Emmitsburg is about two miles from the Adams County, Pennsylvania, line. It is situated in the midst of four streams that, for the most part, originate at the foot of the mountains and then merge south of town before emptying into the Monocacy River. Flowing almost north to south, east of Emmitsburg, is Middle Creek; running in a southeast direction, north of the town, is Flat Run. Toms Creek flows in an easterly direction south of Emmitsburg, as does its tributary, Turkey Run. Along those streams are steep ridges, not unlike those along the south bank of Big Pipe Creek.[30]

Roads then as now run in all directions to and from Emmitsburg. The road the First and Eleventh Corps followed from Frederick to Emmitsburg continued north, ten miles, to Gettysburg. Emmitsburg was laid out along a road that ran east to west, from Taneytown through Emmitsburg, to Monterey Pass in the South Mountain range. That road continued west to Waynesboro, Pennsylvania, west of the South Mountain range. Before the road climbed the mountain to Monterey Pass, on its way to Waynesboro, a road branched off from it and headed north to Fairfield and on to Cashtown.[31]

Reynolds had chosen a position for his First Corps just north of Emmitsburg on the night of 29 June. His troops occupied the high ground above Middle Creek, facing west, overlooking the turnpike from Emmitsburg to Waynesboro, through Monterey Pass in the South Mountain range, and the road that branched off the turnpike and headed to Fairfield and Cashtown. His position protected the left flank of Meade's army from an attack that might emanate from Fairfield or Cashtown, along the eastern base of the mountains. So concerned was Reynolds about an attack against the left flank at Emmitsburg that he ordered his signal officers to man a station on the summit of Carrick's Knob above the town with a telescope so that they could report enemy movement from Fairfield and Cashtown.[32]

In response to Meade's 29 June circular (not Meade's 30 June orders, which he did not timely receive), Reynolds, at 9:45 A.M. on 30 June, ordered the First Corps to move north to Marsh Creek, about seven miles south of Gettysburg, at the intersection of the Emmitsburg Road and a road to Fairfield. After leaving all his supply trains and a brigade of infantry at Emmitsburg, Reynolds sent a note to General Howard informing him that the First Corps was on the move toward Marsh Creek and that "the enemy are reported moving on Gettysburg from Fairfield and Cashtown." He instructed Howard "to be ready to move on his left" in case the enemy moved against the left wing "from Fairfield and the mountain road."[33]

The march of the First Corps to Marsh Creek on 30 June was relatively short. Harry M. Keiffer was a drummer boy in the One Hundred Fiftieth Pennsylvania. During the march, Keiffer remembered, the regiment was halted by its commander, Colonel Langhorne Wister, when it crossed into Pennsylvania so that the men could give "three rousing cheers for the Old Keystone State."[34]

Reynolds halted the leading elements of the First Corps south of Marsh Creek. Brigadier General James S. Wadsworth's First Division, along with Captain James A. Hall's Second Maine Battery, advanced to Marsh Creek, unlimbered, and came into battery, covering the road. The columns left the road and entered the woods along Marsh Creek in a battle line; pickets were sent out ahead. Brigadier General Thomas A. Rowley's Third Division, along with Captain James H. Cooper's Battery B, First Pennsylvania, were sent about a mile out the road toward Fairfield to protect the left flank. Rowley had replaced Doubleday as division commander that morning. Brigadier General John C. Robinson's Second Division, and the remaining batteries of the First Corps, were positioned to the rear as a reserve; there they could respond to any attack against Howard or to any call for assistance from Reynolds.[35]

Buford's two cavalry brigades had galloped close to Gettysburg on the night of 29 June but did not reach town due to the presence of Confederate infantry regiments nearby. Instead of engaging the Confederate infantry, Buford's brigades rode back to Fairfield and Emmitsburg and then onto the road from Emmitsburg to Gettysburg. The columns rode up that road toward Gettysburg, passing through the First Corps from Emmitsburg to Marsh Creek.[36]

By 11:00 A.M. on 30 June, General Buford's two brigades of cavalry entered Gettysburg, about seven miles ahead of the First Corps at Marsh Creek. There, Buford found "everybody in a terrible state of excitement on account of the enemy's advance" on the town. Buford wrote that he directed

Gamble's brigade through the town and westward, out the Chambersburg Pike, where he ran into the enemy. Confederate forces, Buford wrote to Generals Pleasonton and Reynolds, "approached within half a mile of the town when the head of [his] column entered." The enemy's force "was terribly exaggerated by reasonable and truthful but inexperienced men," Buford noted. But on pushing the Confederates back toward Cashtown, he learned from "reliable men that [General] Anderson's [Confederate] Division was marching from Chambersburg by Mummasburg to Hunterstown, Abbottstown, on toward York." Buford related that he had sent parties "in the direction of Cashtown" and "a strong force toward Littlestown." He noted that Colonel Gamble sent word to him that "Lee signed a pass for a citizen this morning at Chambersburg." It was the first information about Lee's whereabouts in several days.[37]

In the meantime, Reynolds penned a message to General Butterfield, bringing Meade up to date with the position of the First Corps. "The corps are placed as follows," he wrote, "two divisions of the First Corps behind Marsh Creek, one on the road leading to Gettysburg and one on the road leading from Fairfield to the Chambersburg Road, at Moritz's Tavern, with the reserve batteries." He further informed army headquarters that the Third Division was "on the road to Chambersburg behind Middle Creek, not placed in position." Reynolds reported that the position he occupied was "the position taken under the orders to march to Marsh Creek [and that he had] not changed it as it might be necessary to dispute the advance of the enemy across this creek in order to take up the position behind Middle Creek ... near Emmitsburg."[38]

In that letter, a handwritten copy of the original that was found in his coat pocket at the time of his death, Reynolds informed his commander of his thoughts regarding the operation. "I think," he wrote, "if the enemy advances in force from Gettysburg, we are to fight a defensive battle in this vicinity, that the position to be occupied is just north of the town of Emmitsburg, covering the plank road to Taneytown." Reynolds wrote that he believed the enemy would "undoubtedly endeavor to turn our left by way of Fairfield and the mountain roads leading down into the Frederick and Emmitsburg Pike near [Mount] St. Mary's College." Reynolds asked Meade if it would not be prudent to assign "an engineer officer to reconnoiter [that] position as [he had] reason to believe that the main force of the enemy is in the vicinity of Cashtown or debauching from the Cumberland Valley above it."[39]

General Meade received Reynolds's letter to Butterfield at his Taneytown headquarters, probably around 11:00 A.M. He had been given copies of all the other dispatches from General Buford that morning. At 11:30 A.M., Meade wrote back to his left wing commander. Interestingly, Meade's letter was written entirely in his own hand, emphasizing the importance Meade placed on it and the close relationship he had with Reynolds.[40]

"The enemy undoubtedly occupy the Cumberland Valley from Chambersburg in force," Meade wrote, "whether the holding of the Cashtown gap is to prevent our entrance, or is their advance against us, remains to be seen." Meade, for the first time, was entertaining the idea that Lee might be collecting his army along the base of the South Mountain range at Cashtown in order to defend that position. In his letter to Reynolds, however, Meade said that he believed that with Buford at Gettysburg and Mechanicsville and a regiment near Emmitsburg, "you ought to be advised in time of [the enemy's] approach." At the time Meade wrote the 30 June letter, he assumed that Reynolds had received his orders to move the First Corps "to Gettysburg." Meade then wrote the most interesting part of the letter: "In case of an advance in force either against you [at Gettysburg] or Howard at Emmitsburg, you must fall back to [Emmitsburg] and I will reinforce you with the corps nearest to you which are Sickles at Taneytown and Slocum at Littlestown." Meade reminded Reynolds that he had previously advised him of the "general position of the army." Meade added: "We are concentrated as my present information of the position of the enemy justifies." The cavalry of the army, he noted, was "pushed out" in "all directions" to feel for the enemy's presence so that he could develop some "positive opinion as to their position." He admonished Reynolds to "get all the information" he could and "post yourself up in the roads and routes of communication [of the enemy]." Meade then wrote a postscript: "If after occupying your present position [at Gettysburg], it is your judgment that you would be in better position at Emmitsburg than where you are, you can fall back without waiting for the enemy or further orders. Your present position was given more with a view to an advance on Gettysburg, than a defensive point."[41]

Meade's letter was the first indication to Reynolds that Meade ordered him to "advance on Gettysburg" but not to defend Gettysburg. It was clear that Meade wanted Reynolds to "post" the First Corps on the "roads and routes of communication" of Lee's forces. That was the Chambersburg to York Turnpike, the turnpike axis. Meade instructed Reynolds to get "all the information" he could. He clarified that the mission was an advance on Gettysburg but that the town was not a position he intended Reynolds to defend. Reynolds's mission was a reconnaissance-in-force. Meade needed "all the information" he could get about the dispositions and intentions of the enemy. By ordering General Howard to march the Eleventh Corps "to Gettysburg in supporting distance" of Reynolds, Meade planned that another corps would be behind and near Reynolds so that the First Corps could fall back on it if vigorously attacked. Meade's handwritten letter of 30 June was found in Reynolds's coat pocket at the time of his death. Meade was receiving his first real taste of operational command.[42]

6

FORCE HIM TO
SHOW HIS HAND

Meade's directive that the First Corps, followed by the Eleventh Corps, "advance on Gettysburg" was not an order directing Reynolds to occupy the town or even hold a position near there; rather, Meade intended for the presence of the First Corps along the turnpike axis to cause the enemy to coalesce and show its intentions. Buford's two cavalry brigades—Gamble's and Devin's—were already at Gettysburg, where the assignment was to screen Reynolds's movement along the turnpike axis.[1]

The key to Meade's strategic thinking on 30 June is found in his letter to Reynolds to "advance on Gettysburg" as well as his order issued on that same date. Meade had no definitive knowledge of the exact whereabouts of all of the corps and divisions of Lee's army; he had only bits and pieces of information. As it stood, he was virtually blind. He knew nothing about the terrain before him. If he could cause the enemy to concentrate and deploy its forces, however, perhaps it could be lured into combat along the Pipe Creek line. If not, the value to Meade of knowing where the enemy was concentrating its forces alone would be immense. Reynolds's operation on 1 July was, in large measure, a reconnaissance in force. Meade had to find a way to cause the enemy to unite and deploy so as to reveal its strength as well as its intentions. That had to be accomplished without endangering the army and its mission of covering Washington and Baltimore, a formidable task.[2]

This author is not unmindful of the conclusions made by other scholars about Reynolds's mission on 1 July. Two highly respected Gettysburg scholars, Edwin Coddington and Harry Pfanz, agree that Meade sent the First and Eleventh Corps under Reynolds forward to Gettysburg, a place where Meade believed the greatest enemy strength appeared to be, and, in the words of one of those scholars, "leaving thereby the decision to bring on a general engagement at Gettysburg to the able and aggressive Reynolds."[3]

There are problems with that contention. Those scholars assert that Meade left to Reynolds the decision to bring on a general engagement against an enemy of unknown size and dispositions at a site fourteen miles ahead of army headquarters, thirty-two miles ahead of the Sixth Corps, twenty miles ahead of the Fifth Corps, and anywhere from ten to sixteen miles ahead of all the other corps. As of 30 June, and even 1 July, none of those corps would be able to assist Reynolds if he ran into trouble. It would take the Sixth Corps at Manchester more than twenty hours of hard marching to reach Gettysburg; the Fifth Corps at Union Mills, more than twelve hours; the Second Corps at Uniontown, six hours; the Twelfth Corps at Littlestown, five hours; and the Third Corps at Bridgeport, five hours. And, if Reynolds determined to engage the enemy at Gettysburg, the battle would be fought at a place Meade knew nothing about, because Meade had no topographical map of Adams County, Pennsylvania. Reynolds did not have a topographical map of Adams County either, so he could have made no assessment of Gettysburg before he arrived there with his First Corps. Meade would write a letter to Reynolds on 1 July (before he was informed that Reynolds had been killed) asking Reynolds to advise him about whether the terrain around Gettysburg presented any advantages for the Army of the Potomac to concentrate there. This request indicated that Reynolds's mission was, to Meade, more a reconnaissance than anything else. Reynolds would never receive that letter. Meade certainly gave Reynolds discretion in his 30 June letter, but that discretion did not extend to bringing on a general engagement at Gettysburg. Meade's order was limited to placing Reynold's First Corps on the turnpike axis in order to cause the enemy to collect and deploy, and then perhaps fight a withdrawing action toward Emmitsburg or return to Emmitsburg without confronting the enemy at all. In either case, Reynolds would be able to send valuable intelligence to Meade.

A popular Civil War author, Stephen Sears, claims that Meade sent Reynolds forward with the First and Eleventh Corps on 1 July without providing any instructions as to what he should do once he arrived there, a contention belied by Meade's 30 June letter to Reynolds. It strains credulity to believe that Meade would have directed Reynolds to move the First and Eleventh Corps forward, without any instructions, knowing there was the possibility that the movement might bring about a clash with an enemy whose size and dispositions he knew nothing about, at a place he knew nothing about, when the remaining five army corps were anywhere from ten to thirty-two miles away and unable thereby to offer any assistance in the event that Reynolds's First and Eleventh Corps were vigorously attacked by forces of greater numbers and firepower.[4]

Another well-known Civil War scholar, Allen Guelzo, opines that Reynolds determined, on his own, "to use the First Corps to measure how much Confederate strength was moving toward Gettysburg; and if that strength was more than the First Corps could handle, he would fall back to Cemetery Hill, where Howard and the Eleventh Corps were waiting." Guelzo adds: "This would, without saying it, also force George Meade's hand, and the other corps of the Army of the Potomac would have to be marched to Gettysburg to fight the great battle there, not in Maryland."[5]

First of all, Meade ordered Reynolds "to Gettysburg"; Reynolds did not embark on the advance on his own. Also, Reynolds did not know there was a Cemetery Hill at Gettysburg before the First Corps arrived there on the morning of 1 July because he did not have a topographical map of Adams County. Likewise, Howard informed Reynolds on 1 July that he would halt his corps at the Wentzes' place, not Cemetery Hill. According to Guelzo, Reynolds's self-determined mission was designed to *force* Meade to give up the Pipe Creek line by engaging an enemy of unknown size and disposition, at a place he had never seen and knew nothing about and far from any support. The contention paints Reynolds as reckless and insubordinate in the extreme. This author has always believed that Reynolds was a consummate soldier and student of war. One has to believe that he was far too capable and professional to undertake any operation for the purpose of frustrating the plans of the commanding general.

Finally, a fifth Civil War scholar, John G. Selby, reaches a conclusion about Meade's mission for Reynolds on 1 July that differs from all the others. He writes: "One can criticize Meade for not aggressively seeking to start a battle with an invading army, but he was also doing nothing less than what winning generals had done time and again in the war: gather as much information as possible on the enemy's whereabouts and intentions before giving battle." Selby then concludes that Meade "remained committed to a reconnaissance in force by the First and Eleventh Corps, and to the possibility of assuming the offensive if the conditions warranted." All of the foregoing, he wrote, "demonstrates [Meade's] preference for information, order, advantage, and yes, caution, before engaging the enemy." The foregoing is entirely correct.[6]

To force the enemy to concentrate and deploy so as to reveal its intentions was what Meade ordered Reynolds and his First Corps—followed by the Eleventh Corps—to do; it is identified as one of the most dangerous tasks in mid-nineteenth-century warfare. The strategy requires using an "Advance Guard," according to Dennis Hart Mahan, professor of military and civil engineering and of the science of war at West Point. Mahan published a book on the use of an advance guard in 1847, entitled *An Elementary Treatise on Advance-Guard, Out-Post and Detachment Service of Troops and the Manner of Posting and Handling Them in the Presence of an Enemy*. Mahan taught military science to Generals Meade, Reynolds, Slocum, Sedgwick, Sykes, Hancock, Howard, and many others in the Army of the Potomac when they were West Point cadets. General Reynolds and Mahan in fact taught strategy and tactics together at West Point just before the war. Likewise, many of Lee's lieutenants studied under Mahan at West Point, and Lee was superintendent of West Point during Mahan's tenure. Much of what Mahan taught was incorporated in the *Revised Regulations of the Army of the United States* of 1861. Leaders in both armies would likely therefore be well versed in the use of a reconnaissance in force.[7]

The use of an advance guard is not unique to American military theorists. Swiss-born, French military theorist Baron Antoine Henri de Jomini used the term "Great Detachment" in his 1838 treatise, *The Art of War*, to describe a similar force. The Prussian military theorist Carl von Clausewitz referred to such a force as an "Advanced Corps" in his great tome, *On War*, published posthumously in 1832. Mahan, Jomini, and Clausewitz describe the composition and use of such an advance force in similar terms. Mahan summarizes the use of such a force best, writing: "When an enemy's position is to be reconnoitered, with a view to force him to show his hand, by causing him to call out his troops; then a large detachment of all arms, adequate to the task of pressing the enemy vigorously, and also of withdrawing with safety when pressed in turn, must be thrown forward."[8]

Mahan, Jomini, and Clausewitz all agree that an Advance Guard, Great Detachment, or Advance Corps must be sufficiently powerful to resist the inevitable attack but also be agile enough to withdraw quickly and safely. After all, the mission of such an advance force is to cause the enemy to concentrate and deploy offensively in its front and to report the enemy's strength and concentration to the army commander. The use of the advance force is for reconnaissance, not to bring on a general engagement. Once the enemy deploys, the advance force must fall back. The advance force must be large enough to delay the enemy's advance, and that, writes Clausewitz, "involves real resistance."[9]

Clausewitz not only concludes that the advance force should be sizable but also diversified: it must contain elements of all branches of service, including infantry, artillery, and cavalry. To him, "a division of 10,000 or 12,000 men, augmented by cavalry," is sufficient for great armies. Mahan, a disciple of Clausewitz, writes that an advance force must be composed of troops from "all arms," and its strength "proportioned to that of the main force [with consideration given to] the more or less resistance of an independent character it may be required to make." Generally speaking, Mahan concludes that the advance force "may vary from a third to a fifth of the total force."[10]

An advance force can be sent forward anywhere from five to twenty miles ahead of the main force, depending on the situation, Clausewitz writes. The farther the advance force moves ahead, of course, the greater the length of time it will cause the enemy forces to fight their way to the main army, assuming the advance force steadily and effectively fends off enemy attacks as it withdraws. If sent ahead five miles, Clausewitz conjectures that it takes the enemy twice as long to reach the main army as the advanced force took reaching the point of deployment. Fifteen to twenty miles ahead, he believes, would take about ten hours to march, and it would take fifteen hours for the enemy to fight its way to the main army.[11]

Withdrawals in the face of the enemy, Clausewitz writes, "must be made slowly as safety will permit." It is hard to conceive of a more complex or dangerous operation than performing the task of an advance force. "For how long such a corps may resist a frontal attack and the start of a turning movement will depend mainly on the nature of the terrain and the proximity of support," concludes Clausewitz. An advance force is always in danger of a flanking movement by the enemy because it will likely be smaller than the collected elements of the enemy. Clausewitz pens a note of caution: "If resistance is stretched over a longer period than normal—whether the result of poor judgment or of self-sacrifice in order to buy time for the army—heavy casualties are bound to follow."[12]

Obviously, the elements of an army chosen as an advance force must be carefully considered for the role. Not only must the troops be well trained and battle-tested, but the commander of the detachment must be highly intelligent, quick thinking, reliable, fearless, and capable of exercising independent judgment, a combination found in few officers.[13]

The use of cavalry alone is unthinkable. Cavalry commands can reconnoiter enemy movements, but they, alone, are not enough to cause the enemy to collect and deploy in large enough numbers so as to fulfill the purpose. Cavalry alone is insufficient to delay a significant enemy advance, particularly an advance by a large body of troops of all arms that covers significant territory. Military theorists agree that it is necessary to use cavalry only in conjunction with an advance force of infantry and artillery.[14]

The purpose of an advance force, in other words, is to march ahead of the main army and into the presence of the enemy so as to compel the enemy to collect its forces and deploy. The commander of the advance force then has some basis to measure the enemy's depth and intentions that he can report to the army commander. In the face of the enemy, the commander of the advanced force must begin a withdrawal that requires the enemy to offer resistance, all the time notifying the commander of the army of the situation. The greater distance the advance force moves ahead of the main army, the more protracted the fighting and the greater need for support from the nearest elements of the main army. A successful operation could well draw the enemy to the main army, bringing on a general engagement there. Clausewitz artfully concludes: "An advance corps derives its operational value more from its presence than from its efforts; from the engagements it might offer rather than from those it actually fights. It was never intended to stop the enemy's movements, but rather, like the weight of a pendulum, to moderate and regulate them so as to make them calculable."[15]

Meade's 30 June letter and order for Reynolds to advance the First Corps "to Gettysburg" was his directive to employ an advance force on his left flank in order to cause the enemy "to [deploy and] show his hand." It covered Meade's overarching intention to develop a defense line along Big Pipe Creek. General Hancock would later refer to Reynolds's operation as a "mask," a term used in the *Revised Regulations of the Army of the United States* of 1861 for such a movement; it could "mask" the army's defensive plans and "unmask" the enemy's positions and intentions. The advance corps was a reconnaissance in force. Reynolds would command that advance corps, an assignment he had never, in his military career, been given before. Whether he could manage the challenge presented by such a task remained to be seen.[16]

Meade made it clear that if the enemy advanced against Reynolds, he must fall back to Emmitsburg, a distance of ten miles. The purpose of the advance on Gettysburg was for Reynolds to post his divisions "in the roads and routes of communications" of the enemy. That meant that Reynolds must advance to the turnpike axis that ran from Chambersburg through Gettysburg. A move to that turnpike axis would place the First Corps in a position separating Hill's corps, then somewhere between Chambersburg and Cashtown, and Ewell's Corps, then north and east of Gettysburg. Rey-

FORCE HIM TO SHOW HIS HAND

nolds placing the First Corps on the turnpike axis would unquestionably force the enemy to collect and deploy. Once that occurred, Reynolds was then directed to withdraw toward Howard's Eleventh Corps, and Meade would reinforce the First and Eleventh Corps as they fell back to Emmitsburg with the corps that were situated nearby, the Third Corps then at Bridgeport and the Twelfth Corps then at Littlestown. While falling back, Reynolds would be able to provide Meade with valuable intelligence all along the way. Meade never ordered any corps of his army to defend an advanced position at any time while he was commander of the Army of the Potomac without having most of the other corps within supporting distance. Never. He certainly did not do so on 30 June. In fact, Meade was preparing a defensive position along Big Pipe Creek and was positioning all the other corps of the army so that they could fall back to it. Meade's operational plan for the left wing of the army was straight out of Clausewitz's treatise and from the tutelage of Meade's and Reynolds's professor Dennis Hart Mahan; it was the classic operational use of an advance corps. The operational plan for the left wing of the army on 1 July was entirely developed and ordered by George Gordon Meade. Meade conceived it, and Meade ordered its execution.[17]

Reynolds's concerns about such an operation were the position and the strength of the left flank and his belief that the enemy might be advancing toward Emmitsburg. Reynolds had been made aware of the vulnerability of his left flank by General Buford. At 12:20 P.M. on 30 June, Buford sent a brief message to Pleasonton and Reynolds: "My extreme left reports a large [enemy] force coming from toward Fairfield, in a direction to strike the Emmitsburg Road this side of Marsh Creek." He then wrote: "Reliable." If true, that was alarming news.[18]

Reynolds wrote to General Howard later in the afternoon on 30 June that "Buford ... sent a regiment to Fairfield, on the road leading from Moritz's Tavern in that direction." Reynolds informed Howard that his headquarters was at Moritz's Tavern; he had sent one division and a battery on the road to Gettysburg, and another was on the road to Fairfield. A third division was held in reserve on the road to Gettysburg. Reynolds relayed to Howard that Buford was near Gettysburg, where he found a regiment of Confederate infantry "advancing on the town." It retired as Buford advanced.[19]

Reynolds also noted that Buford claimed that Anderson's Confederate division was marching on Mummasburg and "passing off in the direction of Berlin." In a postscript to his note to General Howard, Reynolds wrote: "I do not believe the report of their marching on Berlin." He then added:

"The enemy are evidently marching out into this valley, but whether it is for the purpose of going to York or to give us battle, I cannot say." Even with a full cavalry division screening Reynolds's left wing of the army and two other cavalry divisions screening the army to the north and east, the information those cavalry commands could provide was often negligible and contradictory.[20]

By the time Howard received Reynolds's communications, his Eleventh Corps was already on the move into positions at Emmitsburg, having received from Captain Weld a direct order from General Meade to take his Eleventh Corps there. Howard was within supporting distance of Reynolds. He placed his troops "east of the town, picketing the heights to the north, and connecting with Reynolds." The Eleventh Corps occupied the positions along Middle Creek vacated by Wadsworth's and Rowley's divisions of the First Corps that morning. Two of Howard's divisions were held in readiness to resist either an attack from the road leading to Monterey Pass and Waynesboro to the left or to respond to a call from Reynolds for assistance. Howard wrote to Reynolds, stating that he sent "reconnaissances toward Fairfield and Cashtown, also to the left, to the mountains." He then added, evidently frustrated: "I want a map of Adams County [Pennsylvania], if possible. I have nothing."[21]

Meade began aligning his army in preparation for the clash with Lee. He communicated with each of his corps commanders about the positions of all other corps and what intelligence other corps commanders reported. He further admonished his corps commanders to become acquainted with the roads and topography in their area of operations.

Responding to the information supplied by General Buford that the enemy appeared at Fairfield, on the road between Chambersburg and Emmitsburg, Meade's headquarters issued orders to General Sickles at 12:45 P.M. on 30 June to move his Third Corps, then at Bridgeport, "without delay," to Emmitsburg in support of the Eleventh and First Corps. Sickles's men were ordered to "take three days' rations in their haversacks" and "sixty rounds of ammunition." All ambulances were also to accompany the troops. Sickles was ordered to "report to General Reynolds when he arrived at Emmitsburg and to throw out strong pickets on the roads from Emmitsburg to Greencastle [Pennsylvania] and Chambersburg." "The enemy," read the order, "are reported to be in force in Gettysburg." Sickles's troops got under way around 3:00 P.M. on 30 June.[22]

That same day, Meade also ordered General Hancock to move his Second Corps on the morning of 1 July "up to Taneytown, cutting across the rear of Sykes's, so as not to interfere with his movements, if this can be

Brigadier General John Buford. (Library of Congress)

done." All of the corps trains were ordered left behind, "to follow when the roads are clear." As with Sickles's men, the soldiers of the Second Corps were ordered to have "three days' provisions" in their haversacks and "sixty rounds of ammunition." Ammunition trains and ambulances were ordered to move first. Meade's order continued: "Send an officer here to select a point to park your trains ready to move toward Gettysburg or Emmitsburg as circumstances may determine." Hancock was notified that General Sykes had been informed that the Second Corps would support him at Union Mills "in case of the presence of a superior force of the enemy there." The possibility of a move toward Gettysburg was left open by Meade so that Sickles could support Reynolds if he needed the help. Hancock was ordered to communicate with Sykes and be governed by any information indicating enemy presence in front of Sykes. Meade informed Hancock that he believed "the main body of the enemy are on our left, between Chambersburg, Gettysburg, and in that vicinity, and that [he would] not be needed there."[23]

Meade directed General Slocum, commanding the Twelfth Corps at Littlestown, Pennsylvania, to "acquaint [himself] thoroughly with the roads, lanes, and bypaths between yourself and General Reynolds, on your left." He revealed that Reynolds was "at the crossing of Marsh Creek and the [road] from Emmitsburg to Gettysburg." Slocum was ordered to get the corps trains "so parked this afternoon that your ammunition and ambulances are accessible, and the rest of your trains can be left." Slocum was admonished to ascertain all he could of the country between his position and Union Mills and Hanover. The key intelligence Meade reported to Slocum was that "General Reynolds reports the enemy holding Cashtown Pass, between Gettysburg and Chambersburg, in force, moving on Gettysburg."[24]

Finally, Meade wanted to relieve the army of the burden of the immense pontoon trains that traveled along behind the Fifth Corps. He directed the commanding officer of the Engineer Brigade to return the trains, "with the exception of material for 150 feet of bridge," to Washington. Once there, Meade directed the commander to "put [the] trains in order to be sent to any point that may be needed, and report by telegraph to [army] headquarters." Indeed, Meade was preparing for battle.[25]

At 4:30 P.M. on 30 June, Meade summarized the situation facing the Army of the Potomac in a telegram to Halleck. He restated the position of each of his seven corps. Meade then gave Halleck his last understanding of the whereabouts of the enemy. "Our reports," Meade wrote, "seem to place Ewell in the vicinity of York and Harrisburg." He then added: "A. P. Hill moving between Chambersburg and York. Our cavalry drove a regiment out of Gettysburg this A.M." Little, however, seemed to have changed with respect to the position of the enemy over the past twenty-four hours. Meade remained without any definitive information of the enemy's whereabouts on the evening of 30 June, other than the vague reports from Buford. He did note to Halleck that he wanted to rest as many of his troops as possible. "I fear that I shall break down the troops by pushing on much faster, and may have a rest today," Meade wrote.[26]

Meade continued to fume over Sickles's poor performance on the previous day; in the face of a powerful enemy, such performance could be catastrophic. With Seth Williams as his scribe, Meade wrote to Sickles in explicit terms that afternoon: "The commanding general noticed with regret the very slow movement of your corps yesterday. It is presumed you marched at an early hour, and up to 6:00 P.M. the rear of your column had not passed Middleburg, distant from your camp of the night before some 12 miles only." Williams warned that such "was far from meeting the expectation of the commanding general, and delayed to a very late hour the arrival of troops and trains in your rear." He reminded Sickles that the Second Corps, "in the same space of time," marched "double your own."[27]

Despite the noted shortcomings of Sickles's performance as a commander, at this point, Meade's left flank appeared to be secure. The greatest threat of an enemy attack was along that flank. The First, Third, and Eleventh Corps were ordered to positions, or were already in positions, at Emmitsburg and just over the Pennsylvania state line, about five miles north of Emmitsburg, and General Reynolds commanded that wing. Hancock's Second Corps held the center at Uniontown, just east of Meade's Taneytown headquarters. Hancock would move the Second Corps to Taneytown in the morning. North of Taneytown was Littlestown, Pennsylvania, where Slocum's Twelfth Corps was directed to resist any enemy advance and to fall back upon Taneytown and then Big Pipe Creek near Uniontown, where he would be reinforced by the Second Corps. Slocum was also ordered to march to the assistance of the left flank at Emmitsburg by a direct road that ran through Taneytown, if the need arose. Likewise, Slocum was under orders to communicate with Sykes and Sedgwick in the event of enemy activity on their fronts. Anchoring the right flank, Sedgwick's Sixth Corps was approaching Manchester, while Sykes's Fifth Corps was nearing Union Mills, between Littlestown and Westminster, a position that would also allow Slocum and Hancock, if necessary, to fall back on the Fifth Corps if attacked and those corps to take up positions along the south bank of Big Pipe Creek.[28]

As the Sixth Corps approached Manchester, General Sedgwick was alerted about the Confederate sympathies in the town. Two local citizens, Dr. Jacob Shower and George A. Shower, were promptly arrested. Dr. Shower lived on Baltimore Street in Manchester directly across from the Washington Hotel. George Shower owned a general store next to the hotel. They were escorted to Baltimore under guard. General Sedgwick's headquarters occupied a schoolhouse, just south of Manchester, on the road to Westminster, in the midst of his troops. The Sixth Corps went into bivouac in the fields along the road between Manchester and Westminster.[29]

General Sykes's Fifth Corps marched as far as Union Mills on the Baltimore Pike by nightfall. A mill and miller's house were located there on the turnpike and along Big Pipe Creek, about seven miles north of Westminster. Although General Stuart's Confederate cavalry brigades had camped at the site of the mill the night before, the miller's family members were startled by the sheer numbers of Union troops pouring into the area.[30]

"Campfires are burning over all the hills," wrote Miss S. C. Shriver, a sister of William H. Shriver, who lived with her brother and his family on the hill across the Baltimore Pike from the mill. The Shrivers were Confederate sympathizers. They had entertained Generals Stuart and Fitzhugh Lee the night before, and Stuart's three cavalry brigades, responsible for disrupting Meade's communications over the past twenty-four hours, had bivouacked there. Two divisions of the Fifth Corps arrived around 3:00 P.M. One division was commanded by Major General James Barnes, who occupied the Shriver home as his headquarters that night; Brigadier General Romeyn B. Ayres's division was nearby, and General Crawford's division of the Pennsylvania Reserves was near Frizzellburg, not far behind, having marched nearly twenty-five miles. The men broke ranks and began setting up camps. Miss Shriver was astonished and frightened by the size of the Union corps. The supply trains were parked in their fields. All the Shriver's fences quickly disappeared. "Every now and then we hear the report of a gun, which our Provost Guard (stationed in our back yard) tells me is the men killing cattle, of which an immense drove came with the army," wrote Miss Shriver. "I know our Dear Lord will protect us, and our blessed Mother will watch over us," she noted.[31]

Meanwhile, on Meade's left flank, General Reynolds was keenly aware that a major clash with the enemy could occur within the next forty-eight hours. At 8:00 P.M. the signal officers on the summit of Carrick's Knob overlooking Emmitsburg scribbled a note in pencil on onionskin paper to Reynolds at Marsh Creek. They described what they observed from their station above the valley west and north of Emmitsburg and the roads leading there from Fairfield and Monterey Pass until "rain cut short [their] observation." They were able to report "no indications of enemy." Reynolds received that message around 9:00 P.M. on 30 June.[32]

When General Howard had arrived at Emmitsburg on the evening of 29 June, the "Jesuit Fathers" at St. Joseph Female Academy met him and offered their quarters to him. Howard remembered later that he "yielded

FORCE HIM TO SHOW HIS HAND

to the tempting offer of hospitality ... and went to enjoy the neat and comfortable bed which was offered." Howard planned to retire to that same bed on the night of 30 June. At nightfall, a messenger arrived with an oral request from Reynolds for Howard to ride to his headquarters at Marsh Creek. Accompanied by Lieutenant F. W. Gilbreth, his aide-de-camp, and an orderly, Howard set out immediately.[33]

Howard reported to Reynolds at Moritz's Tavern, the two-and-one-half-story brick house that stood on the east side of the turnpike between Emmitsburg and Gettysburg, about one mile south of Marsh Creek. Owned by Samuel Moritz, the house was not used as a tavern in 1863; the owner had ceased paying the necessary assessment. On his arrival, Howard was escorted to a back room at the south end of the house. There Howard found Reynolds, who stood up to greet him. The room was sparsely furnished; it had only a table and a few chairs, remembered Howard. The table was covered with papers, mostly "maps and official dispatches." Reynolds opened with a discussion of Meade's orders to address the troops, reminding Howard to use inspiring, morale-boosting speeches, to promote "every patriotic sentiment" to "arouse to enthusiasm and action [the] whole army." Just as Meade was doing with his corps commanders, Reynolds brought Howard up to date with all the information he had obtained about enemy activity and where all the other corps were situated. Reynolds then reviewed all the numerous dispatches from General Buford and from scouts and alarmed citizens. Those messages uniformly indicated that Lee's army was "in great force" nearby. The two commanders spent the evening "looking over the different maps, discussing the probabilities of a great battle," recalled Howard, "and talking of the part our wing would be likely to play in the conflict." Reynolds discussed with Howard the mission given to the First Corps and the left wing by Meade to move ahead toward Gettysburg and force the enemy to concentrate and deploy.[34]

Howard noted that "Reynolds seemed depressed." He surmised that Reynolds was "probably anxious on account of the scattered condition of [the] army, particularly in view of the sudden concentration of the enemy." At about 11:00 P.M., Howard departed and rode back to his Emmitsburg quarters. When he arrived, he was shocked and surprised when an orderly presented him with an envelope addressed to General Reynolds, as the wing commander, containing Meade's order issued earlier that day for the movement of the army on 30 June. Why it had not reached Reynolds is inexplicable. Howard hurriedly read the dispatches, prepared a note to Reynolds, and sent the entire package off to his wing commander by courier. Before midnight, Reynolds finally received Meade's 30 June order for the movement of the First Corps "to Gettysburg." He undoubtedly understood Meade's directive for him to lead the First Corps to Gettysburg as the "advance corps" of the army.[35]

At 10:30 P.M., Buford sent to Reynolds his most detailed dispatch regarding enemy concentrations, a message Reynolds immediately sent to Meade. Buford wrote that he was "satisfied that A. P. Hill's Corps is massed just back of Cashtown, about 9 miles from [Gettysburg]." He noted that [Major General William D.] Pender's Division of Hill's Corps "came up today." Enemy pickets at the time Buford wrote his dispatch to Reynolds were "within 4 miles of this place, on the Cashtown road." Buford's scouting parties that had scoured the countryside north, northwest, and northeast of Gettysburg reported no enemy force having passed along the road "from Cashtown to Oxford." Still, that road, Buford noted, was "terribly infested with prowling cavalry parties." A courier of Lee's was captured near Heidlersburg, he wrote. Buford added information secured from the captured courier: "Ewell's Corps is crossing the mountains from Carlisle. Rodes's Division being at Petersburg in advance." Petersburg was just north of Heidlersburg. Buford concluded, adding, "Longstreet, from all I can learn, is still behind Hill." Reynolds probably received Buford's dispatch at about the same time as he did Meade's 30 June order. Reynolds unquestionably sent a rider up the Emmitsburg Road to Gettysburg to notify Buford of his pending operation. Reynolds had to make sure, when he arrived there, that he could post the First Corps on the "roads and routes of communication" of the enemy and that he would be able to obtain as much information as possible of the whereabouts of the enemy columns so he could assess where and how to deploy his troops.[36]

June came to an end. Reynolds and the First Corps were at Marsh Creek, just across the Pennsylvania state line, about five miles north of Emmitsburg. Behind Reynolds was Howard's Eleventh Corps at Emmitsburg. Sickles Third Corps was marching to Emmitsburg. Hancock's Second Corps remained at Uniontown. Sykes's Fifth Corps had marched to Union Mills by way of Johnsville, Uniontown, and Frizzellburg, bypassing Westminster to the south; it would march to Hanover in the morning. Sedgwick's Sixth Corps marched from New Windsor through Westminster to within two miles of Manchester, while Slocum's Twelfth Corps was at Littlestown, Pennsylvania; it would march to Two Taverns, a crossroads just northwest of Littlestown, in the morning.[37]

Rain continued to fall through the night of 30 June and into the wee hours of 1 July. Meade found a moment to write to Margaret. He explained to her his belief that the advance of the army had "relieved Harrisburg and Philadelphia and that Lee has now come to the conclusion that he must attend to other matters." Although Meade informed his wife that "all is going on well" and that he, personally, was well, he was, nevertheless, "much oppressed with a sense of responsibility and the magnitude of the great interests entrusted to me." He then noted: "Of course, in time I will become accustomed to this." Closing his brief letter, Meade, as he often did, added: "Love, blessings and kisses to all. Pray for me and beseech our heavenly Father to permit me to be an instrument to save my country and advance a just cause."[38]

While Meade had been preoccupied with discovering the whereabouts of Lee's army and Lee's intentions, the White House and War Department had been inundated with frantic appeals to bolster the defenses of Washington, Baltimore, and Philadelphia. Artillery batteries and infantry were placed at nearly thirty forts located south, west, and north of Washington, blocking all approaches to the city. More than four thousand "able-bodied" African Americans were at work on fortifications outside of Baltimore. Martial law was declared in Baltimore due to "the immediate presence of the rebel army within this department and the State of Maryland." General Halleck even issued orders to General Couch to be prepared to "hold the enemy in check on the Susquehanna till General Meade [could] give them battle." Urgent requests poured into the White House; one of them asked the president to place General McClellan in command of all Pennsylvania troops not attached to Meade's army. Another correspondent suggested that New Jersey and New York "would respond to his call with great alacrity" if McClellan was named commander of their troops.[39]

It seemed as though few people had any confidence at all that Meade's army would, or even could, defeat, much less block, what they believed was Lee's drive to conquer those cities. Yet many officers and men in the army showed little sympathy for those cities, particularly Washington. Wrote a reporter for the *New York Times* traveling with the army: "If NERO could fiddle while Rome was burning, it is believed he finds his counterpart in [Lincoln], who cat-hauls the Army of the Potomac while the rebels are positively knocking at his own doors."[40]

7

ONE CORPS AT EMMITSBURG, TWO AT GETTYSBURG

General Meade was awake throughout the night of 30 June and all through the wee hours of Wednesday, 1 July. He received and sent telegrams and dispatches as a gentle rain pattered down on his headquarters tent along Piney Creek outside of Taneytown. Meade read the telegram from General Halleck approving the "plan of operations"; it was the response to the message he had sent to Halleck at 11:00 A.M. of 29 June! Because the telegraph wires along the Baltimore & Ohio Railroad had been cut, it had taken more than thirty-six hours for Meade to receive a response to his plans.[1]

As if the logistical problems were not worrying enough, Meade continued to be preoccupied with concerns for his left flank. The previous day, he had ordered General Reynolds to move the First Corps to join General Buford's two cavalry brigades that were positioned along the turnpike axis just west of Gettysburg, in an effort to force the enemy to concentrate and to reveal its intentions. That the First Corps would move nearly seven miles north in order to get onto that turnpike axis necessitated close support. Meade had provided for that support in his 30 June orders. Thus, at about 10:00 P.M. on 30 June, he sent an aide to General Howard's headquarters in Emmitsburg with an order directing him to move the Eleventh Corps "to within supporting distance of the [First Corps] at Gettysburg." That aide arrived at Howard's headquarters in the wee hours of 1 July. Meade's idea for the forward movement of the Eleventh Corps was to place it near enough to the First Corps so that Reynolds could fall back on it if the enemy concentrated in overwhelming numbers and vigorously attacked him.[2]

Waiting at Meade's headquarters was Major William Riddle of Reynolds's staff. After delivering dispatches to Meade at 10:00 P.M., 30 June,

Riddle remained there, as was customary, until Meade could send him back to Reynolds with orders of his own. Riddle was given a number of orders and dispatches at about the same early morning hour that Meade sent an aide to General Howard.[3]

Riddle rode through the rain after receiving Meade's orders, arriving back at Moritz's Tavern at about 4:00 A.M. The rain continued pouring down. He found Reynolds sound asleep on the floor of the back room, wrapped in his blanket. Riddle hesitated to disturb the general, but after reading the dispatches, he decided to awaken Reynolds. Among the documents held by Major Riddle was likely a copy of Meade's 30 June orders to advance to Gettysburg along with a copy of his 1 July order to Howard to move the Eleventh Corps in support of Reynolds. Copies of other dispatches relaying information of the whereabouts of the enemy from various commanders, particularly General Buford, were probably included in the packet, too. Riddle awakened Reynolds and handed the documents to the general. Reynolds read the dispatches, stood up, and then walked into the front rooms of the tavern, where all his other staff officers were sleeping on the floor. He walked among his staff, awakening them as was his habit. It was 4:30 A.M.[4]

Back at Taneytown, a heady mixture of both good news and bad news was relayed to Meade by couriers from the four or five telegraphers at the telegraph terminal at Frederick that morning. The War Department informed him that the Baltimore & Ohio Railroad was fully operational again; a mail train had left Baltimore on the morning of 30 June and arrived at Frederick at 1:00 P.M. But then Meade read copies of telegrams from General French at Harper's Ferry to Halleck and from Halleck to French in the early hours of 1 July; he realized that his orders to French had not been obeyed. French notified Halleck that he was unable to telegraph him the day before, but he claimed that an "immense amount of stores [at Harper's Ferry] cannot be removed under at least ten days." Although a brigade of infantry, with artillery and an engineer company, were left behind at Harper's Ferry, French informed Halleck: "I commenced this morning to destroy ammunition. Some of the heavy guns will have to be left." French had violated Meade's and Halleck's explicit instructions. Even though he was ordered by Meade on 29 June to march his command to the Army of the Potomac, French wrote to Halleck: "I am in readiness to move with the remainder of my force, but will await your instructions." His telegram ended: "I cannot communicate with headquarters Army of the Potomac."[5]

Meade must have been beside himself. He read the reply telegram from

Halleck to French. "No ammunition or stores should be destroyed, excepting in the case of absolute necessity," wrote Halleck. "These things should not be abandoned, but defended." Now that telegraphic communications with the Army of the Potomac had been reopened, Halleck informed French he could finally communicate directly with General Meade.[6]

Another package of telegrams arrived at army headquarters from the War Department. Those may well have been carried by Luther Rose of the Military Telegraph Service. Rose recorded in his diary being given "dispatches of the utmost importance" at 1:00 A.M. by the telegraphers at Frederick to be taken to General Meade. He claimed he rode "over thirty miles in four hours and fifteen minutes through strange country in the night." In that package of dispatches, was a curious telegram Secretary Stanton had received from Brigadier General Herman Haupt, chief of the Bureau of United States Military Railroads, whom Meade had known as a classmate at West Point. Haupt had attempted to locate the Army of the Potomac on 29 June in an effort to lend his assistance, but after the Baltimore & Ohio Railroad had been cut by Stuart's Confederate cavalry brigades on 28 June, he sought to travel to Harrisburg to uncover the situation. Unfortunately for Haupt, the Northern Central Railroad bridges had been destroyed between Hanover Junction and Harrisburg by elements of General Ewell's corps, forcing him to travel to Harrisburg by way of Philadelphia and Reading.[7]

In the package was a telegram Haupt wrote to Halleck late at night on 30 June from Harrisburg with information he received from spies employed by the Northern Central and Pennsylvania Central Railroads. "Lee is falling back suddenly from the vicinity of Harrisburg, and concentrating all his forces," Haupt wrote. "York has been evacuated. Carlisle is being evacuated. The concentration appears to be at or near Chambersburg. The object apparently [is] a sudden movement against Meade, of which he should be advised by courier immediately. A courier might reach Frederick by way of [the] Western Maryland Railroad to Westminster." Haupt closed his telegram by noting that the information he provided came from a Colonel Thomas A. Scott, an adviser to Pennsylvania Governor Andrew Curtin. Haupt then wrote: "I think it is reliable."[8]

Another telegram Haupt sent to Halleck at 12:45 A.M. on 1 July was also in the package. In this he wrote that he had just received information that the "point of concentration of Lee's forces was at Gettysburg, not Chambersburg." Haupt then added: "The movement on their part is very hurried.... Meade should, by all means, be informed, and be prepared for a sudden attack from Lee's whole army." That intelligence apparently came from civilian residents of Chambersburg. Haupt claimed that Meade received the message by special courier from Westminster at 3:00 A.M. on 1 July. How he knew that is not known.[9]

Later that morning Haupt wrote yet another telegram to General Halleck commenting on "skirmishing near Harrisburg" and the troops gathered to protect the city. He claimed to possess information that Lee knew of Hooker's removal and replacement and that Meade's communications had been cut. Lee knew as well, Haupt wrote, that "Meade could not at once get his forces in hand, and that, by suddenly concentrating and falling upon Meade, he could be crushed." Yet Haupt did not claim that Lee was concentrating at Gettysburg as he reported in his prior message. Rather, he asserted that Longstreet's corps "passed through Chambersburg . . . in the direction of Carlisle." He then stated, "Hill's corps commenced leaving Chambersburg," in the direction of Gettysburg, and that "Early left Gettysburg for York."[10]

Meade unquestionably was aware of much of the information related by Haupt to the War Department. Similar intelligence had been relayed to Meade through other channels. The problem was that that information had not substantially changed in days. It was also contradictory. Meade believed that Lee was concentrating his army, but he did not know exactly where. Neither did Haupt. That Lee might make a "sudden movement" against Meade's army was already understood by Meade to be a distinct possibility, although it was not a certainty by any stretch of the imagination. Meade was attempting to cause Lee to concentrate his army and advance against him. The information provided by Haupt was useless. Meade probably read the dispatches with some aggravation. Haupt had only a sketchy idea where Meade's army was situated, and he knew little of the course of the campaign to date. That the uninformed Haupt was interjecting himself between Meade and his commanders in Washington—even suggesting movements to be made—must have been troubling to Meade. It would not be the last time Haupt would interfere.[11]

Accompanying Haupt's first dispatch was Secretary Stanton's own "news" to Meade. "It is proper you should know that General French this morning evacuated Maryland Heights, blowing up his magazine, spiking the large cannon, and destroying surplus stores," Stanton wrote to Meade. Stanton continued, writing that French was still at Sandy Hook waiting for orders, and "doubtful what he should do with his force. Please instruct him what you wish him to do." In the dark, early hours of 1 July, George Meade confronted an unpromising situation with respect to General French.[12]

At an early hour, Meade and his staff and engineers, along with General

Henry Hunt, probably General Warren, and a large escort, rode on horse-back in the rain from Taneytown to near Westminster to inspect the full extent of the ground along the south bank of Big Pipe Creek. Hunt, it appears, rode all the way to near Union Mills before returning to Taneytown. While inspecting the contemplated defense lines, Meade wrote to General Halleck at 7:00 A.M. on 1 July. He noted that he was then "nine miles east of Middleburg." That put him between Uniontown and Westminster. To get there, Meade, Hunt, Warren, and their staffs, engineers, and escorts retraced the route between Taneytown and Middleburg at dawn, stopping to examine the bluffs overlooking Big Pipe Creek along the Koons farm where Meade's headquarters were established on the night of 29 June. They then followed the road from Middleburg to Westminster, passing through Uniontown. All along the way, Meade, Hunt, and Warren examined the bluffs overlooking Big Pipe Creek and the roads connecting most of the possible positions along the line the army might occupy. That Meade was examining the extent of the Pipe Creek line on the morning of 1 July illustrates his intention to defend it, not bring on a general engagement with the enemy fifteen miles ahead of it.[13]

While he was outside of Uniontown, Meade acknowledged in his dispatch to Halleck that he received the information from General Haupt but made no comment about it. Instead, he brought Halleck up to date with the positions of the army and of his own strategic thinking. "My positions today," he wrote, "are one corps at Emmitsburg, two at Gettysburg, one at Taneytown, one at Two Taverns, one at Manchester, one at Hanover." He then added: "These movements were ordered yesterday, before receipt of advises of Lee's movements." Meade then informed Halleck of his strategic plans: "The point of Lee's concentration and the nature of the country, when ascertained, will determine whether I attack him or not. Shall advise you further today, when satisfied that the enemy are fully withdrawn from the Susquehanna. If General Couch has any reliable force, I shall call upon him to move it to aid me."[14]

While assessing where and how to position his immense army in the face of an approaching enemy, Meade responded to Halleck's and Secretary Stanton's messages regarding General French at Harper's Ferry. He scribbled a terse reply to Stanton: "French was ordered to send 3,000 of his force to Washington, with all his property, then to move up and join me with the balance." That was it. Obviously, French had failed to follow Meade's direct orders, and Halleck and Stanton must know it. Meade handed the dispatches to an aide and sent him galloping back to the telegraph terminal at Frederick nearly thirty miles south.[15]

Meade's planned advance of the First and Eleventh Corps on the left flank was about to get under way. All around the fields and woods between Moritz's Tavern and Marsh Creek—and south and west of the tavern—the troops were stirring. The weather did not look favorable, being "muggy and disagreeable"; throughout the morning there were intermittent drenching showers. All of that, remembered Captain Weld, made "the roads very bad in some places." Smoke from the innumerable campfires hung close to the ground in the humid and foggy atmosphere, obscuring all but what was near the viewer.[16]

Drums rolled. "Fall in!" yelled officers. "Attention!" The First Corps, twenty-nine infantry regiments and five batteries of artillery, 12,157 officers and men "available for line of battle," according to the muster returns from the previous day, prepared to move ahead. An order from General Doubleday placed the Third Division in the lead and the First Division in the rear, with the artillery brigade following the lead division and ahead of the Second Division. Those were the customary orders; they allowed for the division that led the previous day's march to take a position at the rear of the columns on the ensuing day. Because the First Division occupied both sides of the Emmitsburg Road from Moritz's Tavern all the way north to Marsh Creek, however, Reynolds himself directed the Third Division off the road at the tavern and ordered General Wadsworth's First Division to lead the march of the First Corps for the second day in a row, apparently in order to move the corps forward with greater speed.[17]

The town to which Meade ordered Reynolds to move his First Corps—Gettysburg—was, and still is, the county seat of Adams County, Pennsylvania. Incorporated in 1806, the borough of Gettysburg is located only ten miles north of Emmitsburg, Maryland. By 1863 Gettysburg, and its surrounding Cumberland Township, had 1,325 people living there, including 67 free African Americans. Settled by Scottish and Scottish Irish people in the mid-eighteenth century, Gettysburg abounded with residents named McClellan, McAllister, McKean, McPherson, McKnight, and McIllheny. English, Dutch, and German settlers followed, and the countryside became dotted with names like Trostle, Weikert, Leister, Arendt, Wentz, Herbst, Hummelbaugh, Ziegler, and Wert. Unlike the people in Maryland, the inhabitants of Gettysburg in 1863 were decidedly pro-Union. One of the local newspapers, the *Sentinel*, was a Republican organ. The *Compiler* was the newspaper read by the Democratic minority.[18]

The settling of Gettysburg and Adams County by the Scottish and Scottish Irish, Dutch, and German peoples was told by its churches. Presbyterian churches were the first to be erected in the rural part of the county

Lutheran Theological Seminary, Gettysburg, Pennsylvania.
(Library of Congress)

and in town. Then came the German Reformed Church, Christ Evangelical Lutheran Church, and St. James Lutheran Church, followed by the St. Francis Xavier Roman Catholic Church.[19]

The people of Adams County were vitally interested in education. Gettysburg became the site of the Lutheran Theological Seminary in 1826 and then Pennsylvania College six years later. By 1863, the Lutheran Theological Seminary was housed in a four-story brick building with a distinctive cupola situated on what was aptly called Seminary Ridge on the west end of town just south of the turnpike that ran west from Gettysburg to Cashtown and on to Chambersburg. Pennsylvania College by then featured a beautiful Greek revival four-story brick building, painted white, with an octagonal cupola and a portico supported by four Doric columns, on the north end of town. Several academies and schools, including a female academy, were located in Gettysburg.[20]

In 1863, Gettysburg was a hub of roads and turnpikes. It was situated on the east-to-west Chambersburg to York Turnpike—the turnpike axis—that began at Chambersburg and extended to Cashtown, at the foot of the South Mountain range, and then ran eight miles to Gettysburg. From Gettysburg, the turnpike extended east all the way to York. Gettysburg was also the terminus of the Baltimore Pike, which ran southeast to Westminster and on to Baltimore. Extending south, too, was a road to Taneytown, Maryland, as well as the road to Emmitsburg. Beyond those roads were roads that extended northwest to Mummasburg, Pennsylvania, and north to Carlisle and to Harrisburg. Gettysburg was the terminus of the Hanover Junction, Hanover, and Gettysburg Railroad that connected the town to the Northern Central Railroad at Hanover Junction to the east. A railroad that would eventually run west of Gettysburg to and beyond Fairfield, Pennsylvania, known as the Tapeworm Railroad, was unfinished in 1863.[21]

With all the turnpikes and roads entering and exiting Gettysburg, there were hotels like the three-story Eagle Hotel on Chambersburg Street, the McClellan Hotel on the town square, and the Globe Hotel nearby. There were large buildings like the Fahnestock Brothers store and residence on Baltimore Street, but mostly, the streets were lined by townhouses and storefronts erected next to one another that stood only eight or ten feet from the streets.[22]

Gettysburg is situated between two streams that flow north to south: Marsh Creek on the west and Rock Creek on the east. At Gettysburg, they are six miles apart. Marsh Creek rises south of the Chambersburg Pike in neighboring Franklin Township and flows south; after being joined by a number of smaller streams, including Willoughby Run, it unites with Rock Creek and forms the Monocacy River at the Maryland line. The Adams County countryside is generally undulating, but on the east side of the town of Gettysburg are heights: Cemetery Hill, McKnight's Hill, Culp's Hill, Wolf Hill, and Powers Hill, along or near which runs the Baltimore Pike. As the name suggests, Cemetery Hill is the site of the principal town cemetery. Along the Baltimore Pike on Cemetery Hill stands an iconic brick cemetery gatehouse. Extending south from Cemetery Hill is a low ridge, known as Cemetery—or Granite—Ridge, that extends all the way to two hills that tower over the landscape, known as Big Round Top and Little Round Top. Big Round Top stands about 799 feet above sea level; Little Round Top was not that high, but on its southern, western, and northern faces all the trees had been cut. To the west of town, one mile west of, and mostly parallel to, Cemetery Ridge, is another long ridge, known as Seminary Ridge, that begins northwest of town at Oak Hill and extends south all the way to opposite the Round Tops. On most of those

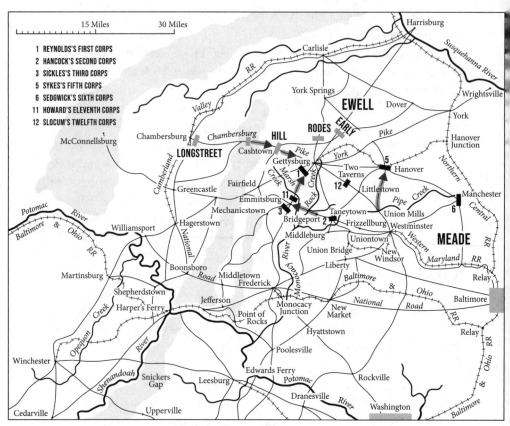

Map 7.1. 1 July 1863: The left wing of Meade's army moves to Gettysburg.

hills and their spur hills and ridges are formations of granite rock. The most notable of those ridges is Devil's Den, just below Little Round Top. Unfortunately for General Reynolds, as for General Meade, the Adams County residential map they were using in the days leading up to the battle failed to show any of those topographical features at all.[23]

Before the First Corps got in motion, it seems breakfast was delivered to Reynolds and his staff by a sixteen-year-old boy named Jacob C. Shriver, the son of Mr. and Mrs. Christian Shriver, who lived in Gettysburg. Reynolds had given Shriver a pass the evening before. Attached to the pass was a request for provisions. Young Shriver delivered meat, potatoes, eggs, and bread, all prepared by his mother, Alice Shriver, to Reynolds and his staff at Marsh Creek just before the columns began their trek to Gettysburg.[24]

At 6:00 A.M. the columns of the First Division of the First Corps prepared to move up the Emmitsburg Road toward Gettysburg; two columns lined up on either side of the road, and the wheeled vehicles, along with mounted officers, came into line in the middle of the road. Reynolds called on Colonel Wainwright to direct Captain Hall's Second Maine Battery, camped near Marsh Creek, to accompany the leading First Division.[25]

General Howard at Emmitsburg wrote to Reynolds at that same hour after arousing the Eleventh Corps and determining the best routes of approach to Gettysburg. The dispatch was received by Reynolds just before the First Division got under way. Howard noted to Reynolds that he "received orders direct from headquarters Army of the Potomac to move within supporting distance of you at Gettysburg." The Eleventh Corps would move forward using two routes: the Emmitsburg Road following the First Corps and the "road past Horner's Mills," in order "to relieve the direct road for [the First Corps] ammunition trains" and to move Howard's own ammunition trains forward more easily. That second route, on which two of Howard's three divisions would march, would allow them to enter Gettysburg on the Taneytown Road. Howard then added: "Unless you desire otherwise, I will encamp near J. Wintz's [sic] place near the crossroads, about 2 miles this side of Gettysburg." Reynolds, it appears, had provided Howard with an 1858 M. S. & E. Converse residential map of Adams County, Pennsylvania, or a similar map, where the frame house of septuagenarian John Wentz was denoted just north of what would become the famous Peach Orchard, across the Emmitsburg Road from the brick house of the Reverend Joseph and Mary Sherfy, about three miles south of Gettysburg. In accordance with Meade's orders, Howard determined to take the Eleventh Corps to the Wentz place so that Reynolds could fall back on it if vigorously attacked.[26]

Reynolds dictated a message to his adjutant general, Captain Edward C. Baird, to be delivered to Howard. He admonished Howard, in accordance with Meade's explicit instructions, that "the movements of all the trains will be subordinate to those of the troops." He then directed all of Howard's "empty wagons, useless horses, etc.," to be sent to the Western Maryland Railroad terminus at Union Bridge, Maryland, three miles south of Middleburg. No orders are extant from Reynolds regarding the disposition of the quartermaster and subsistence wagon trains of the First and Eleventh Corps. Likely, the trains remained at or near Emmitsburg under guard pending subsequent orders. The Twelfth and Fifteenth Vermont Infantry regiments were detailed to protect those trains. Those wagon trains were ultimately directed to Union Bridge.[27]

The wagon trains that accompanied the troops consisted of ambulances, ordnance wagons, and only those quartermaster wagons containing stores absolutely necessary to the mission. The standing orders in the Army of the Potomac called on all other wagon trains to be sent to the rear as the army advanced toward the enemy so that the long columns of wagons would not interfere with the movement of the troops and their immense stores would be protected.[28]

Around 7:00 A.M., Reynolds called for General Doubleday to join him at Marsh Creek. Reynolds carefully went over with Doubleday all the orders and dispatches he had received that morning relating to the movements of the enemy and the latest positions of the other army corps. Doubleday recalled that the dispatches revealed that "the enemy was reported in force at Cashtown and Mummasburg, and that our cavalry was skirmishing with them on the roads leading from Gettysburg to those places." He further remembered that "it was General Reynolds's intention to dispute the enemy's advance, falling back, however, in case of a serious attack, to the ground already chosen at Emmitsburg." That, of course, was precisely what Meade instructed Reynolds to do.[29]

The march of Wadsworth's First Division—only 3,857 officers and men—with Reynolds accompanying it, got under way more than an hour ahead of the remaining two divisions of the First Corps. First on the road was Brigadier General Lysander Cutler's Second Brigade of Wadsworth's division. Why Reynolds did not wait for all three divisions to close up on one another for the march is not known. After all, an advance corps must be composed of a significant force of all arms, as the movement is designed to force the enemy to concentrate against it. Reynolds was impetuous indeed. Perhaps Reynolds did not believe that the enemy was in a position to concentrate forces significant enough that morning to attack the First Corps. Colonel Wainwright claimed that he rode up to Reynolds and asked him, among other things, about the "prospects of a fight." Reynolds remarked, according to Wainwright, that "he did not expect any"; rather, he asserted that the First Corps "was moving up so as to be within supporting distance of Buford, who was pushed out farther." But that did not relieve Reynolds of his duty to bring his maximum strength forward to the "roads and routes of communication" of the enemy in order to force its concentration.[30]

"We moved along very quietly without dreaming of a fight," recalled Wainwright, "and fully expecting to be comfortably in camp by noon." So confident was he of that fact that, "for the first time," he wrote, "I threw my saddlebags into the wagon, and thus left without my supply of chocolate and tobacco, without brush, comb, or clean handkerchief." On up the road, Wainwright's horse, Billy, cast two shoes. He recalled that he "had no hesitation in stopping at a farm house with one of [his] forges until they could be replaced, and even sat there ten or fifteen minutes longer until a heavy shower was over."[31]

The troops marched on. Soon the skies cleared, and the sun beamed bright and hot. The humidity became intense. Recalled a soldier in the Fourteenth Brooklyn: "The men pushed forward along the Emmitsburg Turnpike. Upon reaching a point about two miles from Gettysburg, at a turn of the road, they suddenly beheld a panorama of the hills and valleys lying at the foot of the Blue Ridge spread out before them."[32]

But that bucolic scene was quickly replaced by another less placid one: the flight of refugees. Lieutenant A. P. Smith of the Seventy-Sixth New York remembered marching toward Gettysburg that morning. He wrote of riders momentarily coming in with reports to mounted officers. "Then," he recalled, "came the rush of people from the town—gray-haired old men tottering along; women carrying their children, and children leading each other, while on the faces of all were depicted the indices of the terror and despair which had taken possession of them."[33]

The troops soon understood why refugees were fleeing Gettysburg. Fighting had broken out west of the town. Colonel William Gamble had established a line of battle early that morning with his First Brigade of Buford's cavalry division, dismounted and positioned mostly south of the Chambersburg Pike on a ridge where there was a frame house and a large bank barn of a prominent citizen and congressman named Edward McPherson, just over a mile west of Gettysburg. The ridge bore the name of the owner, McPherson Ridge. Buford's lines had been as far ahead as Herr Ridge, but they had given up much of that ground to numerous approaching Confederate infantry columns. Unlimbering two two-gun sections mostly to the right of Gamble's dismounted troopers along the Chambersburg Pike and one two-gun section on Gamble's left was Lieutenant John F. Calef's Battery A, Second United States.[34]

Reynolds had to have orally communicated with Buford his intentions: that Buford should position one of his two brigades west of Gettysburg, along the turnpike axis (the Chambersburg Pike), and the other brigade on the roads north of Gettysburg so as to screen the approach of the First Corps. No written directives to Buford of Reynolds's intentions exist. When Reynolds arrived on the morning of 1 July with the First Corps, he would then have some knowledge of the proximity of the enemy columns, as they, it was hoped, would be spotted by Buford. Unequivocally, Buford was never instructed to engage the enemy in order to hold Gettysburg. His last orders from General Pleasonton were for his two cavalry brigades to "cover and protect the front, and communicate all information of the enemy rapidly and surely," a mission not changed by Reynolds.[35]

Sometime after 5:00 A.M., Colonel Gamble reported to Buford that the enemy were "coming down from Cashtown in force." Fighting erupted. For just under two hours Gamble's brigade fought a withdrawing action with what was identified by Buford as the leading elements of a full division of A. P. Hill's Confederate corps. Colonel Devin's Second Brigade of Buford's division held a razor-thin line north of Gettysburg. Only a squadron of the Sixth New York Cavalry of Devin's brigade was present on the right of Gamble's troopers, extending the thin line to the Mummasburg Road. By use of skirmishers, vedettes, and pickets, Devin extended his line to the right, all the way to the Carlisle Road and even the Harrisburg Road. Soon Devin faced another threat: an "advance of the enemy's line of battle coming from the direction of Heidlersburg." Devin's troopers were facing the advance of elements of two divisions of Ewell's corps, nearing Gettysburg on two different roads; he was "ordered to retire gradually as the enemy succeeded in getting in range of [his] position[s]." Confederate columns were approaching Gettysburg from the west and north![36]

General Reynolds and his staff, riding "several miles" ahead of Wadsworth's columns, were about two miles south of Gettysburg. One of Buford's staff officers, a scout named Peter Culp, rode up to Reynolds and informed him that a large Confederate force was driving Buford's two cavalry brigades. Reynolds dismounted and directed staff officers and orderlies back to Generals Howard and Sickles to alert them of the circumstances and to urge Howard forward within supporting distance. As was his habit, Reynolds then remounted and, "on a fast gallop," rode ahead toward Gettysburg, his staff struggling to keep up. They rode through the town and emerged on the Chambersburg Pike, riding toward the exploding sounds of gunfire. Reynolds turned to Captain Joseph G. Rosengarten of his staff and directed him to warn citizens to stay in their houses.[37]

Arriving at the Lutheran Theological Seminary building, Reynolds observed Buford in the cupola that was serving as a signal station. Near Buford was acting assistant signal officer Lieutenant Aaron Brainard Jerome, who recalled Reynolds greeting Buford. "What's the matter, John?" Reynolds yelled. "The Devil's to pay!" Buford responded. Buford climbed down from the cupola and conferred with Reynolds for several minutes, telling him what he had observed up to the moment. Buford's troopers had been compelled to fall back from their initial position on Herr Ridge to McPherson Ridge that morning. Reynolds could hear the pounding of continuous small arms and artillery fire and could see, through dense smoke, intermittent flashes from the guns. He could tell that Buford was facing significant enemy forces. Reynolds was informed by Buford of the enemy forces approaching from the north. It was clear that Buford was facing elements of both Hill's and Ewell's corps. Reynolds told Buford to hold on as long as he could and that he would hurry the First Corps forward to his assistance. Yet Reynolds had only Wadsworth's division available to support Buford.[38]

Reynolds turned to Captain Weld and ordered him to ride to Taney-town, thirteen or fourteen miles south, to inform General Meade that "the enemy were coming on in strong force" and that he would "keep them back as long as possible." Reynolds told Weld to notify Meade that two Confederate corps were concentrating at Gettysburg, Hill from the west and Ewell from the north. Weld claimed later that Reynolds told him to tell Meade that he would "barricade the streets" to hold the enemy back as long as possible. Reynolds gave Weld directions to the Taneytown Road, instructing him that he should ride with the greatest speed he could, "no matter if [he] killed [his] horse," and if he did, "to take an orderly's." Weld left Reynolds between 9:30 and 10:00 A.M., riding toward Taneytown. Reynolds galloped back to the town and onto the Emmitsburg Road in order to bring forward Wadsworth's division.[39]

Whatever Reynolds's actual remarks were to Weld, they have to be understood in light of Meade's plans for him to cause the enemy to concentrate and to show its intentions. Once that occurred and Reynolds's First Corps was deployed and the enemy began to concentrate, the First Corps was supposed to withdraw so as to cause the enemy to pursue it, always resisting the enemy's progress. Reynolds had to deploy the entire First Corps in order to make the operation effective. Battling through the streets of Gettysburg and falling back to high ground might be an immediate objective for an advance force, according to Clausewitz and Mahan. Neither the town, nor any nearby height, however, was where Reynolds could finally halt the First Corps as that was not his mission and his command was too far ahead of the army to expect Meade to advance any other assistance. Rather, Reynolds was obligated to continue to withdraw, frequently halting to return fire, then to fall back on Howard's Eleventh Corps and, ultimately, to Emmitsburg, ten miles to the rear.[40]

Buford scribbled a message to Meade ten minutes after Reynolds left to bring up Wadsworth's division. "The enemy forces (A. P. Hill's) are advancing on me at this point, and driving my pickets and skirmishers very rapidly. There is also a large force at Heidlersburg that is driving my pickets at that point from that direction." Buford then noted: "General

Reynolds is advancing, and is within three miles of this point with his leading division." Buford closed, writing: "I am positive that the whole of A. P. Hill's force is advancing." Buford gave the message to a courier who, accompanied by an orderly, went galloping off in the direction of Taney-town.[41]

One of General Sickles's staff officers, Major Tremain, had been in the saddle since the early hours of the morning riding up the Emmitsburg Road. His mission was to report to General Reynolds and receive any orders the left wing commander had for Sickles. Tremain had difficulty locating Reynolds. As the gunfire from Buford's front increased, Tremain finally found Reynolds as he and his staff emerged from the town on the Emmitsburg Road. Tremain introduced himself and reported his mission.[42]

Reynolds asked Tremain how far down the road was Wadsworth. Seeing the head of the column just emerging over an elevation on the road, Tremain replied: "There is General Wadsworth now." According to Tremain, Reynolds appeared to be contemplating setting up his lines along Cemetery Hill, southeast of the town. "That would be a good place," Reynolds uttered to no one in particular, Tremain recalled. Then, after expressing concern about exposing the town to enemy occupation, Reynolds said: "But I doubt if I shall have time to form [on] the other side of the town." According to Tremain, Reynolds appeared to be uncertain of exactly what to do.[43]

General Wadsworth rode up to Reynolds, saluted, and asked: "What are your wishes General Reynolds?" "You had better turn off here," Reynolds responded, pointing to the fields on the western side of the Emmitsburg Road. He ordered his orderlies and Wadsworth's sappers to tear down the post-and-rail fences on the west side of the road to make way for the troops. Reynolds determined to deploy Wadsworth's division.[44]

Across the fields opposite the two-story brick house of Nicholas Codori, which stood on the east side of the Emmitsburg Road, Wadsworth's columns were directed by Reynolds so they could reach Buford's embattled troopers in front of the seminary by the shortest route possible. Sappers were sent ahead of the columns with axes to flatten all the fences that would impede the troops' movement across the fields.[45]

Staff officers and orderlies were sent down the Emmitsburg Road to hurry forward the Third and Second Divisions of the First Corps. Those two divisions were still more than an hour farther down the road. Once informed of the advance of Wadsworth's division, officers rode up and down the columns of those two divisions yelling for the men to "double-quick! double-quick!" Remembered drummer Harry Keiffer, still on the

Emmitsburg Road in the midst of the Third Division columns: "Four miles of almost constant double-quicking is no light work at any time, at least of all on such a day as this memorable first day of July." To add to Keiffer's misery, it became intensely hot.[46]

Reynolds then sent word by a staff officer to General Howard to hurry forward the Eleventh Corps, twenty-six infantry regiments and five batteries of artillery, 12,096 officers and men strong as of the last roll call. That request instructed Howard to take up a position at the Wentzes' place, the site Howard indicated in his dispatch to Reynolds earlier that morning, as Reynolds's request did not order the Eleventh Corps commander to move up to Gettysburg.[47]

Watching Wadsworth's columns move across the fields toward the seminary, Tremain rode up to Reynolds. "I beg your pardon, General Reynolds," he said, "but I suppose I ought to report to General Sickles unless you direct otherwise. My instructions were to communicate with you and ascertain if you had any communication for him." Reynolds responded after pausing a few seconds: "Tell General Sickles I think he had better come up." Tremain recalled how vague the order seemed. Reynolds offered nothing to him about the situation. Tremain then thought: "Perhaps . . . there were more of the enemy to be encountered than our chiefs had arranged for." He turned his horse and galloped back toward Emmitsburg.[48]

As Wadsworth's columns entered the grounds near the seminary, Reynolds led them out into the fields behind Buford's lines, indicating the positions the two brigades of the division should occupy. Reynolds's remaining two divisions were then still far down the Emmitsburg Road, more than an hour away. Driving Buford's troopers were at least two brigades of the division of Hill's corps, commanded by Major General Henry Heth, spread out on either side of the Chambersburg Pike.[49]

North of the Chambersburg Pike, Brigadier General Joseph R. Davis's Confederate brigade had nearly broken through Gamble's thin line of exhausted troopers. Reynolds relieved Lieutenant Calef and his battery and instructed Lieutenant Colonel James M. Sanderson of his staff to bring Captain Hall forward to join him. Hearing Sanderson's urgent directive minutes later, Hall galloped forward and found Reynolds on the Chambersburg Pike along McPherson Ridge. "Put your battery in position on this ridge to engage those guns of the enemy," Reynolds said, pointing to Confederate batteries along Herr Ridge, about one mile west. The six three-inch ordnance rifles of the Second Maine Battery that had accompanied Wadsworth's division from Marsh Creek to Gettysburg were quickly brought into position on the north side of the Chambersburg Pike. At the same time, Colonel Gamble's troopers finally withdrew to the rear to await further orders.[50]

Even though he was fully aware of a large enemy force bearing down from the north, Reynolds then turned to General Wadsworth, who had just galloped up to his commander, and said: "Put a strong support on the right of this battery. I will look out for the left." Wadsworth directed General Cutler to put his brigade, 2,017 officers and men, into line to support Hall's guns on the right; three of Cutler's regiments were sent to positions north of the Chambersburg Pike on both sides of a deep and wide cut through the fields, excavated for purposes of the Tapeworm Railroad roadbed that was still unfinished. The right flank of that brigade would be completely exposed to attack from the north. The remaining regiments in Cutler's brigade were kept south of the pike. Fearing a flanking movement on his left, Reynolds ordered General Doubleday, who just rode onto the battlefield, to attend to the Fairfield Road with the First Brigade of Wadsworth's division, known as the Iron Brigade, commanded by Brigadier General Solomon Meredith. General Howard would write later that night that Reynolds deployed his First Division in a "position [that] was not a good one because both flanks were exposed, and a heavy force [was] approaching from the north [and] rendered it untenable."[51]

On the south side of the Chambersburg Pike, along McPherson Ridge, a large wooded area, known locally as Herbst Woods, stood just south and west of the McPherson buildings. Brigadier General James J. Archer's Confederate brigade occupied the west end of those woods. Accompanied by Sergeant Charles Henry Veil, Reynolds rode back from the site where he placed Hall's battery to meet Meredith's Iron Brigade, sent by General Doubleday to strike Archer's Confederate troops that had reached Herbst Woods. Reynolds sat on his horse at the edge of the woods as Meredith's brigade neared. He sent Lieutenant Colonel John A. Kress of Wadsworth's staff to hurry the Iron Brigade forward. That brigade had 1,829 officers and men as of the muster on 30 June. On the right of the brigade was the Second Wisconsin, and then to the left came the Seventh Wisconsin, the Nineteenth Indiana, and the Twenty-Fourth Michigan. Reynolds directed the two Wisconsin regiments to charge Archer's Confederates in the woods. At the same time, Major Riddle and Captain Craig W. Wadsworth worked to swing the other two regiments of Meredith's brigade to face the northwest so as to enfilade Archer's regiments.[52]

The Iron Brigade recoiled after several Confederate volleys were fired into its ranks but continued its advance toward Herbst Woods. Behind the Second Wisconsin, Reynolds urged the men onward. "Forward, forward

The Death of General Reynolds, *by Alfred R. Waud. (Library of Congress)*

men!" Reynolds yelled. "Drive those fellows out of that. Forward! For God's sake, forward!" Just then, an enemy column in the woods opened fire. Reynolds had turned to look for possible reinforcements when he was struck by a bullet; some of his orderlies were hit as well. Reynolds fell from his horse, landing on his face with his arms outstretched. His powerful black horse galloped off toward the woods. It was 10:15 A.M. The four regiments of the Iron Brigade pressed forward, driving Archer's Confederates all the way back to Willoughby Run and near Herr Ridge, capturing large numbers of the enemy, including General Archer himself.[53]

At that very moment, the right flank of Wadsworth's division was imperiled. Some of General Davis's Confederate brigade poured into the railroad cut and opened a devastating fire into Cutler's brigade and Hall's battery. Wadsworth directed Cutler's troops to fall back to Seminary Ridge, but one regiment, the One Hundred Forty-Seventh New York—and Hall's battery, between the railroad cut and the Chambersburg Pike—never got the orders; they were in danger of being cut off and overwhelmed. Through the smoke, overwhelming numbers of Davis's Confederate forces were moving toward the railroad cut, cutting Cutler's brigade in half. Doubleday ordered the Sixth Wisconsin of Meredith's brigade, which had been held back as a reserve, to move to the right and attack the Confederates threatening Cutler's regiments. Joined by the Fourteenth Brooklyn and the Ninety-Fifth New York, the Sixth Wisconsin stormed ahead, trapping the Confederates in the railroad cut.[54]

Major General Abner Doubleday. (Library of Congress)

Through all the chaos, Reynolds's orderly, Sergeant Charles Henry Veil, dismounted and ran to the general's assistance as the Iron Brigade pushed back Archer's line. Seeing no blood, Veil believed that Reynolds had been stunned by a spent bullet. He picked Reynolds up just as shouts of "Drop him! Drop him!" were heard in the din from Archer's lines. As the enemy line was hurled back, Veil and Captain R. W. Mitchell of Reynolds's staff managed to drag Reynolds out of the field of enemy gunfire only to discover that their commander was dead, the bullet having hit him in the back of the neck and ranged down his spine.[55]

The Second Division of the First Corps was finally seen approaching the field south of the seminary building. Doubleday's aide, Major Jacob F. Slagle, formerly of the One Hundred Forty-Ninth Pennsylvania, was sent by Doubleday to halt the Second Division in a woods near the seminary as a reserve. After Slagle returned to the side of his commander, he recalled Doubleday being informed of the death of Reynolds. It was probably 10:45 A.M. As commander of the First Corps, Doubleday "had to take the whole responsibility which he felt very much," wrote Slagle.[56]

Doubleday intimated to Major Slagle then that "he was not informed of Reynolds's plans." Indeed, Reynolds had earlier that morning told Doubleday that if he was attacked at Gettysburg, he would fall back to Emmitsburg as Meade instructed him. Slagle then recalled Doubleday saying that "all he could do was to fight until he got sufficient information to form his own plans." Meade's carefully directed plans to force the enemy to show its intentions and, it was hoped, draw it back to the selected defense lines of the Army of the Potomac had been nullified. Doubleday later defended himself, writing that the moment Reynolds fell "would have been the proper time to retire, but to fall back might have inflicted lasting disgrace upon the corps, and as General Reynolds, who was high in the confidence of General Meade, had formed his lines to resist the entrance of the enemy into Gettysburg, I naturally supposed that it was his intention to defend the place." Thus, Doubleday determined to continue to fight a battle west and north of Gettysburg, fourteen miles ahead of the army headquarters. If the day had started out badly for Meade, it just got worse.[57]

Underscoring the fact that the First Corps was to serve as an advance corps and not initiate a general engagement so far ahead of the rest of the army, there appears to have been no attempt by Reynolds or his quartermaster and medical director to establish depots for the ambulances or even a park for the supply trains that accompanied the troops, along with a corps hospital or division hospitals, distant from the intended battlefield, and a medical evacuation system, before the troops were brought onto the battlefield as army regulations required. "The wounded were soon drifting to the rear in large numbers, mostly without assistance, unless that of comrades," wrote Captain Louis C. Duncan of the army medical service. Instead, the Lutheran Theological Seminary building and the house of Dr. Charles B. Krauth nearby, both of which literally stood within the First Corps battle lines and received horrific enemy gunfire, along with Christ Evangelical Lutheran Church, St. Francis Xavier Roman Catholic Church, the United Presbyterian Church and Associated Reformed Church, the German Reformed Church, and numerous houses, hotels, and office buildings, all the way down Chambersburg Street to the town square, eventually became First Corps hospitals as the fighting continued and intensified in the afternoon and the need arose. Even the Edward McPherson farm buildings amid the battlefield and the distant Adams County Courthouse were eventually pressed into service. Wrote Captain Duncan: "Some five hundred wounded were collected in these buildings, but many of the most severely wounded were left scattered over the field. For these there was little care during the next two days of battle." Evacuating the wounded without a system whereby ambulances could be driven between depots near the front lines and corps or division hospitals well to the rear was impossible. The First Corps ambulances, for the most part, remained near the seminary until, one by one, they were sent to the rear loaded with what wounded could be taken off the battlefield as the bloody day progressed. Most of the wounded were left where they fell. Such an absence of systematic transportation from the battlefield to well-established hospitals always led to an abnormally high rate of mortality for the wounded.[58]

8

REYNOLDS HAS
BEEN KILLED

Meade arrived back at his Piney Creek headquarters tent outside of Taney-town before eleven o'clock in the morning of 1 July. No news of the fight-ing at Gettysburg had arrived from Buford, Reynolds, or Howard by then. Not knowing Reynolds was dead, Meade dictated to Seth Williams a let-ter to his left wing commander with instructions. The letter clearly illus-trates that Reynolds's mission with the First Corps was a reconnaissance in force. Meade noted in the letter that he was still trying to determine "a more definite point at which the enemy is concentrating." Meade so-licited Reynolds's "views upon the subject, at least so far as concerns [his] position." He referred to Gettysburg as a possible focal point. The concen-tration would occur either east of Gettysburg or "in front" or to the west of it. If that enemy concentration was to the east of Gettysburg, "that point," Meade wrote, "would not at first glance seem to be a proper strategic point of concentration for [his] army." If the enemy concentration was in front, or west, of Gettysburg, Meade noted that he was "not sufficiently well in-formed of the nature of the country to judge of its character for either an offensive or defensive position." Finally, Meade wrote: "The movement of your corps to Gettysburg was ordered before the positive knowledge of the enemy's withdrawal from Harrisburg and concentration was received." If anything, that last sentence indicated a concern—and even an uneasi-ness—about the position of Reynolds's advance force. A copy of the letter was sent to General Howard. The original letter never reached General Reynolds.[1]

Meade had come to a conclusion about his strategic intentions for the army. Not wanting to use Butterfield for such a critical correspondence, Meade dictated to Seth Williams the final touches to his strategic inten-tions in a lengthy order. The directive became known as the Pipe Creek Circular. The body of the order seems to have been formulated hours before. In it, Meade concluded that it was "no longer his intention to assume the offensive until the enemy's movements or position should render such an operation certain of success." Rather, Meade would lure the enemy toward him. "If the enemy assume the offensive and attack," Meade instructed his corps commanders, "after holding [the enemy] in check sufficiently long, to withdraw the trains and other *impedimenta*; and to withdraw the army from its present position and form a line of battle with the left resting in the neighborhood of Middleburg and the right at Manchester, the general direction being that of Pipe Creek."[2]

Meade refined his specific orders to each corps commander. All of Meade's directives were predicated on the enemy assuming the offensive and attacking. In that event, he ordered General Reynolds to "withdraw the force at present at Gettysburg [the First and Eleventh Corps] by the road to Taneytown and Westminster, and, after crossing Pipe Creek, deploy toward Middleburg." The only change Meade made to his previous directives to Reynolds was that, instead of withdrawing to Emmitsburg, he should withdraw toward Taneytown and deploy along the bluffs of Big Pipe Creek where Meade set up his headquarters on 29 June, one mile north of Middleburg. The Pipe Creek line would extend as far west as Middleburg; it would not extend to Emmitsburg. Meade made absolutely no change in Reynolds's mission to "get in the roads and routes of communication" of the enemy to force it to concentrate and reveal its intentions, as he wanted the enemy to assume the offensive against him. Once that happened, Reynolds must withdraw to Taneytown and then Middletown, not Emmitsburg. If the enemy assumed the offensive, Meade directed General Sickles to move the Third Corps from Emmitsburg to Middleburg by way of Mechanicsville or a more direct route.[3]

Meade ordered General Slocum to take overall command of a right wing of the army consisting of the Fifth Corps, then at Hanover, along with his own Twelfth Corps that had moved that morning to Two Taverns. He should withdraw them across Big Pipe Creek and deploy those troops on the high bluffs on either side of the Baltimore Pike below Union Mills in the event of an enemy offensive. He admonished Slocum to connect the left flank of his defense line with the right flank of Reynolds. Slocum was also directed to connect his right flank with that of Sedgwick's Sixth Corps, positioned near Manchester, also a part of Slocum's right wing. Hancock's Second Corps, having arrived at Taneytown at eleven o'clock that morning, was to be held in reserve in the vicinity of Uniontown and Frizzellburg, "to be thrown to the point of strongest attack, should the

REYNOLDS HAS BEEN KILLED

enemy make it." The Artillery Reserve was directed to "move to the rear of Frizzellburg, and be placed in position, or sent to [the various] corps, as circumstances may require, under the general supervision [of General Hunt]." In the meantime, Hunt was ordered to examine the line and select positions for artillery.[4]

In the event Lee went on the offensive and the Pipe Creek line became necessary, Meade's headquarters would be set up at Frizzellburg. General Slocum, as commander of the right wing, would set up his headquarters near Union Mills, and General Reynolds, as left wing commander, would establish his headquarters "near the road from Taneytown to Frizzellburg." To make communications among the corps commanders as rapid as possible, the Signal Corps was ordered to examine the line thoroughly and at once, on the commencement of [the] movement, extend telegraphic communication from Manchester, Union Mills, Middleburg, and the Taneytown Road to Meade's headquarters at Frizzellburg. Meade completed the Pipe Creek Circular around noon.[5]

For the cavalry corps, Meade also had explicit orders; they were issued by General Pleasonton, though. Gregg's division was ordered at 11:55 A.M. to fall back from Hanover to Manchester to more directly protect and operate in concert with Sedgwick's Sixth Corps. General Buford was directed to order his two brigades back to Taneytown and then Middleburg "in case the enemy should advance in force upon you and press you hard." Buford, according to the order, must "dispute every inch of ground, and fall back slowly," sending to Pleasonton's headquarters "all the information" gathered. Kilpatrick's division was ordered to fall back to Manchester from its foray toward Abbottstown, "in case the enemy advance in force upon you and press you hard." As with Buford's troopers, Kilpatrick's were admonished to "dispute every inch of the ground and fall back slowly," sending to headquarters all the information they gathered. Even to General Merritt's brigade of Buford's division, operating along the army's far left and rear, orders were sent directing it to fall back slowly, after the infantry have left Emmitsburg, "in case the enemy advance in force and press you hard," disputing "every inch of ground," sending to army headquarters all the information obtained.[6]

As commander of the Army of the Potomac, Meade had done all that was necessary to direct the widely separated elements of his army back to Pipe Creek. Having received no other reports from Reynolds, Meade prepared a message to General Halleck. He wanted Halleck to comprehend fully the strategy he had chosen. "Ewell is massing at Heidlersburg," Meade wrote. "A. P. Hill is massed between Chambersburg and the mountains." Meade then added: "The news proves my advance has answered its purpose. I shall not advance any, but prepare to receive an attack in case Lee makes one. A battlefield is being selected to the rear, on which the army can be rapidly concentrated, on Pipe Creek, between Middleburg and Manchester, covering my depot at Westminster." Although the message bore the time "12m," it was not sent then. Meade held it back, undoubtedly to await events.[7]

Buford's courier carrying his message written on the battlefield at 10:10 A.M. reached Meade's headquarters just past noon. Captain Weld arrived at Meade's headquarters at about the same time. Weld was escorted to Meade's tent. There he reported Reynolds's words that Hill's and Ewell's corps were advancing in strong force and he would hold them back as long as possible. Weld claimed that when he told Meade that Reynolds would barricade the streets of Gettysburg in order to delay the enemy, Meade responded: "Good! That is just like Reynolds." Meade, Weld recalled, "seemed quite anxious about the matter." According to Weld, Meade let it be known how angry he was with Butterfield. Recalled Weld: "[Meade] roundly damned the Chief of Staff, who he had inherited from his predecessor, for his slowness in getting out orders." It may be presumed that related to specific orders to corps commanders about the Pipe Creek Circular, although there is no direct evidence of it.[8]

Meade was agitated. He scribbled a brief message to General Couch in Harrisburg: "The enemy are advancing on Gettysburg—Hill, from Cashtown; Ewell, from Heidlersburg. Can you throw a force in Ewell's rear, to threaten him, and at the same time keep your line of retreat open? If you can, do so." A courier carried it to Frederick, where it was telegraphed to the War Department in Washington and received there at 5:00 P.M. From there it was relayed to Harrisburg.[9]

Having just completed the Pipe Creek Circular and having been informed of Reynolds being attacked by a significant force at Gettysburg, Meade was seized with alarm about the change he made in the route of withdrawal of Reynolds's and Howard's corps on the left. The last communication Meade sent to Reynolds was that he should withdraw from Gettysburg to Emmitsburg. Meade feared that Reynolds would not get the Pipe Creek Circular in time; after all, he was nearly fourteen miles ahead of army headquarters. Meade had put the left wing in motion before he had completed the Pipe Creek Circular; an adjustment was necessary.[10]

To make sure Reynolds withdrew toward Taneytown and not Emmitsburg would take more than a messenger. On the battlefield, it would take the presence of a large force. The nearest troops Meade could deploy were

General Hancock's Second Corps; they had just arrived at Taneytown at 11:00 A.M. after their march from Uniontown. Meade reasoned that if Hancock could move his corps up the road from Taneytown to Gettysburg and deploy it along the Taneytown Road, Reynolds, on notification from Hancock, could direct his forces to fall back on it.[11]

Meade dictated to Butterfield a message to General Hancock at 12:30 P.M. "The major general commanding," it read, "directs that, in view of the advance of Generals A. P. Hill and Ewell on Gettysburg, and the possible failure of General Reynolds to receive the order to withdraw his command by the route through Taneytown, thus leaving the center of our position open, that you proceed with your troops out on the direct road to Gettysburg from Taneytown." Meade then added: "When you find that General Reynolds is covering that road (instead of withdrawing by Emmitsburg, which it is feared he may do), you will withdraw to Frizzell-burg, as directed in the circular of directions for the positions issued this morning." The Pipe Creek Circular and the subsequent order to Hancock make it abundantly clear that it was Meade's intention all along that Reynolds withdraw back to the main lines of the Army of the Potomac. It appears Meade and Hancock conferred briefly at Meade's headquarters before Hancock got his Second Corps ready to march.[12]

Before Meade began sending the Pipe Creek Circular to his corps commanders, he paused to dictate special orders to General Sedgwick, whose Sixth Corps was situated near Manchester on the far right flank, and to General Slocum, who, by virtue of the Pipe Creek Circular, would command the right wing of the army. To General Sedgwick, Meade noted: "From reports just received [it appears] that the enemy is moving in heavy force on Gettysburg (Ewell from Heidlersburg, and Hill from Cashtown Pass), and it is not improbable he will reach that place before the command under Major General Reynolds (the First and Eleventh Corps), now on the way, can [fully] arrive there." Then, Meade recited to Sedgwick his instructions to Reynolds. "Should such be the case, and General Reynolds finds himself in the presence of a superior force, he is instructed to hold the enemy in check, and slowly fall back." It was a clear recital of Meade's orders to Reynolds to command an advance corps to force the enemy to concentrate so as to "show his hand." Meade informed Sedgwick that if Reynolds was able to so withdraw, "the line indicated in the circular of today will be occupied tonight." Meade then added: "Should circumstances render it necessary for the commanding general to fight the enemy today, the troops are posted as follows for the support of Reynolds's command, *viz*: on his right, at Two Taverns, the Twelfth Corps; at Hanover, the Fifth Corps; the Second Corps is on the road between Taneytown and Gettysburg; the Third Corps is at Emmitsburg." Meade concluded his communication by noting: "This information is conveyed to you that you may leave your corps in readiness to move in such direction as may be required at a moment's notice."[13]

To General Slocum at Two Taverns, Meade sent a similar communication. He first ordered Slocum to move his wagon trains back to Westminster "upon receipt of this order." Meade then instructed Slocum to be prepared to commence the movement indicated in the Pipe Creek Circular, which was enclosed with his instructions, on receipt of intelligence from General Reynolds that he had withdrawn his forces such that it would leave Slocum at Two Taverns exposed to attack. In that event, Slocum was directed to communicate with General Sykes and instruct him to commence his movement in accordance with the Pipe Creek Circular.[14]

Amid all that was facing Meade, he paused to communicate with the wayward General French. Having issued the Pipe Creek Circular and having sent couriers galloping toward Manchester, Hanover, Two Taverns, Gettysburg, and Emmitsburg, Meade found a use for French's command. He forwarded to French the Pipe Creek Circular and instructed him to consult a local map to understand the army's situation. Meade then ordered French to hold Frederick, "camping [his] troops in its immediate vicinity." He also instructed French to hold the railroad and turnpike bridges over the Monocacy River and to protect the Baltimore & Ohio Railroad "from Frederick to a junction with General Schenck, to whom you will communicate your instructions." Then Meade directed French, in no uncertain terms, that if the army was "compelled to withdraw and retire before the enemy," he must be in readiness to move his command "by rail, or march, as may be most practicable and speedy, into the defenses of Washington." In the meantime, Meade stated unequivocally, he must "hold the line of communication to Frederick. Keep it open, and send up from Frederick all stragglers, keeping the town clear and in good order."[15]

Whitelaw Reid, the reporter for the *Cincinnati Gazette*, awoke in Frederick on the morning of 1 July after a long delay on the Baltimore & Ohio Railroad at Relay. After breakfast, he and his fellow newspaper correspondents, Samuel Wilkeson of the *New York Times* and Uriah H. Painter of the *Philadelphia Inquirer*, obtained horses and rode north. "Drunken soldiers were still staggering about the streets," Reid wrote, "looking for a last drink or a horse to steal, before commencing to straggle along the road." The reporters were directed to Taneytown by a courier returning from the army with dispatches to be given over to the telegraphers at Frederick.[16]

Major General George Gordon Meade in front of his headquarters tent.
(Library of Congress)

The reporters reached Taneytown at about the time Meade was forwarding his Pipe Creek Circular to his corps commanders. To Reid, Taneytown was "a pleasant little Maryland hamlet." The presence of the army there, however, made a lasting impression on him. "Army trains blocked up the streets; a group of quartermasters and commissaries were bustling about the principal corner; across the hills, and along the road to the left, as far as the eye could reach, rose the glitter from the swaying points of bayonets, as the steady tramp the columns of our . . . Second Corps were marching [through Taneytown]." Reid believed "something was in the wind."[17]

The reporters rode out the Littlestown Road. "Halt a mile further east, splashed by the hoofs of eager gallopers," Reid wrote. "A large, unpretending camp, looking very much like that of a battalion of cavalry—we turned in, without ceremony, and are at the headquarters of the Army of the Potomac." He noticed that it all seemed quiet at first. Yet, there were "signs of movement." "The baggage was all packed," he noted, "everybody is ready to take the saddle at a moment's notice. Engineers are busy with their maps; couriers are coming in with reports; the trustiest counselors on the staff are with the General." Reid's eyes then turned upon General Meade's wall tent. It was "just like the rest," he wrote. There, he saw Meade, "pen in hand, seated on a camp-stool and bending over a map ... the new 'General Commanding' for the Army of the Potomac." Reid then described Meade: "Tall, slender, not ungainly, but certainly not handsome or graceful, thin-faced, with grizzled beard and moustache, a broad and high but retreating forehead, from each corner of which the slightly curling hair recedes, as if giving premonition of baldness—apparently between forty-five and fifty years of age—altogether a man who impresses you rather as a thoughtful student than a dashing soldier—so General Meade looks in his tent."[18]

Major Riddle of Reynolds's staff suddenly rode into the headquarters along Piney Creek. He carried the sad news that Reynolds had been killed or badly wounded. Riddle had not waited on the battlefield to find out the fate of his commander. Instead, on Doubleday's orders, he galloped first to give word of Reynolds's wounding to General Howard at about 11:30 A.M. and then rode toward Taneytown to relay the news to Meade. With that information, Meade's abandonment of his defense line along Big Pipe Creek was set in motion.[19]

Meade quickly called for General Warren, his chief engineer, an officer he trusted. When Warren arrived at Meade's tent, Meade related what he had just learned about the situation at Gettysburg and of the wounding or possible death of Reynolds. He instructed Warren to ride up to Gettysburg to find out about the situation and to report back to him. As a topographical engineer, Warren was admonished by Meade to examine the ground held by the First and Eleventh Corps, as well as that to which they could fall back. Meade needed to know whether he must move the army to Gettysburg or direct the left wing to retire back to Taneytown. Meade advised Warren that he must perform his task with great speed. Warren mounted up and, with several staff officers and orderlies, galloped down the Littlestown Road to Taneytown and out the road to Gettysburg. Warren would be the first member of Meade's headquarters staff to reach the battlefield.[20]

Generals Meade and Butterfield and a group of staff officers and orderlies galloped up to Hancock's headquarters outside of Taneytown at, probably, about 1:30 P.M. Meade had news for Hancock about the crisis at Gettysburg, and it wasn't good. Meade told Hancock that Reynolds had been killed or badly wounded. He explained that he had no knowledge of Gettysburg or its surroundings, and he needed to know whether it was advisable to move the army there. Meade said to Hancock that he should turn over command of the Second Corps to General Gibbon, ride to Gettysburg, take command there, and then report back to him. That would place Hancock, a major general junior to both Generals Howard and Sickles, in command of the left wing of the army.[21]

Hancock questioned Meade about not only his junior rank but also the rank of Gibbon; his other two Second Corps division commanders, Brigadier Generals Alexander Hays and John C. Caldwell, were senior to Gibbon. To calm Hancock's concerns, Meade showed him the letter he received from Secretary Stanton authorizing him to make whatever changes he desired among the army's officers and that the president would support him. Letter or not, it was a bold move for Meade to elevate Hancock to commander of the left wing of the army even temporarily.[22]

Meade turned to Butterfield and directed him to give to Hancock an order he dictated at 1:10 P.M. In the order Meade first noted that he had "just been informed that General Reynolds has been killed or badly wounded." He then directed Hancock to turn over command of the Second Corps to Brigadier General John Gibbon and "proceed to the front, and, by virtue of this order, in case of the truth of General Reynolds's death, you assume command of the corps there assembled, viz, the Eleventh, First, and Third at Emmitsburg." Meade then added: "If you think the ground and position there a better one to fight a battle under existing circumstances, you will so advise [me] and [I] will order all the troops up. You know [my] views, and General Warren, who is fully aware of them, has gone out to see General Reynolds."[23]

Before the order was handed to Hancock, another messenger from the front arrived and reported to Meade with dispatches. The dispatches included one that was probably written by General Wadsworth after the initial Confederate attacks stalled and a lull in the fighting ensued; it claimed that the enemy was withdrawing. It was relayed to Meade by General Howard. At 1:15 P.M., Meade, buoyed by a sense of hope, dictated to Butterfield a postscript to Hancock's orders: "Reynolds has possession of Gettysburg, and the enemy are reported as falling back from the front of Gettysburg. Hold your columns ready to move."[24]

Of the situation at Gettysburg, Meade knew little. Importantly, he knew nothing of the condition or position of the First and Eleventh Corps. Moreover, Meade had no idea whether Gettysburg offered to the Army of the Potomac advantages of terrain that would make abandoning the line along Big Pipe Creek advisable. If it did, Meade wanted Hancock to so inform him. He invited him to confer with General Warren, who had

Major General Winfield S. Hancock. (Library of Congress)

previously been dispatched to Gettysburg. Meade wanted advice from a reliable corps commander who had not been engaged in the fighting at Gettysburg. Those involved in the fighting would naturally have views that would color their advice. He wanted a competent and independent assessment of the situation. Other corps commanders in the army were capable of making such an assessment, but they were too far away for Meade to speak to them; Sedgwick was at Manchester, Sykes was at Hanover, and Slocum was at Two Taverns. Hancock was at Taneytown, his Second Corps having just arrived there two hours earlier. Although junior to all the other corps commanders, Hancock was readily available. Finally, Hancock was a major general; Warren was not. To exercise command over Howard and Sickles, Meade had to give the assignment to an officer of equal rank, even if he was junior to them.

Why Meade did not go ahead to Gettysburg himself is obvious now. At that moment, he was still planning to defend against an anticipated Confederate advance toward Big Pipe Creek. Until he understood that defending the Pipe Creek line was no longer advisable, his duty was to remain at his headquarters and in communication with his corps commanders. They knew where he was so that he could be notified of any matter needing his attention across his nearly thirty-mile front.

Thirty-nine-year-old Winfield Scott Hancock was making a name for himself in the army. A native of a village north of Norristown, Pennsylvania, he was an 1840 graduate of West Point, probably the youngest in his class. He saw distinguished service in the war with Mexico and then in the campaign against the Seminoles, as well as the Mormon expedition. Hancock was married to the former Almira Russell, whom he met while stationed in St. Louis in 1850; they had two children. When the war broke out, he was serving as chief quartermaster of the garrison at Los Angeles. It was General McClellan who secured for him an appointment as brigadier general of volunteers in September 1861. A brigade commander during the Peninsula and Maryland Campaigns, he was elevated by McClellan to command the First Division of the Second Corps after the mortal wounding of Major General Israel B. Richardson at Antietam. Hancock was promoted to the rank of major general in November 1862 and won praise for his services during the Battles of Fredericksburg and Chancellorsville under General Couch. He was wounded in both engagements. He was named commander of the Second Corps on the resignation of General Couch less than three weeks before. Hancock was a sharp dresser; he always wore starched white collars and cuffs that were noticed by all who saw him. He was proving to be a competent, efficient, and well-liked general officer in the Army of the Potomac.[25]

Hancock began his journey to Gettysburg in an ambulance with a number of his staff officers, including Lieutenant Colonel Charles H. Morgan, chief of staff, and Major William G. Mitchell, assistant adjutant general, Captain I. B. Parker, aide-de-camp, as well as orderlies. With Hancock, too, was a small detachment from the Signal Corps under Captain James S. Hall and Lieutenant David A. Taylor. In the ambulance Hancock was able to read what maps were made available to him of Gettysburg and

Adams County. With him may well have been Lieutenant Alonzo H. Cushing, commander of Battery A, Fourth United States, in the Second Corps Artillery Brigade, and formerly a well-known and well-liked topographical engineer in the Second Corps. Hancock soon called one of his orderlies to bring his and his staff officers' mounts. Mounting their horses, the general and his aides galloped ahead. About four miles south of Gettysburg, Hancock and his staff and aides met an ambulance heading toward Taneytown carrying the body of General Reynolds.[26]

Once Hancock came so near to Gettysburg that he heard the sounds of fighting, he sent his aide, Major Mitchell, ahead to locate General Howard and inform him of his orders and his approach. As Hancock rode closer to Gettysburg, he found the Taneytown Road completely blocked with the extensive wagon trains of the First and Eleventh Corps, making any orderly retreat on that road utterly impossible. It was the first evidence of what appeared to be a disaster at the front.[27]

Back at Taneytown, *Cincinnati Gazette* reporter Whitelaw Reid stood outside Meade's headquarters' tent watching the couriers ride in and out. Suddenly, recalled Reid, "a horseman gallops up and hastily dismounts." It's a familiar face—L. L. Crounse, the well-known chief correspondent of the *New York Times*, with the Army of the Potomac. As Reid and the others were exchanging greetings with Crounse, the *New York Times* correspondent claimed that he just returned from Gettysburg "a little post-village in southern Pennsylvania, ten or fifteen miles away," and that a battle was under way. He could not assess the magnitude of it, but it involved the First Corps and some "unknown force" of the enemy. General Reynolds, he claimed, was already killed, and "there are rumors of more bad news." All of the reporters quickly mounted up and, led by Crounse, galloped down the Littlestown Turnpike to Taneytown, and there they stopped at, probably, the Old Stone Tavern on Frederick Street, where they hastily wrote dispatches to be taken to the telegraph office at Frederick to be forwarded to their newspapers. Amid the enormous columns of Hancock's Second Corps, then marching out on the Taneytown Road, Reid and his fellow correspondents rode up the road to Gettysburg.[28]

Indeed, the situation at Gettysburg was as dire as Crounse intimated. No sooner had Doubleday stalled the morning attacks of General Heth's Division than General Ewell's Confederate corps appeared on his right flank. Doubleday requested General Howard to protect that portion of the line with the Eleventh Corps that had just arrived at Gettysburg. In the meantime, Doubleday directed Brigadier General John C. Robinson to advance his Second Division to a position on the right of Wadsworth's

First Division, extending the First Corps lines all the way to and along the Mummasburg Road. The Third Division, commanded by Brigadier General Thomas A. Rowley, was divided; one brigade—Colonel Roy Stone's—was sent forward to positions north of Herbst Woods, while another—Colonel Chapman Biddle's—was sent to the far left of Wadsworth's lines around 12:30 P.M. Extending the left flank even farther, General Buford directed Colonel Gamble's brigade to the left of Biddle's infantry.[29]

General Howard brought the Eleventh Corps forward at 12:30 P.M., about an hour before General Hancock left Taneytown for Gettysburg. Howard had just been informed by Captain Daniel Hall of his staff that "Reynolds [was] dead and that [he] was senior officer on the field." Major General Carl Schurz, who had been serving as commander of the Second Division, became the Eleventh Corps commander. Brigadier General Alexander Schimmelfennig's Third Division and Brigadier General Francis C. Barlow's First Division were deployed north of Gettysburg, Schimmelfennig's division on the left, Barlow's on the right, extending to the Harrisburg Road. It took more than an hour for the Eleventh Corps to fully reach the battlefield. Colonel Devin's weary brigade of cavalry was finally withdrawn. Unfortunately, Schimmelfennig's left flank and Robinson's right flank never connected. Instead, a yawning gap existed between the two commands. Prudently, as General Howard brought the Eleventh Corps to Gettysburg, he held his Second Division, now commanded by Brigadier General Adolph von Steinwehr, and three batteries of artillery, on Cemetery Hill, an imposing eminence just east of the town. Howard and his chief quartermaster, along with the medical director, established a corps hospital at the 156-acre George Spangler farm just south of the Granite Schoolhouse Road, about a mile or so behind Steinwehr's division stationed on Cemetery Hill. Ambulance depots were established in the town, closer to the battlefield.[30]

Doubleday was under direct assault by elements of General Rodes's Division of Ewell's corps at the time Howard pushed out Schimmelfennig's and Barlow's divisions. At 1:00 and 1:30 P.M., Howard sent riders galloping back to Emmitsburg with written orders for General Sickles to move his Third Corps forward to Gettysburg "immediately." Howard dashed off a note to Meade informing him of the positions of the First and Eleventh Corps. He then confirmed all the previous reports: "Enemy reported to be advancing from York (Ewell's corps). The First and Eleventh Corps are engaged with Hill's forces. Have ordered General Sickles to push forward."[31]

At the same time that Howard sent messengers to General Sickles, he

sent a messenger down the Baltimore Pike to General Slocum informing him that "Ewell's corps is advancing from York" and "the left wing of
the Army of the Potomac is engaged with A. P. Hill's corps." Slocum received Howard's message and replied at 3:35 P.M. that he would move the
Twelfth Corps to within "one mile to the right of Gettysburg."[32]

At 2:45 P.M., General Early's Division and elements of Rodes's Division struck Schimmelfennig's and Barlow's lines. Forty minutes later,
General Pender's Division of Hill's corps appeared opposite Doubleday's
wearied ranks that had all been realigned along Seminary Ridge. The attacks against the remnants of the First Corps and the Eleventh Corps west
and north of Gettysburg became general. The fighting was ferocious. Soon
Schimmelfennig's lines were overwhelmed by Rodes's attacking Confederates, and Barlow's right flank was overlapped by Early's Division.[33]

By then, Sickles had just received Howard's appeals to move to Gettysburg from the two couriers. The first courier brought an oral message
from Howard asking Sickles to move to Gettysburg. The second courier
brought Howard's message on a scrap of paper which read: "General Reynolds is killed. For God's sake, come up. Howard." It had been sent at
3:15 P.M. Sickles responded by writing: "I shall move to Gettysburg immediately." He gave the message to Major Tremain and sent him back to
Gettysburg. He then sent a message to Meade informing him of the dispatches he had received and of the fact that "General Reynolds was killed
early in the action." He explained to Meade that he would "march with my
corps toward Gettysburg immediately, moving on two parallel roads." Ten
minutes later, Sickles wrote to Meade again, stating that he would "leave
one brigade and a battery of artillery on the heights beyond Emmitsburg,
toward Fairfield, and another to the left and rear of Emmitsburg, commanding the approaches by way of Mechanicstown." He evidently understood Meade's and Reynolds's concerns about possible enemy approaches
along that left flank.[34]

At Gettysburg the situation was quickly deteriorating. In little more
than three quarters of an hour after sending the 3:15 P.M. dispatch to
Sickles, Howard sent word to Doubleday that, if he could not hold out
any longer, he must fall back to the heights east of town. By 4:10 P.M.,
Howard's columns began to give way. Indeed, over the next twenty minutes, the lines collapsed, and the battered Union troops, many in a state of
panic, poured back through the streets of Gettysburg. Confusion reigned,
and the detritus of the two corps converged in the streets and alleys of
the town. Although some regiments and batteries in both corps generally
maintained their ranks and fought back the fast-approaching Confeder-

ates in the streets, many did not. "The streets," recalled Major Dawes of the Sixth Wisconsin, "were jammed with crowds of retreating soldiers, and with ambulances, artillery, and wagons. The cellars were crowded with men, sound in body, but craven in spirit, who had gone there to surrender." Thousands of Doubleday's and Schurz's troops were captured by the victorious Confederates.[35]

What Union troops escaped capture fled to Cemetery Hill, east of Gettysburg, where Howard had placed Steinwehr's division. There, Steinwehr's division and the three batteries of artillery formed lines behind stone fences where the broken elements of the First and Eleventh Corps were rallied. It was the sight of the fleeing remnants of the First and Eleventh Corps that General Hancock observed as he rode up the Taneytown Road to Cemetery Hill. So far in advance of the Army of the Potomac had the battle raged that no other corps of the army was closer than five miles away. Meade could have done little to provide support to the First and Eleventh Corps, even if he had been informed of the full extent of the fighting at the time it erupted.[36]

It had been a devastating day for the left wing of the army … and for the army commander, George Gordon Meade. The First and Eleventh Corps had suffered appalling losses. The First Corps left over three thousand officers and men on the field, killed and wounded, and over two thousand captured and missing. General Reynolds was killed and First Corps brigade commanders Brigadier General Gabriel Paul and Colonels Chapman Biddle, Roy Stone, and Langhorne Wister were wounded, and numerous regimental commanders were killed, wounded, and/or captured. The Eleventh Corps lost over two thousand officers and men, killed and wounded, and over fifteen hundred captured and missing. Eleventh Corps division commander Brigadier General Francis C. Barlow was wounded and captured, Eleventh Corps brigade commander General Schimmelfennig was presumed captured, and numerous regimental commanders were wounded and/or captured. The events of 1 July provide a startling example of what happens when an advance corps fails to deploy fully and then fails to withdraw once the enemy concentrates against it. Because of what must be considered General Reynolds's impulsive judgment on the field earlier that morning, Meade's carefully planned use of an advance corps to cause the enemy to concentrate and show its hand completely failed in its execution. As a result, two of the three corps comprising the left wing of the army were shattered. Meade had all the earmarks of a disaster on his hands. Meade faced his first real test as an operational commander.[37]

At the end of the fighting Ewell's Confederate corps held the town of

Gettysburg and extended east all the way to just below Culp's Hill. Rodes's Division held the town from its southern suburbs to its eastern suburbs. Early's Division extended Ewell's lines eastward, below Cemetery and Culp's Hills, and Johnson's Division, after arriving late at night, would be placed in position on the extreme left of Ewell's line after marching to positions below Culp's Hill. Hill's Confederate corps held a line along Seminary Ridge south to near the Henry Spangler farm. Pender's Division occupied Seminary Ridge from the Lutheran Theological Seminary south to the left flank of Anderson's Division, the line of which continued south. Heth's Division was held in reserve. The better part of two of Longstreet's divisions—Hood's and McLaw's—would reach Marsh Creek, west of Gettysburg, that night. All of Hill's, Longstreet's, Johnson's, and Early's troops arrived—or would arrive—at Gettysburg by way of the turnpike axis, the turnpike between Chambersburg and York, that ran through Gettysburg, and by parallel routes just north of it.[38]

9

YOUR MARCH WILL BE A FORCED ONE

One of Meade's staff officers, Major James Cornell Biddle, scion of the famed Biddle family of Philadelphia, wrote a quick letter to his wife while in his tent at Meade's Taneytown headquarters early on the afternoon of 1 July before the news of Reynolds's wounding or death had reached the army commander. Biddle had been in the saddle all through 30 June and was exhausted. "Some of our troops are beyond Littlestown in Pennsylvania," he wrote. "They have come plumb up to the rebel army, and the 4th of July 1863 bids fair to have new memories associated with it. I trust equally as well worth of hereafter honoring, as those for which we now celebrate the day. I am very hopeful of the result. I only wish I had a good map." He concluded his note, writing: "G[eneral] M[eade] has to work very hard and in fact we all have had hard work. I hope they will let me rest today. I do not think we shall leave here, but in all probability the battle will take place here." At that hour, almost everyone at Meade's headquarters still believed that the decisive engagement would be along Big Pipe Creek.[1]

Indeed, the Signal Corps was busy setting up the communications network to aid in the defense of the Pipe Creek line. As if he needed more to do, General Meade called for Captain Lemuel B. Norton, chief signal officer of the army, to report to his headquarters. Norton had been struggling all morning to set up "a [semaphore] signal line between general headquarters, Emmitsburg, and Round Top Mountain," just south of Gettysburg, "but on account of the smokiness of the atmosphere," he was experiencing difficulty. Meade instructed Norton to "examine the [Pipe Creek] line thoroughly, and at once upon the commencement of the movement [to occupy that line], extend telegraphic communication from ... general headquarters, which would be at Frizzellburg, [to] Manchester, Union Mills, Middleburg, and the Taneytown Road." Norton promptly ordered all the signal telegraph wagon trains to Frizzellburg to be "held in readiness to extend the wire at a moment's notice to the points desired by the commanding general."[2]

As the signal telegraph wagon trains, with their enormous spools of wire, were assembling for their movement from Taneytown to Frizzellburg, the movements of the troops, to the casual observer, seemed to be heading in the opposite direction. Brigadier General John Gibbon ordered the Second Corps, then just south of Taneytown, to move out on its march to Gettysburg at about 1:30 P.M. on 1 July. Each regiment was ordered to have a guard in the rear "which was charged to arrest everyone, whether officer or private, who, even for the purpose of getting a drink of water, should step out from his place in the advancing column," recalled Lieutenant Colonel George A. Bruce of the Twentieth Massachusetts. "No interval was allowed between any two units of the corps, whether artillery or infantry." To Bruce it was "the closest marching column we ever had experience of." Importantly, the Second Corps had been ordered to Gettysburg, not to engage the enemy but rather to allow the advance corps—Reynolds's First Corps—and its support—the Eleventh Corps—to fall back on it, and then fall back to Taneytown and the Pipe Creek line.[3]

The heat was intense, reaching nearly ninety degrees; there was no breeze. Adding to the soldiers' discomfort, the Taneytown Road, over the past few days a sea of mud, was now completely dry under the hot sun. The long columns marching alongside the road, and the artillery batteries, mounted officers, and ammunition wagons in the middle of the road, churned up a "cloud of dust so dense and all pervading ... that nothing was anywhere visible." In fact, wrote Lieutenant Colonel Bruce, "the picturesque hills, the rich and fertile valley, the succession of beautiful and productive farms disappeared from sight all at once as if by magic." Soon "the dust settled down upon us, and adhering to the moist skin gave one uniform color of dirty brown to caps, coats, faces, hands, trousers, and shoes. Individual features were obliterated, and it was no longer possible to distinguish file leader from the file closer."[4]

Sergeant George Buckman of the First Minnesota noted in his diary that as his regiment approached the state line of Pennsylvania, "he could see clouds of smoke and distinctly hear the roar of artillery. The people along our route were simply terror stricken. [They gave] anxious and enquiring looks at the troops as they passed rapidly along. Some more thoughtful than the rest had placed tubs of water by the roadside from which the men snatched a cup full and continued on their way."[5]

General Gibbon rode along in the midst of the Second Corps. As the head of the long columns got ever closer to the sound and sight of "bursting shell and clouds of smoke," the disaster that had befallen the First and Eleventh Corps became evident everywhere. The road, Gibbon recalled, was "blocked up with baggage wagons driven to the rear by panic-stricken drivers who with the greatest difficulty could be induced to give up the road to our artillery and ambulances. We finally had to tear down the fences and force the drivers, with drawn pistols, to park the wagons in the fields. Clearing the road this way, vehicles and artillery travelled in the road, whilst the infantry marched, when it could, in the open fields alongside." The sights and sounds of rout and panic were enough to discourage the most stout-hearted patriot.[6]

General Hancock arrived at Cemetery Hill, southeast of Gettysburg, sometime around 3:30 in the afternoon, well ahead of the marching columns of his Second Corps. He observed "a broad, tumultuous stream of panic—stricken men, mingled with caissons, led horses, artillery, ammunition wagons, and ambulances loaded with wounded." It was a scene of "wreck and disorder." Hancock described it himself: "[I] saw our troops retreating in disorder and confusion from the town, closely followed by the enemy." Even more painful to observe were "the disordered groups of fugitives hurrying from the field or skulking behind cover." The Twelfth Corps, positioned about a mile down the Baltimore Pike, southeast of Cemetery Hill, picked up more than fifteen hundred fugitives from Reynolds's and Howard's corps. Steinwehr's division of Howard's corps, along with three artillery batteries, were holding a nearly impregnable position along Cemetery Hill. Hancock quickly perceived that they had to be properly supported on both flanks, though. To the left—or south—of Gettysburg, Buford's two brigades of weary cavalrymen held a thin skirmish line. Hancock apparently rode into Captain James H. Cooper's Battery B, First Pennsylvania Light Artillery, and asked for General Doubleday. Cooper remembered that Hancock's horse was "covered with foam."[7]

Near the gatehouse on Cemetery Hill, General Howard approached Hancock; it was a less than cordial meeting. Hancock saluted Howard and then told him of his assignment. Howard was agitated about being replaced by an officer junior to him. Hancock was not moved; he replied matter-of-factly that General Meade had given him orders and that if Howard wished to examine them, he could do so. Howard backed off. "I do not doubt your word," he said. Rather than dither over rank, Hancock looked at the terrain from Cemetery Hill. Culp's Hill to the east and the Round Tops to the south were formidable, as was Cemetery Hill itself. From Cemetery Hill, a long, gentle ridge extended south toward

The cemetery gatehouse at Gettysburg. (Library of Congress)

the Round Tops. Hancock turned to Howard and said: "I think this is the strongest position by nature on which to fight a battle that I ever saw, and if it meets your approbation I will select this as the battlefield." When Howard agreed, Hancock replied: "Very well, sir, I select this as the battlefield." Hancock prudently made Howard part of the decision-making at the outset of his mission.[8]

At thirty-three years of age, General Howard was the youngest corps commander in the Army of the Potomac. A native of Leeds, Maine, he had been graduated from Bowdoin College in 1849 and then West Point four years later. Before the war, he served as an assistant professor of mathematics at the military academy. After briefly commanding the Third Maine at the outbreak of the war, Howard commanded a brigade at First Bull Run and was elevated to the rank of brigadier general two months later. He commanded a brigade in the Second Corps on the Peninsula, where at Seven Pines he lost his right arm after being severely wounded. He returned to command and led the Second Division of the Second Corps at

Antietam, after which he was elevated to the rank of major general. On the relief of Major General Franz Siegel, Howard was named commander of the Eleventh Corps, a command consisting of a large number of regiments of German-speaking troops, as well as a German-speaking division commander and several German-speaking brigade commanders. Not well liked in the army, Howard's corps was routed by Stonewall Jackson at Chancellorsville, an event that sullied Howard's reputation, as well as that of the Eleventh Corps.[9]

Hancock began an effort to strengthen the Cemetery Hill and Culp's Hill defenses, aided by Howard and General Buford, who was also nearby. Hancock instructed Captain Greenleaf T. Stevens to place his Fifth Maine Battery from the First Corps artillery brigade along a knoll near Culp's Hill known as McKnight's Hill; that knoll would ultimately bear the name Stevens Knoll. Remnants of the First Corps, mainly the Iron Brigade of Wadsworth's battered division, were sent by Hancock to positions along the western summit of Culp's Hill just to the right of Stevens's battery. The bloodied remnants of Rowley's and Robinson's divisions were assigned positions behind stone walls to the left of Steinwehr's division, from Cemetery Hill south, facing west. That night those First Corps troops would be reinforced by the Vermont brigade commanded by Brigadier General George J. Stannard, although two of its regiments had been detached earlier that morning to guard the wagon trains of the First and, probably, the Eleventh Corps to Westminster. The detritus of the fleeing Eleventh Corps were mostly halted, organized as best as could be done, and sent to positions on Cemetery Hill, and between it and Culp's Hill; some were ordered by Hancock to positions facing the Emmitsburg Road, on the western face of Cemetery Hill and Cemetery Ridge. Apart from Steinwehr's troops, the defenders along Cemetery and Culp's Hills and Cemetery Ridge were the remnants of regiments that had been roughly handled and severely depleted earlier that day.[10]

Throughout, Hancock kept an eye on the Confederate forces massing in the distant fields below Cemetery Hill and in the streets of the town. Neither he nor any other commander in the Army of the Potomac knew the extent of Lee's army on the field. Whether all of Hill's and Ewell's corps were present was not known, although each appeared to be present in force. Where Longstreet's corps was located was anybody's guess. Hancock believed that the proximity of the Twelfth Corps to the Baltimore Pike—and the fact that the Third Corps, which he learned was en route to Gettysburg, generally along the Emmitsburg Road, and a wagon road parallel to it—would be enough to stop any assault before nightfall if they

Major General Oliver Otis Howard. (Library of Congress)

reached the field in time. Hancock's own Second Corps, he knew, was nearing Gettysburg on the Taneytown Road.[11]

As instructed by Meade, Hancock called for General Warren, the chief engineer of the army, and the two of them rode along the defenses, examining the terrain. They observed the Round Tops, Cemetery Ridge, Cemetery Hill, and Culp's Hill. Warren generally agreed with Hancock that the positions at Gettysburg were favorable to fight the enemy, but there were difficulties with the terrain that would become obvious over time. Concerned about keeping the Taneytown Road clear for the movement of troops, artillery, and army headquarters, protecting the quartermaster and subsistence stores, General Hancock sent a courier back to General Gibbon ordering him to direct the Second Corps quartermaster and subsistence wagon trains to turn back and proceed to Union Bridge.[12]

Brigadier General John W. Geary, commanding the Second Division in Slocum's Twelfth Corps approaching on the Baltimore Pike, rode ahead to Gettysburg. He found Hancock on Cemetery Ridge. "Geary," Hancock asked, "where are your troops?" Geary responded: "Two brigades are on the road advancing." Pointing to Little Round Top, Hancock asked: "Do you see this knoll on the left? That knoll is a commanding position, and we must take possession of it, and then a line can be formed here (pointing to Cemetery Hill and down Cemetery Ridge to Little Round Top) and a battle fought. If we fail to fight here we will be compelled to fall back about seven miles. In the absence of Slocum, I order you to place your troops on that knoll." Hancock had been given no authority to command any elements of the Twelfth Corps. Given the exigent circumstances, he decided to act.[13]

Geary turned to his aide, Captain Moses Veale, assistant commissary of musters, and barked: "Veale, ride back and order General Greene to double-quick his troops diagonally across the fields and take possession of the knoll (Little Round Top)." Geary's aide rode back down the Baltimore Pike and directed Brigadier General George S. Greene to hurry his Third Brigade forward, followed by Colonel Charles Candy's First Brigade. For a time, those two brigades were the only Union troops in place between the left flank of the First and Eleventh Corps at Cemetery Hill all the way to the northern slope of Little Round Top.[14]

Hancock called for Major Mitchell at about 4:00 P.M. or just thereafter. When Mitchell reported, Hancock told him to ride back to army headquarters, report to General Meade that the remnants of the First and Eleventh Corps held positions that were on high ground that was defensible, and that he (Hancock) suggested the troops could hold the posi-

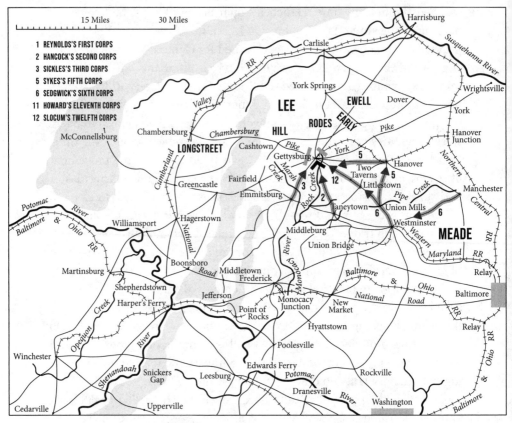

Map 9.1. 1 July 1863: Meade orders the army to Gettysburg.

tions until reinforcements arrived at night. Mitchell dug his spurs into his horse's flanks and galloped back through the cemetery and down the Taneytown Road.[15]

At his Taneytown headquarters, Meade felt the urgency of having Sedgwick's large Sixth Corps closer. It was 4:30 P.M. He dictated orders to General Sedgwick, whose command was at Manchester, thirty-two miles to the east. The orders read: "The major general commanding directs that you move your command up to Taneytown tonight; your train, excepting ambulances and ammunition, to Westminster, and south of the railroad, as ordered." Meade then noted that "General Reynolds was killed at Gettysburg this morning." He directed Sedgwick to notify General Sykes of his movement, as well as the cavalry screening the Sixth Corps.[16]

Reporting to army headquarters earlier that afternoon was Major Hyde and an orderly from General Sedgwick's headquarters. After being offered refreshments by General Williams, Hyde was ushered into General Meade's tent. Meade was "standing behind a table [that was] covered with maps," recalled Hyde. Meade handed Hyde the orders, written on "yellow tissue paper," and then told him to commit to memory the contents of them and destroy them if necessary. Meade asked Hyde if he needed a cavalry escort, and Hyde replied that he could get to Manchester more quickly by himself. It would take Hyde just about four hours to reach Sedgwick's headquarters. Sedgwick would get his Sixth Corps on the road at 10:00 P.M., heading toward Westminster and Taneytown.[17]

Meade sent an urgent order to General Sickles, whose Third Corps had been ordered from Emmitsburg to Gettysburg by General Howard earlier in the afternoon. On reviewing a copy of Howard's order to Sickles, Meade, at 4:45 P.M., informed the Third Corps commander that "General Hancock has been ordered up to assume command of the three corps—First, Eleventh, and Third." Meade then admonished Sickles that he did not "wish the approaches through Emmitsburg left unguarded as they cover our left and rear." Even at that hour Meade still believed that the army would ultimately defend the Pipe Creek line. A large force at Emmitsburg was needed to protect the left flank of that defense line. Meade informed Sickles that he must "hold on until you shall hear from General Hancock, leaving a division at Emmitsburg, as it is a point not to be abandoned excepting in an extremity." Meade was aware of many concerns beyond protecting against enemy approaches through Emmitsburg. The First and Eleventh Corps having fallen back to positions behind the town of Gettysburg, Meade knew then that Sickles's advance of the Third Corps to reinforce Howard needed guidance from Hancock. The entire situation at Gettysburg had changed since Howard ordered Sickles forward. Meade was concerned that Sickles might easily march his corps directly into the presence of the enemy.[18]

Responding to Howard's urgent appeal earlier that afternoon, General Sickles had ordered General Birney to take the First and Second Brigades of the First Division of the Third Corps, and three batteries of artillery, and to proceed to Gettysburg one and one half hours before Meade sent his 4:45 P.M. order. The Third Brigade, commanded by Colonel P. Regis de Trobriand, had been directed to a position at Emmitsburg, along with a battery of artillery, covering the road to Fairfield. Also ordered forward by Sickles at the same time was General Humphreys's Second Division of the Third Corps. Humphreys had left his Third Brigade, commanded by Colonel George C. Burling, along with an artillery battery, at Emmitsburg, also covering the approaches from Fairfield; Humphrey's First and Second Brigades marched toward Gettysburg behind Birney's First Division.

Sickles had forwarded a dispatch to the assistant adjutant general, Seth Williams, at Meade's headquarters, carefully notifying him of all his actions within ten minutes of ordering his corps to move out.[19]

Although composed of only two divisions, the Third Corps was sizable; it consisted of thirty-seven infantry regiments and battalions, along with five batteries of artillery. General Sickles's Third Corps consisted of 13,881 officers and men at the muster the day before.[20]

In a "downpour," likely a localized shower, the soldiers of Birney's division of the Third Corps broke camp and marched "through pasty mud" toward Gettysburg on the Emmitsburg Road. The "clothes of the fatigued men were sticking close to their bodies from the heavy rain and excessive perspiration," recalled one soldier. Often the ranks were ordered to "press forward on the double quick," making the advance even more miserable.[21]

Like the soldiers in the Second Corps, Birney's troops heard the thunder of artillery ahead; it got louder and louder as the march progressed. They knew a battle was raging outside of Gettysburg, and the thought of defending their "homeland" inspired them. Frank Rauscher, a musician in the One Hundred Fourteenth Pennsylvania, remembered other sights as the columns got closer to Gettysburg. "On the Emmitsburg Road," he recalled, "as we approached Gettysburg, we met a long train of country teams, containing women and children and old men, mixed up with an indiscriminate gathering of household furniture and utensils—all fleeing from their homes or driven away by the invaders." The sight of the refugees had an impact on the men. Their "faces grew pale with shame and indignation," remembered Rauscher, "at the idea of our own people being driven from their firesides."[22]

Behind Birney's division marched Humphreys's. Lieutenant Colonel Adolpho Fernandez Cavada, the Cuban-born assistant inspector general and aide to General Humphreys, recalled hearing first that General Reynolds was fighting "against great odds" and was "in danger." He then heard that Reynolds had been killed. "Fatigue, hunger and sickness were all forgotten," wrote Cavada, "when a battle became certain." Although Birney's division had taken the Emmitsburg Road to Gettysburg, Humphreys's division, after crossing Marsh Creek at dark, had been directed by the inspector general of the Third Corps, Lieutenant Colonel Julius Hayden, onto a wagon road that led to the Black Horse Tavern. The tavern was located alongside Marsh Creek on the road between Fairfield and Gettysburg, about five miles upstream.[23]

Darkness found Birney's division at the intersection of the Emmitsburg Road and Millerstown Road, on the Wentz and Sherfy farms, three miles south of Gettysburg, but the head of Humphreys's division, following the wagon road alongside Marsh Creek, got within several hundred yards of the Black Horse Tavern, about three miles northwest of where Birney's division halted. General Humphreys and Lieutenant Colonel Hayden dismounted and cautiously walked toward the Fairfield Road across from the tavern only to find it within the Confederate lines! That is what Meade feared. Humphreys and Hayden returned to the columns of infantry and directed them to "about face" and march in the opposite direction until they reached Pitzer's Schoolhouse on the Millerstown Road. Following the Millerstown Road, the columns reached the Wentz and Sherfy farms. From there, they were finally reunited with Birney's division in the fields around the farm of George Weikert just north of Little Round Top late that afternoon, directed there under orders from General Slocum.[24]

Hancock had to notify Meade formally of the situation at Gettysburg and his recommendations. He directed Captain Parker of his staff to ride back to Taneytown and deliver to Meade a dispatch he had just scribbled, informing the commanding general that "our troops had given up the front of Gettysburg and the town." It was 5:25 P.M. Hancock wrote that he believed the position that the remnants of the First and Eleventh Corps held was a good place to fight the enemy, "although," he added, "[it was] somewhat exposed to be turned by the left." The terrain and the absence of sufficient troops to occupy the broad, open fields between Cemetery Hill and the Round Tops gave Hancock serious concern. "The battle is quiet now," Hancock wrote, "I think we will be all right until night." After assuring Meade he would communicate with General Slocum "in a few moments" and "transfer the command to him," Hancock added: "Howard says that Doubleday's command gave way." Adding the postscript, "General Warren is here," he signed the dispatch and handed it to Parker, who turned his horse and galloped toward Taneytown. Hancock would remain on the battlefield until 8:00 P.M.[25]

Meade received another dispatch on or shortly after 6:00 P.M. That message, sent at 3:20 P.M., was from General Buford at Gettysburg. "I am satisfied that Longstreet and Hill have made a junction," he wrote. "A tremendous battle has been raging since 9:30 A.M., with varying success. At the present moment the battle is raging on the road to Cashtown, and within short cannon range of [Gettysburg]. The enemy's line is a semicircle on the height, from north to west. General Reynolds was killed early this morning. In my opinion, there seems to be no directing person." Indeed, sending the left wing onto the turnpike axis between Cashtown and Gettysburg caused the enemy to show his hand, as Meade anticipated it would, although the cost of the movement was beginning to look terrible. Meade was probably skeptical of Buford's comment about Longstreet's presence at Gettysburg, given what other intelligence he had last received about that corps. Meade, however, must have been displeased over the last sentence of Hancock's message referring to Doubleday's command giving way.[26]

Major Mitchell reached army headquarters outside of Taneytown at about the time Meade received Buford's last message. Mitchell explained the situation at Gettysburg to the army commander. He told Meade that Hancock believed he could hold it until dark and that "he (Hancock) considered Gettysburg the place to fight the coming battle." Meade had just forwarded a cryptic message to General Couch in Harrisburg, informing him that the enemy is "advancing on Gettysburg—Hill from Cashtown; Ewell, from Heidlersburg." Evidence that he was contemplating moving the entire army to Gettysburg, Meade sent a message to Couch, asking if he could "throw a force in Ewell's rear, to threaten him, and at the same time keep your line of retreat open? If you can, do so."[27]

Meade questioned Major Mitchell about the terrain, the placement of the remnants of the First and Eleventh Corps, and the imminent arrival of other elements of the army. Meade concurred with Hancock's decision to concentrate the army at Gettysburg; frankly, he was already committed to moving the army to Gettysburg as a result of the day's actions there. Responding to emergencies on the battlefield over the past nine hours, Generals Reynolds, Howard, and, subsequently, Meade had already directed all but two corps of the army to Gettysburg. The die had been cast.[28]

Meade scribbled a personal note to Generals Hancock and Doubleday just before 6:00 P.M., telling them that "if General Slocum is on the field, and I hope he is, he takes command." He also informed them of his orders to Sickles and that if the Third Corps division left at Emmitsburg is needed, "it can be ordered up tonight." After noting that he ordered Sedgwick forward to Taneytown, Meade added: "It seems to me we have so concentrated that a battle at Gettysburg is now forced on us, and that, if we get all our people, and attack with our whole force to-morrow, we ought to defeat the force the enemy has." The dispatch was likely given by Meade to Major Mitchell, who carried it back to Gettysburg. Meade was ready to concentrate the army at Gettysburg. He was also contemplating going on the offensive once he got there. Meade had formally abandoned the Pipe Creek line.[29]

Meade received a terse dispatch from General Slocum. "A portion of our troops have fallen back from Gettysburg. Matters do not appear well,"

Major General Henry Warner Slocum. (Library of Congress)

wrote Slocum. He let Meade know that his two divisions were in place at Gettysburg, one "on the right of the town," along the Baltimore Pike. Meade must have been relieved to learn that.[30]

A native of Onondaga County, New York, General Slocum was an 1852 graduate of West Point. He was thirty-six years old. He served in Florida and the garrison in Charleston, South Carolina, before resigning his commission in 1856 to practice law in Syracuse. There, he served as county treasurer, a state legislator, and an instructor in artillery in the New York State militia, attaining the rank of colonel. At the outbreak of the Civil War, he was named commander of the Twenty-Seventh New York and fought at First Bull Run. He was then given a brigade in General Franklin's division. When Franklin became commander of the Sixth Corps, Slocum assumed command of Franklin's division, which he led through the Peninsula Campaign and Second Bull Run. After Antietam, Slocum was appointed commander of the Twelfth Corps. His corps suffered severely at Chancellorsville, and as a result of that battle, and General Hooker's retreat across the Rappahannock River, Slocum became an ardent spokesman for Hooker's removal.[31]

The remnants of the First and Eleventh Corps, and now the Twelfth Corps, were at Gettysburg. Elements of the Third Corps were near Gettysburg. Much of that corps, like the Second Corps, was closing in on Gettysburg. Five of Meade's seven corps were already at or near Gettysburg. Meade wrote to General Halleck at that hour: "The First and Eleventh Corps have been engaged all day in front of Gettysburg. The Twelfth, Third, and Fifth have been moving up, and all, I hope, by this time on the field. This leaves only the Sixth, which I will move up tonight. General Reynolds was killed this morning early in the action. I immediately sent up General Hancock to assume command." Although Meade included the Fifth Corps among those already "moving up" (even though it was not at that time), he probably felt justified in so writing as Halleck would not receive the message for more than six hours. The Fifth Corps would be on the move by then. Meade then expressed uncertainty to Halleck about the whereabouts of the enemy. "A. P. Hill and Ewell," he wrote, "are certainly concentrating; Longstreet's whereabouts I do not know." Meade gave Halleck his conclusion: "I see no other course than to hazard a general battle. Circumstances during the night may alter this decision, of which I will try to advise you." Meade informed Halleck that he wanted to strike Hill's and Ewell's corps if at all possible at Gettysburg once he had numerical superiority. Given to a courier, the message was taken by horseback thirty miles south to the Baltimore & Ohio Railroad Station telegraph office in Frederick. There, it was sent over the wires and received at the War Department at 10:20 P.M. Meade's 6:00 P.M. letter to Halleck was a dramatic reversal of the message about the Pipe Creek Circular he had prepared for the general in chief five hours earlier but determined not to send. It was a reversal forced on Meade by what had happened to the First and Eleventh Corps at Gettysburg.[32]

Between 6:30 and 7:00 P.M., Captain Parker arrived at army headquarters near Taneytown. Escorted into the commanding general's tent along Piney Creek, Parker handed Meade General Hancock's written report and recommendation from the battlefield. It confirmed all that Major Mitchell reported. Meade still, though, knew little about the positions of the enemy. He had no real idea of how much of Lee's army had been engaged at Gettysburg and how much of that army had not and, importantly, where the rest of it was located. Other than the road network he could see on the maps, he knew nothing of the terrain at Gettysburg.[33]

With Hancock's assurances, however, Meade boldly started issuing orders. The first order was for General Sedgwick. Meade must have fumed over what he had been informed by Hancock about General Doubleday, who, it appears, was not well liked in the army. According to General Howard, Doubleday may have been ineffective as commander of the First Corps that day. Howard certainly claimed as much in his report to Hancock, although he may have been covering for himself. After all, he was the one who directed Doubleday to fall back that afternoon, although Meade did not know that. It seems that Buford, in a backhanded way, may have expressed similar concerns about Doubleday. Over the signature of General Butterfield, Meade prepared an order for General Sedgwick that Major General John Newton, commanding the Third Division of the Sixth Corps, would "assume command of the First Corps." The order continued: "General Meade wishes him to proceed to the front with all possible dispatch." The first act of Meade in response to Hancock's dispatch that evening was to sack Doubleday! Whether Meade's actions were justified or not, he had little tolerance for failure. War was a life-and-death business, and he had no time or inclination, after reading General Howard's report, to try to uncover all the facts.[34]

Other scholars have written about Meade's treatment of Doubleday. Where Edwin Coddington relegates the matter to a footnote that sets forth the individuals in the army, including Meade, who expressed little or no confidence in Doubleday, Allen Guelzo uses the episode to illustrate that Meade elevated General Newton because he trusted Newton's politics. "Newton," claims Guelzo, "was some twenty heads behind Doubleday in seniority, but he had been a fixture of the McClellanite regime in the Sixth Corps and had played a direct role in undermining Ambrose Burnside after Fredericksburg." According to Guelzo, "To Meade, who had served at Fredericksburg alongside Newton under the arch-McClellanite, William Buel Franklin, Newton was the only other major general he could trust politically." Such a charge is simply baseless. Frankly, Meade did not have confidence in Doubleday, and he had every right, as commander of the army, to name individuals to command positions in whom he had confidence.[35]

Another order of Meade's was directed to General George Sykes, commander of the Fifth Corps, then at Hanover, Pennsylvania. At 7:00 P.M., Meade ordered Sykes to "move up to Gettysburg at once upon receipt of this order." Sykes was directed to communicate directly with General Slocum. "The present prospect," Meade noted, "is that our general engagement must be there." All of Sykes's quartermaster and subsistence trains were ordered to Westminster and Union Bridge. With that order, Meade officially canceled the Pipe Creek Circular, issued only six hours before. Meade had all the nerve and grit necessary to command an army in the field, and he took an enormous risk abandoning the Pipe Creek line in favor of a place he knew nothing about. In the words of General Hunt, Meade was "bold" and "decisive."[36]

Within thirty minutes, Meade prepared another order to General Sedgwick, whose Sixth Corps he had previously ordered to march from Manchester to Taneytown. He informed Sedgwick that a general battle seems to be "impending tomorrow at Gettysburg." It was of "utmost importance," Meade wrote, that "you bring the Sixth Corps forward." Meade knew Sedgwick's corps would have the longest march of all, thirty-two miles. "Stop all [wagon] trains [actually accompanying the troops] that impede your progress or turn them out of the road," Meade wrote. "Your march will have to be a forced one to reach the scene of action, where we shall probably be largely outnumbered without your presence."[37]

Meade let Sedgwick know that he had already ordered General Sykes to move the Fifth Corps from Hanover to Gettysburg and that General Slocum had been ordered to move the Twelfth Corps there from Two Taverns. He informed Sedgwick that General Hancock's Second Corps had been ordered to Gettysburg from Taneytown. Meade finally directed Sedgwick to report to army headquarters "in person before going to the front." Meade concluded with a postscript: "The [quartermaster and subsistence wagon] trains will all go to Westminster and Union Bridge, as ordered."[38]

Meade handed the two dispatches for Sedgwick to Lieutenant Paul A. Oliver, formerly of the Twelfth New York and a staff officer to Butterfield.

Oliver recalled that he started from Meade's headquarters with an orderly at 7:30 P.M. and arrived at Westminster, thirteen miles distant, where he was told that Confederates had entered the town. He found that not to be true, but he recalled that the town of Westminster was in a state of chaos, unquestionably due to the immense wagon trains and cattle herds of the army crowding alongside the Baltimore Pike and into the streets of the town. Just before midnight Oliver reached General Sedgwick, whose enormous columns were approaching Westminster in order to get onto the direct road to Taneytown. Oliver handed Sedgwick Meade's orders. "General," Oliver said, "you must be at Gettysburg by afternoon of tomorrow." After reading the order, Sedgwick turned to Oliver and said: "Say to General Meade I will be at Gettysburg with my corps at four o'clock tomorrow afternoon." Oliver then galloped on up the Baltimore Pike toward Gettysburg, twenty miles distant. As he raced toward Gettysburg early on the morning of 2 July, he recalled that one of his horse's shoes became loose. He procured the services of a local blacksmith, "whose home and fireside I was hastening to defend," and "he took a hammer and fastened a few nails a little tighter." For that, the blacksmith charged Oliver. "These people are more secesh than they are in Maryland," Oliver wrote afterward.[39]

Riding alongside General Sedgwick was General Newton. Sedgwick turned to Newton and informed him that he had just been handed "a dispatch from Meade announcing that a battle had been fought at Gettysburg in which [the First and Eleventh Corps] had been compelled to retire; that the conflict would in all probability be renewed the next day, and it was of the utmost importance that [the Sixth Corps] should be upon the field, as the success of the day might depend upon its presence." Sedgwick then told Newton that he had received another dispatch from Meade that announced "the assignment of General Newton to the command of the First Corps, and directed him to report to the front without delay."[40]

Newton bid Sedgwick goodnight and then, accompanied by two aides, one of whom was Lieutenant Huntington W. Jackson of his staff, and two orderlies, began the ride up the Baltimore Pike to Gettysburg. Sedgwick's Sixth Corps would follow Newton and his entourage.[41]

General Sedgwick was rapidly becoming one of the most popular commanders in the Army of the Potomac. At fifty years of age, he was the oldest major general in the Army of the Potomac. Born in Cornwall Hollow, Connecticut, he was graduated from West Point in 1837 along with Joseph Hooker. He served with both Generals Zachary Taylor and Winfield Scott in the Mexican War. At the outbreak of the Civil War, Sedgwick was commissioned a brigadier general and commanded a division in the

Major General John Sedgwick. (Library of Congress)

Second Corps on the Peninsula, where he was wounded at Glendale. Promoted to the rank of major general, he led his division into the heavy fighting at Antietam, where he was wounded three times and carried off the battlefield. He recovered and was named commander of the Sixth Corps, directing its attacks against Marye's Heights at Fredericksburg, and then at Salem Church, during the Chancellorsville Campaign. A bachelor, Sedgwick was a solid, frontline officer.[42]

The Sixth Corps presented an awe-inspiring spectacle on the march, to be sure. The largest corps in the Army of the Potomac, it boasted of seven brigades in three divisions with thirty-six infantry regiments. It also had eight batteries of artillery and two companies of cavalry, numbering 17,625 officers and men in all at its muster the day before. Stretched out on the road, its columns of infantry alone extended for nearly ten miles.[43]

The leading elements of the Sixth Corps had just entered the Baltimore Pike and were heading south to Westminster when Oliver delivered Meade's last orders to Sedgwick. Those columns had to be halted, turned around, and directed north toward Gettysburg. One soldier recalled the march of the Sixth Corps toward Gettysburg in almost poetic language: "That hot, dry, dusty, moonlit night of 1 July presented a scene of weird, almost spectral impressiveness." He remembered that the road that ran toward Gettysburg

> flowed with unceasing, unbroken rivers of armed men, marching
> swiftly, stolidly, silently. Their garments were covered with dust
> and their gun barrels gleamed with a fierce brilliance in the bright
> moonlight. The striking silence of the march, the dust-gray figures,
> the witchery of the moonbeams made it seem spectral and awesome.
> No drum beat, no trumpet blared, no harsh command broke the
> monotonous stillness of the steady surge forward. From the fields
> along the road came the sighs and drones of full-fed cattle lying in
> the rich pastures, the tinkle of a bell as a cow moved uneasily, the
> mournful call of the whip-poor-will, the chirp of crickets, the buzz
> of night-flying insects. Thousands of ears heard these sounds of the
> night that a few hours later would hear nothing more until that last
> Trumpet.[44]

Sedgwick allowed only a few minutes each hour to breathe the men. A halt was finally called, and "a few fires were kindled and an attempt was made to secure a rude breakfast." Then the yells: "Fall In." Officers kicked over the coffee pots, and the weary march was started again. Many men fell, fainting in their tracks; they were loaded into ambulances until the vehicles were full. Some soldiers were pulled to the side of the road and left until they regained consciousness.[45]

Isaac O. Best of the One Hundred Twenty-First New York, in the Sixth Corps, remembered hearing of the disastrous result of the fighting at Gettysburg from civilians and demoralized soldiers from the front as he marched along in the night. "The night was dark," he recalled, "so that crossing a little stream I got my feet wet, and soon they began to hurt me like the mischief. The dust worked into the shoes and wet socks and irritated the blisters, and to me the miles grew longer and longer and my misery more intense and I longed for daylight."[46]

Surgeon George T. Stevens of the Seventy-Seventh New York, in Sedgwick's Corps, recalled observing at Littlestown "citizens bringing the wounded from the field in their carriages, and many wounded soldiers who could walk were making their way to the [nearest] village." He then noted: "The marching was more rapid. Our friends were waiting for us!" Using few words, Henry Clay Bowman of the Ninety-Third Pennsylvania probably expressed his experience on the night of 1 July best when he entered a few simple notes in his diary: "Pleasant. Wrote Amanda. Orders to march at 8 P.M. Marched at 8; marching all night." Through the wee hours of 2 July, the Sixth Corps marched up the Baltimore Pike ever closer to Gettysburg.[47]

General Sykes's Fifth Corps had marched to Hanover from Union Mills earlier on 1 July, a nearly seventeen-mile trek. In all, the Fifth Corps boasted of thirty-five hard-fighting regiments, ten of which were United States Regulars and nine were Pennsylvania Reserves, along with five batteries of artillery. On receiving Meade's order to march the corps to Gettysburg, Sykes gave the orders to set his columns—15,102 officers and men strong at the muster the day before—on the march toward the site of the fighting at 7:00 P.M. on 1 July.[48]

Private Robert G. Carter, Twenty-Second Massachusetts Infantry, remembered the evening of 1 July for the Fifth Corps. "The bivouac fires … were gleaming in the meadows west of Hanover," he wrote. "Our worn and weary men, having made coffee and eaten some freshly killed beef— yet warm—were just ready to catch a few hours' sleep, when suddenly a mounted courier rode into our lines." At once there were calls all through the bivouac sites to "pack up." The "General" was sounded by drummers. The men got up, packed, and formed into columns. They were then led onto the Hanover Road, where they started marching toward McSherrystown, Pennsylvania, and Gettysburg. "The rapid gait, with the terrible

YOUR MARCH WILL BE A FORCED ONE

march of the day," Carter recalled, "soon began to tell upon our men, and falling out again began. Every effort was made to urge the column on, but no halts were made. It was midnight, and still the weary tramp went on—on through the little villages and hamlets of Pennsylvania. Men, almost fainting, could be seen stealing off by the roadside into the fields and woods, too exhausted to proceed farther." Then Carter remembered: "Soon, by the clear light of the moon, we could distinctly see the form of a courier or staff officer making his way, with difficulty, along the column; could hear a very faint cheering as he announced, and it was passed along, that General McClellan had arrived with 60,000 troops and was again in command of the old army. I never knew who the faker was. But the hitherto inspiring name of 'Little Mac' had lost its magical charm." Jacob Shenkel of the Sixty-Second Pennsylvania, whose columns were distant from Lieutenant Carter's, however, noted that his colonel told the men: "McClellan had been reinstated." To that news Shenkel recalled: "The men cheered louder than I ever heard them." The Fifth Corps would march until they reached Bonaughtown, Pennsylvania, at 12:30 A.M. on 2 July, a nine-mile trek.[49]

General Sickles received Meade's 4:45 P.M. order long after his corps had already reached Gettysburg. A perplexed Sickles wrote back to army headquarters at 9:30 P.M., informing Meade that he had moved the Third Corps forward to Gettysburg before he received Meade's dispatch. He noted that he left two brigades and two batteries at Emmitsburg; he "assumed" the approaches to Emmitsburg from Fairfield should not be "uncovered." He claimed, correctly, that General Howard was in command. "Shall I return to my position at Emmitsburg or shall I remain and report to Howard?" he asked.[50]

Two hours before Sickles scribbled his dispatch to Meade, the army commander wrote to Sickles, ordering all the forces left at Emmitsburg by him to join the Third Corps at Gettysburg "with the greatest dispatch." Meade then admonished Sickles:

The latest information from the field, at 5:25, would indicate that the enemy occupy Gettysburg, and our forces are in position in rear of the town, on the road to Taneytown. The greatest care must be taken in getting on the proper road. It is believed that, after crossing Marsh Creek, there is a road leading into the Gettysburg and Taneytown Road, in rear of our line. The general directs that you take care that you do not come in collision with any force of the enemy in moving up. He expects the division [at Emmitsburg] to be up by daylight tomorrow.[51]

The exchange of orders and messages between Meade and Sickles that afternoon and night illustrate of how difficult it was to command an army the size of the Army of the Potomac that was spread out over a vast expanse of territory when communications were so slow. Once Meade received word of the situation at Gettysburg and resolved to advance the army there, he ordered all of the troops left behind to the front. Emmitsburg would no longer be on his left flank; that line of defense—the Pipe Creek line and the approaches to Emmitsburg from the South Mountain range—had been abandoned.

10

YOU WILL PROBABLY
HAVE A DEPOT AT
WESTMINSTER

As darkness completely covered the landscape on 1 July, Meade finally received some good news. This time it came from an unlikely correspondent, General French. His command, five thousand infantry, seven hundred cavalry, and three batteries of artillery, arrived at Frederick that afternoon. He left four thousand troops at Harper's Ferry as ordered. Six hundred of them would join French's main body soon. He informed Meade that he would "make arrangements for carrying out your instructions" that were received that evening. He also assured Meade that he had picked up two hundred stragglers of the Army of the Potomac in Frederick whom he placed in confinement. Meade had to be relieved that the telegraph terminal at Frederick was secure and that the rail lines and telegraph wires to Baltimore and Washington were protected.[1]

General Meade was exhausted and hungry. Over the past forty-eight hours he had not slept, save for an occasional catnap. He had not had a change of clothes since he took command of the army three days before. He had eaten very little. Meade looked tired, worn, and haggard. It did not appear that rest, fresh clothing, or any sustenance was in his immediate future.[2]

Meade's weariness was not only the result of the outbreak of fighting at Gettysburg. Indeed, all through the day and night of 1 July, Meade grappled with the uncertainties of the fighting, and then the disaster, fourteen miles ahead of his Piney Creek headquarters near Taneytown, but he also faced, and addressed, other enormous problems; he had to feed his men and the army's horses and mules, and he had to supply the men with clothing, shoes, socks, and munitions. He knew that well over one fourth of the army was shoeless. His troops had marched all the way from

Brigadier General Rufus Ingalls. (Library of Congress)

Falmouth, Virginia, to Frederick, Maryland, and then more than thirty miles north of that city. Much of the marching had been over rough terrain and through heavy rains and mud. Most of those marches necessitated the men being on the move more than fifteen hours a day. They were on the march again. Beyond supplies, the men needed rest. There were more than ninety thousand officers and men in the Army of the Potomac, not counting noncombatant support personnel. They had to be supplied and resupplied continuously or the army would disintegrate. Men cannot undergo forced marches and then effectively engage the enemy when they are shoeless and lack adequate clothing and socks. They certainly cannot be expected to fight the enemy when they are not supplied with ample ammunition and are chronically hungry. Here, Meade learned that operational command is vastly more complex than tactical command.[3]

General Ingalls received a dispatch from the telegraph terminal at Frederick around three o'clock in the afternoon of 1 July. Quartermaster General Meigs informed him that all the "booties, socks, and other supplies" previously requisitioned would be sent to Westminster by the Western Maryland Railroad. In that same dispatch, Meigs informed Ingalls that the War Department had ordered General Haupt "to take charge of the repairs of the Northern Central [Railroad] and to work upon the Western Maryland Railroad." It was the first notification received at army headquarters at Taneytown that the War Department would devote the personnel and resources necessary to make Westminster and Union Bridge the supply base for the Army of the Potomac as Meade had requested. That was welcome news, although Westminster was twenty-two miles southeast of Gettysburg. Meigs concluded his dispatch by adding: "If this movement is successful you will probably have a depot at Westminster for a time."[4]

Ingalls responded to Meigs almost immediately. He requested the supplies be forwarded to Union Bridge because so many of the empty wagons from the quartermaster and subsistence wagon trains of the seven infantry corps were being forwarded there. Ingalls, for some reason, then added: "I think we shall rely mainly on Frederick."[5]

Feeding the horses and mules of the Army of the Potomac was a daunting task. Army regulations required each horse to be fed roughly fourteen pounds of hay and twelve pounds of oats every day. For mules, fourteen pounds of hay and nine pounds of oats, corn, or barley were required. Men can go for up to ten days without adequate food, but they become very weak. Horses and mules break down within three days when not fed or when given forage different from their regular diet. Two or three days without any forage for the horses and mules would put them in danger of collapsing; the army would be unable to move. Those horses and mules also regularly needed shoes, calling for an enormous amount of iron for the shoes and nails and coal to burn in the forges. With more than thirty thousand mules and nearly thirty thousand horses to feed every day, and regularly shoe, the task was almost insurmountable. Although Ingalls assured the quartermaster general that the army was well supplied, the situation was very uncertain; supplies had to keep coming to the army. An army the size of the Army of the Potomac burned through a mind-numbing amount of quartermaster, subsistence, and forage stores, and iron and coal every day. At 4:15 P.M. on 1 July, Ingalls would requisition Meigs to forward to the army five hundred thousand more pounds of grain; he would also order twenty thousand more pairs of booties. Incredibly, between 28 June and 1 July, General Ingalls would order fifty thousand pairs of shoes for the army. Due to the strenuous campaigning, Meade's army was staring at enormous supply inadequacies unless regularly resupplied with vast amounts of forage, subsistence stores, clothing, shoes, equipment, iron, coal, and ordnance.[6]

Meade asked Ingalls to bring him up to date on the supply issues facing the army at about 1:00 P.M., 1 July, just after he had issued the Pipe Creek Circular and before news arrived of the fighting at Gettysburg. After reading Ingalls's last dispatch, Meade quickly ordered him to send yet another to Meigs, explicitly directing the quartermaster general to send all the booties, forage, and subsistence stores to Westminster and Union Bridge. Meade did not want the quartermaster general to think that Frederick was a terminus for future shipments. Frederick was too far to the rear, more than thirty miles, as well as exposed to enemy forays from the Cumberland Valley. General French's occupation of Frederick would provide some comfort, but Meade was not apprised that it had already taken place. The roads between Frederick and the army were on the army's left flank, which Meade continued to believe was most vulnerable to attack, and that was the real problem. General Ingalls ended his second dispatch, writing: "I hope General Haupt will cause the prompt repair of the [Western Maryland Railroad]." That was Meade's hope, to be sure.[7]

As Meade became aware of the fighting at Gettysburg, his concern about a base of supply being firmly established became acute. He had no idea of the extent of the fighting or how much of Lee's army was present at or near Gettysburg. Supplies for the army had to be sent to the location nearest to the army that also was the most secure. Westminster and Union Bridge were situated southeast, and directly in the rear, of the Army of the Potomac as it was then aligned in front of Big Pipe Creek. Those towns were at least distant from known enemy positions, and they were connected to Relay, twenty-nine miles southeast, and Baltimore, by railroad lines that were usable. Westminster was about fifteen miles from Taneytown and twenty-two miles from Gettysburg. Union Bridge was closer to Taneytown and about the same distance from Gettysburg as Westminster. Although Meade was unsure what enemy forces might be along his far right flank, he believed then that, with the Fifth and Sixth Corps present at Hanover and Manchester and two cavalry divisions in the area, a supply base at Westminster and Union Bridge would be safe. The twenty-two-mile-long supply line—the Baltimore Pike—from Westminster to Gettysburg would soon present challenges to Meade's efforts to protect wagon and mule pack trains attempting to reach the army, but Meade was not planning on an engagement at Gettysburg at that moment; he was still planning on defending the Pipe Creek line.

Yet another dispatch was forwarded to General Meigs by Ingalls at 7:00 P.M. It is clear that General Meade insisted on it being sent, as he had just received updated intelligence about the fighting at Gettysburg. Ingalls informed Meigs that a "pitched battle" was expected "very soon." After the battle is over, he wrote, "we can then better tell where we want to receive [supplies]. Our teams are now all ordered on the railroad between Union Bridge and Westminster. None go to Frederick. Please therefore send the forage to Union Bridge, but defer sending anything at present to Frederick." Amid all the shocking news coming in from the front, Meade finally put to rest any doubt about his chosen base of supply; it would be Westminster and Union Bridge. It took most of the late morning and early afternoon to make his desires known and understood by the quartermaster general.[8]

On 1 July, a railroad official at Camden Station in Baltimore, the home terminal of the Baltimore & Ohio Railroad, sent a telegram to General Meigs that read: "There are thirty cars of ammunition standing at Frederick for nearly [four] days past, which will not be unloaded. Can we not invoke your action so as to relieve the cars. There has been some delay also in discharging forage and stores but there is much improvement in them today." From all available evidence, it appears that Meade was never notified about this, and those thirty cars of ammunition would remain in the railroad yards at Frederick for a full week after the fighting ended at Gettysburg. That serious mishap may well have been the result of the hurried change in army commanders. It is an example of how even among the highest-ranking officers in the army, important matters fell through the cracks and were forgotten. This particular communication failure could have been disastrous.[9]

Once Meade ordered all of the infantry corps to Gettysburg, Westminster and Union Bridge were transformed. The immense quartermaster and subsistence wagon trains of the First, Second, Third, Fifth, Sixth, Eleventh, and Twelfth Corps, Cavalry Corps, and Artillery Reserve rumbled toward Westminster and Union Bridge all through the afternoon, evening, and night of 1 July, creating a nightmarish traffic jam, as Lieutenant Oliver had discovered. Wagons extended for miles out on the roads from Manchester, Littlestown, Middleburg, Uniontown, Emmitsburg, and Taneytown to Westminster and Union Bridge. Together, those wagon trains were nearly fifty miles long if lined up on a single road. That translated into at least five thousand wagons. Because the army wagons were pulled by six-mule teams, there were at least thirty thousand mules in or en route to the two towns and along the railroad line between them by the end of 1 July. Driving and overseeing each wagon were at least two men, most of them detailed soldiers, making the total number of drivers and teamsters in excess of ten thousand. Alongside the subsistence wagon trains of each infantry corps, the Cavalry Corps, and the Artillery Reserve were vast herds of cattle led by mounted drovers. All of those herds together amounted to more than thirty thousand head of cattle.[10]

J. P. Coburn of the One Hundred Forty-First Pennsylvania had been detailed from his regiment several months before to drive a wagon in the Third Corps quartermaster and subsistence wagon trains. That corps wagon train was about seven miles in length on 1 July. Coburn was one of the very few wagoners in the Army of the Potomac who left a diary. He recalled that on the morning of 1 July the wagons were "hitched up" at Emmitsburg, driven "five miles out on the Emmitsburg Road," and then halted. They were, for a time, following the Third Corps north toward Gettysburg. He recorded that the wagons were then driven "back through Taneytown to Uniontown." Unfortunately, he wrote, the wagons "took the wrong road at Uniontown, halted, 'bout-faced and [were driven] to West-minster where we arrived at 7 A.M., July 2." It took that corps wagon train more than eighteen hours to get from Emmitsburg to Westminster not only because of moving onto the wrong road once but, unquestionably, because of the traffic jam of wagon trains clogging the roads to Westminster and Union Bridge.[11]

Added to all the wagons, mules, cattle, drivers, and teamsters at or near Westminster and Union Bridge were, eventually, seven regiments of infantry performing guard duty with the wagon trains. As corps commanders and quartermasters directed their wagon trains back to those towns, regiments were detached to accompany them. Those seven regiments added at least four thousand officers and men to the crowded towns. The First Corps, and probably the Eleventh Corps, quartermaster and subsistence wagon trains were guarded by the Twelfth and Fifteenth Vermont regiments from Stannard's brigade of the First Corps, as those trains probably moved in tandem. The Third Corps trains were accompanied by the Eighty-Fourth Pennsylvania, while the One Hundred Second Pennsylvania protected the Sixth Corps trains. The wagon trains of the Second,

Fifth, and Twelfth Corps were also accompanied by regiments or battalions detached from each of those commands.[12]

Added to the regiments of infantry in Westminster and Union Bridge were Batteries B and M of the First Connecticut Artillery, sent there to guard the wagon trains. The twelve pieces of ordnance of the First Connecticut were all four-and-a-half-inch rifled siege guns. Colonel Pennock Huey's brigade of Gregg's Second Cavalry Division, consisting of four regiments, was sent to Westminster on 1 July to protect what wagon trains had been sent there and to generally protect the development of Westminster and Union Bridge as a supply base pursuant to orders from Meade issued at 1:30 P.M. Over the next two days, the eight regiments of Colonels Gamble's and Devin's brigades of General Buford's First Cavalry Division would join Huey's brigade at Westminster and Union Bridge to refit and guard the trains, swelling the number of infantry and cavalry regiments there to nineteen. Add the two batteries of Connecticut artillery and the engineers, and nearly twelve thousand troops would eventually be stationed in those two towns protecting the army's quartermaster and subsistence trains and refitting. Westminster and the rail line to Union Bridge became known as "the Camp of Transportation." Commanding the Camp of Transportation was Major William Painter, a career quartermaster.[13]

A sizable group of topographical engineers was sent to Westminster. They were at Meade's headquarters at Taneytown through most of 1 July. According to Gilbert Thompson, a member of the United States Battalion of Topographical Engineers: "We were sent undoubtedly to Westminster not only to guard the trains and picket the roads, but to be ready to lay out a line of defense in case the army fell back." He then added: "This is my opinion; Captain [George H.] Mendell 'had no such instructions,' however." Thompson was correct irrespective of his captain's denial: General Meade would so instruct Captain Mendell in an order issued at 5:00 A.M., 2 July.[14]

The War Department notified General Herman Haupt to report to Baltimore to get the Western Maryland Railroad ready to supply Meade's army and to turn Westminster and Union Bridge into the base of supply for the Army of the Potomac. Haupt had already made his presence known to Meade in a series of telegrams he sent to Secretary Stanton that must have been irritating to the army commander. He was now there to help, and his efforts would prove to be nothing short of remarkable.[15]

Somewhat of a child prodigy, Haupt, a native of Philadelphia, was graduated from West Point at eighteen years of age. He married an Ann Cecilia

Brigadier General Herman Haupt. (Library of Congress)

Keller of Gettysburg, Pennsylvania, three years later, constructed the York
and Wrightsville Railroad, and then became a professor of mathematics
and engineering at Pennsylvania College in Gettysburg. Haupt published
a book on the general theory of bridge construction in 1851. Subsequently,
he fundamentally organized and operated the Pennsylvania Railroad as its
chief engineer, its general superintendent, and a director. In April 1862, at

the urging of Secretary Stanton, Haupt was placed in charge of the United States Military Railroads, rail systems that the government had commandeered for use in the war effort. In that capacity, he had performed ably, rebuilding bridges, repairing trackage, forwarding quartermaster, subsistence, and ordnance stores, bringing back sick and wounded soldiers as well as refugees, and keeping the railroads moving to and from Major General John Pope's Union army. Pope's army met with disaster at Second Bull Run on 30 August 1862. Nevertheless, for Haupt's tireless role setting up, operating, and maintaining the army's principal logistical support system, he was commissioned a brigadier general.[16]

General Haupt would do everything humanly possible to satisfy Meade's and Ingalls's concerns. He left Harrisburg for Baltimore by rail. In Baltimore, he set up his headquarters in the massive five-story brick Eutaw House at the northwest corner of Baltimore and Eutaw Streets. Probably the largest building in Baltimore, and one of the most noted hotels in America, the Eutaw House was located close to the Baltimore & Ohio Railroad terminal, Camden Station. From nearby Calvert Station in Baltimore, Haupt rode on the Northern Central Railroad seven miles north to Relay, and then on the Western Maryland Railroad from Relay to Westminster, where he arrived on the afternoon of 1 July as Meade was dealing with the disaster unfolding at Gettysburg. To make the twenty-nine-mile journey on the Western Maryland Railroad from Relay to Westminster took five hours. Haupt found that the railroad had "numerous small bridges" between Relay and Westminster. All, he concluded, were in danger of being destroyed by "rebel sympathizers." Unfortunately, he did not have the troops at his disposal then to guard all those bridges, although they were on the way with extensive wagon trains of the army. He found that the railroad tracks were "not in good condition." The Western Maryland Railroad had only a single track with "no adequate sidings." In fact, the railroad had no water stations, turntables, or experienced officers. Haupt wrote to Chief Quartermaster Ingalls at Meade's headquarters, giving him his findings. He concluded the message, noting: "There is no telegraph line on that road." It would take at least four hours for that message to reach Ingalls because it was routed through Frederick.[17]

Haupt secluded himself in a covered wagon in Westminster, where he developed an organizational plan of operations. Then, from his headquarters at the Eutaw House in Baltimore, he wrote to General Ingalls a dispatch containing meticulously detailed recommendations. The railroad "trains must be run in convoys of five or six," one behind the other, "with guards sufficient for their protection," wrote Haupt. To protect the bridges,

Haupt wrote that he ordered a "half a dozen men" to guard each bridge "to keep off individuals mischievously inclined." Because there was no telegraph line, "when a convoy [of trains] is dispatched," he warned Ingalls, "no others can be sent until they have returned." Haupt then wrote: "It will be all important, on the arrival of a convoy, to unload each and every car on the main track and send [the empty cars] back immediately. This duty will require the most efficient officer of your staff. The rapidity with which cars can be unloaded will measure the capacity of this road to supply the army." Haupt informed Ingalls that "no extra or special [trains]" would be run on the railroad line because of the risk of them blocking the railroad. He then informed Ingalls that he already "ordered iron, cars, and engines" from the United States Military Railroad yards in Alexandria, Virginia, to be forwarded to Baltimore for use on the Western Maryland Railroad and that he would "increase the business facilities at the depot as rapidly as possible." Haupt told Ingalls to communicate with him at the Eutaw House in Baltimore.[18]

Indeed, Haupt got to work. He ordered one of his most trusted railroad men at the Alexandria yards, Adna Anderson, to join him at Westminster and bring along a force of four hundred railroad men and a train filled with split wood, the fuel needed to operate the wood-burning engines. Haupt also asked Anderson to bring along lanterns, buckets, and other necessary equipment. As the engines boiled water in the production of steam power, the buckets were to be used to hold the water taken from streams and held at ready to fill engine boilers. They would be placed all along the twenty-nine-mile-long right-of-way. On a railroad line that was sufficient to pass only three or four trains a day, Haupt concluded that he could pass thirty trains each day along the tracks between Baltimore and Westminster.[19]

Haupt turned his attention to the line of communication between Meade and the War Department at the same time he was working on the railroad. Even if telegraph wires could be rapidly installed, Haupt believed it would be difficult to use them because of the additional need for them to serve the trains running on the tracks. Consequently, he called on S. M. Shoemaker and the Adams Express Company to assist him in immediately establishing "horse expresses" to "run at intervals of three hours with relays every seven miles, to run day and night." It was the same system that was likely used along the National Road between Frederick and Relay after the Baltimore & Ohio Railroad telegraph wires had been cut on 28 June. Haupt tested his express system and concluded that he could get dispatches from Baltimore to Westminster in three hours. That was two hours shorter than if the messages were carried by train. Haupt forwarded his operational plan for opening communications from Westminster to Quartermaster General Meigs, Chief Quartermaster Ingalls, General Halleck, and Secretary Stanton.[20]

Haupt still needed to get communications from Westminster to General Meade, who, in the late afternoon, he had been notified would likely be at Gettysburg, where a major clash was about to take place. Haupt decided to set up an express system along the Baltimore Pike that would cover the twenty-two miles between those two towns. To implement the express system to Meade's headquarters, James W. Garrett, president of the Baltimore & Ohio Railroad, notified Secretary of War Stanton on the evening of 1 July that he arranged a locomotive to leave Baltimore at 9:00 P.M. to transport to Westminster twelve horses from the Adams Express Company along with a group of "messengers" to ride them. As with the communication network between Westminster and Baltimore, the Adams Express Company would set up relay stations of horse expresses every seven miles between Westminster and Gettysburg. Similarly, those horse expresses would run at three-hour intervals around the clock. Given the hilly country between Westminster and Gettysburg, it would take up to three hours to get a message through that twenty-two miles. Overall, a message would take six hours to get from Baltimore to Gettysburg. Haupt set to work. It would take him considerable time to establish Westminster and Union Bridge as a working supply base and to set up the communications network.[21]

As carloads of horses and the group of messengers rumbled along the rail line through the darkness from Baltimore to Westminster, General Sickles reported to Generals Howard and Slocum on Cemetery Hill at Gettysburg. The three generals set up headquarters on the ground near the cemetery gatehouse. Mrs. Peter Thorn and her daughter lived in the gatehouse cottage. Her husband, the caretaker of the cemetery, was in the army. Mrs. Thorn brought the generals bread and coffee. "Those refreshments have never been forgotten," recalled Howard.[22]

Having accomplished his mission at Gettysburg and having turned command of the forces there over to General Slocum, Hancock left Gettysburg for Taneytown well after dark that night. He arrived at Meade's headquarters at around 10:00 P.M. There, Hancock personally reported his findings and conclusions to Meade. It was probably a short meeting since Meade had already ordered the remaining two corps, Sykes's Fifth Corps and Sedgwick's Sixth Corps, to move to Gettysburg as rapidly as possible.[23]

Sometime after 10:00 P.M., Meade, and his staff and escorts, including the First Pennsylvania Reserve Volunteer Cavalry, along with General Henry Hunt, the army's chief of artillery, and Hunt's aide-de-camp, Lieutenant Charles Bissell, left the Piney Creek headquarters and rode out the road to Gettysburg, guided by Captain W. H. Paine of Meade's engineer staff. The sky was clear and the moon bright, lighting the Taneytown Road for Meade and his entourage all the way to Gettysburg. Meade was mounted on his favorite horse, Old Baldy. Much of the Taneytown headquarters was dismantled, and the wagon train carrying most of the tents, chairs, tables, desks, and baggage followed the commander. Some tents, along with a few members of his staff, assistants, and an escort, were left at Taneytown so that communications with corps commanders who had not been apprised of Meade's departure for Gettysburg, particularly General Sedgwick, would remain open. Meade had waited for a time for Sedgwick, hoping to confer with him. Needing to get to the front, Meade directed General Butterfield to remain behind in the event Sedgwick either sent a reply or appeared in person as Meade had requested in his last order to the Sixth Corps commander.[24]

Behind the Round Tops, Meade stopped at the Second Corps bivouac site to confer with General Gibbon, informing him orders would be forthcoming for the movement of his command forward. Meade arrived at the Gettysburg cemetery just after midnight of 2 July; "He was riding at the head of his escort," recalled General Howard. Meade was met by Howard just inside the gate. Meade dismounted near the gatehouse to the cemetery. "The first words he spoke to me," Howard remembered, "were very kind. I believed that I had done my work well the preceding day; I desired his approval and so I frankly stated my earnest wish. Meade at once assured me that he imputed no blame; and I was as well satisfied as I would have been with positive praise from some other commanders."[25]

Soon Generals Sickles and Warren joined Meade and Howard. General Slocum was also present. Meade asked Howard: "Well, Howard, what do you think, is this the place to fight the battle?" "I told to Meade at once what I thought of the cemetery position," Howard recalled. He told Meade that he believed Cemetery Hill could be held if the enemy attacked the position. "I am confident we can hold this position," Howard said to Meade. With Sickles's Third Corps on the field, and with Buford's cavalry division protecting the left flank, the reinforcements "gave heart to our officers and men," remembered Howard. What Howard did not say to Meade, however, was that at 10:00 P.M., the very time Meade left Taneytown for Gettysburg, he wrote to General Butterfield, commenting that his position on Cemetery Hill "is plenty good for a general battle unless you fear it being turned at considerable distance from Gettysburg."[26]

Slocum was confident the position could be held. "It is good for defense," he is reported to have said to Meade. His batteries held positions along the ridge flanked by Culp's Hill and Wolf's Hill. "It is a good place to fight from, general," remarked Slocum. Meade matter-of-factly responded: "I am glad to hear you say so, gentlemen, for it is too late to leave it." With eyes of a skilled topographical engineer, Meade was not certain if the positions his army would have to occupy really were the best. He was heard to say, almost to himself, "We may fight it out here as well as anywhere else."[27]

Accompanied by "a couple of officers," probably General Hunt and Captain Paine, Meade walked over the Baltimore Pike and stood among the artillery batteries posted on Cemetery Hill. There was a bright moon. He could see in the distance the thousands of campfires of the enemy to the north. The gunfire from the opposing skirmish lines and from snipers in the houses along Baltimore Street in the town was loud and steady, peppering the night. The enemy's lines were described to Meade as closely as the officers collected behind him could discern.[28]

Well before sunrise, Meade, Hunt, and Howard, along with Captain Paine and Lieutenant Bissell, rode along the lines of the army on the left. Meade spotted what General Hancock had written about; there were too few troops in position between Cemetery Hill and Sickles's Third Corps. At Meade's direction, the Second Corps was ordered to move forward from its bivouac site behind the Round Tops to a place along Cemetery Ridge between Cemetery Hill and the right flank of Sickles's Third Corps. That morning, Sickles's corps was directed again to occupy positions on the north slope of Little Round Top, positions held by Geary's division the evening before, and extending up Cemetery Ridge connecting with the left flank of the Second Corps. Captain Paine sketched the area the group inspected. Using that map, Meade directed Payne to sketch onto the map the positions to be occupied by each corps.[29]

Meade and his entourage returned to Cemetery Hill, and as the first rays of the sun appeared, Meade took his field glasses out and examined the areas on the right and left. General Hunt decided to rest on the ground in the cemetery with his back against a tree. Some of Meade's staff officers and aides were nearby. General Slocum appeared and told Meade about a gap that appeared in his lines along Culp's Hill, probably the gap near Spangler's Spring. Hearing Slocum, Meade's adjutant general, Seth Williams, who had been resting near Hunt, got up and walked closer to Meade and Slocum. Meade asked Williams about Hunt's whereabouts, and Williams told Meade that Hunt was resting beneath a tree. "It is no time to sleep now," Meade barked. Hunt replied: "I am not asleep, and heard all that you and General Slocum said." Meade then gave Hunt orders: "Very well, you must attend to this as it is your affair. See that the line is made good with artillery, until the infantry is in position." Hunt promptly brought all the Twelfth Corps batteries forward to the pike to protect the gap of which Slocum spoke. He even brought two Eleventh Corps batteries to bolster that line.[30]

At "the gray of morning," General Newton, his staff officers, and orderlies arrived at Cemetery Hill. "Meade," recalled Lieutenant Jackson, "was on the hill, dismounted, and peering through the still uncertain light to discover the lines of the enemy. The scene was impressive, and one long to be remembered." Newton approached Meade. Lieutenant Jackson recorded the moment. "Meade," he wrote, "[was] tall, slender, and nervous; his hair and whiskers tinged with gray; [he] was pale and careworn. The sleepless and anxious night had left him with great black lines under his eyes."[31]

Meade gave Newton a very cordial welcome and asked him when Sedgwick would be at Gettysburg, but he got no conclusive answer. Newton then asked Meade if he was aware that Doubleday outranked him. Meade responded, "Yes." He then said to Newton that he had authority from the president to make such changes as he desired, and he wanted Newton to command the First Corps. What Newton probably didn't tell Meade was that Doubleday was his classmate at West Point. Newton was directed to the positions of the remnants of the First Corps on Cemetery Hill and Culp's Hill. There, he greeted and spoke with the division and brigade commanders.[32]

Newton was a native of Norfolk, Virginia, and an 1842 graduate of West Point, where he performed well. As a result of his high class rank, Newton was assigned to the Corps of Engineers on graduation. He helped establish the defenses of Washington after being named a brigadier general of volunteers in September 1861. He commanded a brigade in the Sixth Corps on the Peninsula and in the Maryland Campaign in 1862. Newton was given command of a division, and he was conspicuous storming Marye's Heights at Fredericksburg during the Battle of Chancellorsville. Meade believed Newton to be a talented officer and a fine army engineer.[33]

Meade, Howard, and Warren then rode along Culp's Hill to where the Baltimore Pike crosses Rock Creek. War correspondent Whitelaw Reid

Major General John Newton. (Library of Congress)

observed Meade's party: "Two or three general officers, with a retinue of staff and orderlies, come galloping by. Foremost is the spare and somewhat stooped form of the commanding general. He is not cheered, indeed is scarcely recognized. He is an approved corps general, but has not yet vindicated his right to command the Army of the Potomac. By his side is the calm, honest, manly face of General Oliver O. Howard. An empty sleeve is pinned to his shoulder—memento of a hard-fought battle before."[34]

As Meade passed along the Baltimore Pike, Private David Mouat of the

Twenty-Ninth Pennsylvania, of Brigadier General Thomas L. Kane's brigade of the Twelfth Corps, heard that Meade was nearby. It was around 7:00 A.M. Mouat got a glimpse of Meade, who then was talking with General Geary, whose troops were returning to the Twelfth Corps from Little Round Top. He observed Meade point to his regiment and ask Geary the unit designation. Told it was the Twenty-Ninth Pennsylvania, Meade said: "It is a very small one, but order them up. We will want every man today."[35]

Meade told General Slocum that he generally approved of Brigadier General Alpheus Williams's First Division of the Twelfth Corps occupying the heavily wooded slopes of the two eminences known as Culp's Hill with its right near Rock Creek. With Slocum in command of the right wing, Williams was the temporary commander of the Twelfth Corps. Brigadier General Thomas H. Ruger temporarily commanded the First Division. Meade also directed Slocum to place General Geary's division to the left of Ruger's and to the right of Wadsworth's First Corps division, which was holding the line along the western slope of Culp's Hill. The positions held by the regiments of the First and Eleventh Corps from McKnight's Hill, across east Cemetery Hill, and then south, down Cemetery Ridge, were left by Meade as Hancock, Howard, and Slocum had placed them the evening before. Meade directed Paine to note all those positions on his map. He then ordered Paine to make copies of the map and deliver one to each corps commander.[36]

Meade and his fellow officers returned to Cemetery Hill. Meade rode up to General Schurz's positions with a staff officer and orderly. Schurz rode over to Meade and asked how many men were already at Gettysburg. Meade replied: "In the course of the day I expect to have about 95,000 — enough, I guess, for this business." Meade's attention returned to his defenses as he gazed upon them, examining them. General Schurz recalled looking closely at Meade. Schurz recalled Meade's "long-bearded, haggard face, his careworn and tired look." Schurz continued: "[Meade's] mind was evidently absorbed by a hard problem. But this simple, cold, serious soldier, with his business-like air, did inspire confidence. The officers and men, as much as was permitted, crowded around and looked up to him with curious eyes, and then turned away not enthusiastic but clearly satisfied." Meade then, under his breath, said for the second time: "Well, we may as well fight it out here as well as anywhere else." He betrayed his uncertainty about offering the enemy battle at Gettysburg; he was not convinced that the positions could be held.[37]

Meade was especially concerned about his right flank at Cemetery Hill and Culp's Hill. The positions Slocum's Twelfth Corps and Wadsworth's division of the First Corps held on Culp's Hill, and Howard's Eleventh Corps held on Cemetery Hill, protected the Baltimore Pike. That roadway was the line of supply and communication to Meade's army at Gettysburg from the supply base at Westminster; it ran literally along the summit of Cemetery Hill and along the reverse slopes of Culp's Hill just behind the defense lines.

Meade could see how close those defenses were to the Baltimore Pike. At places, the defenses were literally on—and some in the rear of—that turnpike. The terrain might be good, but the army's lifeline ran across it. Any enemy penetration of Meade's defenses there would cut that supply and communications artery. Cutting that artery would be catastrophic; the Army of the Potomac would have to embark on a full-fledged retreat if it could not control the Baltimore Pike. Meade might have taken solace in the knowledge that General Sedgwick's Sixth Corps was coming up the Baltimore Pike, but it was still nine hours away. An enemy break-through along the Baltimore Pike would cut off Sedgwick's corps from the rest of the army. Also east of Gettysburg, not far from the Baltimore Pike, was General Sykes's Fifth Corps, about three hours away. Meade re-solved to concentrate as much firepower as he could reasonably bring to bear in front of the Baltimore Pike and even to try to mount an offensive along that front if possible so as to drive the enemy away from that supply and communications artery. Meade turned to General Hunt and directed him to retrace the lines just inspected to make sure that artillery batteries were posted in the best possible positions. Hunt brought to those positions "about eight" batteries of artillery from the Artillery Reserve. Those bat-teries had accompanied Hunt to Gettysburg from Taneytown after being ordered forward by Meade. The first of July had not gone well for the army, but 2 July gave every indication that it had the making to be even worse.[38]

11

WITHOUT TENTS AND
ONLY A SHORT SUPPLY
OF FOOD

In the predawn darkness, one soldier who awoke in the fields south of Gettysburg recorded 2 July as being "cloudy"; another noted that it was also "close." The humidity was high; the air was thick. A fifer in the First Massachusetts in Sickles's Third Corps, camping in the fields just west of Cemetery Ridge, noted that the morning was "rainy." Another soldier in the Third Corps recalled that the day "dawned close and foggy." All through the night and, with increasing intensity at dawn, pickets and skirmishers from both armies fired at one another; occasionally, there were bursts of artillery fire.[1]

In the early morning of 2 July, several officers and orderlies from General Meade's staff rode south of Cemetery Hill along the Taneytown Road and, just beyond Ziegler's Grove, turned into the yard of the fifty-two-year-old widow Lydia Leister. The Leister house was a very modest, two-room frame structure, painted white, with a stairway that led to a loft. Surrounding the little house was a whitewashed picket fence. The house had just been abandoned. The German-speaking Leister had been living there with her two young daughters, one only three years of age. Her other four children were grown; a son was in the army. Leister and her two little children had left the farm the day before as the fighting intensified west and north of Gettysburg; they probably found refuge with her brother, Dr. David Study, who lived on the Baltimore Pike, and likely fled from the area with them.[2]

Meade's staff officers could tell that the owner of the little house subsisted by working the small farm. The farm consisted of a log barn not far from the house, a small orchard with apple and peach trees, and a hayfield, along with a spring. The little nine-acre farm was defined by a disheveled

General Meade's headquarters at Gettysburg, the Lydia Leister house.
(Library of Congress)

stone fence that ran along the Taneytown Road and across the fields south, west, and north of the house. What little livestock Lydia Leister had was no longer present; it had either been pilfered by hungry soldiers or taken away with her.[3]

The location of the Leister house made it ideal for army headquarters. The house stood along the reverse slope of Cemetery Ridge on the west side of the Taneytown Road. So long and steep was that slope from its crest to the road that the house was not visible from the Confederate lines, more than a mile to the west. It was close enough to the Baltimore Pike for Meade to respond to any emergency from Generals Howard and Newton at Cemetery Hill or to General Slocum farther down the pike at Culp's Hill. The Leister house was close to what was shaping up to be the center of the lines of the Army of the Potomac as they extended south from Cemetery Hill to the Round Tops. Moreover, it was behind the position that would soon be occupied by Hancock's Second Corps. To the left of where the Second Corps would be aligned, Sickles's Third Corps was still in bivouac. Thus, that little "box of a house" owned by Lydia Leister became Meade's headquarters.[4]

As the situation stood at about 7:00 A.M., Geary's division departed Little Round Top. It was supposed to be relieved by Sickles's two divisions, which had been ordered into position along the south end of Cemetery Ridge, extending up Little Round Top. Hancock's Second Corps was to connect with Sickles's right flank, extending the defense line on Cemetery Ridge to Howard's Eleventh Corps on Cemetery Hill. General Steinwehr's division held the left of the Eleventh Corps lines, occupying a position from behind Ziegler's Grove north along the Taneytown Road, in front of the cemetery, facing west. What was left of Generals Robinson's and Doubleday's First Corps divisions supported the defense line of Steinwehr. General Schurz's Eleventh Corps division occupied the center, mostly west of the Baltimore Pike; and General Barlow's division of Howard's corps, commanded by Brigadier General Adelbert Ames after Barlow was badly wounded and captured on 1 July, held the right along East Cemetery Hill, facing north. To the right of Ames's division was Wadsworth's division of the First Corps, along the western slope of Culp's Hill. The Twelfth Corps, still temporarily commanded by General Williams, continued the lines to the right of Wadsworth all along Culp's Hill to Rock Creek. Those defenders consisted of Ruger's division on the right. Geary's division joined Ruger on Ruger's left after it returned from Little Round Top. On the far left, two of Buford's cavalry brigades, Colonels Gamble's and Devin's, still patrolled the Emmitsburg Road, protecting the army's left flank, while General Merritt's brigade of Buford's cavalry division observed the area farther south near Emmitsburg. On the far right, General Gregg's cavalry division patrolled the Hanover Road and Low Dutch Road. General Kilpatrick's cavalry division was on the way from Abbottstown to join Gregg.[5]

Early that morning Meade learned that one of the army corps "left its whole artillery ammunition train behind it." The culprit appeared to have been Sickles's Third Corps. Other corps reported ordnance deficiencies. Meade confided in General Hunt those facts, as well as his concerns that, after the enormous expenditure of ammunition on 1 July, there would not be enough to get the army through the upcoming engagement. Hunt was prepared for such a problem. He had already ordered General Tyler, commander of the Artillery Reserve, to bring forward from Taneytown "every round of ammunition in his trains." He had even formed "a special ammunition column, one hundred wagons in all, attached to the Artillery Reserve, carrying twenty rounds for every gun in the army." He was able to assure Meade that there would be enough ammunition for the upcoming battle, "but none for idle cannonades, the besetting sin of [battery] commanders."⁶

The Second Corps was aroused at its bivouac site along the Taneytown Road, behind the Round Tops, by the drummers beating "the General" before dawn. "We made small fires of twigs to cook our coffee and bacon; [however,] we discovered that we were out of rations," recalled Captain Benjamin Thompson of the Fourth Ohio in Brigadier General Alexander Hays's Third Division of the Second Corps. "I had lost my haversack in the hustle of the day before, and my breakfast, like that of many of my men, consisted of crackers and coffee." That meal was the last he would eat for more than forty-six hours.⁷

Then came the orders: "Fall in." "We got off soon after [daylight]," recalled General Gibbon, "and to facilitate the march and shorten the column, the road was left, as before, to the artillery and ambulances, the infantry marching through the grain and grass fields on each side. In this way our corps reached the field about six o'clock." The columns were led up the Taneytown Road to a place, just south of the Leister house, where General Meade, mounted on Old Baldy in a field just east of the road and south of the house, directed Gibbon, in command of the leading Second Division of the Second Corps, to the positions to be occupied along Cemetery Ridge. Meade told Gibbon the Third Corps would connect with his left.⁸

As General Hancock was riding back to Gettysburg from Taneytown that morning, Gibbon, temporarily in command of the corps, placed Hays's Third Division in line to the left of Steinwehr's Eleventh Corps division, extending from the southwestern slope of Cemetery Hill, down Cemetery Ridge, to the south. The battered divisions of Generals Robinson and Doubleday of the First Corps had been relieved and formed in rear of the Eleventh Corps. To the left of Hays's division, Gibbon placed his own Second Division. Gibbon then directed Brigadier General John C. Caldwell's First Division to hold the left flank of the Second Corps. Gibbon led the five artillery batteries of the corps into line; a battery was placed in Hays's lines; the remaining four were interspersed among the infantry regiments of his own Second Division.⁹

Gibbon reported to Meade at the Leister house. "Reports," recalled Gibbon, "were then constantly reaching [Meade] and everything betokened preparations on both sides for the coming battle." Gibbon recalled Meade saying to him that "Ewell was reported to be concentrating a force on our right." It underscored Meade's prescient concern expressed earlier that morning for his right flank.¹⁰

To the left of Caldwell's division was General Sickles's Third Corps, the bivouac sites of which extended all the way to the base of Little Round Top and into the fields west of Cemetery Ridge. After 7:00 A.M., no other troops were in position to Sickles's left. Geary's division had been pulled out of its position on Little Round Top and advanced to Culp's Hill, Geary having been told earlier by General Slocum that Sickles's Third Corps would occupy Little Round Top and Cemetery Ridge to the north. Sickles's troops, however, had not moved to Little Round Top, and there was no indication that they would do so anytime soon.[11]

Meade was not only busy directing troops into positions but also occupied with communication matters. Before his lines east and south of Gettysburg were even complete, Meade had to make sure that there was an adequate system in place to allow him to communicate with his corps commanders. Meade not only needed precise information about his commanders' locations but also needed to communicate with them where he expected them to be. Apart from written orders or messages—and, at times, oral directives—communications along Meade's three-mile front would be conducted by semaphore flags by day and torches at darkness. Open hills, open fields, and platforms on rooftops, and in trees mostly denuded of branches, were called into service.

All through the early morning hours of 2 July, Meade directed the signal officers who had accompanied him, along with those who had accompanied the corps commanders to Gettysburg, to open signal lines from the headquarters of each corps commander to the Leister house. A signal station had already been established on Cemetery Hill the day before behind the positions held by the remnants of the First and Eleventh Corps. Captain Norton, along with all the signal officers held in reserve, left Taneytown at daylight, under orders from General Butterfield, and arrived at Gettysburg to join Meade at or before 8:00 A.M. As the morning progressed, signal stations were established on Powers Hill, behind the two-story stone Nathaniel Lightner house, the site of Slocum's headquarters to the rear of the right flank of the army on the Baltimore Pike, east of the Taneytown Road; on Culp's Hill, directly behind Wadsworth's division of the First Corps and Greene's brigade of the Twelfth Corps; on Little Round Top, at the far left of the line, above and to the left of the Third Corps positions along and in front of Cemetery Ridge; behind the left flank of the Second Corps positions along the Cemetery Ridge line; and at the Leister house; they would all be operative by 11:00 A.M.[12]

The signal station on Little Round Top was critically important: from the summit of that eminence, which had been mostly cleared of trees along its western and northern faces, there was an unobstructed view of the entire field to the north, all the way to Cemetery Hill. The Leister house and the Second Corps signal station were in plain view. The Union line on Cemetery Hill and Cemetery Ridge was fully visible, as were fields west of Cemetery Ridge and west and southwest of Little Round Top. The entire expanse of the enemy lines along the wooded Seminary Ridge, just under a mile to the west, was in full view. Equally important was the signal station on Cemetery Hill. From that vantage point, signal officers could observe enemy movements all the way from the center of the Confederate lines to almost the enemy's left flank. Messages from all the signal stations were always received at Meade's headquarters, no matter who in leadership was the designated recipient. Under instructions from General Meade, Captain Norton made sure that the signal stations established the day before at Taneytown and Emmitsburg remained open. Those would be needed in the event that the army would have to fall back from Gettysburg.[13]

Even before all signal stations were operative, the Eleventh Corps division and brigade commanders on Cemetery Hill were busy sending information to Meade's headquarters. General Ames, on East Cemetery Hill, reported that his two brigades were in position at 7:30 A.M. Ames's message may not have been encouraging to Meade; Ames reported that his First Brigade, commanded by Colonel Leopold von Gilsa, was "in position to the right and front" but had only 650 men. The Second Brigade, commanded by Colonel Andrew L. Harris, facing the town, had only 500 men. Those brigades had each been reduced to the size of regiments after the fighting on 1 July. More than 1,300 officers and men of those two brigades had been killed, wounded, or captured or went missing on 1 July. General Schurz signaled half an hour later that six of his regiments were deployed on Cemetery Hill behind the stone wall west of the Baltimore Pike; four regiments, he wrote, were "in column in [a] second line" with Captain Hubert Dilger's Battery I, First Ohio, on the left. Those ten regiments and the artillery battery accounted for only 1,500 men. The spare number of troops on Cemetery Hill would not be able to withstand a serious assault, yet they were the first line of defense of the critical Baltimore Pike.[14]

At about 8:00 A.M., General Sykes sent a message from the signal station on Powers Hill to Generals Howard and Meade, informing them of the position of the newly arrived Fifth Corps: "Our line has been contracted, our right rests on Rock Creek. I have massed my troops in rear of our right," wrote Sykes. The Fifth Corps occupied a position behind Slocum's Twelfth Corps on the George Spangler, George Musser, and the Reverend Theodore P. Bucher farms along or near the Blacksmith Shop and

Granite Schoolhouse Roads south of the Baltimore Pike. That was good news to Meade; he was counting on his old corps being available early on 2 July, particularly along the vulnerable right flank.[15]

Meade still knew only few details concerning the whereabouts of the enemy. He knew generally that they were deployed in positions below Cemetery and Culp's Hills, but not in plain sight; most were concealed from view. He knew that enemy forces were in the town of Gettysburg, and he knew that the enemy lines extended south, down the heavily wooded Seminary Ridge. How far the enemy extended down Seminary Ridge was not known. What enemy corps were at Gettysburg was not fully known. Elements of Hill's and Ewell's corps were present on the field. Meade knew these facts from prisoners of war and reports from commanders who fought on 1 July. He believed that Ewell's corps was positioned in front of his right flank. Whether all of Hill's and Ewell's corps were at Gettysburg was not known. Longstreet's corps had not appeared, although it was suspected to be at Gettysburg. The intelligence of the enemy's forces on the field on the morning of 2 July had not materially changed since Meade wrote to Halleck from Taneytown on the previous afternoon. Meade had to believe, though, that Lee would fight him at Gettysburg using everything at his disposal. The mystery that morning, however, was why Lee had not attacked already. For all Meade knew, Lee was still waiting for all his troops to arrive, but he could not count on that. Instead, Meade believed that Lee would launch an attack at any minute, and he acted on that belief all through the morning and afternoon.[16]

Elements of the Army of the Potomac continued to close in on the defense line at Gettysburg. General Tyler's remaining batteries of the Artillery Reserve, eleven in all, were just then about two hours down the Taneytown Road; they would arrive around 10:00 A.M. That meant the artillery ammunition Meade so desperately needed was about to reach Gettysburg. In addition, General Crawford's division of Pennsylvania Reserves, nine regiments, was about six hours from Gettysburg; it would augment the Fifth Corps. General Lockwood's brigade, consisting of Colonel Maulsby's First Maryland, Potomac Home Brigade, and the One Hundred Fiftieth New York, had just arrived in the Union defenses to join the Twelfth Corps along Culp's Hill. The First Maryland, Eastern Shore, regiment was en route.[17]

Beyond aligning and protecting the army, Meade had to feed and supply it, a difficult task even in the best of conditions. The troops' energy and the morale were depleted from lengthy marches through inclement weather. Many were shoeless. All were hungry. The horses and mules of the army were in difficult straits; the animals desperately needed forage, and most needed shoes. Like the men, the cavalry horses, the horses pulling the field artillery and carrying the officers, and the horses and mules pulling the wagon trains that accompanied the troops to Gettysburg were worn out.[18]

Meade's myriad quartermaster and subsistence trains, including the herds of cattle, were at Westminster and Union Bridge, twenty-two miles down the Baltimore Pike. No baggage was allowed at the front. As Quartermaster General Ingalls wrote afterward, "Officers and men went forward without tents and with only a short supply of food."[19]

The War Department had given General Ingalls authority to seize private property if the army was in need. Back on 25 June, General Halleck sent standing orders to the army by telegraph. Wrote the general in chief:

> Under General Orders in force it is the duty of military commanders to take possession of such military supplies as are likely to fall into the hands of the enemy, or which may be necessary for the immediate wants of our own troops in the field of actual hostilities. All horses and beef cattle in such exposed regions should be removed or taken possession and reconverted to government uses. Staff officers should send out, with sufficient escorts, to seize and remove all horses suited for the cavalry, artillery, or wagon trains, giving receipt in which the character of the animals and the service to which [each] is suited. Where not required for immediate use where taken, they should be sent into the nearest depot and turned over to the depot Quartermaster and Commissary. If possible, a Quartermaster and Commissary, or an officer acting in those capacities, should accompany every [foraging] expedition. The vicinity of [any] Rail Rd. in our possession should not be disturbed unless in immediate danger from approaching raids.

The army had total authority to seize whatever it needed from the civilian population. Quartermasters and commissaries throughout the Army of the Potomac were exercising that authority by using foraging teams from their respective commands to seize systematically everything needed; Meade's army was foraging exactly like its enemy.[20]

Thus, behind the lines of the Army of the Potomac at Gettysburg, quartermaster and subsistence details operated to secure from homes, farms, and shops the necessary food, forage, and other articles. Property owners were instructed to file claims for what was taken. Hunger, however, was so acute that many soldiers left the ranks to beg for food from those residents who still occupied their homes or to take what they found.

Many soldiers were apprehended and their officers threatened with discipline for not preventing the men from performing such acts.[21]

Ingalls was addressing the shortages at the front; he determined to assemble mule pack trains to carry supplies the twenty-two miles up the Baltimore Pike from Westminster to the army. He directed that the pack trains would move through the night to minimize the threat of being attacked. Those pack trains would have to be extensive, but the longer they were, the more they were vulnerable to attack. Ingalls ordered the assembly of some wagon trains to carry forward quartermaster stores, such as hay and forage, although he feared losing wagons to an enemy strike. Ingalls's orders were sent down the Baltimore Pike to Westminster by a mounted aide from army headquarters, a three-hour journey. What became problematic was being able to send enough of those necessary stores forward by pack trains and wagons to an army of more than ninety thousand officers and men and nearly thirty thousand horses and mules, all holding or supporting a defense line that was nearly three miles long.[22]

Adequately feeding nearly thirty thousand horses and mules at the front was a Herculean task. Nevertheless, they had to be fed something, and quickly. As the assistant quartermaster general wrote later, "The army either had to supply their animals from the growing crops, or have them perish for want of food." Luckily, early July was the harvest season for fodder crops in south-central Pennsylvania. "During the first and second day [at Gettysburg]," the assistant quartermaster general wrote, "the contents of the barns and stocks were completely stripped of the supply from the preceding year's crop, and during that time the teamsters and others had limited themselves to going in the fields and cutting with knives and sickles, arms full at a time, or picketing their animals in the fields with a 10 to 12 foot rope." That was not enough. "Soon," he noted, "whole fields were occupied by artillery, cavalry, ambulance, and team animals." All the fields of "growing corn, oats, wheat, and grass were being stripped by grazing horses and mules to alleviate their suffering."[23]

All the members of Meade's staff were working around the clock. One of them was his medical director, Surgeon Johnathan Letterman. His task to develop an orderly hospital and medical evacuation system for the army was made hopelessly difficult before he even arrived at Gettysburg just behind the commanding general. Because of the disaster on 1 July and the makeshift defense lines that had to be formed thereafter, the Army of the Potomac would have to depend on hospital and medical evacuation systems that were hurriedly assembled and, frankly, inadequate. Because the fields occupied by Meade's various corps, when they arrived at the defense lines, would all be exposed to enemy fire, "it was impossible," wrote Letterman, "to place hospitals in rear of their divisions," although that is where they were mostly first established. Temporary hospitals, behind their divisions, became "so unsafe," Letterman noted, "that they were [ultimately] obliged to abandon them." Many of the hospitals, he explained later, "were [thereafter] placed entirely out of the enclosure formed by the line of battle."[24]

Second Corps hospitals were overseen by Lieutenant Colonel Richard N. Batchelder, the chief quartermaster, and by the corpulent Surgeon Alexander N. Daugherty, the corps medical director, as that corps was moving toward its positions on Cemetery Ridge on the early morning of 2 July. Nearly all the hospitals were established within sight of the Leister house. The log house, barns, and outbuildings of the widow Catherine Guinn, on the east side of the Taneytown Road, directly across from the Leister house, and the Peter Frey farm, just south of the Guinn farm and on the west side of the road, were seized to become hospitals by the quartermaster and surgeons of General Hays's Third Division of the Second Corps. The tenants living in the two-story stone Peter Frey house were Lydia Leister's nearest neighbors. In addition, the white frame two-story Jacob Hummelbaugh house and barn on the west side of the Taneytown Road, just north of the Granite Schoolhouse Road, and the white frame two-story William Patterson house and log barn, across the Taneytown Road from the Hummelbaugh farm, were taken over as hospitals for the Second Corps; the Hummelbaugh farm was commandeered as a hospital by the quartermaster and chief surgeon of General Caldwell's First Division, and the Patterson farm was used by General Gibbon's Second Division as a hospital. Nearby, the house and barn of Jacob Swisher, also on the west side of the Taneytown Road, were transformed into hospitals by the Third Division of the Second Corps. All the hospitals would be within range of enemy artillery fire. The experienced Letterman had to have known that once the Second Corps came under fire, the confusion of a haphazard medical evacuation and hospital system would be acute; all the hospitals were too close to the battle lines. If one or more hospitals had to shut down due to enemy artillery fire, where the ambulance drivers would take the wounded would be anybody's guess. Letterman was powerless to prevent such a problem.[25]

Magnifying the confused nature of the establishment of the hospitals behind the developing battle lines, the Michael and Sarah Frey farm on the east side of the Taneytown Road, just south of the Granite Schoolhouse Road, and near the Second Corps hospitals, was taken over as a hospital by quartermasters and surgeons of the Third Corps. Farther down on the Taneytown Road, the Leonard Bricker farm, just south of the Black-smith Shop Road, was seized by the Third Corps as was the two-story stone Jacob Weikert house and its barn on the west side of the Taneytown Road, directly behind Little Round Top. East of the Weikert house, across the Taneytown Road, was the Lewis Bushman house, barn, and outbuild-ings, also seized by the Third Corps.[26]

Captain Thomas L. Livermore, of the Fifth New Hampshire, the newly appointed chief of the Second Corps ambulance trains, located his am-bulance park among the Frey, Swisher, and Patterson farms. Livermore's trains consisted of three separate division trains, all moving together. Liv-ermore's trains were made up of about 122 horse ambulances, about four hundred men, more than three hundred horses, and "ten or twelve forage and forge wagons with six-horse teams," all overseen by only thirteen offi-cers. Livermore would send those ambulances forward behind the Second Corps battle lines, along with stretchers and stretcher bearers, as soon as those lines were established. Similarly, ambulance parks were set up by all the other corps in the army at locations near their hospitals, and their ambulances and stretcher bearers were sent forward to positions behind their battle lines.[27]

Although the Eleventh Corps had established a corps hospital on 1 July at the two-story stone George Spangler house and large bank barn, south of the Granite Schoolhouse Road, less than two miles behind Cemetery Hill, many of its wounded, like those of the First Corps, remained in the town of Gettysburg, within enemy lines, on 2 July. The hospitals of the Twelfth Corps were hurriedly established on the night of 1 July along the vulner-able Baltimore Pike, not far from the front lines. The two-story log and stone Abraham Spangler house and outbuildings, on the east side of the Baltimore Pike, were seized by the quartermaster and surgeons of the Sec-ond Division of the Twelfth Corps, while the two-story stone Nathaniel Lightner house and large barn, on the west side of the Baltimore Pike, were also taken over by that division. The Lightner family, Nathaniel, his wife, and their six children, lived, "gypsy-like," in the carpenter shop dur-ing the Union occupation. The quartermaster and surgical teams of the Twelfth Corps seized the George Musser farm on the Baltimore Pike, west of the bridge over Rock Creek, and the Isaac Diehl farm nearby. Even the stone McAllister's Mill, east of the Baltimore Pike, on Rock Creek, nearly one hundred years old then, was pressed into service. Like the Second and Third Corps hospitals along the Taneytown Road, all were dangerously close to the front lines. The quartermasters and surgeons of the First and Eleventh Corps used all those sites to tend to the wounded who escaped capture on 1 July. With the arrival of the Fifth Corps and its placement behind the Twelfth Corps, the hospital and medical evacuation system on either side of the Baltimore Pike would become even more chaotic. Surgeons from the Fifth Corps would share dwellings and barns taken over by the Twelfth Corps that were also occupied by surgeons and wounded from the First and Eleventh Corps. Some Fifth Corps hospitals were established down the road to Bonaughtown; others were set up along the road to Two Taverns.[28]

Supplying field hospitals in the wake of the collapse of the First and Eleventh Corps on 1 July was a chaotic and haphazard task. The quartermasters had to provide those hospitals with necessary tents, straw, bedding, blankets, quilts, sheets, shirts, pillows, pillowslips, towels, beds, boards for beds and coffins, fence rails for fires, cooking apparatus, and subsistence stores for the wounded, as well as extra medical personnel and equipment. The desirable items were almost nonexistent due to the nature of General Reynolds's mission with the First, Eleventh, and Third Corps and the deliberate advance to Gettysburg of the Second and Twelfth Corps—they were all supposed to fall back to the Pipe Creek line—and the hurried advance there of the Fifth and Sixth Corps. Meade had no idea of the exact whereabouts of enemy formations or the situation at Gettysburg through most of 1 July; he ordered all the quartermaster and subsistence trains, save those necessary to accompany the troops, to be sent back to Westminster and Union Bridge as the army marched to Gettysburg. He required by order that the Army of the Potomac have only the bare necessities whenever it advanced to engage the enemy. That was a standing order in the army. Medical wagon trains and ambulances did accompany the marching troops, but most of the wagon trains carrying all the other items necessary to keep the wounded sheltered, warmed, clothed, and fed, or to keep the horses and mules fed, were kept at the rear.[29]

Some medical directors, fearing short supplies, did not follow Meade's orders and took with their respective corps the full allowance of supplies. One of them was the medical director of the Twelfth Corps, Surgeon John McNulty. All other medical officers, in cooperation with their quartermasters, dispatched teams of soldiers to strip from houses, barns, and outbuildings everything they could find from the local citizenry to equip the hospitals, ambulance depots, aid stations, and ambulances and to feed, clothe, and comfort the wounded. They had to forage for their wounded.[30]

From the time the Third Corps arrived at its bivouac sites south of Gettysburg on the night of 1 July, it posted pickets to protect against any enemy attack. General Humphreys's Second Division pickets were well out along the Emmitsburg Road, from just south of the Codori house all the way to the Wentz and Sherfy houses near a large peach orchard of Joseph Sherfy. General Birney's First Division pickets were sent out along a line that extended from the Emmitsburg Road east along generally high, but broken, ground, all the way to the southwestern base of Little Round Top. To the right of Humphreys's division, by dawn, were the pickets of the newly arrived Second Corps. The pickets tore down the fences along the road and piled the rails and posts into a long, makeshift breastwork behind which they kept watch over any enemy movements.[31]

As early as 7:30 A.M., Colonel Hiram Berdan of the First United States Sharpshooters was ordered by General Sickles to send a detachment of one hundred men from his First and Second United States Sharpshooters out into the fields west of the Emmitsburg Road to draw enemy fire so as to gauge its positions and strength along Seminary Ridge. As Berdan's sharpshooters and Confederate skirmishers exchanged gunfire, Sickles ordered Major Tremain of his staff to go to Meade's headquarters and report the location of the Third Corps picket lines as well as the fact that Colonels Trobriand's and Burling's brigades, Captain George B. Winslow's Battery D, First New York, and Captain James Smith's Fourth New York Independent Battery, were nearing Gettysburg from Emmitsburg to join the Third Corps. Tremain was also ordered to express Sickles's concern about the corps quartermaster and ammunition trains on the way up the Emmitsburg Road under the command of Lieutenant Colonel James F. Rusling, the chief quartermaster of the Third Corps, and Captain H. D. F. Young of the Second New Hampshire, the chief ordnance officer of the corps. At the time Tremain left, Sickles had made no effort at all to move his Third Corps into any defensive positions along Cemetery Ridge.[32]

When Tremain returned to Sickles, he accompanied the general and others on a ride out to the picket lines along the Emmitsburg Road and back (east) toward Little Round Top. According to Tremain, the Third Corps bivouac site to the left of the Second Corps, on and in front of Cemetery Ridge, "proved to be on low ground, easily commanded by the land in front, and running off to the left into hill and dale, whose occupants would be at the mercy of the occupants of the 'high ground' at the rear of the extreme left, as well as of the possessors of the elevated land at the immediate front of the extreme left, i.e. the [Sherfy] peach orchard."[33]

What was probably becoming painfully clear to Meade in the early morning hours of 2 July was that the position to which the First and Eleventh Corps had fallen back was really not favorable as a defensive position for the army, although he never spoke of it or wrote about it to General

Halleck or anyone else. It didn't take a topographical engineer to see it, however. Cemetery Hill and Culp's Hill were strong defensive positions, but nothing south of Cemetery Hill offered any real advantages, except Little Round Top. Although in part referring to the lack of troops then on the field, Generals Hancock and Howard said as much when they claimed to Generals Meade and Butterfield, respectively, that the defenses they observed on Cemetery Hill and Culp's Hill on 1 July were subject to being turned on the left. Indeed, General Warren wrote to his wife early in the morning of 2 July, claiming that the army occupied "a position where we cannot be beaten, but fear being turned."[34]

Cemetery Ridge was commanded by the high ground over which ran the Emmitsburg Road, from just below the Codori house to the Sherfy peach orchard, which presented a tactical problem for Meade. General Hunt wrote: "Gettysburg was not a good strategical position for us, and the circumstances under which our army was assembled limited us tactically to a strictly defensive battle." But even then, the ground along Cemetery Ridge was not uniformly desirable; it simply represented all that was available, given the fact that the remnants of the First and Eleventh Corps retreated to Cemetery Hill and Culp's Hill on 1 July, and if the whole army was to defend the place, it had to occupy Cemetery Ridge all the way to Little Round Top.[35]

In addition to the challenge of defending Cemetery Ridge, Meade was concerned by the proximity of the Baltimore Pike to the First, Eleventh, and Twelfth Corps defenses on his right flank. The Baltimore Pike was the army's line of supply and communication from Westminster. Consequently, Meade wanted the troops along his far right flank, namely the Twelfth Corps, then behind hastily constructed breastworks on Culp's Hill, and the Fifth Corps, placed in reserve behind the Twelfth Corps, to, if possible, launch an attack to drive the enemy away from the Baltimore Pike. The Twelfth Corps was positioned to launch such an assault. After his 2 July predawn inspection of the Twelfth Corps positions, Meade believed that such an attack was possible. He left General Warren behind "to reconnoiter the ground, so as to be able to inform him as to the best disposition of the troops for the attack."[36]

What Meade understood was that, on the previous afternoon, General Slocum had directed the First Division of the Twelfth Corps, commanded by General Ruger, through a gap between lower Culp's Hill and Wolf Hill, coursed by Rock Creek, to near the left flank of the enemy. That move may have played a signal role in preventing any Confederate attacks against Meade's right flank on the night of 1 July. At nightfall, the First Division, under the orders from Meade himself, was withdrawn to positions along Culp's Hill, to the right of Wadsworth's division of the First Corps, where it remained on the morning of 2 July when Meade, Howard, Hunt, and Warren inspected them at dawn. Those positions had recently been reinforced by Geary's division that supposedly had been relieved from occupying Little Round Top, under Meade's order, by the Third Corps at 7:00 A.M. If sufficient troops could be moved through that same defile again, an attack might be directed against the enemy far ahead of the Baltimore Pike. If successful, it would give Meade—and the valuable stores he had to protect—some "breathing space." As early as 9:30 A.M., Meade dictated a message from the Leister house to General Slocum over the signature of Seth Williams: "The commanding general desires you will at once examine the ground in your front, and give him your opinion as to the practicability of attacking the enemy in that quarter."[37]

At the time Meade ordered the reconnaissance of the Confederate left by Slocum, he was also receiving disturbing information of movements of enemy troops in that direction. Captain James S. Hall, at the signal station on Cemetery Hill, sent a message to Meade at 9:30 A.M. After examining the enemy lines by means of a telescope, Hall reported that "a brigade of five regiments, from in front of our center," were moving "to our right, accompanied by one four-gun battery and two squadrons of cavalry, at a point southeast of [the] Second Division, Twelfth Corps, and in easy range." Colonel Wainwright's First Corps batteries on Cemetery Hill and Major Thomas H. Osborn's Eleventh Corps batteries nearby opened fire, forcing those moving enemy columns to "seek the cover of ravines to make their movements." Such enemy movements, and artillery fire in response, would increase in frequency as the day progressed. Meade grew concerned that the next enemy attack was going to be directed against his right flank along the Baltimore Pike; there was every reason for him to believe that would happen. Captain Hall then wrote: "A heavy line of enemy's infantry on our right. Very small force of infantry—enemy's infantry—visible in front of our center."[38]

General Butterfield arrived at the Leister house from Taneytown at around 9:30 A.M. Probably the first order Meade dictated to Butterfield was for him "to familiarize himself with the topography of the ground" and "to send out staff officers to learn all the roads." As Meade would later testify: "I had never before been at Gettysburg, and did not know how many roads ran from our position, or what directions they ran." According to Meade, he said to Butterfield: "I wish you to send out staff officers to learn all the roads that lead from this place, ascertain the position of the corps—where their trains are; prepare to familiarize yourself with these details, so that in the event of any contingency, you can, without any order, be ready to meet it."[39]

Shortly after Meade's first message was sent to General Slocum, the army commander dictated a second message to him. This time, General Butterfield signed Meade's message. "The commanding general desires you to make your arrangements for an attack from your front on the enemy, to be made by the Twelfth Corps, supported by the Fifth. He wishes this a strong and decisive attack, which he will order as soon as he gets definite information of the approach of the Sixth Corps, which will also be directed to cooperate in this attack." Meade had no way of knowing the whereabouts of General Sedgwick and the Sixth Corps, except by sending an officer to ascertain the progress of the approach, and report. In fact, at this moment, Sedgwick's Sixth Corps was still nearly five hours away, marching as fast as its foot-sore troops possibly could. Since the previous afternoon, those soldiers had marched a grueling fourteen hours from Manchester.[40]

12

I WISH TO GOD
YOU COULD, SIR

Even while ordering the elements of his right flank to attack if at all possible, Meade continued to address the security of his left flank. From the
Leister house, Meade could not see Sickles's corps due to the long eastern slope of Cemetery Ridge, as well as the presence of the Second Corps
all along that ridge. "No part of the line [of battle] was visible [from the
Leister house]," reported correspondent Whitelaw Reid. Meade met with
Major Tremain but failed to get any positive information about whether
the Third Corps had formed its lines. Meade walked out of the Leister
house and observed his son and aide, Captain George Meade, in the front
yard.[1]

To young Captain Meade that morning, his father seemed "well pleased
with affairs as far as they had proceeded." They struck up a conversation.
Captain Meade recalled that it was probably the first time General Meade
"had an opportunity for private intercourse with anyone since taking command." Meade had taken command on 28 June, his son noted, and on the
morning of 2 July, it was his first opportunity for private discussion in
nearly four days.[2]

After a few "pleasant remarks" to his son, General Meade instructed
Captain Meade to ride to General Sickles and "inquire of him if his troops
were yet in position, and ask him what he had to report." Captain Meade
remembered the general saying: "Now George, you just ride down to Sickles and see what was going on." He then told young Meade where to find
Sickles. Captain Meade rode down the Taneytown Road for just over half a
mile when he came upon the headquarters of the Third Corps, "in a small
patch of woods on the west side of the road." Captain George E. Randolph, chief of artillery of the Third Corps, greeted him. Captain Meade
asked to see General Sickles. Randolph replied that Sickles, being tired

after having been up all night, was resting in his tent nearby. The captain thereupon relayed to Randolph General Meade's request. Randolph told Captain Meade he would visit with Sickles. After a few minutes, Randolph returned and informed Meade that the Third Corps was not in position and that General Sickles was in some doubt as to where he should place his corps. Incredibly, even though Sickles had been given explicit orders by General Slocum about the placement of the Third Corps the evening before, and by means of Captain Paine's map showing the placement of the respective corps as directed by Meade, tendered to the Third Corps commander that morning, Sickles never obeyed those instructions. Captain Meade felt he was in no position to rectify what appeared to be a misunderstanding. Instead, he informed Randolph that he would return to army headquarters and report the exchange to the commanding general.[3]

What young Captain Meade could see was that the Third Corps had not taken up any defensive positions at all, even though, by then, the entire Second Corps was in position to its right. Sickles's corps was still in the bivouac sites just north of Little Round Top extending to the fields to the west, between Cemetery Ridge and the Emmitsburg Road. Neither its artillery batteries nor the infantry "were occupying any special posts selected for defense or offense." What Captain Meade observed disturbed him. "I judged from the tenor of General Meade's message," he later wrote, "that I would find the [Third] Corps in line of battle."[4]

Captain Meade galloped back up the Taneytown Road as fast as his horse would take him. General Meade was still in front of the house, within the little white picket fence, when Captain Meade arrived. Many staff officers and orderlies were present. On hearing Captain Meade describe what had occurred at Sickles's headquarters, General Meade told him, "in his sharp, decisive way," to go back as fast as possible and inform General Sickles that the instructions from the general commanding "were to go into position on the left of the Second Corps; that his right was to connect with the left of the Second Corps; that he was to prolong with his divisions the line of that corps, occupying the position that General Geary had held [on the north slope of Little Round Top] the night before." General Meade told his young aide and son that he should admonish Sickles "that his troops should be in position as quickly as possible."[5]

On Captain Meade's return to General Sickles's headquarters, he observed that the tents were about to be struck. Sickles was mounted and conversing with several mounted staff officers. Young Meade then told Sickles what General Meade had said to him about the placement of the Third Corps. Sickles informed Meade that the Third Corps was moving "and would be in position shortly." Sickles said to Captain Meade something to the effect that General Geary did not occupy any position but, rather, was "massed in the vicinity." That curious remark was fraught with consequence, ultimately.[6]

Later, General Geary would explain to General Meade that after he received notice that he would be relieved by General Sickles, he sent to the Third Corps commander a staff officer "instructed to explain the importance of the position he held, and to ask that, if troops could not be sent at once to relieve him, at least a staff officer might be sent to acquaint himself with the position and be ready to post the troops when they arrived." All Sickles gave as an answer, said Geary, was that he "would attend to it in due time."[7]

As Captain Meade was about to return to army headquarters, Captain Randolph asked him if General Hunt could be directed to the Third Corps to examine the positions he had selected for artillery batteries. Captain Meade thereupon dug his spurs into the flanks of his horse and galloped back up the Taneytown Road to inform the commanding general.[8]

General Meade believed that fighting was imminent. He instructed all of his corps commanders at 11:00 A.M. to examine the roads and communications networks and to "sketch" the positions of "their respective corps, their artillery, infantry, and trains." Meade wanted "to know the roads on or near which the troops are, and where their trains lie, in view of movements in any direction." He required every corps commander to be familiar with the location of the headquarters of every other corps commander. Meade even instructed each corps commander to tender his sketch to a specific staff officer at army headquarters "immediately." Sickles was directed to submit his sketch to Colonel Edmund Schriver of Meade's staff.[9]

After hearing reports from his mounted aides who rode down the Baltimore Pike and the Taneytown Road and onto side roads—and, who, undoubtedly, inquired of Generals Howard and Slocum—Meade was able to identify two farm roads that connected the Baltimore Pike and the Taneytown Road. Neither appeared on the Adams County, Pennsylvania, residential map. The Blacksmith Shop Road left the Baltimore Pike just before it crossed Rock Creek and headed south and then west and entered the Taneytown Road at the base of Little Round Top. The Blacksmith Shop Road connected the extreme right flank of Meade's army with what was developing to be the extreme left flank. Not far from where the Blacksmith Shop Road left the Baltimore Pike, a farm road known as the Granite School House Road left the Blacksmith Shop Road and headed due west, past a schoolhouse, exiting on the Taneytown Road south of the little

Major General Daniel E. Sickles. (Library of Congress)

white frame house of the widow Lydia Leister. The Granite School House Road connected the extreme right flank of Meade's army with what was becoming the center of the army on Cemetery Ridge. Having such internal lines of communication and support was essential to the developing positions at Gettysburg being held. Those two roads enabled Meade not only to communicate with his flanks but to send troops speedily from one end of his lines to the other, all without exposing the troops to enemy observation and fire.[10]

There had been a long—almost interminable—silence from General Slocum on the far-right flank. At around 11:00 A.M., army headquarters received a message from the right wing commander. After acknowledging receipt of Meade's 9:30 A.M. directive, Slocum wrote: "I have already made a better examination of the position in my front than I am able to now that we have taken up a new line. If it is true that the enemy is massing troops on our right, I do not think we could detach enough troops for an attack to insure success. I do not think the ground in my front, held by the enemy, possesses any peculiar advantages for him." General Warren concurred in Slocum's judgment; he found "the ground was rough, being the valley of a considerable stream with dams upon it, that therefore it was favorable to the defense and not to attack, and that artillery could only be moved with difficulty through woods and marshy places." Meade had to accept Slocum's and Warren's conclusions, disappointing though they were.[11]

On Meade's left flank, General Sickles was uneasy; he asked Major Tremain to join him on a visit to Meade's headquarters. Meade received General Slocum's message at about the same time that Sickles and Tremain appeared at army headquarters. During the interview with Meade at the Leister house, Sickles lobbied for his corps to occupy the higher ground along the Emmitsburg Road and the ridges from the Sherfy peach orchard to Little Round Top. Meade told Sickles that his orders were for him to occupy the position held by General Geary's division the night before; he was to prolong the line to the left of Hancock's Second Corps. In so doing, Meade walked with Sickles on the porch of the Leister house and, while there, pointed to Little Round Top, which was in full view, and told Sickles that his left flank was to rest on that summit; his right was to connect with the left flank of Hancock's Second Corps. Sickles persisted. He told Meade that the ground of which he spoke was very good for artillery and requested that Meade send a staff officer forward with him to examine the position. Sickles also asked if he was authorized to post his corps as he deemed most advisable. Meade replied: "Certainly, within the limits of the general instructions I have given you; any ground within those limits you choose to occupy, I leave to you." Meade then turned to General Hunt, who had just returned from an inspection of the right flank of the army, and directed him to accompany Sickles in order to examine the ground of which the Third Corps commander spoke.[12]

Tremain conducted Sickles, Captain Alexander Moore of Sickles's staff, and Hunt on a tour of the Third Corps picket lines. They rode all the way to the Sherfy peach orchard. All along the picket lines, Sickles pointed out to Hunt the ground he proposed to occupy. Indeed, recalled Hunt, "[those ridges] commanded all the ground behind, as well as in front of them, and together constituted a favorable position for *the enemy* to hold." That, Hunt agreed, was a sound reason for Sickles to take possession of it. For all the benefits that the high ground held, however, Hunt quickly concluded that moving Sickles's corps to it "would so greatly lengthen our line—which in any case must rest on [Little] Round Top, and connect with the left of the Second Corps—as to require a larger force than the Third Corps alone to hold it, and it would be difficult to occupy and strengthen the angle [that would be formed by the two Third Corps divisions if the enemy already held the Seminary Ridge woods in force] in its front." Without the Sixth Corps on the field, Meade did not have enough troops to man such a defense line, and even if he did, the line's configuration, not only the angle formed at the Sherfy peach orchard but the line's relationship to the position of the Second Corps to its right would make it untenable.[13]

As the skirmishing west of the Emmitsburg Road slackened, General Hunt directed Sickles to reconnoiter so as to determine the size of Confederate forces in the woods along Seminary Ridge and how far their lines extended south. Just then a cannonade opened up on Cemetery Hill, probably signaling enemy movements toward the Union right. Hunt turned to Sickles and told him he could not wait for the results of the reconnaissance. As Hunt was leaving, Sickles asked him if he could bring his Third Corps forward and occupy a line along the high ground on the Emmitsburg Road and along the ridge lines between the Sherfy peach orchard and the base of Little Round Top. Hunt quickly replied: "Not on my authority; I will report to General Meade for his instructions." Hunt galloped back to the Leister house. There, he told Meade of Sickles's plans to advance to high ground along the Emmitsburg Road. He candidly said that the "position was a good one in itself, offering favorable positions for artillery, but that its relation to other lines were such that [he] could not advise it." Hunt asked Meade "to examine the area himself before ordering its occupation." Meade, recalled Hunt, "nodded assent."[14]

Sickles promptly ordered General Birney to reconnoiter the Millers-town Road to the west as ordered by Hunt. The Millerstown Road marked the left flank of the pickets of Humphreys's division and the right flank of the pickets of Birney's division. Colonel Berdan took another one hundred men from his First and Second United States Sharpshooters, along with two hundred men of the Third Maine as support, and moved out into the no-man's-land between the Emmitsburg Road and the densely wooded, Confederate-occupied Seminary Ridge in order to enter those woods so that they could test the enemy's strength. Berdan's troops were supported by squadrons of dismounted cavalry, and two of Lieutenant Calef's ordnance rifles, from General Buford's two cavalry brigades, then still patrolling the area along the Union left.[15]

General Sickles and Major Tremain returned to the Third Corps headquarters site along Cemetery Ridge. When they arrived, "a lively skirmish fire" opened up in the fields west of the Emmitsburg Road. As Berdan's sharpshooters made contact with the enemy, de Trobriand's and Burling's brigades, and Winslow's and Smith's batteries, finally arrived in the Third Corps positions, having marched from Emmitsburg, and so notified Sickles. Tremain was then ordered by Sickles to return to Meade's headquarters and report the reconnaissance in progress and the arrival of the two Third Corps brigades. Tremain was directed to ask Meade if there were any special orders about the Emmitsburg Road and to report the fact that the Third Corps ammunition train was "at the enemy's mercy."[16]

Major Tremain was ushered into the Leister house. Meade, he recalled, was in "a little room with a low ceiling." The only things that impressed Tremain "were a table, nearly as large as the room, around which five or six people might comfortably take porridge, a geography map of Adams County spread on the table, over which General Meade, spectacled as usual, was studiously bending from his seat, at what in courtesy might be styled in fiction the 'head of the table.'"[17]

Tremain was about to learn something about Meade that Assistant Secretary of War Charles A. Dana once related: "[Meade] was an intellectual man, and agreeable to talk with when his mind was free, but silent and indifferent to everybody when he was occupied with that which interested him." He had plenty on his mind when Tremain entered the room.[18]

Tremain stood at attention, awaiting Meade to recognize him. Meade did not do so. "My situation was becoming embarrassing," recalled Tremain, "not to mention my own mental speculations as to what was going on in the general's heavily burdened mind." Then Meade said: "Well, sir?"[19]

"With all the brevity [he] could command," Tremain stated his mes-

I WISH TO GOD YOU COULD, SIR

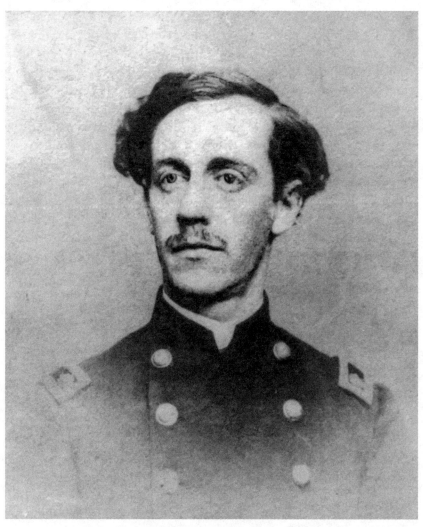

Major Henry Edwin Tremain. (Library of Congress)

sage. Meade returned to the study of the map in silence. Again, recalled Tremain, "the pause became embarrassing." He reported to Meade the reconnaissance that was under way and the lack of protection along the Emmitsburg Road; he then asked if there were any orders for General Sickles. Meade reassured Tremain that there was cavalry to patrol the Emmitsburg Road and that orders had been sent to the Third Corps wagon train. Tremain saluted and left.[20]

Tremain rode with great speed back to General Sickles. When he found the Third Corps commander, Tremain reported all that he had heard. "I was in a state of anxiety," he remembered, "far beyond what I had any right to be." He recalled that General Sickles asked him if Meade said anything else, to which Tremain responded that he had relayed everything.[21]

By noon General Meade had, for all practical purposes, given up launching an offensive operation at Gettysburg unless a clear opportunity was presented for him to do so. The ground his army occupied would not permit it. To attempt an offensive along any segment of the defense lines of the army would involve too much risk. That risk involved not only the army itself, General Hunt later wrote, "but Philadelphia, Baltimore, and Washington." A "strictly defensive battle," however, would be beneficial if a victory was achieved. "The campaign and the invasion, and its moral effect, abroad and at home, North and South," wrote Hunt, "would be of vast importance in a political as well as military sense. The additional risks of an offensive battle were out of all proportion to the prospective gains." Meade's determination to fight a defensive battle at Gettysburg was the only course available to him.[22]

About fifty minutes after the time Meade met with Sickles, messages were received at army headquarters from the signal station at Little Round Top. Lieutenant Jerome reported to General Butterfield, "The rebels are in force, and our skirmishers give way. One mile west of Round Top signal station, the woods are full of them." That indicated that Lee had extended his lines on Seminary Ridge. It might have indicated to Meade the arrival of Longstreet's corps. He could only guess. In little more than thirty minutes, a message was received from the Cemetery Hill signal station that was alarming. Signal officer Captain Paul Babcock Jr. reported "numerous fires, apparently from the burning of wagons southeast from here. A wagon train can be seen in the same direction. Think our trains are being destroyed." If true, that would be calamitous.[23]

General Buford's two cavalry brigades, which had been patrolling the Emmitsburg Road, were played out. Back on the evening of 30 June, Buford had advised General Pleasonton that his men and horses were "fagged out." The horses had not been able to get any grain, and many had thrown shoes. He could get no forage for his horses or food for his men. Even then, Buford's two brigades had fought a determined engagement against vastly superior numbers on 1 July. His men had been in the saddle ever since then. Buford made repeated requests to be relieved and sent to Westminster to refit.[24]

Early in the afternoon, Meade authorized Pleasonton to relieve Buford's division, but he fully expected a replacement command to arrive along the Emmitsburg Road before Buford left for Westminster. Pleasonton relieved Buford, but he never instructed Buford to remain until the replacement arrived. On receiving permission to leave for Westminster, Buford ordered his two worn-out brigades to ride down the Emmitsburg Road, leaving the army without any cavalry force to protect its left flank at all. After being informed that Buford had departed without waiting for a replacement, Meade sent Pleasonton a terse note. Signed by General Butterfield, it read: "The major general commanding directs me to say that he has not authorized the entire withdrawal of Buford's force from the direction of Emmitsburg, and did not so understand when he gave the order to Buford to go to Westminster; that the patrols and pickets upon the Emmitsburg Road must be kept on as long as our troops are in position." Five minutes later, Meade sent another note to General Pleasonton clarifying his previous communication. Also signed by General Butterfield, the second note read: "The [commanding] general expected, when Buford's force was sent to Westminster, that a force should be sent to replace it, picketing and patrolling the Emmitsburg Road. He understood that all your force was up." Only at 1:45 P.M. did Pleasonton order General Gregg to send forward "a regiment ... to picket on the left of our line, lately occupied by General Buford." It would never arrive in time.[25]

Buford later wrote that he ordered his division to head toward Taneytown, on the way to Westminster, after he observed Sickles's Third Corps come into position along the Emmitsburg Road. He claimed that he was "relieved by General Sickles's Corps," but evidently he was not. In any event, the departure of Buford's division occurred at a most inopportune time. The enemy was preparing to move against the left flank of the Army of the Potomac.[26]

At 1:30 P.M., a message was transmitted to army headquarters from Captain Hall, then at the Little Round Top signal station. "A heavy column of the enemy's infantry, about 10,000 strong, is moving from opposite our extreme left toward our right." Then came another ominous message, this time from Lieutenant Jerome on Little Round Top once again. It was sent to General Howard and to Meade. It may have referenced the same enemy movement noted by Captain Hall. "Over a division of the rebels is making a flank movement on our right," it read, "the line extends over a mile, and is advancing, skirmishing. There is nothing but cavalry to oppose them." Not long thereafter, Captain Hall signaled some specifics. Referring to the 1858 residential map of Adams County, Hall noted that the large body of troops was heading northeast on the Herr Ridge Road toward Herr Tavern. They were passing "Dr. [S. E.] Hall's house and a train of ambulances was following them," he reported. They were moving toward Meade's right, and they appeared to be expecting combat. That message indicated Lee was moving troops from his right to his left, possibly, to attack Meade's right.[27]

At around midafternoon, Major Tremain galloped up to army headquarters for the fourth time that day. He recalled that "he went directly to General Meade." Continued Tremain: "There was order and politeness, but an entire absence of ceremony at headquarters. Officers reporting there were sent at once to the commanding general, who was as accessible to all as though [he was] a regimental colonel."[28]

Tremain told Meade that General Birney's reconnaissance had revealed "a concealed column of the enemy" moving to the Union left; skirmishers were covering the movement. That differed from the recent reports from the Little Round Top signal station. Tremain said, "In the opinion of General Sickles more artillery than he had should be posted in order to meet the attack that was expected." General Meade calmly replied, "Generals [are] always expecting attacks on their own fronts." Tremain recalled that he then felt "frosted." Meade added: "If General Sickles needed more artillery in case of attack, the reserve artillery could furnish it." Tremain saluted and then hurriedly walked out of the Leister house, mounted up, and galloped toward the Third Corps lines. Up to that time, Meade had received no information from Sickles that led him to believe the Third Corps was anywhere other than where he explicitly ordered it to be—to the left of the Second Corps and covering Little Round Top.[29]

Meade sat down at his headquarters and drafted a report to General Halleck. He had just gotten word from General Sedgwick that the Sixth Corps was nearing Gettysburg on the Baltimore Pike. Wrote Meade:

> I have concentrated my army at this place today. The Sixth Corps
> is just coming in very much worn out, having been marching since
> 9 P.M. last night.
>
> The army is fatigued. I have today, up to this hour, awaited the
> attack of the enemy, I having a strong position for defensive. I am not
> determined on attacking him till his position is more developed. He
> has been moving on both my flanks apparently, but it is difficult to
> tell exactly his movements. I have delayed attacking to allow the Sixth
> Corps and parts of other corps to reach this place and rest the men.
> Expecting a battle, I ordered all my trains to the rear. If not attacked,
> and I can get any positive information of the position of the enemy
> which will justify me in doing so, I shall attack. If I find it hazardous
> to do so, or am satisfied the enemy is endeavoring to move to my
> rear and interpose between me and Washington, I shall fall back to

my supplies at Westminster. I will endeavor to advise you as often as possible. In the engagement yesterday the enemy concentrated more rapidly than we could, and towards evening, owing to the superior numbers, compelled the Eleventh and First Corps to fall back from the town to the heights this side, on which I am now posted. I feel fully the responsibility resting on me, but will endeavor to act with caution.

Meade's letter, although dated "July 2, 1863, 3 P.M.," would not be received at the War Department until 3 July at 10:20 A.M. That would be due, in part, to the fact that the horse relays from Baltimore to Westminster and from Westminster to Gettysburg would not be operational until later in the night of 2 July. The first express would leave Baltimore at 4:15 P.M. on 2 July. That would mean Meade would be notified of the system being operational only at 10:15 P.M. at the earliest, since it took six hours for the riders to carry messages from Baltimore to Gettysburg. Once Meade's message was sent from army headquarters, it would take another six hours for it to arrive in Baltimore and then be sent by telegraph to the War Department. All of that assumed there were no enemy threats along the Baltimore Pike.[30]

It was just after 3:00 P.M. Miraculously, Lee had not yet launched an attack. Meade called all of his corps commanders to a conference at the Leister house. An aide to Meade was sent to General Sickles informing him that the commanding general wanted to see him at army headquarters. After a while passed without an appearance from General Sickles, a second aide was sent to direct Sickles to Meade's headquarters. After most of Meade's generals arrived and began conversing about their positions, General Warren was given a report that Sickles's Third Corps was not in the position he had been directed to take; rather, the Third Corps was moving to positions far ahead of the army's lines along Cemetery Ridge. Sickles had not yet arrived at army headquarters even though he had been summoned twice to do so. Warren immediately informed General Meade of the report. Momentarily, heavy artillery and small arms fire opened up on the left flank. Sensing the beginning of an attack on the left, Meade ordered General Sykes, who was seated in the Leister house, to return to his Fifth Corps and move it as quickly as possible to the left. Meade's aides were sent out to direct Sykes's troops onto and along the Blacksmith Shop Road to the far-left flank. Meade told Sykes he would meet him on the field. Meade sent word by a staff officer to Sedgwick to place his Sixth Corps in the position vacated by the Fifth Corps on the right flank behind the Twelfth Corps. The meeting broke up; corps commanders and their staff members and orderlies mounted up and galloped back to their commands.[31]

Forty-one years old, General Sykes was a native of Dover, Delaware, and an 1842 graduate of West Point. He served in the Mexican War and on the New Mexico and Texas frontiers before the outbreak of the Civil War. Sykes commanded a battalion of regulars at First Bull Run. Promoted to brigadier general, he commanded a brigade and then a division in General Fitz John Porter's Fifth Corps on the Peninsula, and was then engaged in the fighting at Second Bull Run as commander of a division of mostly regulars. Elevated to the rank of major general just before Fredericksburg, he commanded his division at Chancellorsville but was only slightly engaged. Sykes had a long association with the Fifth Corps as well as with Meade. That Meade directed Sykes to move the Fifth Corps to the left flank before any other corps was likely due to Meade's belief that Sykes and his old corps would fight well for him. Moreover, the Fifth Corps was in a reserve position; it was not holding the front lines protecting the Baltimore Pike when Meade ordered it forward.[32]

For the first time on 2 July, now around 3:30 P.M., Meade determined to leave army headquarters. He had gone out onto the field early in the morning in order to examine the defense lines; that was before he established a headquarters. For a commanding general of an army, leaving his headquarters required a serious reason. The commanding general must always be where his corps commanders and messengers from his government can find him. He has to be accessible to every corps commander and departmental commander at all times so that he can address any emergency that might arise anywhere on the battlefield. Like all his predecessors, Meade required staff officers from every corps commander to be present at his headquarters so that he could send messages to all elements of the army at a moment's notice. Meade now sensed a serious problem on Sickles's front, a problem so serious that it demanded his presence there.

Some scholars have suggested that Meade should have gone over to Sickles personally and made sure the Third Corps was in the position he had ordered it to occupy. James A. Hessler, in his fine book, *Sickles at Gettysburg*, asserts that "while Sickles bears the blame for ultimately acting independent of his orders, the commanding general must share some responsibility for not ensuring that those orders were executed in accordance with his wishes." Edwin Coddington vigorously asserts that Sickles simply disobeyed Meade's orders.[33]

Frankly, it strains credulity to maintain that Sickles did not get suffi-

I WISH TO GOD YOU COULD, SIR

Major General George Sykes. (Library of Congress)

cient instructions from army headquarters about where the Third Corps should be placed. Sickles had been given plenty of explicit orders, but in a startling exhibition of insubordination, he refused to obey them. Likely, not even Meade's personal inspection of the positions of the Third Corps, before it moved forward, would have mattered. As it was, Sickles moved the Third Corps forward precisely at the moment when Meade called the council of his corps commanders. Up until then, Meade had received no information that his orders were not being obeyed.

General Sickles, accompanied by Major Tremain and Captain Moore, finally rode up to join the conference at the Leister house as General Meade was waiting for his horse. Meade told Sickles not to dismount but to ride to the front his corps had taken. "I never saw General Meade so angry," recalled Captain Paine. He spoke to Sickles "in a few sharp words," telling him to retire his line to the position he had been repeatedly ordered to take. Meade said that he would follow with his staff; he then called for General Warren to join him. Sickles, Tremain, and Moore galloped away. Meade sent for Old Baldy, but for some reason, there was a delay in bringing the horse. General Pleasonton told Meade: "Take my horse, General. He is right here." Meade mounted the horse and, with General Warren and a group of staff officers and orderlies, rode toward the front. Riding along the lines of the Second Corps and looking southwest, Meade was astonished to observe that Sickles's corps appeared to be moving into positions nearly a quarter of a mile ahead of the rest of the army.[34]

Sickles had begun his advance away from the positions Meade had instructed him to hold not long before he arrived at the Leister house. General Birney's division had advanced nearly a quarter of a mile; the right flank, held by Brigadier General Charles K. Graham's brigade, extended from the Sherfy peach orchard east toward a large wheat field. The center was held by the brigade of Colonel de Trobriand along generally low ground in front of that wheat field. On Birney's left was Brigadier General J. H. Hobart Ward's brigade at Devil's Den and the base of Little Round Top. Birney's division was not large enough to hold that front. Consequently, regiments would be stripped from multiple brigades to bolster the lines. Even then, there were yawning gaps. The entire division was facing the south; it held broken, rocky ridges all the way to near the base of Little Round Top. The soldiers of the One Hundred Forty-First Pennsylvania in Graham's brigade at the Sherfy peach orchard, and other regiments nearby, were ordered to lie down to minimize the deadly effect of the enemy artillery fire their officers knew would commence at any moment.[35]

Sickles had ordered General Humphreys's division to move directly

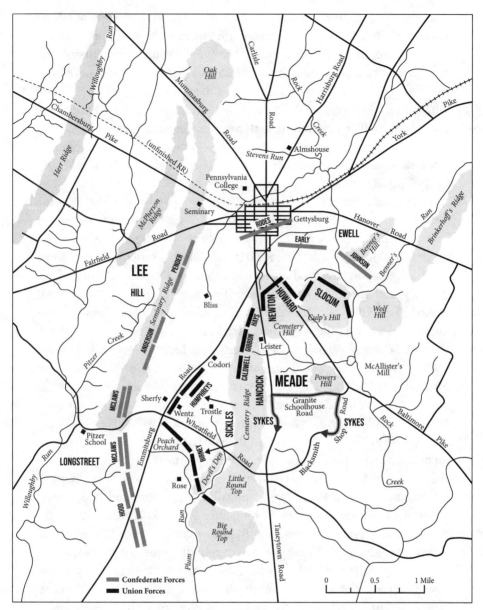

Map 12.1. 2 July 1863, afternoon: The movement of Sickles's Third Corps.

ahead some five hundred yards to a position east of the Emmitsburg Road; its left flank would be situated not far from the peach orchard and its right flank in the air, southeast of the Codori house. Humphreys's left flank would be considerably higher than its right flank, glaring evidence that the high ground that Sickles wanted to seize was not uniformly high but, rather, was a gradual downward slope from the peach orchard to the Codori house. To insure unimpeded troop movement and rapid communications, sappers and pioneers from every regiment in Sickles's corps tore down most of the fence lines in the fields between the positions taken up by the Third Corps and Cemetery Ridge.[36]

When Humphreys began his forward movement, he was unsure of the orders. General Caldwell, commander of the First Division of the Second Corps to Humphreys's right, told Humphreys that he had received no order from Meade to advance. Sickles sent another order to Humphreys, and he thereupon advanced his division ahead of Caldwell's. It must have been a grand spectacle; seemingly endless files of soldiers beneath what looked like countless national colors and blue regimental flags, marching toward the Emmitsburg Road. General Hancock, then with General Caldwell, Colonel Patrick Kelly of the Eighty-Eighth New York, Colonel Richard Byrnes of the Twenty-Eighth Massachusetts, and Colonel St. Clair Mulholland of the One Hundred Sixteenth Pennsylvania, on the left of the Second Corps line, had not received any orders from Meade to advance. Hancock was "resting on one knee leaning upon his sword." He smiled and looked at the officers nearby and said: "Wait a moment, you will soon see them tumbling back." Sickles had never even notified Hancock that he was going to move the Third Corps forward away from Hancock's left flank.[37]

Not satisfied with Humphreys's position, Sickles ordered Humphreys to move all the way up to the Emmitsburg Road close to 3:30 P.M., increasing the gap between his right flank and the left flank of the Second Corps. Already, Sickles's corps was entirely disconnected from the rest of the army. As Humphrey's division was marching toward the Emmitsburg Road, soldiers of the Eleventh Massachusetts in Brigadier General Joseph B. Carr's brigade on the right flank recalled seeing the one-story log house of Peter and Susan Rogers in the distance. One of those soldiers noted that there was "a herd of thirteen or fourteen cows quietly grazing upon the field, flocks of tame pigeons sat upon the dovecots and sheds and the lady inside the cottage was baking bread." That bucolic scene was about to change. To the left of Carr's brigade, around a log house and orchard of shoemaker Daniel H. Klingle, was placed Colonel William R. Brewster's Excelsior Brigade, six regiments from New York City, five of which owed

I WISH TO GOD YOU COULD, SIR

many of their enlistments to Sickles himself. Behind the two brigades at the Emmitsburg Road was placed Colonel George Burling's brigade of six regiments available to respond to any call from the front lines.[38]

Sickles and some of his staff were along the Emmitsburg Road, near the Sherfy peach orchard, when they observed Meade, Warren, and "a small body of horsemen" appear in an open field within easy range of enemy artillery that had begun an intense barrage on the Third Corps lines. Meade and Warren rode toward Sickles. Accompanying Meade were Majors Benjamin C. Ludlow and Biddle, Captains Meade, Addison G. Mason, and Charles E. Cadwalader, Lieutenant Oliver and Captain James Starr, commander of the escort companies of the Sixth Pennsylvania Cavalry. Meade also had signal officers with him to keep abreast of field communications. Captain Norton, Meade's chief signal officer, and his adjutant general, Lieutenant William S. Stryker, were likely a part of the entourage. With Warren were Lieutenants Washington A. Roebling and Ranald S. Mackenzie, along with Captain Chauncey Barnes Reese, of Warren's staff. With both generals were flag bearers and orderlies. As they rode along Humphrey's files of troops, the men of Humphreys's division cheered their new commander. It was their first glimpse of him. Sickles spurred his horse forward to meet the commander.[39]

As Meade, Warren, and Sickles met in the fields, Humphreys's division was still on the move. Looking at Sickles's developing lines, Warren noted that they were "very poorly disposed on that part of the field." Meade asked his Third Corps commander to inform him of the position he intended his corps to occupy. Sickles did so. Then Meade, astonished and angry, told Sickles that the positions to which he had moved the Third Corps were not the line he had been ordered to occupy. Meade turned in his saddle and pointed to the ground between the unoccupied left of the Second Corps and the northern base of Little Round Top, saying, in no uncertain terms, that this was the ground he was to occupy. Addressing the line Sickles established on the Emmitsburg Road, Meade said: "General Sickles, this is neutral ground, our guns command it as well as the enemy's. The very reason you cannot hold it applies to them."[40]

As it stood, Sickles had advanced to a position beyond supporting distance of the rest of the army. It must be presumed that Sickles had provided to Meade's staff a sketch of the position of the Third Corps and its trains in response to Meade's 11:00 A.M. circular order. Sickles had been ordered to tender his sketch to Colonel Schriver of Meade's staff. At 11:00 A.M. Sickles corps had held the line to the left of the Second Corps. He had completely disobeyed his commander's orders. Meade had given him those orders personally in the wee hours of 2 July and had been repeated twice since then, once by Captain Meade and again by General Meade. General Geary had sent a staff officer to alert Sickles of the position his corps was to occupy. Even a sketch of the positions of all the corps of the army had been provided to Sickles. Meade expressed his fear that the enemy would attack before Sickles could get his corps back to Cemetery Ridge. In that event, Sickles would have to meet the enemy all by himself, and then, inevitably, the position would have to be abandoned; he would be lucky to get any of his field artillery out safely.[41]

Sickles told Meade that he regretted that he had occupied positions that did not meet with his commander's approval and that he would withdraw his two divisions back to Cemetery Ridge. "I wish to God you could, sir," Meade replied, "but you see the enemy will not let you withdraw!" He then added, "But you have to come back, and you may as well do it at once as at any other time."[42]

Pointing to Little Round Top, Meade turned in his saddle to General Warren and directed him to ride to the left of Sickles's lines and "examine the condition of affairs" there and, if no troops were posted on that hill, to do whatever was necessary to assemble a sufficient force to defend it. Warren and his aides turned their horses and rapidly galloped toward Little Round Top. Artillery fire was lively on both sides; shells flew overhead and exploded. It was the prelude to an attack.[43]

From almost the moment Meade arrived at Gettysburg, he recognized the importance of Little Round Top. In the early morning hours of 2 July he ordered Sickles's corps to occupy it as it had been over the previous six or eight hours. He even pointed to that eminence while he was on the front porch of the Leister house and, for the second time, personally told Sickles that his Third Corps must form to the left of Hancock's Second Corps, extend the line along Cemetery Ridge, and occupy the northern slope of Little Round Top as it had been occupied the night before.

As Meade and Sickles conferred, General Hunt and his staff and orderlies galloped across the fields not too distant. Sickles's chief of artillery, Captain Randolph, rode out to meet Hunt. Randolph told Hunt that he had been directed to place the batteries of the Third Corps along the new line Sickles established but that he needed more. Hunt observed Meade and Sickles conferring. He believed that Meade may have consented to the advance and, accordingly, sent aides off to bring forward more artillery batteries from the Artillery Reserve then parked along the Granite School House Road on the George Spangler farm opposite Powers Hill.[44]

Just as Sickles turned around to issue orders for a withdrawal of his

Little Round Top. (Library of Congress)

two divisions, Confederate batteries along Seminary Ridge opened an intense fire on the peach orchard salient. Shells burst in and overhead of the files of Sickles's regiments in and near the peach orchard, blowing gaping holes in the lines of prostrate soldiers. Meade swiftly ordered Sickles to keep his lines just where they were; unfortunately, it was too late to move them. The Third Corps was about to be attacked with everything the enemy could bring to bear against it. Meade assured Sickles that he would locate as much support as he could and bring it forward.[45]

Suddenly, an artillery shell fired from a Confederate battery screeched overhead, striking the ground well beyond Sickles and Meade. The "whizzing missile" appeared to frighten Meade's borrowed horse and it became almost uncontrollable. Major Tremain recalled that the horse "reared" and then "plunged; he could not be quieted. "Nothing was possible to be done with such a beast except to let him run; and run he would, and run he did." Meade's staff and orderlies galloped after him until the horse was brought

General Warren on Little Round Top, by Alfred R. Waud. (Library of Congress)

under control. The horse had been bridled with a curb bit but was accustomed to being bridled with a snaffle bit, so General Pleasonton later confessed. Meade always used a curb bit, as did most of the army officers. The shell screeching overhead, and Meade pulling on the curb bit, remarked Tremain, may have caused the horse to panic. Major Biddle noted, however, that "General Meade's horse was shot close to his leg, and the balls flew very thick," the most likely explanation for the cause of the horse's panic. Meade dismounted the horse. An orderly promptly brought Old Baldy to the front, and Meade mounted his favorite war horse.[46]

Over on Sickles's far left flank, General Warren and several of his aides and orderlies, including Lieutenants Roebling and Mackenzie and Captain Reese, galloped up the rocky northern face of Little Round Top. Captain Hall's signalmen were sending semaphore signals, warning of an attack along the left. On reaching the summit of that commanding height, "[my] worst apprehensions were confirmed," Warren later wrote. He could plainly see the entire lines of Sickles's Third Corps before him in the fields below. Although Warren could not see the extent of enemy infantry formations, concealed in the dense woods of Seminary Ridge, he could plainly see the long line of enemy batteries of field artillery in front of those woods that were firing on Sickles's troops. Some of those shells were directed at Little Round Top and burst near Warren and his staff and the signalmen.[47]

Warren quickly sent a message to Captain Smith, four guns of whose Fourth New York Independent Battery were planted along a rocky, boulder-strewn ridge below Little Round Top, known locally as Devil's Den; two of Smith's guns were unlimbered along the low ground 150 yards to the rear. The message called for Smith to fire shells into the distant Seminary Ridge woods southwest of his four guns. At the time Smith received the message, General Hunt rode up to Smith's position to observe the placement of the guns. On Little Round Top, Warren could hear the orders yelled by Smith and his cannoneers to set the fuses for the distance to the targets. Then Smith yelled: "Fire!" The guns boomed and Warren watched the shells' flight. Through his binoculars, he saw the shells burst over and within the distant woods, revealing the gleam of a line of muskets nearly a half mile long, "already arrayed to outflank [Sickles's lines]," Warren wrote later. "There was not a man on [Little Round Top]," he concluded. Hurriedly, Warren sent Lieutenant Mackenzie to find General Sickles and tell him of the extent of the impending Confederate attack and to send a force to defend Little Round Top. In the rock-strewn valley below Warren, General Hunt galloped away from Smith and his cannoneers. As he did, he left the young captain with a disquieting prediction: "You will probably lose your battery!"[48]

Meade had not received any word that General Sykes's Fifth Corps had approached the field. Officers were sent to the rear to hurry Sykes's columns forward. Others were sent all the way down the Baltimore Pike to General Sedgwick to be prepared to hurry the Sixth Corps forward. The situation was already desperate. Within twenty minutes, Mackenzie reported to Warren that Sickles refused to send any help, claiming he needed all the troops he had at the front. Already, Warren could see the long lines of Confederate infantry emerging from the Seminary Ridge woods and heading toward Sickles's exposed and poorly positioned lines. What was terrifying about the sight was that those enemy lines were so long they would overlap Sickles's left, and Little Round Top was without any defenders. Warren scribbled an urgent note to Meade to send some troops to Little Round Top. He handed it to Captain Reese, who galloped down the north slope of Little Round Top. When Reese delivered Warren's message to Meade, the army commander quickly directed Major Ludlow to ride to General Humphreys and tell him to halt his division and guide it toward the left end of Sickles's line. As Humphreys was in the midst of moving his division to the left, word arrived that the Fifth Corps had reached the field and was awaiting Meade's orders. Quickly, Meade ordered Ludlow to return to General Humphreys and tell him to halt his movement and, instead, realign his division along the Emmitsburg Road between the Co-dori house and the Sherfy peach orchard. Excitedly, Ludlow told Humphreys that the Fifth Corps had just arrived. Meade then sent Reese back to Warren with a message that the whole Fifth Corps would be sent to the left![49]

The Army of the Potomac was about to enter into the struggle of its life. What happened on 1 July was difficult enough. Now, the insubordination of a corps commander had placed not only his own Third Corps but the entire army at risk. No cavalry screened the army's left flank. The troops would have to fight as they had never done before, and even that might not be enough, given the sheer magnitude of the attack the enemy was about to unleash against Meade's left. Although Meade was the operational commander of the army, he was about to take tactical command of the fighting on 2 July.

13

THROW YOUR WHOLE CORPS AT THAT POINT

General Meade clearly saw how perilous was the situation for not only the Third Corps but the entire army. That the dire situation was the result of General Sickles's insubordination must have made it maddening to him. Meade did not have enough troops to confront the entire breadth of the attacking force that appeared to extend from the Round Tops all the way to the peach orchard and up the Emmitsburg Road in front of the center of his army and still maintain the defense lines he had established along Cemetery Ridge, Cemetery Hill, and down the Baltimore Pike. General Meade testified before the Joint Committee on the Conduct of the War, eight months after Gettysburg, about that very problem. "The enemy," he said, "threw immense masses upon General Sickles's Corps which, advanced and isolated in that way, it was not in my power to support promptly." To compound the problem, Meade could not use his superior artillery along Cemetery Ridge to fire on the distant Confederate columns as they closed in on Sickles's lines for fear of hitting his own men. Those batteries either had to be moved forward and risk being overwhelmed or remain silent where they were until the enemy was literally on top of them, although by then it might be too late.[1]

Meade had to act swiftly. He directed that Little Round Top be occupied by as large a force as necessary to keep it from falling into enemy hands. Then, if he sent the largest number of troops possible to the front in support of what appeared to be the center of General Birney's Third Corps division, in the large wheat field, it might possibly disrupt the attack and, maybe, arrest its momentum. The center of Birney's division was also closer to Meade's main lines than those lines holding the peach orchard and the Emmitsburg Road, making any force Meade sent there capable of

Major General David Bell Birney. (Library of Congress)

being reinforced by other commands nearby. If his tactic was successful, Meade would then have to contend with the attacking lines approaching the peach orchard and the Emmitsburg Road. Meade determined to follow that course of action; he resolved to send as many divisions as it would take through the large wheat field, framed on the west and east by stony ridges, directly in support of what he believed then was the center of Birney's lines. He would direct the battle himself, and to do so, he would place himself as close to the fighting as was necessary. Meade realized that his casualties would be overwhelming, but he simply had no other viable option.

Sometime after 4:30 P.M., General Meade met General Sykes most likely in the fields north of Little Round Top and west of the intersection of the Taneytown Road and the Wheatfield Shop Road. Sykes's corps had used the Taneytown Road to reach the Union left flank from its previous position behind the Twelfth Corps, west of the Baltimore Pike. Meade pointed to the center of the lines of General Birney's division of Sickles's corps. He could see that Birney's division was not large enough to hold that line and that it would break with the shock of the coming attack. Meade ordered Sykes to "throw [his] whole corps to that point and hold it at all hazards!" Meade assured Sykes he would be in constant communication with him. Major Biddle of Meade's staff was given the assignment of relaying messages from Meade to Sykes and from Sykes to Meade.[2]

Now that Meade ordered General Sykes to deploy the entire Fifth Corps on the field, Sykes was relieved that no blame would attend him for not responding to any call from Sickles; Meade made that clear. Meade demanded that professional soldiers take complete control of the fighting. He eliminated Sickles from any position in the chain of command; Sickles would be lucky if his Third Corps escaped being demolished.[3]

Once Lee launched his attack against Meade's left flank, no one understood more how precarious was the situation of the Third Corps than, frankly, General Sickles. He sent frantic appeals everywhere for reinforcements. For the fifth time, Sickles sent Major Tremain to General Meade, this time to ask for more help. Tremain recalled years later that he found Meade not far from the Taneytown Road "watching a column of troops" that was "marching along the road." Meade was undoubtedly watching the Fifth Corps as it moved onto the battlefield. Tremain remembered that as he began to make his request, "we were well nigh run over, and became separated, by the recklessness of artillery drivers, or the accidental swerving of an artillery caisson." Nevertheless, Tremain recalled that he received Meade's "earnest and fixed attention." The young aide to Sickles "narrated as concisely and comprehensively as possible" all that his commander ordered him to say. "General Meade did not discourage my speech," Tremain recalled. Meade then told him that the Fifth Corps was arriving on the field and more elements of the army would be called upon if necessary. "As I rode away," remembered Tremain, "of one thing I felt assured, and that was that our army commander was then fully alive to the crisis of the situation, and that he was earnestly minded to do everything in his power to uphold our battle lines."[4]

Out in the field, General Sykes called for Brigadier General James Barnes, the sixty-one-year-old commander of the First Division of the Fifth Corps, to ride with him, ahead of his division, to the ground where Meade directed Sykes's troops to form. As Sykes and Barnes reached a site not far from the large wheat field, they observed a general officer and his staff approach them on horseback. It was General Warren, and he pointed to Little Round Top to the left and "urged the importance of assistance in that direction." Recognizing Warren as a trusted member of Meade's staff, Sykes "immediately directed" a staff officer to order Colonel Strong Vincent, commander of the Third Brigade in Barnes's division, "to proceed to that point." Vincent's brigade "moved with great promptness" up the eastern face of Little Round Top and to positions that would protect the southern and southwestern slopes of that eminence from the Confederate attack.[5]

General Warren then observed the approach of Brigadier General Stephen H. Weed's brigade of Brigadier General Romeyn B. Ayres's Second Division of the Fifth Corps, and he rode up to Colonel Patrick O'Rorke of the One Hundred Fortieth New York of Weed's brigade, whom he knew well. Weed had been summoned by Sickles and, not knowing Sykes's determination not to respond to Sickles's calls for reinforcements, had left his command. Warren ordered O'Rorke to march to the left and up the eastern slope of Little Round Top. O'Rorke told Warren that General Weed expected him to follow the orders Weed received from Sickles. "Never mind that, Paddy," said Warren, "bring them up on the double quick—don't stop for aligning. I will take the responsibility." Turning the brigade over to Colonel Kenner Garrard of the One Hundred Forty-Sixth New York, O'Rorke, led by Lieutenant Roebling, directed his regiment to follow him. Pulled and pushed by the cannoneers up Little Round Top behind O'Rorke's New Yorkers was Lieutenant Charles E. Hazlett's Battery D, Fifth United States, the movement ordered by Hazlett himself after conferring with Warren.[6]

A staff officer from General Sykes finally found Weed and told him, without equivocation, to return to the position to which he had been initially directed. Weed rode back to his brigade. General Warren was nearby when he spotted Weed. Warren then led that brigade on the path following Vincent's brigade, O'Rorke's regiment, and Hazlett's guns, up the eastern slope of Little Round Top, where, on the summit, they would fill the line to the right of Vincent's four regiments. As Warren reached the summit of Little Round Top and was conferring with Lieutenant Hazlett, a bullet grazed his neck. Reaching for a bandanna, Warren tied it around his neck to stanch the flow of blood. The wound did not appear to be serious.[7]

According to Lieutenant Colonel David Jenkins of the One Hundred Forty-Sixth New York, in Weed's brigade, General Meade and his staff followed Weed's men up the slope of Little Round Top, stopping at the position of Jenkins's regiment that was directed to hold the right flank of Weed's brigade, along the northwestern slope. From that vantage point, Meade viewed the battlefield just before the fighting broke out. Rifle fire erupted as the Confederate assault force came into view.[8]

Meade and his staff returned to their position near the intersection of the Taneytown Road and the Wheatfield Road to observe the arrival of the rest of the Fifth Corps, which then stretched all the way back up the Taneytown Road behind the army. Meade and some of his staff officers rode down the Taneytown Road a short distance to the two-story stone Jacob Weikert house just behind Little Round Top. The house and grounds had just been commandeered by Fifth Corps surgical teams. Meade was observed by Clyde B. Kernek, the surgeon of the Thirty-Second Massachusetts from the Fifth Corps, as he rode up to the Weikert house. Most of the surgeons "were flustered and speechless" at the sight of Meade and his staff. Surgeon Zabdiel Boylston Adams welcomed the army commander. "General Meade spoke some pleasantries to the men of his old corps," recalled Dr. Kernek. Meade then said: "I expect every man to do his duty—nothing less." Meade then said that he and his staff were thirsty and that is why they visited the hospital. The stewards brought to Meade's officers "cups of cool water." Fifteen-year-old Tillie Pierce, a student at the Young Ladies Seminary in Gettysburg, was working at the Weikert house along with other townspeople. She grabbed a tin cup, filled it with water, and handed it to Meade, apologizing for using such a simple container. "Certainly, that is all right," Meade replied. After some "nervous laughter," Meade and his officers "drank their fill of water." As Meade finished, he handed the cup back to Tillie, thanking her "very pleasantly." Meade turned Old Baldy around. The soldiers at the Weikert house "gave three cheers for General Meade." Meade turned his horse around again and gave Tillie "a nice bow"; he then "saluted the soldiers." Meade and his staff left, returning to their prior position in the fields not far from the intersection of the Taneytown Road and the Wheatfield Road.[9]

Along Birney's far left flank, General Ward's brigade observed columns of Confederate infantry advancing toward Devil's Den at between 4:30 and 5:00 P.M. Captain Smith's four guns of the Fourth New York Independent Battery, on the summit of Devil's Den, poured explosive shells at the dense lines, blowing gaping holes in them. Still, on they came.[10]

The Confederates attacking Ward's brigade and Smith's guns were Brigadier General Henry Benning's four regiments of Georgians and elements of Brigadier General Jerome B. Robertson's Brigade of one Arkansas and three Texas regiments. To the right of Benning's and Robertson's charging lines was a brigade of five regiments of Alabamians commanded by Brigadier General Evander McIvor Law. Benning's, Robertson's, and Law's brigades were from Hood's Division, Longstreet's Corps. Two of Law's regiments were directed toward Devil's Den. Benning's Georgia regiments and one of Robertson's Texas regiments and the Arkansas regiment halted, fired, and then rapidly advanced "with fierce yells," ascending the slope toward Smith's battery and Ward's infantry regiments at Devil's Den; Robertson's and Law's other regiments swarmed toward Little Round Top.[11]

General Ward's regiments at Devil's Den fired devastating volleys and then, with the enemy "only a few rods away," the One Hundred Twenty-Fourth New York charged down the slope. Recalled a private in that regiment: "The conflict at this point defies description. Roaring cannon, crashing riflery, screeching shots, bursting shells, hissing bullets, cheers, shouts, shrieks, and groans were the notes of the song of death which greeted the grim reaper." In the desperate fighting, the One Hundred Twenty-Fourth New York was virtually destroyed.[12]

To the left of Smith's guns, the Fortieth New York advanced against the approaching Texans and Alabamians along the base of Little Round Top, aided by the Fourth Maine. The appearance of the Fortieth New York enabled Smith's cannoneers to slow the enemy with more artillery fire. The regiment was halted by relentless Confederate gunfire, however, and then it retired before the weight of the enemy attack, exposing Smith's battery. Smith somehow maneuvered one of his four guns on the ridge to the rear, although it was disabled. He left behind ten horses killed or disabled. The remaining three guns were abandoned, lending truth to General Hunt's prediction only an hour before. Although the smoke was dense, Meade could observe the desperate fighting from his position near the northern base of Little Round Top.[13]

The attack against Little Round Top, by Edwin Forbes. (Library of Congress)

Above Devil's Den, the Confederate attacks unfolded against the southern and southwestern faces of Little Round Top at about the same time as the attacks struck Devil's Den. At the summit of Little Round Top, Colonel Vincent's brigade had arrived "on the double quick." Two of General Law's Alabama regiments were driving up the southern slope in a desperate effort to seize Little Round Top. To their left, two Texas regiments from Robertson's Brigade advanced up the hill. One of Vincent's men looked down from Little Round Top. "Sickles's corps," he recalled, "was enveloped in sheets of flame, and looked like a vast windrow of fire." Colonel Vincent led his four regiments directly toward the attackers; the Twentieth Maine held the left flank. No sooner were Vincent's regiments in position along the military crest of the hill than the Alabamians were in front of them.[14]

Completely out of Meade's sight, the Alabamians made repeated attacks. Each time they were driven back only to re-form and attack again. The Fifteenth Alabama, in front of Colonel Joshua Chamberlain's Twentieth Maine, moved to its right in an attempt to get on the left flank of the Maine men. Chamberlain quickly ordered the left flank of his regiment "refused," he wrote, "so that it was nearly at right angles with my right." Four distinct times the Alabamians attacked Chamberlain's thin and overextended lines. Each attack led the enemy to within ten paces of the lines of the Twentieth Maine. "The ground," wrote General Barnes, "was strewn with dead and wounded men of both sides, promiscuously mingled. Their ammunition exhausted, they replenished it from the cartridge boxes of the men lying around them, whether friends or foes, but even this resource failed them." Nearly out of ammunition, Chamberlain yelled, "Fix bayonets," then "Charge bayonets!" Out in front of his regiment on foot, with sword upraised, Chamberlain led his men down the southern slope of Little Round Top, finally breaking the Confederate thrusts. To Chamberlain's right, Colonel Vincent fell mortally wounded from a bullet that smashed into his groin.[15]

Rapidly approaching General Weed's brigade and Vincent's right flank were two Texas regiments of Robertson's brigade and one Alabama regiment of Law's. Lieutenant Hazlett, mounted on his horse, had directed his cannoneers to unlimber their six guns and bring them into position. The volleys from the contending lines were fired at one another fewer than ten paces apart. There, Colonel O'Rorke was mortally wounded. In just "a few moments," General Weed fell mortally wounded. As Lieutenant Hazlett dismounted and went to Weed's assistance, he was shot in the head and fell over General Weed. In spite of the severe losses of officers and men, Vincent's and Weed's brigades held.[16]

Lieutenant Roebling recalled that once the senior officers were confident that Little Round Top was secure, he raced down to where he knew General Meade was still situated to report the news. "[I] rode quickly over to General Meade," Roebling recalled, "explained the situation, gave him at least a ray of comfort, and then returned." Meade remained along the northern base of Little Round Top, near the action.[17]

Colonel de Trobriand's brigade, along the southern end of the wheat field, to the right of Ward's brigade, huddled behind a stone-and-rail fence at the foot of a long slope. In that wheat field, at its highest elevation, the artillerymen of Captain George B. Winslow's Battery D, First New York Light, unlimbered their guns facing south.[18]

Just after 5:45 P.M., Confederate columns slammed into de Trobriand's brigade and its artillery support with terrific force. Brigadier General George T. Anderson's brigade of Georgians of Hood's Division—five regiments in all—struck Birney's lines at the Wheatfield from the south and west. Colonel de Trobriand's brigade, in front of the Wheatfield, beat back the initial attacks. The Confederate lines, however, re-formed and attacked again. Winslow's six guns helped hold the attackers at bay; they "mowed them down by the score," recalled one soldier. Yet the attacks did not stop.[19]

Colonel de Trobriand rode up behind the Seventeenth Maine, yelling: "Fall back, right away!" No one heard the order. The Confederates re-formed again and attacked. This time, they got onto the flank and into

Colonel Philip Regis de Trobriand. (Library of Congress)

the rear of de Trobriand's regiments and swept them back up through the Wheatfield until Winslow's guns decimated the oncoming columns. The fighting there, however, was hardly over.[20]

For much of the fighting, Meade and his staff and orderlies were close to General Sykes and his staff. There, Meade "remained in constant communication with all the prominent officers who were engaged there."[21]

For two hours the massed Confederate batteries had zeroed in on Birney's right flank in and near the Sherfy peach orchard and Humphreys's division along the Emmitsburg Road, positions masked from Meade's view by woods, terrain, and dense smoke. The Third Corps troops there would have to defend their positions alone. Only batteries from the Artillery Reserve were brought forward to bolster those lines. A member of the Second New Hampshire, situated at the peach orchard, recalled that "the air was fairly alive with bursting shell and whistling canister; the leaves fell in showers from the peach trees, and the dirt was thrown up in little jets where the missiles were continually striking. A stream of wounded," he continued, "was constantly pouring to the rear, some [artillery] shells skimming along the ground and wounding as many as a half dozen men in their course."[22]

Three South Carolina commands of Brigadier General Joseph B. Kershaw's brigade struck Graham's brigade at the peach orchard, as well as the artillery batteries in place east of the peach orchard, from the southwest. Two brigades, one commanded by General Barksdale, and the other commanded by Brigadier General William T. Wofford, swarmed toward the Sherfy house from the west. Wofford's brigade included five Georgia commands. Barksdale's brigade consisted of four regiments from Mississippi, including the Twenty-First Mississippi, in which Meade's nephew Frank Ingraham had served until he died in the field only eight weeks before. All three brigades were in General McLaws's Division of Longstreet's Corps. Wofford's Brigade was about fifteen minutes behind Barksdale's.[23]

The enemy lines advanced steadily forward from the west as well as the south. The salient of Sickles's lines at the peach orchard was doomed. Some regiments could not hold out any longer for want of men and withdrew. The skirmish lines west of the Emmitsburg Road had given way. The men of the battered One Hundred Forty-First Pennsylvania made their way to the rear; they were hailed by General Sickles, who called out to Colonel Henry Madill: "Colonel! For God's sake can't you hold on?" Tearfully, Madill replied: "Where are my men?" Madill's horse had been killed, and he was carrying the regimental colors. Only twenty of his men emerged from the hellish ordeal with him.[24]

Although Meade received grim reports about the fighting at the peach orchard and along the Emmitsburg Road, there was nothing he could do to assist the troops defending those lines. They were too far forward. Meade had to let the fighting there play itself out; he would address the Confederate attacks as they got closer to his main lines along Cemetery Ridge. If he did otherwise, the reinforcements would simply be sacrificed defending those very positions that Meade knew could not have been held in the first place.

Sickles's lines at the peach orchard salient fell back; the attacking Confederate force there was three lines deep. It was nearly 6:00 P.M. Captain George E. Randolph's Battery E, First Rhode Island, then led by Captain John K. Bucklyn, held a segment of Sickles's line near the two-story frame house of John Wentz, across the Emmitsburg Road from the Sherfy house, its guns directed to the west. The battery was about to be overrun, as were the guns of Captain Nelson Ames of Battery G, First New York, from Captain Robert H. Fitzhugh's Fourth Volunteer Brigade of the Artillery Reserve, and those of Captain James Thompson's Batteries C and F, Pennsylvania Light, from Lieutenant Colonel Freeman McGilvery's First Volunteer Brigade of the Artillery Reserve, in the peach orchard, to the Rhode Islanders' left. McGilvery had directed Thompson's battery up to the peach orchard and placed it in line himself.[25]

Captain Randolph, Sickles's chief of artillery, yelled to the men of the One Hundred Fourteenth Pennsylvania of Graham's brigade in the peach orchard, north of the Millerstown Road: "If you want to save my battery, move forward. I cannot find the general. I give the order on my own responsibility!" Randolph then was shot off his horse with a shoulder wound. Captain Bucklyn, who already had two horses shot out from under him, then went down with a serious wound.[26]

The One Hundred Fourteenth Pennsylvania's commander, Lieutenant Colonel Frederick F. Cavada, was unable to proceed, and he lay in the fields nearby. Command of the regiment fell on Captain Edward R. Bowen, who advanced it alongside the Fifty-Seventh Pennsylvania of Graham's brigade across the Emmitsburg Road and into the fields behind the Sherfy house, momentarily allowing the Rhode Islanders to withdraw the guns, limbers, and caissons that were still capable of being pulled. Even then, forty-one of the eighty-seven horses of the battery had been killed or disabled during the bombardment, and they littered the ground along with the shattered guns, limbers, and caissons of the battery.[27]

It took a mere twenty minutes for that advanced Union line to be overwhelmed. The last of General Graham's regiments to pull back was the One Hundred Fifth Pennsylvania, and it rallied at least eight or ten times before it finally left the field. Withdrawing, those regiments uncovered the left flank of Humphreys's division lined up along the Emmitsburg Road facing west. Confederate batteries then poured a murderous fire into six New York regiments of Colonel Brewster's Excelsior Brigade, holding

Humphreys's left, and the left flank regiments of Carr's brigade of Humphreys's division. Recalled Captain Frank E. Moran of the Seventy-Third New York in Brewster's brigade: "For a few minutes we were in a perfect tornado of bullets and shells from both friends and foes, the open field affording no shelter."[28]

As Barksdale's and Wofford's Confederate infantry lines neared the Third Corps, the artillery fire from Confederate batteries intensified. Countless shells exploded over, in, and among the massed Union ranks, blowing men to pieces and maiming untold others. A soldier in the Seventy-Second New York nearby claimed it was "the heaviest artillery fire the [Third] corps had ever experienced." A private of the Sixty-Eighth Pennsylvania remembered that, like Brewster's regiments, his regiment "was exposed to a terrific artillery fire, the [artillery] battalions of the enemy pouring in a fierce hail of shells." The deafening roar of artillery fire and thick clouds of dark smoke masked much of the scene. "The rebel infantry came rushing at us through the fields west of the Sherfy house," the private recalled, "and once discovered, they had broken through the Peach Orchard and were swarming up the road in our rear." The soldiers in the Seventy-Fourth New York observed the same frightening sight, Sergeant Robert H. Davis remembering: "The enemy [then] charged from [the west], flanking and doubling us up like so many helpless sheep." There, General Graham was wounded in the confused fighting; no one was able to go to his aid because the whole defense line was disintegrating. He would be captured by the enemy.[29]

The soldiers holding the left flank of Humphreys's division could see the Confederates advancing in lines that extended from east of the stone barn of George Rose all the way up the Emmitsburg Road to their left and front. It was about 5:45 P.M. The artillery and small arms fire pelted the Union troops at a constant, unrelenting rate. Recalled one soldier: "All at once our line was swept by an enfilading fire under which no troops could remain and live, and it became necessary to fall back without the range of the deadly hail. We were losing very heavily in our regiment, but fell back in good order, contesting stubbornly every inch of the ground."[30]

Ames's New York battery in the peach orchard was virtually out of ammunition. Four of its guns had been firing toward enemy artillery batteries and infantry formations advancing from the south; two were directed west. Ames could not hold on. Neither could Thompson's battery. Eighteen of Thompson's battery horses littered the ground, dead and maimed. Thompson was able to fire only "a few rounds" when his battery was driven back, losing all the horses of two limbers and one gun. Relief came as Lieutenant Malbone Watson brought his four guns of Battery I, Fifth United States, to a position not far from the peach orchard and opened fire, allowing the weary cannoneers and infantrymen in the peach orchard to withdraw. Ames's men left behind eleven horses killed by enemy artillery fire.[31]

When Watson's battery came into position, it had no support whatsoever. Brought behind the peach orchard salient to buy Randolph's, Ames's, and Thompson's artillerymen and the battered remnants of Graham's brigade time to withdraw, the regulars faced dense Confederate lines of infantry close by and coming fast. Watson's men fired shell, then canister, some twenty rounds, before the enemy was on top of them. The return fire from the enemy ranks was so ferocious Watson's "men and horses were shot down or disabled to such an extent that the battery was [virtually] abandoned." Two guns were extricated. Watson, however, was desperately wounded.[32]

The whole right flank of General Birney's division was collapsing as Meade knew it would. Batteries from Colonel McGilvery's Brigade of the Artillery Reserve, Captains John Bigelow's Ninth Massachusetts, Charles A. Phillips's Battery E, Fifth Massachusetts Light, and Patrick Hart's Fifteenth New York, along with Captain A. Judson Clark's Battery B, First New Jersey, of the Third Corps, perilously clung to positions along undulating ground facing south, extending from just east of the peach orchard to the stony ridge west of the Wheatfield.[33]

Those four artillery batteries faced an impossible situation. As Graham's and Brewster's brigades, and some regiments from Burling's brigade, along with their artillery support, fell back from the Peach Orchard and the Emmitsburg Road, those batteries were without support on their right. Elements of Kershaw's brigade of South Carolinians were directed toward those four batteries and the Wheatfield. Already receiving unrelenting, continuous artillery fire from Confederate batteries, along with intense volleys from Kershaw's approaching infantry lines in their front, they suddenly were also being hit by infantry fire from Barksdale's and Wofford's Confederate brigades on their right.[34]

Horses pulling the limbers and caissons fell in heaps. Colonel McGilvery rode up to Captain Bigelow and told him that "all of Sickles's men had withdrawn and [he] was alone on the field, without support of any kind; limber up and get out!" Bigelow replied that "if [he] attempted to do so, the sharpshooters, on [his] left front, would shoot [all his men] down." Cannoneers tied prolonges to the trails of the guns and to the limbers and then dragged them to the rear, stopping periodically to load and fire the guns when possible. Hart's battery lost thirteen horses and was pulled out.

Clark's New Jersey battery lost seventeen horses. As Captain Phillips was limbering up his six guns, all the horses of his left gun were shot down. The cannoneers pulled the guns to the rear by prolonge. In all, Phillips suffered forty of his battery horses killed. The four batteries were forced to leave four guns behind in the field. By 6:30 P.M., the right flank of Birney's line was nearly finished.[35]

In the Wheatfield, the frenzied fighting continued as Barnes's division of the Fifth Corps, ordered there by Sykes, deployed at around the same time as the fighting reached its height on Little Round Top and Birney's right flank gave way at the peach orchard. At what had been the center of General Birney's division of the Third Corps, General Barnes now directed his two remaining brigades: Colonels Jacob B. Sweitzer's and William S. Tilton's. The first brigade in Barnes's division to arrive on the field, after Vincent's brigade had been ordered to join General Warren, was Colonel Sweitzer's. With only three regiments on the field, Sweitzer was ordered to form a line along the stony ridge on the west side of the Wheatfield, facing west and south.[36]

Colonel Tilton's brigade was directed to the left of Sweitzer's brigade, facing south. General Barnes rode out in front of the two brigades and, after yelling "a few patriotic remarks," led the cheering men through the Wheatfield. As the two brigades advanced, they passed over Colonel de Trobriand's exhausted and thin ranks of men, many of whom were then lying down on the ground, protected by Winslow's guns. Suddenly, the Confederates let loose ferocious volleys and attacked again. Although Sweitzer's and Tilton's brigades held back the attacks, they discovered that enemy forces that had broken through the Peach Orchard salient, namely Kershaw's South Carolinians, were now closing in on them from the west. An aide to Colonel Sweitzer remarked: "Colonel, I'll be—if I don't think we are faced the wrong way; the rebs are up there in the woods behind us on the right!" No sooner than Tilton's brigade faced west to meet that threat than the Confederates in the woods at the south end of the Wheatfield—Anderson's brigade of Georgians—attacked again, striking Tilton's left flank. Nearby General Barnes was wounded, and Colonel Tilton had his horse shot out from under him.[37]

Private Carter of the Twenty-Second Massachusetts in Tilton's brigade described the fighting in the Wheatfield. He recalled "the screaming and bursting of shells, canister, and shrapnel with their swishing sound as they tore through the struggling masses of humanity, the death screams of wounded animals, the groans of their human companions, wounded and dying are trampled underfoot by hurrying batteries, riderless horses and the moving lines of battle, all combined an indescribable roar of discordant elements—in fact, a perfect hell on earth." He recalled his emotions: "the unalterable horror, implacable, unyielding, full of sorrow, heart breaks, untold sufferings, wretched longings, doubt, and fears." He ended: "Nothing could live before such a fire."[38]

The fighting became virtually hand to hand. Sweitzer's brigade put up a desperate fight, now mostly to the left of Tilton's regiments, facing south. The "bullets [were] whistling all the time," wrote Lieutenant John Garden of the Sixty-Second Pennsylvania in his diary, "[Tilton's] brigade [was] driven out of the woods on our right and the enemy flanked us, but we kept our ground until orders came to fall back and then [we] about-faced in order, firing as we fell back, but it was an awful place, many men fell; for a time it looked like a panic!" Lieutenant Garden later added: "The regiment lost four officers killed and nine wounded, 21 men killed and 99 wounded, 75 missing. The brigade—only three regiments—lost 34 officers and 582 men." Although the actual count would be somewhat less, Garden's tabulation reveals how brutal was the fighting. Other brigades thrown into the Wheatfield that bloody afternoon suffered similar losses; some suffered more. Under orders from General Barnes, Sweitzer's and Tilton's brigades slowly fell back; de Trobriand's regiments had virtually disintegrated.[39]

The Fifth Corps regiments thrown into the Wheatfield had done everything possible to blunt the Confederate attack, but it was not enough. They were being fired on from two sides and there were too few men in those commands to handle the attacking forces striking them from the south as well as from the west. Meade would have to send more troops into that "hell on earth" if he was to defeat the attacks or even slow them down.

14

❖

YES, BUT IT IS
ALL RIGHT NOW

Discouraging reports reached General Meade about the fighting in the Wheatfield and from Sickles's lines at the Peach Orchard and along the Emmitsburg Road. The salient at the Peach Orchard had been crushed, and it exposed the right flank of Sickles's and Sykes's troops fighting in the Wheatfield as well as the left flank of Humphreys's troops along the Emmitsburg Road. The left flank of the army was being routed; Meade had little time to address it, and only a few choices. Meade sent a staff officer to summon General Hancock.

In minutes, Hancock reported. Meade was recognizable from a distance because of the large national colors carried by one of his orderlies; those colors designated the location of army headquarters and the army's commander. Meade also tried to stay as long as possible in one location so that all his commanders knew where to find him. The fighting raged across the front from the Emmitsburg Road all the way to Little Round Top. Due to the dense smoke, Meade was able to observe little of it from his position in the field behind the battle lines, but he could definitely comprehend the severe punishment his lines were taking from the flood of wounded, frightened, and demoralized soldiers fleeing to the rear. The remaining two divisions in Sykes's corps were still stretched out along the roads behind the army. Meade ordered Hancock to send a division of his Second Corps to General Sykes. Meade needed a command that could get to the fighting in short order, and it needed to stop or slow down the center of the attack. Once Hancock's mission was accomplished, Meade told him to return for further orders. Hancock saluted and rode off through the dense smoke and deafening roar of the artillery and small arms fire.[1]

Meade then directed an aide, Lieutenant Oliver, down the Granite School House Road to General Slocum's headquarters, requesting reinforcements from the Twelfth Corps. Meade was concerned that the Third and Fifth Corps—even with help from the Second Corps—would not be able to hold the left flank. That act reveals the kind of risks Meade would take on a battlefield. After all, he had already ordered the Fifth Corps to leave the line protecting the Baltimore Pike to reinforce the left flank. Meade would strip more of his forces protecting his line of support and communication to prevent a defeat along the left flank of his army. He would just take his chances and address one crisis at a time. The order was stunning.[2]

When Lieutenant Oliver delivered the order to General Slocum, the Twelfth Corps commander was taken aback. According to Slocum, Meade's order was for him to send to the left flank the entire Twelfth Corps, stripping the right flank—and the Baltimore Pike—of all of its defenders, save the tired and footsore Sixth Corps. Slocum gave orders placing the whole corps in motion. He then sent his adjutant, Lieutenant Colonel Hiram C. Rogers, to General Meade with instructions to inform him that the enemy was in his front, that he deemed it very hazardous to leave the Twelfth Corps entrenchments entirely undefended, and that he hoped Meade would permit him to retain at least a division.[3]

Lieutenant Colonel Rogers soon returned, according to Slocum, saying that "Meade regarded the left as the point of real danger, but if [Slocum] thought it absolutely essential, [he] could retain, not a division, but one brigade." General Greene's Third Brigade of General Geary's Second Division of the Twelfth Corps, which would have formed the rear of the column that was to move to the left and had not left the trenches, was directed by Slocum to remain and extend its lines and "occupy and defend" the front previously occupied by the whole Twelfth Corps.[4]

In the meantime, along Cemetery Ridge, General Hancock rode up to General Caldwell, whose First Division of the Second Corps was closest to the fighting along the left flank, and ordered him to march his command to the left and report to General Sykes. "Caldwell," Hancock said, "you get your division ready." The orders were yelled by regimental and company commanders, and the four hard-fighting brigades of the First Division set out to join their comrades in an effort to hold onto what was left of the center of Birney's division of the Third Corps and Barnes's division of the Fifth Corps in the bloody, swirling Wheatfield.[5]

Probably not far from the position occupied by Meade and his staff, General Caldwell was met by one of General Sykes's staff officers, Lieutenant Colonel Locke, formerly Meade's own assistant adjutant general in the Fifth Corps, who led Caldwell to the position Sykes wished the division to

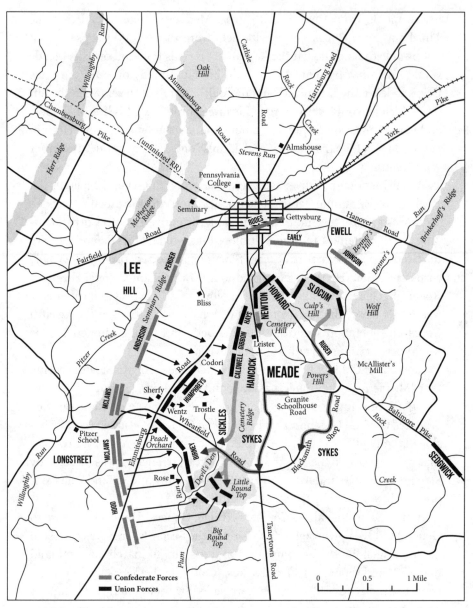

Map 14.1. 2 July 1863, 4:30 P.M. to 8:00 P.M.: Meade fights his battle on the left.

Brigadier General John C. Caldwell. (Library of Congress)

take. The Confederates had nearly overrun the Wheatfield. Caldwell called up Colonel Edward Cross and instructed him to advance his First Brigade into the Wheatfield and toward a wood lot on the left and drive the enemy back. Cross moved his four regiments forward. He then ordered them to halt; they then opened up a "terrific fire" that drove the Confederates back. The enemy, in response, returned continuous volleys of rifle fire. While on his horse, "waving his sword" and cheering on his men, Cross fell mortally wounded, a bullet having pierced his abdomen, passing through his body and exiting near his spine.[6]

Caldwell placed the Second Brigade of his division to the right of Cross's First Brigade. The Second Brigade, commanded by Colonel Patrick Kelly, was known as the Irish Brigade. Three of its regiments were from New York City, one regiment was from Boston, and another was from Philadelphia. Nearly all of the men in those regiments were Irish; most were recent immigrants. The New York commands hardly merited being called regiments: they had suffered terrible losses at Antietam and Fredericksburg. All three were battalions of only two companies each, and all together, they brought onto the field little more than four hundred officers and men. With their rifles at "right shoulder shift," the Irish Brigade advanced as far as it could; the enemy was on its front and flank, only "a few feet apart." "For a moment," wrote one soldier, "it was hand-to-hand." Then they began to fall back.[7]

Caldwell yelled for his Third Brigade under Brigadier General Samuel K. Zook to form behind Kelly's Irishmen. Zook's regiments managed to push back the Confederate columns ahead of them. In minutes, however, General Zook fell mortally wounded. The Wheatfield line was "desperately contested" by the Confederates. So furious was the fighting that the First Brigade of Caldwell's division ran out of ammunition and the Second and Third Brigades were mangled. "Men reeled and fell on every side," remembered a soldier in the One Hundred Fortieth Pennsylvania in Zook's brigade. Orders were given for the brigades to retire, and it was done "generally in good order."[8]

Caldwell ordered his Fourth Brigade, under Colonel John R. Brooke, into the fray. Brooke's brigade drove the enemy back out of the Wheatfield and into the woods on its southern border, but the attack stalled at the base of a steep ridge as Brook was assailed by Anderson's and elements of Kershaw's Confederate brigades on their front and right flank. Caldwell called for support, and General Barnes directed Sweitzer's battered brigade back into the Wheatfield to support the Second Corps division, but

Brigadier General Samuel K. Zook. (Library of Congress)

all of those commands had been severely reduced by heavy casualties and, consequently, could not hold out for long.[9]

Out on the Emmitsburg Road, General Humphrey's line was in peril, even as Caldwell's Second Corps division battled the attacking Confederates in the Wheatfield. General Carr's brigade made up the right flank of Humphrey's division, extending from just south of the Codori house down the Emmitsburg Road to just past the white frame house of Daniel Klingle. Anchoring the right flank of the division was Lieutenant Gulian Verplank Weir's Battery C, Fifth United States, just south of the Codori house. In the center of Humphreys's lines was Lieutenant John G. Turnbull's Batteries F and K, Third United States. Those batteries were from the First Regular Brigade of the Artillery Reserve. On the left of Humphreys's line was Battery K, Fourth United States, commanded by Lieutenant Francis W. Seeley of the Third Corps artillery brigade. To the left of Seeley's guns were the New York regiments of Brewster's brigade.[10]

Meade and his staff had moved up Cemetery Ridge, approaching the left flank of General Gibbon's Second Division of the Second Corps. Meade could see that the Confederate attacks extended all the way up the Emmitsburg Road to opposite the center of the Union lines on Cemetery Ridge. When Hancock reported, Meade ordered him to bring forward a brigade from the Second Corps. Pointing to the fields between the Codori house and barn and the center of the Second Corps line on Cemetery Ridge, Meade commanded Hancock to move forward troops from his corps to those fields so as to connect the exposed right flank of Humphreys's division out along the Emmitsburg Road with the main lines of the Second Corps, some five hundred yards away. Humphreys's right flank was totally in the air. Unless troops were sent to anchor that advanced line with the forces on Cemetery Ridge, Humphreys's line along the Emmitsburg Road would be destroyed.[11]

On Hancock's orders, General Gibbon ordered two regiments from Brigadier General William Harrow's brigade forward to extend into the fields to Humphreys's right. Lieutenant H. L. Christiancy of Humphreys's staff posted the Eighty-Second New York in a line to the right of Carr's brigade, the Eighty-Second's right flank connecting with the Fifteenth Massachusetts in the fields to the right of the Codori house, facing west and northwest. Connecting the right flank of the Fifteenth Massachusetts with the main line of the Second Corps, Christiancy and Gibbon placed Captain T. Frederick Brown's Battery B, First Rhode Island, of the Second Corps artillery brigade, facing northwest.[12]

Meade received word that General Barnes's two Fifth Corps brigades and General Caldwell's four Second Corps brigades, sent to the Wheatfield, had failed to break or even slow down the center of the attacking Confederates, despite heavy casualties on both sides. Even though the smoke on the battlefield was dense, Meade could see that the attacking Confederate lines extended to opposite the center of his defense lines. Only two Second Corps divisions remained on Cemetery Ridge to meet that threat.

Turning to one of his staff officers, Meade ordered him to ride as fast as he could to General Sedgwick and tell him to bring forward the Sixth Corps. That corps, Meade explained, had to be brought into a position where it could respond to crises whether on the far left, in the center, or on the far-right flank. It also meant that the right flank of the army would be stripped of every command, save General Greene's Twelfth Corps brigade on Culp's Hill.

Confederate infantrymen were advancing across the fields from Seminary Ridge toward Humphreys's lines on the Emmitsburg Road. General A. P. Hill's Confederate corps now joined Longstreet's in the attack against Sickles's advanced lines. Out of General Anderson's Division of Hill's corps, the brigades of Brigadier General Cadmus Wilcox, five Alabama regiments, and Colonel David Lang, three Florida regiments, extended the attacks against Humphreys's division up the Emmitsburg Road. To the left of Lang, yet another brigade was forming in front of Seminary Ridge to enter the attack.[13]

With the complete collapse of Graham's brigade at the peach orchard, the left flank of Humphreys's line was exposed, drawing "the enemy's whole attention." Seeley's and Turnbull's batteries opened up on the Confederate lines. Wrote a soldier in the First Massachusetts: "[The enemy] surged in solid masses, only to be hurled back, mangled and bleeding, over the plain again. In some places, they approached so near the batteries that the cannoneers could almost touch them with their rammers before the double-shotted pieces swept scores of them into eternity." Still the enemy columns pressed on, overwhelming Humphreys's regiments. Lieutenant Turnbull's battery fell back with the infantry, suffering tremendous losses. One officer and eight enlisted men were killed, fourteen enlisted men were wounded, and a staggering forty-four horses were killed. Turnbull had to leave four of his guns behind.[14]

Frantically, Humphreys sent aides to General Meade asking for another brigade to bolster his line. Humphreys then received word from General Birney that Sickles had been "dangerously wounded" and that he should "throw back [his] left, and form a line oblique to and in rear of the one [he] then held." Humphreys called for the remnants of Brewster's New

York regiments and the Eleventh New Jersey to form a line facing Barksdale's Mississippi brigade to the south and now Wilcox's Alabama brigade to the west. "All at once," recalled the chaplain of the One Hundred Twentieth New York in Brewster's brigade, "our line was swept by an enfilading fire, under which no troops could remain and live." Humphreys's lines gave way. Seeley's battery remained out along the Emmitsburg Road as long as it could. Already, two of his cannoneers were killed, one officer and nineteen men wounded. Twenty-five of Seeley's horses were killed or disabled.[15]

Meade continued to issue orders amid the overwhelming chaos. He called for Hancock to return. When Hancock arrived, Meade directed him to find yet another brigade from his corps and bring it forward to help hold back the Confederate forces that were breaking through Humphrey's lines and driving through the fields north of the Trostle house and barn. Meade also informed Hancock that he had just learned that Sickles had been badly wounded and taken off the field. He instructed Hancock to take over command of what was left of the Third Corps along with his own Second Corps.[16]

As Carr's brigade withdrew, Lieutenant Weir tried to get his battery out of harm's way. His supply of canister had given out. The enemy was only "a few rods" away, and he ordered his guns limbered up. Only three guns were safely withdrawn; the rest were left on the field because the drivers and horses were all killed or wounded. At the same time, Weir's horse was shot from under him, and as he tried to get up, he was hit by a spent bullet. Still, Weir oversaw the withdrawal of three of his guns. Lieutenant Turnbull was able to get only two of his six guns off the field. Lieutenant Seeley was severely wounded trying to get his battery to fire on enemy infantry that had gotten onto his front and flank. He was taken off the field as his cannoneers tried to fire canister rounds. The infantry having fallen back, what was left of the battery had to retire as well. The Third Corps line along the Emmitsburg Road had completely collapsed.[17]

Meade assessed the deteriorating situation along the Emmitsburg Road. Sickles's peach orchard salient had been crushed, and the enemy battle lines had completely broken Humphreys's division along the Emmitsburg Road. The losses among the infantrymen and their regimental commanders in Humphreys's division was horrific. There seemed to be little in the path of the Confederate lines bearing down on Meade's positions along Cemetery Ridge. More troops were needed to stop what Meade perceived as an imminent enemy breakthrough.

Caldwell's division in the Wheatfield was nearly spent; General Ayres

YES, BUT IT IS ALL RIGHT NOW

finally brought up the remaining two brigades of his Second Division of the Fifth Corps—ten regular United States infantry regiments—deploying them along the north face of Little Round Top, extending from the right flank of Weed's brigade, north, up Cemetery Ridge, facing Plum Run. Caldwell had deep reservations about whether his division could stop the Confederate attacks and, if not, whether he could even extricate it from the Wheatfield. He said as much to General Ayres. Ayres determined to move his two remaining brigades across Plum Run and onto the stony ridge on the left of Caldwell's division.[18]

Although the left flank of General Caldwell's division seemed somewhat secure with the arrival of Ayres's two brigades, the right flank was not; it was being assailed on its front and right flank by enemy troops that had crushed the peach orchard salient. Caldwell suddenly noticed that "all the troops on [his] right had broken and were fleeing to the rear in great confusion." As those troops broke, recalled General Caldwell, "and before I could change front, the enemy in great numbers came in upon my right flank and even my rear, compelling me to fall back or have my command taken prisoners." Caldwell's men fell back "under a very heavy cross-fire, generally in good order, but necessarily with some confusion." Ayres discovered in the dense smoke that "all the troops on [his] right had gone and a large force of the enemy was coming down on [his] rear from the right." Anderson's Georgia brigade and Brigadier General Paul Jones Semmes's brigade of Georgians, from the south, and Kershaw's brigade of South Carolinians and Wofford's brigade of Georgians from the west, had closed in on the Wheatfield. Ayres ordered his two brigades of United States Regulars to "face about and move to the right and rear." They finally rallied north of Little Round Top.[19]

Three divisions from the Second and Fifth Corps had been sent into the Wheatfield by General Meade to bolster General Birney's Third Corps division, only to be shredded or forced to withdraw. From every appearance and report of the fighting thus far, Meade had to have realized that unless something dramatic happened, the whole left flank of the army was going to collapse. He and General Sykes galloped over to be as close to the fighting in the Wheatfield as they could without being unnecessarily exposed to enemy fire.

At the moment of crisis, General Crawford's Third Division of the Fifth Corps moved up the Blacksmith Shop Road and onto the Wheatfield Road that ran north of Little Round Top. The sun had nearly set. Crawford's division consisted of two brigades of Pennsylvania Reserve regiments. They included regiments Meade had himself commanded earlier in the

Brigadier General Samuel Wylie Crawford. (Library of Congress)

war. Recalled a soldier in the Twelfth Pennsylvania: "As we advanced we began to meet wounded men returning. Soon the road was so encumbered with wounded walking to the rear and ambulances going the same way, we had to take to the woods along the side of the road." Incredibly, Crawford's was the fourth division from the army directed to the Wheatfield by Meade. Led by one of Sickles's aides, Captain Moore, Crawford reported to Sykes and Meade. Meade was spotted by some of Crawford's men, so close was he then to the point of attack.[20]

What Crawford could see ahead, through the dense yellowish smoke, was a scene of death and destruction. The troops ahead of Crawford, mostly Caldwell's, had been "unable to withstand the force of the enemy [and] fell back, and some finally gave way." The Wheatfield "was covered with fugitives from all divisions, who rushed through [Crawford's] lines and along the road to the rear." Crawford remembered that "fragments of regiments came back in disorder, and without arms, and for a moment all seemed lost." The enemy's skirmish lines moved steadily through to the eastern edge of the Wheatfield, and the dense lines of the advancing Confederate brigades followed.[21]

In the gathering darkness, Crawford formed two lines of Pennsylvania Reserves in the Plum Run valley, keeping Colonel Joseph W. Fisher's brigade in reserve. Crawford was going into the action with one brigade. The front line was made up of three Pennsylvania regiments, all in the First Brigade commanded by Colonel William McCandless. McCandless's second line consisted of three Pennsylvania regiments, including the First Rifles, or Bucktails. One Bucktail recalled that when he came upon the Plum Run valley and "looked down over the field of carnage, [he] could hear the victorious shouts of the enemy, and when the smoke of the battle lifted momentarily, [he] caught [a] glimpse of fleeing friends and hotly pursuing foes, the general outlook being anything but reassuring." Seizing the flag of the First Pennsylvania, whose color bearer had fallen, General Crawford rushed to the front, yelling, "Forward reserves!" The men moved forward on the "double quick." After halting and firing two volleys, Crawford's Pennsylvania Reserves, "with a ringing cheer," charged the enemy "at a run down the slope, cheering, and driving the enemy back across the space beyond and across [a] stone wall." Along that wall at the eastern end of the Wheatfield, was "a short but determined struggle." To the left of the first lines, Crawford directed his remaining regiments to attack the enemy lines in the valley between Devil's Den and Little Round Top. That last attack appeared finally to blunt the Confederate assaults, the troops of which by then must have been facing a shortage of ammunition and severe losses. Those who remained in the ranks had to have been exhausted.[22]

Northwest of the Wheatfield, Captain Bigelow's men of the Ninth Massachusetts Battery had been pulling their six guns back from their initial position east of the Peach Orchard, firing as they proceeded. One two-gun section on the left had been firing canister at Kershaw's charging South Carolinians; the right two sections had been firing explosive shells at Barksdale's Mississippians, who were bearing down on Bigelow from the southwest and west.[23]

Bigelow's men and guns finally reached the angle in the stone wall at the two-story, whitewashed frame Trostle house and brick bank barn, once Sickles's headquarters. Protected briefly from Barksdale's charging Mississippians by a rise in the ground on the right, Bigelow hoped to limber up his six guns and escape. Just then, Lieutenant Colonel McGilvery rode up and ordered Bigelow to stay where he was; there were no supports, and the area between Little Round Top and the left flank of the Second Corps on Cemetery Ridge was completely unoccupied. Bigelow was ordered to "hold [his] position at all hazards" until that gap in the defense lines on Cemetery Ridge could be filled.[24]

Captain Bigelow had no infantry support. Coming directly at Bigelow's battery from the southwest and west was Barksdale's brigade. The Mississippians were coming fast with bayonets fixed. Only a few rounds of ammunition remained in Bigelow's limber chests and caissons. Nearly half his men and horses had been killed or wounded at their first position east of the peach orchard or along the way to the Trostle farm.[25]

Bigelow ordered his men to roll the guns into position and take all of the ammunition out of the chests and place it near the guns. By the time that was accomplished, the enemy was only fifty yards ahead and poured innumerable volleys into Bigelow's men and horses. The killed and wounded men and horses began to pile up. Bigelow's cannoneers responded, firing explosive shells and then canister into the approaching lines. As the enemy closed in, the left section had to be withdrawn; its position amid some boulders made it impossible to bring those guns to bear on the enemy. One gun was upended by the men while they were moving it over a boulder. Another was driven over a stone wall.[26]

Sitting on his horse, Captain Bigelow was directing the removal of the two-gun section when some of Barksdale's men opened fire. Two bullets hit Bigelow. He fell from his horse but was lifted up on his feet by his men and remained at his post. The charging Mississippians on the right—particularly the Twenty-First Mississippi—were swarming around the re-

*The Trostle house after the battle on 2 July, showing the wreckage of
Bigelow's Ninth Massachusetts Battery. (Library of Congress)*

maining two gun sections. By then all of Bigelow's horses were down. They
littered the ground surrounding the Trostle house and barn. The cannoneers pulled the lanyards and the guns fired double rounds of canister at
the enemy, then only six feet from the muzzles! Some cannoneers were
bayoneted; others were shot down. Bigelow glanced to the rear and saw
the batteries of the artillery reserve coming into place four hundred yards
to the rear along Cemetery Ridge.[27]

Bigelow ordered the cannoneers still standing to get to the rear. Four of
Bigelow's guns were abandoned. Six of the seven sergeants were killed or
wounded. Twenty-eight of the sixty cannoneers were killed or wounded,
and a staggering sixty horses were killed and twenty disabled out of eighty-
eight! The battery had fired three tons of ammunition, including ninety-
two rounds of canister.[28]

Indeed, Lieutenant Colonel McGilvery had frantically assembled an
artillery line about four hundred yards to the rear of Bigelow's shattered
battery, to the left of the Second Corps, on Cemetery Ridge. It was nearly
7:30 P.M. He amassed whatever elements of batteries he could find. What
was left of Watson's United States Battery, Phillips's Battery E, Fifth Mas-

sachusetts, and Thompson's Batteries C and F, Pennsylvania Light, only seven guns, all of which had been dragged back from the line west of the Wheatfield and in and near the Peach Orchard. Those seven guns rapidly opened fire using canister on the attacking Confederates, particularly those concealed in the tall grasses two hundred yards ahead. Soon, Lieutenant Edwin B. Dow brought forward his Sixth Maine Battery of Captain Fitzhugh's brigade of the Artillery Reserve. Then reported Captain James MacKay Rorty and his Battery B, First New York, from the Second Corps artillery brigade.[29]

Farther up Cemetery Ridge, General Hancock rode up to Colonel George L. Willard, commander of the Third Brigade in General Hays's Third Division of the Second Corps, and frantically ordered him to move his brigade by the left flank and come into position "about a quarter of a mile" south of the line it then held behind Ziegler's Grove. At sunset, Willard moved his brigade south along Cemetery Ridge behind Gibbon's lines and the newly formed line of Artillery Reserve batteries. They stopped about five hundred yards east of two Confederate batteries and a column of infantry. It was Barksdale's brigade; it had just overrun Bigelow's battery at the Trostle house and barn. Colonel Willard yelled to his four New York regiments to align in battle formation. General Meade had moved up Cemetery Ridge with his staff and observed Willard form his regiments.[30]

At the command of Colonel Willard, the brigade stepped off from Cemetery Ridge. It was getting dark. Ahead of the brigade was a depression with dense underbrush. Although Willard did not expect the underbrush to be occupied by enemy infantry, it was, and those concealed troops fired on the New Yorkers. Many men fell in the charge. Breaking through the first line of enemy infantry in the underbrush, Willard directed the New Yorkers to re-form their lines. Waving his sword, Willard shouted: "Charge bayonets." As Willard gave the order "Forward," the column, three regiments long, stepped off. They recaptured some abandoned artillery, likely the guns from Turnbull's battery, and then reached a fence line about 350 yards east of the Emmitsburg Road. Suddenly, Confederate batteries in the fields to their left opened fire. The One Hundred Twenty-Sixth New York withdrew with the recaptured guns, but the rest of the brigade continued, crossing Plum Run. Just then, a shell hit Willard, tearing apart his head and face. Colonel Eliakim Sherrill of the One Hundred Twenty-Sixth New York took command and led the brigade forward. The Thirty-Ninth New York was able to recover two of Bigelow's guns from the Twenty-First Mississippi that were left behind at the Trostle house.[31]

Coming off the Granite School House Road and into the fields along the eastern slope of Cemetery Ridge near the Union center were the leading elements of the First Division of the Twelfth Corps led by General Williams himself. Those troops consisted of Colonel Maulsby's First Maryland, Potomac Home Brigade, and the One Hundred Fiftieth New York, under the command of Brigadier General Henry H. Lockwood, along with the brigades of Colonel Archibald L. McDougall and Colonel Silas Colgrove, who temporarily commanded the brigade of General Thomas H. Ruger. It was nearly dark. General Meade saw Williams arrive with his leading regiments and rode over to greet him and the men. Meade then rode at the head of the columns of infantrymen, leading them all the way to Lieutenant Colonel McGilvery's guns. The two regiments formed in line, battalion front, and advanced across the fields for about half a mile, the Marylanders in front, the New Yorkers behind.[32]

McGilvery feared for his line of artillery batteries; they had no infantry support. He predicted the enemy would break that line without the infantry and, in the presence of Meade, who had positioned himself and his staff nearby, asked whether General Williams could bring two of his brigades to the left of Lockwood's Marylanders and New Yorkers to support the artillery line. With Meade's assent, Williams responded in the affirmative, and McDougall's and Colgrove's brigades promptly moved into battle lines along Cemetery Ridge.[33]

Lockwood's Marylanders and New Yorkers, with bayonets fixed, advanced "on the double quick." General Meade was observed along Cemetery Ridge just behind Lockwood's advancing force. The enemy had halted in the yellow sulfurous din. For almost half a mile, the three regiments cleared the fields ahead until they reached the Trostle house and barn. The enemy having given way, three of Bigelow's abandoned guns were retaken. From the rear, Lieutenant Dow sent forward limbers pulled by their six-horse teams so that the guns could be returned to Cemetery Ridge.[34]

Barksdale's brigade advanced about as far as any Confederate command thus far. General Barksdale was mortally wounded and the brigade nearly annihilated. To Barksdale's left, Wilcox's brigade of Alabamians swept through Humphreys's lines all the way to a position near where Barksdale's regiments were stopped, posing yet another serious threat.[35]

There were no other commands coming up behind Ruger's division. Incredibly, General Geary's Second Division of Slocum's corps never reached the left flank. The two brigades General Slocum ordered Geary to march to the left, "by some unfortunate and unaccountable mistake," wrote Slocum afterward, "did not follow [Ruger's] First Division, but took the [Baltimore Pike] toward Two Taverns, crossing Rock Creek." Geary had to have

Brigadier General Alpheus S. Williams. (Library of Congress)

started his columns too far behind Ruger's, and with that, there had to have been a breakdown in the coordination of the staffs of the two division commanders—and those on Slocum's staff—that would have insured that such a serious mishap would not happen. The threat posed by Wilcox's brigade would have to be addressed by using whatever troops were already on the battlefield.[36]

General Meade, while observing these last blows against the left and center of his defense line, called for more reinforcements. As there were no troops behind Ruger's division, he called on General Doubleday's and General Robinson's divisions of Newton's First Corps nearby. Well bloodied on the first day of the fighting at Gettysburg, they had been in a position supporting the defenses held by Steinwehr's division of the Eleventh Corps along Cemetery Hill.[37]

Night was falling, and darkness was setting in. General Hancock observed the threat Wilcox's brigade posed. Behind Lieutenant Evan Thomas's Battery C, Fourth United States, of Captain Dunbar R. Ransom's First Regular Brigade of the Artillery Reserve, brought forward to bolster the left flank of Gibbons's division of the Second Corps, was the First Minnesota. The Minnesotans could see that the remnants of the infantry sent out to halt the attack were being "driven back in some confusion" by Wilcox's hard-charging Alabamians. "What regiment is this?" Hancock yelled. Colonel Colvill replied: "First Minnesota." Pointing to the Confederate lines in the fields ahead, Hancock called out: "Charge those lines."[38]

The First Minnesota dressed ranks and then was ordered to advance. General Meade observed the action from Cemetery Ridge. "Charge!" shouted Colvill. "On the double quick!" The regiment moved straight at the columns of the enemy. Then "[we] poured in our first fire," remembered Captain H. C. Coats. The Alabamians recoiled but then returned heavy volleys. "The fire we encountered," wrote Coats, "was terrible, and although we inflicted severe punishment upon the enemy, and stopped his advance, we there lost in killed and wounded more than two-thirds of our men and officers who were engaged." Colonel Colvill was severely wounded in his right ankle, shoulder, and spine; the regiment's lieutenant colonel and major were also badly wounded. Seven company commanders fell. When the final tally was made, the First Minnesota would record that out "of two hundred and sixty-two men who made the charge, two hundred and fifteen lay upon the field."[39]

The fighting was not over. Out in the fields between the Codori house and General Gibbon's lines along Cemetery Ridge, the Confederate attacks continued. Moving straight at the center of the Second Corps lines was a brigade of three Georgia regiments and a Georgia battalion commanded by Brigadier General Ambrose Ransom Wright. The Georgians struck the Eighty-Second New York and the Fifteenth Massachusetts out along the Emmitsburg Road and in the fields alongside the Codori house. As the New Yorkers and Bay Staters directed their fire at Wright's Georgians, they were fired on by Wilcox's brigade and Confederate batteries. Those two regiments had no support on either the left or the right. In that hideous position, the two regiments were nearly destroyed. As the Eighty-Second fell back, it exposed the left and rear of the Fifteenth Massachusetts. The Bay Staters remained in the fields as long as they could. They finally "retired in some disorder, being pressed so closely that [they] lost quite a number of prisoners, captured by the enemy." Both Colonel George H. Ward of the Fifteenth Massachusetts and Lieutenant Colonel James Huston of the Eighty-Second New York were killed in the action.[40]

Wright's Georgians reached the guns of Brown's Rhode Island battery. All the batteries at the center of the Second Corps lines—Lieutenant Cushing's Battery A, Fourth United States; Captain William A. Arnold's Battery A, First Rhode Island, and Lieutenant George A. Woodruff's Battery I, First United States—fired round upon round of shell and then canister into Wright's depleted ranks. "Will nothing stop these people?" Meade said from his position not too far away. The Nineteenth Maine was then ordered to attack Wright's brigade. The Georgians had almost reached the stone wall on Cemetery Ridge behind which was arrayed Gibbon's division.[41]

As the fighting reached its height along the center of the Second Corps, General Meade was nearby, awaiting, likely with much trepidation, the arrival of Doubleday's and Robinson's troops. He "straightened himself in his stirrups," as did all of his aides, who then got closer to the commander. They "braced themselves ... to meet the crisis." Darkness was settling over the battlefield; that was Meade's last ally. Then Meade heard someone shout: "There they come, general!" Looking to his right, Meade saw General Newton bringing forward the two depleted First Corps divisions on the double quick, their arms at right shoulder.[42]

Meade spurred his horse forward and met Newton and his columns as they turned off the Taneytown Road and into the fields behind Gibbon's division. Waving his hat, Meade yelled: "Come on, gentlemen. Come on!" Meade was exposed perhaps more than was prudent, but not more than the exigencies of the critical hour demanded. To a soldier who commented on how desperate the situation seemed, Meade replied so all around him could hear: "Yes, but it is all right now, it is all right now!" Meade proceeded to lead Newton's troops onto the battlefield.[43]

At that moment, Meade felt a bullet pass through his right trouser leg. He could tell from the sound that it hit the flap of his saddle. Old Baldy came to a standstill; the horse then "staggered a little but recovered." Meade coaxed the horse forward, but he refused, instead lurching to "turn away toward the rear." No amount of coaxing by Meade could get Old Baldy to move. Meade was then heard to remark: "Baldy is done for this time. This is the first time he ever refused to go under fire." General Meade was promptly provided another horse, Blackey, and Old Baldy was led to the rear; the bullet had entered his stomach.[44]

By then, Meade could see that the Nineteenth Maine had swept down on the Georgians, hurling them back toward the Emmitsburg Road. The Maine men moved so far forward that they retook the four twelve-pound Napoleon guns left behind earlier that afternoon by Lieutenant Weir. The guns were sent to the rear.[45]

In compliance with Meade's urgent orders, Sedgwick's Sixth Corps was moving into its positions at dark. General Meade personally ordered Brigadier General Thomas H. Neill's brigade to support what was left of Slocum's corps and Wadsworth's First Corps division along Culps's Hill, on the right flank, where it remained under orders from General Slocum. Sedgwick directed the rest of his corps along the Granite Schoolhouse Road toward the center of the army. Nearing the Taneytown Road, Sedgwick met staff officers of Meade's and conferred with them about the direction of the fighting and the placement of the Sixth Corps. Thereafter, Sedgwick ordered Brigadier General Alexander Shaler's brigade of Brigadier General Frank Wheaton's division to occupy a reserve position along the "left center" of the army to respond to any emergency. Colonels David J. Nevin's and Henry L. Eustis's brigades of Wheaton's division and Brigadier General Joseph J. Bartlett's brigade of Brigadier General Horatio G. Wright's division were ordered forward to positions along the base of the northern slope of Little Round Top, extending their line along Plum Run, north beyond the George Weikert house, led by aides of Generals Meade and Sykes. The lines of the battered Second, Third, and Fifth Corps divisions that had been battling in the Wheatfield had to fall back on these. The Vermont brigade of Brigadier General Albion P. Howe's division, commanded by Colonel Lewis A. Grant, was sent to the far left, along the eastern and southeastern base of Little Round Top to protect the army's extreme left flank. Under Meade's orders, Sedgwick held the brigades of Brigadier Generals A. T. A. Torbert and David A. Russell of Wright's divi-

Harvest of Death. *Dead Union soldiers, probably from the Third Corps, in the fields along the Emmitsburg Road. (Library of Congress)*

sion, in reserve behind Nevin's, Eustis's and Bartlett's brigades to respond to any emergency along the left flank, the center, or the right flank.[46]

The Confederate attacks against the left flank of the army had finally been defeated, but more than twelve thousand of Meade's men and countless horses had fallen in the chaotic fighting. After General Williams placed McDougall's and Colgrove's brigades in position supporting Lieutenant Colonel McGilvery's artillery batteries, he returned to the right of those guns. "It was fast growing dark and the battle was really over," Williams recalled in a letter to his daughters. "I chanced, however, to meet General Meade and a good many other officers on the field and to learn we had successfully resisted all the Rebel attacks and had punished them severely." Williams then wrote: "There was a pleasant gathering in an open field and gratification and gratulation abounded." Williams felt the need to explain his momentary elation at the conclusion of the fighting on the left and center of the army. "One must see these events and anxious scenes," he wrote, "to realize the joy of a successful termination, even of a single day's work, no matter how uncertain may be the morrow."[47]

The assistant adjutant general of the Second Corps, Francis A. Walker, may have best summed up Meade's performance on that extraordinarily bloody afternoon when he wrote: "Few commanders ever showed more resolution in fighting a seemingly lost battle, or stripped other parts of their lines with less hesitation. If one will compare the energy in which this action was conducted by General Meade with the previous experiences of the Army of the Potomac … one cannot fail to acknowledge that never before had the divisions of that army so closely supported each other or been so unreservedly thrown into the fight when and where most needed." Although Meade was the operational commander of the army, he had proven himself to be a fearless tactical commander on 2 July.[48]

For Meade there was little time to recognize what had occurred along the army's left flank, for the roar of heavy gunfire reverberated from the right. Confederate attacks were now directed against Meade's vulnerable line of support and communication, the Baltimore Pike, and he had stripped the forces defending that road of virtually all their strength. Meade had to brace himself again.

15

I SHALL REMAIN IN MY PRESENT POSITION TOMORROW

While the fighting raged on the Union left and center, an intense bombardment of the Union positions on Cemetery Hill and Culps's Hill by Confederate batteries had been under way for more than two hours. Two Confederate brigades were spotted moving out into the fields below Cemetery Hill. They dressed ranks for an advance toward the Union positions on the summit. Those Union positions protected the Baltimore Pike in front of the cemetery gatehouse. On the right of the Confederate attack was a brigade of five Louisiana regiments, known as the Louisiana Tigers, commanded by Brigadier General Harry T. Hays. To the left of Hays's Brigade was a brigade of three North Carolina regiments commanded by Colonel Isaac E. Avery. Both brigades were in General Early's Division of Ewell's corps.[1]

On the left of the Union defense line along Cemetery Hill was the Eleventh Corps brigade commanded by Colonel Harris and, to the right, the brigade of Colonel Gilsa, also from the Eleventh Corps. Harris's and Gilsa's brigades formed the division commanded by Brigadier General Adelbert Ames. Although the number of brigades holding Cemetery Hill seemed impressive, Harris's and Gilsa's brigades were but hollow shells of what they were before 1 July. Colonels Harris and Gilsa had reported to Meade early in the morning of 2 July that their effective strength, combined, was equivalent to the size of two regiments. Beyond their small numbers, most of the troops along Cemetery Hill needed ammunition.[2]

Supporting those two brigades were, on the left of the crest of Cemetery Hill, from the Eleventh Corps artillery brigade, Battery I, First New York, commanded by Captain Michael Wiedrich; on the right, from the First Corps artillery brigade, Battery L, First New York (with Battery E, First New York attached), commanded by Lieutenant George Breck after

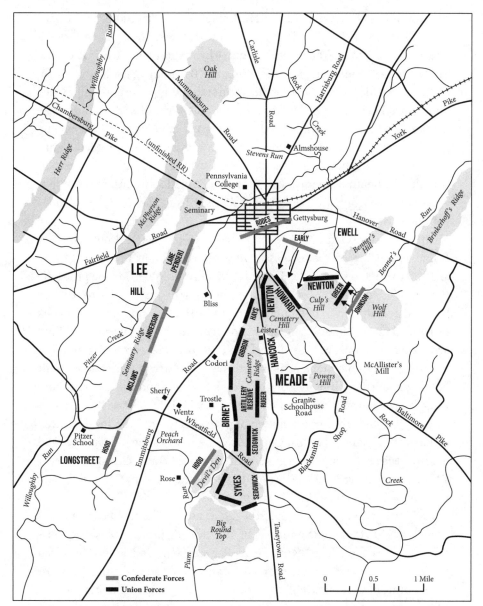

Map 15.1. 2 July 1863, evening: The attack of Lee's army on Meade's right flank.

the wounding of Captain Gilbert H. Reynolds on 1 July; and, in the center of the Cemetery Hill defenses, from the Artillery Reserve, Batteries F and G, First Pennsylvania, commanded by Captain R. Bruce Ricketts. Two more batteries were situated along the Baltimore Pike facing north, from the Artillery Reserve brigades commanded by Captains Elijah Taft and James F. Huntington. It was a formidable array of firepower, but the artillery on Cemetery Hill would not be really effective until the enemy got closer to the crest of the hill. The Fifth Maine battery on McKnight's Hill to the right, however, was in a position where its six twelve-pound Napoleons, behind lunettes, could deliver enfilade fire into any Confederate advance against Cemetery Hill literally from the moment it would get under way.[3]

An aide from General Howard rode up to Meade, still on Cemetery Ridge, requesting immediate assistance. Recalling how few troops Howard had to defend Cemetery Hill and the Baltimore Pike, Meade promptly turned to General Hancock and, for the fourth time in the past three hours, directed him to detach an element of the Second Corps. Hancock ordered General Hays to send a brigade from his Third Division to Howard. Colonel Samuel S. Carroll and his First Brigade were ordered to the right on the double quick. The Eighth Ohio of Carroll's brigade was left holding a skirmish line in front of Hays's division and the Eleventh and First Corps along the west slope of Cemetery Hill.[4]

Believing that there were not enough troops to hold the front vacated by General Slocum's Twelfth Corps, save General Greene's brigade—and hearing the ever-increasing sound of gunfire—Hancock, undoubtedly after conferring with Meade, ordered two regiments from General Webb's brigade of Gibbons's Second Division to the right.[5]

As Hays's and Avery's brigades began to ascend the northeast slope of Cemetery Hill, they came under terrifying enfilade fire of explosive spherical case from the Maine cannoneers at a range of first twelve hundred yards and then eight hundred yards. Avery's brigade advanced toward the summit of Cemetery Hill as steadily as though its regiments were on parade. Stevens's battery fired "the entire contents of the limber chests," explosive shells, solid shot, and canister, at Avery's and Hays's troops, inflicting innumerable casualties. As the assault force neared the summit, they received more murderous artillery and small arms fire. The Louisianans struck Wiedrich's battery on the left of the Union line and were met by "muskets being handled as clubs; rocks torn from the wall in front and thrown, fists and bayonets," so close was the fighting. The attackers seized some of Wiedrich's guns.[6]

Alfred R. Waud sketch of the Fifth Maine Battery firing from McKnight's Hill on the evening of 2 July 1863. Meade observed the fighting from just behind the Fifth Maine Battery. (Library of Congress)

To the right of Wiedrich's guns, Gilsa's brigade extended to low ground not far from Menchy's Spring, just below the Fifth Maine Battery, where the line ended with the Thirty-Third Massachusetts. As Union skirmish lines on the right fell back in places, "clubs, knives, stones, fists, anything calculated to inflict death or pain was resorted to" by Union defenders until the Tar Heels began to fall back. They re-formed, though, and advanced again. Recalled a veteran of the One Hundred Fifty-Third Pennsylvania: "Now advancing, then retreating, this sort of conflict continued for full three quarters of an hour. At one time, defeat seemed inevitable." The Tar Heels reached Ricketts's guns. The death grapple along the stone wall on the left of Cemetery Hill soon extended across much of the Union front. At that time, the Pennsylvania veteran remembered, "our men threw themselves upon the enemy with a resolution and fury that compelled [Avery's North Carolinians] to retire."[7]

As the fighting reached its height along Cemetery Hill, Colonel Carroll arrived with his three Second Corps regiments. The Louisiana regiments had taken several of Wiedrich's guns on Cemetery Hill when Carroll's regiments counterattacked. Although initially halted because of the darkness and converging enemy fire, Carroll's brigade was, in the end, too much for the bloodied attackers to handle; the Louisianans slowly withdrew back down the slope all the way to the foot of the hill. The Fifth Maine Battery's fire into the left flank of the Confederate attack—particularly Avery's brigade—was devastating. Colonel Avery fell mortally wounded, and his regiments were destroyed.[8]

Meade and his staff and aides rode toward the sounds of gunfire on the right. They came to a halt on McKnight's Hill. Meade remained seated on his horse behind and to the right of the Fifth Maine Battery. Through the dense smoke and darkness, Meade briefly viewed the ordeal; he observed the counterattack along the summit of Cemetery Hill that brought the bloodletting to an end.[9]

General Greene's brigade—five New York regiments—were all that remained holding a thin line along the two heights of Culps's Hill. To Meade's right, but out of his view, an attack against Greene's troops arrayed on Culp's Hill was unfolding. Greene's regiments were occupying the breastworks of General Geary's division that had been vacated when the other two brigades of that command were ordered to the left flank of the army. Greene did not have enough troops to defend the breastworks of Ruger's division that had been abandoned when that entire command was ordered to the left. Greene's brigade held the extreme right flank of the Army of the Potomac.[10]

In the darkness, Greene's New Yorkers were assailed by General Johnson's Division of Ewell's corps that included brigades commanded by Brigadier General George H. Steuart, the famed Stonewall Brigade of five Virginia regiments, commanded by Brigadier General James A. Walker, Nicholl's Louisiana Brigade, commanded by Colonel J. M. Williams, and a Virginia brigade commanded by Brigadier General John M. Jones. Those Confederate brigades seized the abandoned breastworks and then concentrated their fire on Greene's regiments.[11]

Greene urgently called for reinforcements from all elements of the Army of the Potomac. Sent by General Hancock, the Seventy-First Pennsylvania arrived on Greene's right flank, but in the darkness, the Pennsylvanians discovered they were too far away to provide the needed support. The attack was so vicious that Greene's lines were in peril of giving way. The Seventy-First Pennsylvania was precipitously withdrawn by its commander, Colonel R. Penn Smith, who feared that the entire regiment would be captured, given its isolated and precarious position. That move left Greene's small brigade to face the attack alone. Greene sent aides back to General Wadsworth, whose First Corps division occupied the west slope

Brigadier General George S. Greene. (Wikimedia Commons)

of Culps's Hill, to Greene's left, with urgent requests for reinforcements, and then to General Howard on Cemetery Hill.[12]

Wadsworth responded by sending to Greene's aid three regiments, all from Generals Meredith's and Cutler's First Corps brigades, regiments that had suffered tremendous losses on 1 July. Howard directed three regiments, all from Colonel George von Amsberg's Eleventh Corps brigade, to hurry to Greene's assistance. Those regiments had also suffered severely on 1 July.[13]

Colonel Rufus Dawes recalled that he ordered his Sixth Wisconsin of General Meredith's brigade into line, facing the front, and yelled: "Forward-run; march!" Down the slope the regiment moved so fast that its sudden appearance in the darkness and through the dense smoke caught the attackers by surprise; the Confederates stood up, fired a volley, but then withdrew down the slope. Two of Dawes's men were killed; both, he recalled, were burned by the guns fired at them, so close were they to the enemy. Before the night was over, the Confederate brigades would attack three more times. Each time General Greene's New Yorkers and their reinforcements held. To withdraw in the face of such gunfire, some of the attackers resorted to stacking the bodies of dead comrades, form-

The defense of Culp's Hill on the night of 2 July 1863, by Edwin Forbes.
(Library of Congress)

ing makeshift breastworks, behind which they found relative safety. The
fighting raged for nearly three hours. Among the wounded in the attacks
was General Jones. When the fighting ended, the Confederates held the
defense works that Ruger's division had abandoned nearly seven hours before. Greene's lines held; their heroic defense of Culp's Hill, aided by the
cover of darkness, proved to be the saving grace for Meade's right flank
and the army. Meade's movement of all of the Twelfth Corps brigades, except Greene's, away from Culp's Hill, could have been disastrous. Greene's
stubborn defense there, though, gave Meade the final victory on 2 July.[14]

As the fighting raged along Culp's Hill, Meade's first act was to send
orders to General Slocum to bring his two divisions back to the Union
right flank and to form along the eastern side of the Baltimore Pike. Slocum responded; over the next hour, General Geary's two brigades of his
division formed on the left, to the right of Greene's battered brigade, and
General Ruger's division on the right, both divisions east of the Baltimore Pike, facing Culp's Hill. There also Slocum directed Lieutenant
Colonel Clermont L. Best of his staff to bring all the artillery batteries of
the Twelfth Corps artillery brigade to the right, where they unlimbered
on high ground west of the Baltimore Pike, facing Culp's Hill, some six
to eight hundred yards from the enemy positions. Likewise, Meade sent
orders to General Sedgwick to be prepared to return to the right whatever elements of the Sixth Corps might be necessary to support Slocum's
Twelfth Corps.[15]

Meade turned his horse around and, with his staff officers and order-lies nearby, rode back to his headquarters. Arriving at the Leister house, Meade could tell that the situation at the hospitals along the Taneytown Road near his headquarters had become frightful. As more and more casualties were brought to them, it became apparent to Dr. Dougherty and to Colonel Batchelder that the Second Corps hospitals had to be moved. Overwhelmed by the numbers of wounded from all the different corps that fought along the left flank and center of the army, as well as Confederate casualties, those hospitals were suffering severe shortages of equipment, medicals, tents, bedding, blankets, and subsistence stores, due to the army's inability to supply the troops at the front by way of the Baltimore Pike from Westminster.[16]

To every one of the hospitals along the Taneytown Road, the wounded and dying from the bloody fields along the left flank and center of Meade's army continued to be brought for care. Lieutenant George G. Benedict, an aide to Brigadier General George J. Stannard, commander of the Vermont brigade in the First Corps, remembered that he "was stopped hundreds of times by wounded men, sometimes accompanied by a comrade but often wandering alone, to be asked in faint tones the way to the hospital of their division, till the accumulated sense of the bloodshed and suffering of the day became absolutely appalling. It seemed to me," he wrote, "as if every square yard of the ground, for many square miles, must have its blood stain."[17]

The chorus of cries from wounded and dying men still strewn across the battlefield, and from every hospital along the Taneytown Road, moaning, groaning, screaming, crying, and uttering the most mournful and hopeless exclamations, was affecting the morale of those troops still in line along Cemetery Ridge. To address that demoralizing problem, Meade called for music. Remembered Captain Benjamin Thompson of the One Hundred Eleventh New York: "All the bands in the army were ordered up and placed between the troops and the hospitals. They played by detachments all night to drown the cries of the wounded and those who were being operated upon." Thompson continued: "They played 'When This Cruel War Is Over' for hours together, and while we sympathized with the sentiment, we execrated the doleful and monotonous music."[18]

Once in the Leister house, Meade dictated a dispatch to General Halleck; it was 8:00 P.M.:

The enemy attacked me about 4 P.M. this day, and, after one of the severest contests of the war, was repulsed at all points. We have suffered considerably in killed and wounded. Among the former are Brigadier Generals Paul and Zook, and among the wounded, Generals Sickles, Barlow, Graham, and Warren, slightly. We have taken a large number of prisoners. I shall remain in my present position tomorrow, but am not prepared to say, until better advised of the condition of the army, whether my operations will be of an offensive or defense character.

Meade could not immediately send the message off to be delivered to the relay riders because gunfire continued on the right, halting the relays down the Baltimore Pike. The Confederates were still too close to the pike.[19]

While Meade was seated at his table in the center of the main room in the Leister house, a group of his aides "came staggering in one after another." Lieutenant Roebling recalled that he "returned to headquarters, too tired to eat, too exhausted to sleep, only to learn that equally severe fighting had raged around Culp's Hill and the Cemetery. We had barely held our own."[20]

Another aide who returned was Colonel Sharpe of the Bureau of Military Information. When Sharpe entered the main room of the house, he observed General Meade seated in front of him. Meade's "chin was resting in his hand, and [he was] evidently deep in thought," recalled Sharpe. One by one, other members of Meade's staff appeared. Everyone, remembered Sharpe, was "covered with dust, and [Sharpe's] face felt as though it had a thick incrustation of mud on it."[21]

A servant, probably John Marley, entered the room and "spread upon the table a few crackers or hard tack, some pieces of bacon, and . . . a little fruit, perhaps cherries," Sharpe recalled. "General Meade looked smilingly although it was rather a dry smile, on our humble repast," remembered Sharpe. Then, "doubtless realizing how worn out we all were," Meade said: "This is one of the occasions when I think a man is justified in taking a drink of whiskey."[22]

Sharpe recalled that Meade was a very abstemious man, rarely drinking any spirituous liquor, and the same was true of every member of his staff. "I will see if there is any whiskey here," Meade said. His servant, John, then produced a bottle of whiskey and set it on the table.

"Colonel Sharpe," Meade said, "Won't you take a glass of whiskey? I think it will do you good." Sharpe replied: "General, I think you ought to take a drink. You need it more than any of us." Meade took the bottle in his hand and held it against the lighted candle on the table to see how much

Colonel George H. Sharpe. (Library of Congress)

whiskey it contained. "There was not enough for one moderate drink," recalled Sharpe.[23]

Taking one last glance at the bottle, Meade replied to Sharpe: "No, I don't think I care for any whiskey. I would like a cup of coffee." When he urged the staff officers to take a drink, all of them refused, although they consumed the hard tack and bacon.[24]

Before Sharpe left, Meade said to him: "I must have more detailed information of the strength of the enemy. Can you get reliable information of the number of troops that were engaged today and whether he had any fresh troops in reserve?" Sharpe asked to be excused and told Meade he would consult with Captain John C. Babcock about the matter. He assured Meade he would return in one or two hours.[25]

Meade sent his staff officers out to all the corps commanders with orders for them to attend a meeting at the Leister house. Generals Hancock and Gibbon were conferring when one of Meade's staff officers approached them; both were summoned to army headquarters. The night was "sultry and starless," remembered Lieutenant Frank A. Haskell of Gibbon's staff, who accompanied his commander to the conference. "The night atmosphere was laden with mist and pervaded by the strange musty smell peculiar to battlefields immediately after battle," wrote Lieutenant Colonel Cavada, whose assigned task was to find and collect as many survivors of General Humphrey's Third Corps division as he could locate. Out in the fields south of the Leister house, the regimental bands continued their music.[26]

When Hancock and Gibbon arrived at the Leister house, they saw ten generals gathered in the room Meade had been using: General Newton, commanding the First Corps; General Birney, commanding the First Division of the Third Corps; General Sykes, commanding the Fifth Corps; General Sedgwick, commanding the Sixth Corps; Generals Slocum and Alpheus Williams from the Twelfth Corps; and General Howard, commanding the Eleventh Corps. In addition, General Warren, the army's chief engineer, and General Butterfield were there, along with Meade. General Hancock arrived as the temporary commander of the Third Corps, and General Gibbon was there as the temporary commander of the Second Corps.[27]

All the generals were dressed in clothes of dark blue. Gibbon recalled that he wore "an old single-breasted blouse with brigadier general's shoulder straps [and] pants stuffed with a long pair of muddy boots and a frayed cap." He then remembered: "I think most of the others were dressed in pretty much the same style." Some wore "top boots." All of them wore

The council of war at Meade's headquarters, 2 July 1863. (Library of Congress)

general officer's swords, but none wore sashes. Most wore black broad-brimmed hats with no decoration save the gold hat cord. General Sykes wore a blue kepi.[28]

The room, recalled General Gibbon, was "not more than 10 or 12 feet square" with "a large four post bed" in one corner, "a small table on one side, and a chair or two." Scattered around the room were about five or six straight-backed, rush-bottom chairs. Generals Meade and Butterfield were sitting at the table. Some generals found chairs; some stood up; others, including Sedgwick and Newton, "lounged on the bed." General Warren, "tired out and suffering from a wound in the neck where a bullet had grazed him, lay down in the corner of the room [at the foot of the bed] and went sound asleep." A handkerchief was tied around his neck to protect his wound. On the table was a "wooden pail of water with a tin cup for drinking," as well as a "candle, stuck to the table by putting the end in tallow melted down from the wick." Some of the generals smoked cigars.[29]

Lieutenant Haskell was struck by the looks of the army commander sitting at the table. He described Meade that night as "a tall, spare man, with full beard, which with his hair, originally brown, is quite thickly sprinkled with gray." Meade, Haskell continued, "has a Romanish face, very large nose, with a white, large forehead, prominent and wide over the eyes, which are full and large, and quick in their movements, and he wears spectacles." Haskell recorded that Meade's *"fibres* are all of the long and sinewy kind. His habitual personal appearance is quite careless, and it would be rather difficult to make him look well dressed." Haskell compared Meade to General Sedgwick, who was lounging on the bed nearby, noting, "He looks, and is, honest and modest," a compliment that truly applied to Meade as well as Sedgwick.[30]

Meade began the discussion by asking each general to report on the condition and position of his corps. Then, each general "made comments on the fight and told what he knew of the condition of affairs." It appeared from the discussion that "the Third Corps had been badly defeated, and rendered, for the time, comparatively useless," remembered General Gibbon. The enemy, he continued, "taking advantage of a portion of the Twelfth Corps sent over to the assistance of our left center after the defeat of the Third Corps [and vacating the defense lines along Culp's Hill] had obtained a footing in a portion of our line on the right." Apart from that, the lines of the army remained intact. The casualties had been devastatingly numerous.[31]

General Newton, it seems, stated that "this was no place to fight a battle in." Gibbon asked Newton, a respected army engineer, about his objections. Newton was uncomfortable with the army's position. His concern echoed that of Meade, Hancock, and Warren on 1 July; the army's flanks could be turned, and the enemy was still dangerously close to the Baltimore Pike, the line of communication and support. Much of that concern, Newton said, arose over the fact that the battlefield had been, in his words, "selected for us." Newton was a practical man, though. "Here we are," Newton said, "now what is the best thing to do?" Everyone in the room appeared to be in favor of remaining in position. General Meade "said very little except now and then to make some comment," recalled General Gibbon. Mostly, Meade listened to the conversation. He never let on to anyone that he had prepared a message to General Halleck that the army would "stay in its present position tomorrow" only a few hours before.[32]

General Butterfield asked if it would be best to formulate some questions, and with Meade's assent, "he took a piece of paper on which he had been making some memoranda and wrote down a question," Gibbon remembered. Butterfield then read the question to the generals: "Should the army remain in its present position or take up some other nearer its base of supplies?" Being the junior member present as Warren had fallen asleep, General Gibbon was expected to answer first. "Remain here, and make such corrections in our position as may be deemed necessary, but take no step which even looks like a retreat," Gibbon said. Most in the room answered in a manner similar to Gibbon.[33]

Butterfield then asked, "If the army remains in its position, should it attack or wait for the enemy to attack?" Gibbon responded emphatically: "The army is in no condition to attack." All the generals agreed. Howard believed that the army should wait until four o'clock the following afternoon and that if, by then, the enemy had not yet attacked, then they should be attacked. Hancock remarked that the only event that would necessitate the army attacking the enemy was if "our communications are cut," a continuing concern of Meade and most of his generals, particularly after enemy forces had seized the breastworks of the two divisions of General Slocum's Twelfth Corps. Sedgwick believed the army should wait "at least one day" before it considered attacking the enemy.[34]

General Birney felt strangely out of sync with the other commanders; his Third Corps had been virtually demolished. Attempting to rally what was left of the Third Corps must have been heartbreaking to General Hancock. Indeed, all of the army's corps, save the Sixth Corps, had been badly damaged. Each commander tried to calculate the effective strength of his corps: the army that boasted of more than ninety thousand effective officers and men on 1 July now had fifty-eight thousand from the estimates of the corps commanders.[35]

The votes having been made and recorded, Meade said quietly: "Such then is the decision." By remaining silent about his own determination to stay and fight it out, Meade allowed his corps commanders to express their resolve to one another and, as a team, determine to hold the line at Gettysburg. Meade was a team player. The Army of the Potomac would remain in its positions from Culp's Hill to Cemetery Hill and down Cemetery Ridge to the Round Tops.[36]

The decision to remain at Gettysburg was very serious on a number of levels. What has never been written about the meeting on the night of 2 July was the generals' discussion of the condition of the army wholly apart from its losses in combat. General Williams wrote to his daughters that the Twelfth Corps had only a single day's rations at Gettysburg; most of the other corps had none. "We had outrun our supplies, and as all the railroad lines which come near us were broken, there were no depots within reach," Williams wrote. The generals seemed to agree at the council of war, Williams noted, that "with beef cattle and flour, which possibly could be got together, we could eke out a few half-fed days." Even more pressing was the problem of feeding the horses and mules, "all which must be fed or the army is dissolved," Williams wrote. Meade had to address the urgent problems of both the lack of subsistence stores and adequate forage for the horses and mules.[37]

Indeed, there had to have been genuine concern among the generals about whether the army could even stay intact. Most of the troops had had nothing to eat, and there were no prospects of anything getting through to them soon. The Baltimore Pike was shut down to large quartermaster wagon trains or mule pack trains due to the presence of heavy Confederate forces holding Union trenches along Culp's Hill. The horses and mules were in worse shape; in one or two days many would become lame or collapse, impairing the army's ability to move at all. Likewise, there was justifiable concern over whether the army had sufficient ordnance. Untold amounts of ammunition had been expended, and much of it wasted and lost, in the past two days of fighting. The army needed to be resupplied with everything.[38]

With the cessation of the heavy fighting on the right flank, the relay riders were called into service on the Baltimore Pike. Still, though, there was repeated gunfire from both sides along that road. While the meeting was in progress, General Meade called for one of his aides. Meade handed the dispatch he had prepared for General Halleck three hours before to the aide with instructions to give it to the first available relay rider and to get it to Westminster and Baltimore, and telegraphed on to Washington, as fast as possible. It was 11:00 P.M., remembered young Captain George Meade. Meade had waited until he had met with his corps commanders before he sent the message to Halleck he had drafted at 8:00 P.M. That message would not be received at the War Department until nearly eighteen hours later, likely evidence of the uncertainties created by the gunfire and the continued presence of the enemy along the Baltimore Pike, the backup of supply trains miles down that road, and the crowding of horses, mules, cattle, wagons, and troops, not to mention the unloading of freight trains and the distribution of vast amounts of quartermaster and subsistence stores to all the corps wagon parks, inside the Camp of Transportation at Westminster and Union Bridge.[39]

Off and on during the meeting, couriers or staff officers would enter the little room and hand Meade dispatches. Meade nevertheless remained largely silent. Gibbon recalled that just before the meeting ended, General Birney engaged General Meade in conversation. Audibly, he heard Meade say to Birney: "General Hancock is your superior and I claim the right to issue the order." To Gibbon, it appeared that Birney had objected to Hancock being named to command the Third Corps. So long as the army was in the presence of the enemy. Meade put an end to the Third Corps, or what was left of it, being led by anyone but a professional soldier.[40]

The meeting ended near midnight, Gibbon approached Meade and informed him of his "doubts about being present," since he was a junior officer to all those at the council of war. Meade liked Gibbon. "That's all right," Meade said, "I wanted you here." The bands continued playing music in the fields nearby. As Gibbon was leaving the Leister house, Meade commented to him that it appeared from the votes in the meeting that the generals all favored acting on the defensive and awaiting an enemy attack. "If Lee attacks tomorrow," Meade said, "it will be on your front." Gibbon asked Meade why he thought that would be the case, and Meade replied: "Because he has made attacks on my left and failed and on my right and failed; now, if he concludes to try it again, he will try the center, right on your front." Taken somewhat aback, Gibbon replied: "Well, General, I hope he does, and if he does, we shall whip him." If Lee attacked the center of Meade's army on 3 July, it would be directed at Gibbon's division of the Second Corps on Cemetery Ridge. That position was less than three hundred yards west of Meade's headquarters.[41]

Born in Philadelphia, Gibbon grew up in North Carolina. He was graduated from West Point in 1847. After service in Mexico and against the Seminoles in Florida, he returned to West Point as an instructor of artillery and quartermaster. There, he wrote a sizable manual of instruction for field artillery. Like Meade, Gibbon had close family members serving in the Confederate armies, including three brothers. After serving as chief of artillery for General Irvin McDowell early in the war, he was made a brigadier general of volunteers on 2 May 1862 and assigned to command what would become known as the Iron Brigade, which he led at Second Manassas and at South Mountain and Antietam. Advanced to division command in General Reynolds's First Corps, Gibbon was badly wounded at Fredericksburg. After recuperating, Gibbon was named commander of the Second Division of the Second Corps. He and Hancock became very close; both of them were liked by General Meade. Both were rising stars in the Army of the Potomac.[42]

As the group of generals and their staff officers were leaving Meade's headquarters, General Gibbon's aide, Lieutenant Haskell, remained behind, talking with some of Meade's aides. He apparently expressed an interest in the whiskey that General Meade and Colonel Sharpe had turned down earlier in the evening. Major Biddle handed the bottle to Haskell, who recalled afterward that he had "a little drink of whiskey."[43]

Brigadier General John Gibbon. (Library of Congress)

It was well after midnight. Skirmishers, and, sometimes, artillery, were still heard, although it was desultory. Those sounds would be heard all through the night. Hancock, Newton, and Gibbon walked their horses through the fields south of the Leister house. Near the small stone farmhouse of Peter Frey, on the west side of the Taneytown Road, still a temporary hospital for Hays's division of the Second Corps, was parked an ambulance from Gibbon's headquarters. Although serving as a Second Corps hospital, the Frey house and yard were also filled with wounded, dying, and dead from the Third and Fifth Corps. There were even Confederate wounded and dying there. Amid the gunfire, the music of the regimental bands in the fields nearby, and the dreadful wails and screams of the wounded from all around the Frey farm and its neighboring farms, the three generals crawled into that ambulance and fell asleep.[44]

Only about two hundred yards away from the three generals, at the Hummelbaugh house, another Second Corps hospital, lay General Barksdale of Mississippi, who fell in the fields between the Trostle house and Cemetery Ridge fighting Colonel Willard's Second Corps brigade. He had been shot through the left breast and his left leg had been hit twice, splintering the bone. He would die there before dawn. Like the Frey properties, the Hummelbaugh house and yard were overwhelmed with casualties from all of the corps that had been committed to the fighting on the left flank, as well as Confederate wounded and dying from those fields. Such was also true of the William Patterson, Michael Frey, Jacob Swisher, and Sarah Patterson farms down the Taneytown Road.[45]

Before Meade retired, Colonel Sharpe returned to the Leister house. Entering the room where the general was still seated at the table, Sharpe handed Meade a report prepared by Captain Babcock of the enemy's order of battle that Babcock had signed for Sharpe. On the evening of 1 July and throughout 2 July, Babcock and other members of the Bureau of Military Information—when not delivering dispatches—had been interrogating prisoners of war, asking their names, regiments, brigades, divisions, and corps, as well as the casualties suffered. In addition, they had been assessing the morale of the enemy.[46]

The report Sharpe gave to Meade read as follows: "Prisoners have been taken today, and last evening, from every brigade in Lee's Army excepting the four brigades of Pickett's Division. Every division has been represented except Pickett's from which we have not had a prisoner. They are from nearly one hundred different regiments."[47]

The intelligence Sharpe provided to Meade was noteworthy. Sharpe claimed after the war that he showed the report to Meade during the council of war and that it convinced Meade to remain at Gettysburg to fight another day. Sharpe even claimed that General Hancock remarked, "We have them nicked," after hearing the report. Meade, however, had already decided to remain at Gettysburg more than four hours before; the participants in the meeting had also reached that conclusion. In addition, no one else who attended the meeting and left a record of the event ever wrote about such an exchange between Sharpe and Meade or of Hancock's remark. General Gibbon and his aide, Lieutenant Haskell, were the only ones, save General Williams, who wrote narratives about the meeting—and Gibbon and Haskell were personally close to General Hancock, even arriving at the meeting with him—and yet they never recorded the Meade and Sharpe exchange or Hancock's comments about Sharpe's intelligence report. That must be dispositive. Sharpe's intelligence may well have convinced Meade that any attack on 3 July would be directed against General Hancock's Second Corps, because Longstreet's corps was holding a portion of the Confederate lines along Seminary Ridge across the fields from Hancock's positions, and Meade knew that Pickett's Division was in Longstreet's corps. If Meade was so convinced, he would have also concluded that Pickett's Division would spearhead the attack.[48]

Meade fell asleep on the bed in the Leister house. It was well deserved. Meade's staff officers, wrote Major Biddle, "from General [Seth] Williams down," went to sleep on the floor. Most of them, like Biddle, did not even have a blanket.[49]

Allen Guelzo claims that Meade called the council of war on the night of 2 July because he may have been "looking for an affirmation for a fall back to Pipe Creek." Dredging up the utterly false allegations made by Generals Butterfield and Sickles before the Joint Committee on the Conduct of the War that Meade wanted to retreat from Gettysburg and even directed Butterfield to draw up plans for it, Guelzo advances that claim even though everything Meade did from the afternoon of 1 July until he met with his corps commanders at the Leister house on the night of 2 July contradict the accusation that he wanted to retreat.[50]

Meade's orders to his corps commanders for forced marches to Gettysburg on 1 July and 2 July, the order of Meade to his topographical engineers to prepare maps of the position of each corps along the defense lines he established at Gettysburg on the morning of 2 July, the orders Meade gave to General Slocum to launch an attack against the Confederate left flank on the morning of 2 July, the establishment of signal stations along every aspect of the defense lines on 2 July, the ferocious tactical battle that Meade directed on the left flank and the center of his lines on the afternoon of 2 July, Meade's orders to move troops back to the right flank of the army on the evening of 2 July, Meade's dispatch to General Halleck at 3:00 P.M. on 2 July, wherein he stated that "I have today, up to this hour, awaited the attack of the enemy, [and] I have a strong position for defense. If not attacked, and I can get positive information of the position of the enemy which will justify me in doing so, I shall attack," and, finally,

Meade's dispatch to General Halleck at 8:00 P.M. of 2 July, written two hours before the council of war, that "I will remain in my present position tomorrow" all completely belie Guelzo's assertion.

Given the desperate and costly fighting on 2 July, it was essential for Meade to consult with all of his corps commanders and for the corps commanders to consult with one another. After all, troops had been shuffled from one flank of the army to the other all through the fighting on the afternoon and evening of 2 July. There was a need for Meade and his corps commanders to discuss the situation of the army and of each corps of the army with respect to the alignment and realignment of troops, as well as the need for subsistence, quartermaster, and particularly ordnance stores. There was also a need to discuss casualties and the effective strengths of each corps after the desperate fighting that afternoon and night. All of that, of course, was what was discussed.

16

TRYING TO FIND
A SAFE PLACE

If General Meade slept at all, he was up early on 3 July, because at 4:00 A.M., the four artillery batteries of Lieutenant Edward Muhlenberg's Twelfth Corps artillery brigade, situated west of the Baltimore Pike, opened fire on the Confederate positions along Culp's Hill. Early on, a Confederate attack against the right flank of the Twelfth Corps was repulsed. Then, reinforced by Shaler's and Neill's Sixth Corps brigades, and two regiments from Wadsworth's division of the First Corps, Ruger's First Division and two brigades of Geary's Second Division of the Twelfth Corps assaulted General Johnson's Confederate division that held the defense works along Culp's Hill it had seized the evening before. The fighting would continue for six hours.[1]

Meade heard the booming volleys of gunfire from the Leister house and received reports of the progress of the attack throughout the morning hours. "Headquarters," wrote correspondent Whitelaw Reid, "presented a busy scene. Meade was receiving reports in the little house, coming occasionally to the door to address a hasty inquiry to someone in the group of staff officers under the tree." Reid related, "Quick and nervous in his movements, but calm, and as it seemed to me, lit up with the glow of the occasion, [Meade] looked more the general, less the student." With Meade was General Pleasonton, "polished and fashionable-looking," and General Warren, while being "calm, absorbed, earnest as ever," was "constantly in consultation with the Commander." Reid continued: "Orderlies and aides were momentarily dashing up with reports and off with orders; the signal officers were bringing in the reports telegraphed by the signal flags from different crests that overlooked the fight. The rest of the staff stood ready for any duty, and outside the little garden fence a great group of horses stood hitched. Reports coming back to Meade indicated a general success on the right flank. The Twelfth Corps regained all the defense works that

286

The repulse of the Confederate attack of Culp's Hill on the morning of 3 July 1863, by Edwin Forbes. (Library of Congress)

had been lost. Once again, the Baltimore Pike appeared to be safe in the area controlled by the Twelfth Corps.[2]

Firmly believing the enemy would attempt to strike the center of his lines, Meade immediately sought to bolster the defenses on Cemetery Ridge. Already in line along Cemetery Ridge was the Second Corps. On the right, in front of Ziegler's Grove and extending south, was General Hays's Third Division. To Hays's left was General Gibbons's Second Division. Brought into the line to the left of Gibbons's division the evening before were four regiments of Brigadier General George J. Stannard's Third Brigade of the First Division, First Corps, all Vermont commands. General Caldwell's battered and depleted First Division of the Second Corps filled the line to the left of Stannard's brigade among the guns of the Artillery Reserve brought there the day before.[3]

Extending from right to left, and positioned in and among the three Second Corps divisions, were four batteries from the Second Corps artillery brigade: Lieutenant Woodruff's Battery I, First United States; Captain Arnold's Battery A, First Rhode Island; Lieutenant Cushing's Battery A, Fourth United States; and, at the far left, Captain Rorty's Battery B, First New York. Lieutenant Brown's Battery B, First Rhode Island, suffered terrible losses on the evening of 2 July. What guns, limbers, and caissons were salvaged by Brown's cannoneers were in place to the left of Webb's brigade and Cushing's battery.[4]

No sooner had the fighting ended along Culp's Hill than Meade sent a staff officer to General Slocum directing him to send all the troops he could spare to reinforce the Cemetery Ridge line. General Robinson's division of the First Corps was ordered by Meade to move into line in reserve along Cemetery Hill; it had been massed in a position to reinforce the Twelfth Corps earlier that morning. The four New York regiments of Colonel Sherrill's brigade that had fought in the fields along Plum Run, north of the Trostle farm, on 2 July rejoined the right flank of the Second Corps the evening before. Two brigades of the battered First Division of the Third Corps were ordered to form a reserve to the rear of the Second Corps. General Shaler's brigade of the Sixth Corps, after fighting with the Twelfth Corps at Culp's Hill, would be directed by Meade to a reserve position behind and to the right of the Second Corps and in the rear of what was left of the Third Corps. Colonel Henry Eustis's brigade of the Third Division of the Sixth Corps was ordered by Meade to move from the base of Little Round Top to the rear of the Second Corps.[5]

Meade was also considering of other moves he might make. What appears to have captured his attention was the possibility of a flanking operation against the enemy's right flank if an attack against the Union center was attempted, knowing that the Fifth Corps and some elements of the Sixth Corps occupied positions on the far-left flank. To bolster the left flank, Meade ordered Brigadier General Joseph J. Bartlett's brigade to support the Fifth Corps. Brigadier General A. T. A. Torbert's brigade of the First Division of the Sixth Corps was ordered to the right center of the defense lines, where it would hold a position supporting the First and Second Corps. Meade also ordered Brigadier General David A. Russell's brigade of the First Division of the Sixth Corps to the rear of the Fifth Corps on the extreme left, in reserve. Accompanying Russell's brigade was Brigadier General Horatio G. Wright, commanding the First Division of the Sixth Corps, who assumed command of that brigade and Colonel Lewis A. Grant's Vermont brigade situated along the southern base of Little Round Top.[6]

As the attacks along Culp's Hill on the right flank were under way, Confederate artillery batteries, across the fields from the positions of the Second Corps along Cemetery Ridge, opened fire. At the same time, Confederate sharpshooters entered the house and large bank barn of farmer William Bliss on the west side of the Emmitsburg Road, directly across from the position of General Hays's division, and opened fire on the Union troops along Cemetery Ridge. Although a Union attack by four companies of Major John T. Hill's Twelfth New Jersey of the Second Brigade of

Brigadier General Alexander Stewart Webb. (Library of Congress)

Hays's division against the Bliss house and barn had been carried out the day before, they were unable to hold the position. The attack was renewed at 7:30 A.M. by five companies of the Twelfth New Jersey, but again, they were forced to withdraw.[7]

General Hays then ordered Colonel Thomas A. Smyth, the commander of the Second Brigade of Hays's division, to send another regiment to take the Bliss properties. Smyth rode up to the Fourteenth Connecticut and ordered its regimental commander, Major Theodore G. Ellis, to send four companies to seize the barn. Led by a captain, they came under withering fire from artillery and the sharpshooters but managed to seize the barn. Major Ellis yelled for the remaining companies of his Fourteenth Connecticut to form battle lines and rush forward. They seized the Bliss house. Once he received the orders to fire the structures, Ellis and his men torched them, and flames and black smoke soon poured out of the house and barn.[8]

At the same time, Confederate artillery batteries opened fire on the center of the Second Corps defense lines, held by the four Pennsylvania regiments of Brigadier General Alexander Stewart Webb's Philadelphia Brigade of Gibbons's division, less than three hundred yards west of Meade's headquarters at the Leister house. It was then 8:00 A.M. General Hunt had come over to speak with Lieutenant Cushing about the location of the reserve ammunition train. General Webb joined the conference. Suddenly, a shell struck an open limber in Cushing's battery. With a deafening report, the limber was blown to pieces, sending flaming fragments into the open chests of two more limbers of the battery. Both exploded. Frightened, some of the horses attached to the limbers broke free and ran headlong across the fields toward the Confederate lines.[9]

Artillery shells shrieked by the Leister house: "One passed not two feet from the door and buried itself in the road three or four yards in front [of a group of aides and reporters]," wrote correspondent Whitelaw Reid. "General Meade came to the door and told his staff that the enemy had our range" and that they should "go up the slope fifteen or twenty yards to the stable." Everyone did as the general asked, but then they came under even more intense fire from enemy guns.[10]

At least eight times, Confederate artillery opened fire on the positions of the Second Corps. The fire was returned by all the Union batteries along Cemetery Ridge. Finally, at about 11:00 A.M., the artillery fire ceased. An eerie quiet settled over the landscape.[11]

The cessation of artillery fire gave troops along Cemetery Ridge the opportunity to cook a meager breakfast; even the officers seized on the moment. In a little peach orchard just west of the Leister house, General Gibbon's staff officers put together a breakfast around 11:00 A.M. on 3 July. Earlier that morning, one of the officers rode down the Taneytown Road with an orderly and "procured" a "few chickens, some butter, and one huge loaf of bread, which was last bought of a soldier," wrote Lieutenant Haskell, "because he had grown faint carrying it, and was afterwards rescued with much difficulty, and after a long race from a four-footed hog, which had got hold of and had actually eaten a part of it."[12]

John, a servant and cook at Gibbon's headquarters, prepared a repast of stewed chicken, potatoes, toast, and butter. Although most of the officers who tasted the chicken stew questioned the age of the chickens and whether the water used to make the coffee "might have come from near a barn," they enthusiastically ate the simple meal. The table was the top of a mess chest. Two stools were saved for the generals; everyone else sat on the ground with their legs crossed "like the picture of a smoking Turk, and held [their] plates upon [their] laps."[13]

General Gibbon rode down to the Leister house and dismounted. Entering the house, he found General Meade "looking worn and haggard." Gibbon asked him if he had any breakfast. Meade said, "No," and Gibbon urged him to come to his headquarters and share his. Meade "at first objected," recalled Gibbon, saying that he must remain at his headquarters, "prepared to receive the reports which were constantly coming in and act on them." Gibbon responded, telling Meade that his mess was close to the Leister house and in plain sight of it, and it wouldn't take but a few minutes to eat what was prepared. Gibbon said that he would leave word with Meade's staff where the general would be. Finally, he urged Meade to eat some hot food because he (Meade) needed to "keep up his physical strength." Meade yielded to Gibbon's urging and rode to the little peach orchard, accompanied by a member of his staff.[14]

There, Meade sat on one of the stools; seated on the other stool was General Hancock. Gibbon sat on the ground. Hancock wore a black felt hat with the general officer's gold cord and an "undress coat only buttoned in the upper front." Soon General Newton arrived with General Pleasonton. They sat on blankets; their aides sat with Gibbon's staff officers. "And fortunate to relate," recalled Lieutenant Haskell, "there was enough cooked for us all, and from General Meade to the youngest second lieutenant, we all had a most hearty and well relished dinner."[15]

As always among army officers, there was banter. With lighted cigars, they first talked of incidents of the fighting the day before and "of the probabilities of today." Then General Newton playfully spoke of General Gibbon as "this young North Carolinian" who "was becoming arrogant and above his position because he commanded a corps." Gibbon quickly snapped back, saying that "General Newton had not been long enough in such a command—only since yesterday—to enable him to judge of such things."[16]

Meade changed the subject, speculating that if Lee attacked his left, he was ready; General Hancock believed that Lee would attack that afternoon, and it would be against the Second Corps. No doubt agreeing with Hancock's speculation, Meade told Hancock that he was returned to command of the Second Corps and Gibbon would retake command of his Second Division.[17]

Meade then turned his attention to the issue of how best to use the Provost Guards of the army. He believed they were all good men, and it would be best to have them in the ranks when Lee attacked, as the skulkers "would be good for but little even in the ranks." Then and there, Meade gave the order for all Provost Guards to "at once temporarily rejoin their regiments." Hearing that, General Gibbon called for Captain Wilson B. Farrell of the First Minnesota, who commanded the Provost Guard of Gibbon's division. When Farrell arrived, Gibbon instructed him to order all his men to rejoin their regiments for the day.[18]

Having eaten and given the orders, General Meade stood up and called for his horse. He bid all of the officers good-bye, mounted up, and rode over to visit the lines of Hays's division. Thereafter, Generals Newton and Hancock left the mess and returned to their commands. Accompanied by General Warren, Meade then rode along Cemetery Ridge inspecting the lines of Gibbon's division, Stannard's brigade, the remnants of Caldwell's division, and what was left of the Third Corps. He passed the long line of artillery batteries from the Second Corps and the Artillery Reserve brought forward the evening before.[19]

Meade stopped briefly at General Sedgwick's headquarters along the north base of Little Round Top to confer with him about preparations for the expected attack in the afternoon. Meade and Warren then rode all the way up to the summit of Little Round Top. Taking out his binoculars, Meade examined the enemy lines; he observed an ever-growing line of Confederate artillery batteries unlimbering out in the fields in front of Seminary Ridge, facing the center of the Union lines, a sure indication of a coming assault. He also surveyed the rough ground west of Little Round Top, spotting Confederate troops. The divisions of Generals Hood and McLaws of Longstreet's corps still held those positions—Devil's Den, the Wheatfield, and the fields just south of the Trostle farm—after seizing them the afternoon before. Any attempt to strike the right flank of an attack against the center of Meade's forces on Cemetery Ridge would have to contend first with the Confederate divisions arrayed along that rough terrain. Meade and Warren raced at a gallop back down the north slope of Little Round Top and headed for the Leister house. Meade knew exactly what the enemy was about to unleash: a relentless artillery bombardment of the Second Corps lines, followed by a massive infantry assault. That is what he had anticipated would occur the evening before.[20]

Lieutenant Haskell was resting on the ground near Generals Gibbon and Hancock in the little peach orchard not far from the Leister house. He looked at his watch; it was 12:55 P.M. Suddenly, from the Confederate right flank near the Sherfy peach orchard, the same grove of peach trees that was fought over the day before, two shots were fired from the guns of Major B. F. Eshleman's Washington Artillery of New Orleans. The shells arched across the sky, hit the ground, and then bounded toward Gibbon's lines. The first shell crashed into the fire pit and mess tins of Cushing's battery, while the second plowed down the stacks of muskets of the Nineteenth Massachusetts nearby. All the infantrymen along the Second Corps lines hit the ground or looked for cover behind the low stone wall that defined the defense lines along the crest of Cemetery Ridge. To the dismay of some of the frontline soldiers, the mess wagons that had finally arrived on the field from Westminster turned promptly around and headed back to the Taneytown Road without stopping to feed the men.[21]

Within seconds, the lanyards were pulled on what may have been as many as 150 Confederate guns. Shells arched toward the Union lines, burst in the air, plowed the earth, and slammed into guns, limbers, caissons, horses, and men. On Cemetery Ridge, all the Union batteries—about 100 guns in all—replied. "The earth shook beneath our very feet, and the hills and woods seemed to reel like a drunken man," wrote Sergeant Frederick Fuger of Cushing's battery. "The splash of bursting shells and shrapnel," he recalled, "and the fierce neighing of wounded artillery horses, made a picture terribly grand and sublime." From his position in the little peach orchard near Generals Gibbon and Hancock, Lieutenant Haskell recalled:

> The thunder and lightning of these two hundred and fifty guns, and their shells, whose smoke darkens the sky, are incessant, all pervading, in the air above our heads, on the ground at our feet, remote, near, deafening, ear-piercing, astounding; and those hail stones are massy iron charged with exploding fire ... the projectiles shriek long and sharp, - they hiss, - they scream, - they growl, - they sputter, - and all sounds of life and rage; and each has its different note, and all are discordant. Was ever such a chaos of sound before.

"Men and horses," wrote one cannoneer on Cemetery Ridge, "were being torn to pieces on all sides. Every few seconds a shot or shell would strike in among our guns, but we could not stop for anything. We could not even close our eyes when death seemed to be coming."[22]

Lieutenant Woodruff's battery in front of Ziegler's Grove was taking severe losses, wrote Lieutenant Haskell:

> The great oaks ... heave down their massy branches with a crash, as if the lightning had smote them. The shells swoop down among the battery horses, standing there apart, - a half dozen horses start, - they tumble, - their legs stiffen, - their vitals and blood smear the ground. And these shot and shells have no respect for men either. We see the poor fellows hobbling back from the crest, or unable to do so, pale and weak, lying on the ground, with the mangled stump of an arm or leg, dripping their life blood away, or with cheek torn open, or shoulder smashed. And many, alas!, hear not the roar as they stretch upon the ground, with upturned faces, and open eyes, though a shell should burst at their very ears. Their ears, and their bodies, this instant are only mud.[23]

When the bombardment began, Meade was in the fields not far from the Leister house, conferring with General Hancock and a group of other officers. With the sound of gunfire and the bursting of shells, Hancock and his staff and orderlies mounted up and rode back down the lines to the left flank of the Second Corps. Meade returned to the Leister house, where Generals Seth Williams and Daniel Butterfield remained with a large number of staff officers and orderlies, along with their horses, "exposed without any particular necessity to the very severe fire." Meade's aides repeatedly urged him to move the headquarters to a less exposed position. Meade refused, claiming that he needed to be where he could be found.[24]

Samuel Wilkeson, a reporter from the *New York Times*, sat inside the Leister house not far from General Meade. Wilkeson's son had been mortally wounded on 1 July commanding a United States artillery battery in the Eleventh Corps. Having first heard a bird "warbling," Wilkeson recalled, "a shell screamed over the house, instantly followed by another and another, and in a moment the air was full of the most complete artillery prelude to an infantry battle that was ever exhibited." He wrote that "every size and form of shell ... shrieked, whirled, moaned, and whistled and wrathfully fluttered over our ground." Every second, two, and often six, shells burst and screamed over or around the Leister house at the same time. "They burst in the yard—burst next to the fence on both sides, garnished as usual with the hitched horses of aides and orderlies," he wrote. "The fastened animals reared and plunged in terror. Then one fell, then another—sixteen lay dead and mangled before the fire ceased, still fastened by their halters." An ambulance sped by through the exploding shells driven at full speed and pulled by a horse galloping on three legs. A shell had torn off one of its hind legs.[25]

It was not only the horses tethered outside the Leister house that suffered. "Soldiers in Federal blue," wrote Wilkeson, "were torn to pieces in the [Taneytown] Road, and died with the peculiar yells that blend the extorted cry of pain with horror and despair. Not an orderly—not an ambulance—not a straggler was to be seen upon the plain swept by this orchestral death, thirty minutes after it commenced."[26]

Amid the pandemonium, a shell tore apart the steps to the Leister house. Another smashed one of the pillars holding up the porch. "A spherical case shell burst opposite the open door, and another ripped through the low garret. The remaining pillar went almost immediately to the howl of a fixed shot that Whitworth must have made," wrote Wilkeson. The bombardment was unrelenting. Shells tore through the two lower rooms of the house. One hit the chimney but failed to explode; many shells rained down, exploding into the yard. General Williams missed being hit by two inches.[27]

All around Meade, his staff, and the orderlies flew splinters of wood and falling tree limbs. Meade himself was nearly hit by a shell as it screamed past him while he was standing in the doorway. He stepped outside and began pacing up and down the fenced yard in the rear, appearing oblivious to the missiles of death falling everywhere.[28]

According to Captain Meade, his father noticed that some of his staff officers and orderlies were "edging around to the lee side of the house, believing they could avoid being in the line of fire." Among them, it seems, were Colonel George Sharpe, General Williams, and Lieutenant Henry W. Perkins, an aide to General Butterfield. Meade took this moment to relate a Mexican War tale. "'Gentlemen,' Meade said, as shells rained down everywhere, 'are you trying to find a safe place? You remind me of the man who drove the ox-team which took ammunition for the heavy guns on to the field at Palo Alto. Finding himself within range,' Meade continued, 'he tilted up his cart and got behind it. Just then General [Zachary] Taylor came along, and seeing this attempt at shelter, shouted, 'you damned fool, don't you know you are no safer here than anywhere else?' The driver replied, 'I don't suppose I am, general, but it kind of feels so.'" One trait that Meade evidently possessed was absolute coolness under fire.[29]

The bombardment proved to be so destructive and unrelenting that Meade finally agreed to move to a barn across the Taneytown Road. "I went into the cellar of our Headquarters," wrote Major Biddle, "with some dozen of our staff, and remained there till the rebels charged on our bat-

Meade's headquarters, the Leister house, showing the effects of the Confederate artillery bombardment, including the dead horses of Meade's staff officers in the fields around the house and in the Taneytown Road on 3 July 1863. (Library of Congress)

teries." Once Meade arrived at the barn, he found it as exposed to enemy fire as the Leister house. While at the barn, an incoming shell exploded after smashing through the boarding, sending fragments in all directions. One of the fragments, a piece of shell about two inches in diameter, hit General Butterfield just below the heart. He was immediately taken back to the Leister house, where he was placed on the bed in the main room. A surgeon was summoned. He was ultimately sent elsewhere due to the exposure of the Leister house to enemy fire. Being informed that the signal officer on Powers Hill along the Baltimore Pike, near the site of General Slocum's headquarters, could readily communicate with the Leister house, Meade agreed to move his headquarters to General Slocum's headquarters at the Leightner house on Powers Hill, leaving a signal officer behind at the Leister house.[30]

When the bombardment had been under way for more than an hour,

Meade sent orders to all the corps, division, and brigade commanders and artillery officers to cease firing in order to save ammunition. General Hunt rode up the lines, also ordering all the artillery batteries to cease firing. In the place of Brown's battered Rhode Island battery, Captain Andrew Cowan brought forward his First New York Independent Battery from the Sixth Corps, placing it in position to the left of Cushing's battery and Webb's Philadelphia Brigade, supporting Colonel Norman J. Hall's Third Brigade and Brigadier General William Harrow's First Brigade of Gibbon's division.[31]

As Meade was relocating his headquarters, the last great drama was unfolding in the fields west of Cemetery Ridge. At 2:50 P.M., more than 10,500 Confederate infantrymen dressed ranks along Seminary Ridge and, on command, stepped off on their march toward the Second Corps lines on Cemetery Ridge at route step, 110 paces per minute. At times, the assault force was hidden within deep swales in the fields and by the dense, yellow sulfurous smoke that hung close to the ground in the still air and eighty-seven degrees' heat. Meade got word of the approaching assault force within minutes after it was spotted by the Union front lines: General Hancock sent Lieutenant Mitchell of his staff to Meade with word that "the enemy was advancing to the assault on my front."[32]

On and on they came. Indeed, as Colonel Sharpe had intimated to Meade the night before, fifteen of the regiments in the assault force were from the three Virginia brigades of Major General George E. Pickett's Division of Longstreet's corps. The rest of the assault force were regiments and battalions from Alabama, Tennessee, Mississippi, and Virginia, but mostly from North Carolina, of Brigadier General J. Johnston Pettigrew's and Major General Isaac R. Trimble's Divisions of Hill's corps. Many of the regiments and battalions in those two divisions were but remnants of what they were before the clash of arms began on 1 July. Nevertheless, the attacking force extended for just under a mile from flank to flank.[33]

With what artillery was still serviceable along Cemetery Ridge, and what batteries were brought to the front from the Sixth Corps, and the Artillery Reserve, a perfect storm of shell was poured into attacking Confederate lines. Men in the attacking regiments were blown out of the ranks, torn to shreds, and dismembered. While inspecting the right flank of the Second Corps, General Hancock became alarmed that some regiments he had posted across the Taneytown Road on Cemetery Hill had left or been taken away. He rode to the Leister house to ask Meade to send troops to that area, but as neared the house he found it deserted and rode back to the battle lines.[34]

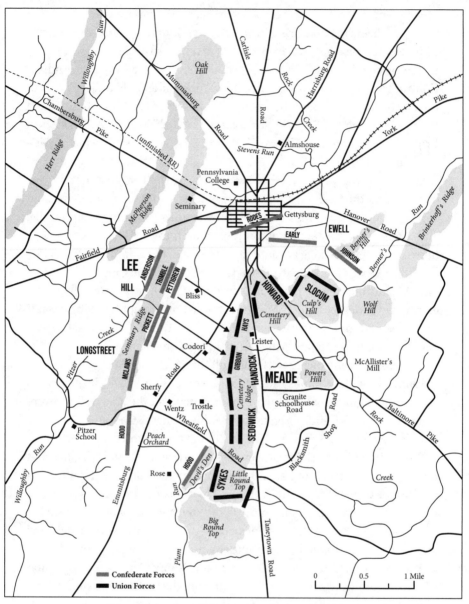

Map 16.1. 3 July 1863, midafternoon: Meade's army
repulses Lee's attack on the center.

Still, on the enemy came, making several "left obliques" before and just after they crossed the Emmitsburg Road and neared the Second Corps defense lines on Cemetery Ridge, allowing them to mass their ranks directly toward the center of Hancock's lines. Looking at the files of infantry coming ever closer to the Union lines, General Hunt, then at the "extreme front," recalled in a letter to his wife, "the display of secesh battle flags was splendid and scary." General Hunt was mounted on his favorite horse, Billy, amid the artillery batteries near the center of General Gibbon's division. "The mare," Hunt wrote afterward, "had already had her throat cut by a piece of shell." The Confederate lines halted and fired volleys of musketry, killing and wounding countless defenders of Cemetery Ridge. So continuous were the volleys being fired into the ranks of the Second Corps that the sheer volume of bullets resembled a hailstorm. "Within a space of two minutes," recalled General Hunt, "[Billy] was shot in the neck, the chest, the left fore shoulder, the right knee, and the head which brought the poor fellow down."[35]

As the Confederate assault force advanced closer, the Union cannoneers loaded their guns with canister. Some guns were loaded with three rounds of the deadly projectiles. At the command "commence firing," the guns were fired "at will," and the canister tore gaping holes in the Confederate ranks. Colonel Franklin Sawyer, commander of the Eighth Ohio in Colonel Carroll's brigade of Hays's division on Cemetery Ridge, remembered the scene, viewed from his position looking down the Second Corps line from the right flank. Many of the infantrymen in the attacking force, he wrote, were "bent in a half stoop as they marched up the slope, as if to protect their faces and dodge the balls." When the artillery opened fire on them, Sawyer recalled:

> Arms, heads, blankets, guns, and knapsacks were thrown in the air. Their track, as they advanced, was strewn with dead and wounded. A moan went up from the field, distinctly to be heard amid the storm of battle, but on they went, too much enveloped in smoke and dust now to permit us to distinguish their lines or movements, for the mass appeared more like a cloud of moving smoke and dust than a column of troops. Still it advanced amid the now deafening roar of artillery and then storm of battle.[36]

Some of the attacking Confederates got over the low stone wall and into Generals Gibbons's and Hays's lines on Cemetery Ridge. They were met with steady, repeating volleys of musketry and then ultimately with clubbed muskets and bayonets. Hopelessly outnumbered and without any

The repulse of Pickett's division on 3 July 1863, by Edwin Forbes.
(Library of Congress)

support, those Confederates were either shot down or surrendered. General Hancock would later note that he could account for thirty-three battle flags captured by the Second Corps there.[37]

As the fighting reached its apex, General Hancock, while riding a borrowed bay horse near General Stannard's Vermont brigade, received a bullet in his thigh, an extremely painful and bloody wound. Assisted from his horse by his aides, Captain H. H. Bingham and Lieutenant I. B. Parker, he continued giving orders while lying on his back, directing regiments to be sent to assist General Webb at the center of the defense line about two hundred yards north of where he was wounded. Before he was placed in an ambulance, Hancock dictated a note to General Meade that read: "Tell General Meade that the troops under my command have repulsed the enemy's assault and that we had gained a great victory." He gave it to his aide, Lieutenant Mitchell, to be taken to Meade.[38]

At the time Meade established his headquarters at Powers Hill, he directed the signal officer there to communicate his arrival to all the other headquarters of corps commanders and to the Leister house. Due to the heavy artillery fire, the signal officer at the Leister house had left. That put General Meade in a most difficult position; he was unable to effectively communicate with anyone at the site of the attack! He quickly mounted up and rode back to the Leister house. Along the way he met several of his staff officers who had lost their horses. Among them was his son, Captain Meade, who informed his father that his horse had been killed. Indeed, sixteen dead horses of Meade's staff officers and orderlies littered the ground around the Leister house where they had been tethered or lay in the middle of the Taneytown Road.[39]

Meade directed his son to take the horse of an orderly and to follow him. Accompanying Meade as well was Lieutenant Ranald Mackenzie. Confederate artillery fire, by then, had largely ceased, replaced by pounding musketry volleys, mostly fired from the Union ranks. Meade rode through a large number of Confederate prisoners who were being directed to the rear. Meade and his staff officers stopped "a little to the right and [rear] of Cushing's battery and about fifteen or twenty yards in the rear of the stone wall where General Hays's division of the Second Corps was posted." The first officer Meade met at the front was Lieutenant John Egan, the left section commander in Woodruff's battery, whose two guns had been directed by Woodruff to assist Cushing's battery that had been virtually demolished by the bombardment. Woodruff and Cushing were classmates at West Point. Cushing had been killed and Woodruff mortally wounded. Just then General Hays rode along the lines, "trailing a rebel flag." Meade asked Egan: "Have they turned?" Egan responded: "Yes. See, General Hays has one of their flags." Meade replied, with some anger: "I don't care for their flag. Have they turned?" Egan then said: "Yes, sir, they are just turning." Egan recalled that Meade was "mighty cross." From the locations of his three headquarters sites, Meade had been unable to observe any of the attack, and he returned to the Second Corps lines because he had lost communication with the front. He had every right to be "cross."[40]

Meade could see the wreckage at the center of Gibbon's division's lines. More than two thousand mangled bodies of Confederate soldiers lay alongside and in front of the stone wall from Woodruff's battery to below the position of Cushing's battery, at the center of the line. Twenty-nine of Lieutenant Cushing's battery horses lay dead; thirty-six were wounded. Seven officers and men in that battery had been killed and thirty-three wounded. All of the limbers had been shot to pieces or exploded, and all of the artillery pieces had been dismounted or the carriages destroyed. The losses were similar in Arnold's and Brown's Rhode Island batteries nearby, as well as Woodruff's battery, in front of Ziegler's Grove, and Rorty's New York battery to the left of Gibbon's lines. The dead and wounded from Webb's brigade and those brigades to its left and right littered the ground. All of it was testimony of the intensity of the bombardment and the savagery of the fighting at the center of that line.[41]

Lieutenant Haskell observed Meade. "He rode up, accompanied only by

Damaged caisson and dead battery horses near a grove of trees, the wreckage of Cushing's battery, by Edwin Forbes. (Library of Congress)

his son, his aide-de-camp and escort, if select, not large for a commander of such an army," Haskell recalled. Meade, he remembered, "was no bedizened hero of some holy day review, but he was a plain man, dressed in a serviceable summer suit of dark blue cloth, without badge or ornament, save the shoulder straps of his grade, and a light, straight sword of a general, a general staff officer." Haskell continued: "He wore heavy, high top boots and buff gauntlets; and his soft black felt hat was slouched down over his eyes. His face was very white, not pale, and the lines were marked, and earnest, and full of care."[42]

Meade rode up to Haskell and asked him in a sharp, eager voice: "How is it going here?" Haskell replied: "I believe, General, the enemy's attack is repulsed." Meade could observe enemy files that appeared to be falling back, but the fields were still clouded in smoke, and gunfire continued. He could not tell what was occurring on the left flank of the Second Corps at all. Haskell repeated that the attack had been repulsed, and Meade uttered: "Thank God." He then waved his hand and said, "Hurrah," so Haskell wrote after the war. Meade's son yelled three "Hurrahs."[43]

Haskell told Meade that General Gibbon had been wounded in the shoulder and that General Caldwell, whose division occupied the far left flank, was in command of the Second Corps. Meade responded: "No matter; I will give my orders to you and you will see them executed." He then told Haskell that "the troops should be reformed as soon as possible and that they should hold their places as the enemy might be mad enough to attack again." He then added: "If the enemy does attack, charge him in the flank and sweep him from the field, do you understand?" Meade then rode away.[44]

Meade and his aides rode over to Cemetery Hill to get a better view of the field. There, Meade was approached by Lieutenant Mitchell, who presented to him the joyful message of victory from General Hancock, as well as the news that the Second Corps commander had been wounded. That was the first word from any senior officer on the battlefield that a "victory was won." After hearing Hancock's news, Meade told Lieutenant Mitchell: "Say to General Hancock that I regret exceedingly that he is wounded and that I thank him for the Country and for myself for the service he has rendered today." On Cemetery Hill, Meade was reunited with most of his staff officers.[45]

While Meade was on Cemetery Hill, he likely received from General Gregg, whose cavalry division screened the army's right flank, the news that a determined attack by General Stuart's Confederate cavalry, spearheaded by Brigadier Generals Fitzhugh Lee's and Wade Hampton's brigades, had been repulsed, Gregg's division having been reinforced by a brigade of Michigan cavalry regiments commanded by General Custer of Kilpatrick's division. The attack appeared to have been coordinated with the assault against the Union center.[46]

Meade and his staff officers and orderlies, joined by Generals Warren and Pleasonton, rode back to the battle lines and then galloped south toward Little Round Top to confer with General Sykes. It was about 4:30 P.M. In the midst of Meade's entourage, the national colors were prominently displayed. As Meade rode by the long lines of the dirty and bloodied ranks of soldiers along Cemetery Ridge, he was cheered by them. The cheering turned into a sustained ovation for Meade all the way down the lines. The Confederate batteries, for a moment, opened a bombardment as what was left of the bloodied assault columns were falling back; some were still firing back at the Union lines. Amid the Confederate return fire, Meade's horse was shot with a musket ball and his son's horse was killed by an exploding shell, the second horse young Captain Meade lost that day.[47]

Meade rode to the left of his line "with the determination," he would later testify, "of advancing on my left, and making an assault on the enemy's lines." Major Generals Crawford, Sykes, and Sedgwick met Meade's entourage, and together they rode up to the site held by the One Hundred Forty-Sixth New York, not far below the crest of the northwestern slope of Little Round Top.[48]

General Pleasonton claimed later that he urged Meade then to "order a general advance of his whole army in pursuit of the enemy." Such advice—and there is a total absence of corroborating evidence that Pleasonton said anything at that moment—would not have impressed Meade, a cold prac-titioner of war. What Pleasonton said to Meade, if anything, is a matter of speculation. Meade did turn to General Sykes and order him to make an "armed reconnaissance" across the ground west of Little Round Top. Sykes thereupon ordered General Crawford to use his division for the operation. Around 5:30 P.M., General Crawford ordered Colonel McCandless, com-manding the First Brigade of the Pennsylvania Reserves, accompanied by Colonel Nevin's brigade and Brigadier General Joseph J. Bartlett's bri-gade, of the Sixth Corps, to move forward.[49]

At the same time, two cavalry brigades, the regular brigade commanded by Brigadier General Wesley Merritt of Buford's First Cavalry Division, and another brigade commanded by Brigadier General Elon J. Farns-worth of Kilpatrick's Third Cavalry Division, pursuant to orders given by General Pleasonton, attacked the Confederate concentrations in the fields west and south of Little Round Top.[50]

McCandless's, Nevin's, and Bartlett's reconnaissance ran into signifi-cant Confederate resistance, mostly the brigade commanded by Brigadier General Henry L. Benning of Hood's Division. The Confederates with-drew, and it became clear that Hood's and McLaws's divisions of Long-street's corps, which had held the area, had fallen back to higher ground along the Emmitsburg Road and were constructing breastworks. To attack those breastworks would have been suicidal. Likewise, any attack would require the entire Sixth Corps, and possibly elements of the Fifth Corps. The brigades of those two corps were scattered all across the Union lines. Indeed, as Lieutenant Roebling recalled after the war, the organization of the army was now chaotic disarray: "Single regiments were scattered about, not knowing where their brigades were. Brigades had lost their divisions. It was essential that this universal mix-up be straightened out. To assemble all of them would take hours, and darkness was approaching." It also began raining that evening.[51]

Merritt's and Farnsworth's cavalry attacks on the left of McCandless's infantry movement were met with Confederate resistance from Brigadier General George T. Anderson's brigade commanded by Major Henry D. McDaniel, but then they withdrew. Farnsworth was killed, and the two

Union brigades withdrew in the darkness after suffering significant losses. Meade abandoned any idea of an attack, a decision that probably relieved Generals Sykes and Sedgwick. He must have understood from observing those two operations that the enemy, though it may have been defeated, was not demoralized; there was plenty of fight left in those troops. Lee's army remained a dangerous opponent.[52]

Meade composed a message to General Halleck at 8:35 P.M.:

> The enemy opened at 1 P.M. from about 150 guns, concentrated upon my left and center, continuing without intermission for about three hours, at the expiration of which time he assaulted my left center twice, being upon both occasions handsomely repulsed with severe loss to him, leaving in our hands nearly 3,000 prisoners; among the prisoners, Brigadier General Armistead and many colonels and officers of lesser rank. The enemy left many dead upon the field and a large number of wounded in our hands.
>
> The loss upon our side has been considerable. Major General Hancock and Brigadier General Gibbon were wounded. After the repelling of the assault, indications leading to the belief that the enemy might be withdrawing, an armed reconnaissance was pushed forward from the left, and the enemy found to be in force. At the present hour all is quiet. My cavalry here have been engaged all day on both flanks of the enemy, harassing and vigorously attacking him with great success, notwithstanding they encountered superior numbers, both cavalry and infantry. The army is in fine spirits."

The message was received at the War Department on 4 July at 6:10 A.M.[53]

17

OUR TASK IS NOT
YET ACCOMPLISHED

Meade was forced to relocate his headquarters again in the late hours of 3 July. The Leister house was overflowing with wounded, as were all the houses, barns, and outbuildings up and down the Taneytown Road. Even though a consolidated Second Corps hospital had been set up along Rock Creek, on the night of 2 July, the hospitals along the Taneytown Road continued to receive casualties from the battlefield. Meade's staff officers found a location for the headquarters "in a little wood" on the Baltimore Pike.[1]

As reported by correspondent Whitelaw Reid, Meade rode up to the new headquarters site, "calm as ever, and called for paper and aides; he had orders already to issue." Then "a band came marching over the hill-side; in the night air its notes floated out—significant melody—'Hail to the Chief.'" Samuel Wilkeson, the *New York Times* correspondent, who was standing nearby, said to Meade: "Ah! General Meade, you're in very great danger of being President of the United States." Then another reporter exclaimed: "No! Finish well this work so well begun and the position you have is better and prouder than President." Meade offered no response.[2]

Meanwhile, Meade drafted the first circular he would issue from his new headquarters: "General Headquarters, until further orders, are established on the Baltimore Pike about a mile below the position occupied by Major General Slocum during the recent engagement as his headquarters." Meade then added: "Corps commanders will send an orderly with the bearer of this circular to acquaint himself with the exact location of headquarters." Although that circular was sent to each corps commander by a staff officer and orderly, Meade would begin sending and receiving messages using the signal station on Powers Hill nearby, weather conditions permitting.[3]

General Meade occupied "a little wall tent," from which he dictated orders and received dispatches. General Ingalls used a "covered wagon" to sleep and write dispatches. The rest of the officers at headquarters, "majors, colonels, generals, and all, had slept on the ground and [in the early morning of 4 July] were now standing about the campfires, hands full of fried pork and hard bread, making their breakfasts in a style that a year ago would have astonished the humblest private in the Army of the Potomac."[4]

Using his writing table in the covered wagon, General Ingalls prepared a telegram to Quartermaster General Meigs early on the morning of 4 July. "The enemy has been defeated," he wrote. "I trust now that the Army of the Potomac may be regarded as capable of fighting. Our supplies are coming up. We marched and fought this battle without baggage or wagons."[5]

General Ingalls was also busy requisitioning horses from General Meigs that day. Read Ingalls's first such telegram: "The loss of horses in these severe battles has been great in killed, wounded, and worn down by excessive work. General Meade and staff lost sixteen in killed yesterday. I think we shall require two thousand—2,000—cavalry and 1,500 artillery horses as soon as possible to recruit the army. Both these arms have done glorious service. I hope you have enough to make up deficiencies." Where all those horses Ingalls requisitioned would be sent would depend on the location of the Army of the Potomac at the time the replacement horses were assembled.[6]

At the time Ingalls wrote that requisition, he could only estimate the extent of the loss of horses in the army. In the months after the campaign ended, a clear picture of those losses would emerge. On 4 July, however, it appeared as though the army suffered the loss of nearly fourteen hundred horses killed. The numbers of horses that were injured, had broken down, or had become unserviceable was not known, although it was probably understood, on 4 July, based on experience, that it would be about six or eight times the number killed. Indeed, by the time the army would conclude the campaign and recross the Potomac River, nearly ten thousand horses would be broken down and unserviceable and nearly two thousand more would be abandoned. That would bring the total number of horses lost in the Army of the Potomac to nearly fourteen thousand, a staggering figure. The officers and men handling horses, whether in the artillery, cavalry, or quartermaster service, could tell on 4 July that most of those animals would likely not make it over the next three or four days.[7]

A low-pressure weather front rapidly moved into the region. On the night of 3 July, the clouds were described by a Confederate officer as "fast scudding." By 3:00 A.M. on 4 July, it started to rain, and as the morning progressed, the rain fell steadily. Just after noon, the rain would fall in blinding sheets.[8]

On the night of 3 July and the early morning hours of 4 July, Lee's army was repositioned. The left flank, Ewell's corps, withdrew from the bases of Culp's Hill and Cemetery Hill, as well as the town of Gettysburg, to occupy a defense line along Oak Ridge and Seminary Ridge all the way to the Fairfield Road on the northwestern and western side of the town. Ewell's left flank was anchored on Oak Hill. To Ewell's right, Hill's corps strengthened its position along Seminary Ridge from the Fairfield Road all the way south to the left flank of Longstreet's corps, held by McLaws's Division. To McLaws's right, Hood's Division extended the line on Seminary Ridge all the way to where it is crossed by the Emmitsburg Road. There the line was refused to protect the right flank. General Stuart's cavalry brigades protected both flanks. The remnants of Pickett's Division were ordered to guard the nearly four thousand Union prisoners at Marsh Creek, well behind the defense lines.[9]

From one end of the line to the other, artillery batteries held positions supporting the infantry. All along the defense line, the troops constructed formidable breastworks made of logs taken from fence lines, and from barns and outbuildings that had been dismantled, packed with mounds of earth. Thick clouds of smoke from innumerable campfires behind the enemy lines hung close to the ground, concealing from view much of Lee's defenses. Skirmish lines were established in the fields ahead of the defense line. In front of that defense line, the Confederates set on fire all the houses and outbuildings on the edge of the town that could be used to conceal Union sharpshooters. At dawn on 4 July, at least twelve columns of dense, black smoke arose from those burning structures.[10]

Having detected Lee's movements, Meade called on General Howard to send elements of the Eleventh Corps into Gettysburg because its divisions were positioned closest to the town. Howard ordered Colonel Harris's brigade of General Ames's division forward into town in the wee hours of 4 July. Joining Harris's brigade was the Fifty-Eighth New York of General Schurz's division. A signal station was established in the clock tower of the Adams County Courthouse on Baltimore Street. Some of the wounded—both Union and Confederate—left behind after the Confederate evacuation of the town were sent to First Corps hospitals along the Baltimore Pike and to the Eleventh Corps hospital at the George Spangler farm, among other sites. Surgeons, nurses, and orderlies were also brought forward to houses and buildings in the town to work alongside surgeons and

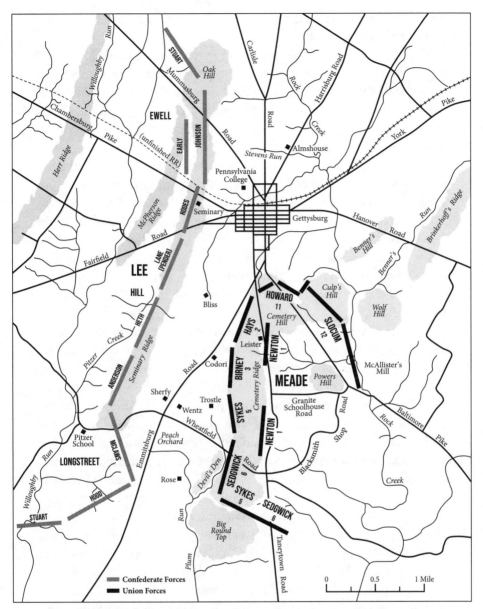

Map 17.1. 4 July 1863: Lee's re-formed defense lines at Gettysburg.

Confederate Forces
Union Forces

0   0.5   1 Mile

aides from the First and Eleventh Corps who had remained behind to care for their wounded on 1 July.[11]

The movement of Meade's forces forward into town and closer to all the newly established enemy positions prompted a vigorous response from the enemy, for Lee likely believed that Meade would launch an attack early that morning. Artillery fire broke out all along the Confederate lines, piercing the dawn with deadly blasts. The smoke hung close to the ground in the heavy, humid air.

The Sixth Corps Signal Station on Little Round Top sent Meade the first indication that elements of Lee's army were on the move. At 6:45 A.M. on 4 July, Lieutenants J. S. Wiggins and N. Henry Camp sent the following: "The wagon trains of the enemy are moving toward Millerstown on the road leading from Gettysburg to the Fairfield Road. Enemy show a very heavy line of skirmishers, extending from our extreme left to the brick house on our right. Look out for our flag." Those wagon trains appeared to have been moving along the Herr Ridge Road, proceeding south to the Fairfield Road.[12]

From 3:00 A.M. on 4 July and throughout the day, Lee was moving his lengthy wagon and ambulance trains onto the Chambersburg Pike and the Fairfield Road. All the quartermaster, subsistence, ordnance, and ambulance wagon trains of Hill's and Longstreet's corps were directed to the Chambersburg Pike from their wagon parks at all the division and brigade hospital sites west and southwest of Gettysburg, using, for part of the movement, the Herr Ridge Road. Hill's and Longstreet's corps wagon and ambulance trains, along with those of General Stuart's cavalry division, would be led west, along the Chambersburg Pike, through the Cashtown Pass, and on to Williamsport, protected by Generals Fitzhugh Lee's, Hampton's, and, notably, Imboden's cavalry brigades. Hampton's brigade was commanded by Colonel Lawrence S. Baker after Hampton was wounded on 3 July. Those wagon and ambulance trains of Ewell's corps were directed to the Fairfield Road, by way of the Herr Ridge Road, from the wagon parks at division and brigade hospitals of that corps north and northwest of Gettysburg protected by Generals Jones's and Robertson's cavalry brigades, then positioned near Fairfield. They would first protect an immense reserve wagon train of quartermaster and subsistence stores that had been parked on the road between Cashtown and Fairfield once it got under way toward Monterey Pass and Williamsport at 3:00 A.M. So long were all those wagon and ambulance trains assembling west of Gettysburg that it would take nearly fifteen hours for all of them to come into line and begin moving up the Chambersburg Pike and the Fairfield

Road. All together, Lee's quartermaster, subsistence, ordnance, and ambulance wagon trains were fifty-seven miles in length.[13]

At 7:00 A.M., General Meade sent his first report of the day to General Halleck. "This morning," he wrote, "the enemy has withdrawn his pickets from the positions of yesterday. My own pickets are moving out to ascertain the nature and extent of the enemy's movements. My information," Meade added, "is not sufficient for me to decide its character yet—whether a retreat or maneuver for other purposes."[14]

At 8:25 A.M. on 4 July, Meade was handed a letter that had been received from the enemy lines under a white flag. Addressed to Major General George [G.] Meade, it read:

> General: In order to promote the comfort and convenience of the officers and men captured by the opposing armies in the recent engagements, I respectfully propose that an exchange be made at once.
>
> Should this proposition be acceptable, please indicate the hour and point between the lines of the armies where such an exchange can be made.
>
> Very respectfully, your obedient servant,
> R. E. Lee
> General

General Halleck had already stopped all prisoner exchanges back on 25 May 1863. Meade had nothing to decide in the matter. He found a piece of stationery, and wrote a response:

> General R. E. Lee,
> Commanding Army of Northern Virginia:
> I have the honor to acknowledge the receipt of your communication of this date, proposing to make an exchange at once of captured officers and men in my possession, and have to say, most respectfully, that it is not in my power to accede to the proposed arrangement.
>
> Very respectfully,
> Geo. G. Meade
> Major General, Commanding[15]

Believing that Lee was then retreating back to the Cumberland Valley on his line of support and communication, Meade sent a dispatch to General French at Frederick ordering him to "proceed immediately and seize and hold the South Mountain passes with such force as in your judgment is proper and sufficient to prevent the enemy's seizing them, to cover his retreat." Meade also ordered French to reoccupy Maryland Heights.[16]

Within three hours, Meade changed his mind. Although wagons appeared to be moving to the rear of Lee's army on the roads to Fairfield and Cashtown, there were no sightings of Lee's troops abandoning the formidable defense lines established the previous night. It appeared to Meade that Lee was luring him into an attack on those defenses. Meade immediately notified General French that, "more recent developments indicate that the enemy may have retired to take a new position and await an attack from us." Meade countermanded his previous order for French to seize the South Mountain passes and reoccupy Maryland Heights.[17]

At noon, Meade apprised Halleck again of the circumstances at Gettysburg. "The position of affairs," Meade wrote, "is not materially changed from my last dispatch at 7:00 A.M. The enemy apparently has thrown back his left, and placed guns and troops in position in rear of Gettysburg, which we now hold. The enemy has abandoned large numbers of his killed and wounded on the field." Meade then presented to Halleck the basic facts regarding any movement of his army that day. "I shall require some time," Meade wrote, 'to get up supplies, ammunition etc. [and] rest the army, worn out by long marches and three days' hard fighting. I shall probably be able to give you a return of our captures and losses before night, and return of the enemy's killed and wounded in our hands."[18]

The two armies were a study in contrast. Lee's army foraged in Maryland and Pennsylvania for two weeks before the fighting erupted at Gettysburg. Although reports received at Meade's headquarters during the early phases of the campaign indicated that large herds of cattle, flocks of sheep, and numerous horses, as well as other quartermaster and subsistence stores that had been purchased, impressed, and confiscated from civilians in those states, were being sent to the rear and across the Potomac River by Lee's army, much of the livestock and stores obtained were kept with the army to feed and equip the troops and feed the horses and mules during the campaign.[19]

As each of Lee's corps arrived at Gettysburg, the divisions of those corps (and, in some cases, brigades) methodically established hospitals two to three miles behind the battle lines. Around those hospitals were parked all the division (or brigade) wagon trains containing the quartermaster and subsistence stores and medical supplies. Also, each division (or brigade) brought its own herds of cattle and flocks of sheep. Thereby, Lee's army was able to feed the troops fresh meat, and feed the horses and mules the needed hay and grain, at sites just behind the battle lines.[20]

Meade's army was less fortunate. When the battle began at Gettysburg, the First and Eleventh Corps were far not only from army headquarters but from the other five corps. All five corps had to be rushed to the site of the fighting. At the same time, under standing orders of the army, those corps had to send all their quartermaster and subsistence wagon trains, herds of cattle, and their medical wagons (except those absolutely necessary for the immediate needs of the troops at the front) to Westminster and Union Bridge. There, twenty-two miles southeast of Gettysburg, was established what became known as the Camp of Transportation. The Camp of Transportation had been established, however, to serve the Pipe Creek line, only seven miles distant. When General Meade arrived on the battlefield in the wee hours of 2 July, the battered First and Eleventh Corps occupied high ground, but the Baltimore Pike, the road from Gettysburg to the Camp of Transportation, ran across and just behind that high ground, causing shipments of ammunition, subsistence stores, forage, and even medical supplies to be halted for much of the time the army held those positions due to enemy attacks and threats of attack.

The contrast was striking. Lee's troops, although defeated on the battlefield, had been steadily if meagerly fed, as had his horses and mules. In victory, Meade's troops had not been fed for days; his horses and mules, likewise, had not been fed. The horses and mules were in danger of collapse. The wounded in Union hands were suffering terribly from the lack of food and medicines as well as tents. Many lay on the ground totally exposed to the driving rain and unable to move. Some were in danger of drowning. They were all too far from the army's base of supply. Given that Meade's army was fighting to defend its homeland, the situation was filled with irony. Such was the bitter fruit of General Reynolds's failed reconnaissance in force on 1 July.

Lee had positioned his army at Gettysburg only nine miles east of the base of the South Mountain range, mountains that towered seven hundred feet above the valley floor. Behind the army were two roads, the Chambersburg Pike and the Fairfield Road, that led across that mountain range, through Cashtown Pass and Monterey Pass, respectively, and directly to Lee's line of supply and communication, the Cumberland Valley Turnpike to Williamsport, Maryland, and the Valley Turnpike in Virginia, across the Potomac River from Williamsport.[21]

Although both armies expended extensive amounts of ammunition in the three days of fighting, Meade had substantial ammunition at, or being sent to, the Camp of Transportation to refill soldiers' cartridge boxes and refill the artillery limbers and caissons, but it had to be brought to the army at Gettysburg all the way from Westminster. Meade was short of ammunition at the front. Unbeknown to Meade, Lee, with characteristic forethought, had ordered a train of reserve ammunition that was on track to meet elements of his army at Williamsport on 5 July, although Lee had not been informed of its whereabouts in more than a month.[22]

On 4 July, General Halleck received from General Haupt a telegram from Relay, north of Baltimore. Haupt wrote that "one of our engines proceeded over the Gettysburg Railroad to within seven miles of Gettysburg where a burned bridge obstructed further progress." He then noted that nineteen bridges were destroyed between Harrisburg and Hanover Junction on the Northern Central Railroad. Half of Haupt's "bridge crews" were sent to Harrisburg by way of Baltimore and Philadelphia to work south—the other half to work north. Haupt claimed that the Gettysburg Railroad from Hanover Junction "is of the very poorest description, with curves of 300 feet radius round which ordinary engines with flanged drivers cannot run."[23]

That was unwelcome news to Meade. Reports on 4 July indicated that there were 14,529 Union wounded in and around Gettysburg, along with nearly 7,000 Confederate wounded in Union hands, many of whom, if possible, needed to be sent to Baltimore or Washington. Likewise, more than 5,000 nonwounded Confederate prisoners of war were in Union hands at Gettysburg. They had to be sent to Baltimore and then to prisoner of war camps elsewhere. All could have been sent by the Gettysburg Railroad to Hanover Junction and then by the Northern Central Railroad to Baltimore, but that was no longer possible. Large numbers of prisoners of war were already on the road to Westminster on 4 July.[24]

With the Gettysburg railroad out of service, the Baltimore Pike was the only means available to get the wounded and prisoners of war to Baltimore. The presence of ambulances and spring wagons filled with wounded, as well as thousands of prisoners of war on foot, on that road would hamper the transporting of ammunition, quartermaster and subsistence stores, and medical supplies to the army. Similarly, the return of empty wagons to the Camp of Transportation at Westminster would also be impeded. On 4 July, hundreds, maybe thousands, of prisoners of war were marched from Gettysburg to Westminster. J. P. Coburn, a wagoner with the One Hundred Forty-First Pennsylvania, was with the wagon trains of the Third Corps at Westminster that day. As the rain poured down, he wrote in his diary, "Thousands of Rebel prisoners has [sic] passed through here today."[25]

Even as the fighting raged on 3 July, Meade's corps commanders sent urgent orders to their ordnance officers, quartermasters, and commissar-

Hanover Junction on the Northern Central Railroad. (Library of Congress)

ies of subsistence for shipments of ammunition, forage for the horses, subsistence stores for the men, and medical supplies to be sent to the front. For much of the morning, though, the fighting along the right flank of the army at Culp's Hill had shut down the Baltimore Pike, the only direct route from the Camp of Transportation at Westminster to Gettysburg. By the end of the day, Jonathan Letterman, the medical director of the army, met with Meade to obtain permission to order to Gettysburg all of the wagons containing tents and medical supplies. At the time Meade allowed only

Marching prisoners of war to Westminster, Maryland, by Edwin Forbes.
(Library of Congress)

half of those wagons forward, so concerned was he then that fighting along the right flank would be renewed.[26]

Getting adequate supplies shipped to Westminster was also a problem. At Westminster, General Haupt demanded railroad trains delivering supplies to the army be unloaded as rapidly as possible, so that they could return to Baltimore to load up again. Those trains were entering and leaving Westminster on the single track of the Western Maryland Railroad in convoys of five trains at a time, one behind the other.[27]

On 3 July, General Meade issued a circular to all corps commanders of the Army of the Potomac: "The Major General Commanding directs that all ammunition wagons be sent to the Depot in the vicinity of Westminster as fast as they are emptied." That the commander of the army believed it necessary for him to issue such an order reveals how much ammunition he understood the army had expended or lost during the three days of fighting and how dangerous that situation was at the front.[28]

That same day, Captain H. A. Lacey, the quartermaster of the Eleventh

Corps at Westminster, sent a message to Lieutenant Colonel T. A. Meysenburg, General Howard's assistant adjutant general: "I find great difficulty in getting forage this morning, not a pound was in the hands of the quartermaster of this station." He then wrote about the transportation of the Fifth Corps being nearby and that he could "only obtain today one day's forage for the animals that are entirely out." He reassured his corps commander that the chief quartermaster at Westminster "is doing all he can to obtain a sufficient supply." When the Baltimore Pike reopened after the fighting ceased at Gettysburg on the afternoon of 3 July, Captain Lacey, under orders from General Ingalls, finally sent forage to the Eleventh Corps by means of mule pack trains. All the other corps quartermasters in the army sent to their corps that day what supplies of forage they could get by mule pack trains as well. Those trains were slow moving; they would not arrive at Gettysburg until long after dark.[29]

By 4 July, the situation at Westminster had somewhat improved, although the drenching rains created problems transporting the supplies to Gettysburg. At Gettysburg, the situation was grim. General Patrick went "down to the front" from his headquarters on the Baltimore Pike that morning. There, he penned in his diary: "Everybody was without anything to eat and waiting for subsistence." Even General Hunt wrote to his wife, Mary, on 4 July: "I will take good care of myself hereafter, am pretty well, but very hungry. Our supplies are out, but I will buy a breakfast somewhere." General Doubleday's aide, Major Jacob F. Slagle, wrote to his brother that he nothing to eat on 1 July and nothing to eat "except a few broken crackers" from 1 July until 4 July. Luther Furst of the Thirty-Ninth Pennsylvania may have summed up the problem best when he wrote in his diary on 4 July: "Our rations were out two days ago and we have not been able to draw any. Last night I picked up a beef bone which served for my supper."[30]

Back at Westminster, Captain Lacey was able to forward to the Eleventh Corps fifteen thousand pounds of forage and two days' supply of grain by wagons early on 4 July. He made no mention of forwarding subsistence stores for the men, however, as feeding the horses at that moment was of paramount importance. Lacey gave explicit instructions as to how each wagon train must proceed to Gettysburg. "On the march," he wrote that day, "Quartermasters of the Divisions must remain at the head of [their] Division [trains]; Brigade Quartermasters at the head of their Brigade trains, and Regimental Quartermasters at the head of the trains of their respective Regiments, unless circumstances may require their temporary presence along the line of their trains." He then added that the sergeants

Supply Train, *by Edwin Forbes. (Library of Congress)*

must always "remain at the rear of the Regimental train, and the Chief Quartermaster of the Corps may be found at all times at the head of the Corps train." Those orders also applied to quartermasters leading mule pack trains. The same instructions were given by the chief quartermaster of each corps in the army to all their subordinates.[31]

Later in the day the situation substantially improved, even with the continuous, drenching rainfall. Captain Lacey was able to send to the Eleventh Corps at the front on the afternoon of 4 July "forty thousand pounds of forage, being two days rations for the Corps animals in the Ammunition Train, Artillery and Staff horses—four thousand pounds was to report to General Howard's headquarters." He then added: "I also sent forward, in obedience to orders of Med[ical] Director, the Medical Wagons and Commissary Wagons for only to Officers." Still, there were no subsistence stores shipped to the troops. All seven corps in the army, and the cavalry corps, likely received shipments similar to those sent to the Eleventh Corps. Thus, over 350,000 pounds of forage alone was sent up the Baltimore Pike to Gettysburg by means of pack mule and wagon trains to feed the army's horses on 4 July. That same day, Colonel Henry F. Clark, the chief commissary of the army, managed to bring up to Gettysburg from Westminster thirty thousand rations to be delivered to the hospitals, but most of the frontline soldiers received little until after the forage and hospital rations were delivered.[32]

The quartermasters and ordnance officers of all seven infantry corps in the Army of the Potomac, as well as the cavalry corps, were sending mule pack and wagon trains forward to Gettysburg from Westminster all through the day and night. Along with those mule pack and wagon trains were, eventually, uncountable head of cattle. The amount of forage, subsistence stores, and ammunition needed by the army was astonishing. Those mule pack trains and wagon trains stretched the entire length of the Baltimore Pike from Westminster to Gettysburg, twenty-two miles, and even then, there were an equal number of miles of all kinds of trains waiting to get on the road at any given time. The mule pack trains and wagon trains and herds of cattle heading to Gettysburg had to occupy one side of the Baltimore Pike, and the empty mule pack trains and wagon trains, along with ambulance trains of wounded and large groups of prisoners of war on foot heading to Westminster, had to occupy the other side of the road, in order for the mule pack trains and wagon trains heading to Gettysburg to move as rapidly as possible.

Help transporting the wounded came from the Adams Express Company, the same business that operated the horse relays between Gettysburg and Baltimore. The superintendent of the company, S. M. Shoemaker, wrote to Secretary of War Stanton on 4 July proposing the Adams Express Company to organize a "hospital corps" to bring "food and comforts to the front" along with "spring wagons to bring the wounded." Stanton notified Shoemaker at 5:25 P.M. that day that the proposal was "heartily approved." General Haupt was "instructed to furnish such transportation by rail as he can without interfering with the transportation of any supplies." Stanton admonished Shoemaker that his wagons must be sent to Westminster by "the common road" and that the Army of the Potomac has "1,100 ambulances with from two to four horses each 'that his men can use.'"[33]

At Westminster, General Haupt demanded that railroad trains delivering supplies to the army be unloaded as rapidly as possible, so that they could return to Baltimore to load up again. Those trains were entering and leaving Westminster on the single track of the Western Railroad in convoys of five trains at a time, one behind the other, at intervals of eight hours. Haupt managed to get fifteen trains per day operating each way between Baltimore and Westminster. That meant that Haupt was able to pass 140 cars per day each way, carrying two to four thousand wounded with each trip. Haupt projected that "by 11 o'clock" P.M. on 4 July, "about

2,000 tons of supplies should have been forwarded, since yesterday morning, to Meade's army." Haupt arranged for fifteen hundred tons of supplies to be delivered to Westminster per day on the Western Maryland Railroad.[34]

At his headquarters along the Baltimore Pike at Gettysburg, Meade sat down with General Seth Williams and prepared a general order for the army at 4:15 P.M. on 4 July. Over the signature of General Williams, Meade's order read:

> The commanding general, in behalf of the country, thanks the Army of the Potomac for the glorious result of the recent operations.
>
> An enemy, superior in numbers, and flushed with the pride of a successful invasion, attempted to overcome and destroy this army. Utterly baffled and defeated, he has now withdrawn from the contest. The privations and fatigue the army has endured, and the heroic courage and gallantry it has displayed, will be matters of history, to be ever remembered.
>
> Our task is not yet accomplished, and the commanding general looks to the army for greater efforts to drive from our soil every vestige of the presence of the invader.
>
> It is right and proper that we should, on all suitable occasions, return our grateful thanks to the Almighty Disposer of events, that in the goodness of His providence He has thought fit to give victory to the cause of the just.[35]

Ever since the fighting ended on 3 July, every corps in the Army of the Potomac had been engaged in the grisly task of burying their dead. According to the official return of casualties, 3,155 of Meade's officers and men had been killed in the fighting. On 4 July, Meade, by circular, ordered all of his corps commanders to detail burial parties "to bury all the enemy's dead in the vicinity of their lines." They were also ordered to keep "correct accounts of the numbers buried" and report them "through corps headquarters, to the assistant adjutant general." The order further directed that all arms and accoutrements collected be turned into the ordnance officers, along with detailed reports of "the numbers and kinds of each." Meade, in a second circular, ordered his corps commanders to "report the present position of the troops under their command and their immediate front, location, etc., amount of supplies on hand and the condition of them." Then Meade wrote: "The intention of the major general commanding is not to make any present move, but to refit and rest today. The opportunity must be made use of to get the commands well in hand, and ready for such duties as the general may direct. The lines as held are not to be changed without orders, the skirmishers being simply advanced, according to instructions given, to find and report the position and lines of the enemy."[36]

Meade had to find a way to exploit the major victory on the battlefield his generalship obtained for the Army of the Potomac. The question was not as easily answered as one might expect. Before he could even contemplate a pursuit of Lee's army, he had to make sure it was, in fact, retreating rather than lying in wait along Seminary Ridge, luring Meade to attack.

Meade had studied military strategy and tactics under Dennis Hart Mahan at West Point. Mahan was a disciple of Clausewitz. Meade, a linguist as well as a scholar of strategy and tactics—and as a former student of Dennis Hart Mahan—was well acquainted with Clausewitz's teachings, including those relating to the pursuit of a defeated enemy. Meade was well equipped to meet the challenge after Gettysburg.

Both of the contending armies, Clausewitz writes, "are already physically tired when they go into battle, since the movements directly preceding an engagement are usually of a strenuous kind. A prototypical struggle on the battlefield," he continues, "calls for exertions that complete the exhaustion." Meade and his army were living those words. Clausewitz then notes: "Moreover, the winning side is in almost as much disorder and confusion as the losers, and will, therefore, have to pause so that order can be restored, stragglers collected, and ammunition distributed." He continues:

> Each of the thousands [of] men under [the general's] command needs food and rest and longs for nothing so much as a few hours free of danger and fatigue. The voices of [those thousands of men] is what is heard in the general's council; it is conducted up a channel of senior officers who urge these human needs on the general's sympathy. The general's own energies have been sapped by mental and physical exhaustion, and so it happens that for purely human reasons less is achieved than is possible.[37]

Meade had just fought and won the largest and most costly land battle ever fought on the North American continent, and his army needed food and rest as well as reorganizing.

The manner of the pursuit of the enemy presented to Meade yet another question. According to Clausewitz, there are "three gradations" of pursuing an enemy after it has been defeated on the battlefield. "The first," he writes, "consists of merely following the enemy; the second in exerting pressure on him; and the third, in a parallel march to cut him off." Jomini offers similar theories on pursuing a defeated enemy.[38]

Clausewitz cautions against merely pursuing a defeated enemy. "This kind of pursuit would suffice to exhaust the effect of the superiority gained in the battle. In addition, the victor will capture everything the loser cannot take with him: sick and wounded, stragglers, baggage, and wagons of all kinds." Arguing against a direct pursuit, Clausewitz writes, "In itself, however, merely following the enemy will not accelerate the break up of [the enemy's] forces, while pressure and parallel marches will."[39]

Clausewitz cautions against ever following a defeated army through mountains. Pursuing Lee's defeated army into the mountains, like the South Mountain range, would inevitably lead to the loss of all that Meade's victory had gained. Lee's army would have the advantage of high ground with every attack, and small elements of Lee's defeated army could, in the mountains, hold back much larger commands of Meade's on the narrow roads that Meade's troops would have to use in pursuit. In addition, the pressure of flanking operations, particularly the use of cavalry, in such a pursuit through mountain passes would have been severely restricted.[40]

"Finally," writes Clausewitz, "the third and most effective degree of pursuit takes the form of marching parallel with the enemy toward the immediate goal of his retreat." Every defeated army has an "immediate goal for his retreat," Clausewitz notes. That may be because the site is where the defeated army will have to cross a river or where it might expect reinforcements. In any event, a pursuit along a parallel course may prompt the defeated force to speed up the retreat, a result the victorious army would wish to see happen, because the faster a retreating army moves, the more it suffers disintegration.[41]

If Meade could ascertain that Lee was truly retreating rather than luring the Army of the Potomac to attack, he knew that Lee would retreat on his lines of communication and support and that the "immediate goal" would have to be Williamsport on the Potomac River. If Meade knew Lee was retreating, he would not directly pursue Lee's army through the South Mountain range; his only means of pursuit would be on a parallel course. Such a pursuit would also place Meade's army in position to continue to cover Baltimore and Washington. Meade would use cavalry, however, to apply pressure on Lee's flanks. He still had to make sure that his men and horses and mules were properly fed before he embarked on any pursuit. If he did not, any such pursuit would collapse.

To move on a parallel route, Meade's army would have to cover a considerably greater distance to arrive at Lee's "immediate goal" than Lee's army. Lee's army was retreating southwest along the hypotenuse of a triangle, whereas Meade's course would have to follow the other two sides.

For Lee's army, the total distance to Williamsport would be about forty-four miles; for Meade's army, it would be sixty-four miles. Still, following a parallel course was Meade's only option. Meade's immediate concern on 4 July was discerning Lee's exact intentions.

As early as 1:30 P.M., Meade had made up his mind about how he would pursue Lee's army should it withdraw to its lines of supply and communication in the Cumberland Valley. "As soon as it can be definitely ascertained that Lee is retiring into the valley, I shall move rapidly in a southern direction," Meade wrote to General Couch. Meade sent a message to General William F. Smith of Couch's force not long thereafter asserting that he was "of the opinion that the enemy is retreating via Fairfield and Cashtown, but [he was] not certain on his present information." Meade continued: "Should the enemy be retreating, [I] will pursue by way of Emmitsburg and Middletown, on the left flank." Stephen Sears writes that during 4 July, "Meade immersed himself in matters of military housekeeping, and, unlike, General Lee, seemed to devote little thought to his course of action." As Meade's letters to Generals Couch and Smith of 4 July reveal, he not only thought about his course of action but determined that day exactly how he would move the army. It must be noted, too, that obtaining from Westminster sufficient forage for nearly thirty thousand starved horses and subsistence for nearly sixty thousand starved men was no small "housekeeping" matter.[42]

In the meantime, Meade decided to put pressure on Lee's army's flanks were it falling back to its line of supply and communications in the Cumberland Valley. On the early afternoon of 4 July, Meade ordered General Pleasonton, his cavalry chief, to direct General Buford, then with Colonels Devin's and Gamble's cavalry brigades at Westminster, to move to Frederick, where they would be joined by General Merritt's brigade of regulars, coming from Gettysburg. Once joined at Frederick, they would proceed along the National Road through Turner Pass in the South Mountain range to Williamsport, Lee's immediate goal.[43]

Pursuant to Meade's direction, Pleasonton ordered General Kilpatrick's cavalry division to proceed from Gettysburg to Emmitsburg, where it would be joined by Colonel Pennock Huey's brigade of General Gregg's cavalry division, which would move there from Westminster. Together, those commands would move to Monterey Pass, one of the passes Lee's army would have to use to retreat to the Cumberland Valley and to Williamsport.[44]

Colonel J. Irvin Gregg's cavalry brigade of General Gregg's division was ordered by Pleasanton, after consulting with Meade, to move to Hunterstown, and then through Cashtown Pass, to Greenwood, Pennsylvania, on what would be the right flank of Lee's army should it use the Chambersburg Pike to get onto the Cumberland Valley Turnpike in order to reach Williamsport.[45]

Soaking rain and smoke not only from campfires but from also fires set deliberately behind and along Lee's lines to cover his movements, adversely affected visibility, reducing thereby the ability of Meade's signal stations to observe Confederate movements. Not until 5:15 P.M. was another message sent to Meade regarding the movement of the enemy. This time it came from Lieutenant P. A. Taylor at the courthouse signal station in Gettysburg: "Three regiments of cavalry and four wagons passed along our front 2½ miles from town, halted on the hills northwest from the college building, and were joined by two more regiments, a battery of artillery, and two ambulances coming from behind the hills. The column is now moving toward the Chambersburg road. Dense smoke has been seen all day behind the hills in the direction of Cashtown."[46]

Taylor sent another message to Meade at 7:15 P.M. "A train of thirty-three wagons just passed from near Herr's Tavern toward the Fairfield Road," the message read. "Several smaller trains have been seen during the day in the same direction." Taylor continued, stating: "The column of cavalry reported this P.M. moving toward Chambersburg Pike, halted behind the woods north of the Seminary, head of column rising on the Tapeworm Road. It is still there at this hour; horses grazing." Before then, Meade had received no word that any of Lee's defense line either had been or was being abandoned. Meade remained unsure of Lee's intentions.[47]

On the night of 4 July, Meade called a meeting of his corps commanders at his headquarters tent. The rain was pouring down in sheets. Recalled General Butterfield: "We were almost drowned out of headquarters down in the woods." The meeting was moved to a house nearby that had been used by Brigadier General Thomas Neill as his headquarters. That house was, most likely, the one owned by George Musser and his wife, Elizabeth, because it was directly across the Baltimore Pike from the position taken by Neill's brigade, on the extreme right flank of the army. Present at the meeting were Generals Birney, who was restored to command of the Third Corps after the wounding of General Hancock, and Generals Sedgwick, Howard, Sykes, Warren, Newton, Slocum, and Pleasonton. Even the wounded General Butterfield was present. In addition, Brigadier General William Hays was present; he had been appointed to command the Second Corps by General Meade on 3 July after the wounding of Generals Hancock and Gibbon that afternoon. Forty-four years old, Hays was an

1836 graduate of West Point and a veteran of the Mexican War, as well as of the battles on the Virginia Peninsula, Antietam, Fredericksburg, and Chancellorsville, where he was captured but then released two weeks later. Hays had already reported to Meade the condition and situation of the Second Corps earlier on 4 July.[48]

Meade opened the meeting by stating that his instructions were to cover Washington and Baltimore. There is no record that he shared any of the messages he had written to Generals Couch and Smith with his corps commanders. He did ask the generals what each believed was the course the army should take. General Slocum believed that the army should move as far as Emmitsburg and, if the enemy had not gone from Gettysburg, hold on there and push out a force at once with a view of preventing the enemy from crossing the Potomac. Both Generals Sedgwick and Howard argued to "remain at Gettysburg until certain the enemy is moving away."[49]

Meade presented four questions to the assembled generals: First, "Shall this army remain [at Gettysburg]?" Second, "If we remain, shall we assume the offensive?" Third, "Do you deem it expedient to move towards Williamsport through Emmitsburg?" Fourth, "Shall we pursue the enemy if he is retreating on his direct line of retreat?"[50]

Most of the generals agreed that the army should remain at Gettysburg until they received positive information that the enemy was retreating. None of were in favor of attacking Lee at Gettysburg. Most believed that the army should follow a parallel course in order to confront Lee at Williamsport, and all agreed that the army should not directly follow the enemy, save for cavalry, or some infantry, as a show of force. Just as at the meeting in the Leister house on 2 July, what determinations Meade had made in writing, but not shared with those present, were confirmed by most, if not all, the generals in attendance.[51]

Edwin Coddington asserted that Meade "was seeking advice when perhaps it was not necessary, and he was exposing himself to the charge that he lacked moral courage." Meade's reason for calling the meeting with his corps commanders was simple. "I never called those meetings councils; they were [using a word chosen by Jomini in *The Art of War*] 'consultations,'" he testified later, "and they were probably more numerous and more constant in my case, from the fact that I had just assumed command of the army, and felt that it was due to myself to have the opinions of high officers before I took action on matters which involved such momentous issues."[52]

Most of the officers and men in Meade's army had not been fed; even worse, the horses of the army had not been fed. Ammunition had not been restored. The army was in no shape to mount a lengthy pursuit of the enemy until adequate provisions and ammunition were received at the front. Too, Meade's army was sprawling; it was holding a more than three-mile front across varying geography that made coordination difficult. The commanders on the flanks knew little or nothing of the situation on the opposite flank or the center. Commanders of the center knew little about the situation on either flank. If Meade expected all the elements of his army to coordinate their efforts, all the corps commanders had to consult among themselves and, all together, consult with the army commander. It is the way commanders of great armies have exercised command throughout history and today. Meade was a team player, and that team effort was what had been lacking in past campaigns and battles fought by the Army of the Potomac. Jomini writes that councils of war "can be useful only when concurring in opinion with the commander." On the nights of 2 July and 4 July that is precisely what occurred, and what Meade expected. As such, those councils assured Meade, in the words of Jomini, "that his lieutenants, being of his opinion, [would] use every means to insure success." Major Biddle wrote a letter to his wife not long after the meeting: "Everything works homogenously, and the corps commanders appear very satisfied with Meade. I think there is more unity among them than ever before."[53]

18

I SHALL CONTINUE MY
FLANK MOVEMENT

The dawn of 5 July was rainy; it had poured rain continuously all through the night. Some subsistence stores finally began to reach the army and were being distributed to the troops. For the first time since 1 July many of Meade's officers and men were getting something to eat. That morning, Meade wanted to relieve General Butterfield as chief of staff and asked General Humphreys to take Butterfield's place. Humphreys wished to think about it. In the meantime, Meade asked Generals Pleasonton and Warren to assist him during the pursuit of the enemy: Butterfield was not in a position to serve in such a role due to his wound.[1]

Meade was anxious for information about the movements by Lee's army. As early as 5:40 A.M. on 5 July, a dispatch was sent to Meade at his Baltimore Pike headquarters by Captain James S. Hall at the Courthouse signal station in Gettysburg. "The enemy," it read, "have evacuated the positions they held yesterday. No indications of the enemy anywhere, only on the Chambersburg road and in small force." Captain Hall added: "Their batteries have disappeared from the hills near the Seminary. Prisoners report that the enemy has gone to Hagerstown."[2]

Not long after Hall's dispatch, another arrived from Lieutenants William H. Hill and Isaac S. Lyon on Little Round Top. The dispatch was directed to General Sykes but also forwarded to Meade. "Though the atmosphere is smoky," it read, "yet many of the points which yesterday composed the enemy's front and reserve lines can be distinctly seen. At these points not a single object can be seen moving on either line, which leads to the belief that the enemy have left our front."[3]

Signal officer Captain E. C. Pierce gave Meade another sighting of Lee's defense lines that morning. At 8:40 A.M., Pierce wrote: "We can see no signs of the enemy on our left front." He did spot "quite a heavy body of troops" on the Herr Ridge Road and "a few wagons." With respect to General Ewell's troops, who occupied Lee's left flank, from the Seminary Ridge to Oak Hill the day before, Pierce concluded that they "have disappeared." Pierce could spot no artillery. Ten minutes later, Pierce wrote that the "heavy body of troops he spotted on Herr Ridge Road was moving to the left, toward Fairfield Road."[4]

Lee's army had, indeed, evacuated the Seminary Ridge defense lines. The movement began late on the night of 4 July and progressed through the morning of 5 July. By the time the troops began forming columns on either side of the Fairfield Road, all the quartermaster, subsistence, and ordnance wagon trains and ambulance trains of Ewell's corps, nearly twenty miles in length, had passed up the Fairfield Road behind the gigantic reserve quartermaster and subsistence train that left Fairfield at 3:00 A.M. on 4 July and was already at Hagerstown and Williamsport. Most of Lee's troops moved out under cover of darkness and dense smoke from campfires and fires intentionally set to create a smokescreen. Rain fell in sheets, turning the Fairfield Road into a quagmire.[5]

The first of Lee's troops to enter the Fairfield Road was the corps commanded by General Hill. That movement began at about 5:00 P.M. on 4 July. The left flank of that corps, because it had been positioned along the Seminary Ridge defense line, rested on the Fairfield Road; the right flank touched the left flank of Longstreet's corps. Behind Hill's corps came Lee's headquarters wagon train on or about 1:00 A.M. on 5 July, and then Longstreet's corps. As Longstreet's columns began their movement from the far right flank of the Seminary Ridge defense line toward the Fairfield Road at dawn, 5 July, Ewell's corps evacuated its position on the left flank and moved to a position east of Willoughby Run Road, straddling the Fairfield Road, three miles west of Gettysburg and mostly out of view of Meade's signal stations. Ewell's corps formed a screen for Longstreet's corps to move into line on the Fairfield Road. Finally, at about 11:00 A.M., 5 July, Ewell's corps moved onto the Fairfield Road behind Longstreet's.[6]

The rear guard of the long columns was the brigade of Georgia infantry regiments in General Early's Division of Ewell's corps, commanded by Brigadier General John B. Gordon. Gordon's columns were screened by three companies of Colonel White's Thirty-Fifth Battalion of Virginia cavalry.[7]

In the middle of Longstreet's columns, between McLaws's and Hood's Divisions, were the remnants of Pickett's Division, guarding more than four thousand Union prisoners of war. One of those prisoners was Sergeant R. N. Martin of the Sixty-Second Pennsylvania, who had been captured in the fighting for the Wheatfield on 2 July. Observing Lee's army pass by, Martin remembered the endless "trains of wagons, artillery, and cattle, stolen horses, hogs, etc."[8]

Unbeknown to Meade, significant events had occurred overnight. Under orders from General French, an expedition led by Major Shadrock Foley of the Fourteenth Pennsylvania Cavalry, using detachments from his regiment, the Thirteenth Pennsylvania Cavalry, and from two others, the First New York (Lincoln) Cavalry and the First West Virginia Cavalry, about three hundred troopers in all, set out from Frederick and, on reaching the south bank of the Potomac River at Falling Waters on the night of 4 July, destroyed Lee's only pontoon bridge. Lee's army had left the bridge behind in order to get dispatches as well as wagon trains across the river in the event that the fords were erased due to high waters; at the time it was destroyed, it was dismantled and guarded by a small contingent of engineers and infantrymen. Foley's cavalry commands were then stationed at Frederick. Foley's regiment was attached to Brigadier General William W. Averill's command in the Department of West Virginia; the other cavalry commands Foley used were from regiments formerly in General Milroy's occupation forces at Winchester, Virginia, during the previous month. They had escaped to Harper's Ferry when General Ewell's corps seized Winchester on 14 June; those veterans of Milroy's debacle were derisively called by some in the army "the debris of Winchester." Foley's successful operation, however, would make an immense difference in Meade's ability to confront Lee north of the Potomac River. Meade would not be informed of the success, though, until 7:00 P.M. on 5 July.[9]

At the same time as Foley's men were destroying the pontoon bridge, General Kilpatrick's cavalry division, along with Colonel Huey's brigade of General Gregg's cavalry division, after leaving Westminster and passing through Emmitsburg, reached the summit of the South Mountain range at Monterey Gap. In a wild electrical storm, General Custer's brigade attacked the quartermaster, subsistence, and ordnance wagon trains and ambulance trains of mostly Rodes's Division of Ewell's corps protected there only by a company of Maryland cavalry and one artillery piece, seizing more than 287 wagons and capturing more than thirteen hundred officers and men. Information about that success would not be delivered to Meade until his army was marching toward Middletown and Frederick on 7 July. Kilpatrick moved his troopers, along with their captured wagons and prisoners, to Boonsboro, on the west side of the South Mountain range and, on 5 July, was completely out of contact with army headquarters.[10]

Meade was further unaware that Lee's enormous reserve wagon train of quartermaster and subsistence stores that led Ewell's corps wagon and ambulance trains out of Fairfield had already entered Hagerstown at 11:00 P.M. on 4 July. In addition, the wagon and ambulance trains of Generals Hill's and Longstreet's corps, and General Stuart's cavalry division, guided by Generals Imboden's and Fitzhugh Lee's, and Colonel Baker's, cavalry brigades, along the Chambersburg Pike and the Cumberland Valley Turnpike, would enter Williamsport on the afternoon of 5 July.[11]

Across the Potomac River from Williamsport, Lee's long-awaited reserve ammunition wagon train would arrive at about 2:00 P.M. on 5 July. Although Lee may have lost his pontoon bridge, he would have ample ammunition for his field artillery and infantrymen once his army arrived at Hagerstown and Williamsport.[12]

Meade knew that Lee's defeated army was retreating. The question raised that morning, however, was whether Lee was retreating toward Fairfield, a town located at the base of the South Mountain range nine miles west of Gettysburg, in order for his army to congregate along those heights and lure Meade to attack him there or whether he was, in fact, retreating to the Cumberland Valley and back to Virginia. For a defeated army to retreat to heights and fortify them was a favored strategy of both Clausewitz and Jomini.[13]

Assessing Lee's intent was no small matter. Everything, including the life of the army, and possibly the war, depended on Meade's correct judgment. Visibility was restricted due to the lingering smoke and pounding rains. If Lee was moving his army to Fairfield in order for all its elements to congregate along the South Mountain range, Meade had to be prepared for a confrontation there that might become protracted; his primary mission was still to protect Baltimore and Washington. That meant Meade must have a significant element of his army pursue Lee's retreating forces and keep all of his remaining corps within supporting distance of the pursuing force, and then he would have to ensure that the Gettysburg Railroad was operational from Hanover Junction to Gettysburg and that the Northern Central Railroad was open from Baltimore to Hanover Junction. It also meant that he would have to send all the wagon trains of quartermaster, subsistence, and ordnance stores from the Camp of Transportation at Westminster and Union Bridge to Gettysburg: that railhead would have to become the army's base of supply.

The reason for that was because of the fundamental mission General Halleck gave Meade when he assumed command; first and foremost, Meade had to protect Baltimore and Washington. Those orders remained in effect. Meade had to consider the possibility that Lee might move his army back to Gettysburg and continue his foraging operations if the Army of the Potomac moved toward Middletown before positive information of Lee's intent was discovered. Lee could then choose a position for his army to occupy and force Meade to attack him there. That would nullify everything gained in three days of fighting at Gettysburg and open up Baltimore and Washington to raids by Lee's army. The military and political fallout from such an event would be catastrophic to Lincoln, Meade, the army, and the Union cause. General Halleck, from his desk at the War Department in Washington, was desperately concerned about that very possibility. Halleck would respond to a dispatch of Meade's regarding the movements of the army on 5 July by writing simply, "So long as you move men to cover Baltimore and Washington from Lee's main army, [those cities] are in no danger from any force the enemy may detach for a raid."[14]

If Meade were to conclude positively that Lee's intention was to return to Virginia, he would move the army on parallel routes toward Lee's army but east of the South Mountain range, where he could then use the macadamized National Road to cross over that mountain range and reach a position to confront Lee directly. To embark on that operation, Meade would have to use Frederick, Maryland, as his base of supply, with the Baltimore & Ohio Railroad as his means of forwarding supplies to the army from Baltimore and Washington to Frederick. Telegraphic communications with Washington, D.C., would be reopened at the Baltimore & Ohio Railroad station. All of Meade's quartermaster, subsistence, and ordnance wagons would have to move from the Camp of Transportation at Westminster and Union Bridge to Frederick, then on to Middletown. Meade could not make a mistake in judgment, or days would be spent by all the elements of Meade's army correcting their movements, and worse yet, an opening might be given to the enemy to move back toward Gettysburg, threatening Baltimore and Washington.

Meade sat down with General Seth Williams and dictated a circular to all the corps commanders early on the morning of 5 July. In that circular, Meade ordered the entire Army of the Potomac to move south along routes parallel to Lee's army, but on the eastern side of the South Mountain range. Meade directed all the elements of the army to the initial destination of Middletown, Maryland, a town on the National Road nine miles west of Frederick, in the valley between the Catoctin Mountains and the South Mountain range. The First, Sixth, and Third Corps were directed by Meade to move "by Emmitsburg" and then to Mechanicstown, Lewistown, Hamburg, and on to Middletown. The Fifth and Eleventh Corps were ordered to proceed "by the left hand" Taneytown Road, "through Emmits-burg," Creagerstown, Utica, and Highknob Pass, to Middletown. Those five corps would cross over the Catoctin Mountains south of Emmitsburg, fol-lowing the two most direct routes to Middletown. The Twelfth and Second Corps were directed to Taneytown, Middleburg, Woodsboro, and "through Frederick" to Middletown, thereby avoiding, as much as possible, conges-tion on the two narrow roads being used by the other five corps.[15]

What corps wagon trains and cattle herds were with the army at Gettys-burg would follow their respective corps; all the wagon trains and cattle at the Camp of Transportation at Westminster and Union Bridge, however, would have to move to Middleburg and on to Middletown by way of Fred-erick. That would separate all those necessary stores from the troops until they could reunite at Middletown. The Artillery Reserve would bring up the rear by way of Taneytown and Middleburg, and through Frederick, to Middletown. The Twelfth and Second Corps, the Artillery Reserve, and all the wagon trains would traverse much of the same countryside that they did on 29 June.[16]

Meade informed his corps commanders that army headquarters on the night of 5 July would be at Creagerstown, between Emmitsburg and Fred-erick. The army, Meade ordered, "will assemble at Middletown" on the evening of 7 July.[17]

The battalion of regular engineers at Westminster was ordered to Middletown by way of Frederick. Meade ordered the medical director of the army, Jonathan Letterman, to establish a general hospital at Gettys-burg to care for all the wounded who could not be moved with the army.[18]

Finally, Meade ordered General Sedgwick, without relinquishing com-mand of his Sixth Corps, to assume command and direct the movements of the corps forming the right wing—the First, Sixth, and Third Corps. Similarly, Meade ordered General Slocum to command the left wing, the Twelfth and Second Corps. General Howard was ordered to command the center, the Fifth and Eleventh Corps.[19]

Meade stated in the circular that the movement was to start immedi-ately. The "Headquarters train," he wrote, "will move at once." Meade waited, however, to send the circular to each of his corps commanders until later in the day; he apprehended that he might have to suspend the movements if Lee's forces appeared to be gathering along the South Mountain range at Fairfield rather than retreating to the Potomac River and on to Virginia.[20]

To obtain the necessary information about Lee's intentions, Meade ordered General Sedgwick to move the Sixth Corps forward from its position at the base of the Round Tops and follow the retreating enemy along the Fairfield Road. Sedgwick, in turn, ordered General Wright, commander of the First Division of the Sixth Corps, to lead the reconnaissance in force. The purpose of Sedgwick's mission was to discover Lee's intentions, not to bring on engagement. The mission was similar to that given to General Reynolds on 1 July; Sedgwick was to deploy his corps and put pressure on the enemy in order to cause it to reveal Lee's intentions. It was a show of force on Lee's rear. Neither Meade nor any of his corps commanders wanted to pursue Lee's army directly through the South Mountain range, if Lee was in fact retreating to Virginia. Direct pursuits through mountains are rarely successful, and importantly, the army would be unable to resupply itself with forage and subsistence stores if it were to pursue the enemy directly because it would be constantly moving farther from any base of supply.[21]

At 8:30 A.M., Meade prepared a dispatch to General Halleck. "The enemy retired, under cover of the night and heavy rain, in the direction of Fairfield and Cashtown," he wrote. "All my available cavalry are in pursuit, on the enemy's left and rear. My movement will be made at once on his flank, via Middletown and South Mountain Pass." After discussing having to leave many of his wounded at Gettysburg and employing "citizens to bury the dead" because his own men were unable to complete that grim task, Meade informed Halleck that his headquarters for the night of 5 July would be at Creagerstown, Maryland, midway between Gettysburg and Frederick. Halleck would not receive that dispatch until twelve hours later.[22]

General Herman Haupt claimed in his report of his operations and in his reminiscences published in 1901 that he visited with Meade and General Pleasonton at Meade's headquarters on the Baltimore Pike around noon on 5 July, for a stated purpose of discussing a change in the army's base of supply. Neither the report nor the reminiscences contain any details concerning moving the supply base; instead, Haupt writes in his reminiscences that he tried to encourage Meade to move the army faster or he would allow Lee's army to cross the Potomac River before the Army of the Potomac could confront it. He claims that he left the meeting discouraged about the prospects of Meade moving fast enough and that he traveled to Washington to meet with General Halleck about the matter. It appears that a meeting with Meade took place, but it is doubtful that all of what Haupt wrote about it was factual. Meade, first of all, was totally preoccupied with preparing the orders for the army to move; he would have had little time to listen to Haupt discuss him moving the army faster and, likely, would have declined talking about Haupt's concerns. Haupt, having been far from the battlefield, had no idea what the army had been through over the preceding four days or any information about the dispositions of Meade's and Lee's armies; it was rude and disrespectful for him to have lectured Meade as he claimed he did. Neither Meade, nor anyone present with him at the time, ever wrote anything about the Haupt meeting. Haupt did forward a letter to General Halleck in which he wrote: "I fear that while Meade rests to refresh his men, and collect supplies, Lee will be off so far that he cannot intercept him." This was the second time Haupt had interjected himself between Meade and Halleck. In both instances, he knew nothing of the circumstances confronting Meade. Despite that, his back-channel communications with Halleck likely tainted Meade's reputation with Halleck and President Lincoln.[23]

In battle alignment, Wright's division, followed by the other two divisions of the Sixth Corps, moved out into the bloody fields below Little Round Top. At 12:30 P.M., Meade sent General Warren to General Sedgwick with written instructions. Those instructions to Sedgwick were clear: "All the information I can obtain proves withdrawal of the enemy through Cashtown and Fairfield road. Push forward your column in a westerly direction." Meade then added: "Fire on his force. If rear guard, it will be compelled to return; if not, you will find out." Meade then informed Sedgwick of his overarching concern: "Time is of great importance, as I cannot give [the] order for a movement [in any direction] without explicit information from you." Warren would accompany Sedgwick all the way to Fairfield.[24]

Recalled Jacob W. Haas of the Ninety-Sixth Pennsylvania, in Wright's division: "The whole corps seemed to move [forward from the base of Little Round Top] and halted in the wheat field until 1:00 P.M., when we moved forward. I think 'the Rebs' have gone. The stench is horrible from the dead carcasses lying around." Hess then added: "Moved forward by columns and line of battle at times, skirmishing along [the way]."[25]

As Sedgwick's corps got closer to the rear guard of Lee's army along the Fairfield Road, the Sixth Corps artillery batteries unlimbered and opened fire. Artillery fire was returned. The enemy forces, though, continued their withdrawal down the Fairfield Road. It was the last hostile exchange between the two armies at Gettysburg. Sedgwick continued pursuing the rear of Lee's army toward Fairfield.[26]

One of Haas's fellow soldiers in the Ninety-Sixth Pennsylvania, Henry Keiser, recorded in his diary what he observed on the afternoon of 5 July as he followed the rear guard of the Lee's army toward Fairfield:

We followed slowly, feeling our way carefully as we went. It rained all afternoon and was very muddy. Every barn we passed was converted into a Rebel hospital and had the red flag floating over it. While we were halting near one (a large barn full of wounded Rebs) I ran over to see how it looked. It was sickening to look at. The barn floor and every place in the barn where a person could be layed [sic] was filled with wounded Rebels, and outside the barn, on the south side, I seen [sic] piles of hands, feet, legs, and arms, at least two feet high.[27]

Sedgwick's Sixth Corps pursued Lee's retreating army all the way to within two miles of Fairfield. It was late in the afternoon. Sedgwick could distinctly see the rear elements of the enemy and their wagon trains passing through the town toward Monterey Gap. The enemy rear guard opened fire, and Sedgwick called for Captain George W. Adams to bring forward his Battery G, First Rhode Island Light Artillery, and open fire. By evening, Adams's six guns had fired 162 rounds of shell at the enemy. Sedgwick then called on General Wright to move his division forward, pushing the enemy out of the town toward the Emmitsburg-Waynesboro Turnpike or onto the Maria Furnace Road, both roads heading to Monterey Gap. Warren left Sedgwick to report back to Meade at Gettysburg.[28]

Meade wrote to Sedgwick at 7:30 P.M., informing him that he had ordered General Newton's First Corps and General Birney's Third Corps to hold their forces "in readiness" in case they were needed. Meade then noted: "Believing the enemy were in full retreat, and for the Potomac, I have authorized the issue of the [circular] order of march, and several corps have moved, but, as they cannot get very far today, they can be recalled if the information obtained through your operations should justify the same." It seems, however, that General Butterfield actually forwarded the circular order of 5 July to all the corps commanders without obtaining Meade's authority. Evidently, Meade wanted to wait to issue the circular order of march until much later in the day so that if he suddenly had to address the threat of the enemy collecting along the South Mountain range, the various corps of the army would be nearby. Meade kept Butterfield's actions to himself, not wishing to communicate what had occurred to his corps commanders.[29]

Warren reported back to Meade later that evening; he told him of the large enemy force at Fairfield. That prompted Meade to issue an order to all the corps commanders suspending any further movements under the circular of 5 July. He issued another order to all his corps commanders informing them that "Headquarters will be to-night at the same place

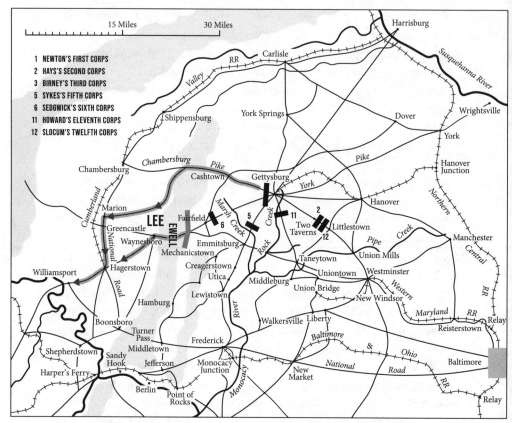

Map 18.1. 5 July 1863 to 6 July 1863: Lee begins his retreat; Meade uses
Sedgwick's Sixth Corps to probe. The First and Third Corps
remain at Gettysburg in support of the Sixth Corps.

as last night instead of Creagerstown." General Meade then sent another
dispatch to General Sedgwick at 2:00 A.M. on 6 July: "After conversation
with General Warren," Meade wrote, "I think under existing circumstance
you had better push your reconnaissance so as to ascertain, if practicable,
how far the enemy has retreated, and also the character of the Gap, and
practicability of carrying same."[30]

Meade's headquarters remained along the Baltimore Pike at Gettysburg. That night, Meade found a moment to write a letter to Margaret.
"I hardly know when I last wrote to you," he wrote, "so many and such stirring events have occurred. I think I have written since the battle, but I am
not sure." Meade continued: "It was a grand battle, and is in my judgment
a most decided victory, though I did not annihilate or bag the Confederate
army." He wrote of the enemy retiring "in great haste into the mountains"

and how they left "their dead unburied and their wounded in the field." Meade then told Margaret about his own perceptions of the enemy's generals' thinking. "They awaited one day," he wrote, "expecting that, flushed with success, I would attack them when they would play their old game of shooting at us from behind breastworks—a game we played this time to their entire satisfaction." He then lapsed into his feelings about his troops. "The men behaved splendidly," he wrote, "I really think they are becoming soldiers. They endured long marches, short rations, and stood one of the most terrific cannonading I ever witnessed." Then, with a touch of sadness, he continued: "Baldy was shot again, and I fear will not get over it. Two horses that [Captain] George [Meade] rode were killed, his own and the black mare." Recalling the fighting of 2 July, Meade then wrote, "I had no time to think of either George or myself, for at one time things looked a little blue; but I managed to get up reinforcements in time to save the day." Before he signed his name, Meade ended the letter probably thinking about all that occurred on 5 July: "The most difficult part of my work is acting without correct information on which to predicate action." That is always one of the greatest problems confronting the operational commander.[31]

Pursuant to Meade's direct orders, General Sedgwick at Fairfield sent forward from his corps the brigade of infantry commanded by General Neill in conjunction with a brigade of cavalry commanded by Colonel John B. McIntosh of Gregg's cavalry division, which was then at Emmitsburg, to test the enemy's positions and intentions along the Maria Furnace Road at the base of the South Mountain range in the wee hours of 6 July. "I believe from the immense numbers of camp-fires seen last evening," wrote Sedgwick to Meade, "that the enemy will hold the gaps strongly."[32]

With General Sykes's Fifth Corps at Marsh Run on the Emmitsburg Road, only five miles north of Emmitsburg, under orders to move to Moritz's Crossroads, General Howard's Eleventh Corps at Emmitsburg, and General Newton's First Corps and General Birney's Third Corps at Gettysburg, Meade had ample forces nearby to address any attempts by the enemy to congregate along the South Mountain range at Fairfield and possibly strike Sedgwick's corps. At the same time, General Hays's Second Corps was at Two Taverns, only five miles southeast of Gettysburg, while General Slocum's Twelfth Corps had reached Littlestown, only five miles ahead of Hays's corps.[33]

Meade was awake all through the early morning hours of 6 July. Notified that Sedgwick had directed General Newton's First Corps and General Birney's Third Corps to move to Emmitsburg, Meade intervened, halting those commands and directing the two commanders to inform Sedgwick of their precise locations. Meade then notified Sedgwick that he had just received word that Colonel J. Irvin Gregg's brigade of cavalry passed through Cashtown Pass and that Gregg reported that there was "no opposition." Concern that an enemy force might try to strike Sedgwick from Cashtown was finally put to rest. "All evidence," Meade wrote to Sedgwick, "seems to show a movement to Hagerstown and to the Potomac." Meade's only remaining concern was the main body of Lee's army moving through Monterey Gap ahead of Sedgwick. "Whenever I am satisfied that the main body [of the enemy] is retiring from the mountains, I shall continue my flank movement," Meade wrote to Sedgwick.[34]

Early in the morning of 6 July, Meade dictated orders to Brigadier General H. W. Benham to forward to Harper's Ferry the three pontoon bridges that traveled with the army until Meade directed them to return to Washington on the eve of the battle of Gettysburg. By midafternoon, one bridge would be on its way to Harper's Ferry by means of the Chesapeake & Ohio Canal; another would be forwarded by means of the Baltimore & Ohio Railroad on 7 July. A third would be forwarded on 7 July by means of the National Road. By nightfall, General Seth Williams would notify Benham that Meade wanted two bridges at Berlin on the railroad line, just downstream from Harper's Ferry; the other bridge would be placed at Sandy Hook on the railroad line, across the Potomac River from Harper's Ferry.[35]

At 2:00 P.M., Meade wrote to General Halleck bringing him up to date on the movement of the army. "Yesterday," Meade wrote, "I sent General Sedgwick with the Sixth Corps in pursuit of the army toward Fairfield, and a brigade of cavalry toward Cashtown." With characteristic honesty, Meade then wrote: "General Sedgwick's report indicating a large force of the enemy in the mountains, I deemed it prudent to suspend the movement to Middletown until I could be certain that the enemy were evacuating the Cumberland Valley." Meade then added, "I find great difficulty in getting reliable information, but from all I can learn I have reason to believe the enemy is retreating, very much crippled, and hampered with his trains." He continued: "General Sedgwick reported that the gap at Fairfield was very formidable, and would enable a small force to hold my column in check for a long time." Meade then gave Halleck the good news: "I have accordingly resumed the movement to Middletown, and expect by tomorrow night to assemble the army in that vicinity."[36]

Colonel McIntosh scribbled a message to army headquarters at 3:45 P.M. on 6 July, stating that he advanced his cavalry brigade toward the rear of Lee's retreating army about two miles west of the summit of

Monterey Gap. There, he engaged the enemy for about two hours. "The bulk of Lee's army," he wrote, "passed on to the Waynesboro Pike yesterday from Fairfield. They passed through Fountain Dale and Monterey, and I think were moving to Hagerstown."[37]

Through General Warren, Meade notified General Neill that he was detaching his brigade from General Sedgwick's corps for the purpose of having Neill "watch closely the movement of the enemy's rear guard." Meade also advised Sedgwick to send a battery of rifled guns to accompany Neill. He finally wrote that Colonel McIntosh's brigade of cavalry must also report to Neill.[38]

Meade was finally resigned to the fact that Lee was retreating to the Potomac River, and he wrote to General Sedgwick, ordering him to hold his position until dark on 6 July, then withdraw the Sixth Corps, "except Neill's brigade and a rifled battery," and, on 7 July, along with the First and Third Corps, "execute the order of march of 5 July." All the other corps were ordered to resume the march set forth in the 5 July circular at 4:00 A.M. on 7 July.[39]

Meade at last went to sleep. Earlier in the day, General Halleck directed Meade to assume general command of all troops of General Couch's Department of the Susquehanna. On learning of his command over those forces, Meade had ordered Brigadier General William F. Smith to move his large division of six brigades, then in the Cumberland Valley, to Gettysburg to "protect the hospitals" and government property there. In a subsequent order, Meade directed that Smith's command join the Army of the Potomac as soon as "developments show no necessity" for his force to remain at Gettysburg.[40]

On 6 July at 7:00 P.M., President Lincoln wrote a letter to General Halleck from "The Soldier's Home." "I left the telegraph office a good deal dissatisfied," he wrote. "You know I did not like the phrase in [Meade's 4 July] Orders No. 68, I believe, 'Drive the invaders from our soil.'" Lincoln then told Halleck that he read a dispatch that told of enemy wounded being taken across the Potomac River on flats, yet no Union commander wrote of plans to stop it. More importantly, Lincoln read a dispatch from General Pleasonton stating that, at General Meade's direction, "the main army is halted because it is believed the rebels are concentrating." Then Lincoln wrote: "These things all appear to me to be connected with a purpose to cover Baltimore and Washington and to get the enemy across the river again without a further collision, and they do not appear connected with a purpose to prevent his crossing and to destroy him." Meade had no knowledge of the letter at the time it was forwarded to Halleck. The letter represented the first time Lincoln regarded "destroying" Lee's army as Meade's objective.[41]

Coddington adjudges Meade to be overly cautious; he claims that Meade missed an opportunity of striking Lee at Fairfield. Stephen Sears echoes Coddington, claiming that Meade should have directed a "strike force" of "one or two brigades, or even a division, of Sedgwick's fresh Sixth Corps" toward Monterey Gap. "Should Lee be forced to fight [at Monterey Gap]," Sears continues, "the rest of [Meade's] army might fall upon [Lee's] rear." Both commentators, however, oversimplify the situation confronting Meade. Meade had no idea where all of Lee's army was located, other than it was either collecting along the eastern face of the South Mountain range or was west of it. Sears does not explain how Meade would have located Lee's rear or how he would get "the rest of [his army]" in a position to attack Lee. If Meade had made such a move, it would have opened the way for Lee to move against Sedgwick's small force east of the mountains and then interpose his army between Meade's army and its base of supply and communication, because Lee would have had no other of Meade's forces in his front to contest him. Meade, it must be reiterated, had no intention of striking Lee's army at Fairfield, nor did any of Meade's corps commanders. With a small number of troops, Lee could defend against any attack by Meade, because he was holding Monterey Pass in the South Mountain range above Fairfield. Meade and all his generals had correctly ruled out pursuing Lee's army directly through the mountains.[42]

As to Meade's delay of the movement of the army, it was ordered because it appeared then that Lee's army was, in fact, concentrating in the mountains above Fairfield. That being the case, Meade had no choice but to halt the movement of the army. He could not march the army toward Frederick and Middletown and allow the enemy to advance back toward Gettysburg, completely unopposed. Until Meade knew that Lee's army was, in fact, across the mountains and heading toward Hagerstown and the Potomac River, he had to keep the army in position to resist any enemy movements from Fairfield toward Gettysburg.

Coddington also criticizes Meade for pursuing Lee's retreating army by the use of the Sixth Corps. According to Coddington, smaller cavalry commands could have been used. Meade's use of the Sixth Corps was for the same purpose as his use of the First Corps on 1 July. It was a reconnaissance in force, or the operational use of an advance corps. Meade used the Sixth Corps to try to get Lee to show his intentions, not to bring on an engagement that might involve all of both armies. To do that, Meade needed a sizable force of all arms, infantry, cavalry, and artillery. Only a large force of all arms would provoke an enemy to call out sufficient forces to contest such an advance. Once that happened, Sedgwick was to notify Meade that all of Lee's army was in front of him and then pull the Sixth Corps back. Just as Coddington—and Sears—-misdiagnose Reynolds's mission on 1 July, they misdiagnose Sedgwick's mission on 5 July and 6 July.[43]

At 10:00 P.M. on 6 July, Meade's headquarters received a dispatch from General Smith stating that his division was at Newman's Pass, three miles west of Cashtown. It was a purely informational dispatch. General Warren replied for Meade, informing Smith that the "army is concentrating at Middletown rapidly, and will all be gone [from Gettysburg] tomorrow." After notifying Smith to open communications with General Neill, whose brigade was following the enemy from Fairfield toward Waynesboro, Warren wrote: "As your note requires no special action, I do not wake General Meade to reply, as he is now refreshing himself with the first quiet sleep he has had since he came in command, if not for many nights before." By dawn the next day, Meade would order Smith to move his division south toward Hagerstown and join the Army of the Potomac in its coming confrontation with Lee's army.[44]

The day of 7 July 1863 would go down as the date of one of the most grueling marches in the annals of the Army of the Potomac. All day long, through driving rains and deep mud, the weary officers and men of the army trudged along on their way toward Middletown. Meade's headquarters that day were moved from Gettysburg to Frederick, thirty miles. The First Corps marched from Emmitsburg to Hamburg in the Catoctin Mountain, thirty miles; the Second Corps from Two Taverns to Taneytown, eleven miles; the Third Corps moved from Gettysburg to Mechanicstown, twenty-one miles; the Fifth Corps, from Moritz's Crossroads, by way of Emmitsburg, to Utica, twenty-one miles; the Sixth Corps, from Emmitsburg to Hamburg, thirty miles; the Eleventh Corps, from Emmitsburg to Middletown, thirty-two miles; the Twelfth Corps, from Littlestown to Walkersville, twenty-five miles; and the Artillery Reserve, from Littlestown to Woodsboro, twenty miles.[45]

Luther Furst of the Thirty-Ninth Pennsylvania in Sedgwick's Sixth Corps wrote of the dreadful march to Hamburg on 7 July. He and some of his men "put up at a farmer's house just to get out of the pouring rain." They were also there to "purchase food for our horses." He wrote how the horses "have stood the trip admirably." But, he penned, "They have gone several times without grain for 60 hours, having nothing but a little grass." It would not take much longer for those horses to break down completely. Jacob Haas of the Ninety-Sixth Pennsylvania in the Sixth Corps passed

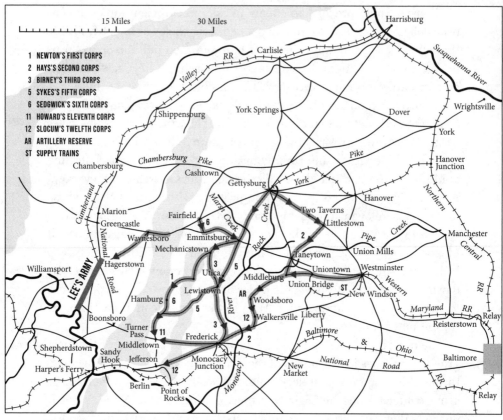

Map 18.2. 6 July 1863 to 8 July 1863: Meade's army pursues on Lee's flank.

through Emmitsburg, Mechanicstown, and Lewistown, then crossed over the Catoctin Mountains to Hamburg. Echoing many of his fellow soldiers, Haas penned in his diary on 7 July: "All very short of rations. Three crackers apiece. Commenced to rain and continued all night. All suffered from hunger, fatigue, and exposure."[46]

Such suffering was evident throughout Meade's army. Captain Francis Donaldson of the One Hundred Eighteenth Pennsylvania in the Fifth Corps wrote, after spending the night of 7 July on the march: "We have marched night and day since the battle, but owing to the fearful condition of the roads could not make headway. My boots have been worn out for some time and I am now barefoot nearly." Another Fifth Corps soldier, Corporal John Parker of the Twenty-Second Massachusetts, recalled that the roads were completely cut up by artillery and cavalry, turning them into "one immense hog-wallow the entire distance." When darkness overtook the columns in the pouring rain, nothing along the roads could be

In Pursuit of Lee, *by Edwin Forbes. (Library of Congress)*

distinguished. Parker wrote: "The men fell out by the scores; the commands melted away and sought shelter wherever they could find it—a confused, muddled-up, completely lost body of men." For Captain William Kepler of the Fourth Ohio in the Second Corps, the problem was hunger. On the morning of 7 July, he wrote, "The entire army seemed to be in motion; we arrived at Taneytown at noon; in the afternoon it rained very hard; we were out of rations and obtained provisions from the civilians." Major Rufus Dawes of the Sixth Wisconsin in the First Corps penned: "Our men have toiled and suffered as never before. Almost half our men have marched barefooted for a week." One officer, Captain Charles Morey of the Second Vermont, got to the point with few words: "We marched from Emmitsburg MD to the top of South Mountain, terrible rainy and dark in evening, awful suffering, mud terrible, rain all night."[47]

There were troubles even with the wagon trains, moving from Westminster to Middletown, in the driving rain. Wagoner J. P. Coburn wrote in his diary on 7 July that the wagon "trains left Westminster with expectation that we were to report to Frederick City." Instead, just as happened on 1 July, he and his captain "march[ed] about 14 miles and the train halted and then we have to counter-march 7 miles to Uniontown." Coburn then noted: "Captain says he will not lose sight of the Brigade wagons again while with the trains."[48]

Even with all the hardships, the soldiers in the Seventy-Fourth New York in the Third Corps, on their weary way from Emmitsburg to Mechanicstown, "were extravagant in their praise of General Meade," recalled Private Robert H. Davis. "We was [*sic*] satisfied with his generalship. It inspired us with renewed courage, believing our country had at last found more than a match for General Lee."[49]

Amid all the movement of troops toward Frederick and Middletown, Meade continued to address the bewildering number of deficiencies the army was facing. The day before the army got under way, Meade directed General Hunt to assign batteries from the Artillery Reserve to the artillery brigades of the various army corps "to replace losses and deficiencies." Those corps artillery brigade batteries had suffered terrible losses of guns, limbers, caissons, horses, ammunition, and cannoneers at Gettysburg. To replace horses, Meade directed General Ingalls to take horses from the army wagon trains "to supply deficiencies" in the artillery. Ingalls, in turn, notified General Meigs that the army needed two thousand cavalry and fifteen hundred artillery horses "as soon as possible." The army was desperate for enough horses to pull its field artillery and mount its cavalry regiments.[50]

Quartermaster General Montgomery Meigs made frantic efforts to supply horses, fodder, shoes, stockings, subsistence stores, and other articles necessary for the life of the Army of the Potomac. He claimed to General Ingalls on 5 July that he could obtain twelve hundred horses from Washington, D.C. He then sent telegrams to the commanders of horse depots and horse rehabilitation centers in Boston, New York, Philadelphia, Baltimore, Harrisburg, Indianapolis, Detroit, and Chicago, directing them to forward horses to make up for the deficiencies in Meade's army. To speed up the transporting of horses from those depots and rehabilitation centers, General Haupt sent telegrams to the presidents of the railroads in those eight cities and others informing them of the army's desperate situation.[51]

On 6 July, General Meigs notified General Ingalls that "2,000 cavalry horses have left Washington for Frederick, and that several cars, from 100 to 275 horses in each car [are] on their way to the army." He also informed Ingalls that "a few hundred [horses] more will be gathered from the trains at the depot. Two hundred fifty arrived [in Washington] last night and will be forwarded as soon as shod and fed." He then wrote: "Three hundred start from Detroit today and tomorrow; 275 from Boston, by special train last night." Later that day, Meigs informed Ingalls that "tomorrow 5,000 fresh horses will be on their way to Frederick from Boston, New York, Philadelphia, Baltimore, Harrisburg, Indianapolis, and Detroit." He then added, "170 more will be sent tomorrow from Chicago." Although the response to Meigs's order was remarkable, most of those horses were coming from so far away that they would never arrive in time to make up for Meade's immediate needs.[52]

Forage was also desperately needed. Although the Camp of Transportation forwarded large amounts of forage to Gettysburg on 4 July and 5 July, it was not enough to take care of the immediate needs and also provide enough to support the horses for the grinding marches to Frederick and Middletown over the next three days.

Colonel D. H. Rucker, assistant quartermaster general in Meigs's office, telegraphed General Ingalls that he ordered of 750,000 pounds of grain and 250,000 pounds of hay to be sent to Frederick. Still, there were nearly forty thousand horses and mules to feed in Meade's army after all the losses. Rucker claimed that he collected eight hundred cavalry horses in addition to the sixteen hundred already in transit.[53]

Shoes and socks for the troops were in short supply; horses were also in need of shoes. Some of Meade's corps commanders were reporting that more than half of their men were shoeless. Rucker wrote to Ingalls telling him that he ordered twenty-five thousand pairs of booties and twenty-five thousand pairs of stockings, along with a plenteous supply of horseshoes and nails. Again, the question was whether any of those desperately needed articles could be delivered to the soldiers in time.[54]

Not only were the horses hungry for forage and hay, but the troops were starved. On 5 July, Colonel Clarke, the commissary of subsistence of Meade's army forwarded to the railroad yards in Washington a demand for 100,000 "marching rations." On 5 July, a response was sent claiming that the rations ordered would be loaded in railroad cars to be sent to Frederick in the morning. Another 100,000 were to be sent on 6 July. The superintendent at the railroad yards was summarily notified: "You had better send another 100,000 also." Although the news was welcome, distributing those rations to the hungry men would take days, because most of them were then marching through rough terrain in driving rain to destinations far from Frederick.[55]

As if all the shortages of horses, fodder, and subsistence stores were not enough, there were also shortages of ammunition. All the corps commanders were ordered to "be careful in expending ammunition, both artillery and infantry," Meade wrote, "as we are now drawing upon our reserve trains."[56]

On the afternoon of 7 July, General Meade and his staff and escorts arrived at Frederick, where they established the headquarters of the Army of the Potomac at the United States Hotel across Market Street from the Baltimore & Ohio Railroad station, the supply and telegraph center for the army as it prepared to advance due west toward Lee's army at Williamsport. Joining Meade were Generals Pleasonton and French along with their staffs. They were all spotted at the hotel by diarist Jacob Engelbrecht at 3:30 P.M. Moments after Meade arrived, "a deputation of ladies" visited with him and showered him with "wreaths and bouquets." The streets were "crowded with people" wanting a glimpse of the victor at Gettysburg.[57]

No sooner did Meade arrive at the United States Hotel than the telegraph terminal in the Baltimore & Ohio Railroad station across Market Street received a message from General Halleck notifying Meade that he had just been appointed a brigadier general in the regular army "to rank from July 3, the date of your brilliant victory at Gettysburg." Meade sent a note back to Halleck within the hour. "Please convey to the President," Meade wrote, "my grateful thanks for this honor, and receive for yourself my thanks for the kind manner [with which] you have conveyed the notification."[58]

Meade also advised Halleck that General Buford reported to him that day that his cavalry division had attacked Williamsport the day before, hoping to seize all of Lee's wagon and ambulance trains parked along the bottomland between Williamsport and the Potomac River and extending out the Cumberland Valley Turnpike and Hagerstown Road. Buford informed Meade that his attack was unsuccessful; he found Williamsport "guarded by a large force of infantry and artillery," and "heavy forces were coming into Williamsport all night."[59]

Indeed, Buford had been repulsed at Williamsport. At the same time, General Kilpatrick's cavalry division had also been repulsed as it attacked Lee's wagon and ambulance trains, and those trains' escorts, as they were rumbling down Potomac Street in Hagerstown at the same time on 6 July as Buford's division attacked at Williamsport.[60]

Clearly, the defeat at Gettysburg had failed to demoralize Lee's army; it likely increased its resolve. The army remained a dangerous foe, or as Clausewitz famously stated, it was like a "wounded lion." Confronting Lee's army would not be easy.

Later that day, another message was received from Halleck. This time, Halleck forwarded to Meade a communication he received from President Lincoln that read: "We have certain information that Vicksburg surrendered to General Grant on the 4th of July. Now, if General Meade can complete his work, so gloriously prosecuted thus far, by the literal or substantial destruction of Lee's army, the rebellion will be over."[61]

Undoubtedly pleased to hear of the fall of Vicksburg, Meade had to have been concerned about the president believing that Lee's army could be "destroyed." Literally, or even substantially, destroying an army as large and as sophisticated as Lee's—now even further strengthened by the supplies it obtained in its operations in Pennsylvania—was hardly realistic. Yet that is where Lincoln appeared to have set the bar for success.

19

I FOUND HE HAD RETIRED IN THE NIGHT

From his quarters in the United States Hotel in Frederick, Meade penned a letter to Margaret early in the morning of 8 July. "I arrived here yesterday," he wrote. "The army is assembling at Middletown. I think we shall have another battle before Lee can cross the river, though from all accounts he is making a great effort to do so." He then added: "For my part, I have to follow and fight him, I would rather do it at once in Maryland than to follow into Virginia." Meade explained to her that he had received her letters and "rejoiced that you are treated with such distinction on account of my humble services." Meade added: "I claim no extraordinary merit for this last battle, and would prefer waiting a little while to see what my career is to be before making any pretensions. I did and shall continue to do my duty to the best of my abilities, but knowing as I do, that battles are often decided by accidents, and that no man of sense will say in advance what their result will be, I wish to be very careful in not bragging before the right time."[1]

Meade informed his wife that young George "is very well, though both of us are a good deal fatigued with our recent operations." He then explained to Margaret the bald truth of what the campaign and battle had done to him. "From the time I took command," he wrote, "til today, now over ten days, I have not changed my clothes, have not had a regular night's rest, and many nights not a wink of sleep, and for several days did not even wash my face and hands, no regular food, and all the time in a great state of anxiety. Indeed, I think I have lived as much in this time as in the last thirty years."[2]

Meade gave Margaret the good news that "'Old Baldy' is still living and apparently doing well. The ball passed within half an inch of my thigh,

Major General George Gordon Meade. (Library of Congress)

passed through the saddle and entered Baldy's stomach. I did not think he could live, but the old fellow has such a wonderful tenacity of life that I am in hopes he will."[3]

On the morning of 8 July, the First Corps was at Hamburg and under orders to move by way of the National Road to Turner Pass in the South Mountain range. The Second Corps had only gotten as far as Taneytown on 7 July and was under orders to move to Frederick. The Third Corps was at Mechanicstown and would move "to a point three miles southwest of Frederick." The Fifth Corps was at Utica and was ordered to move to Middletown. The Sixth Corps was at Hamburg and was ordered to move to Middletown. The Eleventh Corps reached Middletown on 7 July and was ordered to Turner Pass; General Schurz's division was ordered to advance to Boonsboro. The Twelfth Corps was at Walkersville and was under orders to move to Jefferson, just south of Frederick. The Artillery Reserve was situated at Woodsboro and would move to Frederick.[4]

Colonel J. Irvin Gregg's cavalry brigade was galloping from Chambersburg, Pennsylvania, to Middletown. Smith's division of the Department of the Susquehanna was at Altodale, Pennsylvania, and was under orders by Meade to march to Waynesboro, north of Hagerstown. Meade's headquarters would move from Frederick to Middletown.[5]

Once again, the marching was not easy. Lieutenant Washington A. Roebling sent a message to General Warren on the morning of 8 July, telling him he went over both gaps in the mountains. "The roads," he wrote, "are frightful. [The Sixth Corps batteries] have been trying all day to get over. It will take until tomorrow noon before [they] are entirely across, and then the horses will be unfit for use." Henry Keiser of the Ninety-Sixth Pennsylvania penned in his diary on the afternoon of 8 July: "It commenced raining at two last night and did not leave off until two this afternoon, raining hard all the time." He then added, "Our rations have run out, and half the boys have not eaten anything since last night." General Newton wrote to army headquarters, asserting that the artillery of the Sixth Corps and Third Corps would "consume at least all day in getting [to Middletown]. This delay has been in consequence of the extremely bad roads over the mountain." Newton claimed later that day that he would "leave behind the Vermont Brigade, about 1,700 strong, because they have already made one march today, without rations. They may follow after rations are issued." General Howard's Eleventh Corps reached Turner Pass, but Howard sent a message to Meade: "My men are suffering for want of shoes." He also wrote to General Ingalls: "One half of the effective strength of the corps cannot march for want of shoes and stockings.

Dragging Up the Guns, *by Alfred R. Waud. (Library of Congress)*

Draw 3,000 pairs of shoes and 5,000 pairs of stockings ... and forward them to this place. The remainder of the corps will march as soon as provisions arrive."[6]

On 8 July, some portion of the road from Mechanicstown to Frederick over which marched the One Hundred Twenty-Fourth New York in the Third Corps "was macadamized and covered only with a slight coating of thin mud and shallow pools of slush," recalled Charles Weygant, "but in other places the road was deep, and several of my men who had lost one of their shoes 'away down underground' and thrown away the other, kept their pants rolled above their knees and declared they would 'wade it through bare-footed sink or swim.'"[7]

Weygant then remembered:

We were [to the people of Frederick] the most unsoldierly, sorry looking victorious veteran army it has been the lot of any human being of this century to look upon. For two days we had been spattering each other with mud and slush, and soaked with rain which was falling in torrents. Our guns and swords were covered with rust; our pockets were filled with dirt; muddy water oozed from the toes of the footmen's government shoes at every step, ran out of the tops of the horsemen's boots, and dropped from the ends of the fingers, noses, and chins of all.[8]

General Meade and his staff and escorts were often seen riding along the seemingly endless columns of troops. One soldier in the Twenty-Second Massachusetts in the Fifth Corps, on the way to Middletown from

Utica, was suffering from chronic diarrhea and "was compelled to fall out for a few minutes." As he did so, General Meade and his staff rode across the fields and overtook the "straggler."

"What are you doing here, sir, so soon out of camp? What command do you belong to?" barked Meade.

"I belong to the Twenty-Second Massachusetts, First Division, Fifth Army Corps. I was obliged to fall out, General, and am joining my command," the soldier replied.

"What are you straggling for?" Meade asked. "Didn't you know, sir, that it is punishable by death?"

"Yes, sir, but I am not straggling," the soldier answered.

"Don't you call being out of ranks and cutting off this bend through the field 'straggling,' sir?" asked Meade.

"But, General, I have chronic diarrhea, and was just . . . . "

"Stop it, sir! Don't talk! Move on! And if you are caught outside of the marching column again, I will arrest you!"

The soldier fell back in the ranks, and Meade and his staff rode off alongside the marching columns of soldiers.[9]

While Meade's army struggled through the rain and mud to get to Middletown on 8 July, Lee's army already arrived at Hagerstown and Williamsport. Lee's troops had suffered over the past two days, just like Meade's men. Torrential rains, mud, hunger, and exhaustion plagued them all the way from Gettysburg.

Lee was aware when he arrived at Hagerstown on 7 July that his bridge over the swollen Potomac River had been destroyed. He also knew that his long-awaited ammunition train had reached the southern bank of the Potomac River across from Williamsport. Ever since the army's quartermaster and subsistence wagon trains and ambulance trains reached Williamsport on 5 July, wagons and ambulances had been ferried across the Potomac River on flats attached by a rope to a cable stretched across the river. That effort continued around the clock as Lee's army had nearly five thousand wagons and ambulances pulled by nearly thirty thousand horses and mules. After dropping off the wagons and ambulances, the return trips of the flats brought the wagons filled with the much-needed ammunition to Williamsport. Soon, Lee's men took boats out of the Chesapeake & Ohio Canal basin at Williamsport and converted them into ferry boats in order to speed up the efforts.[10]

Lee wasted no time once he arrived at Hagerstown. He immediately issued orders that "all needful arrangements be promptly made for an engagement [with the enemy] which may be expected at any time. Additional ammunition has been received at Williamsport, and all required will be processed in the different commands respectively." Because Lee's artillery batteries had suffered a devastating loss of horses, just as Meade's had, Lee directed that "animals needed in the artillery will be taken wherever found in the hands of officers and men unauthorized to be mounted and by impressments if necessary in the country, the animals to be paid for."[11]

Lee's immediate goal was to establish a defense line. He was aware that Meade's army would be approaching on the National Road. In fact, on 8 July, Howard's Eleventh Corps and Sykes's Fifth Corps had reached Middletown, only twenty-three miles from Williamsport. Newton's First Corps was only two miles behind the Fifth Corps. Farther behind were Sedgwick's Sixth Corps and Birney's Third Corps. Hays's Second Corps and Slocum's Twelfth Corps had just reached Frederick. All would be at Middletown or Boonsboro by the end of that day. Screening the approach of Meade's army were Buford's and Kilpatrick's cavalry divisions along the National Road and the Williamsport-Boonsboro Road outside of Boonsboro.[12]

Colonel Edward P. Alexander, one of Lee's trusted engineers and artillery commanders, believed on 8 July that Lee's army had only about forty-eight hours before Meade's army would be in front of it. Screening Lee's army were five brigades of cavalry and five batteries of artillery from Stuart's cavalry division situated on the National Road, between Funkstown and Beaver Creek, and along the Williamsport-Boonsboro Road, from College of St. James to a position about four miles west of Boonsboro.[13]

West and south of Hagerstown, Lee and his staff engineers and his three corps commanders and their staff engineers, as well as Colonel Alexander and Major Jedediah Hotchkiss, laid out a defense line of breastworks and gun emplacements from Hagerstown all the way to Downsville near the Potomac River. The engineers patched together a defense line along a dominant but broken ridge known as Salisbury Ridge. East of Salisbury Ridge were boggy lowlands drained by Antietam Creek, from Hagerstown to just south of Funkstown, and by a stream known as Marsh Run, from Funkstown to well south of the Williamsport-Boonsboro Road. Salisbury Ridge rises to nearly 150 feet above, and about one mile west of, Marsh Run. The defense line would extend for nearly nine miles. It would be known as the Downsville line.[14]

An accomplished engineer, Lee directed the layout of the defense line. Any attempt by Meade's army to assault Lee's positions along Salisbury Ridge would require Meade's troops to cross through muddy bottomlands, wade across Marsh Run, crest several small ridges, and then ascend nearly half a mile of undulating, rocky slopes before reaching the Confederate works, all the time under fire. Gun emplacements were constructed across the ridge. So sophisticated were the artillery emplacements that no matter where an assault would be directed against Lee's army there, it would run into crossfire from Confederate artillery. Likewise, the flanks of the defense line were secure; Lee's right flank was anchored on bluffs near the Potomac River, and his left flank was anchored on high ground overlooking Hagerstown, supported and screened by Stuart's cavalry division. The Downsville line would be completed by the morning of 10 July.[15]

No sooner had Lee gotten the Downsville line under construction than he directed his engineers to build a bridge across the Potomac River at Falling Waters. He ordered each corps commander to direct their pioneer teams to Williamsport to assist in the effort.[16]

At mid-afternoon on 8 July, Meade wrote to Halleck what he had learned from the army's scouts. He had been advised that Lee's wagon trains were crossing the Potomac River at Williamsport "very slowly." He added: "So long as the river is unfordable, the enemy cannot cross." Meade then wrote: "From all I can gather, the enemy extends from Hagerstown to Williamsport, covering the march of their train. Their cavalry and infantry pickets are advanced to the Hagerstown and Sharpsburg Pike, on the general line of the Antietam." Meade's intelligence of Lee's positions was largely correct. "We hold Boonsboro," Meade continued, "and our pickets, 4 miles in front, toward Hagerstown, are in contact with the enemy's pickets. My army is assembling at Middletown slowly." Meade wrote about the fact that "the rains of yesterday and last night have made all the roads, but pikes, almost impassable. Artillery and wagons are stalled; it will take time to collect them together. A large portion of the men are barefooted." Meade informed Halleck that "the spirit of the troops was high" and that they were "ready and willing to make every exertion to push forward." He then added: "The very first moment I can get the different commands, the artillery and cavalry, properly supplied and in hand, I will move forward."[17]

Meade then addressed to Halleck some realities his army faced. "Be assured," Meade wrote, "I most earnestly desire to try the fortunes of war with the enemy on this side of the river, hoping through Providence and the bravery of my men to settle the question, but I should do wrong not to frankly tell you of the difficulties encountered." Meade then raised his concerns about the message Halleck sent him from President Lincoln. Wrote Meade: "I expect to find the enemy in a strong position, well covered with artillery, and I do not desire to imitate his example at Gettysburg, and assault a position where the chances were so greatly against success. I wish in advance to moderate the expectations of those who, in ignorance of the difficulties to be encountered, may expect too much. All that I can do under the circumstances I pledge this army to do."[18]

Obviously prodded by the president, Halleck wrote back to Meade on 8 July, claiming to have "reliable information that the enemy is crossing at Williamsport." Halleck added: "The opportunity to attack his divided forces should not be lost. The President is urgent and anxious that your army should move against him by forced marches."[19]

Meade responded swiftly, stating, matter-of-factly, "My information as to the crossing of the enemy does not agree with that just received in your dispatch." Meade reiterated that Lee's army was "in position between Funkstown and Williamsport" and that he had just received information that the enemy "has driven my cavalry forces in front of Boonsboro." Meade then addressed the president's demand that the army move against the enemy by forced marches. "My army," wrote Meade, "is and has been making forced marches, short of rations, and barefooted. One corps marched yesterday and last night over 30 miles." He ended his terse note, writing, "I take occasion to repeat that I will use my utmost efforts to push forward this army."[20]

When Halleck received Meade's dispatch, he wrote yet another message to the army commander. "Do not understand me as expressing any dissatisfaction; on the contrary, your army has done most nobly." He then wrote: "It is telegraphed from near Harper's Ferry that the enemy have been crossing [the Potomac River] for the last two days. It is also reported that they have a bridge across." Halleck then added: "If Lee's army is so divided by the river, the importance of attacking the part on this side is incalculable."[21]

Meade had no such information that Lee's army was crossing the Potomac River. In fact, what Meade had learned was that Lee's forward units were pressing against his forward units, west of Boonsboro. That gave him confidence that Lee was attempting to develop defenses and that the forward units were being used to keep Meade's forward units at bay. There was no indication that Lee's army was crossing the river. Beyond that, if Halleck was demanding that Meade divide his forces to attack some elements of Lee's army on the Virginia side, he was asking the impossible, because the bridge over the Potomac River at Harper's Ferry had been destroyed by French's troops on 7 July. In addition, Meade's pontoon bridges had only just arrived at Sandy Hook that day, across the Potomac from

Harper's Ferry, more than sixteen miles southwest of Middletown. Once at Sandy Hook, any force Meade would send across the Potomac River would then have more than twenty miles more to march just to get into a position to attack an enemy force that was south of the river. There was no means by which Meade could get any element of his army across the Potomac unless he directed it to fall back to Sandy Hook.[22]

As a learned and experienced military commander, Meade also understood that to attack an enemy army required the use of all the forces at his disposal. Clausewitz refers to that axiom as "economy of force." If Meade knew that Lee had divided his force, he would have certainly continued his march toward Boonsboro—as he was doing—with the idea of striking what enemy force was north of the Potomac, using everything under his command.[23]

Meade dictated to Seth Williams a circular to all his corps commanders for 9 July. He directed the Sixth Corps to move by the National Road from Middletown to Boonsboro. The Fifth Corps was ordered to move from Middletown "on the old Sharpsburg road to the crossing of the road through Fox's Gap with the road between Rohrersville and Boonsboro." The Twelfth Corps was to move from Middletown "to Rohrersville." The Third Corps was directed "to follow the Fifth Corps." The Second Corps was directed from Middletown "to follow the Twelfth Corps." The Eleventh Corps was ordered "to take a position in the rear of the Sixth Corps," and the First Corps was ordered "to occupy Turner Pass." The Artillery Reserve was directed to take the National Road from Middletown "and encamp with the Fifth Corps." Meade's headquarters would be established "near the Mountain House" on the National Road in Turner Pass. There, the Engineer Battalion would "encamp with the army headquarters." Across the National Road from the Mountain House were the ruins of the stone Washington Monument that the Signal Corps had taken over as a signal station. From that site was an uninterrupted, panoramic view of the Cumberland Valley, Boonsboro, Hagerstown, and even Williamsport. Meade wanted to be near that signal station. Signal stations had been established by orders from Meade between Frederick and Turner Pass on 7 July. On 8 July, communication was opened between Turner Pass and Boonsboro, as well as Elk Ridge, four miles from Boonsboro.[24]

Meade ordered that all necessary supplies received at Frederick "must be sent forward to the troops." He ordered all the wagons of quartermaster and subsistence stores parked in the Middletown Valley along the roads taken by their respective corps. "No trains," Meade commanded, "will accompany the troops except ammunition and medicine wagons and ambulances."[25]

Having desired General Humphreys to serve as his chief of staff ever since Meade had been named army commander, Meade finally got his way. On 8 July, Meade formally relieved General Butterfield as chief of staff. Generals Pleasonton and Warren, who had been acting as joint chiefs of staff, were returned to their prior positions. Pleasonton remained as commander of the cavalry corps, while Warren remained on Meade's staff as chief engineer. Meade elevated Humphreys to be his chief of staff. The next day, Meade named General French as commander of the Third Corps, relieving General Birney. Since 7 July, French's two brigades had been attached to that corps.[26]

The morning of 9 July was cloudy. For the first time in days there was no rain. Soldiers described the day as "close." It would become intensely hot and humid. Meade dictated a dispatch at Middletown to be sent to General Halleck at 11:00 A.M. "The army is moving in three columns," Meade stated, "the right column having in it three corps. The line occupied to-day with the advance will be on the other side of the mountains, from Boonsboro to Rohrersville." He then noted: "Two corps will march without their artillery, the animals being completely exhausted, many falling on the road." He explained to Halleck that his forward units had driven back the enemy's infantry from Boonsboro toward Hagerstown, a sign that Lee had not crossed the Potomac River. "I am still under the impression," Meade wrote, "that Lee's whole army is between Hagerstown and Williamsport." Meade then gave Halleck a glimpse of his strategic plan: "I propose to move on a line from Boonsboro toward the center of the [enemy's defense] line from Hagerstown to Williamsport, my left flank looking to the river and my right toward the mountains, keeping the road to Frederick in my rear and center."[27]

When Halleck received Meade's dispatch, he quickly "changed his tune." No longer would he argue for Meade to divide his army. Instead, because he was a military historian and scholar of military strategy and tactics, he probably recalled Clausewitz's axiom about "economy of force." He wrote to Meade at 3:00 P.M. "The evidence that Lee will fight north of the Potomac seems reliable. In that case, you will want all your forces in hand." With some humility, Halleck added: "Don't be influenced by any dispatch from here against your own judgment." That must have created a sense of relief in Meade, who by now was likely exasperated with the armchair generals in Washington. Perhaps it also reflected Halleck's understanding

Union troops marching through Middletown, Maryland, by Alfred R. Waud.
(Library of Congress)

that President Lincoln, who lacked formal military training, would not try to suggest Meade's next move.[28]

As it stood, on the night of 9 July, the headquarters of the army was at Turner Pass. There, too, were the First and Eleventh Corps. At nearby Fox's Gap were elements of the Third Corps; two brigades were at Middletown, having marched that day from Frederick. The Fifth and Sixth Corps were at Boonsboro and the Second and Twelfth Corps were at Rohrersville.[29]

Meade issued a circular to all his corps commanders for the movement on 10 July. The Twelfth Corps, followed by the Second Corps, were ordered to move at daylight, passing through Keedysville to Bakersville. The Fifth Corps was ordered to the bridge on the Antietam Creek on the road from Boonsboro to Williamsport. The Third Corps was directed to follow the Fifth Corps and take a position near the bridge over the Antietam. The Sixth Corps, followed by the First Corps, was directed to proceed along the Hagerstown Pike and take position on the north side of Beaver Creek.

The Eleventh Corps was to take up a position on the northwest side of Boonsboro, where it could support any of the other six corps. The Artillery Reserve was to position itself on the west side of Boonsboro. Meade instructed the corps commanders to "keep themselves in communication with the columns on the right and left, and be prepared to move forward if the developments of the day should require."[30]

By day's end of 10 July, Meade had positioned his entire army to confront the enemy. Given the horrific conditions and impediments he and his troops faced since leaving Gettysburg, Meade's effort, and that of the army, was nothing short of remarkable. The soldiers who left diaries recorded on 10 July that there was "considerable skirmishing with the enemy" as they advanced west of Boonsboro. Luther Furst of the Thirty-Ninth Pennsylvania in the Sixth Corps recorded: "The artillery has opened and indications prove as if they were going to make a stand. Reported that they are fortifying." Then he ended his entry with a note of concern. "It is thought that we ought not to risk a battle here as we have not over 50,000 efficient troops and the enemy equal that, if not more, with advantage of position and troops concentrated."[31]

Halleck correctly believed that Meade was literally going straight at Lee. At 9:00 P.M. on 10 July, Halleck wrote to the army commander: "I think it will be best for you to postpone a general battle until you can concentrate all your forces and get up your reserves and reinforcements." There were reinforcements en route to Meade's army from Harpers Ferry and Washington. Meade thought little of their value as combat-ready troops. Nevertheless, Meade must have received Halleck's dispatch with puzzlement. Halleck had gone from wanting forced marches to asking Meade to postpone any attack.[32]

On 11 July, Meade cautiously advanced his army to a position where the right flank of the Army of the Potomac—Howard's Eleventh Corps—rested just west of Funkstown, on the road from Hagerstown to Funkstown. The left flank of the army—Slocum's Twelfth Corps—was at Jones's Crossroads, where the Hagerstown-Sharpsburg Turnpike crosses the Williamsport-Boonsboro Road. The center of the army faced Marsh Run, generally aligned along the Hagerstown-Sharpsburg Turnpike. To the left of Howard's Eleventh Corps was Newton's First Corps. To Newton's left was Sedgwick's Sixth Corps, and to Sedgwick's left was Sykes's Fifth Corps. Hays's Second Corps formed on the left flank of Sykes's corps and the right flank of Slocum's Corps. All the troops were ordered to construct breastworks in front of their positions in order to defend the lines should the enemy attack. Meade sent his cavalry brigades toward Williamsport on the Williamsport-Boonsboro Road and, on the right, toward Hagerstown, Chewsville, and Leitersburg, making sure that any advance of the enemy would be detected. Meade's army was facing the enemy, and for many officers and men in the army, the situation was unsettling. Colonel Wainwright, the First Corps artillery chief, wrote in his diary that day: "Lee has not crossed into Virginia yet.... If he does not clear out soon, we shall have another fight. It would nearly end the rebellion if we could actually bag this army, but, on the other hand, a severe repulse of us would give them all the prestige at home and abroad which they lost at Gettysburg, and injure our morale greatly. I trust, therefore, that Meade will not attempt it, unless under circumstances which will make our chances of success at least four out of five."[33]

On 12 July, Meade received a dispatch from one of his staff officers, Lieutenant Ranald Mackenzie, then at Sandy Hook with one of the pontoon trains. "The [Potomac] river," it read, "has fallen 18 inches in the last twenty-four hours, and is still falling. A citizen states that he is acquainted with the river here, and that he judges from its appearance at this place, that the fords near Shepherdstown and Williamsport are now practicable for infantry." Meade realized then that he had to launch an attack or Lee's army would escape.[34]

At 4:30 P.M. of 12 July, Meade sent a message to Halleck. "Upon advancing my right flank across the Antietam this morning, the enemy abandoned Funkstown and Hagerstown and my line now extends from [Hagerstown] to Fair Play." A cavalry advance on the right revealed "the enemy to be strongly posted on the Hagerstown and Williamsport Road about 1½ miles from Hagerstown. On the left, the cavalry advance showed them to be in position back of St. James College and at Downsville." Meade then described the Downsville line. "Their position," he wrote, "runs along high ground from Downsville to near Hagerstown. This position they are entrenching. Batteries are established on it." Meade then shared with Halleck his intentions. "It is my intention," he wrote, "to attack them tomorrow, unless something interferes to prevent it, for the reason that delay will strengthen the enemy and will not increase my force." The message was transmitted by telegraph back to Frederick and, from there, to Halleck's office in Washington. Halleck received it at 8:00 P.M.[35]

Meade may have shared his intentions with one or more of his senior corps commanders. If he did, his plan was probably not received with enthusiasm. If Meade ordered an attack against the Downsville line, he would have to have the enthusiastic cooperation of all of his corps commanders to have a chance at it being successful. An attack against Lee's

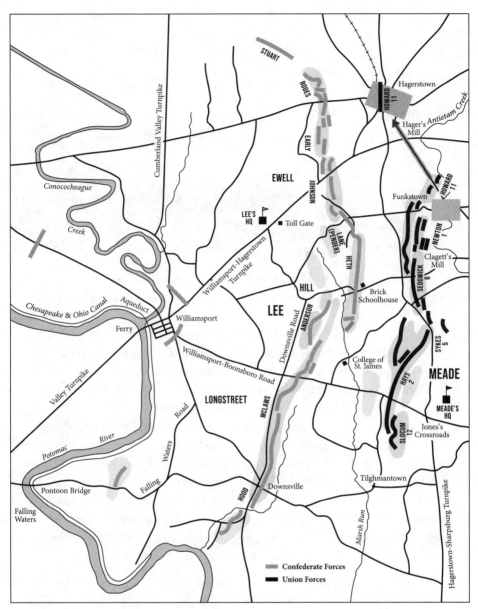

Map 19.1. 12 July 1863 to 14 July 1863: Lee's Downsville
line and Meade's approach.

The Downsville line, Lee's elaborate defense line between Hagerstown and Downsville, showing gun emplacements, by Edwin Forbes. (Library of Congress)

defenses at Williamsport would require the determined efforts of all involved, given the wetlands, creek, and long slope the troops would have to negotiate under concentrated small arms and artillery fire.

General Meade, along with Generals Humphreys and Warren, rode out to examine "the enemy's position and entrenchments as closely as practicable soon after coming up with [the enemy]," recalled Humphreys. "Wherever seen, the position was naturally strong, and was strongly intrenched," he wrote. "It presented no vulnerable points, but much of it was concealed from view.... Its flanks were secure and could not be turned."[36]

At the end of the day, Meade developed second thoughts. "It was my desire to attack the enemy in that position," he later testified, "although I had had no opportunity [before writing to Halleck] of examining critically and closely the enemy's position." Meade offered his rationale:

> In view of the important and tremendous issues involved in the result, knowing that if I were defeated the whole question would be reversed, the road to Washington and to the north open, and all the fruits of my victory at Gettysburg dissipated. I did not feel that I would be right in assuming the responsibility of blindly attacking the enemy without any knowledge of his position. I therefore called a council of war of my corps commanders, who were the officers to execute this duty, if it was determined upon, and laid before them the precise condition of affairs.[37]

In addition, Meade discovered that Lee's army had been resupplied with ammunition. Moreover, Meade must have been concerned about whether his army, after all it had been through, was even capable of making a successful assault against Lee's formidable defenses. Writing about those who criticized Meade for not attacking Lee's defenses on 13 July, Edwin Coddington insightfully notes: "[Meade's critics] failed to realize that after the battle [of Gettysburg] Meade no longer possessed a truly effective instrument for the accomplishment of his tasks." Coddington continues: "The army needed a thorough reorganization with new commanders and fresh troops." That would not happen until the spring of 1864. Coddington is absolutely correct.[38]

Meade's concerns about attacking Lee's defense lines undoubtedly mirrored those expressed by Lieutenant Haskell, who had occasion to view those defenses. "I felt the probability of defeat strongly at the time," he wrote to his family, "when we all supposed a conflict would certainly ensue; for always before a battle—at least it so appears to me—some dim presentiment of results, some unaccountable foreshadowing pervades the army." Haskell concluded, writing, "When [those presentiments] are general, I think they should not be wholly disregarded by the commander." Apparently, many officers and men in the army felt the same way as Haskell.[39]

The council met at 8:00 P.M. at Meade's headquarters tent about five miles behind the lines. In attendance was General Wadsworth of the First Corps. It appears that General Newton, then the First Corps commander, was ill. General Hays was present as the Second Corps commander, and General French was present as the Third Corps commander. None of those commanders had led an army corps in battle, and those three corps had suffered tremendous losses of officers and men at Gettysburg. Also present were General Sykes of the Fifth Corps, General Sedgwick of the Sixth Corps, General Howard of the Eleventh Corps, and General Slocum of the Twelfth Corps. With the exception of the Sixth Corps, all the other corps, particularly the Fifth and Eleventh Corps, had suffered enormous losses at Gettysburg. In addition, General Humphreys was present as Meade's chief of staff, and General Warren was there as Meade's chief engineer. General Pleasonton was also present.[40]

Meade testified that he "represented to those generals, so far as [he] knew it, the situation of affairs." Meade continued:

I told them that I had reason to believe, from all I could ascertain, that General Lee's position was a very strong one, and that he was prepared to give battle and defend it if attacked; that it was not in my power, from a want of knowledge of the ground, and from not having had time to make reconnaissances, to indicate any precise point of attack; that, nevertheless, I was in favor of moving forward and attacking the enemy and taking the consequences; but that I left it to their judgment, and would not do it unless it met with their approval.

"The opinion of the council," Meade testified later, "was very largely opposed to any attack without further examination." Apparently, only Generals Wadsworth and Howard were in favor of attacking. Those two corps commanders and their corps were not the forces Meade would have used for any attack. All the rest of the corps commanders were opposed to an attack, and the opposition, save General French, consisted of all the senior major generals who would have to lead their respective corps in any assault. "In view of the opinion of my subordinate officers," Meade testified, "I yielded, or abstained from ordering an assault." Meade did, however, give directions "for such an examination of the enemy's position as would enable us to form some judgment as to where he might be attacked with some degree and probability of success."[41]

On the rainy morning of 13 July, Meade and General Humphreys rode along the fields over which the reconnaissance in force would advance, observing, in detail, the ground occupied by the enemy and by the attacking forces. Meade then advanced divisions from the Second, Fifth, Sixth, and Twelfth Corps forward toward the Downsville line, in an effort to uncover a weak point. By the end of the day, Meade wrote to General Halleck:

> In my dispatch of yesterday, I stated that it was my intention to attack the enemy to-day, unless something intervened to prevent it. Upon calling my corps commanders together and submitting the question to them, five out of the six were unqualifiedly opposed to it. Under these circumstances, in view of the momentous consequences attending a failure to succeed, I did not feel myself authorized to attack until after I had made more careful examination of the enemy's position, strength, and defensive works. These examinations are now being made. So far completed they show the enemy to be strongly intrenched on a ridge running from the rear of Hagerstown past Downsville to the Potomac. I shall continue these reconnaissances with the expectation of finding some weak point, upon which, if I succeed, I shall hazard an attack.[42]

On receipt of Meade's dispatch, at 6:40 P.M., General Halleck wrote back to Meade three hours later. He very likely presented the matter to

Meade and his generals after Gettysburg, left to right: Generals Warren, French, Meade, Hunt, Humphreys, and Sykes. (Library of Congress)

President Lincoln. If so, Lincoln undoubtedly became aggravated at the delay and wanted to urge Meade to attack even though neither he nor Halleck knew anything about the situation facing Meade and his army. Halleck wrote: "You are strong enough to attack and defeat the enemy before he can effect a crossing. Act upon your own judgment and make your generals execute your orders. Call no council of war. It is proverbial that councils of war never fight. Re-enforcements are pushed on as rapidly as possible. Do not let the enemy escape."[43] Only three days before Halleck had asked Meade to postpone any attack until all the reinforcements had joined the army. Even though most of those reinforcements still had not arrived, he was demanding that Meade attack.

All through the night of 13 July and the wee hours of 14 July, Lee's army evacuated the Downsville line under cover of darkness, heavy rain, and dense smoke. On Lee's left flank, Ewell's corps left the breastworks and gun emplacements behind Hagerstown and moved to Williamsport, where they waded through the Chesapeake & Ohio Canal viaduct over Conococheague Creek and then waded across the Potomac River, the waters having fallen in depth enough to do so. On the right flank, Longstreet's corps evacuated the trenches and marched down the muddy Falling Waters Road and, at Falling Waters, crossed the Potomac on an eight-hundred-foot pontoon bridge that Lee's engineers had constructed over the preceding sixty-eight hours using the remnants of the pontoons from the bridge that had been destroyed on 4 July and actually constructing their own pontoons from scratch, making them watertight by using tar from melted barn roofing and dismantling barns and warehouses for the bridging and trestlework. Behind Longstreet's corps came Hill's corps at daylight.[44]

Meade directed a reconnaissance in force against the enemy's positions at 9:00 A.M., 14 July, consisting of the entire army. That movement developed the fact that Lee's army had abandoned the Downsville line and was crossing or had crossed the Potomac River.[45]

Meade ordered that the retreating Confederate army be pursued. One regiment of General Kilpatrick's cavalry division galloped toward Williamsport; the other elements of the division followed along the Falling Waters Road, where they collided with the rear guard of Lee's army, General Pettigrew's Division of Hill's corps. In an attack carried out by three Michigan regiments of General Custer's brigade, General Pettigrew was mortally wounded, and nearly two thousand prisoners, mostly those who had fallen out of the ranks, were captured. Custer's command was unable to do anything to prevent the last elements of Lee's army from crossing into Virginia.[46]

Many officers in the reconnaissance in force who observed Lee's abandoned defenses left diary entries about their observations. One of them was Colonel Wainwright. "These were by far the strongest I have seen yet," he wrote, "evidently laid out by engineers and built as if they meant to stand a month's siege." Wainwright continued: "The parapet was a good six feet wide on top, and the guns, which were very thick, were all placed so as to get a perfect crossfire and sweep their whole front." Indeed, Meade observed those defenses that morning, too, and he later testified that having examined those positions "[brought] me clearly to the opinion that an attack, under the circumstances which I had to proposed to make it, would have resulted disastrously to our arms." When asked for the reasons for that opinion, Meade said: "It is founded upon the strength of [the enemy's] position. I will say that if I had attacked the enemy in the position which they then occupied—he having the advantage of position

and being on the defensive, his artillery in position, and his infantry behind parapets and rifle-pits—the very same reasons and causes which produced my success at Gettysburg would have operated in his favor there,
and be likely to produce success on his part."[47]

At 11:00 A.M., Meade wrote a dispatch to General Halleck, likely knowing it would not be well received. "On advancing my army this morning,
with a view of ascertaining the exact position of the enemy and attacking
him if the result of the examination should justify one, I found on reaching
his lines, that they were evacuated. I immediately put my army in pursuit,
the cavalry in advance."[48]

At 1:00 P.M., Halleck responded to Meade's dispatch sent two hours
before: "The enemy should be pursued and cut up, wherever he may have
gone. This pursuit may or may not be upon the rear or flank, as circumstances may require. The inner flank towards Washington presents the
greatest advantage. Supply yourself from the country as far as possible.
I cannot advise details, as I do not know where Lee's army is, nor where
your pontoon bridges are."

After admitting he knew nothing about where Lee's army was or even
where Meade's pontoon bridges were, Halleck went one step too far:
"I need hardly say to you that the escape of Lee's army without another
battle has created great dissatisfaction in the mind of the President, and
it will require an active and energetic pursuit on your part to remove the
impression that it has not been sufficiently active heretofore."[49]

Meade was not a petulant man. Halleck's response, however, had to
have been maddening to Meade. He had pushed his army to the limits of
its endurance. Luther Furst of the Thirty-Ninth Pennsylvania said it all
in his diary entry on 14 July: "Our soldiers are very much fatigued, feel
sore and in need of clothes and rest. Our horses are getting poor and hundreds are dying every day." Moreover, Meade's reluctance to assault Lee's
defense line was because of his belief that it could not be taken and that
a bloody repulse would have undone all that was gained by the victory at
Gettysburg.[50]

Meade sat down in his tent at 2:30 P.M. and wrote a letter back to Halleck: "Having performed my duty conscientiously and to the best of my
ability, the censure of the President conveyed in your dispatch of 1:00 P.M.
this day, is, in my judgment, so undeserved that I feel compelled most respectfully to ask to be immediately relieved of command of the army."[51]

At 4:30 P.M., Halleck scribbled a note back to Meade. He had received
Meade's letter of resignation an hour and twenty minutes before. He undoubtedly talked with Lincoln about the news, and together, they crafted

the response. "My telegram, stating the disappointment of the President at the escape of Lee's army," Halleck wrote, "was not intended as a censure, but as a stimulus to active pursuit. It is not deemed a sufficient cause for your application to be relieved [from command of the army]." Unquestionably, Halleck's earlier remarks in the 1:00 P.M. dispatch setting forth the "dissatisfaction in the mind of the President" and his "impression that [the army] has not been sufficiently active heretofore" were not only totally unjustified but inexcusable. It seems that Meade was even angrier at the president and Halleck's claim that he needed a "stimulus to an active pursuit."[52]

Meade penned a letter to Margaret:

I found Lee in a very strong position, intrenched. I hesitated to attack him, without some examination of the mode of approaching him. This morning, when I advanced to feel his position and seek for a weak point, I found he had retired in the night and was nearly across the river. I immediately started in pursuit, and my cavalry captured two thousand prisoners, two guns, several flags, and killed General Pettigrew. On reporting these feats to General Halleck, he informed me that the President was very much dissatisfied at the escape of Lee. I immediately telegraphed I had done my duty to the best of my ability, and that the expressed dissatisfaction of the President I considered undeserved censure, and I asked to be immediately relieved. In reply he said it was not intended to censure me, but only to spur me on to an active pursuit, and that it was not deemed sufficient cause for relieving me. This is exactly what I expected; unless I did impracticable things, fault would be found with me. I have ignored the senseless adulation of the public and the press, and I am now just as indifferent to the censure bestowed without just cause.

I start tomorrow to run another race with Lee.[53]

According to Lincoln's secretary, John Hay, the president was "deeply grieved" by Meade's last dispatch. "We had only to stretch forth our hands and they were ours. And nothing I could say or do would make the army move," Hay reported Lincoln saying. Navy Secretary Gideon Welles penned in his diary that Lincoln told him that "he had dreaded, yet expected, this; that there has seemed to him for a full week a determination that Lee should escape with his force and plunder. There is bad faith somewhere. Meade has been pressed and urged, but only one of his generals was for an immediate attack, was ready to pounce on Lee; the rest held back. What does this mean, Mr. Welles? Great God! What does it mean?"[54]

The evening of 14 July, Lincoln wrote a letter to Meade. "As you had learned, I was dissatisfied," Lincoln wrote. "I have thought it best to kindly tell you why. I am very—very—grateful to you for the magnificent success you gave the cause of the country at Gettysburg; and I am sorry now to be the author of the slightest pain to you." Referring to Meade's dispatches to Generals Couch and Smith on 4 July, Lincoln wrote: "There appeared to be evidence that you, General Couch, and General Smith, were not seeking a collision with the enemy, but were trying to get him across the river without another battle." Concluding his letter, Lincoln wrote: "Again, my dear General, I do not believe you appreciate the magnitude of the misfortune involved in Lee's escape. He was within your easy grasp, and to have closed upon him would, in connection with our other late successes, have ended the war. As it is, the war will be prolonged indefinitely.... Your golden opportunity is gone and I am distressed immeasurably because of it."

Although Lincoln folded the letter and put it in an envelope, addressed to General Meade, he must have reconsidered his words and decided not to send it. The unsent letter was found years later after the deaths of both Lincoln and Meade and became part of the body of so-called evidence that continued to damage Meade's reputation, damage that is perpetuated to this day.[55]

Contrary to Lincoln's charges in the unsent letter, Meade's letters to Generals Couch and Smith addressed his determination to move against Lee using a parallel course; they were hardly written to inform those generals that he wanted to avoid a "collision with the enemy" and that he was "trying to get [the enemy] across the river without another battle." Lincoln simply had no concept whatsoever of how retreating armies are pursued. Likewise, Meade had no "golden opportunity" on 13 July. His crippled, hungry, and exhausted army was facing the prospects of assaulting Lee's elaborate and virtually impregnable defenses. Meade observed them; Lincoln did not. Those positions can be observed today. To make that assault against any segment of Lee's defense lines would have required the assault force to move nearly a mile across open, undulating ground, wading a swollen stream, and then moving up a slope, the summit of which was more than 150 feet above the surface of the stream, all the while under the concentrated artillery and small arms fire from a well-positioned enemy of almost equal size as Meade's.

Publicly, Lincoln stated in a cabinet meeting on 17 July, that Meade "has committed a terrible mistake." Echoing Lincoln's criticism, much of the contemporary disparagement came from civilian members of the Lincoln administration, Gideon Welles, Edwin M. Stanton, and Charles Dana, to name the prominent critics. All those criticisms were directed to Meade's failure to attack on 13 July and Meade's "want of decision and self-reliance in an emergency," as well as his "missed opportunity." There were some in the army who criticized Meade for not attacking on 13 July, too, and their comments were not unlike those of the civilian officials in Lincoln's administration.[56]

With respect to whether Meade should have attacked Lee's defense lines on 13 July, Edwin Coddington provides a somewhat contradictory assessment. "Meade should have heeded his own counsel [to attack Lee on 13 July]," writes Coddington, "which was so ably seconded by his two valued advisors, Warren and Humphreys." General Humphreys, however, was not enthusiastic about attacking Lee. He believed that a reconnaissance in force would have been useful, and that is what Meade directed his army to perform on 13 and 14 July. "If we had made the attack," Humphreys testified, "there is no doubt that we should have lost very severely." Sedgwick, Slocum, Sykes, and Hays agreed with Humphreys's assessment. That is where the argument should end. Coddington continues: "Meade's unfortunate moment of hesitation [to attack Lee on 13 July] gave his reputation a blow from which it never fully recovered. [Meade's] detractors attached to it," Coddington concludes, "a significance out of proportion to its true meaning, and Lincoln never forgave him for not venturing an attack of some sort when he seemed [to Lincoln] to have the opportunity." Coddington's analysis there is correct.[57]

Sadly, the blow to Meade's reputation leveled by President Lincoln, General Halleck, and others is how history has remembered him, even after out-generaling Robert E. Lee to claim a decisive victory in the largest land engagement ever fought on the North American continent and the first victory of the Army of the Potomac since the war began. One wonders, though, what Meade's detractors, including Lincoln, Welles, Stanton, and Dana, would have said had Meade attacked Lee's defense lines on 13 July and suffered a bloody and crippling repulse, which likely would have occurred. We will never know.

EPILOGUE

On 15 July, General Meade marched his tired, hungry, and depleted army to Sandy Hook and Berlin, Maryland, the sites of the placement of the army's pontoon bridges across the Potomac River. Meade's headquarters were established at Berlin. Two pontoon bridges spanned the river there. On 17 July, the army crossed the Potomac River into Virginia. As Meade's army was under way, four days of riots that took place in New York City in response to the enforcement of the draft had finally ended.[1]

Despite his victory at Gettysburg, Meade had become the subject of biting criticism from Lincoln as well as those who were Lincoln's closest advisers, including Secretary of War Edwin M. Stanton. All the criticism centered around Meade pursuing Lee's retreating army too slowly; not intending to engage Lee in another battle north of the Potomac River but rather allowing Lee to escape back to Virginia; and not blindly attacking Lee's formidable defense lines on 13 July, thereby giving Lee the opportunity to escape in the wee hours of 14 July.[2]

Much of the criticism emanated from Lincoln's notion that Lee's army, somehow, could have been destroyed if Meade had only vigorously pursued the enemy and then blindly attacked it when the Army of the Potomac came face to face with it on 13 July. Incredibly, no civilian official from inside Lincoln's administration ever gave Meade credit for out-generaling General Robert E. Lee at Gettysburg and thereby delivering the first victory of the Army of the Potomac since its formation in November 1861. Few historians have done so either.[3]

Many of Meade's corps commanders and their staff officers heard of Lincoln's expectation that Meade destroy the enemy. Lieutenant Frank Haskell was one of those officers who wrote to his family about Lincoln's expectations: "We shall probably cross into Virginia tomorrow, and then God only knows the rest.... The purpose is—to destroy the Rebel Army. The details of this destruction are not arranged. Look to the Polititians

Bridges across the Potomac River at Berlin, Maryland, and supply trains ready to cross. Part of Meade's army crossed the Potomac River on the two bridges at Berlin. (Library of Congress)

[*sic*] at Washington for all such matters. They can fix it. Shoemakers, Quacks, and the like know these things—Generals in the field do not."[4] Such comments from a lowly lieutenant made no difference. He likely represented, though, how most general officers felt about the matter. But we really don't know. What we do know is that the criticism reached such a level that the Joint Committee on the Conduct of the War in Congress conducted hearings on Meade's generalship in the Gettysburg Campaign in the spring of 1864. Those testifying against Meade were, of course, General Sickles and his allies, Generals Birney, Butterfield, and Pleasonton. General Doubleday also got in on the act, still smarting after Meade had replaced him as commander of the First Corps on 1 July. Since then, many historians have marched in step with Meade's contemporary critics, asserting all of the same allegations about Meade's "failings" as did Lincoln

and his confidants. For all those critics, the high probability of an attack on 13 July being repulsed with heavy casualties does not enter the equation. It seems as though Lincoln and his confidants cared nothing about that. Politics trumped every consideration. So, too, with many historians.[5]

Meade did have his supporters; they were all in the army. Some of them testified for him before the Joint Committee on the Conduct of the War. Generals Humphreys, Warren, Wright, Hancock, Sedgwick, Hays, and Sykes, all of whom counseled Meade against a blind attack against Lee's defense lines on 13 July, were among them.

It did not take General Halleck long to understand the truth of the matter. He evidently realized that the criticism of Meade's performance was both unwarranted and not truthful; it was born out of expectations that were totally unrealistic. He also understood that the criticism was damaging not only to Meade but to the Union cause. On 28 July 1863, Halleck wrote to Meade, who was then with the army at Warrenton, Virginia:

> Your fight at Gettysburg met with universal approbation of all military men here. You handled your troops in that battle as well, if not better, than any general has handled his army during the war. You brought all your forces into action at the right time and place, which no commander of the Army of the Potomac has done before.
>
> And now a few words, in regard to subsequent events. You should not have been surprised or vexed at the President's disappointment at the escape of Lee's army. He thought that Lee's defeat was so certain that he felt no little impatience at his unexpected escape. I have no doubt, general, that you felt the disappointment as keenly as anyone else. Such things occur to us without any fault of our own. Take it altogether, your short campaign has proved your superior generalship, and your merit, as you will receive, the confidence of the Government and the gratitude of the country. I need not assure you, general, that I have lost none of the confidence which I felt in you when I recommended you for the command.[6]

One prominent general who presented not altogether favorable testimony before the Joint Committee on the Conduct of the War, Henry Jackson Hunt, Meade's chief of artillery, later became a staunch supporter of Meade's generalship during the Gettysburg Campaign. Hunt was an unlikely spokesman for Meade. Meade had severely scolded Hunt; in fact, shortly after the army had crossed the Potomac River and reentered Virginia, Meade claimed that Hunt had mismanaged the movement of the ammunition wagon trains of the Artillery Reserve during the Battle of

Gettysburg, a duty Hunt had never been given, because the Artillery Reserve was commanded by General Tyler.[7]

On 21 July, Hunt wrote a letter to Meade's chief of staff, General Humphreys, requesting that the general commanding relieve him of his duties as chief of artillery "as soon as his arrangements permit." Hunt continued: "Under existing orders and practices the position is not one that I can hold with any advantage to the service, consistently with self-respect." Angrily, Meade threatened to muster Hunt out of the army, stripping him of his rank. Hunt became incensed and refused to withdraw his letter of resignation. General Humphreys interfered and negotiated a resolution. It seems that Meade apologized to Hunt, who then withdrew his request to be relieved of his duties.[8]

The Hunt resignation episode is important because he, of all officers, had every right to join the chorus of Meade critics. Yet that is not what occurred. On 12 January 1888, sixteen years after General Meade died, Hunt, then living at the Soldiers' Home in Washington, wrote a letter to Brevet Major General Alexander Stewart Webb about Meade's generalship during the Gettysburg Campaign. It read in pertinent part:

> Now, I was no means a favorite with Meade; he rarely consulted me as a Chief of Artillery is consulted—or, e.g.,—he consulted the Chief of Engineers or of staff, etc.
>
> I am under no sort of obligation to him that would lead me to sustain him if wrong, nor have I any occasion for ill-feeling or malice towards him—i.e., there was no close personal relations between us, such as there was with Humphreys and Gibbon and yourself that could or would in any respect whatever sway my judgment. We differed on some points, i.e., sometimes I was vexed, once I *demanded* to be relieved—so I could be impartial—I think.
>
> Now, Webb, as I have studied this battle because I have written about it and had to study it, Meade has grown and grown upon me....
>
> Meade was suddenly placed in command. From that moment *all* his acts and intentions, as I can judge of them, were just what they *ought* to have been, except perhaps in his order to attack at Falling Waters on the morning of the 13th, and especially on the 14th of July, when his Corps Commanders reported against it, and I was *then* in favor of the attack, so I can't blame him. He was *right* in his orders as to Pipe Creek; *right* in his determination under certain circumstances to fall back to it; *right* in pushing up to Gettysburg after the battle commenced; *right* in remaining there; *right* in making his battle a

purely defensive one; *right*, therefore in taking the line he did; *right* in not attempting a counter attack at *any* stage of the battle; *right* as to his pursuit of Lee. Rarely has more skill, vigor, or wisdom been shown under such circumstances as he was placed in, and it would, I think, belittle his grand record of that campaign by a formal defense against his detractors, who will surely go under as will this show story.[9]

Why Lincoln and his confidants never saw Meade's achievement in the Gettysburg Campaign as Hunt and other professional soldiers did was because, in Hunt's words, "the hopes and expectations [of Lincoln and others] excited by the victory of Gettysburg were as unreasonable as the fears that had preceded it."[10]

ACKNOWLEDGMENTS

It takes many dedicated people to produce a book. That is certainly the case here. No single person has done more to help me make this book a reality than my dear wife, Genevieve. She, too, believed in the compelling story of General Meade and wanted to see his cause in print; she proofread chapters and typed chapters and was tireless in formatting all the chapters, prologue, epilogue, bibliography, and endnotes. Done, I know, out of love—I am a fortunate man. I love her more than I can say. My three children, Annie Louise, Philip, and Thomas, were patient throughout the writing of this book and its formatting stages. They spent so much time on the battlefields of Gettysburg while I was researching the book that they began to refer to it as their backyard. I know they felt neglected at times, but I also know they cheered me on as I was getting close to being finished. I love them all.

Outside of my family, others helped immensely in the production of this book. My longtime, patient, and faithful chief of staff, Sharon Howard, typed all of the chapter drafts, sharing some of those duties with Genevieve. Likewise, Lyndon Howard prepared all the maps. Speaking of patience, Lyndon has it in spades. Maps are always difficult, and yet, without a moment's hesitation, he tackled them all, including many retakes that were necessitated by my errors. Sharon and Lyndon are great; I am most thankful.

Every book needs a champion, a person who is its advocate from the beginning of its writing until its publication. Advocates are rare, particularly in my field, as few individuals have a working knowledge of not only the Campaign and Battle of Gettysburg but also the historiography of those events. Peter Carmichael is one of those wonderful individuals who not only has a marvelous grasp of the Gettysburg story—and the Meade story—but also of how historians have treated Gettysburg and Meade. Peter has been an incredible support. I am so grateful for his advocacy for this project, his thoughtful and insightful suggestions, and, above all, his long-standing friendship.

Beyond an advocate, a writer needs a publisher, and no publisher is better than the University of North Carolina Press for books such as this one. The editorial director at Chapel Hill, Mark Simpson-Vos, has been enthusiastic about this project from the beginning. No author could have a better director of his press than Mark. I am most grateful.

Many other individuals have helped make this book a reality, too many to name. The late Jay Luvaas at the Army War College at Carlisle, Pennsylvania, is one I must mention. I spent many hours with Jay talking about George Meade. One day he handed me an "Abstract" written by one of his students about Meade's generalship during the Campaign and Battle of Gettysburg, entitled "The Operational Art of George Gordon Meade." The writer, Lieutenant Colonel David A. Rolston, did a fabulous job. Frankly, his manuscript not only changed my thinking about

Meade but convinced me to write this book! I have since learned that Rolston, a full colonel, died at the age of seventy-one in Yorktown, Virginia, in 2016, a decorated veteran of the Vietnam War and Operation Desert Shield. I am indebted to him, and I thank God for his remarkable service to my country and for the service of all the others like him.

One of my mentors is Edward M. "Mac" Coffman, the retired professor of military history at the University of Wisconsin. Mac and I became great friends, and it was he who introduced me to Dennis Hart Mahan, the West Point professor who wrote the book *The Outpost*, about the operational use of an advance corps. That was earth-shattering in terms of understanding Meade at Gettysburg. He gave me a copy of Mahan's book, and the two of us discussed its tenets at our weekly lunches at our favorite barbeque joint in town. I dearly love Mac and am grateful for our hours talking history together.

Many wonderful folks shared with me diaries of their ancestors who fought in the Army of the Potomac under General Meade; Jim Cobb and Philip Maxson are among them. Thank you.

The Horse Soldier at Gettysburg, and its proprietors, the Small family, have always helped me to locate unpublished diaries, and they did so for this book. Steve Lichti of Martinez, California, provided me with the remarkable letter of J. F. Slagle, recounting his experience as a staff officer to General Doubleday during the Gettysburg Campaign. What a letter! Heritage Auctions in Dallas, Texas, gave me a copy of the fabulous letter of Colonel Paul Oliver, a staff officer to General Butterfield.

Beyond all those great people are institutions that made archival resources available to me: The New York State Library; the United States Army Military History Institute; the Southern Historical Collection at the University of North Carolina; Gettysburg College; the Gettysburg National Military Park; the Hagerstown–Washington County Historical Society; Yale University; the Historical Society of Oak Park and River Forest, Illinois; the Historical Society of Pennsylvania; the Virginia Historical Society; the Virginia Baptist Historical Society; the American Civil War Museum; the Library of Congress; and the National Archives. I am very grateful for all their help and resources.

Finally, I must say a word about my late father, Henry Pell Brown. During World War II, he was a captain in command of companies A and B, 636 Tank Destroyer Battalion, in the Thirty-Sixth Division. He saw action in North Africa, Sicily, Italy, and southern France, where he was badly wounded. He often spoke of the bloody campaign from Salerno to the Rapido and Gari Rivers, Monte Cassino, and Anzio, as well as the liberation of Rome. I recall with great fondness my many talks with him. He spoke only about the mechanics of war, never about himself. From him, I first learned about blind attacks against well-established enemy positions, pursuits of retreating armies through mountains, overextended supply lines, the central importance of quartermasters, and why some generals were "great" to those they commanded and others were not. What he explained to me about war will always remain with me.

Kent Masterson Brown
Lexington, Kentucky

NOTES

Abbreviations

ACWM	American Civil War Museum
AHI	*American History Illustrated*
B&L	*Battles and Leaders of the Civil War*
CR	*Carroll Record*
F&MC	Franklin & Marshall College
GC	Gettysburg College
GM	*Gettysburg Magazine*
GNMP	Gettysburg National Military Park
HWCHS	Hagerstown–Washington County Historical Society
HA	Heritage Auctions
HS	The Horse Soldier Shop
HSOP&RF	Historical Society of Oak Park and River Forest, Illinois
HSP	Historical Society of Pennsylvania
JC	James Cobb Collection
JCCW	Joint Committee on the Conduct of the War
JMSI	*Journal of Military Service Institute*
KMB	Kent Masterson Brown Collection
LOC	Library of Congress
MOLLUS	Military Order of the Loyal Legion of the United States
NA	National Archives
NAR	*North American Review*
NYSL	New York State Library
OR	*The War of the Rebellion: A Compilation of the Official Records of the Union and Confederate Armies*
PH	*Pennsylvania History*
PMHB	*Pennsylvania Magazine of History and Biography*
PSA	Pennsylvania State Archives
PM	Philip Maxson Collection
RR	*Rebellion Record*
RG	Record Group
RU	Rutgers University
SL	Steve Lichti Collection
SHC	Southern Historical Collection, University of North Carolina
USAMHI	United States Army Military History Institute
USGS	United States Geological Survey
VBHS	Virginia Baptist Historical Society
VHS	Virginia Historical Society

WHS   Wisconsin Historical Society
YUL   Yale University Library

Prologue

1. Fry, "McDowell's Advance to Bull Run," *B&L*, 1:181–93, 194.

2. Warner, *Generals in Blue*, 290–91.

3. McClellan, "Peninsular Campaign," *B&L*, 2:160–81.

4. Ibid.; Johnston, "Manassas to Seven Pines," *B&L*, 2:202–19.

5. Imboden, "Stonewall Jackson in the Shenandoah," *B&L*, 2:282–301; Longstreet, "Seven Days," *B&L*, 2:396–405; Johnson and Buel, "Opposing Forces in the Seven Days Battles," *B&L*, 2:313–17.

6. Warner, *Generals in Blue*, 376–77.

7. Pope, "Second Battle of Bull Run," *B&L*, 2:449–500; Johnson and Buel, "Opposing Forces at Second Bull Run," *B&L*, 2:497–500.

8. McClellan, "From the Peninsula to Antietam," *B&L*, 2:545–55; Walker, "Jackson's Capture of Harper's Ferry," *B&L*, 2:604–18.

9. Cox, "Battle of Antietam," *B&L*, 2:630–60.

10. Ibid.; Johnson and Buel, "Opposing Forces in the Maryland Campaign," *B&L*, 2:598–603.

11. Warner, *Generals in Blue*, 57–58.

12. Longstreet, "Battle for Fredericksburg," *B&L*, 3:70–95.

13. Ibid.; Johnson and Buel, "Opposing Forces at Fredericksburg," *B&L*, 3:143–47.

14. Warner, *Generals in Blue*, 233–35; Couch, "Chancellorsville Campaign," *B&L*, 3:233–38.

15. Johnson and Buel, "Opposing Forces in the Chancellorsville Campaign," *B&L*, 3:233–38.

16. Long, *Civil War Day by Day*, 384–85. The first names of the new draft were drawn on Saturday, 11 July, and appeared in the newspapers on Sunday, 12 July. Riots broke out on Monday, 13 July, as Meade's army arrived in front of Lee's defense lines.

Chapter 1

1. George G. Meade to Mrs. George G. Meade, 8, 10 May 1863, George G. Meade Papers, HSP; Meade, *Life and Letters of George Gordon Meade*, 1:371–74.

2. Agassiz, *Meade's Headquarters*, 358–59.

3. Meade, *Life and Letters of George Gordon Meade*, 1:1–18, 51–198, 199–215; Cleaves, *Meade of Gettysburg*, 3–4, 355.

4. Meade, *Life and Letters of George Gordon Meade*, 1:216–301 (the narrative about Meade's wounds and recovery is found at 300–301).

5. Ibid., 301–8.

6. Ibid., 309–22.

7. George G. Meade to Mrs. George G. Meade, 29 September, 9 November, 2 December 1862, George G. Meade Papers, HSP; Meade, *Life and Letters of George Gordon Meade*, 1:314–15, 325–26, 334–35. All the commanders of the First Corps went to army headquarters to bid farewell to McClellan. That included Rey-

nolds as commander of the First Corps, Major General Abner Doubleday as commander of the First Division, Brigadier General John Gibbon as commander of the Second Division, and Meade as commander of the Third Division, which consisted of the Pennsylvania Reserves.

8. Meade, *Life and Letters of George Gordon Meade*, 1:337–38, 341–43, 350.

9. Frederick Law Olmstead to E. L. Godkin, 15 July 1863, in Page, "After Gettysburg, Frederick Law Olmstead on the Escape of Lee," *PMBH* 75:437.

10. Byrne and Weaver, *Haskell of Gettysburg*, 93.

11. Ibid., 93–94.

12. Porter, *Campaigning with Grant*, 247.

13. Major General Samuel Wylie Crawford was the individual who stated that Meade told him the men were calling him a "damned old google-eyed snapping turtle." Styple, *Generals in Bronze*, 156; Agassiz, *Meade's Headquarters*, 57, 73; Lowe, *Meade's Army*, 255; Porter, *Campaigning with Grant*, 247–48; Acken, *Inside the Army of the Potomac*, 289, 313, 318, 371, 393; Gen. H. J. Hunt to Gen. A. S. Webb, 12 January 1888, in Powell, *Fifth Army Corps*, 558–59.

14. Agassiz, *Meade's Headquarters*, 25.

15. Meade, *Life and Letters of George Gordon Meade*, 1:16–17; Cleaves, *Meade of Gettysburg*, 18, 19, 29, 47, 49.

16. Moore and Drake, *Leaves*, xiii.

17. Ibid., xiii, xiv, 26, 55; George G. Meade to Mrs. George G. Meade, 1 February 1863, George G. Meade Papers, HSP; Meade, *Life and Letters of George Gordon Meade*, 1:353; George G. Meade to Mrs. George G. Meade, 3 December 1863, George G. Meade Papers, HSP; Meade, *Life and Letters of George Gordon Meade*, 2:159. Meade received a letter from his niece, Charlotte Ingraham, who wrote that "all her brothers and one brother-in-law lie on the battlefield." Meade then added, "She says her parents are at Port Gibson, completely ruined, and that they have all to begin anew the world. Is not this terrible?" See also Elizabeth Meade Ingraham to My Dear George, 23 July 1863, in Moore and Drake, *Leaves*, 58.

18. Cleaves, *Meade of Gettysburg*, 52, 357; Warner, *Generals in Gray*, 341–42.

19. Meade, *Life and Letters of George Gordon Meade*, 1:213.

20. George G. Meade to Mrs. George G. Meade, 16 December 1862, George G. Meade Papers, HSP; Meade, *Life and Letters of George Gordon Meade*, 1:337–38; Miller, *Photographic History of the Civil War*, 4:312, 314; Johnston, "Record of 'Baldy,' Gen. Meade's Horse," George G. Meade File, GNMP; Raff, *Horse in the Civil War*, 61–64; Agassiz, *Meade's Headquarters*, 8–9.

21. Couch, "Chancellorsville Campaign," *B&L*, 3:156–71; Johnson and Buel, "Opposing Forces in the Chancellorsville Campaign," *B&L*, 3:237–38; Bigelow, *Campaign of Chancellorsville*, 473–75 (Bigelow's record of casualties at Chancellorsville is very close to those recorded by Johnson and Buel: Confederate, 12,821, and Union, 17,278); Jackson, "Sedgwick at Fredericksburg and Salem Heights," *B&L*, 3:227–32.

22. Hebert, *Fighting Joe Hooker*, 17, 19–21, 25–35, 38–40, 50, 72, 91–145, 152–63, 169–71; Winslow, *General John Sedgwick*, 2; Nichols, *Toward Gettysburg*, 211–13. General Sedgwick was a lifelong bachelor; Reynolds was engaged to a Catherine Hewitt at the time of the Gettysburg Campaign. See also Sister Mary Louise to

Sister Ramona for Sister Rose Theodore, 27 August 1976, Daughters of Charity, St. Joseph's Provincial House, Emmitsburg, Md. (Gen. J. F. Reynolds's fiancée), John F. Reynolds Papers, F&MC; William Riddle to Lt. Bouvier, 4 August 1863, John F. Reynolds Papers, F&MC; Ellie Reynolds to Brother, 5 July 1863, John F. Reynolds Papers, F&MC; and Viola, *Memoirs of Charles Henry Veil*, 35–36.

23. Couch, "Chancellorsville Campaign," *B&L*, 3:171; George G. Meade to Mrs. George G. Meade, 8 May 1863, George G. Meade Papers, HSP; Meade, *Life and Letters of George Gordon Meade*, 1:371–72.

24. Marszalek, *Commander of All Lincoln's Armies*, 5, 11–13, 15–27, 42–49, 75–104, 106–18, 122–28.

25. Marszalek, *Commander of All Lincoln's Armies*, 129–54; Welles, *Diary of Gideon Welles*, 7 July 1863, 1:363–64; Burlingame, *Lincoln's Journalist*, 288.

26. Marszalek, *Commander of all Lincoln's Armies*, 133, 154, 172–73, 183; Welles, *Diary of Gideon Welles*, 26 July 1863, 1:384.

27. George G. Meade to Mrs. George G. Meade, 8 May 1863, George G. Meade Papers, HSP; Meade, *Life and Letters of George Gordon Meade*, 1:371–73; Hebert, *Fighting Joe Hooker*, 226–27; Benjamin, "Hooker's Appointment and Removal," *B&L*, 3:241, 243n2. Edwin Coddington claimed that Benjamin's article "was quite untrustworthy" but never explained why. Coddington, *Gettysburg Campaign*, 664n30. Edward J. Nichols also questioned Benjamin's statements but gave no reasons either. Nichols, *Toward Gettysburg*, Appendix, 222–23. Benjamin admitted having given the wrong date for Meade's acceptance of command and that he was writing from memory. All that being said, there remains plenty in Benjamin's article to accept. He was certainly present at army headquarters when Hooker was relieved of command and Meade given command of the army, and much of what he writes about are events he remembered. Charles F. Benjamin to J. G. Rosengarten, 7 August 1883, John F. Reynolds Papers, F&MC. He also knew Colonel James A. Hardie, a prominent actor in the drama, well and spoke with him many times about his role in the change of commanders. Benjamin even wrote the privately published *Memoir of James Allen Hardie* in 1877. The discussions among Lincoln, Halleck, and Stanton were obviously not held in Benjamin's presence, but they were the subject of published commentaries before he wrote his article for *B&L* and favorably measure up to what is known about those discussions.

28. Benjamin, "Hooker's Appointment and Removal," *B&L*, 3:241; Gorham, *Life and Public Services of Edwin M. Stanton*, 2:99; Weld, *War Diary and Letters of Stephen Minot Weld*, 21 December 1862, 154–55.

29. George G. Meade to Mrs. George G. Meade, 10, 20 March 1863, George G. Meade Papers, HSP; Meade, *Life and Letters of George Gordon Meade*, 1:373–74, 379–80.

30. George G. Meade to Mrs. George G. Meade, 8, 10 May 1863, George G. Meade Papers, HSP; Meade, *Life and Letters of George Gordon Meade*, 1:371–74.

31. Hunt, "First Day at Gettysburg," *B&L*, 3:258.

32. Johnson and Buel, "Opposing Forces in the Chancellorsville Campaign," *B&L*, 3:233–37.

33. Hunt, "First Day at Gettysburg," *B&L*, 3:259; *OR*, 25(2):320, 574; Joseph

Hooker to Major General Halleck, 6 June 1863, 3:00 P.M. (received 3:30 P.M.), *OR*, 27(1):33; Joseph Hooker to Major General Halleck, 12 June 1863, 8:30 A.M. (received 8:45 A.M.), *OR*, 27(1):36. Hooker blamed Stoneman for rendering many of his horses unserviceable during his raid in Suffolk.

34. Hunt, "First Day at Gettysburg," *B&L*, 3:259; *OR*, 25(2):574; Johnson and Buel, "Opposing Forces at Gettysburg," *B&L*, 3:440; Brig. Gen. R. N. Batchelder to Gen. Alexander S. Webb, 8 March 1895, Alexander S. Webb Papers, box 4, folder 004-0072, YUL. According to Batchelder, the wagon trains of the Army of the Potomac moved with their respective corps until they crossed the Potomac River at Edwards Ferry. From there to Frederick they moved in one train; they were divided again at Frederick. "There were about 4,000 six-mule wagons, and 1,000 ambulances, the length of the [train] being about fifty miles," he wrote.

35. "Gen. G. H. Sharpe Dead," *New York Times*, 15 January 1900; Fishel, *Secret War for the Union*, 286–97; *OR*, 25(2):167.

36. Fishel, *Secret War for the Union*, 153–54, 286–87, 290–93.

37. Ibid., 314–33, 375–79; *OR*, 25(2):367–77.

38. Hunt, "First Day at Gettysburg," *B&L*, 3:258; Johnson and Buel, "Opposing Forces at Gettysburg," *B&L*, 3:440.

39. *OR*, 27(1):140.

40. Joseph Hooker to His Excellency, the President of the United States, 5 June 1863, 11:30 A.M., *OR*, 27(1):30.

41. *OR*, 27(2):293–94, 305; Fishel, *Secret War for the Union*, 428. Fishel quotes a dispatch from Colonel Sharpe to General Butterfield, 7 June 1863, Bureau of Military Information Papers, RG 393, NA.

42. Danl. Butterfield to Major General Sedgwick, 6 June 1863, 10:30 A.M. and John Sedgwick to General Butterfield, 6 June 1863, 11:15 A.M., *OR*, 27(3):12–13; Danl. Butterfield to Commanding Officer, Cavalry Corps, 7 June 1863; *OR*, 27(3): 27–28; Joseph Hooker to Major General Halleck, 6 June 1863, 3:00 P.M. (received 3:30 P.M.), *OR*, 27(1):32–33; Hunt, "First Day at Gettysburg," *B&L*, 3:261; *OR*, 27(2):313.

43. *OR*, 27(1):902–6; *OR*, 27(2):679–85; Hunt, "First Day at Gettysburg," *B&L*, 3:261–63.

44. A. Pleasanton to General Williams, 10 June 1863, 4:30 P.M. (received, War Department, 9:00 P.M.), *OR*, 27(3):47–48; *OR*, 27(2):43, 92–93, 547–48.

45. *OR*, 27(2):16–39, 52, 93–94, 440–44, 461–63, 500–502, 548–50.

46. Ibid., 442, 464.

47. Ibid., 357, 613, 687–92.

48. Ibid., 358, 613, 692.

49. Edwin Stanton to Hon. Simon Cameron, 10 June 1863, *OR*, 27(3):54–55; General Orders No. 186, War Department, Adjt. Gen's Office, 24 June 1863, *OR*, 27(3):299.

50. *OR*, 27(1):141.

Chapter 2

1. Joseph Hooker to His Excellency, the President of the United States, 5 June 1863, 11:30 A.M., *OR*, 27(1):30; A. Lincoln to Major General Hooker, 5 June 1863,

4:00 P.M., *OR*, 27(1):31; H. W. Halleck to Major General Hooker, 5 June 1863, 4:40 P.M., *OR*, 27(1):31–32.

2. Joseph Hooker to His Excellency, the President of the United States, 10 June 1863, 2:30 P.M. (received 5:10 P.M.), *OR*, 27(1):34–35; A. Lincoln to Major General Hooker, 10 June 1863, 6:40 P.M., *OR*, 27(1):35; between 11 June, at 12:40 P.M., and 16 June, at 7:00 A.M., General Hooker sent eleven telegrams to President Lincoln, *OR*, 27(1):37–44; Joseph Hooker to His Excellency Abraham Lincoln, President, 16 June 1863, 11:00 A.M., *OR*, 27(1):45.

3. A. Lincoln to Major General Hooker, 16 June 1863, 10:00 P.M., *OR*, 27(1):47.

4. Joseph Hooker to Major General Halleck, 17 June 1863, noon, *OR*, 27(1):48–51; Joseph Hooker to Major General Halleck, 19 June 1863, *OR*, 27(1):51–52; H. W. Halleck to Major General Hooker, 22 June 1863, *OR*, 27(1):54; H. W. Halleck to Major General Hooker, 22 June 1863, 3:15 P.M., and Joseph Hooker to Major General Halleck, 22 June 1863, 4:45 P.M., *OR*, 27(1):55.

5. Welles, *Diary of Gideon Welles*, 23 June 1863, 1:340; Joseph Hooker to Major General Halleck, 24 June 1863, *OR*, 27(1):55–56; Seth Williams to Major General W. H. French, 24 June 1863, *OR*, 27(3):291–92; Edwin M. Stanton to Brig. Gen. B. F. Kelly, 24 June 1863, *OR*, 27(3):299.

6. Nevins, *Diary of Battle*, 29 June 1863, 229; George G. Meade to Mrs. George G. Meade, 13 June 1863, George G. Meade Papers, HSP; Meade, *Life and Letters of George Gordon Meade*, 1:385; Nichols, *Toward Gettysburg*, Appendix, 220–21; Weld, *War Diary and Letters of Stephen Minot Weld*, 208. Weld wrote that Reynolds went to Washington on 31 May. Weld recollected later: "I was with General Reynolds when he received the order appointing Meade to the command of the army. He said he was very glad of it and he spoke most highly of Meade. He then told me, confidentially, that the command had been offered to him, but he had refused it." Weld, *War Diary and Letters of Stephen Minot Weld*, 227n1.

7. B. [Babcock] to Major General Hooker, 24 June 1863, *OR*, 27(3):285–86.

8. *OR*, 27(1):143; Nevins, *Diary of Battle*, 25 June 1863, 224; Diary of Lieutenant John R. Garden (62nd Pennsylvania), 25 June 1863, 59–60, KMB; Diary of Corporal James W. Johnson (29th Pennsylvania), 25 June 1863, 19, HS; Diary of Charles T. Hunter (142nd Pennsylvania), 25 June 1863, KMB. All the diarists recorded a drizzling rain on 25 June.

9. *OR*, 27(1):143.

10. Ibid.; Nevins, *Diary of Battle*, 26 June 1863, 224; Diary of Lieutenant John R. Garden (62nd Pennsylvania), 26 June 1863, 60–61, KMB; Diary of Corporal James W. Johnson (29th Pennsylvania), 26 June 1863, 21, HS; Diary of Charles T. Hunter (142nd Pennsylvania), 26 June 1863, KMB; Bardeen, *Little Fifer's War Diary* (1st Massachusetts), 26 June 1863, 211. All the diarists recorded a drizzling rain on 26 June.

11. Joseph Hooker to Major General Halleck, 27 June 1863 (received 2:55 P.M.), *OR*, 27(1):60.

12. Joseph Hooker to Major General Halleck, 27 June 1863, 1:00 P.M. (received 3:00 P.M.), *OR*, 27(1):60.

13. Williams, *Lincoln and the Radicals*, 201–4; Zachariah Chandler to wife, 20

May 1863, Zachariah Chandler Papers, LOC; Benjamin, "Hooker's Appointment and Removal," *B&L*, 3:240–41; Hebert, *Fighting Joe Hooker*, 228–29.

14. Warner, *Generals in Blue*, 446–47; Hessler, *Sickles at Gettysburg*, 31–32, 43–45; Bardeen, *Little Fifer's War Diary*, 211–12.

15. Butterfield, *Biographical Memorial of General Daniel Butterfield*, 7–9, 76, 111–15; Warner, *Generals in Blue*, 62–63; Hessler, *Sickles of Gettysburg*, 42.

16. George G. Meade to Mrs. George G. Meade, 26 January, 13 February 1863, George G. Meade Papers, HSP; Meade, *Life and Letters of George Gordon Meade*, 1:350–51, 354.

17. *OR*, 27(1):143–44; Nevins, *Diary of Battle*, 27 June 1863, 225; Diary of Lieutenant John R. Garden (62nd Pennsylvania), 27 June 1863, 61, KMB; Manley Stacey to Father (111th New York), 27 June 1863, Manley Stacey Civil War Letters, HSOP&RF; Diary of James W. Johnson (29th Pennsylvania), 27 June 1863, 21, HS; Diary of Charles T. Hunter (142nd Pennsylvania), 27 June 1863, KMB. All the diarists and the letter writer record heavy rain on the night of 26 June and 27 June being cloudy but pleasant.

18. Williams, *History of Frederick County, Maryland*, 1:250, 374–75, 380–81, 384–85; Adams, *Civil War in Frederick County, Maryland*, 9–10; Hueting, "Meade Receives Command of the Army of the Potomac."

19. *OR*, 27(1):143; Adams, *Civil War in Frederick County, Maryland*, 40; Hueting, "Meade Receives Command of the Army of the Potomac."

20. Benjamin, "Hooker's Appointment and Removal," *B&L*, 3:241.

21. Warner, *Generals in Blue*, 204–5; Benjamin, *Memoir of James Allen Hardie*, viii, 1–35, 57.

22. Benjamin, "Hooker's Appointment and Removal," *B&L*, 3:241; Benjamin, *Memoir of James Allen Hardie*, 37–38.

23. Benjamin, "Hooker's Appointment and Removal," *B&L*, 3:242; Benjamin, *Memoir of James Allen Hardie*, 38, 40.

24. Ibid.

25. Sickles, "Further Recollections of Gettysburg," *NAR*, 152:259; Smith, *Famous Battery and Its Campaigns*, 97–98.

26. Benjamin, "Hooker's Appointment and Removal," *B&L*, 3:242. The original Baltimore & Ohio Railroad Station and the United States Hotel still stand across the street from each other on the corner of Market and All Saints Streets.

27. George G. Meade to Mrs. George G. Meade, 29 June 1863, George G. Meade Papers, HSP; Meade, *Life and Letters of George Gordon Meade*, 2:11–12; Powell, *Fifth Army Corps*, 500n1. Lieutenant Colonel Locke recalled years later that Hardie appeared at his tent at 2:00 A.M. Meade's letter, however, was written on the day after the event and is, consequently, used here as the authoritative time of Hardie's arrival at Meade's headquarters.

28. H. W. Halleck to Maj. Gen. George G. Meade, 27 June 1863, *OR*, 27(1):61.

29. Benjamin, "Hooker's Appointment and Removal," *B&L*, 3:242–43, 243n2; Benjamin, *Memoir of James Allen Hardie*, 38–39.

30. Benjamin, "Hooker's Appointment and Removal," *B&L*, 3:242–43; Benjamin, *Memoir of James Allen Hardie*, 39.

31. Jas. A. Hardie to Maj. Gen. H. W. Halleck, 28 June 1863 (received 5:30 A.M.), *OR*, 27(3):373.

32. Taylor, *Gouverneur Kemble Warren*, 4–8, 19–44, 49–105, 119–21. Written from memory by General Warren, the manuscript he composed about the episode refers to Meade coming to his tent at 2:30 A.M. Warren was mistaken about the time. Meade, who wrote a letter to his wife on 29 June 1863 about being named commander of the army, records being awakened by Hardie at 3:00 A.M. That, of course, is the best evidence, as it was written closest to the time of the event. Meade must have approached Warren around 5:30 A.M.

33. Ibid., 119–20.

34. Warner, *Generals in Blue*, 562–63.

35. Benjamin, "Hooker's Appointment and Removal," *B&L*, 3:243; Benjamin, *Memoir of James Allen Hardie*, 40; Hyde, *Following the Greek Cross*, 140.

36. Geo. G. Meade to General H. W. Halleck, 28 June 1863, 7:00 A.M. (received 10:00 A.M.), *OR*, 27(1):61–62.

37. Powell, *Fifth Army Corps*, 500n1; Warner, *Generals in Blue*, 492–93.

38. Benjamin, *Memoir of James Allen Hardie*, 40; *OR*, 27(1):143–44; Diary of Lieutenant John R. Garden (62nd Pennsylvania), 28 June 1863, 62; KMB, Diary of Charles T. Hunter (142nd Pennsylvania), 28 June 1863, KMB; Bardeen, *Little Fifer's War Diary* (1st Massachusetts), 28 June 1863, 212; Diary of James L. Howie (141st Pennsylvania), 28 June 1863, JCC. All of the diarists recorded that it rained all day on 28 June 1863.

39. *OR*, 27(1):143–44.

40. Ibid.; Benjamin, "Hooker's Appointment and Removal," *B&L*, 3:243.

41. Dilts, *Great Road*, 80–129, 140–50, 154–69, 185–201.

42. Warner, *Generals in Blue*, 245–46.

43. Ibid., 361–62; Sparks, *Inside Lincoln's Army*, 11–19.

44. Charles F. Benjamin to J. G. Rosengarten, 7 August 1883, John F. Reynolds Papers, F&MC; Benjamin, "Hooker's Appointment and Removal," *B&L*, 3:243.

45. Charles F. Benjamin to J. G. Rosengarten, 7 August 1883, John F. Reynolds Papers, F&MC; Benjamin, "Hooker's Appointment and Removal," *B&L*, 3:243.

46. Benjamin, "Hooker's Appointment and Removal," *B&L*, 3:243.

47. Ibid.

48. *New York Times*, 25, 27 June 1863.

49. *OR*, 27(3):333–72.

50. O. O. Howard to General John F. Reynolds, 26 June 1863, 5:10 P.M., *OR*, 27(3):336.

51. J. S. Robinson to Colonel Asmussen (Reynolds's endorsement), 27 June 1863, *OR*, 27(3):352.

52. Chas W. Asmussen to Major General Butterfield, 28 June 1863, 11:00 A.M., *OR*, 27(3):372.

53. Benjamin, "Hooker's Appointment and Removal," *B&L*, 3:243.

54. General Orders, No. 66, Headquarters, Army of the Potomac, 28 June 1863, *OR*, 27(3):373–74.

55. General Orders, No. 67, Headquarters, Army of the Potomac, 28 June 1863, *OR*, 27(3):374.

56. Jas. A. Hardie to Maj. Gen. H. W. Halleck, 28 June 1863, 2:30 P.M. (received 3:20 P.M.), *OR*, 27(3):374.

57. Benjamin, "Hooker's Appointment and Removal," *B&L*, 3:234; Hyde, *Civil War Letters by General Thomas W. Hyde*, 87.

58. Gibbon, *Personal Recollections of the Civil War*, 128–29.

59. Ibid., 129.

60. Howard, *Autobiography of Oliver Otis Howard*, 1:395–96.

61. *New York Times*, 2 July 1863; Benjamin, "Hooker's Appointment and Removal," *B&L*, 3:243.

Chapter 3

1. *New York Times*, 2 July 1863; Meade, *Photographs of Union and Confederate Officers*, 10. The names of Meade's twelve aides-de-camp during the Gettysburg Campaign were: Lieutenant Colonel Joseph Dickinson, assistant adjutant general; Major James C. Biddle; Major Benjamin Ludlow; Captain William Jay; Captain John C. Bates; Captain Charles Cadwalader; Captain Emlen N. Carpenter; Captain Ulrich Dahlgren; Captain Addison G. Mason; Captain George Meade; Captain James Starr; and First Lieutenant Frederick Rosencrantz. See also Coughenour, "Assessing the Generalship of George G. Meade during the Gettysburg Campaign," *GM*, 28:30–33; Heitman, *Historical Register and Dictionary of the U.S. Army*, 1:70; Tsouras, *Major General George H. Sharpe*, 136, quoting "Sharpe: A Great Man," *Inter Ocean Courier* (Chicago), 21 January 1900.

2. Meade, *With Meade at Gettysburg*, 20–21.

3. Warner, *Generals in Blue*, 240–41; Humphreys, *Andrew Atkinson Humphreys*, 186–87.

4. Humphreys, *Andrew Atkinson Humphreys*, 186–87. Meade denied offering Humphreys the position of chief of staff in a letter to a G. G. Benedict in 1870; see George Gordon Meade to G. G. Benedict, 16 March 1870, as published in the *Philadelphia Weekly Press*, 11 August 1886. Clearly, Meade's memory failed him then. General Humphreys testified about Meade offering him the post during his appearance before the Joint Committee on the Conduct of the War on 21 March 1864. Hyde, *Union Generals Speak* (Humphreys Testimony, JCCW), 183–84. As testimony closer in time to the event, it is the best evidence.

5. Warner, *Generals in Blue*, 242; Longacre, *Man behind the Guns*, 153–55.

6. Orders, Headquarters, Army of the Potomac, 28 June 1863, *OR*, 27(3): 374–75.

7. *OR*, 27(3):329, 334–35, 336, 350–51, 352, 360, 363, 370, 372, 384. Meade's information was supplied by Stahel's cavalry division and Howard's Eleventh Corps Signal Station at Turner Pass, as well as by mounted scouting parties sent into the Cumberland Valley; beyond that, Reynolds First Corps made some reports. Those were the only forces of the Army of the Potomac in a position to observe enemy movements west of the South Mountain Range. Apart from Meade's left wing, Couch's Department of the Susquehanna sent to the War Department a raft of dispatches regarding elements of Lee's army nearing Harrisburg, Carlisle, Gettysburg, and York. It must have been bewildering to the new commander. The intelligence Meade was receiving was not far off the mark. By 28 June, Lee had

started the advance of Rodes's Division of Ewell's corps from Carlisle to Harrisburg; Early's Division was at York. Hill's corps was at Chambersburg with Longstreet's corps just behind. Indeed, Lee's army was situated along, or just north of, the Chambersburg-to-York turnpike; its front was more than fifty miles long; *OR*, 27(2):307, 316.

8. From the orders Meade issued on the night of 28 June directing the army to move north, it is clear that he was using what were called "county residential maps" of Frederick and Carroll Counties, Maryland, and Adams County, Pennsylvania. His orders reference residences along the routes by the name of the residents so that they would be understood as mileposts for the commanders of his corps. There were some popular residential maps of those counties that would have been made available to the army by the War Department. The "Map of Frederick County, Md.," is one of them. It states that it was "accurately drawn from correct instrumental surveys of all the county roads, etc. by Isaac Bond, CE.," and was published by E. Sachse & Co. of Baltimore in 1858. Meade undoubtedly used that map. The map not only provided all the roads and railroad routes but set forth all the names and homes of all the residents in the county. Towns and villages were mapped and illustrated as detailed insets with names of all residents, as well as hotels and stores. For Carroll County, Meade unquestionably used "Martenet's Map of Carroll County, Maryland." Much like the Frederick County map, its title claims that it was "drawn from actual surveys by S. J. Martenet and assistants." The map was published by Simon Martenet, surveyor and civil engineer, in Baltimore in 1862. Like the Frederick County map, Martenet's map of Carroll County included all the roads and railroads and the name and location of every resident along said roads. Hotels and shops were set forth by the name of the proprietor. Towns and villages were mapped as detailed inserts with the resident's homes included. For Adams County, Pennsylvania, Meade would have used the "Map of Adams Co., Pennsylvania." It was "made from surveys by G. M. Hopkins, C.E.," and was published by M.S.&E. Converse in Philadelphia in 1858. Like the two Maryland maps, the Adams County Map has all the residences of the county set out along all the roads and in the towns and villages with the name of the residents. All the roads and railroads are set forth in detail. Importantly, none of those residential maps are topographical; they do not illustrate hills or ridges. The Frederick County, Maryland, and Adams County, Pennsylvania, maps provided only outlines of the South Mountain Range and the Catoctin Mountains. The War Department provided large numbers of these maps for use by corps and division commanders.

9. DePeyster, *Gettysburg and After*, 99. The topographical engineer officer referenced by dePeyster was identified only as "Brevet Colonel W. H. P."

10. "Martenet's Map of Carroll County, Maryland, 1862"; Warner, *Carroll County, Maryland*, 39–42; Haupt, *Reminiscences of General Herman Haupt*, 214.

11. Rufus Ingalls to General M. C. Meigs, 28 June 1863, 6:00 P.M., *OR*, 27(3): 378.

12. H. W. Halleck to Maj. Gen. George G. Meade, 28 June 1863, 1:00 P.M., *OR*, 27(1):62; H. W. Halleck to Major General Couch, 28 June 1863, 12:45 P.M., *OR*, 27(3):385.

13. H. W. Halleck to Major General Meade, 28 June 1863, 12:30 P.M., *OR*, 27(1):62.

14. *OR*, 27(2):692–95.

15. H. W. Halleck to Major General Meade, 28 June 1863, 3:00 P.M., *OR*, 27(1): 63; M. C. Meigs to General Ingalls, 28 June 1863, 4:05 P.M., *OR*, 27(3):378.

16. Cowan to Major Eckert, 28 June 1863 (received 7:20 P.M.), *OR*, 27(3): 381–82.

17. Although there is no direct evidence that courier relays were set up along the National Road from Frederick to Baltimore, there is circumstantial evidence. Meade, writing to Halleck on 29 June at 11:00 A.M., noted: "I send this by courier with the hope and expectation that it will reach you safely"; Geo. G. Meade to Maj. Gen. H. W. Halleck, 29 June 1863, 11:00 A.M., *OR*, 27(1):66–67. Clearly, the dispatches from Frederick were being carried by couriers to Relay, where they could be telegraphed to Washington. Dispatches from Washington were received by the telegraph at Relay and then carried to Frederick by couriers. Because of the great distance between Frederick and Relay, no courier would be able to carry a message at breakneck speed all the way. The horse would break down. Consequently, dispatches must have been carried by couriers in relays in order to get to the destination as rapidly as possible. As noted in a later chapter, the Adams Express Company was used for such a purpose after Meade became engaged at Gettysburg; Haupt, *Reminiscences of General Herman Haupt*, 215. Adams Express Company, which would operate the courier relays from Gettysburg to Baltimore, was a business engaged in forwarding packages on the railroads. Founded in the great depression of 1835, it was formally created in 1854. Only nine years old, the Adams Express Company was a visible partner of the Baltimore & Ohio Railroad and was able to assemble a system of express riders quickly.

18. D. N. Couch to the President of the United States, 28 June 1863, 7:40 P.M., and D. N. Couch to Colonel Frick, 28 June 1863, *OR*, 27(3):385; M. A. Reno to Major General D. N. Couch, 28 June 1863, *OR*, 27(3):387–88; Henry Palmer to Major General Couch, 28 June 1863, *OR*, 27(3):389; D. N. Couch to Hon. E. M. Stanton, 28 June 1863 (received 2:30 P.M.), *OR*, 27(3):390.

19. Geo. G. Meade to Maj. Gen. H. W. Halleck, 28 June 1863, 4:45 P.M. (received 6:05 P.M.), *OR*, 27(1):65.

20. S. Williams to Major General French, 28 June 1863, 6:00 P.M., *OR*, 27(3): 378; Wm. H. French to General S. Williams, 28 June 1863, 9:30 P.M., *OR*, 27(3): 382.

21. C. G. Sawtelle to General R. Ingalls, 28 June 1863, 7:00 P.M., *OR*, 27(3):380.

22. Geo. G. Meade to General H. W. Halleck, 28 June 1863, 7:25 P.M., *OR*, 27(1):66.

23. Geo. G. Meade to Major General Halleck, 28 June 1863, 8:15 P.M. (received 10:20 P.M.), *OR*, 27(1):64–65.

24. Hyde, *Union Generals Speak* (Meade Testimony, JCCW), 103.

25. Orders, Headquarters, Army of the Potomac, 28 June 1863, *OR*, 27(3): 375–76.

26. Ibid.

27. Ibid.

28. M. C. Meigs to General Ingalls, 28 June 1863, 10:30 P.M., *OR*, 27(3):379.

29. "An Account of the McConaughy Family," David McConaughy Papers, GC; Fishel, *Secret War for the Union*, 495. For a fine article on David McConaughy, see Hempel, "Gone and Nearly Forgotten: David McConaughy, the Man behind the Soldiers' National Cemetery and the Gettysburg National Military Park," *GM*, 34: 86–97.

Chapter 4

1. George G. Meade to Mrs. George G. Meade, 29 June 1863, George G. Meade Papers, HSP; Meade, *Life and Letters of George Gordon Meade*, 2:11–12; Diary of Jacob Shenkel (62nd Pennsylvania), 29 June 1863, USAMHI; Diary of Henry Clay Bowman (93rd Pennsylvania), 29 June 1863, PM; Diary of Charles T. Hunter (142nd Pennsylvania), 29 June 1863, KMB; Manley Stacey to Father (111th New York), 29 June 1863, Manley Stacey Civil War Letters, HSOP&RF; Diary of Colonel Henry J. Madill (141st Pennsylvania), 29 June 1863, USAMHI; Bardeen, *Little Fifer's War Diary* (1st Massachusetts), 212. All the diarists and the letter writer recorded a drizzling rain on and off through the day of 29 June 1863.

2. Special Orders, No. 175, Headquarters, Army of the Potomac, *OR*, 27(3):373; Special Orders, No. 98, Headquarters, Cavalry Corps, 28 June, 1863, *OR*, 27(3): 376; Warner, *Generals in Blue*, 108–10, 148–49, 266–67.

3. Orders, Headquarters, Army of the Potomac, *OR*, 27(3):375–76.

4. Special Orders, Headquarters, Cavalry Corps, 29 June 1863, *OR*, 27(3):400–401.

5. Ibid.

6. Ibid.

7. Ibid.

8. Billings, *Hard Tack and Coffee*, 336; Diary of Corporal James W. Johnson (29th Pennsylvania), 29 June 1863, HS.

9. Billings, *Hard Tack and Coffee*, 337–38; Hyde, *Civil War Letters by General Thomas W. Hyde*, 88–89.

10. *OR*, 27(1):151; Orders, Headquarters, Army of the Potomac, *OR*, 27(3):375–76. The First Corps marched from Frederick to Emmitsburg on the Old Frederick and Emmitsburg Road, now generally U.S. 15. The Eleventh Corps marched parallel to the First Corps. The Second Corps left Frederick on the Old Frederick and Emmitsburg Road and then marched east on the Liberty Road to Liberty. It then marched north on present-day Md. Rt. 75 to Johnsville and turned northeast to Union Bridge. The Second Corps then followed the Green Valley Road to present-day Md. Rt. 84 to Uniontown. The Fifth Corps followed the Second Corps, halting at Liberty. The Third Corps left Walkersville, north of Frederick, on present-day Md. Rt. 194, to the Forks of Pipe Creek, and then marched east on the Middleburg Road to Middleburg. It turned north on the Crouse Mill Road to Taneytown. The Twelfth Corps generally followed the Third Corps, halting at the Forks of Pipe Creek. The Sixth Corps began its march at Hyattstown, southeast of Frederick, and marched on the present-day Green Valley Road to Monrovia. There, it turned east on the National Road, present-day U.S. 40 to Mount Airy. At Mount Airy, the

Sixth Corps marched north on the Ridge Road, halting at Sams Creek after probably marching northwest along what is now called the Sams Creek Road.

11. Quynn, *Diary of Jacob Engelbrecht*, 29 June 1863, 2:972.

12. *New York Times*, 2 July 1863; Warner, *Generals in Blue*, 312.

13. Reid, "Battle of Gettysburg," *RR*, 7:85; Andrews, "Press Reports the Battle of Gettysburg," *PH*, 31:185–86.

14. "Map of Frederick County, Md.," by Isaac Bond, 1858; "Martenet's Map of Carroll County, Maryland," by S. J. Martenet, 1862. The description of the countryside is also derived from the thorough examination of the region by the author.

15. Geo. G. Meade to Maj. Gen. H. W. Halleck, 29 June 1863, 11:00 A.M., *OR*, 27(1):66–67.

16. Ibid.

17. W. H. Halleck to Major General Meade, 29 June 1863, 10:35 A.M., *OR*, 27(1):66.

18. Danl. Butterfield to Major General French, 29 June 1863, *OR*, 27(3):401–2.

19. Dawes, *Service with the Sixth Wisconsin Volunteers*, 157–58; *OR*, 27(1):155; John Hamilton to Col. John B. Bachelder, 27 June 1882, in Ladd and Ladd, *Bachelder Papers*, 2:890. See also J. P. Taylor to Jno. Bachelder, Esq., 13 July 1882, in Ladd and Ladd, *Bachelder Papers*, 2:897–99.

20. Bardeen, *Little Fifer's War Diary* (1st Massachusetts), 211–12; Eddy, *History of the Sixtieth Regiment, New York Volunteers*, 257–58; Young, *What a Boy Saw in the Army* (84th Pennsylvania), 279.

21. Weld, *War Diary and Letters of Stephen Minot Weld*, 228–29; "Martenet's Map of Carroll County, Maryland," by S. J. Martenet, 1863. The Carroll County Map shows a Joe Linn Hotel in the crossroads village of Middleburg. It stands on the north side of the road just west of the intersection of the road from Middleburg to Taneytown, the Crouse Mill Road. That is the hotel used by Meade. A two-story stone house, it still stands in Middleburg. Meade used it to get out of the rain and catch up on his correspondence while his headquarters tents were being set up about one mile up the road to Taneytown.

22. S. Williams to Commanding Officer, Sixth Corps, 29 June 1863, 5:35 P.M., *OR*, 27(3):398.

23. H. W. Slocum to Maj. Gen. George G. Meade, 29 June 1863, 6:20 P.M., *OR*, 27(3):398.

24. Danl. Butterfield to General M. R. Patrick, 29 June 1863, *OR*, 27(3):398; Sparks, *Inside Lincoln's Army* (Diary of General M. R. Patrick, 30 June 1863), 266.

25. Manley Stacey to Father, 30 June 1863 (111th New York), Manley Stacey Civil War Letters, HSOP&RF.

26. S. Williams to Commanding Officer, Fifth Corps, 29 June 1863, 6:45 P.M., S. Williams to Commanding Officer, Third Corps, 29 June 1863, 7:00 P.M., *OR*, 27(3):399.

27. *OR*, 27(1):144.

28. Warner, *Carroll County, Maryland*, 46, 50, 54–57.

29. *New York Times*, 2 July 1863.

30. John F. Reynolds to Major General Butterfield, 29 June 1863, 3:15 P.M., *OR*, 27(3):397.

31. Koons, "History of Middleburg," *Carroll Record*, 1895, George G. Meade File, GNMP.

32. Ibid.

33. Ibid.

34. *OR*, 27(2):317, 444, 467–68.

35. Ibid., 695; Geo. G. Meade to Maj. Gen. H. W. Halleck, 29 June 1863, 11:00 A.M., *OR*, 27(1):66–67.

36. *OR*, 27(2):201–2, 695; Miss S. C. Shriver to Lizzie (Mrs. Thomas J. Myer), 29 June 1863, William H. Shriver Papers, LOC. Miss Shriver describes Generals Stuart and Fitzhugh Lee occupying her home at Union Mills on the night of 29 June 1863.

37. *OR*, 27(1):367; Hyde, *Union Generals Speak* (Hancock Testimony, JCCW), 206.

38. Circular, Headquarters, Army of the Potomac, 29 June 1863, *OR*, 27(3):402.

39. Clausewitz, *On War*, 117.

40. George H. Sharpe to D. McConaughy, 29 June 1863, "An Account of the McConaughy Family," David McConaughy Papers, GC.

41. Danl. Butterfield to Col. G. H. Sharpe, 29 June 1863, *OR*, 27(3):399.

42. S. M. Felton and Thomas Kimber Jr. to Hon. E. M. Stanton, 29 June 1863 (received 11:10 A.M.), *OR*, 27(3):409.

43. George G. Meade to Mrs. George G. Meade, 29 June 1863, George G. Meade Papers, HSP; Meade, *Life and Letters of George Gordon Meade*, 2:13–14.

44. Clausewitz, *On War*, 119.

Chapter 5

1. Diary of Henry Clay Bowman (93rd Pennsylvania), 30 June 1863, PM; Diary of Charles T. Hunter (142nd Pennsylvania), 30 June 1863, KMB; Diary of Jacob Shenkel (62nd Pennsylvania), 30 June 1863, USAMHI; Diary of Corporal James W. Johnson (29th Pennsylvania), 30 June 1863, HS; Diary of Lieutenant John R. Garden (62nd Pennsylvania), 29, 30 June 1863, KMB; Diary of Henry Kaiser (96th Pennsylvania), 30 June 1863, USAMHI; Bardeen, *Little Fifer's War Diary* (1st Massachusetts), 212. All the diarists wrote about the rain that fell virtually all day. Jno. Buford to General Reynolds, 30 June 1863, 5:30 A.M., *OR*, 27(1): 922; Orders, 30 June 1863, *OR*, 27(3):416.

2. S. Williams to Maj. Gen. John F. Reynolds, 30 June 1863, 7:40 A.M., *OR*, 27(3):417.

3. Koons, "History of Middleburg," *Carroll Record*, 1895, George G. Meade File, GNMP.

4. Ibid.; Hunt, "First Day at Gettysburg," *B&L*, 3:273–74, 290–91.

5. Hunt, "First Day at Gettysburg," *B&L*, 3:273–74, 290–91.; Littlestown Quadrangle, Carroll County, Maryland, Quadrangle Atlas 14, https://pubs.er.usgs.gov/publication/70047508; Manchester Quadrangle, Carroll County, Maryland, Quadrangle Atlas 15, https://pubs.er.usgs.gov/publication/70047498; Taneytown and Emmitsburg Quadrangle, Carroll County, Maryland, Quadrangle Atlas 16, https://pubs.er.usgs.gov/publication/7004751; Union Bridge and Woodsboro Quadrangle,

Carroll County, Maryland, Quadrangle Atlas 17, https://pubs.er.usgs.gov/publica tion/70047512.

6. Koons, "History of Middleburg," *Carroll Record*, 1895, George G. Meade File, GNMP; Hunt, "First Day at Gettysburg," *B&L*, 3:273–74; "Martenet's Map of Carroll County, Maryland," by S. J. Martenet, 1862.

7. Hunt, "First Day at Gettysburg," *B&L*, 3:273–74; "Martenet's Map of Carroll County, Maryland," by S. J. Martenet, 1862.

8. Hunt, "First Day at Gettysburg," *B&L*, 3:274.

9. Hunt, "Second Day at Gettysburg," *B&L*, 3:290–91.

10. Ibid., 291; Hunt, "First Day at Gettysburg," *B&L*, 3:274.

11. *OR*, 27(3):402. The road from Middleburg to Taneytown is now called the Crouse Mill Road. It enters the Frederick Pike about one mile south of Taneytown.

12. Reid, "Battles of Gettysburg," *RR*, 7:87–88; "Meade's Headquarters," Historical Marker Database. "Martenet's Map of Carroll County, Maryland," by S. J. Martenet, 1862. Martenet notes the sites of the Benjamin Shunk farm and the nearby farms of Samuel Null, John and Jacob Thompson, and John Keviner. Diary of J. P. Coburn (141st Pennsylvania), 30 June 1863, USAMHI. Coburn, a wagoner, records moving through Taneytown on 30 June and stopping "on the York Road." Coburn's regiment was in the Third Corps. Diary of James L. Howie (141st Pennsylvania), 20, 30 June 1863, JC. Howie writes about marching a mile "beyond Taneytown" on 29 June and then "returning to Taneytown in a westerly direction" on the march to Emmitsburg on 30 June. That would put the Third Corps on the Null, Thompson, and Keviner farms next to the Shunk farm. Klein, *Just South of Gettysburg*, 226.

13. Klein, *Just South of Gettysburg*, 226.

14. *OR*, 27(1):201. The signal station would have been established at Trinity Lutheran Church across the street from Meade's first headquarters in the Lutheran Parsonage on Emmitsburg Street in Taneytown. The steeple of the Trinity Lutheran Church provided the most unobstructed view toward Emmitsburg of any site in Taneytown.

15. Quynn, *Diary of Jacob Engelbrecht*, 30 June 1863.

16. George G. Meade to Major General Couch, 30 June 1863, 10:45 A.M., *OR*, 27(1):67–68.

17. Circular, Headquarters, Army of the Potomac, 30 June 1863, *OR*, 27(3):415.

18. J. W. Garrett to Hon. E. M. Stanton, 29 June 1863 (received 11:55 P.M.), *OR*, 27(3):410.

19. J. A. Early to Colonel, 30 June 1863, accompanying a letter from Jno. Buford to an unnamed recipient (probably John Reynolds), 30 June 1863, *OR*, 27(3):414; Weld, *War Diary and Letters of Stephen Minot Weld*, 30 June 1863, 229. Before Reynolds's Corps began its short march to Marsh Creek in the early morning hours of 30 June, Weld was sent to Meade's headquarters with dispatches. The message from Buford to Reynolds was one of the dispatches he carried.

20. Jno. Buford to unnamed recipient, 30 June 1863, *OR*, 27(3):414.

21. Orders, Headquarters, Army of the Potomac, 30 June 1863, *OR*, 27(3):416; Weld, *War Diary and Letters of Stephen Minot Weld*, 30 June 1863, 229. Weld

noted that after he delivered the dispatches to Meade on the morning of 30 June, he was given orders from Meade to deliver to Generals Howard and Reynolds. Those were supposed to be the marching orders for 30 June 1863, but it seems that the orders to Reynolds were left behind by mistake.

22. Orders, Headquarters, Army of the Potomac, 30 June 1863, *OR*, 27(3):416.

23. Ibid.

24. Klein, *Just South of Gettysburg*, 212. Maggie Muhring, a thirteen-year-old girl, left a wartime journal wherein she recorded the burial of the soldier in the Presbyterian graveyard on 1 July 1863. She noted that he died of exhaustion.

25. Ibid., 222–23.

26. Gibbon, *Personal Recollections of the Civil War*, 131.

27. Howard, *Autobiography of Oliver Otis Howard*, 1:404–5. It seems that the 30 June 1863 marching orders for Reynolds were mistakenly not given to Captain Weld. Howard recalled that they were given to him around midnight, 30 June–1 July 1863. Howard sent them forward to Reynolds immediately as they were addressed to him. Reynolds received the order probably around one or two o'clock in the morning of 1 July 1863. Warner, *Generals in Blue*, 396–97; Weld, *War Diary and Letters of Stephen Minot Weld*, 229, 230, 234; Nevins, *Diary of Battle*, 140, 149, 191, 218; Biddle, *First Day of the Battle of Gettysburg*, 18; Viola, *Memoirs of Charles Henry Veil*, 35–36; E. R. to Brother, 5 July 1863, John F. Reynolds Papers, F&MC; William Riddle to Lt. Bouvier, 4 August 1863, John F. Reynolds Papers, F&MC.

28. *OR*, 27(1):201.

29. Order, Headquarters, Army of the Potomac, 30 June 1863, *OR*, 27(3): 414–15.

30. Williams, *History of Frederick County, Maryland*, 1:324–25.

31. Ibid.; "Map of Frederick County, Md.," by Isaac Bond, 1858; "Martenet's Map of Carroll County, Maryland," by S. J. Martenet, 1862.

32. *OR*, 27(1):201, 243; John F. Reynolds to Major General Butterfield, 30 June 1863, *OR*, 27(3):417–18. Lt. Wiggins Hamp, Signal Officer, to Maj. Gen. Reynolds, 30 June 1863, 8:00 P.M., "Official Papers Found on the Body of Maj. Gen. John F. Reynolds, Comdg. Right Wing of A. of P., July 1, 1863," Eleventh Corps Papers, RG 393, No. 14, vol. 2, 1863, NA.

33. Edward C. Baird to Major General Howard, 30 June 1863, 9:45 A.M., *OR*, 27(3):418.

34. Kieffer, *Recollections of a Drummer Boy*, 135.

35. Edward C. Baird to Major General Howard, 30 June 1863, 9:45 A.M., *OR*, 27(3):418.

36. *OR*, 27(1):926.

37. Jno. Buford to General Pleasonton, 30 June 1863, *OR*, 27(1):923.

38. John F. Reynolds to Major General Butterfield, 30 June 1863, "Official Papers Found on the Body of Maj. General John F. Reynolds, Comdg. Right Wing of A. of P., July 1, 1863," Eleventh Corps Papers, RG 393, No. 14, vol. 2, 1863, NA (letter also published at *OR*, 27(3):417–18).

39. Ibid.

40. George G. Meade to John F. Reynolds, 30 June 1863, "Official Papers Found on the Body of Maj. General John F. Reynolds, Comdg. Right Wing of A. of P.,

July 1, 1863," Eleventh Corps Papers, RG 393, No. 14, vol. 2, 1863, NA (letter also published at *OR*, 27[3]:419–20).

41. Ibid.

42. Ibid.

Chapter 6

1. Orders, Headquarters, Army of the Potomac, 30 June 1863, *OR*, 27(3):416.

2. Ibid.; Mahan, *Elementary Treatise on Advance-Guard, Out-Post*, 83.

3. Edwin Coddington writes: "To challenge the enemy without recklessly exposing his army, Meade worked out a beautiful strategic pattern based upon a realistic appraisal of geographical factors and intelligence reports. He boldly thrust out two infantry corps (the First and Eleventh) under perhaps his ablest general (Reynolds) to a place where the greatest enemy strength seemed to be concentrating." He then adds: "Thus he left the question of a general engagement at Gettysburg to the able and aggressive Reynolds." Coddington, *Gettysburg Campaign*, 237–38, 240. Harry Pfanz is less certain about Meade's intentions but generally agrees with Coddington. He acknowledges that Meade "was preparing contingency plans in case the Confederate army attacked, and he was looking for an opportunity to bring the enemy to battle if he could do so to an advantage." That was clearly true. Pfanz then adds: "Meade relied on Reynolds's judgment and probably would have endorsed any decision he made." Pfanz, *Gettysburg: The First Day*, 46, 49.

4. Stephen Sears argues: "It was clear enough that on 1 July Reynolds was to march to Gettysburg with the Eleventh Corps in close support. What was not made clear was what he was supposed to do when he got there." Sears, *Gettysburg*, 158. Most recently, Sears notes: "Wing Commander Reynolds rode that morning (1 July) with the First Corps with no further instruction than to march to Gettysburg." Sears, *Lincoln's Lieutenants*, 550.

5. Allen Guelzo presents a completely different picture. "Reynolds," he claims, "would use the First Corps to measure how much Confederate strength was moving toward Gettysburg, and if that strength was more than the First Corps could handle, he would fall back to Cemetery Hill, where Howard and the Eleventh Corps were waiting. This would, without saying it, also force George Meade's hand, and the other corps of the Army of the Potomac would have to be marched to Gettysburg to fight the great battle there, not in Maryland." Guelzo, *Gettysburg: The Last Invasion*, 126–129.

6. Selby, *Meade: The Price of Command*, 24–26.

7. Heitman, *Historical Register and Dictionary of the U.S. Army*, 1:684. Mahan began teaching at West Point on 1 January 1832. His tenure extended until well into the Civil War. War Department, *Revised Regulations of the Army of the United States*, 1861, §§ 719, 720.

8. De Jomini, *Art of War*, 217–24; Clausewitz, *On War*, 308–11; Mahan, *Elementary Treatise on Advance-Guard, Out-Post*, 112.

9. De Jomini, *Art of War*, 217–21; Mahan, *Elementary Treatise on Advance-Guard, Out-Post*, 112; Clausewitz, *On War*, 308–11.

10. Clausewitz, *On War*, 310; Mahan, *Elementary Treatise on Advance-Guard, Out-Post*, 83–84, 112.

11. Clausewitz, *On War*, 310.

12. Ibid., 309.

13. Mahan, *Elementary Treatise on Advance-Guard, Out-Post*, 86.

14. Clausewitz, *On War*, 310–11; Mahan, *Elementary Treatise on Advance-Guard, Out-Post*, 83–84.

15. Clausewitz, *On War*, 311.

16. Hyde, *Union Generals Speak* (Hancock Testimony, JCCW), 207; Mahan, *Elementary Treatise on Advanced-Guard, Out-Post*, 83; "To keep an enemy in ignorance of the state of our forces and the character of our position is one of the most indispensable duties of war. It is in this way that we oblige him to take every possible precaution in advancing; forcing him to feel his way, step by step, and to avoid risking his own safety in hazarding those bold and rapid movements which, when made against a feeble, or an unprepared enemy, lead to the most brilliant results" (223); "This object is effected by placing between the position occupied by the main force, and the presumed direction of the enemy, a body detached from the main force, but acting always with reference to it, termed an Advance Guard" (224). War Department, *Revised Regulations of the Army of the United States*, 1861 § 720.

17. Orders, Headquarters, Army of the Potomac, 30 June 1863, *OR*, 27(3):416.

18. Jno. Buford to General Pleasonton, 30 June 1863, 12:20 P.M., *OR*, 27(1):922.

19. John F. Reynolds to Major General Howard, 30 June 1863, *OR*, 27(3):417.

20. Ibid.

21. O. O. Howard to Major General Reynolds, 30 June 1863, *OR*, 27(3):419.

22. S. Williams to Commanding Officer, Third Corps, 30 June 1863, 12:45 P.M., *OR*, 27(3):422.

23. S. Williams to Commanding Officer, Second Corps, 30 June 1863, 1:00 P.M., *OR*, 27(3):422–23.

24. S. F. Barstow to Commanding Officer, Twelfth Corps, 30 June 1863, *OR*, 27(3):420–21.

25. S. Williams to Commanding Officer, Engineer Brigade, 30 June 1863, 4:00 P.M., *OR*, 27(3):423.

26. Geo. G. Meade to Maj. Gen. H. W. Halleck, 30 June 1863, 4:30 P.M., *OR*, 27(1):68–69.

27. S. Williams to Commanding Officer, Third Corps, 30 June 1863, *OR*, 27(3):420.

28. Orders, Headquarters, Army of the Potomac, *OR*, 27(3):416.

29. Klein, *Just South of Gettysburg*, 217–21; "Martenet's Map of Carroll County, Maryland," by S. Martenet, 1862. The schoolhouse is found on the map on the east side of the road to Westminster, about one mile south of Manchester.

30. Klein, *Just South of Gettysburg*, 217–21; Fowler, "Union Mills Homestead," *AHI* (July 1968): 22–30; Miss S. C. Shriver to Lizzie (Mrs. Thomas J. Myer), 29 June 1863, William H. Shriver Papers, LOC; *OR*, 27(1):595.

31. Miss S. C. Shriver to Lizzie (Mrs. Thomas J. Myer), 29 June 1863, William H. Shriver Papers, LOC.

32. *OR*, 27(1):201; Lt. Wiggins Hamp, Signal Officer, to Maj. Gen. Reynolds,

30 June 1863, 8:00 P.M., "Official Papers Found on the Body of Maj. Gen. John F. Reynolds, Comdg. Right Wing of A. of P., July 1, 1863," Eleventh Corps Papers, RG 393, No. 14, vol. 2, 1863, NA.

33. Howard, *Autobiography of Oliver Otis Howard*, 1:402–3.

34. Ibid., 403–4.

35. Ibid., 404–5.

36. Jno. Buford to Major General Reynolds, 30 June 1863, 10:30 P.M., *OR*, 27(1):923–24. No dispatch from Reynolds to Buford dated 1 July 1863 is found in the *Official Records*. Reynolds had to have directed a staff officer to notify Buford of his movement to Gettysburg because it appears that Buford knew Reynolds was coming there and that Reynolds knew Buford was expecting him.

37. Orders, Headquarters, Army of the Potomac, 30 June 1863, *OR*, 27(3):416, 418, 419, 420–21, 422–23.

38. George G. Meade to Mrs. George G. Meade, 30 June 1863, George G. Meade Papers, HSP; Meade, *Life and Letters of George Gordon Meade*, 2:18.

39. *New York Times*, 1, 2 July 1863; *OR*, 27(3):431, 433, 435–38.

40. *New York Times*, 2 July 1863.

Chapter 7

1. Diary of Charles T. Hunter (142nd Pennsylvania), 1 July 1863, KMB; Bardeen, *Little Fifer's War Diary* (1st Massachusetts), 216; Weld, *War Diary and Letters of Stephen Minot Weld*, 1 July 1863, 229; Diary of Nathaniel Rollins (2nd Wisconsin), 30 June–1 July 1863, WHS; Diary of James L. Howie (141st Pennsylvania), 1 July 1863, JC; Diary of Abner B. Frank (12th Illinois Cavalry), 1 July 1863, USAMHI. Most diarists recorded that it rained on and off during the night of 30 June and the early morning hours of 1 July 1863; H. W. Halleck to Major General Meade, 30 June 1863, *OR*, 27(1):68.

2. Orders, Headquarters, Army of the Potomac, 30 June 1863, *OR*, 27(3):416; Howard, *Autobiography of Oliver Otis Howard*, 1:404.

3. William Riddle to Lt. Bouvier, 4 August 1863, John F. Reynolds Papers, F&MC.

4. Ibid.

5. Wm. H. French to H. W. Halleck, 30 June 1863 (received 11:05 A.M.), *OR*, 27(3):428.

6. H. W. Halleck to Major General French, 30 June 1863, 2:15 P.M., *OR*, 27(3):428.

7. Diary of Luther Rose (Military Telegraph Service), 1 July 1863, Luther Rose Papers, LOC. Luther Rose noted in his diary that he was commended by Secretary Stanton for his delivery of the package of dispatches to Meade on the morning of 1 July 1863. Haupt, *Reminiscences of General Herman Haupt*, 208–12.

8. Haupt, *Reminiscences of General Herman Haupt*, 212; Edwin M. Stanton to Major General Meade, 30 June 1863, 11:30 P.M., *OR*, 27(1):69; Robt. C. Schenck to Major General Halleck, 30 June 1863, midnight, *OR*, 27(3):427.

9. Haupt, *Reminiscences of General Herman Haupt*, 212, 214.

10. Ibid., 212–13.

11. Ibid., 214.

12. Edwin M. Stanton to Major General Meade, 30 June 1863, 11:30 P.M., *OR*, 27(1):69.

13. Geo. G. Meade to Maj. Gen. H. W. Halleck, 1 July 1863, 7:00 A.M. (received 4:00 P.M.), *OR*, 27(1):70. Hunt, "Second Day at Gettysburg," *B&L*, 3:291. Meade unquestionably used Hunt to advise him about the suitability of the Pipe Creek Line. He would also have used the chief engineer of the army, General Warren, although Warren's letters indicate that he was away from headquarters only "in the evening." Taylor, *Gouverneur Kemble Warren*, 121. Meade and Warren were close, and Meade would have called on his chief engineer to view the proposed line of defense.

14. Geo. G. Meade to Maj. Gen. H. W. Halleck, 1 July 1863, 7:00 A.M. (received 4:00 P.M.), *OR*, 27(1):70.

15. Geo. G. Meade to Hon. E. M. Stanton, 1 July 1863, 7:00 A.M. (received 3:40 P.M.), *OR*, 27(1):70.

16. Weld, *War Diary and Letters of Stephen Minot Weld*, 229.

17. *OR*, 27(1):151, 243–44; Nevins, *Diary of Battle*, 232.

18. 1886 History, *Adams County, Pennsylvania*, 57–78, 144, 185, 237.

19. Ibid., 196–201.

20. Ibid., 121–35.

21. Ibid., 55–56.

22. "Map of Adams County, Pennsylvania," by M. S. & F. Converse, 1858.

23. 1886 History, *Adams County, Pennsylvania*, 48, 52, 236–37.

24. Shriver, "History of the Shriver Family," September 1926, 1, John F. Reynolds File, GNMP.

25. *OR*, 27(1):244; Nevins, *Diary of Battle*, 232.

26. O. O. Howard to Major General Reynolds, 1 July 1863, 6:00 A.M., *OR*, 27(3):457; "Map of Adams County, Pennsylvania," by M. S. & F. Converse, 1858. The dispatch was signed by General Howard; it was found in Reynolds's pocket at the time of his death. "Official Papers Found on the Body of Maj. General John F. Reynolds, Comdg. Right Wing of A. of P., July 1, 1863," Eleventh Corps Papers, RG 393, No. 14, vol. 2, 1863, NA.

27. E. C. Baird to General [Howard?], 1 July 1863, *OR*, 27(3):457; *OR*, 27(1):156.

28. *OR*, 27(1):221–24. Wrote General Ingalls: "No baggage was allowed in front. Officers and men went forward without tents and with only a short supply of food. A portion only of the ammunition wagons and ambulances was brought up to the immediate rear of our lines. This arrangement, which is always made in this army on the eve of battle and marches in the presence of the enemy, enables experienced and active officers to supply their commands without risking the loss of trains or obstructing roads over which the columns march."

29. Ibid., 244; Biddle, *First Day of the Battle of Gettysburg*, 18.

30. *OR*, 27(1):244, 265–66; Busey and Martin, *Regimental Strengths at Gettysburg*, 20; Smith, *History of the Seventy-Sixth Regiment, New York Volunteers*, 236–37; Nevins, *Diary of Battle*, 232.

31. Nevins, *Diary of Battle*, 232.

32. Tevis and Marquis, *History of the Fighting Fourteenth*, 82.

33. Smith, *History of the Seventy-Sixth Regiment, New York Volunteers*, 236.

34. *OR*, 27(1):926–27, 934–35. Buford wrote in his after-action report: "By daylight on July 1, I had gained positive information of the enemy's position and movements, and my arrangements were made for entertaining him until General Reynolds could reach the scene." Buford had earlier placed Gamble's brigade as far ahead as Herr Ridge. For two hours, Gamble's troopers had been engaged with the enemy, steadily falling back to McPherson Ridge. Colonel Gamble reported that his first position was one mile ahead of the seminary. That places them along Herr Ridge. *OR*, 27(1):934.

35. J. G. Rosengarten to Col. Samuel P. Bates, 13 January 1871, Reynolds file, GNMP (original in HSP). Rosengarten claims that Buford was directed by Reynolds on the night of 30 June to "feel the enemy" on the morning of 1 July. Special Orders, No. 99, Headquarters, Cavalry Corps, 29 June 1863, *OR*, 27(3):400–401. The 29 June orders by Pleasonton were the last orders issued to Buford. There are no further orders to Buford on the record.

36. *OR*, 27(1):927, 934–35, 938–39; Flavius J. Bellamy to Parents (3rd Indiana Cavalry) 3 July 1863, Flavius J. Bellamy Papers, LOC.

37. Biddle, *First Day of the Battle of Gettysburg*, 23; Charles H. Veil to D. McConaughy, Esq., 7 April 1864, David McConaughy Papers, GC. Veil recalled Reynolds and his staff being "several miles" ahead of Wadsworth's division. Viola, *Memoirs of Charles Henry Veil*, 28; Weld, *War Diary and Letters of Stephen Minot Weld*, 229, 231; *OR*, 27(1):1031; Joseph G. Rosengarten to M. Jacobs, 5 October 1863, John F. Reynolds Papers, F&MC; Hintz, "Dinna Forget," *GM*, 31:93.

38. Viola, *Memoirs of Charles Henry Veil*, 28; Jerome, "Buford in the Battle of Oak Ridge," 3; *OR*, 27(1):244, 923–34, 934–35.

39. Weld, *War Diary and Letters of Stephen Minot Weld*, 229–30, 232.

40. Clausewitz wrote that when an advance corps withdraws in the face of an enemy, "any good natural position that is available should be used." Clausewitz, *On War*, 309. Mahan wrote: "Whilst in position, the advance guard should take advantage of the natural, or other obstacles on its front and flanks." As it retires slowly before the enemy, the advance guard should unite with the troops in reserve and make a good stand. Mahan, *Elementary Treatise on Advance-Guard, Out-Post*, 84–85.

41. Jno. Buford to General Meade, 1 July 1863, 10:10 A.M., *OR*, 27(1):924.

42. Tremain, *Two Days of War*, 10.

43. Ibid., 10–11.

44. Ibid., 12.

45. Ibid.

46. Keiffer, *Recollections of a Drummer Boy*, 137–38.

47. *OR*, 27(1):151; Historical Society of Pennsylvania, *Reynolds Memorial*, 22; *OR*, 27(1):151. In fact, as the Third Division of the First Corps was marching across the fields toward the Lutheran Theological Seminary buildings well before noon, an aide from Reynolds's staff met Howard on the Emmitsburg Road and informed him that Reynolds desired him to halt the Eleventh Corps in the area of the Wentz

and Sherfy houses. Reynolds clearly intended to fall back on the Eleventh Corps if attacked. Howard, "Gen'l. O. O. Howard's Personal Recollections of the War of the Rebellion," *National Tribune* (Washington, D.C.), 27 November 1884.

48. Tremain, *Two Days of War*, 13–14.

49. *OR*, 27(2):637–39.

50. Ibid., 637; *OR*, 27(1):359; James A. Hall to J. Bachelder, 29 December 1869, in Ladd and Ladd, *Bachelder Papers*, 1:385–89; Maine Gettysburg Commission, *Maine at Gettysburg*, 16; Ladd and Ladd, *John Bachelder's History of the Battle of Gettysburg*, 204, 212–13.

51. *OR*, 27(1):244, 266–67, 278–79; Maine Gettysburg Commission, *Maine at Gettysburg*, 19; Busey and Martin, *Regimental Strengths at Gettysburg*, 21; O. O. Howard to Maj. Gen. Meade, 1 July 1863, Eleventh Corps Papers, RG 393, Pt. 2, E 5312, Letters Sent, NA. See Nelson, "Reynolds and the Decision to Fight," *GM*, 23:31–50. Nelson's article is a fine examination of Reynolds's decision-making on 1 July.

52. *OR*, 27(2):637–38; *OR*, 27(1):244–45, 265–66, 267–68, 273–74, 278–79, 927; Busey and Martin, *Regimental Strengths at Gettysburg*, 21.

53. Viola, *Memoirs of Charles Henry Veil*, 28–18; Charles H. Veil to D. McConaughy, 7 April 1864, David McConaughy Papers, GC; J. G. Rosengarten to Col. Samuel P. Bates, 13 January 1871, Reynolds file, GNMP (original in HSP); Ellie Reynolds to Brother, 5 July 1863, John F. Reynolds Papers, F&MC; William Riddle to Lt. Bouvier, 4 August 1863, John F. Reynolds Papers, F&MC; Veil, "An Old Boy's Personal Recollections and Reminiscences of the Civil War," 1–3, John F. Reynolds File, GNMP; *OR*, 27(1):244.

54. *OR*, 27(1):244–46; Dawes, *Service with the Sixth Wisconsin Volunteers*, 158–59; Tevis and Marquis, *History of the Fighting Fourteenth*, 82–85; Smith, *History of the Seventy-Six Regiment, New York Volunteers*, 237–40.

55. Charles H. Veil to D. McConaughy, 7 April 1864, David McConaughy Papers, GC; Veil, "An Old Boy's Personal Recollections and Reminiscences of the Civil War," John F. Reynolds File, GNMP; J. G. Rosengarten to Col. Samuel P. Bates, 13 January 1871, Reynolds file, GNMP (original in HSP).

56. J. F. Slagle to Brother, 13 September 1863, SL. Slagle's letter is nineteen pages long. It is one of the most detailed letters about the fighting on 1 July in existence. A native of Pittsburgh, Slagle was a member of the Allegheny County bar and solicitor of the city of Pittsburgh after the war. He helped recruit a company of the One Hundred Forty-Ninth Pennsylvania but was detailed as judge advocate of the Third Division of the First Corps on the staff of General Doubleday. It was in this position that Slagle was serving during the Gettysburg Campaign. All staff officers became battlefield aides to the general they served.

57. Ibid.; *OR*, 27(1):246. Doubleday was the unfortunate victim of Reynolds's abandonment of his original orders from Meade. Doubleday understood Reynolds's original orders: "to dispute the enemy's advance ... falling back, however, in case of a serious attack, to the ground already chosen at Emmitsburg." *OR*, 27(1):244. When Reynolds fell, he was in the act of fighting a tactical engagement west of Gettysburg. Doubleday had no choice but to try to carry out what Reynolds had initiated.

58. War Department, *Revised Regulations for the Army of the United States*, 1861: "Before the action, the Quartermaster of the division makes all the necessary arrangements for the transportation of the wounded. He establishes the ambulance depots in the rear, and gives his assistants the necessary instructions for the service of ambulance wagons and other means of removing the wounded" (§735). "The medical director of the division, after consultation with the Quartermaster General, distributes the medical officers and hospital attendants at his disposal, to the depots and active ambulances. He will send officers and attendants, when practicable, to the active ambulances, to relieve the wounded who require treatment before being removed from the ground. He will see that the depots and ambulances are provided with the necessary apparatus, medicines, and stores. He will take post and render his professional services at the principal depot" (§738). "The wounded in the depots and the sick are removed, as soon as possible, to the hospitals that have been established by the Quartermaster General of the army on the flanks or rear of the army" (§740).

The obligation to establish and organize the hospitals and ambulance depots for the three First Corps divisions fell squarely on Reynolds and his chief quartermaster if Reynolds had intended to stay and fight west of Gettysburg. Those hospitals and ambulance depots should have been established, staffed, and outfitted as the First Corps was approaching the battlefield. It appears that little was done in advance of the fighting, illustrating that Reynolds's original intention was not to stay and fight there. Duncan, *Medical Department of the United States Army in the Civil War*, 237; Coco, *Vast Sea of Misery*, 5–22. Dr. James Fulton, the surgeon of the One Hundred Forty-Third Pennsylvania Infantry of the First Corps, recalled the chaos on 1 July. He first occupied a small stone house literally on the battlefield but was then told to "go into town." Once he reached the town, he found that "[the corps staff and numerous surgeons and attendants] had taken possession of the Catholic Church, the Courthouse, and a great many private houses for the wounded." Then he wrote: "We had nothing upon which to feed our wounded, save such as we begged from house to house; that being an exceedingly slow proceeding, the women of the city being so frightened they kept in their cellars, out of the way of the shot and shell; they consequently could cook nothing for their own families, to say nothing about us." He finally confessed: "We were reduced to sad straits. Our provision train was far to the rear, and might just as well been a thousand miles away for all the good it was to us. We had little beef extract, and but little of it. We could by going to the houses get a little apple butter, sometimes a little rusk or bread. In this condition we worked along the first and part of the second day." Dr. James Fulton, "A Surgeon's Story of the Battle of Gettysburg," *National Review* (Washington, D.C.), 20 October 1878.

Chapter 8

1. S. Williams to Major General Reynolds, 1 July 1863, *OR*, 27(3):460–61.
2. Circular, Headquarters, Army of the Potomac, 1 July 1863, *OR*, 27(3): 458–60.
3. Ibid.
4. Ibid.

5. Ibid.

6. Ibid.

7. George G. Meade to General Halleck, 1 July 1863, 12:00 P.M., *OR*, 27(1): 70–71.

8. Jno. Buford to General Meade, 1 July 1863, 10:10 A.M., 27(1):924; Weld, *War Diary and Letters of Stephen Minot Weld*, 229–33.

9. George G. Meade to General Couch, 1 July 1863, 12:00 P.M. (copy received, War Department, 5:00 P.M.), *OR*, 27(3):458.

10. George G. Meade to General [Reynolds], 30 June 1863, 11:30 A.M., *OR*, 27(3): 420.

11. Danl. Butterfield to Commanding Officer, Second Corps, 1 July 1863, 12:30 P.M., *OR*, 27(3):461. General Hancock reported that the Second Corps arrived at Taneytown at 11:00 A.M. on 1 July. See *OR*, 27(1):367.

12. Danl. Butterfield to Commanding Officer, Second Corps, 1 July 1863, 12:30 P.M., *OR*, 27(3):461; Hancock, *Reminiscences of Winfield S. Hancock*, 185–86.

13. S. Williams to Commanding Officer, Sixth Corps, 1 July 1863, *OR*, 27(3):462.

14. Danl. Butterfield to Commanding Officer, Twelfth Corps, 1 July 1863, *OR*, 27(3):462.

15. S. Williams to Major General French, 1 July 1863, *OR*, 27(3):462–63.

16. Reid, "Battles of Gettysburg," *RR*, 7:85.

17. Ibid., 87.

18. Ibid., 87–88.

19. *OR*, 27(1):702; Ellie Reynolds to Brother, 5 July 1863, John F. Reynolds Papers, F&MC. Major Riddle spoke with Ellie Reynolds at General Reynolds's funeral in Lancaster, Pennsylvania. He told her that he was carrying orders at the time and did not know Reynolds was killed.

20. Taylor, *Gouverneur Kemble Warren*, 121–25.

21. *OR*, 27(1):367–68; Hancock, *Reminiscences of Winfield S. Hancock*, 186.

22. *OR*, 27(1):367; Hancock, *Reminiscences of Winfield S. Hancock*, 186–88; Gibbon, *Personal Recollections of the Civil War*, 132–33.

23. Danl. Butterfield to Major General Hancock, 1 July 1863, 1:10 P.M., *OR*, 27(3):461.

24. Jas. S. Wadsworth to General Doubleday or General Howard, 1 July 1863, 12:10 P.M., *OR*, 27(3):463; Danl. Butterfield to Major General Hancock, 1 July 1863, 1:10 P.M., postscript, 1:15 P.M., *OR*, 27(3):461.

25. Warner, *Generals in Blue*, 202–4.

26. *OR*, 27(1):367–68, 376; Hancock, *Reminiscences of Winfield S. Hancock*, 188; Brown, *Cushing of Gettysburg*, 202–3.

27. Hancock, *Reminiscences of Winfield S. Hancock*, 188–90; Tucker, *Hancock the Superb*, 132; Brown, *Cushing of Gettysburg*, 202–3.

28. Reid, "Battles of Gettysburg," *RR*, 7:88.

29. *OR*, 27(1):246–47.

30. Ibid., 702–3; *OR*, 27(3):463; Howard, *Autobiography of Oliver Otis Howard*, 1:412; Coco, *Vast Sea of Misery*, 105–7.

31. *OR*, 27(1):702–3; D. E. Sickles to Major General Howard, 1 July 1863, 3:15

P.M., *OR*, 27(3):463; O. O. Howard to Major General Meade, 1 July 1863, 2:00 P.M., *OR*, 27(3):457–58.

32. *OR*, 27(1):703; T. A. Meysenburg to Major General Slocum, 1 July 1863, 1:00 P.M., *OR*, 27(3):463; H. W. Slocum to General Hancock or General Howard, *OR*, 27(3):465.

33. *OR*, 27(1):703.

34. D. E. Sickles to Major General Howard, 1 July 1863, 3:15 P.M., *OR*, 27(3):463; D. E. Sickles to General Williams, 1 July 1863, 3:15 P.M., *OR*, 27(3):464; Tremain, *Two Days of War*, 18–19.

35. *OR*, 27(1):704; Dawes, *Service with the Sixth Wisconsin Volunteers*, 178.

36. *OR*, 27(1):704.

37. Ibid., 173–74, 182–83. The casualty figures for the First and Eleventh Corps in the *Official Records* are for the three days fighting at Gettysburg. Those two corps suffered most of their losses on the first day. *OR*, 27(1):173–74, 182–83.

38. *OR*, 27(2):358, 445, 469–78, 504, 555, 607.

Chapter 9

1. Jim "to my own darling little wife," 1 July 1863, James Cornell Biddle Letters, George G. Meade Collection, HSP.

2. *OR*, 27(1):202. Norton wrote nearly three months after 1 July that his conference with Meade was "in the evening," but it had to have been held earlier in the afternoon. By seven o'clock that evening, all but two of Meade's seven army corps would be at, en route to, or about to be ordered to Gettysburg.

3. Bruce, *Twentieth Regiment Massachusetts Volunteers*, 269.

4. Ibid., 269–70.

5. Sergeant George Buckman Diary (1st Minnesota), 1 July 1863, *Minneapolis Star Tribune*, 30 June 2013.

6. Gibbon, *Personal Recollections of the Civil War*, 132.

7. *OR*, 27(1):368; Hancock, "Gettysburg: Reply to General Howard," http://www.worldcat.org/title/gettysburg-reply-to-general-howard/oclc; Walker, *History of the Second Army Corps*, 266–67; Hancock, *Reminiscences of Winfield S. Hancock*, 188–89; Tucker, *Hancock the Superb*, 132; J. H. Cooper to "Mac," 14 June 1886, Winfield S. Hancock Papers, USAMHI.

8. Halstead, "Incidents of the First Day at Gettysburg," *B&L*, 3:285. Major E. P. Halstead, adjutant general of the First Corps, was with Hancock and Howard when they met on Cemetery Hill. His version of the meeting stands out as the best of the few narratives extant. However, Halstead's claim that Hancock stated to Howard that he would "second any order you have to give" not only does not fit with Hancock's character but does not make sense with the rest of the narrative. Meade gave Hancock explicit authority, and he would never surrender that to anyone else. See Hancock's testimony before the Joint Committee on the Conduct of the War. Hyde, *Union Generals Speak* (Hancock Testimony, JCCW), 200–201. Hancock testified that he told Howard he had orders to take command and that Howard "acquiesced." General Howard's version is not believable, as in it he gives the orders to Hancock. Howard, *Autobiography of Oliver Otis Howard*, 1:418. See General

Doubleday's report, noting Hancock directly informing him that he (Hancock) had been placed in command of the two corps on Cemetery Hill. *OR*, 27(1):252.

9. Warner, *Generals in Blue*, 237–38.

10. *OR*, 27(1):230–31, 266–67, 361, 368.

11. Winf'd S. Hancock to General Butterfield, 1 July 1863, 5:25 P.M., *OR*, 27(1): 366–69.

12. *OR*, 27(1):368; Hancock, "Gettysburg: Reply to General Howard."

13. Hancock, "Gettysburg: Reply to General Howard"; Veale, *109th Regiment Pennsylvania Veteran Volunteers*, 11.

14. *OR*, 27(1):368, 825; Hancock, *Reminiscences of Winfield S. Hancock*, 191; Walker, *History of the Second Army Corps*, 168–269; Veale, *109th Regiment Pennsylvania Veteran Volunteers*, 11.

15. Winf'd S. Hancock to General Butterfield, 1 July 1863, 5:25 P.M., *OR*, 27(1): 366; Hancock, "Gettysburg Reply to General Howard"; Hancock, *Reminiscences of Winfield S. Hancock*, 191; Walker, *History of the Second Army Corps*, 168–269.

16. Danl. Butterfield to Major General Sedgwick, 1 July 1863, 4:30 P.M., *OR*, 27(3):465.

17. Hyde, *Following the Greek Cross*, 142; Hyde, *Civil War Letters*, 90. Hyde was clearly the messenger who carried Meade's first of two orders to Sedgwick to move the Sixth Corps to Taneytown. In his book, Hyde claims he carried the second order. As noted hereinafter, Lieutenant Paul A. Oliver of General Butterfield's staff carried the second order to move the Sixth Corps to Gettysburg. Two messages written by Butterfield on 2 July 1863, at 2:40 A.M. and 5:30 A.M., confirm Oliver as the messenger carrying the order for Sedgwick to move his corps to Gettysburg and notifying General Newton of his appointment to command the First Corps. Danl. Butterfield to Major General Meade, 2 July 1863, 2:40 A.M., *OR*, 27(3):483; Danl. Butterfield to Major General Sedgwick, 2 July 1863, 5:30 A.M., *OR*, 27(3): 484–85. Oliver's letter to "My Dear Sam," written only six days after he delivered the order, confirms that he carried the order for Sedgwick to march his corps to Gettysburg and that Newton would command the First Corps. Paul A. Oliver to My Dear Sam, 8 July 1863, HA.

18. Danl. Butterfield to Commanding Officer, Third Corps, 1 July 1863, 4:45 P.M., *OR*, 27(3):466.

19. *OR*, 27(1):482, 519–20, 530–31.

20. Ibid., 151.

21. Diary of James L. Howie (141st Pennsylvania), 1 July 1863, JC; Bardeen, *Little Fifer's War Diary* (1st Massachusetts), 216; Craft, *History of the One Hundred Forty-First Regiment, Pennsylvania Volunteers*, 117; Rauscher, *Music on the March*, 86.

22. Rauscher, *Music on the March*, 86.

23. *OR*, 27(1):530–31; Diary of Adolfo Fernandez de la Cavada, 1 July 1863, GNMP; Report by Major Charles Hamline, Assistant Adjutant General on General Humphrey's staff, 11 August 1863, typescript, Daniel E. Sickles file, GNMP, original in HSP.

24. *OR*, 27(1):482, 531; Humphreys, *Andrew Atkinson Humphreys*, 187–92.

25. Hancock, "Gettysburg: Reply to General Howard"; Hancock, *Reminiscences of Winfield S. Hancock*, 192; Winf'd S. Hancock to General Butterfield, 1 July 1863, 5:25 P.M., *OR*, 27(1):366, *OR*, 27(1):368.

26. Jno. Buford to General Pleasonton, 1 July 1863. 3:20 P.M., *OR*, 27(1):924–25.

27. Hancock, "Gettysburg: Reply to General Howard"; Hancock, *Reminiscences of Winfield S. Hancock*, 191; George G. Meade to General Couch, 1 July 1863, 12 noon, *OR*, 27(3):458.

28. Hancock, *Reminiscences of Winfield S. Hancock*, 191; *OR*, 27(1):368.

29. George G. Meade to Major Generals Hancock and Doubleday, 1 July 1863, 6:00 P.M., *OR*, 27(3):466.

30. H. W. Slocum to General Meade, 1 July 1863, 5:00 P.M., *OR*, 27(3):466.

31. Warner, *Generals in Blue*, 451–52.

32. George G. Meade to Maj. Gen. H. W. Halleck, 1 July 1863, 6:00 P.M., *OR*, 27(1):71–72.

33. Hancock, *Reminiscences of Winfield S. Hancock*, 191–92.

34. S. Williams to General Sedgwick, 1 July 1863, *OR*, 27(3):465. Although the order from Meade to Sedgwick to direct General Newton to assume command of the First Corps does not bear a time of issuance, it had to have been written after Meade received the written message from Hancock, as that message contained Hancock's note that "Doubleday's command gave way." The order from Meade to replace Doubleday was signed by General Seth Williams.

35. Coddington, *Gettysburg Campaign*, 275, 690–91n82; Guelzo, *Gettysburg: The Last Invasion*, 224–26.

36. Danl. Butterfield to Commanding Officer, Fifth Corps, 1 July 1863, 7:00 P.M., *OR*, 27(3):467; Hunt, "Second Day at Gettysburg," *B&L*, 3:301.

37. Danl. Butterfield to Major General Sedgwick, 1 July 1863, 7:30 P.M., *OR*, 27(3):467–68.

38. Ibid.

39. Paul A. Oliver to My Dear Sam, 8 July 1863, HA; Hyde, *Following the Greek Cross*, 142–43; Winslow, *General John Sedgwick*, 98–100; Mark, *Red: White: and Blue Badge*, 213.

40. Jackson, "Battle of Gettysburg," *Military Essays and Recollections*, 10:168.

41. Ibid.

42. Warner, *Generals in Blue*, 430–31.

43. *OR*, 27(1):151; R. N. Bachelder to Gen. Alexander S. Webb, 8 March 1895, Alexander S. Webb Papers, box 4, folder 004-0072, YUL.

44. Paul A. Oliver to My Dear Sam, 8 July 1863, HA; Mark, *Red: White: and Blue Badge*, 216.

45. Mark, *Red: White: and Blue Badge*, 213.

46. Best, *History of the 121st New York State Infantry*, 87.

47. Stevens, *Three Years in the Sixth Corps*, 240; Diary of Henry Clay Bowman (93rd Pennsylvania), 1 July 1863, PM.

48. *OR*, 27(1):151, 595.

49. Carter, *Four Brothers in Blue*, 298; Diary of Jacob Shenkel (62nd Pennsylvania), 1 July 1863, USAMHI.

50. D. E. Sickles to Major General Butterfield, 1 July 1863, 9:30 P.M., *OR*, 27(3):468.

51. Danl. Butterfield to Commanding Officer at Emmitsburg, 1 July 1863, 7:30 P.M., *OR*, 27(3):467.

Chapter 10

1. Wm. H. French to Brigadier General Williams, 1 July 1863, *OR*, 27(3):473.

2. George G. Meade to Mrs. George G. Meade, 8 July 1863, George G. Meade Papers, HSP; Meade, *Life and Letters of George Gordon Meade*, 2:132–33.

3. *OR*, 27(1):151; Rufus Ingalls to M. C. Meigs, 1 July 1863, 4:15 P.M., Records of the Quartermaster General, RG 92, Consolidated Correspondence File, NA.

4. M. C. Meigs to Brig. Gen. R. Ingalls, 1 July 1863, 11:20 A.M., *OR*, 27(3):472.

5. Rufus Ingalls to M. C. Meigs, 1 July 1863, 4:15 P.M., Records of the Quartermaster General, RG 92, Consolidated Correspondence File, NA.

6. War Department, *Revised Regulations for the Army of the United States, 1861*, §§ 1121, 1122. Rufus Ingalls to M. C. Meigs, 1 July 1863, 4:15 P.M., Records of the Quartermaster General, RG 92, Consolidated Correspondence File, NA.

7. Rufus Ingalls to M. C. Meigs, 1 July 1863 (received 2 July 1863, 4:26 A.M.), Records of the Quartermaster General, RG 92, Consolidated Correspondence File, NA. The letter is dated "July 1st, 1863," although below the date it reads: "Hd.Qrs. A.P., Taneytown, Md., June 30/63." The letter had to have been written on the afternoon of 1 July because General Meigs's letter to Ingalls, dated "July 1, 1863—11:20 A.M.," was the first notification by Meigs to Ingalls that General Haupt had been ordered to repair the Western Maryland Railroad and open a depot at Westminster.

8. Rufus Ingalls to M. C. Meigs, 1 July 1863, 7:00 P.M., Records of the Quartermaster General, RG 92, Consolidated Correspondence File, NA.

9. W. P. Smith to M. C. Meigs, 1 July 1863, 2:20 P.M., Records of the Quartermaster General, RG 92, Consolidated Correspondence File, NA. On 10 July 1863, W. P. Smith would record those thirty freight cars of ammunition were still standing at Frederick. W. P. Smith to M. C. Meigs, 10 July 1863, Records of the Quartermaster General, RG 92, Consolidated Correspondence File, NA.

10. Gen. R. N. Bachelder to Gen. Alexander S. Webb, 8 March 1895, Alexander S. Webb Papers, box 4, folder 004-0072, YUL; Klein, *Just South of Gettysburg*, 101–3. Klein quotes recollections written by Dr. J. W. Hering of Westminster, Maryland, wherein he noted that there were "about 5,000 army wagons parked in Westminster and its immediate vicinity." With those wagons, recalled Dr. Hering, "there were 30,000 mules."

11. Diary of J. P. Coburn (141st Pennsylvania), 1 July 1863, USAMHI.

12. *OR*, 27(1):156, 160, 163.

13. Ibid., 168, 926–30, 970–71; *OR*, 27(3):471–72, 484.

14. Diary of Gilbert Thompson (Battn. of U.S. Topographical Engineers), 1 July 1863, Gilbert Thompson Papers, LOC; Danl. Butterfield to Captain Mendel, 2 July 1863, 5:00 A.M., *OR*, 27(3):484.

15. *OR*, 27(1):22–24.

16. Warner, *Generals in Blue*, 217–18; Haupt, *Reminiscences of General Herman Haupt*, xiii–xxxi.

17. Haupt, *Reminiscences of General Herman Haupt*, 214–16; "Stereoview of the Eutaw House by William M. Chase."

18. Haupt, *Reminiscences of General Herman Haupt*, 214–15, 546; *OR*, 27(1): 22–23.

19. Haupt, *Reminiscences of General Herman Haupt*, 213; *OR*, 27(1):22–23.

20. Haupt, *Reminiscences of General Herman Haupt*, 215.

21. Ibid.

22. Howard, *Autobiography of Oliver Otis Howard*, 1:419.

23. *OR*, 27(1):115, 368–69; Hyde, *Union Generals Speak* (Meade and Hancock Testimony, JCCW), 124–25, 212–13, 295.

24. *OR*, 27(1):115, 232; Meade, *With Meade at Gettysburg*, 69; Nicholson, *Pennsylvania at Gettysburg*, 2:785–97; John Hamilton to Col. John B. Bachelder, 27 June 1882, in Ladd and Ladd, *Bachelder Papers*, 2:890. Hamilton, formerly the sergeant major of the First Pennsylvania Reserve Volunteer Cavalry, informed Bachelder that his regiment escorted Meade from Taneytown to Gettysburg on the night of 1 July 1863.

25. Howard, *Autobiography of Oliver Otis Howard*, 1:422–23; Meade, *With Meade at Gettysburg*, 69, 95.

26. *OR*, 27(1):115; Howard, *Autobiography of Oliver Otis Howard*, 1:422–24; Meade, *With Meade at Gettysburg*, 95; Hunt, "Second Day at Gettysburg," *B&L*, 3:291–93; Shultz and Mingus, "Sunrise Hours at Gettysburg, July 2, 1863," *GM*, 56:14, 22; O. O. Howard to Maj. Gen. Butterfield, 1 July 1863, 10:00 P.M., Eleventh Corps Papers, RG 393, Pt. 2, E 5312, Letters Sent, NA.

27. Gibbon, *Personal Recollections of the Civil War*, 133; Howard, *Autobiography of Oliver Otis Howard*, 1:422–23.

28. Meade, *With Meade at Gettysburg*, 95; Cleaves, *Meade of Gettysburg*, 140; Howard, *Autobiography of Oliver Otis Howard*, 1:423.

29. Meade, *With Meade at Gettysburg*, 96; Howard, *Autobiography of Oliver Otis Howard*, 1:423.

30. *OR*, 27(1):115–16; Meade, *With Meade at Gettysburg*, 96.

31. Jackson, "Battle of Gettysburg," *Military Essays and Recollections, MOLLUS*, 10:168–69. Although Jackson's article contains some factual errors, what is used of it herein appears reliable because he was present with Newton on the road to Gettysburg and on Cemetery Hill when Newton met Meade.

32. Ibid.

33. Warner, *Generals in Blue*, 344–45.

34. *OR*, 27(1):115; Meade, *With Meade at Gettysburg*, 96; Hunt, "Second Day at Gettysburg," *B&L*, 3:291–92; Reid, "Battles of Gettysburg," *RR*, 7:89.

35. Mouat, "Three Years in the 29th Pennsylvania," 29th Pennsylvania Papers, HSP.

36. Meade, *With Meade at Gettysburg*, 96; *OR*, 27(1):758–59.

37. Schurz, *Reminiscences of Carl Schurz*, 3:20–21.

38. *OR*, 27(3):486–87; Harman, "The Gap: Meade's July 2 Offensive Plan,"

77–78, 82. Illustrative of how concerned Meade was with protecting the Baltimore Pike, he directed General Slocum, along with General Sykes, to launch an attack against the Confederate left flank early on the morning of 2 July in an effort to force the enemy away from the Baltimore Pike; *OR*, 27(1):872.

Chapter 11

1. Diary of Stephen A. Wallace (153rd Pennsylvania), 2 July 1863, roll #4028, PSA; Bardeen, *Little Fifer's War Diary* (1st Massachusetts), 217; Marbaker, *History of the Eleventh New Jersey*, 96; Blake, *Three Years in the Army of the Potomac*, 205.

2. Meade, *With Meade at Gettysburg*, 96; Smith, *Farms at Gettysburg*, 40–41.

3. Smith, *Farms at Gettysburg*, 40–41.

4. Ibid.

5. *OR*, 27(1):261, 368–69, 482, 592, 663, 705, 759, 915–16, 987.

6. Hunt, "Second Day at Gettysburg," *B&L*, 3:297–99; Kirkwood, *Too Much for Human Endurance*, 88–89, quoting James Freeman Huntington, "Notes of Service with the Light Artillery at Chancellorsville and Gettysburg," *Sunday Observer* (Marietta, Ohio), 4 August 1918.

7. Kepler, *History of the Three Months' and Three Years' Service of the Fourth Regiment Ohio Volunteer Infantry*, 126; Thompson, "Personal Narrative of Experiences in the Civil War," 33–34, GNMP.

8. Gibbon, *Recollections of the Civil War*, 133; Meade, *With Meade at Gettysburg*, 96–97.

9. Gibbon, *Recollections of the Civil War*, 133–34.

10. Ibid., 133.

11. *OR*, 27(1):369, 825.

12. Ibid., 202; Brown, *Signal Corps in the War of the Rebellion*, 360. The signal station on Cemetery Hill was established late in the afternoon of 1 July. A signal station had been set up in the cupola of the Lutheran Seminary as fighting erupted early that morning; it was then moved to the Adams County Court House as the Union lines collapsed west and north of Gettysburg late that day. Those signal stations had reported to the Cemetery Hill signal station where General Howard's headquarters had been established.

13. Brown, *Signal Corps in the War of the Rebellion*, 360, 363.

14. A. Ames to Lieutenant Colonel Meysenburg, 2 July 1863, 7:30 A.M., *OR*, 27(3):485, C. Schurz to [unknown], 2 July 1863, 8:00 A.M., *OR*, 27(3):486; *OR*, 27(1):182.

15. George Sykes to General Howard, 2 July 1863, *OR*, 27(3):486; Kirkwood, *Too Much for Human Endurance*, 81.

16. In a message sent to General Sedgwick by General Butterfield at 5:00 A.M., General Meade gave a synopsis of all he knew about the positions of the enemy and what elements of Lee's army he believed were on the field. "A. P. Hill and Longstreet," it read, "are supposed to be concentrated in front of Gettysburg. Ewell—it is not known definitely where he is, but may be on our right flank. His headquarters were at Berlin night before last." That is all Meade knew. Dnl. Butterfield to Major General Sedgwick, 2 July 1863, 5:30 A.M., *OR*, 27(3):484–85.

17. Hunt, "Second Day at Gettysburg," *B&L*, 3:294.

18. *Report of Major General D. H. Rucker, Assistant Quartermaster General, U.S. Army, December 29, 1868*, 7–10. Records of the Quartermaster General, RG 92, Consolidated Correspondence File, NA.

19. *OR*, 27(1):221–22.

20. "By Telegraph from Washington, June 25/63," General and Special Orders Received and Issued, Eleventh Corps Papers, RG 393, Pt. 2, E 5323, box 1, NA.

21. *Report of Major General D. H. Rucker, Assistant Quartermaster General, U.S. Army, December 29, 1868*, 5–10. Records of the Quartermaster General, RG 92, Consolidated Correspondence File, NA; *General Order, July 6, 1863*, Headquarters Eleventh Corps, General and Special Orders Received and Issued, Eleventh Corps Papers, RG 393, Pt. 2, box 1, NA. General Howard wrote: "The attention of officers is called to the great amount of straggling soldiers going about the country visiting houses in advance on the flank and in rear of the troops. The whole blame is due to the regimental officers. I know they can stop it. Hereafter when stragglers are found from a company, the officers in command shall be made to suffer for this shameful neglect of duty or utter incompetency."

22. *OR*, 27(1):222.

23. *Report of Major General D. H. Rucker, Assistant Quartermaster General, U.S. Army, December 29, 1868*, 5–8. Records of the Quartermaster General, RG 92, Consolidated Correspondence File, NA.

24. Letterman, *Medical Recollections*, 155.

25. Coco, *Vast Sea of Misery*, 61–67.

26. Ibid., 66–70.

27. Livermore, *Days and Events*, 239–41, 243.

28. Coco, *Vast Sea of Misery*, 74–77, 105–7; Duncan, *Medical Department of the United States Army*, 236–39, 251–53, 253–54.

29. *Report of Major General D. H. Rucker, Assistant Quartermaster General, U.S. Army, December 29, 1868*, 3. Records of the Quartermaster General, RG 92, Consolidated Correspondence File, NA; Letterman, *Medical Recollections*, 154–57; Duncan, *Medical Department of the United States Army*, 234–39; *OR*, 27(1):221–22.

30. *Report of Major General D. H. Rucker, Assistant Quartermaster General, U.S. Army, December 29, 1868*, 1–2, 7–10. Records of the Quartermaster General, RG 92, Consolidated Correspondence File, NA; Letterman, *Medical Recollections*, 157.

31. *OR*, 27(1):416, 482, 543.

32. Ibid., 515, 519, 570–71, 587; Stevens, *Berdan's United States Sharpshooters*, 302–3; Tremain, *Two Days of War*, 42, 48; Rusling, *Men and Things I Saw in Civil War Days*, 4.

33. Tremain, *Two Days of War*, 42–43.

34. Taylor, *Gouverneur Kemble Warren*, 130.

35. Hunt, "Second Day at Gettysburg," *B&L*, 3:303.

36. Taylor, *Gouverneur Kemble Warren*, 122.

37. S. Williams to Commanding Officer, Twelfth Corps, 2 July 1863, 9:30 A.M.; *OR*, 27(3):486; Harman, "The Gap: Meade's July 2 Offensive Plan," 77–78, 82.

38. Jas. S. Hall to General Meade, 2 July 1863, 9:30 A.M., *OR*, 27(3):486–87; *OR*, 27(1):233, 358.

39. Hyde, *Union Generals Speak* (Meade Testimony, JCCW), 295–96.

40. Danl. Butterfield to Commanding Officer, Twelfth Corps, 2 July 1863, *OR*, 27(3):486.

Chapter 12

1. Meade, *With Meade at Gettysburg*, 100; Meade, "Memorandum of George Meade," 1, Alexander S. Webb Papers, box 7, YUL; Reid, "Battles of Gettysburg," *RR*, 7:94.

2. Meade, *With Meade at Gettysburg*, 100; Meade, "Memorandum of George Meade," 1, Alexander S. Webb Papers, box 7, YUL.

3. Meade, *With Meade at Gettysburg*, 100–101; Meade, "Memorandum of George Meade," 1, Alexander S. Webb Papers, box 7, YUL.

4. Tremain, *Two Days of War*, 37; Meade, "Memorandum of George Meade," 1, Alexander S. Webb Papers, box 7, YUL.

5. Meade, *With Meade at Gettysburg*, 101–2; Meade, "Memorandum of George Meade," 2, Alexander S. Webb Papers, box 7, YUL.

6. Meade, *With Meade at Gettysburg*, 102; Meade, "Memorandum of George Meade," 2–3, Alexander S. Webb Papers, box 7, YUL.

7. George Gordon Meade to G. G. Benedict, 16 March 1870, reprinted in *Philadelphia Weekly Press*, 11 August 1886.

8. Meade, *With Meade at Gettysburg*, 102; Meade, "Memorandum of George Meade," 3, Alexander S. Webb Papers, box 7, YUL.

9. Circular, Headquarters, Army of the Potomac, 2 July 1863, 11:00 A.M., *OR*, 27(3):487; Hunt, "Second Day at Gettysburg," *B&L*, 3:297.

10. "Map of Adams County, Pennsylvania," by G. M. Hopkins, 1858.

11. H. W. Slocum to Major General Meade, 2 July 1863, 10:30 A.M. (received 11:00 A.M., *OR*, 27(3):487; Taylor, *Gouverneur Kemble Warren*, 122.

12. Meade, "Memorandum of George Meade," 4–5, Alexander S. Webb Papers, box 7, YUL; Tremain, *Two Days of War*, 43; Meade, *With Meade at Gettysburg*, 105–6.

13. Tremain, *Two Days of War*, 43–44; Hunt, "Second Day at Gettysburg," *B&L*, 3:301–3.

14. Hunt, "Second Day at Gettysburg," *B&L*, 3:301–3; Tremain, *Two Days of War*, 45–46.

15. *OR*, 27(1):507, 515; Stevens, *Berdan's United States Sharpshooters*, 303.

16. Tremain, *Two Days of War*, 44–46, 48–49; *OR*, 27(1):519, 570, 581.

17. Tremain, *Two Days of War*, 49.

18. Dana, *Recollections of the Civil War*, 189–90.

19. Tremain, *Two Days of War*, 49.

20. Ibid., 49–50.

21. Ibid., 50.

22. Hunt, "Second Day at Gettysburg," *B&L*, 3:303.

23. Lieutenant Jerome to General Butterfield, 2 July 1863, 11:55 A.M.; Captain Babcock to General Butterfield, 2 July 1863, 12:35 A.M., *OR*, 27(3):488.

24. Jno. Buford to General Pleasonton, 30 June 1963, *OR*, 27(1):923; Jno. Buford to General Pleasonton, 30 June 1863, 10:40 P.M., *OR*, 27(1):923–24; see also *OR*, 27(1):927–28.

25. Daniel Butterfield to Commanding Officer, Cavalry Corps, 2 July 1863, 12:50 P.M. and 12:55 P.M.; A. Pleasonton to Brigadier General Gregg, 2 July 1863, 1:45 P.M., *OR*, 27(3):490.

26. *OR*, 27(1):927–28.

27. Captain Hall to General Butterfield, 2 July 1863, 1:30 P.M.; A. B. Jerome to General Howard, 2 July 1863, no time given; Captain Hall to General Butterfield, 2 July 1863, 2:10 P.M., *OR*, 27(3):488. The movement of the large force on the Herr Ridge Road may well have been a ruse. Lee may have intended that movement to be seen from the Little Round Top signal station because Lee was well aware of its presence and, possibly, many of the signals being sent. If so, Lee was trying to get Meade to move more of his troops to the right so as to weaken the left.

28. Tremain, *Two Days of War*, 54.

29. Ibid., 54–55.

30. S. M. Shoemaker to Hon. E. M. Stanton, 2 July 1863 (received 3:45 P.M.), *OR*, 27(3):494; George G. Meade to Maj. Gen. H. W. Halleck, 2 July 1863, 3:00 P.M. (received 3 July 1863, 10:20 A.M.), *OR*, 27(1):72.

31. Meade, *With Meade at Gettysburg*, 108–9; Tremain, *Two Days of War*, 59–62.

32. Warner, *Generals in Blue*, 492–93.

33. Hessler, *Sickles at Gettysburg*, 150; Coddington, *Gettysburg Campaign*, 349–58.

34. Meade, *With Meade at Gettysburg*, 108; Tremain, *Two Days of War*, 61–62, 65–66; William H. Paine to George Meade, 22 May 1886, GL, 78, George G. Meade Papers, HSP.

35. Meade, *With Meade at Gettysburg*, 112; *OR*, 27(1):483, 493, 499, 500–501, 502–3, 504, 519–20; Craft, *History of the One Hundred Forty-First Regiment*, 120.

36. *OR*, 27(1):532.

37. Meade, *With Meade at Gettysburg*, 112–13; Nicholson, *Pennsylvania at Gettysburg*, 2:623.

38. *OR*, 27(1):531–32; Blake, *Three Years in the Army of the Potomac*, 206.

39. Tremain, *Two Days of War*, 62; Jim to my own darling wife, 8 July 1863, James Cornell Biddle Letters, George G. Meade Collection, HSP; Paul [Oliver] to My Dear Sara, 8 July 1863, HA; James C. Biddle to George Meade, 18 August 1880, 10 July 1886, GL, 27, 33, James Cornell Biddle Letters, George G. Meade Collection, HSP; James Starr to George Meade, 7 February 1880, GL, 891, George G. Meade Collection, HSP; Jorgensen, "Securing the Flank: How Three Aides Helped Warren Save Little Round Top," *GM*, 45:84–91; Diary of Adolfo Fernandez de la Cavada, 2 July 1862, GNMP; Meade, *Photographs of Union and Confederate Officers*, 2A.

40. Tremain, *Two Days of War*, 63; Meade, *With Meade at Gettysburg*, 114; James C. Biddle to George Meade, 18 August 1880, GL, 27, George G. Meade Collection, HSP.

41. Meade, *With Meade at Gettysburg*, 114; *OR*, 27(3):487. General Sickles

launched a campaign in the newspapers refuting the fact that specific orders had been given to him to align the Third Corps along Cemetery Ridge, to the left of the Second Corps, extending up Little Round Top, with an article in the *New York Herald* on 12 March 1864. Although written over the name Historicus, it was readily apparent that Sickles either wrote it himself or supervised its writing. The article claimed that Sickles had no orders at all! *OR*, 27(1):128–36. In a letter to Henry Tremain, dated 30 June 1867, Sickles repeated his claim that "no orders or disposition for the battle of Thursday, July 2, were communicated by Gen'l Meade to Gen'l Sickles until the engagement between Longstreet and Sickles on the left began, when Meade, for the first time, made a reconnaissance in person of the position." Sickles further claimed that his "dispositions to resist Longstreet's attack were defensive—and not made until the maneuvers of the enemy on our left and his demonstrations for attack had been communicated to General Meade and orders solicited—yet none received." Finally, Sickles claimed that, after waiting until the latest moment for orders, and when the formation of Longstreet's columns of attack had undressed, further delay would have been criminal. "I took position on the ridge and toward Round Top as far as I could prolong my weak line." Daniel E. Sickles to Henry Tremain, 30 June 1867, Daniel E. Sickles File, GNMP.

None of those assertions were truthful. Frankly, no corps in the Army of the Potomac received more attention from General Meade than the Third Corps. Three times Meade had given Sickles instructions as to the placement of the Third Corps, twice personally. Even a sketch showing the position of the Third Corps had been provided to Sickles early in the morning. Beyond that, Meade ordered Sickles to prepare a sketch of the position the Third Corps was to take and tender it to Meade. If that was not enough, General Geary notified him of the position and asked him to send a staff officer to Little Round Top so he could familiarize himself with the site.

Sickles's allegations were inexcusable. General Meade actually sent to General Halleck the article in the *New York Herald*, asking for a court of inquiry or for authority to publish such official documents as necessary for his defense. Halleck asked Meade to ignore Sickles entirely. *OR*, 27(1):127–28, 137. Meade did as Halleck requested.

42. James C. Biddle to George Meade, 18 August 1880, GL, 27, George G. Meade Collection , HSP; Biddle, "Meade and Sickles at Gettysburg," *Philadelphia Weekly Press*, 14 July 1886; Meade, *With Meade at Gettysburg*, 114; "The Gettysburg Fight, the Second Day's Battle, and Gen. Sickles Part in It," *New York Sun*, 28 June 1891.

43. Meade, *With Meade at Gettysburg*, 118; Biddle, "Meade and Sickles at Gettysburg," *Philadelphia Weekly Press*, 14 July 1886; Taylor, *Gouverneur Kemble Warren*, 125–26; Col. Washington A. Roebling to Col. Smith, 5 July 1913, Warren Papers, NYSL. Roebling agreed with Captain Meade and Major Biddle that General Meade raised the question of Little Round Top being unoccupied and ordered Warren to place troops there. Although Roebling claimed Meade directed Warren to ride over to Little Round Top, to see if it was unoccupied, and, if so, to attend to it, he recalled that the event occurred in Meade's headquarters. Clearly, Roebling's memory failed him on that point. Meade was in the field at the time he directed Warren to ride to Little Round Top. In his testimony before the Joint Committee

on the Conduct of the War, Warren testified: "I then went, by General Meade's direction, to [what he called] 'Bald Top.'" Hyde, *Union Generals Speak* (Warren Testimony, JCCW), 168.

44. Hunt, "Second Day at Gettysburg," *B&L*, 3:303; Kirkwood, *"Too Much for Human Endurance,"* 88–89.

45. Meade, *With Meade at Gettysburg*, 115.

46. Tremain, *Two Days of War*, 64–66; Jim to my own darling wife, 8 July 1863, James Cornell Biddle Letters, George G. Meade Collection, HSP.

47. Jorgenson, "Securing the Flank: How Three Aides Helped Warren Save Little Round Top," *GM*, 45:84–91; Taylor, *Gouverneur Kemble Warren*, 123, 126–27.

48. *OR*, 27(1):588; Taylor, *Gouverneur Kemble Warren*, 123, 127; Jorgenson, "Securing The Flank: How Three Aides Helped Warren Save Little Round Top," *GM*, 45:84–91; Hunt, "Second Day at Gettysburg," *B&L*, 3:305.

49. Jorgenson, "Securing the Flank: How Three Aides Helped Warren Save Little Round Top," *GM*, 45:84–91; Humphreys, *Andrew Atkinson Humphreys*, 193; Meade, *With Meade at Gettysburg*, 119; Meade, *Life and Letters of George Gordon Meade*, 2:82–83. Lt. Ranald S. Mackenzie to Major General Meade, 22 March 1864, Meade, "Memorandum of George Meade," 5, Alexander S. Webb Papers, box 7, YUL.

Chapter 13

1. Hyde, *Union Generals Speak* (Meade Testimony, JCCW), 108. The inability of the superior Union artillery to be used against the Confederate attack on Sickles's advanced positions along the Emmitsburg Road and between the Peach Orchard and Devil's Den was raised by General Gibbon, a noted artilleryman, in Gibbon, "Another View of Gettysburg," *NAR*, 152:415, 712. Gibbon testified before the Joint Committee on the Conduct of the War about his fear of hitting his own men with artillery fire. Hyde, *Union Generals Speak* (Gibbon Testimony, JCCW), 279.

2. *OR*, 27(1):592. General Sykes noted that he was instructed by Meade to "throw [his] whole corps *to that point* and hold it at all hazards" (emphasis added). As Meade was on the field at the time, he must have conversed with Sykes at a site close enough to the Wheatfield for Sykes to understand exactly where to deploy his divisions. Meade wrote that he "rode out to the extreme left to await the arrival of the Fifth Corps." *OR*, 27(1):116. That the First and Second Divisions of the Fifth Corps used the Granite Schoolhouse Road to get to the left flank was made clear by the report of Brigadier General James Barnes: "The column was immediately formed, and moved rapidly up by the Taneytown road to the ground assigned to the Division." Brigadier General Romeyn B. Ayres, commanding the Second Division, reported that his command was "preceded by the First Division." Jim to my own darling wife, 8 July 1863, James Cornell Biddle Letters, George G. Meade Collection, HSP. Major Biddle wrote that he and six other staff officers rode with Meade all the way to the lines General Sickles established and then gave Sickles "instructions."

3. *OR*, 27(1):592.

4. Tremain, *Two Days of War*, 71–76. Tremain recalled that the meeting with Meade took place near the Taneytown Road at the Leister house. Tremain's mem-

ory failed him here. Meade would have been in the field near where the Fifth Corps would enter the battlefield so he and General Sykes could confer; that was near the intersection of the Blacksmith Shop–Wheatfield Road and the Taneytown Road.

5. *OR*, 27(1):592, 600–601; Warner, *Generals in Blue*, 20.

6. *OR*, 27(1):593, 651; Taylor, *Gouverneur Kemble Warren*, 128–29; Brown, *Signal Corps in the War of the Rebellion*, 366–67.

7. *OR*, 27(1):593, 651; Taylor, *Gouverneur Kemble Warren*, 128–29; Brown, *Signal Corps in the War of the Rebellion*, 366–677; Norton, *Attack and Defense of Little Round Top*, 132.

8. David Jenkins to Mr. A. P. Case, 7 January 1864, in Ladd and Ladd, *Bachelder Papers*, 1:73–74.

9. Kernek, *Field Surgeon at Gettysburg*, 38–39; Alleman, *At Gettysburg*, 50–51.

10. *OR*, 27(1):588; Smith, *Famous Battery*, 103; Kauffman, *Inscriptions on Monuments, Markers and Plaques*, 27.

11. *OR*, 27(2):393–427.

12. *OR*, 27(1):493–94; Weygant, *History of the One Hundred Twenty-Fourth New York*, 173–77.

13. *OR*, 27(1):494, 526, 588–89; Smith, *Famous Battery*, 104–5; Floyd, *History of the Fortieth (Mozart) Regiment*, 202.

14. *OR*, 27(1):602–3, 622–23; Gerrish, *Army Life*, 106–7; Kauffman, *Inscriptions on Monuments, Markers and Plaques*, 35.

15. *OR*, 27(1):593, 603, 617–18, 622–25; Nash, *History of the Forty-fourth Regiment New York Volunteer Infantry*, 144–47; Judson, *History of the Eighty-third Regiment Pennsylvania Volunteers*, I (chapter XIV), 1–7; Norton, *Strong Vincent and His Brigade at Gettysburg*, 8–11.

16. *OR*, 27(1):651–52; *OR*, 27(2):391, 404–6, 411–12.

17. Smith, *Washington Roebling's Civil War*, 147, quoting Washington Roebling, "Life of John A. Roebling, C.A.," 314, Roebling Collection, MS box 10, folders 23–26, RU.

18. Houghton, *Campaigns of the Seventeenth Maine*, 92; *OR*, 27(1):587.

19. Kaufman, *Inscriptions on Monuments, Markers, and Plaques*, 26–28; Silliker, *Rebel Yell and the Yankee Hurrah*, 101.

20. Silliker, *Rebel Yell and the Yankee Hurrah*, 101.

21. Meade, *Did General Meade Desire to Retreat at the Battle of Gettysburg?*, 5.

22. *OR*, 27(1):504–5, 523–24, 573–75; Haynes, *History of the Second Regiment New Hampshire Volunteers*, 139.

23. *OR*, 27(2):358, 367–69; Pfanz, *Gettysburg: The Second Day*, 246, 314.

24. Craft, *History of the One Hundred Forty-First Regiment, Pennsylvania Volunteers*, 123; Diary of Colonel Henry J. Madill (141st Pennsylvania), 2 July 1863, USAMHI.

25. *OR*, 27(1):583–84, 589–90, 881–82, 889–90, 900–901; Lewis, *History of Battery E, First Regiment Rhode Island Light Artillery*, 198, 200–202.

26. *OR*, 27(1):502–3, 589–90; Lewis, *History of Battery E, First Regiment Rhode Island Light Artillery*, 202, 211.

27. *OR*, 27(1):497, 502–4, 589–90.

28. Ibid., 484, 500–501, 551, 554; Scott, *History of the One Hundred and Fifth*

Regiment of Pennsylvania Volunteers, 82–83; Marbaker, *History of the Eleventh New Jersey Volunteers*, 98–99; Moran, *Philadelphia Weekly Times*, 22 April 1882.

29. Robert H. Davis Handwritten Memoir (74th New York), 56, HS; Brown, *History of the Third Regiment Excelsior Brigade, 72nd New York Volunteer Infantry*, 104; Hays, *Under the Red Patch*, 195.

30. Van Santvoord, *One Hundred and Twentieth Regiment New York State Volunteers*, 74.

31. *OR*, 27(1):659–60, 889–90, 900–901.

32. Ibid., 659–60.

33. Ibid., 585–86, 884–89; Hanifen, *History of Battery B, First New Jersey Artillery*, 68–77; Baker, *History of the Ninth Mass. Battery*, 56–60; Cowles, *History of the Fifth Massachusetts Battery*, 623–25.

34. *OR*, 27(1):884–88.

35. Bigelow, *Peach Orchard*, 55; *OR*, 27(1):585–86, 884–89; Kauffman, *Inscriptions on Monuments, Markers and Plaques*, 26.

36. *OR*, 27(1):607–8, 610–13.

37. Ibid., 599–605, 610–13; Diary of Lieutenant John Garden (62nd Pennsylvania) 2 July 1863, KMB.

38. Carter, *Four Brothers in Blue*, 311; Col. Wm. S. Tilton to Brig. Gen James Barnes, 14 March 1864, James Barnes File, GNMP; J. B. Sweitzer, Comndg. Brig. to General, 8 April 1864, James Barnes File, GNMP.

39. Diary of Lieutenant John Garden (62nd Pennsylvania), 2 July 1863, KMB.

Chapter 14

1. Beale, *Battle Flags of the Army of the Potomac at Gettysburg*, 2; Biddle, "Meade and Sickles at Gettysburg," *Philadelphia Weekly Press*, 14 July 1886; Meade, *With Meade at Gettysburg*, 123; *OR*, 27(1):379. Nicholson, *Pennsylvania at Gettysburg*: 2:623. Meade made it clear to Hancock that he did not want him to order Caldwell's division to aid Sickles's Third Corps. He wanted Hancock to send Caldwell's division directly to Sykes.

2. *OR*, 27(1):759, 773–74.

3. Maj. Gen. Henry W. Slocum to Messrs. T. H. Davis & Co., 8 September 1875, Samuel P. Bates Papers, PSA.

4. Ibid.; *OR*, 27(1):759, 774; New York Monuments Commission, *In Memoriam, George Sears Greene*, 41–43.

5. Nicholson, *Pennsylvania at Gettysburg*, 2:623; Kauffman, *Inscriptions on Monuments, Markers and Plaques*, 16.

6. *OR*, 27(1):379. Caldwell wrote: "Before reaching the position designated for me, I met a staff officer (I think the adjutant general of General Sykes)." Colonel Locke was Sykes's assistant adjutant general; Child, *History of the Fifth Regiment*, 204; Muffly, *Story of Our Regiment*, 536; Kauffman, *Inscriptions on Monuments, Markers and Plaques*, 18.

7. *OR*, 27(1):379, 386, 387–88; Mulholland, *Story of the 116th Regiment, Pennsylvania Volunteers*, 125.

8. *OR*, 27(1):379, 393–94; Stewart, *History of the One Hundred and Fortieth Regiment, Pennsylvania Volunteers*, 105.

9. *OR*, 27(1):379–81.

10. Ibid., 531–33, 543, 551–54, 558–59.

11. Ibid., 370, 416–17, 419–20, 478, 533. Although Hancock and Gibbon simply refer to the fact that Gibbon directed the Eighty-Second New York and Fifteenth Massachusetts to the Emmitsburg Road and the Codori fields along with Battery B, First Rhode Island, the order to do so must have come from Meade. Ibid., 370, 416, 419. Meade would have seen the gap between Humphreys's right flank and Gibbon's left flank immediately, and in terms of elements of one corps moving to support elements of another corps, it would have been Meade, as army commander, who issued those orders or gave his assent to do so. Certainly, that is what he did all through the afternoon.

12. Ibid.; Ford, *Story of the Fifteenth Regiment, Massachusetts Infantry*, 226–90; Rhodes, *History of Battery B, First Regiment Rhode Island Light Artillery*, 200–201.

13. *OR*, 27(2):288–608.

14. *OR*, 27(1):533; Cudworth, *History of the First Regiment, Massachusetts Infantry*, 395.

15. *OR*, 27(1):533, 543, 568, 591; Van Santvoord, *One Hundred and Twentieth Regiment, New York State Volunteers*, 74; Marbaker, *History of the Eleventh New Jersey Volunteers*, 98.

16. *OR*, 27(1):370; Meade, *With Meade at Gettysburg*, 126.

17. *OR*, 27(1):532–33, 575–76, 590–91, 880.

18. Ibid., 634–35.

19. Ibid., 379–80, 634–35.

20. Ibid., 653–54; Hardin, *History of the Twelfth Reserve Volunteer Corps*, 153. That Crawford's Third Division used the Blacksmith Shop Road to reach the left flank was made clear by the Testimony of General Crawford before the Joint Committee on the Conduct of the War. He described the path of the Blacksmith Shop Road all the way to "the right of Little Round Top." He also stated in his report that he was led to the left flank by a different route than the First and Second Divisions. Hyde, *Union Generals Speak* (Crawford Testimony, JCCW), 342–43.

21. *OR*, 27(1):653–54; Hardin, *History of the Twelfth Regiment, Pennsylvania Reserve Volunteer Corps*, 153.

22. *OR*, 27(1):653–54; Minnigh, *History of Company K, 1st (Inft.) Penn'a. Reserves*, 24–25; Thompson, *History of the Bucktails*, 266, 269–70; Hardin, *History of the Twelfth Regiment, Pennsylvania Reserve Volunteer Corps*, 154–55.

23. *OR*, 27(1):882; Baker, *History of the Ninth Mass. Battery*, 59–60; Bigelow, *Peach Orchard*, 16–18, 55–56.

24. *OR*, 27(1):882, 886; Baker, *History of the Ninth Mass. Battery*, 60–61; Bigelow, *Peach Orchard*, 18–19.

25. *OR*, 27(1):882, 886; Bigelow, *Peach Orchard*, 56–57; Baker, *History of the Ninth Mass. Battery*, 60–61.

26. *OR*, 27(1):882–86; Baker, *History of the Ninth Mass. Battery*, 62–63; Bigelow, *Peach Orchard*, 56–57.

27. Bigelow, *Peach Orchard*, 57–58.

28. Ibid.; 60–61; Baker, *History of the Ninth Mass. Battery*, 215.

29. *OR*, 27(1):882–83.

30. Ibid., 371, 472–73.

31. Ibid., 371, 473, 475–76; Kauffman, *Inscriptions on Monuments, Markers and Plaques*, 23.

32. *OR*, 27(1):773–74, 778, 783; Bartlett, *Dutchess County Regiment*, 31; Meade, *With Meade at Gettysburg*, 126–27.

33. *OR*, 27(1):773–74, 804–6, 809. Meade had to have ordered or given his assent to McDougall's and Colgrove's brigades moving into battle lines to the left, as he was in the midst of the movement of Williams's division onto Cemetery Ridge.

34. *OR*, 27(1):804, 809; Bartlett, *Dutchess County Regiment*, 31–32; Kauffman, *Inscriptions on Monuments, Markers and Plaques*, 58.

35. *OR*, 27(2):618.

36. *OR*, 27(1):759, 773–74.

37. Ibid., 261, 290, 371, 759, 773–74.

38. Ibid., 371, 419, 424–25; Searles, *History of the First Regiment Minnesota Volunteer Infantry*, 344.

39. *OR*, 27(1):425; Searles, *History of the First Regiment Minnesota Volunteer Infantry*, 344–45; Meade, *With Meade at Gettysburg*, 127.

40. *OR*, 27(2):623, 617, 419–20, 423, 426; Ford, *Story of the Fifteenth Regiment Massachusetts Volunteer Infantry*, 267–68.

41. Rhodes, *History of Battery B, First Rhode Island Light Artillery*, 201–3; *OR*, 27(1):478; Smith, *History of the Nineteenth Regiment, Maine Volunteer Infantry*, 75–76.

42. Meade, *With Meade at Gettysburg*, 126–27.

43. Ibid.

44. Meade, *With Meade at Gettysburg*, 126–27; Johnston, "Record of 'Baldy' Gen. Meade's Horse," George G. Meade File, GNMP; Geo. Meade to Mr. Bachelder, 6 May 1882, in Ladd and Ladd, *Bachelder Papers*, 2:852–58. Captain Meade recalled "Old Baldy" being wounded while General Meade was leading Newton's two divisions onto the battlefield and that General Meade rode "Blackey" thereafter.

45. Ibid.; *OR*, 27(1):420, 422; Smith, *History of the Nineteenth Regiment, Maine, Volunteer Infantry*, 75–76.

46. *OR*, 27(1):663, 665, 671, 678, 680–81; Kauffman, *Inscriptions on Monuments, Markers and Plaques*, 42, 43, 44, 45; James Bowen to Col. J. B. Bachelder, undated, in Ladd and Ladd, *Bachelder Papers*, 2:973–76. Bowen, a captain in the Thirty-Seventh Massachusetts, claimed the Sixth Corps did not arrive at Gettysburg until 6:00 P.M., 2 July 1863, although General Sedgwick reported to General Meade earlier in the afternoon.

47. A. S. W. to My Dear Daughters, 6 July 1863, in Quaife, *From the Cannon's Mouth*, 228–29. General Williams claimed he recognized Meade as he returned to Cemetery Ridge after the attack. Meade, he recalled, was with "a large collection of generals and other officers in an open field." A. S. Williams to Jno. Bachelder, Esq., 21 April 1864, in Ladd and Ladd, *Bachelder Papers*, 1:163–66. See also A. S. Williams to Mr. Jno. B. Bachelder, 10 November 1865, in Ladd and Ladd, *Bachelder Papers*, 1:212–23. In that letter, Williams recalled: "On riding back (well into

the dusk of the evening) I found in an open field General Meade in quite a crowd of general and staff officers discussing the operations and occurrences of the afternoon." For Union casualties on the left flank on 2 July 1863, see *OR*, 27(1):175–87. Just the casualties on the left flank on 2 July 1863 represented nearly 60 percent of all Union casualties in the Battle of Gettysburg.

48. Walker, "Meade at Gettysburg," *B&L*, 3:409.

Chapter 15

1. *OR*, 27(2):480, 484–85, 486–87.

2. *OR*, 27(1):713–14, 715–16, 722, 724, 740.

3. Ibid., 363–65, 751–52, 894–95.

4. Ibid.

5. *OR*, 27(1):427, 432, 434.

6. *OR*, 27(2):480, 484–85; *OR*, 27(1):361, 749; Kieffer, *History of the One Hundred Fifty-Third Regiment*, 87, 141–42.

7. *OR*, 27(1):22, 724; Kieffer, *History of the One Hundred Fifty-Third Regiment*, 86–87.

8. *OR*, 27(1):457; *OR*, 27(2):484–85.

9. Meade, *With Meade at Gettysburg*, 132–33.

10. New York Monuments Commission, *In Memoriam, George Sears Greene*, 44–48.

11. *OR*, 27(2):504, 509–12, 513, 518–19, 531–32.

12. *OR*, 27(1):427, 432; Ward, *History of the One Hundred and Sixth Regiment*, 196.

13. New York Monuments Commission, *In Memoriam, George Sears Greene*, 47.

14. Dawes, *Service with the Sixth Wisconsin Volunteers*, 181–82; New York Monuments Commission, *In Memoriam, George Sears Greene*, 46–47.

15. *OR*, 27(1):663, 759, 761.

16. Livermore, *Days and Events*, 258–59.

17. Benedict, *Army Life in Virginia*, 171–72.

18. Maust, *Grappling with Death*, 115, quoting Thompson, *Personal Narrative of Experiences in the Civil War (111th New York)*, 39, GMNP.

19. George G. Meade to Major General H. W. Halleck, 2 July 1863, 8:00 P.M. (received 3 July 1863, 5:15 P.M.), *OR*, 27(1):72.

20. Smith, *Washington Roebling's Civil War*, 147, quoting Washington Roebling, "Life of John A. Roebling, A.C.," 314, Roebling Collection, MS box 10, folders 23–26, RU.

21. Tsouras, *Major General George H. Sharpe*, 147, quoting Edwards, "Unselfishness of Meade," *Daily Press* (Sheboygan, Wis.), 21 June 1910. It seems that Sharpe gave similar speeches in Kingston and Mount Vernon, New York. *Daily Freeman* (Kingston, N.Y.), 18 January 1899; *Daily Argus* (Mount Vernon, N.Y.), 21 November 1908. There is a ring of truth about the whiskey story, but given Meade's return to the Leister House, it had to have occurred after 8:00 P.M. Sharpe evidently spoke with Meade and some of Meade's staff officers in the Leister house before all the corps commanders and aides arrived, since no other participants in the conference recorded Meade's exchange with Sharpe. Indeed, Sharpe's narrative of the

exchange with Meade about the whiskey bottle makes no mention of all the corps commanders being in the room. In fact, the article presents Meade as being virtually alone and seated at a table by himself in a contemplative state.

22. Ibid.

23. Ibid.

24. Ibid.

25. Ibid.

26. Gibbon, *Recollections of the Civil War*, 140.

27. Ibid.; Byrne and Weaver, *Haskell of Gettysburg*, 132.

28. John Gibbon to Anonymous, 12 September 1879, John Gibbon file, GMNP.

29. Gibbon, *Recollections of the Civil War*, 140; Byrne and Weaver, *Haskell of Gettysburg*, 134.

30. Byrne and Weaver, *Haskell of Gettysburg*, 132.

31. Gibbon, *Recollections of the Civil War*, 140.

32. Ibid., 140–41.

33. Ibid., 141–42.

34. Ibid., 142–43.

35. Ibid., 143–44.

36. Ibid., 142.

37. Quaife, *From the Cannon's Mouth*, 229–30.

38. Ibid.

39. George G. Meade to Major General H. W. Halleck, 2 July 1863, 8:00 P.M. (received 3 July 1863, 5:15 P.M.); Meade, *With Meade at Gettysburg*, 137.

40. Gibbon, *Recollections of the Civil War*, 144.

41. Ibid., 145.

42. Warner, *Generals in Blue*, 171–72.

43. Byrne and Weaver, *Haskell of Gettysburg*, 144.

44. Gibbon, *Recollections of the Civil War*, 145.

45. Coco, *Vast Sea of Misery*, 64–67.

46. Fishel, *Secret War for the Union*, 526–27; Tsouras, *Major General George H. Sharpe*, 148–49.

47. Fishel, *Secret War for the Union*, 521n48, 526–28; Tsouras, *Major General George H. Sharpe*, 148–49. Fishel states that he observed the report Sharpe gave to Meade but that it was a photocopy; he believed that the original was among the items stolen from the records collection of the Bureau of Military Information in the National Archives.

48. Fishel, *Secret War for the Union*, 528–29; Tsouras, *Major General George H. Sharpe*, 148–49.

49. Jim to My own darling wife, 6 July 1863, James Cornell Biddle Letters, George G. Meade Collection, HSP.

50. Guelzo, *Gettysburg: The Last Invasion*, 354–55.

Chapter 16

1. *OR*, 27(1):761, 775, 780–81, 827–30.

2. Reid, "Battles of Gettysburg," *RR*, 7:97; *OR*, 27(1):761.

3. *OR*, 27(1):349–50, 369, 372–74. The Thirteenth, Fourteenth, and Sixteenth

Vermont of Stannard's Brigade were on Cemetery Ridge; the remaining regiments, the Twelfth and Fifteenth Vermont, were detailed to guard the wagon trains of the First Corps in Westminster.

4. Ibid., 477–78.

5. Ibid., 290, 485, 663, 681, 682, 781, 785.

6. Ibid., 665, 668, 671, 674, 678.

7. Ibid., 470.

8. Ibid., 467; Page, *History of the Fourteenth Connecticut*, 142–47; Affidavit of Wilbur D. Fiske, 9 October 1887, Fourteenth Connecticut File, GNMP, 438.

9. *OR*, 27(1):437; Fuger, "Cushing's Battery at Gettysburg," JMSI, 41:407; Aldrich, *History of Battery A, First Rhode Island*, 210.

10. Reid, "Battles of Gettysburg," *RR*, 7:98.

11. *Buffalo Evening News*, 29 May 1894.

12. Byrne and Weaver, *Haskell of Gettysburg*, 144–45.

13. Ibid., 145.

14. Gibbon, *Personal Recollections of the Civil War*, 146; Byrne and Weaver, *Haskell of Gettysburg*, 146.

15. Byrne and Weaver, *Haskell of Gettysburg*, 146.

16. Ibid.

17. Ibid., 146–47.

18. Ibid., 147.

19. Meade, *With Meade at Gettysburg*, 146.

20. Ibid.

21. Byrne and Weaver, *Haskell of Gettysburg*, 147; Wise, *Long Arm of Lee*, 677; Owen, *In Camp and Battle*, 248–49; *Buffalo Evening News*, 29 May 1894; Waitt, *History of the Nineteenth Massachusetts*, 234–35; Rhodes, *History of Battery B, First Regiment, Rhode Island*, 208.

22. Fuger, "Cushing's Battery at Gettysburg," JMSI, 41:408; Byrne and Weaver, *Haskell of Gettysburg*, 150; *Buffalo Evening News*, 29 May 1894.

23. Byrne and Weaver, *Haskell of Gettysburg*, 151.

24. Winfield S. Hancock to My Dear Sir, 31 December 1868, W. S. Hancock File, GNMP; Reid, "Battles of Gettysburg," *RR*, 7:101.

25. Reid, "Battles of Gettysburg," *RR*, 7:101.

26. Ibid.

27. Ibid.

28. Meade, *With Meade at Gettysburg*, 148.

29. Ibid., 148–49; Butterfield, *Biographical Memorial of General Daniel Butterfield*, 128.

30. Meade, *With Meade at Gettysburg*, 150; Jim to my own darling wife, 8 July 1863, James Cornell Biddle Letters, George G. Meade Collection, HSP; Butterfield, *Biographical Memorial of General Daniel Butterfield*, 127.

31. Meade, *With Meade at Gettysburg*, 150–51; Brown, "'Double Canister at Ten Yards,'" 293–99.

32. Johnson, *Story of a Confederate Boy*, 204; Clark, *Histories of Several Regiments and Battalions from North Carolina*, 2:365; Brown, *Cushing of Gettysburg*,

244; Winfield S. Hancock to My Dear Sir, 31 December 1868, W. S. Hancock File, GNMP.

33. *OR*, 27(2):284, 289–290, 308, 320–21, 359–60, 385–87, 608, 643–44, 650–51, 666–67, 671–72.

34. Winfield S. Hancock to My Dear Sir, 31 December 1868, W. S. Hancock File, GNMP.

35. Henry Hunt to My Dear Mary, 4 July 1863, Henry Hunt Papers, LOC.

36. Sawyer, *Military History of the 8th Ohio*, 131; *OR*, 27(1):478–81.

37. Winfield S. Hancock to My Dear Sir, 31 December 1868, W. S. Hancock File, GMNP; H. H. Bingham to Dear Sister, 18 July 1863, W. S. Hancock File, GNMP.

38. H. H. Bingham to Dear Sister, 18 July 1863, W. S. Hancock file, GNMP; Maj. William G. Mitchell to Maj. Gen. Winfield S. Hancock, 10 January 1866, in Ladd and Ladd, *Bachelder Papers*, 1:231–32.

39. George G. Meade to Jno. B. Bachelder, 4 December 1869, in Ladd and Ladd, *Bachelder Papers*, 1:378–80.

40. Ibid.; Lt. John Egan to George Meade, Jr., 8 February 1870, in Ladd and Ladd, *Bachelder Papers*, 1:389–90.

41. Records of the Adjutant General's Office, "Muster Rolls Pertaining to Battery A, 4th United States Artillery," 30 June to 31 July 1863, RG 94, NA; Returns from Regular Army Artillery Regiments, 4th Artillery, July 1863, Roll 29, Fourth Regiment, January 1861 to December 1870, RG 94, NA; Rhodes, *History of Battery B, First Rhode Island*, 214; Aldrich, *History of Battery A, First Rhode Island*, 219.

42. Byrne and Weaver, *Haskell of Gettysburg*, 173–74.

43. Ibid., 174.

44. Ibid., 174–75.

45. Major William G. Mitchell to Major General Winfield S. Hancock, 10 January 1866, in Ladd and Ladd, *Bachelder Papers*, 1:231–32.

46. *OR*, 27(1):916.

47. Meade, *With Meade at Gettysburg*, 152–53; George G. Meade to Jno. B. Bachelder, 4 December 1869, in Ladd and Ladd, *Bachelder Papers*, 1:378–80.

48. Meade, *With Meade at Gettysburg*, 153–54; Case, "Taking and Holding of Little Round Top," New York Monuments Commission, *Final Report on the Battlefield of Gettysburg*, 3:971.

49. George G. Meade to Major General Halleck, 3 July 1863, 8:35 P.M. (received July 4, 6:10 A.M.), *OR*, 27(1):74–75; Meade, *With Meade at Gettysburg*, 153–55; Hyde, *Union Generals Speak* (Pleasonton Testimony, JCCW), 111, 139; "Report of Lieutenant Colonel Charles H. Morgan," in Ladd and Ladd, *Bachelder Papers*, 3:1366; *OR*, 27(1):654–55, 657–58, 671.

50. *OR*, 27(1):943, 1005.

51. "Report of Lieutenant Colonel Charles H. Morgan," in Ladd and Ladd, *Bachelder Papers*, 3:1365–66; Harman, "Did Meade Begin a Counteroffensive after Pickett's Charge?"; *OR*, 27(2):423–24; Smith, *Washington Roebling's Civil War*, 148, quoting Washington Roebling, "Life of John A. Roebling, C.A.," 315–16, Roebling Collection, MS box 10, folders 23–26, RU; Diary of Henry Clay Bowman

(93rd Pennsylvania) 3 July 1863, PM; Diary of Jacob W. Haas (96th Pennsylvania), 3 July 1863, USAMHI.

52. *OR*, 27(1):657–58; 27(2):402–3.

53. George G. Meade to Major General Halleck, 3 July 1863, 8:35 P.M., *OR*, 27(1):74–75.

Chapter 17

1. Reid, "Battles of Gettysburg," *RR*, 7:98; Livermore, *Days and Events*, 258–59; Muffly, *Story of Our Regiment*, 460; Maust, *Grappling with Death*, 118–23.

2. Reid, "Battles of Gettysburg," *RR*, 7:98.

3. Circular, Headquarters, Army of the Potomac, 4 July 1863, Twelfth Corps Papers, RG 393, NA.

4. Reid, "Battle of Gettysburg," *RR*, 7:98.

5. Rufus Ingalls to Gen. M. C. Meigs, 4 July 1863, Records of the Quartermaster General, RG 92, Consolidated Correspondence File, NA.

6. Ibid.

7. Report of Captain L. H. Pierce to Gen. M. C. Meigs, 11 September 1863, Records of the Quartermaster General, RG 92, Consolidated Correspondence File, NA.

8. Oats, *The War*, 237; Imboden, "Confederate Retreat," *B&L*, 3:423; Diary of Lieutenant John R. Garden (62nd Pennsylvania), 4 July 1863, KMB; Diary of Corporal James W. Johnson (29th Pennsylvania), 4 July 1863, HS; Diary of Abner B. Frank (12th Illinois Cavalry), 4 July 1863, USAMHI; Diary of Lieutenant Wilson N. Paxton (140th Pennsylvania), 4 July 1863, USAMHI.

9. *OR*, 27(2):370, 372, 412, 416–17, 423–24, 426–27, 448, 471, 490, 495, 505, 513, 519, 557, 569, 580, 588, 590, 593, 608, 734–35.

10. Ibid., 376, 381, 389, 430, 432; Berkeley, *Four Years in the Confederate Artillery*, 52. Cannoneer Henry Robinson Berkeley of the Amherst-Nelson (Virginia) Battery counted "ten or twelve dwelling houses on fire between our line and the town."

11. *OR*, 27(1):716, 731; *OR*, 27(3):516, 532; Brown, *Signal Corps in the War of the Rebellion*, 369.

12. *OR*, 27(3):514.

13. Brown, *Retreat from Gettysburg*, 103–6, 118–20.

14. Geo. G. Meade to Major General Halleck, 4 July 1863, 7:00 A.M. (received 7:20 P.M.), *OR*, 27(1):78.

15. R. E. Lee to Maj. Gen. George [G.] Meade, 4 July 1863, 6:35 A.M. (received 8:25 A.M.) and George G. Meade to General R. E. Lee, 4 July 1863, 8:25 A.M., *OR*, 27(3):514.

16. Daniel Butterfield to Major General French, 4 July 1863, *OR*, 27(3):517–18. Some have argued that the foregoing message to General French was triggered by a message to Meade from General Couch, stating: "Unquestionably, the rebels have fortified the passes in South Mountain. Such information was given me a week ago from Gettysburg." D. N. Couch to General George G. Meade, 4 July 1863 (received, War Department, 12:40 P.M.), *OR*, 27(3):515. That message would likely not have reached Meade before he wrote to General French. Aside from whether Meade had received that communication, Meade knew he had to protect Frederick

and its rail and telegraphic connections to Washington, as it would become the Army of the Potomac's base of supply. He was well aware how important it was to keep the enemy from seizing the passes in the South Mountain range.

17. Daniel Butterfield to Major General French, 4 July 1863, 10:20 A.M., *OR*, 27(3):518.

18. George G. Meade to Major General Halleck, 4 July 1863, 12:00 P.M. (received 5 July 1863, 3:50 P.M.), *OR*, 27(1):78.

19. L. B. Pierce to Major General Couch, 26 June 1863, 10:00 P.M., *OR*, 27(3): 345; J. S. Robinson to Colonel Asmussen, 27 June 1863, *OR*, 27(3):352; Chas. Asmussen to Major General Butterfield, 28 June 1863, 11:00 A.M., *OR*, 27(3):372; Brown, *Retreat from Gettysburg*, 24–36.

20. Brown, *Retreat from Gettysburg*, 50–65.

21. TopoZone.com, https://www.topozone.com/pennsylvania/adams-pa/; Lake, *Atlas of Adams Co.*, 35; dePeyster, *Gettysburg and After*, 87.

22. Imboden, "Confederate Retreat," *B&L*, 3:425; *OR*, 27(2):488; Williams, "Fifty-Fourth Regiment," *NC Regiments*, 3:270–71.

23. H. Haupt to Major General Halleck, 3 July 1863 (received 10:20 A.M.), *OR*, 27(3):511.

24. Rufus Ingalls to General M. C. Meigs, 4 July 1863, 8:10 P.M., *OR*, 27(3):520; Report from Edward P. Vollum to M. C. Meigs, 17 August 1863, Records of the Quartermaster General, RG 92, Consolidated Correspondence File, NA. Edward P. Vollum, the medical inspector of the U.S. Army, reported that there were 13,603 Union wounded and 6,739 Confederate wounded in Union hands. The final tally of Union wounded was 14,529, according to the Return of Casualties of the Union Forces at Gettysburg. *OR*, 27(1):187. The total wounded in Union hands was a staggering 20,342. Add to that the wounded that would be uncovered along the routes taken to pursue Lee's army, and "in round numbers," the numbers from both sides taken care of by Union surgical and medical teams was nearly 35,000. The number of Confederates buried by Union burial parties exceeded 3,500, and "about 2,000" Union soldiers were buried.

25. Diary of J. C. Coburn, 4 July 1863 (141st Pennsylvania), USAMHI.

26. Captain H. A. Lacey to Lieutenant Colonel T. A. Meysenburg, A.A.G., 3 July 1863, Eleventh Corps Papers, RG 393, Letters Received, NA. The correspondence from Captain Lacey to the headquarters of the Eleventh Corps represents the only record extant of any corps in the Army of the Potomac requisitioning and being delivered forage and subsistence stores on 3, 4, and 5 July 1863 from the Camp of Transportation at Westminster. All seven corps and the cavalry corps were desperate for provisions. Lacey's correspondence with the headquarters of the Eleventh Corps reveals the desperate need for forage for the horses and subsistence stores for the men and the frantic attempts to fulfill those needs. *OR*, 27(1):196.

27. H. Haupt to E. M. Stanton, 4 July 1863 (received 4:20 A.M.), *OR*, 27(3): 521–22.

28. Circular, Headquarters Army of the Potomac, 3 July 1863, Eleventh Corps Papers, RG 393, Letters Received, NA.

29. Captain H. A. Lacey to Lieutenant Colonel T. A. Meysenburg, A.A.G., 3 July 1863, Eleventh Corps Papers, RG 393, Letters Received, NA.

30. Captain H. A. Lacey to Lieutenant Colonel C. W. Asmussen, Chief of Staff, 4 July 1863, Eleventh Corps Papers, RG 393, Letters Received, NA; Sparks, *Inside Lincoln's Army*, 268; Henry Hunt to My Dear Mary, 4 July 1863, Henry Hunt Papers, LOC; J. F. Slagle to Brother, 13 September 1863, SL; Diary of Luther C. Furst (39th Pennsylvania), 4 July 1863, USAMHI.

31. Captain H. A. Lacey to Lieutenant Colonel C. W. Asmussen, Chief of Staff, 4 July 1863, Eleventh Corps Papers, RG 393, Letters Received, NA.

32. Captain H. A. Lacey to Lieutenant Colonel T. A. Meysenburg, A.A.G., 3 July 1863, Eleventh Corps Papers, RG 393, Letters Received, NA; Diary of Lieutenant John R. Garden (62nd Pennsylvania), 4 July 1863, KMB; Diary of Jacob W. Haas (96th Pennsylvania), 4 July 1863, USAMHI.

33. J. M. Shoemaker to Hon. E. M. Stanton, 4 July 1863, and Edwin M. Stanton to S. M. Shoemaker, 4 July 1863, 5:25 P.M.; Special Order, Edwin M. Stanton, 4 July 1863, 5:50 P.M.; M. C. Meigs to Brigadier General Haupt, 4 July 1863, 5:45 P.M.; H. Haupt to General Ingalls, 4 July 1863, *OR*, 27(3):521, 523–24.

34. H. Haupt to E. M. Stanton, 4 July 1863, 4:30 P.M.; H. Haupt to Major General Halleck, 4 July 1863 (received 12:35 P.M.); H. Haupt to Major General Halleck, 4 July 1863 (received 4:20 P.M.); H. Haupt to Major General Halleck, 4 July 1863, 11:00 A.M. (received 11:15 A.M.), *OR*, 27(3):521–22, 523.

35. General Orders No. 68, Headquarters Army of the Potomac, 4 July 1863, 4:15 P.M., *OR*, 27(3):519.

36. Return of Casualties of Union Forces at Gettysburg, *OR*, 27(1):187; Circular, Headquarters Army of the Potomac, 4 July 1863, *OR*, 27(3):519–20; Circular, Headquarters Army of the Potomac, 4 July 1863, *OR*, 27(3):520.

37. Clausewitz, *On War*, 263–64.

38. Ibid., 267; Jomini, *Art of War*, 242.

39. Clausewitz, *On War*, 267; Jomini, *Art of War*, 242.

40. Clausewitz, *On War*, 267, 352–54.

41. Ibid., 268–70.

42. Dan'l Butterfield to Major General Couch, 4 July 1863, 1:30 P.M., *OR*, 27(3):515; S. Williams to General William F. Smith, 4 July 1863, *OR*, 27(3):517; Sears, *Gettysburg*, 474.

43. *OR*, 27(1):916–17, 928, 939, 943.

44. Ibid., 970–71, 993–94, 998, 1005–6.

45. Ibid., 977–78.

46. P. A. Taylor to General Meade, 4 July 1863, 5:15 P.M., *OR*, 27(3):516.

47. P. A. Taylor to General Meade, 4 July 1863, 7:15 P.M., *OR*, 27(3):516.

48. Hyde, *Union Generals Speak* (Butterfield Testimony, JCCW), 259–61; Warner, *Generals in Blue*, 224–25; William Hays to General S. Williams, 4 July 1863, *OR*, 27(3):515. The George and Elizabeth Musser house still stands on the west side of the Baltimore Pike, above Rock Creek. It is the site where Ms. Peter Thorn stayed during the battle after her residence in the cemetery gatehouse was surrounded by troops and came under fire. The Musser house has been unoccupied for many years and is in a dilapidated state. A private company operates a quarry behind the house.

49. Hyde, *Union Generals Speak* (Butterfield Testimony, JCCW), 259.

50. Ibid., 259–60.

51. Ibid., 260–61.

52. Coddington, *Gettysburg Campaign*, 544; Hyde, *Union Generals Speak* (Meade Testimony, JCCW), 128; Jomini, *Art of War*, 58.

53. Jomini, *Art of War*, 58; Jim to My own darling wife, 6 July 1863, James Cornell Biddle Letters, George A. Meade Collections, SHP.

Chapter 18

1. Diary of Henry Keiser (96th Pennsylvania), 5 July 1863, USAMHI; Diary of Jacob Haas (96th Pennsylvania), 5 July 1863, USAMHI; Diary of Lieutenant John R. Garden (62nd Pennsylvania), 5 July 1863, KMB; Diary of Henry Clay Bowman (93rd Pennsylvania), 5 July 1863, PM.

2. Captain James S. Hall, Signal Officer to General Meade, 5 July 1863, 5:40 A.M., *OR*, 27(3):532.

3. William H. Hill and I. S. Lyon, Signal Officers, to General Sykes, 5 July 1863, *OR*, 27(3):532.

4. Captain E. C. Pierce, Signal Officer, to Captain Norton, 5 July 1863, 8:40 A.M., *OR*, 27(3):532.

5. *OR*, 27(2):699; Brown, *Retreat from Gettysburg*, 78–79.

6. *OR*, 27(2):360–61, 448–49, 608–9; Alexander, *Fighting for the Confederacy*, 267; Brown, *Brown's Civil War*, 226.

7. *OR*, 27(2):448, 471, 493, 558; Brown, *Brown's Civil War*, 226; John Warwick Daniel Journal, 20, John Warwick Daniel Papers, box 23, VHS.

8. R. N. Martin to My Dear Aunt and Cousin, HS; Gantt, "Gettysburg Prisoners," 4 July 1863, KMB.

9. Beach, *First New York Cavalry*, 269; *OR*, 27(1):489; Wm. H. French to Major General Butterfield, 5 July 1863 (received 7:00 P.M.), *OR*, 27(3):538.

10. J. Kilpatrick to Major General Pleasonton, 5 July 1863 (received 1:45 P.M.), *OR*, 27(1):988; and see *OR*, 27(1), 993–94, 998, 999, 1000.

11. Wm. H. French to Major General Halleck, 5 July 1863 (received 9:15 P.M.), *OR*, 27(3):546. General French received word that "five hundred wagons (rebel), guarded by about 150 infantry, 150 cavalry, three pieces of inferior-looking artillery, and from 3,000 to 5,000 head of cattle passed through Hagerstown last night after 11 o'clock to about 4 o'clock." Obtained from civilian informants, that dispatch represents the only sighting known to exist of the time Lee's reserve trains entered Hagerstown.

12. *OR*, 27(2):487–88; Worsham, *One of Jackson's Foot Cavalry*, 104; Williams, "Fifty-Fourth Regiment," *North Carolina Regiments*, 3:270–71; John Paris Diary, 15 June to 5 July 1863, Paris Papers, UNC-SHC.

13. Clausewitz, *On War*, 271–72, 352–54, 429–32; Jomini, *Art of War*, 180–82.

14. H. W. Halleck to Major General Meade, 5 July 1863, *OR*, 27(1):79–80.

15. Circular, Headquarters Army of the Potomac, 5 July 1863, *OR*, 27(3): 532–33.

16. Ibid.

17. Ibid.

18. Ibid.

19. Ibid.

20. Ibid.

21. Geo. G. Meade to General Sedgwick, 5 July 1863, 12:30 P.M., *OR*, 27(3):535; *OR*, 27(1):663.

22. Geo. G. Meade to Maj. Gen. H. W. Halleck, 5 July 1863, 8:30 A.M. (received 8:40 P.M.), *OR*, 27(1):79.

23. *OR*, 27(1):23; Haupt, *Reminiscences of General Herman Haupt*, 223–29. In a reminiscence published more than thirty-eight years after the conclusion of the battle, General Haupt claims he appeared at Meade's headquarters along the Baltimore Pike around noon on 5 July. He writes that he found Meade and General Pleasonton "seated at a small table in a farm house near Rock Creek." Haupt asserts that he asked about "future movements so that [he] could arrange for [Meade's] supplies." According to Haupt, "I supposed Meade would march at once to the Potomac and cut off Lee's retreat." To that, writes Haupt, Meade responded, claiming that "he could not start immediately. The men required rest." Incredibly, Haupt claims that he questioned Meade: "I ventured to remark that the men had been well supplied with rations; that they had been stationary behind the stone walls during the battle; that they could not be footsore; that the enemy before and after the battle had been in motion more than our army; that it was but little more than a day's march to the [Potomac] river, and that if advantage were not taken of Lee's present condition, he would escape." Haupt writes that Meade responded to his remarks by saying that Lee had no pontoon bridges and that the Potomac River was swollen. Haupt continues by saying he argued with Meade about how his engineers could construct a pontoon bridge in short order to cross the river. Haupt then notes that he could not get Meade to cease being concerned about feeding his men.

Haupt's account claims he left Meade's headquarters around noon "much discouraged" and "communicated the situation to General Halleck that very day, asserting that "Lee's army will reach the Potomac before Meade can possibly overtake them." According to Haupt, he took a locomotive to Washington and met with Halleck the next day about the matter.

Edwin Coddington writes about the Haupt visit with Meade with some skepticism about what was in fact said. First of all, Coddington has Haupt visiting Meade on 4 July, not 5 July, the date Haupt wrote of the visit. Coddington claims that Haupt's report "thoroughly depressed President Lincoln and increased his fear that Meade would let Lee slip away and thus lose a superb chance to end the war right then and there on the slopes of Seminary Ridge." Coddington, *Gettysburg Campaign*, 545–47, 812n56. First of all, neither Meade nor any of his corps commanders had any intention of attacking Lee's army on Seminary Ridge. Haupt claims that he visited with Meade in order to arrange to send his army supplies, yet he never discusses that with Meade; instead, he launches into a monologue about how Meade's men were well fed and could not be footsore and how they only fought behind stone fences. Yet Haupt had no personal knowledge of any of the battle events or of the condition of Meade's army. The meeting probably did not last more than a few minutes. Meade was preoccupied with getting his army under way on 5 July and would not have had time to listen to Haupt's remarks. Moreover,

Haupt's remarks to Meade, if actually spoken, would have been insulting, if not insubordinate. They would have angered Meade. Most significantly, no records by reporters, by Meade's staff officers, by Meade, by General Pleasonton, who Haupt says was in the meeting, or by Halleck, mention the meeting. Of paramount consideration is that Meade had already prepared orders for his army to move at the very time Haupt claims that he met with him.

24. Geo. G. Meade to General Sedgwick, 5 July 1863, 12:30 P.M., *OR*, 27(3):535.

25. Diary of Jacob Haas (96th Pennsylvania), 5 July 1863, USAMHI.

26. *OR*, 27(1):663, 666.

27. Diary of Henry Keiser (96th Pennsylvania), 5 July 1863, USAMHI.

28. *OR*, 27(1):695.

29. Geo. G. Meade to Commanding Officer, Sixth Corps, 5 July 1863, 7:30 P.M., *OR*, 27(3):537; Hyde, *Union Generals Speak* (Meade Testimony, JCCW), 114; Crounse, "Escape of Lee's Army," *RR*, 7:346. L. L. Crounse, the *New York Times* reporter assigned to the Army of the Potomac, wrote that Meade issued the Circular order of march of 5 July was issued sometime "between the hours of ten o'clock A.M. and six P.M." on 5 July.

30. Orders, Headquarters Army of the Potomac, 5 July 1863, Twelfth Corps Papers, RG 393, NA; Geo. G. Meade to Major General Sedgwick, 6 July 1863, 2:00 A.M., *OR*, 27(3):554.

31. George G. Meade to Mrs. George G. Meade, 5 July 1863, George G. Meade Papers, HSP; Meade, *Life and Letters of George G. Meade*, 2:125.

32. John Sedgwick to Brig. Gen. S. Williams, 6 July 1863, *OR*, 27(3):555.

33. *OR*, 27(1):145–46.

34. S. Williams to Commanding Officer, First Corps, 6 July 1863, 7:40 A.M., *OR*, 27(3):557; Geo. G. Meade to General [Sedgwick], 6 July 1863, 9:00 A.M., *OR*, 27(3):558.

35. Danl. Butterfield to General Benham, 5 July 1863, *OR*, 27(3):547; H. W. Benham to Gen. S. Williams, 6 July 1863, 1:00 A.M., *OR*, 27(3):564; H. W. Benham to General S. Williams, 6 July 1863, 1:30 A.M. (sent from War Department, 10:15 A.M.), *OR*, 27(3):564; H. W. Benham to General S. Williams, 6 July 1863, 4:45 A.M. (sent from War Department, 10:30 A.M.), *OR*, 27(3):565; H. W. Benham to General S. Williams, 6 July 1863, 9:15 A.M., *OR*, 27(3):565; H. W. Benham to General S. Williams, 6 July 1863, 3:45 P.M., *OR*, 27(3):565; M. C. Meigs to General Ingalls, 7 July 1863, 2:40 P.M. (received 3:20 P.M.), *OR*, 27(3):590–91.

36. Geo. G. Meade to Maj. Gen. H. W. Halleck, 6 July 1863, 2:00 P.M. (received 9:20 P.M.), *OR*, 27(1):80–81.

37. J. B. McIntosh to Col. A. J. Alexander, AAG, 6 July 1863, 3:45 P.M., *OR*, 27(3):560–61.

38. G. K. Warren to General Neill, 6 July 1863, *OR*, 27(3):562.

39. G. K. Warren to Maj. Gen. John Sedgwick, 6 July 1863, *OR*, 27(3):561–62.

40. H. W. Halleck to Major General Meade, 5 July 1863, *OR*, 27(1):79–80; Geo. G. Meade to Major General Couch, 6 July 1863, 4:40 P.M., *OR*, 27(3):578–79; S. Williams to General William F. Smith, 6 July 1863, *OR*, 27(3):579; G. K. Warren to General William F. Smith, 6 July 1863, *OR*, 27(3):579.

41. A. Lincoln to Major General Halleck, 6 July 1863, 7:00 P.M., *OR*, 27(3):567.

42. Coddington, *Gettysburg Campaign*, 550–51; Sears, *Gettysburg*, 476.

43. Ibid.

44. G. K. Warren to General Smith, 6 July 1863, 10:00 P.M., *OR*, 27(3):581; A. Pleasonton to Brig. Gen. William F. Smith, 7 July 1863, 5:00 A.M., *OR*, 27(3):585.

45. *OR*, 27(1):146.

46. Diary of Luther Furst (39th Pennsylvania), 7 July 1863, USAMHI; Diary of Jacob Haas (96th Pennsylvania), 7 July 1863, USAMHI.

47. Acken, *Inside the Army of the Potomac*, 292; Parker, *History of the Twenty-Second Massachusetts*, 350; Kepler, *History of the Fourth Ohio*, 134; Dawes, *Service with the Sixth Wisconsin*, 185; Diary of Capt. Charles Morey (2nd Vermont), 7 July 1863, USAMHI.

48. Diary of J. P. Coburn (141st Pennsylvania), 6 July 1863, USAMHI.

49. Robert H. Davis Handwritten Memoir (74th New York), 69, HS.

50. Order, Headquarters Army of the Potomac, 5 July 1865, *OR*, 27(3):542.

51. M. C. Meigs to General Ingalls, 5 July 1863, *OR*, 27(3):543–44; M. C. Meigs to Brig. Gen. R. Ingalls, 6 July 1863, 5:00 P.M., *OR*, 27(3):569.

52. M. C. Meigs to Brig. Gen. R. Ingalls, 6 July 1863, 12:45 P.M., *OR*, 27(3):568–69; M. C. Meigs to Brig. Gen. R. Ingalls, 6 July 1863, 5:00 P.M., *OR*, 27(3):569. H. Haupt to The Presidents of the following Railroads, 6 July 1863, *OR*, 27(3):568. The following railroad executives were contacted by Haupt: Boston & Worcester, Boston; New Haven, Hartford & Springfield, Hartford; Camden & Amboy, New York; Philadelphia, Wilmington & Baltimore, Philadelphia; Cleveland & Toledo, Cleveland; Pittsburgh, Columbus & Cincinnati, Steubenville, Ohio; Pennsylvania Central, Philadelphia; Indiana Central, Dayton, Ohio; Cleveland & Pittsburgh, Cleveland; New Jersey Railroad Transportation Company, New York; New York & New Haven, New York; and Southern Michigan, Toledo, Ohio.

53. D. H. Rucker to Brig. Gen. R. Ingalls, 6 July 1863, 9:30 P.M., *OR*, 27(3):569.

54. Ibid.

55. A. P. Porter to Col. A. Beckwith, 5 July 1863, *OR*, 27(3):552.

56. Circular, Headquarters Army of the Potomac, 5 July 1863, *OR*, 27(3):542.

57. Quynn, *Diary of Jacob Engelbrecht*, 7 July 1863, 2:974; George G. Meade to Mrs. George G. Meade, 8 July 1863, George G. Meade Papers, HSP; Meade, *Life and Letters of George G. Meade*, 2:132–33; Delaplane, "General Meade Acclaimed in Frederick for Victory at Gettysburg," *The News* (Frederick, Md.), 7 July 1973.

58. H. W. Halleck to Maj. Gen. George G. Meade, 7 July 1863, 3:00 P.M., *OR*, 27(1):82; Geo. G. Meade to Maj. Gen. H. W. Halleck, 7 July 1863, 4:00 P.M. (received 5:00 P.M.), *OR*, 27(1):82.

59. Geo. G. Meade to Maj. Gen. H. W. Halleck, 7 July 1863, 3:10 P.M. (received 4:45 P.M.), *OR*, 27(1) 81–82; *OR*, 27(1):928.

60. *OR*, 27(1):928, 995–96.

61. H. W. Halleck to Major General Meade, 7 July 1863, *OR*, 27(1):83.

Chapter 19

1. George G. Meade to Mrs. George G. Meade, 8 July 1863, George G. Meade, HSP; Meade, *Life and Letters of George Gordon Meade*, 2:132.

2. Ibid., 132–33.

3. Ibid., 133.

4. *OR*, 27(1):146.

5. Ibid.

6. W. A. Roebling to General G. K. Warren, 8 July 1863, *OR*, 27(3):606; Diary of Henry Keiser (96th Pennsylvania) 8 July 1863, USAMHI; John Newton to Brig. Gen. S. Williams, 8 July 1863, 9:00 A.M., *OR*, 27(3):602; O. O. Howard to General S. Williams, 8 July 1863, *OR*, 27(3):604; O. O. Howard to Lieutenant-Colonel LeDuc, 8 July 1863, 6:00 A.M., *OR*, 27(3):601.

7. Weygant, *History of the One Hundred and Twenty-Fourth Regiment*, 196.

8. Ibid., 197.

9. Parker, *History of the Twenty-Second Massachusetts Infantry*, 351.

10. Julius Lineback Diary (26th North Carolina), 6 July 1863, Lineback Papers, vol. 2, UNC-SHC; Imboden, "Confederate Retreat," *B&L*, 3:425–26.

11. Robert H. Chilton to Robert E. Rodes, 7 July 1863, Rodes Papers, vol. 51, ANV, ACWM.

12. Imboden, "Confederate Retreat," *B&L*, 3:425–26.

13. Alexander, *Fighting for the Confederacy*, 269; *OR*, 27(2):703; *OR*, 27(3):985.

14. Hotchkiss, *Make Me a Map*, 159–60; Alexander, *Fighting for the Confederacy*, 269–70. Salisbury Ridge remains a dominant feature of the landscape between Hagerstown and Downsville. It is observed by looking west from St. James School.

15. Brown, *Retreat from Gettysburg*, 293–95; Alexander, *Fighting for the Confederacy*, 270.

16. Alexander, *Fighting for the Confederacy*, 271.

17. Geo. G. Meade to Maj. Gen. H. W. Halleck, 8 July 1863, 2:00 P.M. (received 2:55 P.M.), *OR*, 27(1):84.

18. Ibid.

19. H. W. Halleck to Maj. Gen. Meade, 8 July 1863, *OR*, 27(1):84.

20. Geo. G. Meade to Maj. Gen. H. W. Halleck, 8 July 1863, 3:00 P.M. (received 3:20 P.M.), *OR*, 27(1):85.

21. H. W. Halleck to Major General Meade, 8 July 1863, *OR*, 27(1):85.

22. H. W. Benham to General S. Williams, 8 July 1863, 2:30 P.M., *OR*, 27(3):603.

23. Clausewitz, *On War*, 213.

24. Circular, Headquarters Army of the Potomac, 8 July 1863, *OR*, 27(3):601.

25. Ibid.

26. *OR*, 27(1):488–89, 536; Hyde, *Union Generals Speak* (Humphreys Testimony, JCCW), 198.

27. Diary of Jacob Haas (96th Pennsylvania), 8 July 1863, USAMHI; Koogle Diaries, 9 July 1863, HWCHS. Koogle's diaries are most useful; he meticulously recorded the weather in Washington County, Maryland, every day. George G. Meade to Maj. Gen. H. W. Halleck, 9 July 1863, 11:00 A.M. (received 12:10 P.M.), *OR*, 27(1):86–87.

28. H. W. Halleck to Maj. Gen. George G. Meade, 9 July 1863, 3:00 P.M., *OR*, 27(1):88.

29. *OR*, 27(1):146.

30. Circular, Headquarters Army of the Potomac, 10 July 1863, *OR*, 27(3):626–27; Koogle Diaries, 10 July 1863, HWCHS.

31. Diary of Luther Furst (39th Pennsylvania), 10 July 1863, USAMHI; Diary of Henry Keiser (96th Pennsylvania), 10 July 1863, USAMHI.

32. H. W. Halleck to Major General Meade, 10 July 1863, 9:00 P.M., *OR*, 27(1):89.

33. Geo. G. Meade to Maj. Gen. H. W. Halleck, 11 July 1863, 4:00 P.M. (received 5:30 P.M.), *OR*, 27(1):90–91, 147; Nevins, *Diary of Battle*, 259.

34. Ranald S. MacKenzie to Brig. Gen. G. K. Warren, 12 July 1863, *OR*, 27(3):669.

35. Geo. G. Meade to Maj. Gen. H. W. Halleck, 12 July 1863, 4:30 P.M. (received 8:00 P.M.), *OR*, 27(1):91.

36. Humphreys, *Gettysburg to the Rapidan*, 6.

37. Hyde, *Union Generals Speak* (Meade Testimony, JCCW), 116.

38. Ibid., 118, and (Humphreys Testimony, JCCW), 198–99; Coddington, *Gettysburg Campaign*, 573.

39. Byrne and Weaver, *Haskell of Gettysburg*, 183.

40. Hyde, *Union Generals Speak* (Meade Testimony, JCCW), 116–17; (Warren Testimony, JCCW), 175; (Humphreys Testimony, JCCW), 199–201; (Wadsworth Testimony, JCCW), 233–34; and (Sedgwick Testimony, JCCW), 329–30.

41. Hyde, *Union Generals Speak* (Meade Testimony, JCCW), 117.

42. Hyde, *Union Generals Speak* (Humphreys Testimony, JCCW), 200; Geo. G. Meade to Maj. Gen. H. W. Halleck, 13 July 1863, 5:00 P.M. (received 6:40 P.M.), *OR*, 27(1):91–92.

43. H. W. Halleck to Maj. Gen. George G. Meade, 13 July 1863, 9:30 P.M., *OR*, 27(1):92.

44. *OR*, 27(2):448–49, 472, 558–59, 609, 639–40, 705; Scheibert, *Seven Months*, 120; Harris, "Civil War Diary," VBHS; Casler, *Four Years*, 179.

45. Hyde, *Union Generals Speak* (Meade Testimony, JCCW), 118.

46. *OR*, 27(1):997–1001.

47. Nevins, *Diary of Battle*, 261–622; Hyde, *Union Generals Speak* (Meade Testimony, JCCW), 118.

48. George G. Meade to Maj. Gen. H. W. Halleck, 14 July 1863, 11:00 A.M. (received 12:10 P.M.), *OR*, 27(1):92.

49. H. W. Halleck to Major General Meade, 14 July 1863, 1:00 P.M., *OR*, 27(1):92; 50. Diary of Luther Furst (30th Pennsylvania), 14 July 1863, USAMHI; Hyde, *The Union Generals Speak* (Meade Testimony, JCCW), 118–19; Coddington, *The Gettysburg Campaign*, 573.

51. George G. Meade to Maj. Gen. H. W. Halleck, 14 July 1863, 2:30 P.M. (received 3:10 P.M.), *OR*, 27(1):93.

52. H. W. Halleck to Major General Meade, 14 July 1863, 4:30 P.M., *OR*, 27(1):93–94.

53. George G. Meade to Mrs. George G. Meade, 14 July 1863, George G. Meade Papers, HSP; Meade, *Life and Letters of George Gordon Meade*, 2:135.

54. Hay, *Letters of John Hay*, 1:85; Beale, *Diary of Gideon Welles*, 14 July 1863, 1:374–75.

55. Basler, *Collected Works of Abraham Lincoln*, 6:327–28.

56. Beale, *Diary of Gideon Welles*, 1:374–75; Thomas and Hyman, *Stanton*, 275.

57. Coddington, *Gettysburg Campaign*, 569; Hyde, *Union Generals Speak* (Humphreys Testimony, JCCW), 201. A. Wilson Greene wrote a very fine—and fair—assessment of Meade's pursuit of Lee. Greene, "Meade's Pursuit of Lee."

Epilogue

1. Circular, Headquarters Army of the Potomac, 14 July 1863, and Circular, 17 July 1863, Henry J. Hunt Papers, LOC; Long, *Civil War Day by Day*, 384–85. According to Meade's Circular of 14 July, the movement of the Army of the Potomac toward Sandy Hook and Berlin would begin on 15 July. The army would cross the pontoon bridges on 17 July. The riots in New York City over the draft broke out on 13 July.

2. Hay, *Letters of John Hay*, 1:85; Beale, *Diary of Gideon Welles*, 14 July 1863, 1:374–75; Thomas and Hyman, *Stanton*, 275; Basler, *Collected Works of Abraham Lincoln*, 6:327–28.

3. H. W. Halleck to Major General Meade, 7 July 1863, *OR*, 27(1):83; Basler, *Collected Works of Abraham Lincoln*, 6:327–28; H. W. Halleck to Major General Meade, 14 July 1863, 1:00 P.M., *OR*, 27(1):92.

4. Frank A. Haskell to Family, 17 July 1863, in Byrne and Weaver, *Haskell of Gettysburg*, 202.

5. Hyde, *Union Generals Speak*.

6. Ibid.; H. W. Halleck to Major General Meade, 28 July 1863, *OR*, 27(1):104–5; Geo. G. Meade to Major General Halleck, 31 July 1863, *OR*, 27(1):108–10.

7. Longacre, *Man behind the Guns*, 180; Hyde, *The Union Generals Speak* (Hunt Testimony, JCCW), 301–20.

8. Henry J. Hunt to General A. A. Humphreys, 26 July 1863; A. A. Humphreys to Dear Hunt, 27 July 1863; Henry J. Hunt to My Dear General Humphreys, 22 July 1863, Henry J. Hunt Papers, LOC; Longacre, *Man behind the Guns*, 180.

9. H. J. Hunt to Bvt. Maj. Gen. Alexander S. Webb, 12 January 1888, Powell, *Fifth Army Corps*, 558–59.

10. Hunt, "Third Day at Gettysburg," *B&L*, 3:382–93.

BIBLIOGRAPHY

Archival Sources

Albany, N.Y.
  New York State Library
    Gouverneur Kemble Warren Papers
Carlisle, Pa.
  United States Army Military History Institute
    Diary of J. P. Coburn
    Diary of Abner B. Frank
    Diary of Luther C. Furst
    Diary of Henry Keiser
    Diary of Col. Henry J. Madill
    Diary of Charles Morey
    Diary of Jacob Shenkel
Chapel Hill, N.C.
  Southern Historical Collection
    Julius Lineback Papers
    John Paris Papers
Dallas, Tex.
  Heritage Auctions
    Major Paul A. Oliver Letter
Gettysburg, Pa.
  Gettysburg College
    David McConaughy Papers
  Gettysburg National Military Park
    James Barnes File
    Diary of Adolfo Fernandez de la Cavada
    Fourteenth Connecticut File
    W. S. Hancock File
    George G. Meade File
    Daniel E. Sickles File
    Benjamin W. Thompson, "Personal Narrative of Experiences of the
      Civil War"
  The Horse Soldier Shop
    Robert H. Davis, handwritten memoir
    Diary of Corporal James W. Johnson
Hagerstown, Md.
  Hagerstown–Washington County Historical Society
    John Koogle Diaries

Harrisburg, Pa.
   Pennsylvania State Archives
      Samuel P. Bates Papers
      Diary of Stephen A. Wallace
Lancaster, Pa.
   Franklin & Marshall College
      John F. Reynolds Papers
Lexington, Ky.
   Kent Masterson Brown Collection
      George Gantt, "The Gettysburg Papers"
      Diary of Lieutenant John R. Garden
      Diary of Charles T. Hunter
   James Cobb Collection
      Diary of James L. Howie
   Philip Maxson Collection
      Diary of Henry Clay Bowman
Madison, Wis.
   Wisconsin Historical Society
      Diary of Nathaniel Rollins
Martinez, Calif.
   Steve Lichti Collection
      J. F. Slagle Letter
New Brunswick, N.J.
   Rutgers University Library
      Washington A. Roebling Papers
New Haven, Conn.
   Yale University Library
      Alexander S. Webb Papers
Oak Park and River Forest, Ill.
   Historical Society of Oak Park and River Forest
      Manley Stacey Civil War Letters
Philadelphia, Pa.
   Historical Society of Pennsylvania
      George Meade Collection
         James Cornell Biddle Letters
         Charles Cadwalader Letters
         Gettysburg Letters
         George G. Meade Papers
         The 29th Pennsylvania Papers
Richmond, Va.
   Virginia Baptist Historical Society
      Henry H. Harris Diary
   Virginia Historical Society
      John Warwick Daniel Papers
   American Civil War Museum

Army of Northern Virginia Collection
   Robert E. Rodes Papers
Washington, D.C.
  Library of Congress
    Flavius J. Bellamy Papers
    Zachariah Chandler Papers
    Henry J. Hunt Papers
    Alfred Pleasonton Papers
    Luther Rose Papers
    William H. Shriver Papers
    Gilbert Thompson Papers
  National Archives
    First Corps Papers, RG 393
    Second Corps Papers, RG 393
    Third Corps Papers, RG 393
    Fifth Corps Papers, RG 393
    Sixth Corps Papers, RG 393
    Eleventh Corps Papers, RG 393
    Twelfth Corps Papers, RG 393
    Cavalry Corps Papers, RG 393
    Bureau of Military Information Papers, RG 393
    Records of the Quartermaster General, Consolidated Correspondence File,
      RG 92
    Records of the Adjutant Generals Office, Muster Rolls Pertaining to
      Battery A, 4th United States Artillery, June 30, 1863, to July 31, 1863,
      RG 94
    Returns from Regular Army Artillery Regiments, 4th Artillery, July 1863,
      RG 94

Government Publications

Heitman, Francis Bernard. *Historical Register and Dictionary of the U.S. Army.*
  2 vols. Ann Arbor: University of Michigan, 1903. Reprint ed., 1966.
War Department. *Revised Regulations of the Army of the United States.* 1861.
*War of the Rebellion: A Compilation of the Official Records of the Union and
  Confederate Armies.* 128 vols. Washington, D.C., 1880–1901.

County Histories

Adams, Charles S. *The Civil War in Frederick County, Maryland.* Rev. ed.
  Shepherdstown, W.Va., 1996.
Adams County, PA, 1886 History. Chicago: Warner, Beers,1886. Reprint ed.,
  Knightstown, Ind.: Book Mark, 1980.
Klein, Frederic Shriver. *Just South of Gettysburg: Carroll County, Maryland
  in the Civil War.* Historical Society of Carroll County, 1963.
Lake, D. J. *Atlas of Adams Co., Pennsylvania.* Philadelphia: I. W. Field, 1872.
Warner, Nancy M. *Carroll County, Maryland: A History, 1837–1976.* Carroll
  County Bicentennial Committee, 1976.

Williams, T. J. C., and Folger McKinsey. *History of Frederick County, Maryland: From the Earliest Settlements to the Beginning of the War between the States, Continued from the Beginning of the Year 1861 down to the Present Time.* 2 vols. Hagerstown, Md.: L. R. Titsworth, 1910.

Newspapers

Buffalo Evening News
Daily Argus (Mount Vernon, N.Y.)
Daily Freeman (Kingston, N.Y.)
Daily Press (Sheboygan, Wis.)
Inter Ocean Courier (Chicago)
National Tribune (Washington, D.C.)
The News (Frederick, Md.)
New York Herald
New York Sun
New York Times
Philadelphia Weekly Press
Philadelphia Weekly Times
Star Tribune (Minneapolis, Minn.)
Sunday Observer (Marietta, Ohio)

Maps

Bond, Isaac. "Map of Frederick County, Md., 1858."
Hopkins, G. M. "Map of Adams County, Pennsylvania," 1858.
Martenet, S. J. "Martenet's Map of Carroll County, Maryland, 1862."
M. S. & E. Converse. "Map of Adams County, Pennsylvania, 1858."

Military Treatises

Clausewitz, Carl von. *On War.* Edited by Michael Howard and Peter Paret. Princeton, N.J.: Princeton University Press, 1976.
de Jomini, Baron Antoine Henri. *The Art of War.* Mechanicsburg, Pa.: Stackpole Books, 1992.
Mahan, D. H. *An Elementary Treatise on Advance-Guard, Outpost, and Detachment Service of Troops, and the Manner of Posting and Handling Them in the Presence of an Enemy.* New York: John Wiley, 1861.

Memorial Addresses

Biddle, Chapman. *The First Day of the Battle of Gettysburg: An Address Delivered before the Historical Society of Pennsylvania, on the 8th of March, 1880.* Philadelphia: J. B. Lippincott, 1880.
Nicholson, John Page, ed. *Pennsylvania at Gettysburg: Ceremonies at the Dedication of the Monuments Erected by the Commonwealth of Pennsylvania to Major General George G. Meade, Major General Winfield S. Hancock, Major General John F. Reynolds, and to Mark the Positions of the Pennsylvania Commands Engaged in the Battle.* 2 vols. Gettysburg, Pa.: W. S. Ray, 1904.
Veale, Moses. *The 109th Regiment Pennsylvania Volunteers: An Address*

Delivered at the Unveiling of Their Monument on Culp's Hill Gettysburg, Pennsylvania, September 11, 1889. Philadelphia: James Beale, 1890.

Published Letters and Diaries

Acken, Gregory J., ed. *Inside the Army of the Potomac: The Civil War Experience of Captain Francis Adams Donaldson.* Mechanicsburg, Pa.: Stackpole Books, 1998.

Agassiz, George R., ed. *Meade's Headquarters, 1863–65: Letters of Col. Theodore Lyman from the Wilderness to Appomattox.* Boston: Atlantic Monthly Press, 1922.

Bardeen, C. W. *The Little Fifer's War Diary.* Syracuse, N.Y.: C. W. Bardeen, 1910.

Basler, R. *The Collected Works of Abraham Lincoln.* 9 vols. New Brunswick, N.J.: Rutgers University Press, 1953.

Benedict, George G. *Army Life in Virginia: The Civil War Letters of George G. Benedict.* Edited by Eric Ward. Harrisburg, Pa.: Stackpole Books, 2002.

Berkeley, Henry Robinson. *Four Years in the Confederate Artillery: The Diary of Henry Robinson Berkeley.* Edited by William H. Runge. Chapel Hill: University of North Carolina Press, 1961.

Burlingame, Michael, ed. *Lincoln's Journalist: John Hay's Anonymous Writings for the Press, 1860–1864.* Carbondale: Southern Illinois University Press, 1999.

Favill, Josiah M. *A Diary of a Young Army Officer.* Army of the Potomac Series. Baltimore: Butternut and Blue, 2000.

Ford, Chauncey Worthington. *A Cycle of Adams Letters.* 2 vols. New York: Houghton Mifflin, 1920.

Hay, Clara S., ed. *Letters of John Hay and Extracts from Diary.* 3 vols. Washington, D.C.: n.p., 1908.

Hotchkiss, Jedediah. *Make Me a Map of the Valley: The Civil War Journal of Stonewall Jackson's Topographer.* Edited by Archie P. McDonald. Dallas, Tex.: Southern Methodist University Press, 1973.

Hyde, Gen. Thomas W. *Civil War Letters.* Lt. Col. J. W. Hyde: privately printed, 1933.

Ladd, David L., and Audrey J. Ladd, eds. *The Bachelder Papers: Gettysburg in Their Own Words.* 3 vols. Dayton, Ohio: Morningside Press, 1994.

Lowe, David W., ed. *Meade's Army: The Private Notebooks of Lt. Col. Theodore Lyman.* Kent, Ohio: Kent State University Press, 2007.

Moore, Sue Burns, and Rebecca Blackwell Drake, eds. *Leaves: The Diary of Elizabeth Meade Ingraham, the Rebel Sister of General George Meade.* Raymond, Miss.: Champion Hill Heritage Foundation, 2019.

Nevins, Allan, ed. *A Diary of Battle: The Personal Journals of Col. Charles S. Wainwright, 1861–1865.* New York: Harcourt, Brace, and World, 1962.

Quaife, Milo M., ed. *From the Cannon's Mouth: The Civil War Letters of General Alpheus S. Williams.* Detroit, Mich.: Wayne State University Press, 1959.

Quynn, William R., ed. *The Diary of Jacob Engelbrecht.* 2 vols. Frederick, Md.: Historical Society of Frederick County, 2001.

Silliker, Ruth L., ed. *The Rebel Yell and the Yankee Hurrah: The Civil War*

BIBLIOGRAPHY 437

Journal of a Maine Volunteer, Private John W. Haley, 17th Maine Regiment.
Camden, Me.: Down East Books, 1985.

Sparks, David S., ed. *Inside Lincoln's Army: The Diary of General Marsena Rudolph Patrick, Provost Marshal General, Army of the Potomac.* New York: Thomas Yoseloff, 1964.

Weld, Stephen Minot. *War Diary and Letters of Stephen Minot Weld: 1861–1865.* 2nd ed. Boston: Massachusetts Historical Society, 1979.

Welles, Gideon. *Diary of Gideon Welles, Secretary of the Navy under Lincoln and Johnson.* 3 vols. New York: Houghton Mifflin, 1911.

Published Memoirs

Alexander, E. P. *Fighting for the Confederacy: The Personal Recollections of General Edward Porter Alexander.* Edited by Gary Gallagher. Chapel Hill: University of North Carolina Press, 1989.

Alleman, Matilda Pierce. *At Gettysburg; or, What a Girl Saw and Heard of the Battle: A True Narrative by Mrs. Tillie Pierce Alleman.* New York: W. Lake Borland, 1889. Reprint ed., Baltimore: Butternut and Blue, 1989.

Benjamin, Charles F. *Memoir of James Allen Hardie, Inspector General, United States Army.* Washington, D.C.: Privately published, 1877.

Billings, John D. *Hard Tack and Coffee; or, The Unwritten Story of Army Life.* Boston: George M. Smith, 1887.

Blake, Henry N. *Three Years in the Army of the Potomac.* Boston: Lee and Shepard, 1865.

Brown, Campbell. *Campbell Brown's Civil War: With Ewell and the Army of Northern Virginia.* Edited by Terry L. Jones. Baton Rouge: Louisiana State University Press, 2001.

Byrne, Frank L., and Andrew T. Weaver, eds. *Haskell of Gettysburg: His Life and Civil War Papers.* Madison: State Historical Society of Wisconsin, 1970.

Carter, Robert Goldthwaite. *Four Brothers in Blue; or, Sunshine and Shadows of the War of the Rebellion: A Story of the Great Civil War from Bull Run to Appomattox.* Austin: University of Texas Press, 1978.

Casler, John O. *Four Years in the Stonewall Brigade.* Dayton, Ohio: Morningside Press, 1981.

Dana, Charles A. *Recollections of the Civil War with the Leaders at Washington and in the Field in the Sixties.* New York: D. Appleton, 1902.

de Peyster, J. Watts. *Gettysburg and After: Battle at Gettysburg and at Williamsport and Falling Waters.* New York: MacDonald, 1867.

Gerrish, Rev. Theodore (Late a Member of the 20th Maine Vols). *Army Life: A Private's Reminiscences of the Civil War.* Portland, Me.: Hoyt, Fogg and Donham, 1882.

Gibbon, Brig. Gen. John. *Personal Recollections of the Civil War.* New York: G. P. Putnam's Sons, 1928.

Haupt, Gen. Herman. *Reminiscences of General Herman Haupt.* Reprint ed. New York: Arno Press, 1981.

Johnston, David E. *The Story of a Confederate Boy in the Civil War.* Portland, Ore.: Glass and Prudhomme, 1914.

BIBLIOGRAPHY

Kernek, Clyde B., M.D. *Field Surgeon at Gettysburg: A Memorial Account of the Medical Unit of the Thirty-Second Massachusetts Regiment.* Indianapolis: Guild Press of Indiana, 1993.

Kieffer, Harry M. *The Recollections of a Drummer Boy.* Boston: James Osgood, 1883.

Letterman, Jonathan, M.D. *Medical Recollections of the Army of the Potomac.* Reprinted in *Medical Recollections of the Army of the Potomac by Jonathan Letterman, M.D., and Memoir of Jonathan Letterman, M.D., by Lt. Col. Bennett A. Clements.* Knoxville, Tenn.: Bohemian Brigade, 1994.

Livermore, Thomas L. *Days and Events, 1860–1866.* Boston: Houghton Mifflin, 1920.

Mark, Penrose J. *Red, White, and Blue Badge.* Harrisburg, Pa.: Aughinbaugh Press, 1911.

Porter, Gen. Horace. *Campaigning with Grant.* Reprint ed. Secaucus, N.J.: Blue and Grey Press, 1984.

Rusling, Gen. James F. *Men and Things I Saw in Civil War Days.* New York: Eaton and Mains, 1899.

Sauers, Richard A., ed. *Fighting Them Over: How the Veterans Remembered Gettysburg in the Pages of "The National Tribune."* Baltimore: Butternut and Blue, 1998.

Schurz, Carl. *The Reminiscences of Carl Schurz.* 3 vols. New York: McClure, 1907.

Sheibert, Justus, *Seven Months in the Rebel States during the North American War.* Translated by Joseph C. Hayes. Tuscaloosa, Ala.: Confederate Publishing, 1958.

Tremain, Henry Edwin. *Two Days of War: A Gettysburg Narrative and Other Excursions.* New York: Bonnell, Silver, and Bowers, 1905.

Viola, Herman J., ed. *The Memoirs of Charles Henry Veil: A Soldier's Recollections of the Civil War and the Arizona Territory.* Library of the American West. New York: Orion Books, 1993.

Worsham, John H. *One of Jackson's Foot Cavalry: His Experience and What He Saw during the War, 1861–1865.* New York: Neale, 1912.

Young, Jesse Bowman. *What a Boy Saw in the Army: A Story of Sight-Seeing and Adventure in the War for the Union.* New York: Hunt and Eaton, 1894.

Autobiographies and Biographies

Brown, Kent Masterson. *Cushing of Gettysburg: The Story of a Union Artillery Officer.* Lexington: University Press of Kentucky, 1993.

Butterfield, Julia Lorrilard. *A Biographical Memorial of General Daniel Butterfield.* New York: Grafton, 1904.

Cleaves, Freeman. *Meade of Gettysburg.* Norman: University of Oklahoma Press, 1960.

Gorham, George C. *Life and Public Services of Edwin M. Stanton.* 2 vols. Boston: Houghton Mifflin, 1899.

Hancock, A. R. *Reminiscences of Winfield S. Hancock by His Wife.* New York: Charles L. Webster, 1887.

Hebert, Walter H. *Fighting Joe Hooker.* Indianapolis, Ind.: Bobbs-Merrill, 1944.

Hessler, James A. *Sickles at Gettysburg*. New York: Savas Beatie, 2009.

Howard, Gen. Oliver Otis. *Autobiography of Oliver Otis Howard*. 2 vols. New York: Baker and Taylor, 1907.

Humphreys, Henry H. *Andrew Atkinson Humphreys: A Biography*. Philadelphia: John C. Winston, 1924.

Longacre, Edward G. *The Man behind the Guns: A Biography of General Henry J. Hunt, Commander of Artillery, Army of the Potomac*. New York: A. S. Barnes, 1977.

Marszalek, John. *Commander of All Lincoln's Armies: A Life of General Henry W. Halleck*. Cambridge, Mass.: Belknap Press of Harvard University Press, 2004.

Meade, George, ed. *Life and Letters of General George Gordon Meade*. 2 vols. New York: Charles Scribner's Sons, 1913.

———. *With Meade at Gettysburg*. Philadelphia: John C. Winston, 1930.

Nichols, Edward. *Toward Gettysburg: A Biography of John F. Reynolds*. State College: Pennsylvania State University Press, 1958.

Smith, Diane Monroe, *Washington Roebling's Civil War: From the Bloody Battlefield at Gettysburg to the Brooklyn Bridge*. Guilford, Conn.: Stackpole Books, 2019.

Taylor, Emerson Gifford. *Gouvernor Kemble Warren: Life and Letters of an American Soldier*. Boston: Houghton Mifflin, 1932.

Thomas, Benjamin, and Harold Hyman. *Stanton: The Life and Times of Lincoln's Secretary of War*. New York: Alfred A. Knopf, 1962.

Tsouras, Peter G. *Major General George H. Sharpe and the Creation of American Military Intelligence in the Civil War*. Philadelphia: Casemate, 2018.

Tucker, Glenn. *Hancock the Superb*. New York: Bobbs-Merrill, 1960.

Warner, Ezra J. *Generals in Blue: Lives of the Union Commanders*. Baton Rouge: Louisiana State University Press, 1952.

———. *Generals in Gray: Lives of the Confederate Commanders*. Baton Rouge: Louisiana State University Press, 1952.

Winslow, Richard E. *General John Sedgwick: A Story of a Union Corps Commander*. Novato, Calif.: Presidio Press, 1982.

Regimental Histories

Aldrich, Thomas M., *The History of Battery A, First Rhode Island Light Artillery, in the War to Preserve the Union, 1861–1865*. Providence, R.I.: Snow and Farnham, 1904.

Baker, Levi W. *History of the Ninth Massachusetts Battery*. South Framingham, Mass.: Lakeview, 1888.

Best, Isaac O. *History of the 121st New York State Infantry*. Chicago: Lieut. Jas. H. Smith, 1921.

Brown, Sgt. Henri Le Fevre. *History of the Third Regiment Excelsior Brigade, 72nd New York Volunteer Infantry, 1861–1865*. Jamestown, N.Y.: Journal Printing, 1902.

Brown, J. Willard. *The Signal Corps in the War of the Rebellion*. Boston: U.S. Signal Corps Association, 1896. Reprint ed., Baltimore: Butternut and Blue, 1996.

Bruce, Bvt. Lt. Col. George A. *The Twentieth Regiment of Massachusetts Volunteer Infantry, 1861–1865.* Boston: Houghton, Mifflin, 1906.

Child, Maj. William M., M.D. *A History of the Fifth Regiment of the New Hampshire Volunteers in the American Civil War, 1861–1865. In Two Parts.* Bristol, N.H.: R. W. Musgrove, 1893.

Clark, Walter, ed. *Histories of the Several Regiments and Battalions from North Carolina in the Great War, 1861–1865.* 5 vols. Raleigh, N.C.: E. M. Uzzell, 1901.

Cook, S. G., M.D., and Charles E. Benton, eds. *The "Duchess County Regiment" (150th Regiment of the New York State Volunteer Infantry) in the Civil War, as Told by Its Members; Based upon the Writings of Rev. Edward O. Bartlett, D.D.* Danbury, Conn.: Danbury Medical, 1907.

Cowles, Luther E. *Fifth Massachusetts Battery, Organized October 3, 1861, and Mustered Out June 12, 1865.* Boston: published by the author, 1902.

Craft, David. *History of the One Hundred Forty-First Regiment, Pennsylvania Volunteers.* Towanda, Pa.: Reporter-Journal, 1885.

Cudworth, Warren H. *History of the First Regiment (Massachusetts Infantry) from the 9th of May, 1861, to the 25th of May, 1864, including Brief References to the Operations of the Army of the Potomac.* Boston: Walker, Fuller, 1866.

Davis, Charles E. *Three Years in the Army: The Story of the Thirteenth Massachusetts Volunteers from July 16, 1861, to August 1, 1864.* Boston: Estes and Lauriat, 1894.

Dawes, Rufus R. *Service with the Sixth Wisconsin Volunteers.* Marietta, Ga.: E. R. Alderman and Sons, 1890.

Eddy, Richard. *History of the Sixtieth Regiment of New York Volunteers from the Commencement of Its Organization in July, 1861, to Its Public Reception at Ogdensburg as a Veteran Command, January 7th, 1864.* Philadelphia: Crissy and Markley, 1864.

Floyd, Sgt. Fred. C. *History of the Fortieth (Mozart) Regiment of the New York Volunteers, Which Was Composed of Four Companies from New York, Four Companies from Massachusetts, and Two Companies from Pennsylvania.* Boston: F. H. Gilson, 1909.

Ford, Andrew E. *The Story of the Fifteenth Regiment, Massachusetts, Volunteer Infantry in the Civil War, 1861–1864.* Clinton, Mass.: Press of W. J. Coulter, Courant Office, 1898.

Frederick, Gilbert, D. D. *The Story of a Regiment; Being a Record of the Military Services of Fifty-Seventh New York State Volunteer Infantry in the War of the Rebellion, 1861–1865.* Chicago: C. H. Morgan, 1895.

Hanifen, Michael. *History of Battery B, First New Jersey Artillery.* Ottawa, Ill.: Republican-Times, 1905.

Hardin, Brig. Gen. U. S. Army (Ret.), M.D. *History of the Twelfth Regiment, Pennsylvania Reserve Volunteer Corps (41st Regiment of the Line) from Its Muster into the United States Service, August 10th, 1861, to Its Muster Out, June 11, 1864, Together with Biographical Sketches of its Officers and Men and a Complete Muster-Out Roll.* New York: published by the author, 1890.

Hays, Gilbert Adams. *Under the Red Patch: Story of the Sixty-Third Regiment*

Pennsylvania Volunteers, 1861–1864. Pittsburgh, Pa.: Published by the Sixty-
Third Pennsylvania Volunteers Regimental Association, 1908.

History Committee. *History of the Nineteenth Regiment Massachusetts Volunteer
Infantry.* Salem, Mass.: Salem Press, 1906.

Houghton, Edwin B. *The Campaigns of the Seventeenth Maine.* Portland, Me.:
Short and Loring, 1866.

Hyde, Gen. Thomas W. *Following the Greek Cross; or, Memories of the Sixth
Army Corps.* Boston: Houghton Mifflin, 1895.

Judson, A. M. *History of the Eighty-Third Regiment Pennsylvania Volunteers.*
Erie, Pa.: B. F. H. Lynn, 1881.

Kepler, William M. *History of Three Months and Three Years of Service from
April 16th, 1861, to June 22d, 1864, of the Fourth Regiment Ohio Volunteer
Infantry in the War for the Union.* Cleveland, Ohio: Leader Printing, 1886.

Kernek, Clyde B., M.D. *Field Surgeon at Gettysburg: A Memorial Account of the
Medical Unit of the Thirty-Second Massachusetts Regiment.* Indianapolis:
Guild Press of Indiana, 1993.

Kiefer, Rev. W. R. *History of the One Hundred and Fifty-Third Regiment
Pennsylvania Volunteers Infantry Which Was Recruited in Northampton
County, Pa., 1862–1863.* Easton, Pa.: Chemical Publishing, 1909.

Lewis, George. *History of Battery E, First Regiment Rhode Island Light Artillery,
in the War of 1861 and 1865, to preserve the Union.* Providence: Snow &
Farnham, 1892.

Maine Gettysburg Commission. *Maine at Gettysburg: Report of Maine
Commissioners.* Portland: The Lakeside Press, 1898.

Marbaker, Sgt. Thomas D. *History of the Eleventh New Jersey Volunteers from
Its Organization to Appomattox to Which Is Added Experiences of Prison Life
and Sketches of Individual Members.* Trenton: MacCrellish and Quigley, 1898.

Minnigh, Capt. and Bvt. Maj. H. N. *History of Company K, 1st (Inft) Penn'a
Reserves, "The Boys Who Fought at Home."* Duncansville, Pa.: "Home Print,"
1891.

Muffly, Adjt. J. W., ed. *The Story of Our Regiment: A History of the 148th
Pennsylvania Volunteers Written by the Comrades.* Des Moines, Iowa: Kenyon
Printing, 1904.

Mulholland, Col. and Bvt. Maj. Gen. St. Clair A. *The Story of the 116th Regiment
Pennsylvania Volunteers in the War of the Rebellion: The Record of a Gallant
Command.* Philadelphia: F. McManus Jr., 1906.

Nash, Capt. Eugene Arus. *A History of the Forty-Fourth Regiment New York
Volunteer Infantry in the Civil War, 1861–1865.* Chicago: R. R. Donnelley and
Sons, 1911.

New York Monuments Commission. *In Memoriam, George Sears Greene Brevet
Major-General, United States Volunteers, 1801–1899.* Albany, N.Y.: J. B. Lyon,
1909.

Oates, William C. *The War between the Union and the Confederacy and Its Lost
Opportunities with a History of the 15th Alabama Regiment and the Forty-
Eight Battles in Which It Was Engaged.* Dayton, Ohio: Morningside Press,
1974.

Owen, William Miller. *In Camp and Battle with the Washington Artillery of New Orleans*. Boston: Ticknor, 1885.

Page, Charles D. *History of the Fourteenth Connecticut, Vol. Inf'y*. Meridian, Conn.: The Horton, 1906.

Parker, John L., and Robert G. Carter. *Henry Wilson's Regiment: History of the Twenty-Second Massachusetts Infantry, the Second Company Sharpshooters, and the Third Light Battery, in the War of the Rebellion*. Boston: Regimental Association, Press of Rand Avery, 1887.

Powell, William H. *The Fifth Army Corps (Army of the Potomac): A Record of the Operations during the Civil War in the United States of America, 1861–1865*. New York: G. P. Putnam's Sons, 1896.

Rauscher, Frank. *Music on the March, 1862–65, with the Army of the Potomac*. Philadelphia: Wm. F. Fell, 1892.

Rhodes, John H. *The History of Battery B, First Regiment Rhode Island Light Artillery, in the War to Preserve the Union, 1861–1865*. Providence, R.I.: Snow and Farnham, 1894.

Sawyer, Franklin. *A Military History of the 8th Regiment Ohio Vol. Inf'y, Its Battles, Marches, and Army Movements*. Edited by George A. Groot. Cleveland, Ohio: Fairbanks, 1881.

Scott, Kate M. *History of the One Hundred and Fifth Regiment of Pennsylvania Volunteers: A Complete History of the Organization, Marches, Battles, Toils, and Dangers Participated in by the Regiment from the Beginning to the Close of the War, 1861–1865*. Philadelphia: New World, 1877.

Searles, Jasper N., and Matthew F. Taylor. *History of the First Regiment Minnesota Volunteer Infantry, 1861–1864, with Maps and Illustrations*. Stillwater, Minn.: Easton and Masterman, 1916.

Smith, Abram P. *History of the Seventy-Sixth Regiment, New York Volunteers; What It Endured and Accomplished; Containing Descriptions of Its Twenty-Five Battles; Its Marches; Its Camp and Bivouac Scenes; with Biographical Sketches of Fifty-Three Officers, and a Complete Record of the Enlisted Men*. Cortland, N.Y.: printed for the publisher, 1867.

Smith, Capt. James E. *A Famous Battery and Its Campaigns, 1861–'64*. Washington, D.C.: W. H. Loudermilk, 1892.

Smith, John Day. *The History of the Nineteenth Regiment of the Maine Volunteer Infantry, 1862–1865*. Minneapolis, Minn.: Great Western, 1909.

Stevens, Capt. C. A. *Berdan's United States Sharpshooters in the Army of the Potomac, 1861–1865*. St Paul, Minn.: Price-McGill, 1892.

Stewart, Robert Laird, D.D. *History of the One Hundred and Fortieth Regiment, Pennsylvania Volunteers*. N.p.: Published by the Authority of the Regimental Association, 1902.

Survivors' Association. *History of the 118th Pennsylvania Volunteers, Corn Exchange Regiment from Their First Engagement at Antietam to Appomattox*. Philadelphia: J. L. Smith, Map Publisher, 1905.

Tevis, C. V. *The History of the Fighting Fourteenth*. New York: Brooklyn Eagle, 1911.

Thomson, O. R. Howard, and William H. Rauch. *History of the "Bucktails"*

Kane Rifle Regiment of the Pennsylvania Reserve Corps (13th Pennsylvania Reserve, 42nd of the Line). Philadelphia: Electric Printing, 1906.

Van Santvoord, C., D.D. *The One Hundred and Twentieth Regiment New York State Volunteers: A Narrative of Its Services in the War for the Union.* Rondout, N.Y.: Kingston Freeman, 1894.

Waitt, Ernest Linden. *History of the Nineteenth Regiment, Massachusetts Volunteer Infantry, 1861–1865.* Salem, Mass.: Salem Press, 1906.

Walker, Francis A. *History of the Second Army Corps in the Army of the Potomac.* New York: Charles Scribner's Sons, 1886.

Ward, Joseph R. C., D.D.S. *History of the One Hundred and Sixth Regiment Pennsylvania Volunteers, 2d Brigade, 2d Division, 2d Corps, 1861–1865.* Philadelphia: F. McManus Jr., 1906.

Weygant, Charles H. *History of the One Hundred Twenty-Fourth N.Y.S.V.* Newburgh, N.Y.: Journal Printing, 1877.

Willson, Mrs. Arabella M. *Disaster, Struggle, Triumph: The Adventures of 1000 "Boys in Blue" from August, 1862, to June, 1865.* Albany: Argus, 1870.

Wise, Jennings Cropper. *The Long Arm of Lee; or, The History of the Artillery of the Army of Northern Virginia with a Brief Account of the Confederate Bureau of Ordnance.* 2 vols. Lynchburg, Va.: J. P. Bell, 1915.

Secondary Sources

Beale, James. *The Battle Flags of the Army of the Potomac at Gettysburg, Penna., July 1st, 2d, and 3d, 1863.* Philadelphia: James Beale, 1888.

Bigelow, Maj. John, Jr. *The Campaign of Chancellorsville: A Strategic and Tactical Study.* New Haven, Conn.: Yale University Press, 1910.

Bigelow, Capt. John. *The Peach Orchard Gettysburg, July 2, 1863, Explained by Official Reports and Maps.* Minneapolis, Minn.: Kimball-Storer, 1910.

Brown, J. Willard. *The Signal Corps in the War of the Rebellion.* Boston: U.S. Signal Corps Association, 1896.

Brown, Kent Masterson. *Retreat from Gettysburg: Lee, Logistics, and the Pennsylvania Campaign.* Chapel Hill: University of North Carolina Press, 2005.

Busey, John W., and David G. Martin. *Regimental Strengths at Gettysburg.* Baltimore: Gateway, 1982.

Coco, Gregory A. *A Vast Sea of Misery: A History and Guide to the Union and Confederate Field Hospitals at Gettysburg, July 1–November 20, 1863.* Gettysburg, Pa.: Thomas, 1988.

Coddington, Edwin B. *The Gettysburg Campaign: A Study in Command.* New York: Charles Scribner's Sons, 1968.

Dilts, James D. *The Great Road: The Building of the Baltimore and Ohio, the Nation's First Railroad, 1828–1853.* Stanford, Calif.: Stanford University Press, 1993.

Duncan, Capt. Louis C. *The Medical Department of the United States Army in the Civil War.* Reprint ed. Gaithersburg, Md.: Olde Soldier Books, 1987.

Fishel, Edwin C., *The Secret War for the Union: The Untold Story of Military Intelligence in the Civil War.* New York: Houghton Mifflin, 1996.

Guelzo, Allen C. *Gettysburg: The Last Invasion*. New York: Alfred A. Knopf, 2013.

Humphreys, Andrew A. *From Gettysburg to the Rapidan*. New York: Charles Scribner's Sons, 1883.

Hyde, Bill, ed. *The Union Generals Speak: The Meade Hearings on the Battle of Gettysburg*. Baton Rouge: Louisiana State University Press, 2003.

Kauffman, G. F. *Inscriptions on Monuments, Markers, and Plaques on the Battlefield of Gettysburg, Pennsylvania*. York, Pa.: Kauffman, 1970.

Kirkwood, Ronald D. *"Too Much for Human Endurance": The George Spangler Farm Hospitals and the Battle of Gettysburg*. El Dorado Hills, Calif.: Savas Beatie, 2019.

Ladd, David L., Audrey J. Ladd, eds. *John Bachelder's History of the Battle of Gettysburg*. Dayton, Ohio: Morningside House, 1997.

Long, E. B., with Barbara Long. *The Civil War Day by Day: An Almanac, 1861–1865*. Garden City, N.Y.: Doubleday, 1971.

Maust, Roland R. *Grappling with Death: The Union Second Corps Hospital at Gettysburg*. Dayton, Ohio: Morningside House, 2001.

Meade, George. *Did General Meade Desire to Retreat at the Battle of Gettysburg?* Philadelphia: Porter and Coates, 1883.

———. *Photographs of Union and Confederate Officers in the Civil War in America: Collection of Bvt. Lt. Col. George Meade U.S.A.* Philadelphia: Civil War Library and Museum, 1996.

Miller, Francis Trevelyan. *Photographic History of the Civil War*. 10 vols. New York: Review of Reviews, 1911.

Moore, Frank, ed. *The Rebellion Record: A Diary of American Events*. 11 vols. New York: G. P. Putnam, 1861–63, and D. Van Nostrand, 1864–68.

Norton, Oliver W. *Strong Vincent and His Brigade at Gettysburg, July 2, 1863*. Chicago: N.p., 1909.

Pfanz, Harry W. *Gettysburg—The First Day*. Civil War America Series. Chapel Hill: University of North Carolina Press, 2001.

———. *Gettysburg: The Second Day*. Civil War America Series. Chapel Hill: University of North Carolina Press, 1967.

Porter, Gen. Horace. *Campaigning with Grant*. Secaucus, N.J.: Blue and Grey Press, 1984.

Raff, Lyne. *My Heart Is Too Full to Say More: The Horse in the Civil War*. N.p.: Art Horse Press, 2010.

Sauers, Richard A., ed. *Fighting Them Over: How the Veterans Remembered Gettysburg in the Pages of "The National Tribune."* Baltimore: Butternut and Blue, 1998.

Sears, Stephen W. *Gettysburg*. New York: Houghton Mifflin, 2003.

———. *Lincoln's Lieutenants: The High Command of the Army of the Potomac*. Boston: Houghton Mifflin Harcourt, 2017.

Selby, John G. *Meade: The Price of Command, 1863–1865*. Kent, Ohio: Kent State University Press, 2018.

Smith, Timothy H. *Farms at Gettysburg: The Fields of Battle*. Gettysburg, Pa.: Thomas, 2007.

Styple, William B. *Generals in Bronze: Interviewing the Commanders of the Civil War*. Kearny, N.J.: Belle Grove, 2005.

Williams, T. Harry. *Lincoln and the Radicals*. Madison: University of Wisconsin Press, 1960.

Articles in Journals, Periodicals, and Collected Works

Andrews, J. Cutler. "The Press Reports: The Battle of Gettysburg." *Pennsylvania History* 31 (1964): 176.

Benjamin, Charles F. "Hooker's Appointment and Removal." In *Battles and Leaders of the Civil War*, vol. 3, edited by Robert W. Johnson and Clarence C. Buel, 239–43. New York: Thomas Yoseloff, 1956.

Brown, Kent Masterson. "'Double Canister at Ten Yards': Captain Andrew Cowan at Gettysburg." *Filson Club Historical Quarterly* 59 (1985): 293–326.

Case, Lieut. A. P., "The Taking and Holding of Little Round Top." In *Final Report on the Battlefield of Gettysburg*, vol. 3, edited by New York Monuments Commission, 969–72. Albany: J. B. Lyon Co., 1900.

Couch, Gen. Darius N. "The Chancellorsville Campaign." In *Battles and Leaders of the Civil War*, vol. 3, edited by Robert U. Johnson and Clarence C. Buel, 154–71. New York: Thomas Yoseloff, 1956.

Coughenour, Col. Kavin. "Assessing the Generalship of George G. Meade during the Gettysburg Campaign." *Gettysburg Magazine* 28 (January 2003): 27–39.

Cox, Jacob D. "The Battle of Antietam." In *Battles and Leaders of the Civil War*, vol. 2, edited by Robert U. Johnson and Clarence C. Buel, 630–60. New York: Thomas Yoseloff, 1956.

Crounse, L. L. "The Escape of Lee's Army." In *Rebellion Record*, vol. 7, edited by Frank Moore, 345–47. New York: G. P. Putnam, 1864.

Fry, James B. "McDowell's Advance to Bull Run." In *Battles and Leaders of the Civil War*, vol. 1, edited by Robert U. Johnson and Clarence C. Buel, 181–93. New York: Thomas Yoseloff, 1956.

Fuger, Frederick. "Cushing's Battery at Gettysburg." *Journal of Military Service Institution of the United States* 41 (November–December 1907): 404–10.

Fulton, Dr. James A. "A Surgeon's Story of the Battle of Gettysburg on Pennsylvania Soil." *National Tribune*, October 20, 1878.

Gibbon, Major General John. "Another View of Gettysburg." *North American Review* 152 (1891): 704–13.

Greene, A. Wilson. "Meade's Pursuit of Lee: From Gettysburg to Falling Waters." In *The Third Day of Gettysburg and Beyond*, edited by Gary Gallagher, 162–201. Chapel Hill: University of North Carolina Press, 1994.

Halstead, E. P. "Incidents of the First Day at Gettysburg." In *Battles and Leaders of the Civil War*, vol. 3, edited by Robert U. Johnson and Clarence C. Buel, 284–85. New York: Thomas Yoseloff, 1956.

Hempel, Katherine. "Gone and Nearly Forgotten: David McConaughy, the Man behind the Soldiers' National Cemetery and the Gettysburg National Military Park." *Gettysburg Magazine* 34 (January 2006): 86.

Hintz, Kalina Ingham. "'Dinna Forget': The Gettysburg Monuments to General John F. Reynolds." *Gettysburg Magazine* 31 (July 2004): 89–111.

Hunt, Gen. Henry J. "The First Day at Gettysburg." In *Battles and Leaders of the Civil War*, vol. 3, edited by Robert U. Johnson and Clarence C. Buel, 255–84. New York: Thomas Yoseloff, 1956.

———. "The Second Day at Gettysburg." In *Battles and Leaders of the Civil War*, vol. 3, edited by Robert U. Johnson and Clarence C. Buel, 289–313. New York: Thomas Yoseloff, 1956.

———. "The Third Day at Gettysburg." In *Battles and Leaders of the Civil War*, vol. 3, edited by Robert U. Johnson and Clarence C. Buel, 369–85. New York: Thomas Yoseloff, 1956.

Imboden, John D. "The Confederate Retreat from Gettysburg." In *Battles and Leaders of the Civil War*, vol. 3, edited by Robert U. Johnson and Clarence C. Buel, 420–29. New York: Thomas Yoseloff, 1956.

———. "Stonewall Jackson in the Shenandoah." In *Battles and Leaders of the Civil War*, vol. 2, edited by Robert U. Johnson and Clarence C. Buel, 282–301. New York: Thomas Yoseloff, 1956.

Jackson, Col. Huntington W. "The Battle of Gettysburg." In *Military Essays and Recollections*, 10:147–84. Reprint ed. Wilmington, Del.: Broadfoot, 1992.

———. "Sedgwick at Fredericksburg and Salem Heights." In *Battles and Leaders of the Civil War*, vol. 3, edited by Robert U. Johnson and Clarence C. Buel, 224–32. New York: Thomas Yoseloff, 1956.

Jerome, Aaron B. "Buford in the Battle of Oak Ridge: The First Days Fight at Gettysburg a.m. Wednesday, 1st July, 1863." In *Gettysburg and After: Battle of Oak Ridge at Williamsport and Falling Waters*, edited by J. Watts de Peyster, 153. Gaithersburg, Md.: Olde Soldier Books, 1987.

Johnston, Joseph E. "Manassas to Seven Pines." In *Battles and Leaders of the Civil War*, vol. 2, edited by Robert U. Johnson and Clarence C. Buel, 202–19. New York: Thomas Yoseloff, 1956.

Jorgenson, Jay. "Securing the Flank: How Three Aides Helped Warren Save Little Round Top." *Gettysburg Magazine* 45 (July 2011): 84–91.

Longstreet, James. "The Battle for Fredericksburg." In *Battles and Leaders of the Civil War*, vol. 3, edited by Robert U. Johnson and Clarence C. Buel, 70–95. New York: Thomas Yoseloff, 1956.

McClellan, George B. "From the Peninsula to Antietam." In *Battles and Leaders of the Civil War*, vol. 2, edited by Robert U. Johnson and Clarence C. Buel, 282–301. New York: Thomas Yoseloff, 1956.

———. "The Peninsular Campaign." In *Battles and Leaders of the Civil War*, vol. 2, edited by Robert U. Johnson and Clarence C. Buel, 160–81. New York: Thomas Yoseloff, 1956.

Nelson, L. Patrick. "Reynolds and the Decision to Fight." *Gettysburg Magazine* 23 (July 2000): 31–50.

Page, Evelyn, ed. "After Gettysburg: Frederick Law Olmstead on the Escape of Lee." *Pennsylvania Magazine of History and Biography* 75 (October 1951): 436–46.

Pope, John. "The Second Battle of Bull Run." In *Battles and Leaders of the Civil War*, vol. 2, edited by Robert U. Johnson and Clarence C. Buel, 449–500. New York: Thomas Yoseloff, 1956.

Reid, Whitelaw. "The Battles of Gettysburg." In *Rebellion Record*, vol. 7, edited by Frank Moore, 84–128. New York: G. P. Putnam, 1864.

Sickles, Gen. Daniel E. "Further Recollections of Gettysburg." *North American Review* 152 (1891): 257–86.

Walker, Gen. Francis A. "Meade at Gettysburg." In *Battles and Leaders of the Civil War*, vol. 3, edited by Robert U. Johnson and Clarence C. Buel, 406–19. New York: Thomas Yoseloff, 1956.

Newspaper Articles

Brown, Curt. "Sgt. Buckman's Diary: The 150-Year-Old Story of Gettysburg and the First Minnesota." *Star Tribune* (Minneapolis), June 30, 2013.

Delaplane, Judge Edward S. "General Meade Acclaimed in Frederick for Victory at Gettysburg." *The News* (Frederick, Md.), July 7, 1973.

"Gen. G. H. Sharpe Dead." *New York Times*, January 15, 1900.

"George Gordon Meade to G. G. Benedict, March 16, 1870." *Philadelphia Weekly Press*, August 11, 1886.

"The Gettysburg Fight, the Second Day's Battle, and Gen. Sickles' Part in It." *New York Sun*, June 28, 1891.

Koons, James H. "History of Middleburg." *Carroll Record* (Taneytown, Md.), October 19, 1895.

Moran, Francis E. "A New View of Gettysburg." *Philadelphia Weekly Times*, April 22, 1882.

"Unselfishness of Meade." *Daily Press* (Sheboygan, Wis.), June 21, 1910.

Online Sources

Hancock, Winfield S. "Gettysburg: Reply to General Howard." https://www.worldcat.org/title/gettysburg-reply-to-general-howard/oclc/44680213.

Harman, Troy D. "Did Meade Begin a Counteroffensive after Pickett's Charge?" *Gettysburg Seminar Papers: The Third Day: The Fate of a Nation*. http://npshistory.com/series/symposia/gettysburg_seminars/12/essay9.pdf.

———. "The Gap: Meade's July 2 Offensive Plan." *Gettysburg Seminar Papers: The Most Shocking Battle I Have Ever Witnessed: The Second Day at Gettysburg*. http://npshistory.com/series/symposia/gettysburg_seminars/11/essay3.pdf.

Hueting, Jim. "Meade Receives Command from the Army of the Potomac." *Gettysburg Daily*, October 13, 2009. https://www.gettysburgdaily.com/meade-receives-command-of-the-army-of-the-potomac-gettysburg-lbg-jim-hueting/.

Littlestown Quadrangle, Carroll County, Maryland, Quadrangle Atlas 14. https://pubs.er.usgs.gov/publication/70047508.

Manchester Quadrangle, Carroll County, Maryland, Quadrangle Atlas 15. https://pubs.er.usgs.gov/publication/70047498.

"Meade's Headquarters." Historical Marker Database, https://www.hmdb.org/m.asp?m=2996.

"Stereoview of the Eutaw House by William M. Chase." *Photographicus Baltimorensis* (blog), October 3, 2010. https://19thcenturybaltimore

.wordpress.com/2010/10/03/stereoview-of-the-eutaw-house-by-william
-m-chase/.

Taneytown and Emmitsburg Quadrangle, Carroll County, Maryland, Quadrangle
Atlas 16. https://pubs.er.usgs.gov/publication/7004751.

Topozone.com, https://www.topozone.com/pennsylvania/adams-pa/.

Union Bridge and Woodsboro Quadrangle, Carroll County, Maryland,
Quadrangle Atlas 17. https://pubs.er.usgs.gov/publication/70047512.

INDEX

Page numbers in italics refer to maps, figures, and captions.

Abbottstown, Pa., 96, 137, 192

Adams County, Pa., 94, 119–20; courthouse of, 134, 308, 408n12; maps of, 57, 100, 101, 106, 122, 123, 145–46, 208, 212, 215, 388n8; topography of, 121–22

Adams Express Company, 61, 182–83, 319, 389n17

advance guard, advance force, 102–5, 112, 124, 127, 149, 396n16, 399n40

African Americans, 52–53, 113, 119

alcohol, 17, 281; Meade and, 274, 276, 418–19n21; overimbibing of, 70, 74, 91, 140

Aldie, Va., *23*, 28–29

Alexandria, Va., 2, *23*, 182

ambulance wagons, 145, 169–70, 310–11, 352, 401n58; attacks on, 328–30, 346; depots for, 133, 134, 147; movement of, 106, 107, 108; trains of, 19, 69, 123, 158, 319. *See also* medical service

Ames, Adelbert, 192, 195, 266

ammunition, 177, 196, 202, 212, 240, 256–57, 297, 321, 344, 373–74, 406n9; Confederate supplies of, 330, 352, 353, 363; at Harper's Ferry, 115–16; personal complement of, 106, 107; shortages of, 5, 192–93, 236, 248, 266, 345; wagon trains for, 107–8, 123, 158, 290, 313–19, 398n28. *See also* ordnance

Anderson, George T., 236, 242, 248, 253, 304

Anderson, Richard H., 22, 96, 105, 150, 251

Antietam Campaign, 3, 14, 46, 55, 145, 154–55, 164, 167, 169, 248, 281, 324–25. *See also* Battle of Antietam

Antietam Creek (Pa. and Md.), 3, 353–54, 358, 360

Arcadia (Robert McGill House, Frederick County, Md.), 34–35, 37, 43, 52

Archer, James J., 130–31, 133

Army of Northern Virginia, 7, 13, 21, 47, 62, 82, 311; artillery of, 28, 48, 62; cavalry of, 59, 112; crosses Potomac, 24, 28, 59; intelligence on, 19, 22, 25, 61, 67, 76, 77, 79–80, 99, 100; Meade and, 4–5, 72, 81; numbers of, 21, 56, 62; reorganization of, 20–21. *See also* Lee, Robert E.; *and names of officers and units of*

Army of the Potomac, 18, 55, 65, 75, 95, 70, 99, 116; artillery of, 22, 24, 64, 69, 170; cavalry of, 18, 22, 29, 66–67, 71, 96, 97, 108, 124; chief quartermaster of, 46, 183, 197, 401n58; chief topographical engineer of, 142, 157; covers Washington and Baltimore, 25, 71–72, 84; engineers and bridge trains of, 64, 96; at Frederick, 28, 34; headquarters of, *53*, 61, 73; Hooker and, 14, 17, 26, 30, 39, 49–50; Lee's army and, 5, 56, *75*, 76; logistic of resupply of, 5, 44, 57, 85, 174–83; Meade ordered to command, 4, 35, 37–38, 65; orders to, 64–65, 90–91, 124; organization and general officers of, 19, 35, 41, 46; payday and paymasters of, 77, 90; pre-Meade history of, 1–4, 13, 20; quartermaster corps and general of, 46, 61;

Army of the Potomac (*continued*)
size and position of, 18–19, 27, 109,
112, 118; state of troops of, 88, 90,
91, 108–9; telegraph system of,
44–45, 59–60, 115; transfer of command of, 28, 35, 41, 43, 49–51, 81;
wagon trains of, 19, 24, 59, 67, 69,
70, 74, 75, 77. *See also* left flank,
left wing, of Army of the Potomac;
right flank, right wing, of Army of
the Potomac; *and names of officers
and units of*
Arnold, William A., 262, 287, 301
artillery, 18, 22, 24, 55, 64, 67, 95, 104,
113, 129, 153, 170, 179; of Army of
Northern Virginia, 21, 28, 48, 62;
on Cemetery Hill, 149, 185, 186;
horse, 21, 59; Meade in, 7. *See also*
Artillery Reserve, Army of the
Potomac; Hunt, Henry Jackson;
ordnance; *and names of units*
Artillery Reserve, Army of the Potomac, 19, 21, 77, 178, 344; at Gettysburg, 224, 238–39, 241–42, 250,
258, 261, 268, 287, 292, 297; Hunt
and, 224, 373–74; movements of,
28, 70, 74, 75, 79, 137, 177, 189, 196,
332, 341, 350, 356, 359; Tyler and,
18, 77, 192, 374
Avery, Isaac E., 266, 268–70
axis, Chambersburg-to-York turnpike,
for Lee, 47–48, 56, 64, 77–78, 82,
92, 97, 104, 150; Buford on, 114,
125; Meade and Reynolds and, 99,
100, 105, 161–62
Ayres, Romeyn B., 110, 232, 252–53,
413n2

Babcock, John C., 19, 20, 28, 52, 276,
283. *See also* Bureau of Military
Information
Ballenger Creek, Md., 32, 34, 52
Baltimore, 23, 28, 44, 49–50, 57, 72,
83, 88–90, 109, 113, 121, 344; communication networks from, 60–61,
173, 182, 183, 217, 280, 389n17;

Haupt's headquarters in, 179, 181;
Meade's orders to cover, 25, 38, 43,
71, 75, 84, 99, 322, 325, 330–31,
339; National Road and, 44, 46;
railroads and, 58, 85, 91, 173, 177,
181; threats to, 81, 214, 331. *See also*
Baltimore & Ohio Railroad; Baltimore Pike
Baltimore & Ohio Railroad, 37, 44,
46, 63, 140, 164, 177, 181–83, 314,
331, 338, 345–46, 385n26, 389n17;
destruction along, 59–60, 70–71,
78, 116; in Frederick and Frederick
County, 34–35, 51; repaired, 61, 89,
115; telegraph along, 114, 165
Baltimore Pike, 57, 79, 121, 148, 167,
177, 189–91, 194, 196, 229, 231,
265, 272, 278, 280, 286, 314, 317,
324; Blacksmith Shop Road and,
208; Confederates and, 274, 313;
Eleventh Corps and, 192, 195; hospitals along, 200–201, 308; Meade
and headquarters on, 185–87,
306–7, 320, 327, 333, 336; protection of, 195, 218, 245, 266, 268,
408n38; right flank along, 204,
208; Rock Creek and, 186, 259;
Sixth Corps and, 167, 169–70, 216,
227; as supply and communications
line, 183, 197, 198, 203, 217, 274,
318–19; Twelfth Corps and, 153,
155, 157, 164, 203, 287; Union Mills
and, 110, 136; Westminster and,
273, 315
Barksdale, William, 11, 238, 240, 241,
252, 256, 258, 259, 283
Barlow, Francis C., 147–49, 192, 247
Barnes, James, 110, 232, 235, 242, 243,
245, 248, 249, 413n2
Barnesville, Md., 28–29, 32
Bartlett, Joseph J., 263, 264, 288, 304
Batchelder, Richard N., 199, 273,
383n34
Battle of Antietam, 3, 14, 55, 145, 154–
55, 164, 169, 248, 281, 325; Meade
at, 7–8, 13, 14

Battle of Chancellorsville, 4, 6, 18, 26, 37, 52, 55, 92, 145, 155, 164, 186, 218, 325, 381n21; Hooker and, 6, 13, 14, 17, 20, 25, 30; Lee and, 20–21; Meade and, 6, 8, 13. *See also* Chancellorsville Campaign

Battle of Fredericksburg, 3, 4, 19, 21, 32, 35, 39, 55, 145, 169, 186, 281; Meade at, 8, 166

Battle of Glendale, 2, 169; Meade wounded at, 7

Battle of South Mountain, 2–3, 34

Benjamin, Charles F., 41, 44, 46, 382n27

Berlin, Md., 78, 90, 105, 338, 371, *372*, 408n16, 431n1

Biddle, James Cornell, 223, 231, 281, 284, 295, 326, 413n2; as Meade's aide-de-camp, 52, 151

Bigelow, John, 241, 256–59, *257*, 381n21

Big Pipe Creek, 94, 136; as defensive line, 83–84, 104–5; Meade inspects, 117–18; Meade's army along, 76–77, 79, 90. *See also* Pipe Creek line

Birney, David Bell, 212, 216, *230*, 251, 276, 279–80, 357, 372; commands First Division, Third Corps, 159–61; commands Third Corps, 18, 21, 324, 335, 337, 353

blacksmiths, 61, 77, 167

Blacksmith Shop Road, Gettysburg, 208, 217, 253, 414n4, 416n20; farms on, 195–96, 200

Boonsboro, Md., 23, 47, 67, 329, 350, 353–54, 356, 358–59

Brewster, William R., 222, 239–41, 250–52

Bridgeport, Md., *84*, 90, 100, 105–6, *122*

Brown, T. Frederick, 250, 262, 287, 297, 301

Buford, John, *107*, 124, 147, 155, 165, 399n34; attacks by, 22, 346; dispatches and reports from, 82, 89, 90, 97, 105–6, 108, 111–15, 126–28,

138, 161–62, 393n19, 397n36; First Cavalry brigades of, 18, 29, 44, 66, 75, 99, 179, 184, 192, 212, 214, 304, 353; at Gettysburg, 97, 135, 153; at Lutheran seminary, 126, 129; orders to and movements of, 67, 76, 114, 125, 137, 214–15, 323, 399n35; reconnoiters Gettysburg to Cashtown, 95–97; Reynolds and, 125–27

Bull Run, Va., 7, 24. *See also* First Battle of Bull Run; First Manassas, battle of; Second Battle of Bull Run; Second Manassas, battle of

Bureau of Military Information, 19, *20*, 52, 80, 274, 283, 419n47. *See also* Babcock, John C.; McEntee, John; Sharpe, George H.

Burling, George C., 159, 202, 212, 223, 241

Burnside, Ambrose, 3–4, 8, 14, 19, 41, 46, 166

Butterfield, Daniel, 32, *33*, 47, 53, 96, 194, 203, 214, 295, 296, 324, 327; as chief of staff, 39, 41, 64, 80, 357; as Fifth Corps commander, 8, 32; at Leister house, 204, 276–79, 294, 327; Meade's relationship with, 64, 135, 138, 284, 335, 372; Oliver and, 166, 404n17; takes dictation, 55, 80, 139, 143, 165, 215, 408n16; at Taneytown, 142, 184

Cadwalader, Charles F., 52, 223, 387n1

Caldwell, John C., 193, 222, 245, *247*, 415n1; commands First Division, Second Corps, 143, 199, 248, 287, 292, 302; in Wheatfield, 250–53, 255, 415n6

Calef, John F., 125, 129, 212

Camp of Transportation, 179, 280, 313–15, 330–32, 345, 423n26

Carlisle, Pa., 47, 48, 126, 387–88n7; Confederate army and, 61, 65, 82, 112, 116, 117; roads to, 76, 121, 126

Carpenter, Emlen N., 52, 387n1

Carr, Joseph B., 222, 240, 250, 252

clothing: Army of the Potomac lacks, 5, 44, 58, 88, 174, 345; blankets and, 58, 201, 273, 284; supplies of, 59, 63, 89, 173, 175, 176. *See also* shoes

coal, supplies of, 44, 58, 63, 175, 176

Coburn, J. P., 178, 314, 343, 393n12

Coddington, Edwin, 165, 218, 325, 340–41, 363, 370, 382n27, 395n3, 426n23; on Meade's orders to Reynolds, 99–100

Codori, Nicholas, house of, 128, 202–3, 222, 228, 250, 261–62, 416n11

Colgrove, Silas, 259, 264, 417n33

Confederacy, 11, 62; Confederate sympathizers and, 62, 83, 109–10, 366

Couch, Darius N., 17, 60, 71, 91; commands Department of the Susquehanna, 25, 66, 72, 113, 339; commands Second Corps, 18, 21, 145; dispatches from, 61, 65, 387n7, 422n16; Meade and, 18, 58; Meade's messages to, 88–89, 138, 162, 323, 325, 369

couriers and dispatch riders, 63, 112, 127, 142, 146, 157, 171, 217, 280, 389n17; express riders as, 61, 182–83, 319, 389n17; Halleck and, 62, 72, 164–65; Meade's, 53, 72, 89, 138, 140, 148, 164–65, 170

Crampton's Gap, Md., 2, 356, 358

Crawford, Samuel W., 196, 253, *254*, 255, 303, 304, 381n13, 416n20; Pennsylvania Reserves division of, 43, 110

Creagerstown, Md., 64, 67, 332, 333, 336

Crounse, L. L., 76, 146, 427n29

Culpeper, Va., 21, 22, 24, 26

Culp's Hill, 121, 189, 274, *272*, *287*, 288; Baltimore Pike and, 280, 315; Confederates hold, 150, 280, 286, 308; defenses of, 203–4, 278, *279*; Greene's brigade on, 251, 270–72; Hancock on, 153, 155, 157; Slocum on, 185, 186, 191, 196; Wadsworth's

and Williams's Divisions on, 188, 192

Cumberland Valley, 97, 176, 311, 323, 330, 338–39, 356, 387n7; Lee's army in, 24, 47, 48, 56, 67, 85, 96, 97

Cumberland Valley Turnpike, 313, 324, 330, 346

Curtin, Andrew, 24, 47, 116

Cushing, Alonzo H., 146, 262, 287, 290, 293, 297, 301–2

Custer, George Armstrong, 67, 303, 329, 366

Cutler, Lysander, 124, 130–31, 271

Dawes, Rufus R., 73, 149, 271, 343

Department of the Susquehanna, 25, 66, 339, 350, 387n7

Devil's Den, 122, 220, 227, 234, 235, 255, 292, 413n1

Devin, Thomas C., 67, 99, 126, 147, 179, 192, 323

Dickinson, Joseph, as senior aide to Meade, 52, 387n1

Doubleday, Abner, 8, 95, 131, *132*, 119, 142, 165, 186, 381n7; commands First Corps, 94, 133, 192, 193, 261, 262; Meade and, 165–66, 372; Reynolds and, 124, 130, 133, 400n57; Slagle as aide to, 317, 400n56; troops of, break under Confederate attacks, 146–48, 161, 162, 405n34

Double Pipe Creek, 73, 75, 83

Downsville, Md., 353–54, 360, *361*, *362*, 364–66, 429n14

draft for Union army, 4, 371, 380n16; riots over, 431n1

Dranesville, Va., 13, 29, 32

Early, Jubal Anderson, 89, 90; division of, 22, 48, 65, 148, 266, 328; at Gettysburg, 148, 150, 117; movements of, 76, 78, 117, 388n7

Edwards Ferry, Potomac River, 28, 29, 32, 43, 59, 71, 383n34

Eighty-Second New York, 250, 262, 416n11

Elementary Treatise on Advance-Guard ..., An (Mahan, 1861), 102, 399n40

Eleventh Corps, Army of the Potomac (Howard; Schurz), 13, 21, 44, 100–101, 119, 127, 139, 164, 165, 271, 313, 350, 353, 390n10; artillery of, 186, 204, 266, 268, 294; casualties of, 149, 403n37; on Cemetery Hill, 157, 159, 161, 162, 188, 189, 192, 194, 195, 203, 266; Emmitsburg and, 71, 75, 106, 337; forage and stores received by, 317–18, 423n26; Hill attacks, 147, 148; hospital and wounded of, 200–201, 308, 310; Howard commands, 276, 363; on left wing, 94, 143; movement of, 25, 28, 29, 32, 43, 48, 56, 146, 341; numbers of, 70, 129; orders to, 64, 129, 136, 308, 331–32, 356, 359, 399–400n47; position of, 143, 147, 157, 202; reconnaissance in force by, 101–2, 105; retreat of, 149, 153, 155, 167; Second Division of, 192–93, 261; as support for First Corps, 90, 98, 114–15, 123, 127, 152, 395n4, 395n5; at Turner Pass, 250, 258, 387n7; wagon trains of, 123, 146, 178. *See also* Howard, Oliver Otis; Schurz, Carl; *and names of units of*

Emmitsburg, Md., 63, 70, 71, *88*, 90, 94, 96, 97, 106, 109–10, 118–19, 123, 136–39, 143; Buford's cavalry and, 67, 95, 192; Carrick's Knob and, 14, 94; Eleventh Corps and, 79, 112, 390n10; falling back to, 100, 104–5, 124, 127, 133, 400n57; First Corps and, 64, 69, 72–76, 79, 98, 390n10; Howard at, 111, 114, 123; left flank at, 87, 92, 172; during pursuit of Lee, 323, 325, 329, 331–32, 337, 341–43; roads to, 57, 85, 94, 177; signal station at, 151, 195, 393n14; telegraph and, 87, 92; Third Corps and, 79, 112, 129, 140, 147–48, 159–60, 162, 171–72, 212, 393n12

Emmitsburg-Gettysburg Road, 57, 108, 112, 119, 121, 127–28, 155, 160, 202–3, 213–15, 222–23, 238–40, 258, 337, 390n10, 399–400n47, 413n1, 416n11; Buford's cavalry on, 95, 192; Confederate line and, 304, 308; Eleventh Corps on, 94, 123; First Corps on, 92–96, 129; First Division, First Corps on, 122–23; at Gettysburg, 123, 207, 210–13, 229, 231; Humphreys's division and, 220, 227–28, 244, 250–52; Marsh Creek and, 95, 105, 160; Pickett's Charge and, 299–300; Third Corps and, 157, 241, 244, 252, *264*; Union counterattack on, 262–63

Engelbrecht, Jacob, 70, 88, 346

engineers, 115, 179, 184, 186, 329, 332; civil, 7, 102, 180, 388n8; Confederate, 329, 353–54, 366; wagon trains of, 64, 70, 75, 77, 79, 87. *See also* Haupt, Herman; pontoon bridges; topographical engineers; United States Battalion of Topographical Engineers

Eustis, Henry L., 263, 264, 288

Ewell, Richard S., 65, 76, 78, 147, 388n7; advancing in force on Meade's right, 138, 146–48; Early's Division under, 150, 266, 328; at Gettysburg, 126–27, 139, 149–50, 155, 164, 196, 308, 328; Heth's Division under, 146; Johnson's Division under, 150, 270; reported locations and movement of, 47, 48, 56, 62, 82, 88–90, 108, 112, 137, 138, 148, 162, 193, 408n16; Rodes's Division under, 150, 329; Second Corps of, 20–26, 61, 104, 116, 329, 365; wagon trains of, 310, 328, 330

Fairfield, Pa., 106, 121, 328, 337, 341; Buford's cavalry at, 67, 75–76, 82, 95, 105; Gettysburg road to, 160–61, 308, 310–11, 334; Lee's retreat and, 323, 324, 330, 332–35, 338–39,

Fredericksburg, Va., 3, 4, 21, 22, 24, 26. *See also* Battle of Fredericksburg

French, William H., 140, 176, 311–12, 329, 346, 355, 357, 363–64, *365*, 422n16, 425n11; Harper's Ferry and, 28, 173; Meade and, 62–63, 72–73, 115–18, 140

Frey, Peter, 199, 200, 282, 283

Frizzellburg, Md., 110, 112, 137, 151–52; roads to, 57, 83; Second Corps and, 64, 71, 136, 139

Funkstown, Md., *353, 355,* 359–60

Furst, Luther, 317, 341, 359, 367

Gamble, William, 67, 99, 129–30, 147, 179, 192, 323, 399n34; fights on Chambersburg Pike, 96, 125–26, 129

Geary, John W., 157, 185, 188, 204, 272, 286; Sickles and, 194, 208, 210, 224, 412n41

Gettysburg, Pa., 86, 119, 179–80; Chambersburg-York turnpike and, 56, 77–78, 82, 120, 121; churches in, 119–20; Confederate troops in, 61, 65, 95, 106, 108, 139, 149, 155; Emmitsburg Road to, 94, 95; hotels and stores in, 121, 134; as Lee's potential destination, 48, 82, 90, 116–17, 135; railroads and, 121; refugees from, 125, 160, 181; road network and, 56–57, 76, 84, 120–21, 165; schools in, *120,* 120; Sharpe's scouts at, 76, 80; snipers in, 185; streets of, 121, 138, 148–49, 185; terrain and topography of, 100, 121–22. *See also* Adams County, Pa.; maps; *and names of cemeteries, roads, houses, buildings, farms, and topographical features of*

Gibbon, John, 8, 9, 199, 281, *282,* 374, 413n1; at Cemetery Ridge, 193, 250, 258, 261–62, 287, 299, 301, 416n11; commands Second Corps, 143; commands Second Division, Sec-ond Corps, 91, 292, 381n7; Hancock's orders to, 157, 268; at Leister house, 276–81, 282, 284; on march, 152–53; Meade and, 50, 91, 184, 291; wounding of, 302, 305, 324. *See also* Second Corps, Army of the Potomac

Gilsa, Leopold von, 195, 266, 269

Glendale, Va.: battle of, 2, 169; Meade wounded at, 7

God, 110; Meade refers to, 66, 81, 224, 302, 320

Graham, Charles K., 220, 238–41, 251, 274

Granite Schoolhouse Road, 147, 196, 199, 200, 413n2

Grant, Ulysses S., 11, 346

Greencastle, Pa., 28, 56, 62, 80, 106

Greene, George S., 157, 194, 245, 251, 268, 270–72, *271*

Gregg, David McMurtrie, 76, 179, 192, 215, 329, 337; Division of, 18, 22, 29, 44, 67, 78, 79, 137, 303, 323; reports on Stuart's location, 82–83

Gregg, J. Irvin, 323, 338, 350

Guelzo, Allen, 101, 165–66, 284–85, 395n5

Haas, Jacob W., 334, 341–42

Hagerstown, Md., 48, 61, 62, 67, 356; Ewell's infantry at, 24, 365; Lee at, 72; Lee's defenses at, 353–54, *362,* 376; during Lee's retreat, 327–28, 330, 338–41, 346, 352, 425n11; Longstreet and, 47, 48, 56, 76; Meade advances on, 359–60; Union cavalry at, 44, 67

Hagerstown-Sharpsburg Turnpike, 354, 358–359

Hall, James A., 95, 123, 129, 131

Hall, James S., 145, 204, 215–16, 327

Halleck, Henry W., *16,* 17, 108, 113, 412n41; French and, 115–16; as general in chief, 14, 38; Hardie's communication with, 39, 41, 49;

Herr Ridge, 125–26, 129, 131, 215, 310, 328, 399n34, 411n27

Heth, Henry, 78, 129, 146, 150

Hewitt, Catherine (Kate), 92, 381n22

Hill, Ambrose Powell, 3, 161; Buford's cavalry and, 127–29; at Cashtown Pass, 88, 92, 104, 112; Chambersburg and, 82, 104, 108, 117, 137; at Gettysburg, 126, 139, 147–48, 164, 251; movement of, 48, 62, 78, 138; Third Corps of, 20, 21, 24, 26, 56, 76, 112, 155, 297, 328, 330, 366, 388n7, 408n16. *See also* Third Corps, Army of Northern Virginia

historiography, 99–101, 165–66

Hood, John Bell, 21, 62, 150, 234, 236, 292, 304, 308, 328

Hooker, Joseph ("Fighting Joe"), 6, *15*, 20, 21, 35, 46, 58, 59, 62, 73, 117; Battle of Chancellorsville and, 13, 164; briefs Meade on Lee's forces, 43–44, 47–48; commands Army of the Potomac, 4, 18, 39, 41, 49; friends and allies of, 30, 32; gathers intelligence, 19, 22, 26, 28, 48; Halleck and, 26–27; headquarters of, 21, 25, 27, 29, 34, 39, 47, 50, 52; leave taking of, 50, 51, 70–71; Lincoln and Halleck meet with, 14, 17, 28; protects Washington, *23*, 25; reorganizes cavalry, 66–67; resignation of, 30, 49; Stoneman and, 18, 383n33; wounded at Antietam, 8, 14

horses, 123, 173, 175, 383n33; for ambulance wagons, 200, 319; breaking down of, 196, 280, 307, 341, 350, 367, 389n17; captured by Lee's army, 24, 48, 62, 312, 329, 352; couriers and express riders and, 61, 127, 164, 182–83, 217, 319, 389n17; feed and forage for, 5, 176, 198, 201, 279–80, 312–18, 322–23, 325, 345, 423n26; losses and resupply of, 5, 234, 238, 239–42, 251–52, 256–57, *257*, 264, 293–95, *296*, 299,

300–303, *302*, 307, 344–45, 353; need for, 44, 353; officers,' 118, 124, 130–31, *131*, 146, 153, 207–8, 220, 225–26, 282, 286, 337; shoes for, 124–25, 167, 197, 214, 345. *See also* Old Baldy

hospitals, 133–34, 198–201, 233, 308, 318–19, 322, 339, 401n58; Confederate, 310, 312, 335; of Eleventh Corps, 147, 201, 308; of Second Corps, 273, 282–83, 306. *See also* ambulance wagons; medical service

Howard, Oliver Otis, 13, 95, 97, 102, 105, 126, 135, 148, *156*, 165, 318, 398n26, 409n21; attends war councils, 279, 324–25, 363–64; on Cemetery Hill, 189, 191–92, 268, 271, 393n5, 403n8, 408n12; commands Eleventh Corps, 18, 21, 43, 64, 70, 75, 79, 90, 276, 387n7; injuries of, 154, 187; on Lee's army, 47–48, 56; Meade and, 50–51, 184–85; orders to, 114, 308, 332; in pursuit of Lee, 332, 337, 350–51, 353, 359; Reynolds and, 91–92, 106, 111, 123, 129, 147, 399–400n47; as senior officer on field, 143, 147, 153; Wentzes' place and, 101, 123. *See also* Eleventh Corps, Army of the Potomac

Huey, Pennock, 179, 323, 329

Humphreys, Andrew Atkinson, *53*, 53, *54*, 55, 222, *365*, 374; as chief topographical engineer, 39, 55; commands Second Division, Third Corps, 53, 159; examines Lee's Downsville line, 362, 364; at Gettysburg, 227–28; on march to Gettysburg, 160, 161; as Meade's chief of staff, 55, 327, 357, 363, 387n4; opposes attacking Lee's defenses, 370, 373

Hunt, Henry Jackson, 55, *86*, 137, 208, 297, 317, 344, *365*; as chief of artillery, 184, 373; on Gettysburg, 203, 214; makes inspections,

184, 192, 212, 215, 228; Confederate attack on, 215–18, 228, 231, 264;
Emmitsburg and, 159, 172; moves
on Gettysburg, 119, *122*, 122–25;
reinforcement of, 231, 245, 263,
270, 288, 413n2, 416n20; Reynolds
as commander of, 92, 109; Sickles
and, 210, 226–27, 231; vulnerability
of, 161, 176

Leister, Lydia, 190–91, 199, 210
Leister house, as Meade's Gettysburg
headquarters, 190–95, *191*, 199,
204–6, 210–12, 216–20, 224, 273–
76, 281–86, 290–97, *296*, 300–301,
306, 325, 413n4, 418n21
Letterman, Johnathan, 198–99, 315,
332
Lewistown, Md., 64, 67, 69, 331, 342
Liberty, Md., 64, 67, 69, 70, 74, 75, 90,
390n10
Lincoln, Abraham, 30, 32, 80, 331,
339; Halleck and, 17, 355, 382n27;
Hooker and, 4, 14, 25–29, 35, 62;
McClellan and, 3, 81, 113; Meade
and, 37, 41, 143, 186, 334, 340, 346–
47, 354–55, 359, 364–65, 367–72,
426n23; politics and, 373, 375; as
president and commander in chief,
1, 2, 38
Linn, Joe, 73, 74, 391n21
Little Round Top, 121–22, 188, 192,
194, 195, 203–4, *225*, *226*, *235*, 242,
255, 310; base of, 194, 208, 220,
234, 288, 334; Chamberlain at,
235–36; eastern slope of, 232, 233;
north slope of, 157, 185, 226, 253,
263, 292, 304; occupied, 157, 194,
229, 412–13n43; Sickles and, 202,
207, 210–11, 223–24, 412n41; signal
station on, 214–16, 411n27; southern slope of, 235–36; Warren and,
227, 233, 292; Weikert farm and,
161, 200, 233
Littlestown, Pa., 67, 76, 83, 90, 96, 151,
170, 341; roads to, 57, 141, 142, 177;

Slocum's Twelfth Corps and, 79, 97,
100, 105, 108, 109, 112, 337, 341
Littlestown (York) Turnpike, 87, 146,
151
Locke, Frederick T., 37, 43, 245,
385n27
Longstreet, James: commands First
Corps, 20–22, 26, 62, 150; at
Gettysburg, 161, 196, 214, 234,
238, 251, 284, 292, 297, 304, 308,
412n41; during Lee's retreat, 310,
328, 330, 366; locations and movement of, 24, 47, 56, 62, 76, 78, 82,
88, 90, 92, 112, 117, 150, 155, 164,
388n7, 408n16. *See also* First Corps,
Army of Northern Virginia
Ludlow, Benjamin C., 52, 223, 227–
28
Lutheran Theological Seminary,
Gettysburg, *120*, 120, 126, 133–34,
150, 399n47

Mackenzie, Ranald S., 223, 226–27,
301, 360
Mahan, Dennis Hart, 102–3, 105, 127,
321, 395n7, 399n40
Manassas Junction, Va., 21, *23*, 27
Manchester, Md., 81, 90, 109–10, 112,
118, 136–40, 144, 151, 159, 166,
176–77, 205; Big Pipe Creek and,
83, 138; Confederate sympathizers
in, 109–10; roads to, 57, 177; Sixth
Corps and, 79, 100, 158
maps, 43, 64; of Adams County, Pa.,
100, 101, 106, 122–23, 145–46, 208,
212, 215, 388n8; of Carroll County,
Md., 79, 388n8, 391n21, 396n29; of
Frederick County, Md., 57, 388n8;
of Gettysburg battle, 221, 246, 267,
298, 309; of Lee's retreat and pursuit, 336, 342, 361; Paine sketches,
185, 188, 207; of pre-battle movements, 23, 75, 84, 122, 158; used by
Meade and Reynolds, 56, 57, 64,
122, 165

Marsh Creek, 105, 110, 112, 119, 121, 123, 129, 150, 160–61, 171, 308, 393n19; First Corps and, 79, 90, 95, 96; Reynolds at, 108, 111, 122, 124

Martinsburg, Va. (now W. Va.), 22, 24, 25, 28, 44

Marye's Heights, Fredericksburg, Va., 3, 11, 13, 169, 186

Maryland, 37, 44, 47, 88, 101, 113, 119, 121, 167, 388n8; Army of Northern Virginia in, 4, 7, 24, 25, 48, 312, 348; Lee's 1862 campaign in, 2–3, 35, 145, 186

Maryland Heights, 24, 28, 29, 72, 117, 312

Mason, Addison G., 52, 223, 387n1

Maulsby, William P., 34, 196, 259

McClellan, George B., 3, 46, 55, 145, 166; as commander of Army of the Potomac, 7, 41; Meade and, 6, 8, 380–81n7; Peninsula Campaign of, 1–2, 35; rumors of, 73, 81, 113, 171

McDougall, Archibald L., 259, 264, 417n33

McDowell, Irvin, 1, 3, 281

McEntee, John, 19, 20, 52

McGilvery, Freeman, 239, 241, 256–57, 259, 264

McIntosh John B., 337–39

McKnight's Hill (Stevens Knoll), 121, 155, 188, 268–70, 269

McLaws, Lafayette, 21, 62, 238, 292, 304, 308, 328

McPherson, Edward, 125, 130, 134, 152

McPherson Ridge, 125, 126, 130, 399n34

Meade, George Gordon

—as commander, Army of the Potomac, 41, 49, 51, 117; concentrates his forces at Gettysburg, 162, 164; Hooker briefs, 43–44, 47–48; Howard and, 184–85; informs Halleck of situation at Gettysburg, 164–65; inspires troops, 89, 111, 160; leaves for Gettysburg, 183–84; logistics and, 173–83; makes his

original dispositions at Gettysburg, 185–86, 188; obeys orders to be, 4, 35, 37–38, 65; operational command of, 98, 105, 149; Pipe Creek Circular of, 135–41, 165, 166, 176; plans to draw Lee into battle, 63–64; receives intelligence on Lee's army, 48, 79–80, 82, 89–90; responds to Reynolds, 96–97; shares intentions and plans with Halleck, 71–72; strategy of, 79–81, 85, 87, 99, 100, 118; studies maps, 56, 57, 64, 79, 83, 142, 159

—criticisms of: as lacking moral courage, 4; of pursuit of Lee after Gettysburg, 5, 334, 339–40, 346–47, 354–55, 359, 364–65, 367–73, 426n23; by reporters, 6; because of resentment, 73; as short tempered, 9; as timid, 64

—headquarters of, 50, 53; aides-de-camp of, 52, 387n1; at Arcadia, 34, 37; on Baltimore Pike, 306–7; chief of staff of, 39, 41; escort of, 73, 77, 87, 183–84; at Koons's farm near Middleburg, 77, 80, 82, 83; at Piney Creek, 87, 114, 135, 142, 165, 173, 184; staff officers of, 9, 19, 39, 41, 46, 52–53, 53, 73, 83, 117, 142, 151, 183–84; at Taneytown, 79, 87, 90, 96, 114, 136; tent of, 141, 142, 159; train of, 71, 77, 79, 87, 184

—military career of, 6–7, 17, 46; as capable tactical commander, 5, 51; commands Fifth Corps, 18, 21, 28, 52; confidence of officers in, 50, 91; horses of, 12, 12–13, 39, 53, 71, 220, 225–26, 262, 263, 270, 273, 292, 303, 417n44; at West Point, 7, 46, 102

—personal life of: African American servant of, 52–53, 274; corresponds with wife, 6, 8, 18, 32, 53, 65, 66, 81, 112–13, 348; early life of, 6–7; fluency of, in French, 9; politics and, 12; siblings of, 7, 11–12; wife and children of, 11

Meade, George Gordon (*continued*)
—physical appearance and personal characteristics of, 8–9, *10*, 39, 50, 73, 142, 186, 188, 277–78; abstemiousness of, 274; agitation of, 138; carefulness of, 101; constitution of, 173; coolness of, 295; decisiveness of, 166; as devout Christian and family man, 11, 12, 66, 81, 113, 224, 302, 320; dutifulness of, 4; eyesight of, 8, 278; harshness of, 6; Howard on, 50–51; modesty of, 9; sense of responsibility of, 113; vigor of, 76; wounds of, 7
Meade, George (Meade's son), 11, 39, 52, 295, 348, 412n43, 417n44; horses killed, 300–301, 303, 337; as Meade's aide-de-camp, 52, 302; Sickles and, 206–8, 223
Meade, Margaretta ("Margaret") Sergeant (Meade's wife), 11, 66; Meade writes to, 6, 8, 18, 32, 53, 65, 66, 81, 112–13; sister of, 11–12
Mechanicstown, Md., 64, 67, 69, 148, 331, 341, 350, 351; Buford's reserve brigade at, 76, 97
medical service, 133, 315; medical directors and, 147, 198–99, 201; medical evacuation and, 134, 198–99, 201; medical supplies and, 273, 312–14, 332, 401; wagon trains of, 70, 75, 77, 87, 201, 313, 318. *See also* ambulance wagons
Meigs, Montgomery, *60*, 65, 344; Haupt and, 183, 406n7; Ingalls and, 59, 63, 65, 175–77, 307, 345, 406n7; Meade and, 63, 88; as U.S. Army quartermaster general, 59, 63
Meredith, Solomon, commands Iron Brigade, 130, 131, 271
Merritt, Wesley, 66, 67, 137, 192, 304, 323
Mexican War, 13, 35, 41, 46, 55, 92, 145, 167; Meade in, 7
Middleburg, Md., 64, 67, 75, 77, 79, 109, 118, 123, 136, 138, 332, 391n21;

confluence of Pipe creeks at, 83; Meade's headquarters near, 72, 73, 80, 82, 83; roads to, 57, 74, 85, 87, 177, 390n10, 393n11; telegraph and, 137, 151
Middle Creek (Emmitsburg, Md.), 94, 96, 106
Middletown, Md., 43–44, 77, 136, 323, 329, 331–33, 338, 340–41; cavalry at, 44, 67; Eleventh Corps at, 29, 32, 48; during pursuit of Lee, 343–45, 348, 350–54, 356–58, *358*; roads to, 56, 332
Millerstown Road, 160–61, 212, 239
Milroy, Robert H., 22, 24, 329
Mitchell, Lieutenant, on Hancock's staff, 297, 300, 303
Mitchell, William G., 145–46, 157–58, 162, 165
Monocacy Junction, Md., 34, 44, 56, 70
Monocacy River, 71, 83, 89, 94, 121, 140; mouth of, 28, 29, 32, 43, 70
Monterey Gap, 67, 329, 335, 338–39, 340. *See also* Monterey Pass
Monterey Pass, 94, 106, 110, 310, 313, 323, 340. *See also* Monterey Gap
Moore, Alexander, 211, 220, 255
Moritz's Tavern, 96, 105, 111, 115, 119
mud, 5, 152, 274, 276, 335; Burnside's Mud March and, 3–4; marching through, 28, 29, 71, 88, 160, 174, 341, 343, 351–53, 366; Meade and, 39, 41
mules, 1, 44, 56; captured by Confederates, 24, 59; feed and forage for, 173, 175, 196–97, 198, 201, 279–80, 31–13, 322, 345; pack trains of, 177–78, 198, 281, 317–19; pull wagon trains, 197, *318*, 319, 352, 383n34, 406n10
Mummasburg, Pa., 82, 89, 96, 105, 121, 124
Mummasburg Road, 121, 126, 147
music, musicians, 69, 160, 169, 273, 276, 281, 283, 306; drummers, 95, 119, 128, 170, 193; fifers, 73, 190

Musser, George, 195, 324; farm of, 200, 424n48

National Road, 44, 46, 59, 61, 182, 323, 331, 338, 350, 353, 356, 389n17, 390n10
Neill, Thomas H., 263, 286, 324, 337, 339, 341
Nevin, David J., 263–64, 304, 350
New Jersey, 7, 19, 25, 81, 113
newspapers, 14, 47; of Gettysburg, 119; on Meade, 6, 76; reporters and correspondents of, 71, 140–41, 113. See also *Cincinnati Gazette*; *New York Times*; *and names of reporters and correspondents*
Newton, John, 186, *187*, 191, 262–63, 282, 291–92, 407n31, 417n44; career of, 186; commands First Corps, 165–66, 167, 261, 276, 363, 404n17, 405n34; in councils of war, 276–77, 278, 324; in pursuit of Lee, 335, 337, 350, 353, 359
New Windsor, Md., 58, 64, 75, 78, 83, 91, 112; mills in, 76; Sixth Corps and, 70, 71, 73, 90; Third Brigade of Third Cavalry Division ordered to, 67
New York, 14, 35, 37, 39, 46, 92, 164; emergency troops raised in, 25, 81, 113; state militia of, 19
New York City, 14, 19, 30, 222–23, 248, 344; draft riots in, 371, 380n16, 431n1
New York Times, 47; reporters and correspondents of, 71, 76, 113, 140, 146, 294, 306, 427n29
Ninety-Sixth Pennsylvania, Sixth Corps, 334–35, 341–42, 350
Ninth Massachusetts Battery (Bigelow), 241, 256, 257
Northern Central Railroad, 58, 61, 65, 88, 91, 116, 121, 181, 175, 314, *315*, 330
Norton, Lemuel B., 151, 194–95, 223, 403n2

Oak Hill, 121, 308, 328
Old Baldy, *12*, 12, 13, 39, 71, 184, 220, 226; shot in stomach, 263, 337
Oliver, Paul A., 166–67, 169, 177, 223, 24–45, 378, 404n17
One Hundred Forty-First Pennsylvania, 178, 220, 238, 314
One Hundred Forty-Sixth New York, 232, 233, 304
On War (Clausewitz, 1832), 102, 399n40
ordnance: deficiencies of, 192, 280; officers of, 202, 314, 319–20; supplies and stores of, 44, 56, 58, 176, 181, 285; wagons for, 19, 24, 69, 123, 310–11, 328–29, 330–31
O'Rorke, Patrick, 232–33, 236

Paine, W. H., 184–85, 188, 207, 220
Parker, I. B., 145, 161, 165, 300
Patrick, Marsena Rudolph, *53*, 74, 317; as provost marshal general, 19, *45*, 46, 73
Patterson, William, farm of, 199, 200, 283
Peach Orchard, 202–3, 210–11, 228, 229, 231, 253, 256, 258, 293; Confederate barrage on, 225, 238; Graham's brigade in, 220, 238–41, 251; Humphreys's division and, 220, 222; Sickles and, 220, 223, 225, 238–39, 244, 252, 413n1; Wentz's house and, 123, 202; withdrawal from, 241–42
Pender, William D., 112, 148, 150
Peninsula Campaign, Va., 1–2, 7, 14, 35, 39, 55, 145, 154, 164, 169, 186, 218, 325
Pennsylvania, 24, 25, 198; Cumberland Valley of, 47, 56; emergency troops for, 81, 113; governor of, 47, 116; Lee invades and plunders, 4, 48, 61–62, 312, 347; state line of, 95, 109, 112, 152
Pennsylvania Reserves, 43, 110, 170,

196, 255, 304; Meade as commander of, 7, 8, 253, 381n7

Pettigrew, J. Johnston, 297, 366, 388

Pfanz, Harry, 99–100, 395n3

Philadelphia, 53, 88, 151, 214, 248, 281, 344; Haupt and, 116, 179, 314, 428n52; Meade's connections to, 6, 11; relief of, 80, 91, 112–13

Phillips, Charles A., 241, 242, 257

Pickett, George E.: charge of, 284, 297, *298*, 299–300, *300*; division of, 21, 62, 78, 283, 308, 328

Piney Creek, Md., Meade's headquarters at, 87, 114, 135, 142, 165, 173, 184

Pipe Creek Circular, 135–41, 165–66, 176

Pipe Creek line, 83, 84, 99, 101, 136; Hunt on, 85, 87; idea abandoned, 142, 162, 166, 172; Meade's intended defense of, 118, 159, 177. *See also* Big Pipe Creek

Pleasonton, Alfred, 22, 66, *68*, 78, 323, 339; Buford and, 96, 105, 125–26, 214–15, 399n35; commands cavalry corps, 18, 21, 357; in councils of war, 324, 363; headquarters of, 21, 77, 137; Meade and, 65, 67, 220, 226, 286, 291, 303–4, 327, 333, 346, 372

Plum Run, 253, 255, 258, 263, 288

Point of Rocks, Md., 29, 32, 34–35, 71

pontoon bridges, 3, 22, 28; wagon trains for, 70, 75, 77, 79, 87–88, 108

Poolesville, Md., 28, 32, 44, 59, 63, 70; Hooker's headquarters at, 29, 34

Pope, John, 2, 3, 7, 181

Port Gibson, Miss., 11, 381n17

Potomac River, 24, 25, 32, 34, 44, 72, 332, 338, 339, 355, 360, 366, 426n23; Army of the Potomac crosses, 28–29, 43, 307, 373, 383n34; bridges across, 329, 352, 354–55, *372*; Downsville and, 353, 364; Fitzhugh Lee crosses, 59,

65; Lee crosses, 2, 48; Lee moves toward, 21, 28, 340; Lee recrosses, 3, 5, 48, 325, 333, 335, 357; Point of Rocks and, 29, 71; Sandy Hook and, *356*, 371; Williamsport and, 313, 322, 330, 346, 352, 354

Powers Hill, Gettysburg, 121, 194, 195, 224, 296, 300, 306

prisoners of war, 274, 283, 305, 311; Confederates as, 19, 82, 90, 112, 301, 314, *316*, 319, 366, 368; intelligence provided by, 19, 90, 196; officers as, 7, 131, 149, 192, 240, 325; Union, 3, 24, 149, 262, 308, 328–29

Prospect Hall, Frederick County, Md., *34*, 34, 39, 44, 47, 66

Provost Guards, 73, 74, 77, 110, 292

provost marshal, 19, 46, 48, 50, 73, 77. *See also* Patrick, Marsena Rudolph

quartermaster general of U.S. Army, 59, *60*, 63, 88, 175–77, 307, 344; assistant, 198, 345; department of, 13, 61. *See also* Meigs, Montgomery

quartermaster officers, 141, 145, 178–79, 197, 199, 200, 314, 317–19; of Eleventh Corps, 147, 201; of First Corps, 133, 201; regimental, 69, 317. *See also* quartermaster and subsistence stores; wagons

quartermaster and subsistence stores, 19, 44, 57, 59, 69, 88, 123, 157, 175–79, 280, 285, 331; captured or foraged by Lee's army, 48, 78; Confederate, 62, 310–12, 328–30, 352; Fifth Corps, 110, 166; First Corps, 123, 133; at Frederick, 345, 356; rail transport of, 181, 330; Third Corps, 202, 314; at Union Bridge and Westminster, 197, 201, 330; wagon trains of, 24, 124, 166, 198, 313. *See also* Camp of Transportation; Union Bridge, Md.; wagons; Westminster, Md.

railroads, 7, 37, 55, 72, 85, 116, 121, 177, 181, 314; army supply by, 44, 58, 63, 181, 330; Baltimore and, 58, 72, 85, 91, 173; bridges for, 61, 140; Frederick and, 51, 70, 344, 383n34; Harrisburg and, 61, 84, 121, 126; repair of, 175, 176, 179, 182–83, 406n7; Stuart destroys, 24, 78; Union Bridge and, 58, 72–74, 76, 83, 91, 123, 175, 316. *See also* Haupt, Herman; *and names of individual railroad companies*

Randolph, George E., 206–8, 224, 239, 241

Rappahannock River, 3, 4, 6, 14, 17, 21, 22, 164

reconnaissance in force, Reynolds's Gettysburg mission as, 97–102, 104, 135

Reese, Chauncey Barnes, 223, 226–28

refugees from Gettysburg, 125, 160, 181

Reid, Whitelaw, 71, 140; on Army of the Potomac headquarters, 141–42; Gettysburg and, 146, 206, 286, 290, 306; on Meade, 142, 186–87

Relay (Washington Junction), Md., 37, 44, 50, 70, 71, 140, 176, 181; telegraph lines through, 60–61, 72, 89, 182, 389n17

Revised Regulations of the Army of the United States (Mahan, 1861), 102, 104, 396n16, 401n58

Reynolds, John Fulton, 28, 48, 56, 73, *93*, 102, 110, 111, 123, 129; as bachelor, 14, 92; Buford and, 96, 112; commands First Corps, 18, 21, 43, 64, 69, 71, 75, 79, 90; death of, 96, 98, *131*, 131, 133, 142, 146–49, 158, 160–61, 164; dispositions by, 96, 105–6; historians on, 99–101; Meade clarifies Gettysburg orders to, 97–99; Meade's conversation with, 46–47; Meade's orders and communications to, 94, 99, 100, 135; Meade's relationship with, 7, 8, 38, 92, 94, 97; orderlies of, 128,

133; sends news of movement of Lee's corps, 76, 82; staff officers of, 115, 126; to withdraw to Taneytown, 136, 138. *See also* First Corps, Army of the Potomac

Richmond, Va., as capital of Confederacy, 1, 2, 3, 13, 26

Riddle, William, 114–15, 130, 142, 402n19

right flank, right wing, of Army of the Potomac, 78, 79, 81; Slocum to command, 136–37, 139, 188

Robertson, Beverly H., 21, 24, 310

Robertson, Jerome B., 234, 235, 236

Robinson, John C., 95, 146–47, 155, 192–93, 261–62, 288

Rock Creek, 121, 186, 188, 192, 195, 200, 203, 208, 259, 306, 424n48, 426n23

Rockville, Md., 59, 72, 78

Rodes, Robert E., 62; Division of, 20, 22, 61, 76, 78, 82, 112; at Gettysburg, 147–48, 150; on retreat to Virginia, 329, 388

Roebling, Washington A., 223, 226, 232, 236, 274, 304, 350, 412n43

Rohrersville, Md., 356, 357, 358

Rorty, James MacKay, 258, 287, 301

Rosengarten, Joseph G., 126, 382n27, 399n35

Round Tops, Gettysburg, 121, 153–54, 157, 161, 184–85, 191, 193, 229, 279. *See also* Little Round Top

Rowley, Thomas A., 95, 106, 147, 155

Ruger, Thomas H., 188, 192, 203, 259, 261, 272, 286

rumor, rumors, 73, 80–81, 146

Sandy Hook, Md., 29, 34, 355–56, 360, 371, 431n1

sappers and pioneers, 128, 222, 354

Schenck, Robert C., 27–28, 59, 72, 78, 85, 140

Schimmelfennig, Alexander, 147–49

Schurz, Carl, 147, 149, 188, 192, 195, 308, 350

Scott, Winfield, 1, 7, 13, 14, 55, 167
scouts, 19, 64, 111, 354, 387n7;
    Buford's, 75, 82, 89, 112, 126;
    Sharpe's, 22, 28, 76, 80. *See also*
    Buford, John; Bureau of Military
    Information; Sharpe, George H.
Sears, Stephen, 323, 100–101, 340, 341,
    393n4
Second Battle of Bull Run (Second
    Bull Run), 2, 7, 14, 39, 164, 181,
    218. *See also* Second Manassas,
    battle of
Second Cavalry Division (Gregg), 18,
    22, 29, 44, 67, 76, 78–79, 137, 179,
    192, 303, 323, 329, 337. *See also*
    Gregg, David McMurtrie; *and
    names of officers and units of*
Second Corps, Army of Northern Vir-
    ginia (Ewell), 13, 20, 24–26, 61, 65,
    126
Second Corps, Army of the Potomac
    (Hancock; Gibbon), 13, 21, 25, 50,
    71, 109, 136, 140, 145; artillery bri-
    gade of, 146, 250, 258, 262, 266,
    287, 416n11; march of, 64, 74, 90,
    152; movement of, 28, 29, 32, 56,
    70; Taneytown and, 90, 106, 141; at
    Uniontown, 75, 90, 91, 100; wagon
    trains of, 178–79; *See also* Gibbon,
    John; Hancock, Winfield Scott;
    and names of officers and units of
Second Division (Geary), Twelfth
    Corps, 259, 270; on Culp's Hill, 194,
    204, 272, 286; on Little Round Top,
    157, 188, 192
Second Division (Gibbon), Second
    Corps, 50, 91, 297
Second Division (Humphreys), Third
    Corps, 53, 223, 240, 250; Emmits-
    burg Road and, 222, 227–28, 238,
    250, 252; left flank of, 25–51, 212,
    222, 244; line breaks, 252, 259;
    marches to Gettysburg, 159–61;
    pickets of, 201–2
Second Division (Robinson), First
    Corps, 95, 128–29, 133, 146–47

Second Maine Battery (Hall), 95, 123,
    129
Second Manassas, battle of, 13, 281.
    See also Second Battle of Bull Run
Secretary of War, 29, 38. *See also* Stan-
    ton, Edwin M.
Sedgwick, John, 14, 21, 22, 158, 167–
    69, *168*; aides to, 41, 69, 73; at
    Chancellorsville, 4, 13; Confederate
    cavalry spotted by, 59, 63; in coun-
    cils of war, 276–79, 324–25, 363;
    at Gettysburg, 263, 303; headquar-
    ters of, 158–59, 292; Hooker and,
    17–18; at Manchester, 109–10, 136,
    144, 158; Meade and, 18, 73–74,
    184, 216, 251, 292, 370; Meade's
    orders to, 64, 79, 90, 139, 162, 165,
    166–67, 169, 183, 263, 272, 332–34,
    336, 339, 404n17; Newton and,
    167, 186, 405n34; in pursuit of Lee,
    334–41, *336*; as right wing com-
    mander, 332; at West Point, 102,
    167. *See also* Sixth Corps, Army of
    the Potomac
Seeley, Francis W., 250, 251, 252
Seminary Ridge, 120–22, 131, 148, 321,
    328, 426n23; Confederate batteries
    along, 225–26, 292; Confederate
    line along, 150, 195–96, 202, 211–12,
    214, 227, 284, 308; Confederates
    advance from, 251, 297. *See also*
    Lutheran Theological Seminary
Seminole War, 7, 53, 55, 145, 281
Seven Days Battles, 2, 13, 39
Shaler, Alexander, 263, 286, 288
Sharpe, George H., *19*, 20, *275*, 295,
    297; Meade and, 52, 80, 274, 276,
    283–84, 418–19n21; scouts of, 22,
    28, 76. *See also* Bureau of Military
    Information
Sharpsburg, Md., 3, 24, 47, 356. *See
    also* Hagerstown-Sharpsburg
    Turnpike
sharpshooters, 202, 212, 288, 290,
    308
Shenandoah Valley, Va., 2, 22, 24

Shepherdstown, Va. (now W. Va.), 24, 28, 360

Sherfy, Joseph: house of, 123, 160–61, 202, 238–40, 400–401n47; Peach Orchard and, 202–3, 210–11, 220, 223, 228, 238, 293

shoes: Army of the Potomac lacks, 5, 44, 58, 88, 90, 173–74, 196, 345, 350–51; for horses, 124, 167, 175, 197, 214; supplied to Union troops, 69, 89, 176, 344

Sickles, Daniel E., *31*, 37, 108, 126, 128, 143, 148, 160, 171–72, 184, *209*, 220, 251–52; commands Third Corps, 43, 69, 74, 75, 79, 87, 90; Confederates attack, 225–27, 229, 231, 235, 241, 244; disobeys orders, 218, 229; fails to occupy Little Round Top, 185, 192, 194, 202, 206–8, 210–11, 216; forward position of, 217, *221*, 222, 238; Humphreys and, 159, 221–23, 227–28; Meade reprimands and admonishes, 74–75, 109, 159, 207, 223–24; Meade's orders to, 106, 129, 136, 147, 159, 162, 210; Meade's relationship with, 30, 32, 284, 372, 411–12n41; movement of, 64, 69, 75, 79, 90, 112; Slocum and, 183, 194, 207. *See also* Third Corps, Army of the Potomac; Tremain, Henry E.

Signal Corps: telegraph system and, 44–45, 87, 91, 92, 137, 151–52; wagon train of, 70, 75, 77, 87. *See also* Hall, James S.; Norton, Lemuel B.; signal stations

signal stations, 24, 70, 324; on Carrick's Knob, 94, 110; at Gettysburg, 126, 194–95, 204, 214–16, 284, 308, 310, 324, 327–28, 408n12, 411n27; semaphore and, 151, 194, 226; in Taneytown Lutheran Church steeple, 87, 393n14; in Turner Pass, 356, 387n7

Sixth Corps, Army of the Potomac (Sedgwick), 13, 18, 22, 44, 50, 63, 64, 69, 70, 78, 79, 91, 139, 165, 169, 176, 178, 186, 363; at Gettysburg, 245, 251, 263, 272, 286, 288, 297, 304, 310, 332–36, *336*, 417n46; Manchester and, 79, 90, 100, 109–10, 136–39, 166; marches to Gettysburg, 169–70, 183, 189, 205, 216, 227; movement of, 21, 25, 28–29, 32, 44, 56, 63, 71, 73, 75, 159, 390–91n10; New Windsor and, 71, 73, 78, 90; numbers of, 69, 70, 169; orders to, 64, 73–74, 79, 158, 166–67, 183, 184, 404n17; in pursuit of Lee, 339–41, 350, 353, 356, 358–59. *See also* Sedgwick, John; *and names of officers and units of*

Sixth Pennsylvania Cavalry, 52, 73, 223

Sixth Wisconsin, First Division, First Corps, 73, 131, 149

Sixty-Second Pennsylvania, Fifth Corps, 171, 243, 328

skirmishers, 126–27, 185, 190, 202, 214, 216, 282, 310, 321

Slagle, Jacob F., 133, 317, 400n56

Slocum, Henry Warner, 74, 102, 148, 161–64, *163*; commands Twelfth Corps, 17, 18, 21, 29, 44, 64, 70, 164; at Gettysburg, 164, 183–86, 188, 191, 194–95, 203, 259, 263, 276, 324–25; headquarters of, 137, 244, 296, 306; Meade's orders to, 79, 90, 108–9, 140, 148, 188, 204–5, 245, 272, 288, 332; movement of, 74, 75, 79, 90, 97, 108, 112, 140, 144; in pursuit of Lee, 337, 353, 359, 363, 370; as right wing commander, 136–37, 139, 188, 210; Sickles and, 183, 194, 207. *See also* Twelfth Corps, Army of the Potomac

Smith, James E., 37, 202, 212, 227, 234

Smith, William F., 323, 325, 339, 341, 351, 369

South Mountain range, 2–3, 28, 44, 57, 58, 78, 121; eastern base of, 75, 82, 94; Lee's army to west of, 47, 97;

passes through, 34, 85, 94; western base of, 67, 76

Spangler, George, farm of, as hospital, 147, 195, 200, 224, 308

Stahel, Julius, 29, 32, 47, 66, 387n7

Stannard, George J., 155, 178, 273, 287, 292, 300, 419–20n3

Stanton, Edwin M., 38, 382n27, 397n7; French and, 117, 118; Haupt and, 116–17, 179, 181; Hooker and, 17, 35, 62; as Meade critic, 379, 371; as secretary of war, 29, 30, 80, 118, 143, 183, 319. *See also* War Department

Steinwehr, Adolph von , 63, 192, 193; on Cemetery Hill, 147, 149, 153, 155, 261

St. Francis Xavier Roman Catholic Church, Gettysburg, 120, 134

stragglers, 91, 140, 295, 321–22, 409n21; in Frederick, 74, 173; Meade and, 64, 352

Stuart, J. E. B., 79; captures wagon trains, 72, 78; cavalry division of, 21, 59, 70; cuts rail and telegraph lines, 24, 78, 116; location of, 22, 48, 63, 65, 78, 81–83, 110; movement of, 24, 65

Susquehanna River, 56, 61, 79, 88, 113; Lee and, 43, 63, 71, 80, 91, 118

Sweitzer, Jacob B., 242–43, 248

Swisher, Jacob, farm of, 199, 200, 283

Sykes, George, 102, 106, 108–10, 144, 158, 218, *219, 365*, 370; commands Fifth Corps, 43, 64, 69, 74, 75, 79, 90, 112, 170, 276, 363, 414n4; in councils of war, 276–77, 324, 363, 373; at Gettysburg, 195–96, 203, 217–18, 227–28, 231–33, 237, 242, 244–45, 253, 288, 303–4, 414n4; headquarters of, 34, 37, 52; Meade's orders and dispatches to, 64, 74, 90, 91, 166, 183, 217, 304, 408n38, 413n2; in pursuit of Lee, 337, 353, 359; Slocum and, 109, 140. *See also* Fifth Corps, Army of the Potomac

Taneytown, Md., 64, 67, 69, 118, 141–42, 178, 194, 343, 390n10, 407n24; Artillery Reserve and, 64, 79, 189, 192, 332; cavalry and, 67, 137, 215; Hancock and Second Corps and, 90, 106, 109, 136, 138–39, 142–45, 147, 332, 341, 350, 402n11; Meade's headquarters at, 79, 87, 88, 90, 92, 96, 109, 114, 135, 151, 158, 162, 165, 179, 183–84, 393n14; reporters at, 140–41, 146; Reynolds and First Corps and, 136–39; roads to, 57, 77, 83, 85, 94, 96, 121, 177–78, 391n21, 393n11; Sedgwick and Sixth Corps and, 158, 159, 166, 404n17; Sickles and Third Corps and, 64, 69, 71, 75, 79, 97, 393n12; Signals Corps and, 194–95; Slocum and Twelfth Corps and, 64, 70, 71, 90, 332

Taneytown Road, 87, 127, 136, 196, 290, 332; Blacksmith Shop Road and, 208, 414n4; blocked by wagon trains, 146, 153, 157; Captain Meade on, 206–8; Confederate barrage on, 295–96, *296*, 301; at Gettysburg, 191–92, 194, 199–200, 262–63, 282, 293, 297; to Gettysburg, 57, 121, 123, 158, 171, 184, 190; Hancock and Second Corps and, 139–40, 149, 152, 157, 193; hospitals along, 200, 273, 283, 306; Leister house and, 191, 199, 413n4; telegraph and, 137, 151–52; Wheatfield Road and, 231, 233–34

Tapeworm Railroad, 121, 130, 131

Taylor, Zachary, 7, 13, 167, 295

telegraph lines: along Baltimore & Ohio Railroad, 44, 46, 182, 331, 345–46; disruption of, 59–61, 63, 70, 72, 76, 78, 88, 89, 114–17, 182, 389n17; between Emmitsburg and Taneytown headquarters, 87, 92; quartermaster department and, 61, 88, 152; repair of, 61, 89, 91, 173, 331; along Western Maryland Railroad, 58, 181–82

178, 197, 201, 280, 313, 330–32. *See also* Camp of Transportation

Union Mills, Md., 57, 76, 79, 118, 137, 151; Meade's defense line at, 83, 85, 136; Stuart and, 78, 110, 392n36; Sykes's Fifth Corps and, 71, 90, 100, 108–10, 112, 170

Uniontown, Md., 64, 72, 73, 118, 343; roads to, 85, 177, 178; Second Corps and, 69, 75, 78, 90, 91, 100, 109, 112, 136, 139, 390n10

United States Battalion of Topographical Engineers, 39, 53, 57, 179, 356; Meade in, 7, 11

United States Congress, 4; Joint Committee of, on the Conduct of the War, 30, 229, 284, 372–73, 387n4, 403n8, 413n43, 413n1, 416n20; members of, 11, 12, 30

Utica, Md., 64, 67, 332, 341, 350, 352

Veil, Charles Henry, 130, 133, 399n37

Vincent, Strong, 232–33, 235–36, 242

Virginia, 5, 12, 44, 48; 1861–63 battles in, 1–4

Virginia Peninsula, 1–2, 14. *See also* Peninsula Campaign

Wadsworth, James S., 95, 106, 119, 124–31, 143, 146–47, 155, 192, 194, 204, 263, 270–71, 286, 399n37; in councils of war, 363–64; on Culp's Hill, 188–89. *See also* First Division (Doubleday; Wadsworth), First Corps

wagons, 67, 74, 108, 141, 177, 310–11; ambulance, 19, 69, 106–8, 123, 133–34, 145, 147, 158, 169–70, 200, 319, 328–30, 346, 352, 401n58; ammunition and ordnance, 19, 24, 69, 107–8, 123, 158, 290, 313–19, 328–31, 398n28; of Army of the Potomac, 19, 24, 59, 67, 69, 70, 74, 75, 77, 123–24; captured by Confederates, 24, 59, 78; on Cashtown Road, 310, 312; of Eleventh Corps,

123, 146, 178; Emmitsburg and, 94, 123, 178, 202, 213; empty, 91, 123, 124; of engineers, 64, 70, 75, 77, 79, 87; of Fifth Corps, 179, 317; of First Corps, 123, 133, 178, 420n3; headquarters, 71, 77, 87; infantry guards of, 56, 178–79; of Lee's army, 62, 310, 328–30, 346, 352, 425n11; medical, 70, 75, 77, 87, 201, 313, 318; mules and, 197, *318*, 319, 352, 383n34, 406n10; for quartermaster and subsistence stores, 19, 24, 69, 123–24, 157, 166, 175, 177–78, 198, 280, 313; of Second Corps, 107–8, 178–79; of Signal Corps, 70, 75, 77, 87, 152; traffic jams of, 146, 153, 157; Union Bridge and Westminster and, 91, 123, 157, 166, 175, 178–79, 197, 201, 280, 313, 330–32; Wilcox's, 62, 251, 252, 259, 261–62

Wainwright, Charles S., 123–24, 204, 360, 366

Walkersville, Md., 56, 64, 69, 341, 350, 390n10

War Department, 2, 25, 28, 29, 55, 80–81, 175, 179, 197, 331; communication between Meade and, 89, 115–16, 138, 165, 182, 217, 280, 305; Hooker and, 26, 35, 49; intelligence on Lee's movements and, 28, 61–62, 387–88n7; maps and, 57, 388n8. *See also* Secretary of War; Stanton, Edwin M.

Warren, Gouverneur Kemble, 39, *40*, 145, 161, *226*, *365*; analyzes position at Gettysburg, 142–43, 157, 184, 186, 203–4, 210, 224, 226–27, 232–33, 412–13n43; in councils of war, 276, 278, 324, 363; declines being Meade's chief of staff, 39, 41; inspects Big Pipe Creek with Meade, 118, 398n13; Meade and, 217, 220, 223, 228, 286, 292, 303, 335–36, 341, 370, 373, 386n32, 398n13; in pursuit of Lee, 327, 334, 339, 350, 357, 362; wounded, 233, 274, 277

Warrenton, Va., 3, 8, 373
Washington, D.C., 1, 2, 21, 26, 27, 59, 70, 72, 73, 108; Baltimore & Ohio Railroad and, 44, 71; covered by Meade's army, 25, 71–72, 75, 84, 99; defenses of, 113, 140, 186; Hooker and, *23*, 24, 25; Meade ordered to protect, 38, 43, 57; rumors in, 80–81; telegraph lines to, 60–61, 88, 89, 91, 138, 173. *See also* Halleck, Henry W.; Lincoln, Abraham; Secretary of War; United States Congress; War Department; White House
Waynesboro, Pa., 48, 94, 106, 341, 350
weather: cloudy, 385n17; driving rain, 5, 313, 343, 345; drizzle, 28, 29, 43, 66, 384n8, 384n10, 390n1; gentle rain, 87, 114; heavy rain, 3, 125, 160, 174, 308, 317, 328, 324, 333, 343, 351, 352, 365, 385n17; hot and humid, 125, 129, 152, 357; intermittent rain, 87; pleasant, 385n17; pounding rain, 330; pouring rain, 70, 115, 314, 324, 327, 341, 342; rain, 71, 81, 82, 88, 110, 112, 115, 118, 342, 352, 354, 391n21, 392n1; visibility and, 87, 110, 324, 328, 330, 365. *See also* mud
Webb, Alexander Stewart, 268, 287, *289*, 290, 300, 374
Weed, Stephen H., 232–33, 236, 253
Weir, Gulian Verplank, 250, 252, 263
Weld, Stephen Minot, 76, 89, 92, 106, 119, 384n6, 394n27; carries messages to Meade, 127, 138, 393n19, 393–94n21
Welles, Gideon, 17, 368–69, 370
Wentz, John, house and farm of, 101, 123, 129, 160–61, 202, 239, 399–400n47
Western Maryland Railroad, 74, 76, 85, 116, 175, 179, 181, 182, 316; as means of resupply, 58, 85, 91, 320; repair of, 176, 406n7; Stuart and, 65, 72, 78–79, 83; Union Bridge

and, 91, 123; Westminster and, 58, 72–74, 76, 79, 83, 85, 116, 175, 181, 316
Westminster, Md., 57, 73, 88, 90, 117–18, 140, 217, 280, 314–15, *316*, 318, 323, 330, 420n3; Baltimore Pike and other roads to, 57, 79, 85, 110, 118, 121, 136, 169, 177, 198, 203, 273, 396n29; as base of supply, 65, 85, 138, 167, 175–77, 179, 183, 189, 320; cavalry and, 67, 76, 78, 83, 214–15, 323, 329; Eleventh Corps and, 317, 423n26; Fifth Corps and, 90, 109, 166, 317; Meade moves army to, 63, 71; Pipe Creek line and, 85, 118, 176; railroad to, 58, 72–74, 76, 79, 83, 85, 116, 175, 177, 181–82, 316, 319–20, 406n7; Sixth Corps and, 79, 110, 112, 158–59, 167, 169; Stuart and, 65, 78–79, 83; wagons trains and, 155, 158, 166–67, 177–79, 197, 201, 280, 313, 316, 319, 331–32, 343, 406n10. *See also* Camp of Transportation; Carroll County, Md.; Western Maryland Railroad
West Point, U.S. Military Academy at, 14, 32, 102; Army of the Potomac officers as graduates of, 13, 35, 39, 41, 46, 52, 55, 66, 67, 102, 145, 164, 167, 186, 218, 301, 325; Meade at, 7, 46, 102, 116, 179, 321; teachers at, 53, 55, 92, 102, 154, 281, 321, 395n7
Wheatfield, the, 220, 229, 231–32, 241, 244, 258, 263, 292, 329, 334; Birney and Barnes attacked in, 236–37, 242–43, 245; Caldwell counterattacks in, 248, 250–53; Crawford counterattacks in, 253, 255
White House, 81, 113. *See also* Lincoln, Abraham
Wiedrich, Michael, 266, 268–69
Wilcox, Cadmus, wagons of, 62, 251–52, 259, 261–62
Wilkeson, Samuel, 71, 140, 294–95, 306
Williams, Alpheus S., *260*, 284; at Gettysburg, 259, 264, 279, 417–

INDEX